P9-CRU-147

Never Stop Running

Never Stop Running

Allard Lowenstein and the Struggle to Save American Liberalism

WILLIAM H. CHAFE

BasicBooks
A Division of HarperCollins*Publishers*

Designed by Craig Winer

93 94 95 96 ◆/RRD 9 8 7 6 5 4 3 2 1

Library of Congress Cataloging-in-Publication Data

Chafe, William Henry.
    Never stop running : Allard Lowenstein and the struggle to save American liberalism / William H. Chafe.
        p.   cm.
    Includes bibliographical references and index.
    ISBN 0-465-00103-3
    1. Lowenstein, Allard K.   2. Liberalism—United States—History—20th century.   3. United States—Politics and government—1945–1990.   4. Legislators—United States—Biography.   5. United States. Congress. House—Biography.   I. Title.
E840.8.L68C47   1993
328.73'092—dc20   93-9475
                                                                                                          CIP

To Aunt Dot and Uncle John

Contents

Preface

Writing about Allard Lowenstein has been the most challenging and exciting task I have undertaken as a professional historian. I had the good fortune to know Lowenstein briefly during his first race for Congress in 1966. A graduate student at Columbia at the time, I was actively involved in the West Side reform Democratic movement, especially with its work in support of civil rights and in opposition to American involvement in the war in Vietnam. Although I was not a Lowenstein supporter in that congressional contest, I had the opportunity to witness his magnetic appeal to the young, his charismatic, almost magical ability to weave a rhetorical web that quickly enwrapped an audience. I also was able to see the whimsy, humor, and idiosyncratic qualities of dress and presentation—the shirttail always hanging out, for example—that identified him as so special in his followers' eyes. It was a personal exposure to Lowenstein that, however brief, has proven enormously helpful in this undertaking.

But that encounter did not lead to the writing of this book. Rather, I came to this project because it seemed an ideal way to explore further the most critical questions that have defined my career as a historian. I had spent almost twenty years writing about discrimination and protest in America. One focus of that research was the way gender has functioned in American society as a pivotal means of assigning people to roles of subordination, and how women have challenged that gender system, especially during the last three decades. I have written also about the civil rights movement and the students who, together with their parents and teachers, insisted on toppling the structure of legal segregation—only to discover that more institutional and economic sources of oppression remained to buttress and perpetuate racism. More recently, I have tried to come to grips with how issues of gender, race, and class can illuminate the history of postwar America, and especially the interior dynamics of how America functions, how power is allocated, and how change may happen.

As I pursued these concerns, two separate but related themes kept recurring. First, I discovered that I enjoyed writing about individual lives. I had done a long biographical sketch of Eleanor Roosevelt on the occasion of her centenary and briefer ones of the characters who were most important in my other work. Drawing these portraits, delving into family and personal backgrounds, and tracing nuances of motivation and emotion provided more gratification and challenge than any other kind of historical writing I had done.

But just as important, I observed how the issues I was most concerned with always revolved around one question: Could people achieve change, or progress toward equality, by working within existing social and political structures? Or was it necessary, to alter American society on such fundamental questions as race, class, and gender, to go *outside* the existing system and attack the root sources of discrimination in values, institutions, and economic structures?

Feminists certainly divided over this issue in the 1970s. While liberal women's rights activists saw their goal as the integration of women into existing structures, radical and socialist feminists believed they had to challenge the very foundation of "things as they are" to secure freedom. Civil rights activists faced the same dilemma. Their movement was torn between two conflicting goals: to obtain equal treatment as individuals before the law, regardless of race; and to advance collectively as a group toward obtaining a larger, more proportionate share of economic, political, and social resources. One course presumed a continuation of existing social and economic arrangements, with the goal of assimilating individual black people and women; the other proposed a fundamental alteration of these arrangements, with collective progress for oppressed groups as the objective. It all came back to the basic question of liberal activism: Can one resolve problems of social injustice through incremental reform, or is something more drastic necessary?

To some the question may seem irrelevant or the answer self-evident.

Those reared on faith in the New Deal were convinced that reform from within the existing political and social system offered the only path to change. Liberalism was a given, so internalized a part of a political belief system that no alternatives could emerge as consciously considered options. Others, especially those who have seen Ronald Reagan and George Bush define liberalism—the "L" word—as a modern-day scarlet letter, may consider any critique of liberalism from the left as romantic self-indulgence. Surely, they might say, at a time when communism and other "left" alternatives have largely self-destructed, it is clear that liberalism is the only left-of-center option available, and even then, must be defended against right-wing assault. Yet these stances deny historical agency and recognition to a generation of activists reared in the sixties and seventies for whom the issue of incremental reform versus more radical structural change constituted the defining question of an era. It was an issue so central in importance that it could shape one's entire approach to political engagement. Nor is the underlying problem time-limited. In some form, it has occupied each generation of political activists.

Undertaking a biography of Allard Lowenstein has offered me the opportunity not only to address this pivotal issue but to respond to the challenge of writing about a complicated and extraordinary individual. I have never enjoyed researching and writing a book as much as this one. Nor, I think, have I ever learned as much about myself and the world I have grown up in.

Such a venture would never have been possible without the aid of hundreds of people. I am grateful first of all to the Lowenstein family—Jenny, Tom, Frank, Kate, Larry, Marie, and Dorothy. They have known from the beginning that there would be parts of this book they would not like. Yet they have persisted in their cooperation, providing every measure of assistance I have requested. There are also the countless Lowenstein friends and associates whose willingness to be interviewed for this book represents a generosity I cannot acknowledge in words. Many of these individuals have put their innermost thoughts and experiences before me. I only hope that I have treated them, and their experiences, with the respect and care they deserve. Because there are so many of these individuals, to mention a few would do an injustice to the many. But I hope all will know how much their assistance has meant.

From the very beginning, I have also been the beneficiary of superb library and research support. Richard Schrader, John White, Tim West, and David Multke-Hansen of the Southern Historical Collection at the University of North Carolina have offered help at every turn. Fran Weaver, the now-retired curator of the Lowenstein Papers, honored her lifetime of friendship with Al Lowenstein by organizing the papers in as comprehensive and informative a manner as one could imagine. Ronald Grele and the Columbia Oral History Project staff have transcribed virtually all the tapes as part of their Allard Lowenstein Oral History Project. Their expertise, counsel, and support have been instrumental in making this book possible. Most important, little of my research would have been possible without the extraordinary commitment to preserve the historical record of Allard Lowenstein himself. With a care and devotion that might well astonish those who knew only the chaotic state of his suitcase and his office files, Lowenstein kept virtually every piece of paper he received or wrote upon from the age of ten onward.

I also am deeply indebted to those who have provided the time, financial support, and camaraderie to make this book happen. The first part of the book was written at the Center for Advanced Study in the Behavioral Sciences at Stanford University in the company of as distinguished and friendly a group of scholars as I can imagine. While there in 1989–90, I was the recipient of a John Simon Guggenheim Fellowship, as well as support from the National Endowment for the Humanities and the Andrew Mellon Foundation. Duke University has been unstinting in providing research support from the beginning, as has the Duke Center for Documentary Studies. I am particularly grateful to Vivian Jackson for her cheerful assistance, Grace Guyer for doing such a fine job in overseeing preparation of the manuscript, and Patrick Wilkinson for all his help with last-minute research questions. The final version of the manuscript was prepared at the Rockefeller Foundation Study and Conference Center in Bellagio, Italy. I am deeply grateful for the opportunity to work there amid such natural beauty and inspiring companionship. A special thanks to those, both at Stanford and Bellagio, who tramped through the hills with me each day after lunch, marshaling the energy and insight to get back to work.

As much as anyone I know, I have been blessed with friends who have been willing to spend hours reading and commenting on my work. At an early stage, John Demos was very helpful in giving me insight on the psychological dimensions of Lowenstein's life. John Dittmer and Clayborne Carson generously offered assistance relating to civil rights history and Mississippi. Estelle Freedman and her colleagues in the Stanford biography seminar gave helpful comments on the early chapters. My greatest debt is to those who have read the entire manuscript. With care and precision, they have identified the areas that I needed to change and improve, and although I have not always taken their advice, this book is measurably better because of them. Nancy Hewitt, Steve Lawson, John D'Emilio, and Sydney Nathans are friends who know what it means to be critics, and critics who know what it means to be friends. In this list also belongs Steve Fraser. As an editor he has been all that one could hope for, and as a historian and critic, a person of acute insight. Jane Judge has been very helpful in overseeing final production of the manuscript.

Finally, I want to thank my family. Writing a book like this creates a range of emotions and discoveries. There are all those things I have learned about myself because of Al Lowenstein, and all the things I have come to appreciate even more about those I care for most. Wisdom sometimes come with age, and a part of wisdom is to realize how cherished are our human connections, and how important it is to acknowledge and nurture them. To my wife Lorna and my children Christopher and Jennifer, I offer my gratitude for making this—and all ventures—possible and worthwhile. In the course of writing this book, I have also become more aware of those qualities that endure in our lives and connect us to our pasts—the cycles of tides and of seasons, the location of family homesteads that sing of past generations. This book was written mostly on an island where my family—or part of it—has been for many years. Because of the book, I have a new appreciation for that place. I am proud, therefore, to dedicate this book to Aunt Dot and the memory of Uncle John—two people who have made it possible for us to be the next generation to carry on with the tides and the seasons.

Chapel Hill, North Carolina
September 1993

Introduction

Allard Lowenstein was one of the pivotal figures who shaped American political culture during the post–World War II era. Although neither a chief executive nor a cabinet member, he touched the lives of thousands of people who became active in running America's public business. Many of his disciples have continued to play major roles in American politics— Senators Bob Kerrey, Tom Harkin, Paul Wellstone, and Bill Bradley, to name just a few. For at least two generations of Americans born before 1960, Allard Lowenstein was a name synonymous with engagement, political commitment, and the transformative belief that young people, infused with idealism, could help America become as close to a perfect democracy as possible.

In large part, Lowenstein's influence reflected the degree to which he embodied and exemplified the tradition of liberal activism in postwar America. Franklin Roosevelt was his first political hero, and much of Lowenstein's own political credo went back to the social democratic policies of the 1930s—a belief in a humane and compassionate government that has a moral responsibility to provide shelter, food, and clothing where necessary and to promote a mutual regard among American citizens for each others' rights and well-being. But Lowenstein also played a major role in supporting the second part of what the journalist Godfrey Hodgson has called America's "liberal consensus"—a vigilant anticommunism that after World War II went hand in hand with, and indeed, seemed inextricably connected to the belief in social reform.[1]

Thus, for example, the national student movement that Lowenstein helped to form became a primary combatant in the ideological cold war with the Soviet Union. Under his direction, it dedicated itself as fiercely to fighting *against* Marxist student groups abroad as it did to fighting *for* racial justice at home. During the 1950s and 1960s, when Lowenstein was urging college students to find their political voices and change their society, he always gave equal attention to the importance of fighting "leftists" who might infiltrate and subsequently subvert democratic reform.

Partly because of his anticommunism, Lowenstein was a profound individualist. Not only did he believe in the sanctity of individual over group identity and allegiance—each person, he insisted, should be defined as a distinctive being, not as a Jew or a black or a Catholic—but he also was convinced that only individuals make the difference in society, that each person has the responsibility to shape history. Lowenstein, one observer said, was "like the Just Man among the Jews," a singular prophet whose responsibility it was to defend the faith against those who would pervert and destroy it. The "faith" in this instance was the American democratic process and its capacity for internal reform. Foremost among its "enemies," in turn, were groups committed to a collectivist ideology that were bent on snuffing out individual will and personal freedom.

Because he so passionately cared about abolishing racism, preserving individualism, and fighting communism, Lowenstein became a liberal political hero. His own life provided a model for others to follow. One of the first Americans to protest loudly and vigorously against the apartheid regime in South Africa (his book *Brutal Mandate* was published in 1962), he became an arch critic of America's policy of opposition to African nationalism. At home, Lowenstein carried forward his battle against racism by mobilizing white students at Stanford and Yale to enlist in the civil rights struggle, urging them to journey to Mississippi in 1963 and 1964 to join their black comrades in the fight for the ballot and self-determination. Later in the 1960s, Lowenstein waged a single-minded campaign to end the war in Vietnam; once again he was galvanizing students, this time to "dump Johnson." Largely responsible for making possible the 1968 presidential candidacy of Eugene McCarthy, Lowenstein quickly won a reputation as a Pied Piper who could sway thousands of youthful followers, persuading them to fulfill his own commitment to making American democracy work. Throughout the late 1960s and 1970s, Lowenstein pursued his vision, as a one-term congressman and then perennial candidate for Congress, as a U.N. ambassador during the Carter administration, and as a private citizen still rallying young people to his cause. He persisted in that quest until his death in the late winter of 1980.

Yet if Allard Lowenstein's life offers a window through which to examine the history of postwar liberal activism, he was by no means a typical liberal. He may have ended up taking the same position on most issues as Hubert Humphrey, but he conveyed a political message far less predictable. At the heart of Lowenstein's liberalism was a tension. He lived on the edge of conventional liberalism, torn between complacent New Deal–type homilies and a radical challenge to all comfortable and entrenched institutions. In effect, Lowenstein walked a line between these two options through much of his life—seeking to achieve reform within the system, but frequently being willing to challenge established institutions and authorities as well.

At every stage of his political development, Lowenstein grappled with the dilemma of how far to go in questioning existing political arrangements. Initially, the issues were the fraternity system in the nation's colleges and "Jim Crow" in North Carolina; then came apartheid in South Africa, the Student Nonviolent Coordinating Committee's commitment to transform Mississippi, and the antiwar movement's debate over its tactics in confronting the government. Repeatedly, Lowenstein performed a balancing act, inciting students, on the one hand, to rebel against prevailing policies, and on the other hand, resisting with every ounce of his energy the eventual decision by some to become radicals. Although Lowenstein almost always came down on the side of working *inside* the system, he never stopped flirting with the idea of outright rebellion.

At least in part, Lowenstein's impulse to "live on the edge" reflected his own generational dilemma. He came of age at the onset of the cold war and thus internalized most of the assumptions of an earlier cohort of liberals reared on suspicion of communism. Yet he anticipated, and in some ways helped to crystallize, the more radical disillusionment of the generation to follow. Throughout his late twenties and early thirties, Allard Lowenstein prodded, spurred, and inspired younger students to seize the opportunity—and responsibility—to challenge the status quo and remake the world. In effect, Lowenstein became a tribune who tried to convey liberal idealism from one generation to another. Yet in doing so, he almost inevitably offered mixed messages, both of which were authentic. To those in positions of authority, Allard Lowenstein often seemed like a Communist agitator, and he was denounced as such. To more radical members of the new generation, on the other hand, he sometimes appeared to be a spokesman for the "establishment" and was called by some a CIA agent. Who, then, was Allard Lowenstein? A democratic insurgent or an agent of social control? A top-down manipulator, seeking to act *for* but not *with* oppressed people, or a populist able to identify with and join the ranks of those who were victims of oppression? Precisely because that tension was always there, Allard Lowenstein defies categorization as an ordinary liberal; yet the way he resolved the tension tells us a great deal about the limits—and possibilities—of reform within the liberal tradition.

The other powerful reality about Allard Lowenstein is that very few questions about his political career can be answered without exploring his private life as well. It was a life as rich, as complex, and as turbulent as even the most creative novelist might imagine. A man surrounded by friends (his address book contained thousands of names, most of them recipients of at least one postcard from him every year), Lowenstein was also intensely lonely. He deeply craved, yet was profoundly afraid of, the kind of intimacy that requires sharing confidence and love. The product of an immigrant family that seemed a textbook example of success and togetherness, he in fact could never talk about the most important issues of his life with his father and brothers. He was Jewish but went to Protestant churches. He came from New York but chose to go to college in Chapel Hill, North Carolina. A person who spent most of his political life in the ethnic hothouse of New York's polyglot communities, he fantasized about living in a midwestern small town full of Protestant farmers. Although he courted countless young women and eventually married one of them, his closest companions were men, and from adolescence onward, he struggled with the issue of whether or not he might be homosexual. In his appeal to the young, he often inspired devotion and worship; yet these same emotions could turn to hatred and alienation when the magic of the moment, or the intensity of the crusade, had passed.

Many if not most of Lowenstein's political decisions reflected private insecurities and concerns. And his primary mode of political organizing—seeking out, inspiring, and engulfing the young—emerged directly from his deepest and most powerful personal needs. The connection of the personal and political helps to explain why his triumphs could be so inspiring, and to underscore why his failures were so painful. In the ultimate irony, that connection led a devoted former protégé to walk into his office one day in 1980 and shoot him to death. Thus, if Lowenstein was a liberal hero, he was also a tragic one.

In what follows, it sometimes has seemed best to treat the private and the public narratives of Allard Lowenstein's life separately. Each can stand on its own. Yet the key to understanding this extraordinary person is to recognize that, ultimately, a dialectic was at work. The dynamics of Lowenstein's personal story shaped and defined his political story, even as the events of his public career created the stage on which he sought to work out his private dilemmas. This, then, is a life that offers a vantage point on an era of liberal activism—and also illuminates the struggles of a person who tried desperately to find himself in an often hostile and confusing world. Both stories speak powerfully to the abiding strength and tragedy of the human spirit, as well as to the changes our society has gone through in the past half-century on some of the most important issues confronting us.

1
Secrets

O<small>N</small> J<small>ANUARY</small> 16, 1968—<small>HIS THIRTY-NINTH BIRTHDAY</small>—A<small>LLARD</small> L<small>OWEN</small>-stein stood poised on the threshold of one of the great triumphs of twenti-eth-century political history. Eight months earlier, he and a small group of followers had set out to topple Lyndon Johnson from the presidency. Out-raged morally and politically by the Vietnam War, Lowenstein and his friends had struck upon the grandiloquent notion that if they could only galvanize the unrest and dissatisfaction of ordinary citizens about the war, they could actually force the president of the United States to step aside. It was a fantasy so bizarre that most realistic politicians dismissed it as egomaniacal hubris. Yet just two months into Al Lowenstein's fortieth year, President Lyndon Johnson announced that he would not seek reelec-tion. As much as anyone else, Allard Lowenstein had made that decision possible. He had come a long way from the near anonymity of his entry into the world on January 16, 1929, on the eve of the Great Depression.

On that day, the name on the roster of newborns at the Newark hospital read "Baby Lowenstein." Neither the father, Gabriel, nor the mother, Au-gusta, could decide which side of the family to honor in naming this, their third son. Eventually, they settled on Allard, a name that Lowenstein him-self described, in a moment of sardonic humor, as being appropriate to his appearance. "I was a duck," he used to say. "Mallard without the *M*."

1

Later, he discarded his given middle name, Augustus, in favor of Kenneth, a far more conventional, "American" name, perhaps seeking to remake his image and identity. A little more than a year after his birth, his mother died from breast cancer. Shortly after that, Gabriel remarried and the family moved to New York. Gabriel's new wife, Florence, was the only mother Allard ever knew. In fact, no one ever told him that he had another, natural mother until he discovered it himself more than a decade later.[1]

Although the circumstances of Allard Lowenstein's birth and naming may not themselves carry enormous significance, they highlight some of the abiding themes of his life—insecurity and doubt about his own self-worth, a passionate quest for acceptance as an "American," and persistent unease about the secret, hidden aspects of his life. To a remarkable extent, these private questions were tied to, and informed, the public roles that Lowenstein chose to play during his extraordinary career, even as they drove his effort to find a personal identity in a society that has most often preferred conventional patterns of labeling to tolerance for individual diversity.

CHILDHOOD

Allard's father, Gabriel, came to the United States from Lithuania in the great Jewish migration from Eastern Europe just after the turn of the century. Born in 1889, he was active in the anticzarist revolutionary movement as a teenager and in 1905 was arrested for helping to organize his community's participation in the general strike of that year. Released from prison on the condition that he leave the country, Gabriel fled to America in 1906 to join his brother William, who was already there. After a few brief jobs, he quickly learned English and became a devoted student. He entered college at the age of nineteen, receiving his B.S. degree from Columbia in 1913, then a Ph.D. in biochemistry in 1917.[2]

Gabriel's first love was academia. Shortly after receiving his Ph.D., he became an instructor of biochemistry at the College of Physicians and Surgeons at Columbia University. By all accounts, he was a brilliant scientist, dedicated to his students, to his discipline, and to the institution that had made possible his career. "He was always a teacher," his daughter-in-law Marie Lowenstein observed. "He taught all his life. In conversation he was teaching." The library at the Lowenstein home, bursting with literary classics, was an inspiration, recalled one childhood friend of

Allard's. But it was by no means clear that Gabriel's appointment at Columbia would continue, and with a new wife and baby, he worried about whether he could support a family on a teacher's salary of $2,200.[3]

According to family legend, Gabriel Lowenstein chose to sacrifice his career preference to provide a better life for his children. "When I was young," he later wrote Allard, "I didn't have all the milk and honey that God has provided. . . . I had to struggle, fight, think hard, try to earn a living . . . to borrow, to work, and to repay." Gabriel felt keenly his own status as an outsider. He spoke with a thick accent, experienced profound ambivalence about his Jewishness, and regretted, in his daughter's words, "coming to this country and not feeling comfortable in many situations because he didn't know [the social graces]." And so he was determined that his own children would not have to suffer such liabilities, deciding that the only way to provide them with the advantages he had not enjoyed was to give up his academic career. His brothers were already faring well in the restaurant business, so Gabriel joined them, committed to making his fortune in order that his children might become whatever they wished to be. "If you knew how to [play tennis, dance, and] do everything well," he told his daughter, "[then] there was never a situation that you would be in [where] you would be uncomfortable."[4]

Having made that commitment, Gabriel Lowenstein—always called "Doc" thereafter because of his academic achievements—was forced to live with the consequences. The centerpiece of his dreams, his beloved Augusta, died one year after Allard was born. By all accounts, theirs had been a wonderful relationship. The daughter of immigrants who were garment workers, Augusta Goldberg had earned her high school diploma, then married Gabriel. "He was so devoted to her," Augusta's sister noted, "that if she started to wash the floor from one side of the room, he would get down on his knees on the other side to wash his half." Now she was gone, the victim of breast cancer that ravaged her both physically and psychologically. Augusta had been delighted with her new child. "He was the fattest of all," she wrote seven months after his birth. "He is the smartest too. We may yet have a very prominent member in our Lowenstein family." But by then the cancer had taken over her body. Forced to wean Allard, she wrote in her diary, "Son, the mental anguish I went through in separating our two united selves you will never understand. . . . A God looking on must have realized the cruelty of the affair. To rob a mother of the joy of real motherhood, and a baby of the pleasure of his mother's food." As her condition worsened, only the chance to watch Allard mitigated her pain, seeing him "climb up the whole flight of stairs, cooing so sweetly, saying words, in short, unfolding like a little bud. . . . You won't care a hoot . . . when you're grown. But then you're my baby and how dear to me." At the time of her death, Allard was one year old, his brother Larry seven, and his brother Bert eleven.[5]

Although Gabriel was now making a substantial income, he had to provide for his family, create a new home, and devote himself to a job that was, at best, a second choice for his life's career. He remarried quickly, to the deep consternation of Augusta's parents. The family then moved from Newark to New York—largely, his son Larry said, as a means of "wiping out the past"—and threw himself into the task of building a material base for the next generation to use in its search for fulfillment. Jenny Littlefield, Al's former wife, remarked that, in a sense, Gabriel had lost both his first two loves, the career as a scientist that he thrived on, and the woman he cherished. Al used to comment on his own sense of his father's disappointment. "How sad it was, for Papa to end up slicing roast beef," he said.[6]

Florence, the woman Gabriel married so that his sons might have a mother, had taught English to new immigrants. They met at Madison House, a social settlement on the Lower East Side for which Gabriel had been a member of the board and subsequently served as president. Florence loved her work, especially the joy of teaching small children, and prided herself on her vocabulary, her grammar, and her penmanship, boasting frequently of the compliments she received for these and using— sometimes ostentatiously—her favorite "big" words. She also cared deeply about her Jewishness. She tried to keep a kosher household, notwithstanding Gabriel's contempt for religious ritual. Even after Allard helped destroy that possibility by insisting on drinking milk with his meat, she preserved Passover as a period when strict religious observances would be maintained. At such times, Al told his wife Jenny, Gabriel "would sit at the other end of the table pooh-poohing [the whole process] . . . talking about how he was an atheist and how ridiculous it all was." Clearly, the situation was not optimal for creating an ideal family life.[7]

The greatest problem, perhaps, involved Bert, the oldest son, who was twelve when his father remarried. Although Florence was "extraordinarily loving to them all," according to family members, Bert "hated" his stepmother, resented her presence, and loathed her "hovering" ways. To make matters worse, Bert was the apple of his father's eye, "*the* favorite," Marie

Lowenstein said, "from the moment he was born." Bert appeared to be a "genius." He skipped the first and second grades and so excelled at science that a faculty member at Fieldston who had taught Robert Oppenheimer called Bert "his most brilliant student." Gabriel refused to countenance anyone interfering with Bert; he allowed "no disciplinary action, nothing," a family member recalled. "The sun rose and set on Bert. Bert was going to be everything Doc wasn't—in his own mind." He entered Harvard, finished in three years, made Phi Beta Kappa, and then attended Harvard Medical School. "Dad would have sacrificed every one of us for Bert," Florence later wrote; that preference, together with the circumstances surrounding Florence's sudden entry into the family, guaranteed that one of the most important people in the family—the eldest son—would always be at odds with his stepmother.[8]

The situation was somewhat better, but not greatly, when it came to Larry, who was four years younger than Bert. Seven years old at the time of his mother's death, Larry must have been profoundly shaken by the experience. Yet in retrospect he had no recollection of it; rather, he adapted to the loss of his mother by distancing himself emotionally from the situation. Instead of hating his stepmother, as Bert did, he evidently responded to her presence with "indifference." Although an excellent student, he had little of Bert's flair, taking a more stolid, detached posture toward the world. Occasionally, he doted on his father—"like a nursemaid," Florence once wrote. But toward his stepmother he showed no affection at all. "[He] neglects me as much as he caters to Dad," she complained.[9]

That, of course, left Allard and his sister Dorothy, born two and a half years later. As far as Florence was concerned, Dorothy later recalled, "Al was . . . her son." Florence had married Gabriel when Allard was an infant. She raised him as her own, shaped him in a way that was not possible with either Bert or Larry, and cherished him as though he were her firstborn. "*Our* baby no longer uses the bottle for his milk," she noted when he was nineteen months old. And then the next month she exulted, "He calls for *Mama;* I am glad of that because I feel *necessary.*" Late in the fall of 1930, Florence Lowenstein wrote in her diary that the baby would wake her in the middle of the night and not let Gabriel relieve her. "Often is the time that Gabriel wishes to but Allard persists. He wants the Mother."

Allard apparently reciprocated the emotions, especially as a youngster. "Maybe because he was the youngest, he was the child that accepted her the most," according to Jenny Littlefield. Marie Lowenstein agreed. "The reason Florence so adored Al," she said, "is that Al was the only child who . . . treated her kindly." He even enjoyed a warmer relationship with her than did her own daughter, Dorothy, who fought with her mother frequently. As if that were not enough, Allard quickly came to share the role of "favorite" initially occupied by Bert. Indeed, within a few years, Allard had superseded his eldest brother as the centerpiece of Gabriel's world. By the time Allard was five, his oldest brother had gone off to college, and by the time he was nine, when the family moved to the affluent suburb of Harrison, New York, Larry had left as well. Now literally as well as figuratively, Allard was the focal point of the household, the child upon whom both Florence and Gabriel could lavish their dreams, hopes, and aspirations. He was to be both the vehicle for realizing their individual fantasies of parental fulfillment and the tangible evidence—perhaps the only evidence—of the worth of their union. It was not a light burden.[10]

THE FAMILY STRUGGLE

The entire family enterprise during Allard's childhood hinged on keeping hidden from him the secret of his mother's death. Augusta was the "forgotten" woman. "Doc told me," Marie Lowenstein later said, "that he had decided that in order for them to have a closer family, he had deliberately wiped Augusta out of their lives." So painful, perhaps, was the memory, so vivid the sense of loss, so strong the passion for the appearance of normality, that only complete repression would suffice. Yet inevitably, the process was not easy. The older boys were fully aware of their real mother and had to be pledged to silence. Moreover, all the children remained in contact with their natural mother's family, visiting their Goldberg grandparents and aunts and uncles—"relatives from the old country," they were called—on a regular basis. Hence, Augusta's family became complicit as well. The grandparents, for example, would hide photographs of Augusta and Gabriel whenever Allard came to visit—all in service to the myth that Florence and Gabriel comprised the natural roots of the entire Lowenstein family tree. Otherwise, it was assumed, the family could not be viewed as whole.[11]

Inevitably, the myth shattered and the truth emerged. Lowenstein offered different versions of the story of his discovery. He told his sister Dorothy that on one of his visits to his Goldberg grandparents, the pictures had not been put away. When Allard—seven or eight at the time—asked about the woman in the photograph with his father and a tiny baby, his grandmother tried to dissemble; but after walking around the city for days, Lowenstein said, he eventually put the pieces together. With others, he placed the age of his discovery at eight or nine and said he had found the truth when he saw that the Gabriel Lowenstein entry had been torn from a "Who's Who" volume on American Jews. Upon locating the entry, he learned that his father had been married to Augusta. Whatever the actual process of discovery, Al appears to have come to the realization that Florence was his stepmother at the age of thirteen, not eight or nine. He told his Aunt Ruth, Augusta's sister, in a phone call and a letter in 1944 that he had unearthed the truth two years earlier. But even then he framed the issue with such high drama that his discovery of the secret became almost as momentous as the secret itself. He had told only one other person besides Ruth of his new knowledge, he said, and he would now keep his own awareness a secret.

Despite some discrepancies, all the stories share important threads, most notably, how explosive Al felt his discovery to be. He was afraid to confront his father, he told Dorothy, "because he felt that if my father and everybody else didn't talk about it, they didn't *want* to talk about it [and it must be] . . . very painful or something." At age fifteen, Al wrote his Aunt Ruth, testing one explanation for this silence. "No one has ever told me," he said, "because they didn't want me hurt. I still think they made the *right* decision." But that decision meant that Al had to become an accomplice in the secret, keeping his knowledge from them lest they suffer as well. "I know that if people in general ever discover that I know these things . . . all of them from Dad and Mother on down would be terribly hurt and for nothing. . . . It is . . . not because of myself that I want this whole business kept quiet. . . . When I first found out for sure, I was naturally shocked and hurt and really lost. . . . [Now], my hurt and pain and shock has long since gone." But if others found out that he knew, everyone who had tried so hard to protect him would be devastated. To resolve the situation, according to family lore, Al eventually "went home and told his mother that he had found out, but that he loved her, and nothing else could change that." He never spoke with his father about the matter, however, because of the pain it would cause Gabriel. "[It was a] very touching . . . effort on the part of a fairly small child to make something right for someone else," Jenny Littlefield commented, "as opposed to worry[ing] about himself." Later in his life, one measure of how close Al felt to certain friends was whether he told them about his natural mother.[12]

Yet the most significant aspect of Lowenstein's discovery was his realization that the central figure of power and authority in his life was both the author of the conspiracy of silence and the one person he could never talk to about it. According to Sandy Friedman, Al's oldest friend from childhood, Gabriel had always been a demanding, sometimes harsh father. He did not hug or kiss. Nor was he a figure to be confronted or to confide in, especially about issues that, by his own dictates, were taboo. Hence, Al's impassioned letter went to Aunt Ruthie, the wonderful woman whom he now knew to be his real mother's sister. Gabriel could never offer unconditional love; Aunt Ruthie was the personification of it. Thus he could write to her, knowing she would understand.[13]

But did she understand enough? His insistence that his primary concern was not to hurt anybody in the family may very well have been genuine. But it is almost a cliché in the therapeutic community that individuals with a particularly strong emotional need will often say the opposite of what they mean. Thus, the statement, "I have plenty of friends," means, "I have no friends." Given Lowenstein's fear of his father, this effort to reach out to Aunt Ruth may have been the only way he could get the issue on the table. Thus, there was another way to read his letter—a desperate cry to Ruth to tell the others because he was in such pain and needed his father to acknowledge that fact. Ruth, the all-giving aunt, might have read his true intentions and served as the vehicle for his desire to communicate with his father. In that light, the message, "Don't tell anybody. I don't want to hurt people," really meant, "Tell everybody. I am hurting." But Ruth did as Allard asked, not perhaps as he wished. The result was a tacit decision not to confront conflict and to repress fundamental feelings that, if expressed, might explode out of control.

Ironically, the story was not yet over, since Allard then became an accomplice in keeping the truth from his younger sister. Not until she was sixteen—five years after Allard discovered the truth—was she told, and only then because Larry's fiancée Marie was so stunned by the secret Larry had told her that she insisted Dorothy be informed. Even distant acquaintances knew that Bert and Larry's mother was not Dorothy's mother, she pointed out. Imagine what would happen if Dorothy learned the truth accidentally, or in a cruel manner. So Al was chosen to impart the news. Later, Dorothy learned that her mother had been so overwrought prior to the disclosure that she had gone to a psychologist, fearful that the earth-shattering revelation would cause Dorothy never to like her brothers again. In fact, Dorothy said, she had always wondered why her parents never celebrated their anniversary. "Every kid," she commented, "thinks they're adopted or something." But for years after everyone else knew the truth, she had been kept in the dark. As Marie Lowenstein later noted, "The contradictions in [that] family were absolutely incredible."[14]

The pretense of wholeness and happiness might have made sense if other family relationships had been smooth or harmonious. Yet nothing could have been further from the truth. From the beginning, it seemed, Gabriel had conceived of his marriage in purely utilitarian terms. If he was not quite employing Florence to take care of his children, it certainly seemed that way to some people. The two had little in common intellectually, a fact Florence frequently alluded to in her correspondence with Allard. "Dad and I are hitting it off very well," she commented sardonically in one letter. "I say nothing!" On another occasion, she expressed astonishment that, upon returning from a few weeks' trip to Cape Cod, she was allowed to talk and was even listened to at home. She desperately wanted approval and equal treatment, but more often than not, when she allowed herself to hope it might be forthcoming, she was disappointed. "All the time Dad was reading this article [out loud,]" she wrote Allard, "I kept thinking, 'how nice of him to think of me.' [Then] he said, 'some day, when Dorothy has time, read this to her.' . . . Back where I started from." Far more in love with Gabriel than he would ever be with her, the only way she could find solace or touch his heart was through the children, a formula that, in the Lowenstein family circumstances, simply compounded the pressures and problems that already existed.[15]

For the children themselves, the family dynamics more often than not led to domestic strife. "There were almost nightly fights," Dorothy recalled. "I can picture the logistics of the whole thing. My [parents'] room was to the left . . . and Al and I were to the right. . . . Al would be up and I would be in bed, and the fight would start. . . . We would run in, and he would go to my mother and I would go to my father. We would try to kid them out of it. You know, tweak their cheeks, things of that sort. . . . It was a very difficult thing to live with, this big shouting match that would go on at night, and quite nasty."[16]

Although Dorothy remembered the quarrels happening primarily from the time she was seven until she was sixteen, Al recalled hearing them as far back as when he was three. Money was often the issue: Florence would be trying to keep up with the country club set that Gabriel had introduced the family to; Gabriel in turn would decry her as a "bottomless pit . . . with no business sense . . . [who] couldn't [even] handle an allowance." When the issue was not money, it was religion, ethnic intermarriage—something about which Florence had strong views—or how to handle the children. In all likelihood, the parents did not fight every night. Frequently, Gabriel would go to bed right after dinner, exhausted from a long day's work. But whatever the case, the marriage from its inception reflected an absence of love, mutual respect, and shared interests. It also taught the obvious lesson that personal conflict is deeply painful and should be avoided at all costs.[17]

By contrast, Allard's relationships with his maternal grandparents and aunts were warm, nurturant, and affectionate. Beginning well before he learned the truth about his mother, he developed a close bond with the Goldbergs, going out of his way to endear himself to them, as they had obviously endeared themselves to him. He wrote them in detail when he went away to camp, sent them telegrams on important occasions like anniversaries, and luxuriated in their warm, spontaneous responses. "[Your anniversary telegram] meant more to us than you can possibly imagine," his grandmother Goldberg wrote him at camp. "If you do nothing else ever, you have done as much and more than any one could do to make us happy. You will have to forgive Grandpa and me if we sound old and sentimental. We love you. You never need to tell us you love us. You have demonstrated it time and time again." It was Allard's Aunt Ruthie who commiserated with him about "the secret," who urged him not to blame his mother and father, and who helped reinforce his sense of worth and goodness. Even as an adult, Allard would visit Ruth whenever he was in or around New York. "She'd serve him rye bread, you know," Jenny Littlefield recalled, "and it's as though they'd talk to each other in Yiddish, although they didn't. They'd sit on the sofa and she'd take care of him and he must have felt like he was a prized little boy again, without the conflict. Never any conflict with Aunt Ruthie. . . . That was when he was most comfortable . . . with his Jewishness." It was conflict-free Jewishness. At the Goldbergs, there seemed to be acceptance, appreciation, and warmth; at home, there was pressure, intensity, and conflict. The polarity was striking.[18]

The pressure took different forms, depending on where it came from. Allard's stepmother hovered constantly, overseeing each meal and activity as though it represented a final examination on the success of her stewardship. Allard was her pride and joy. She exulted in her maternal role (something she could never do with Bert and Larry), often sharing with Allard her pleasure in being able to single him out for special praise. "When he entered the room," she once wrote him in a portrait of himself, "there was a bright, light feeling that came with him. His round limpid pools, his eyes, expressed the great joy each person was to experience with him. . . . He had an olive complexion, an esthetic oval face, a high intelligent forehead, and a very sweet expression about a rosebud mouth. How fortunate to be born with an intelligent mind in so fine a body." In fact, there was nothing exceptional in Lowenstein's appearance—as a child he was lean, had a cowlick that fell over his forehead, and otherwise was quite ordinary—but to his stepmother, he looked like a Roman patrician.

To compound the pressure such praise conveyed, Florence sent a second message emphasizing how much pleasure she derived from her friends' praise of Allard, especially when they commented on "what an interesting, delightful conversationalist" he was. Yet, there was still something missing. "It's too bad," she once wrote, "that you and I who see so many things eye to eye and have so much understanding . . . have never been able to unburden ourselves to each other wholeheartedly." Even the "perfect" boy fell short of providing total satisfaction.[19]

Gabriel, on the other hand, applied pressure in a more staccato, less nuanced manner. "He wanted his children to excel in everything," Marie Lowenstein recalled, and he brooked no exceptions. When Larry came home from school with a 98 on his math exam, Gabriel responded, perhaps with a half-hidden smile, "So, where are the other two points?" All the children were ordered to master the basic athletic skills, to dress well, to learn the social graces, and to outachieve each other. "I insist that you play tennis every day," he wrote Allard, "and that you take a swim every day. . . . Are your shoes shined? Are your laces tied? . . . Consider your words and start a regime of self-constraint . . . at least as far as your speech is concerned. . . . Slow up. . . . Keep your room in order . . . go to bed early . . . watch your dress." The injunctions were endless, the demands insistent. While some saw humor and love in Gabriel's perfectionism, others saw only the heavy hand of despotic authority. "[Dad] felt that [Al] was so incredible," Dorothy said, "that he wanted him not to be [just] the best, but the best of the best . . . which is the same way he felt about Bert, and so he was, I guess, pushing even harder."[20]

The two kinds of pressure converged when Allard became the centerpiece of family dinners. At night, Gabriel presided over a seminar on the day's activities. Each child was expected to perform, to participate in a battle of wits with everyone else at the table. In the early years, Bert and Gabriel would dominate, with the conversation focusing on scientific matters. But politics was always a topic as well. Gabriel, playing devil's advocate, would tease and provoke Allard into sharpening his arguments, all the while enjoining him to remain poised, speak in measured tones, and listen respectfully to all other opinions. The only one partly left out was Larry. Resentful sometimes that, in his sister's words, "[Al] was treated by everybody . . . [as] the little genius," Larry would intentionally adopt a more conservative political stance or act annoyed at Al's "brilliance." "It's easy to sit back and criticize with thick glasses, statistics, [and] notebooks," Larry once wrote Al after a conversation about World War II. "I will not tolerate any talk by little babies like you about military strategy."[21]

At no other time was the accent on performance more evident than when guests were in the home. On such occasions, Allard was trotted out like a prodigy. "Al was supposed to recite at the dinner table," Jenny Littlefield observed, "and carry on political treatises." Sometimes he would be asked to give the population of a city, at other times to name all the state capitals or deliver an assessment of Julius Caesar. In the early years, Florence insisted that he dress up in "little Lord Fauntleroy" outfits, as if to underline, via costuming, the role Allard was expected to play for his audience. Eventually, Allard became sufficiently outraged at the scripted role that he drew the line and said, "No more, finished." But if he refused to dress up or perform his lines exactly as written, he always remained a vibrant presence at family gatherings, vigorously enlivening political debates with his wit and passion, all the while using his humor and eloquence to keep attention focused on himself. Thus if he rejected some of the pressure that informed the roles assigned him by his parents, he reveled in the actual fencing of the conversational repartee.[22]

The same sense of delight infused his play, much of which consisted of engaging his sister Dorothy in one-on-one battles. When they lived in the city, their social life often entailed "making dates" with friends, whether to go to the theater or to play. In spite of the Depression, the Lowensteins were very well off and lived in a fashionable neighborhood near Central Park. But unlike their counterparts in ethnic and working-class areas, the children in those elegant apartment buildings did not gather spontaneously on the street to engage in sports or expeditions. Instead, their social interactions were formally organized, in the style of their parents.

The same arrangements prevailed—even more so—when the family moved to the suburbs. Schoolmates were far removed, and only one other family on the street had children of the same age. Suburban life at the beginning of World War II was different from that of the Levittowns that sprang up after the war. Houses were more isolated—not ringed in concentric circles with common play space, as they would be later—and the informal practice of going in and out of the next-door neighbor's house that became synonymous with 1950s suburban life was relatively nonexistent. Consequently, Allard and Dorothy spent hours devising their own recreation. They used a special sleeping porch in the Harrison house as a playroom; sometimes they would crawl across the tile roof from their rooms to get to it. One of their games involved sectioning off the playroom by national boundaries, then dividing up soldiers, cannons, and ships among the competing powers to fight their own version of World War II. The cannons fired spaghetti as ammunition, and the two armies would battle sometimes for days. But Al always won, just as he always won his favorite game of all, Politics. A board game like Monopoly, Politics included a map of the United States; players tried to win those states with the most electoral votes. In that game, too, Dorothy reported, "I don't know anybody who ever beat Al." Even as a young child, Al kept notebooks filled with political data.[23]

The young Lowenstein's school life obviously reflected a similar drive to excel. Because his parents were wealthy and concerned about giving their children every advantage, each youngster was sent to private school. All four attended the Ethical Culture School during the elementary grades; Larry and Al went to Horace Mann for high school (Bert and Dorothy went to Fieldston). Al resented private school, sensing the elitism and privilege of such a setting, but at Ethical Culture, he lived in an environment suffused with the progressive political values of Algernon Black, founder of the school. There, according to his sister Dorothy, "social awareness and liberal thought . . . [were] the bywords." By the time Allard was ready for second grade, his teachers had already identified him as a brilliant student and advanced him immediately to the third grade, moving him ahead of his class by one year. Allard handled the adjustment "with exceeding rapidity and ease," his teachers said. "Socially he is moderately successful, more so when he is in charge and managing. He sets high standards for himself [and shows] perseverance [that is] unusual." Although later evaluations would note a certain disorder and fussiness in his personal manners, as well as "careless habits of speaking" (traits that, to Allard's consternation, his father would be obsessive about), he seemed effectively to carry out, in his early school years, his parents' injunction to succeed.[24]

Thus, despite the enormous conflicts that buffeted Lowenstein during his formative years, a substantial core of positive experiences remained.

He thrived in school, honed his competitive edge both in sibling rivalry with Larry and Dorothy and in intellectual combat with his father, and somehow managed to strike a balance between the insistent demands and conflicts of his parents and the simpler, more affectionate security of his Goldberg family relatives.

In a play he wrote in 1937, Allard reflected his own sense of the family dynamics that were shaping him. Called "A Day with Bodo," the drama describes a medieval fiefdom presided over by the feudal lord Bodo, who has three children at home, including a daughter who always cries. Awakened early one morning by his intrusive mother Ermentrude, who insists that he get up because his father is waiting (and besides, she has arisen early to make his breakfast), the young son Wido prepares to ride off with his father to visit the peasants doing their chores. When Wido remarks that "it's awful hot, ain't it," Bodo says, "I don't like your language." The son then responds, "All right, then, it's terribly hot, isn't it." After similar exchanges over not having his shirt tucked in and other misdemeanors, Wido comments, "I told you Papa was a better worker [than others]. He [gets] along perfectly. . . . Papa never lets his tongue slip. . . . No excuses." The duo return home to a meal carefully prepared by Ermentrude, who asks Bodo how work was. "Tiring but successful," he replies. "I can't eat any more. I'm going to bed."[25]

The eight-year-old had depicted with acute accuracy a home life awash with many tensions and some rewards. But for the moment, he seemed able to stay afloat and resist the undertow, finding sufficient satisfaction in his positive relationships and other activities to sustain and animate his enthusiasm for life.

POLITICS AND A WAY OF LIFE

One of those activities was politics. In addition to enjoying the board game that he played with his sister, Allard was passionately committed to expressing his political commitments and rallying support for his causes. At the age of seven, he and his sister were circulating leaflets for Franklin Roosevelt's reelection on the corner of Central Park West and Eighty-first Street. Two years later, he was doing the same for the Republican side during the Spanish civil war. As editor of the school newspaper at Ethical Culture, the sixth-grader initiated a fund-raising drive for the Spanish Republicans. The goal had been $5, the final sum a glorious total of $18.26. This money, his editorial said, was raised "for a noble cause . . . [showing] that Americans are interested in preserving democracy and fighting fascism." The same issue of the school paper urged students to telegraph their congressman demanding the immediate lifting of the arms embargo on Republican Spain. When the Fascist forces eventually triumphed, Lowenstein wept bitterly, calling it one of the worst moments of his entire life. In every election from 1936 onward, state or national, Lowenstein plotted the races, calculated the odds, and pleaded for his candidates. With friends, he debated how much aid the Allies should give to the Soviet Union after the Germans invaded in 1941; to the editor of *The Nation* he wrote letters demanding harsher criticism of Francisco Franco and greater support for progressive candidates like the American Labor party's gubernatorial nominee. In almost all these ventures, Lowenstein defended the underdog, the outcast, the less established cause.[26]

At least in part, these allegiances could be traced to Lowenstein's home environment. Gabriel Lowenstein had been an ardent socialist and political activist, especially in his youth. He joined the supporters of Morris Hilquit and Eugene Debs during their campaigns in New York and helped organize workers in the garment industry when the International Ladies' Garment Workers Union was breaking down barriers of ethnicity and gender with its explosive unionizing efforts of the 1910s. Besides his political talk at dinner every night, Gabriel's record of union organizing and support for socialism helped explain his son's identification with the Spanish Republicans and with the American Labor party in New York.

Yet Allard clearly went beyond his family's politics, even at the tender age of thirteen. Gabriel bitterly denounced Al's hero, Fiorello LaGuardia—"your angel"—for causing the Harlem race riot of 1943 by appeasing the "hoodlums, gangsters and muggers." "I despise . . . these people," he wrote Allard, "who have never done a day's [honest] work in their lives . . . and who think they can solve the world's problems by making wild statements." Nor was Al's brother Larry any less critical, calling his brother's candidate for governor "a well-meaning fifth columnist" and accusing Al of using "communistic statements as your authority." Thus, family political convictions told only part of the story.[27]

More important was Al's own feeling of marginality, his sense of being different from—and inferior to—the mainstream norm. Notwithstanding his stepmother's idyllic portrayal of his good looks, others saw him as "physically a kind of weakling . . . [who] thought of himself as extremely homely." Allard had thick "Coca-Cola" glasses that seemed to magnify his eyes, a friend recalled, and "his most characteristic posture was to sit with his finger pressed against the tip of his nose [as if] he was trying to do away with about half an inch of his nose . . . or press it upward." As a youngster, he was interested in neither sports nor more conventional peer group activities. In fact, the friend noted, "Allard was thought to be quite peculiar."[28]

Lowenstein's sensibility toward outsiders also reflected his ambivalence about being a Jew. Despite Florence's religiosity ("To me," she wrote, "Passover means Allard to a large extent"), the young Lowenstein seemed to identify more with his father's agnosticism than with his mother's devotion. One night Gabriel said, "Oh, God," and six-year-old Allard said, "Daddy, why do you appeal to God, you don't believe in him." But Allard also felt deeply the searing pain of being stigmatized as a Jew. "That's such an important part of Al's identity conflicts," Jenny Littlefield said. "The sense of isolation out there [in Harrison] where all the neighbors were Christians [and] they were the only car in miles with a Roosevelt bumper sticker." World War II was being fought; Nazism was at its peak, and anti-Semitism and the Holocaust were sweeping Germany. Even in suburban Westchester, Al was ridiculed and beaten up by some of the Gentiles in the community. He might make jokes later about "being a little Jewish boy from the West Side," but the experience of being a victim was "a great source of pain to him." "I don't know if I have a way of understanding how horrible . . . that kind of thing must have been," Jenny Littlefield said, or how important it was to show "that you're okay, that you can be accepted by them." His friend Sandy Friedman agreed. "[Allard] felt a very powerful sense of inferiority in some ways . . . and then there was the whole thing about being a Jew . . . [and] whatever he was doing with his nose had something to do with that."[29]

Perhaps most important, there were the "outcasts" in his own world—the servants in his household, the workers in the cafeteria chain his father owned. Rex Freeman was a black chauffeur and handyman in the Lowenstein home in Harrison. He befriended Al and Dorothy and played games with them. He became, in effect, both a playmate and part of the extended family. When he went off to join the army in World War II, he wrote regularly to both children. But his letters to Allard were searing indictments of the horror of racism in the South. After describing the murder of a black man who dared to sit in the front of a bus, Freeman said: "Colored soldiers and the colored race . . . have nothing whatsoever to fight for here in Georgia or the south generally. . . . I'm afraid I can't feel the same toward my country again. . . . Looking at the situation through the eyes of the Negroes of Georgia, we have absolutely nothing to fear from the Japs or the Germans."

Their correspondence was remarkable. Somehow a bond had already developed between this twelve-year-old and a household employee more than twice his age, with the result that the two had an astonishingly candid exchange about an issue that few other black and white Americans could even talk to each other about. "I have always felt that I could speak freely to you," Freeman wrote, and so when Al asked him directly to comment on race relations in the armed forces, Freeman responded, appreciating "deeply the fact that you are interested and have the guts to speak up for what you think is right and lash out against injustice." Al had invited Freeman to reveal his "bitterness of soul." "At such times," Freeman wrote, "one must unburden oneself to someone, and who would understand conditions or me better than you? I wouldn't dare utter some of the things I confided to you to anyone else." As extraordinary as the communication itself was Lowenstein's ability to generate trust, to evoke from others shared confidences and the faith that these would be neither violated nor betrayed. It was a role he would play over and over again.[30]

Thus, in the end, Lowenstein's political sympathies reflected his own personal experiences as much as his father's predilections. "Allard's tremendous compassion for, and empathy with the [oppressed]," his best friend concluded, "came from a feeling of himself as an underdog." And so, he reached out and identified with those who were similarly on the margins or in rebellion, whether the scrappy anti-Fascists in the Spanish civil war, the black and Hispanic women who worked at the steam tables in his father's cafeteria, or the chauffeur who shared with a twelve-year-old his deepest pain at being treated like a nonperson.[31]

That explanation helps to illuminate at least partially Lowenstein's writing and politics during his high school years. Horace Mann was a staid, socially conservative, and politically complacent school. Despite a student body full of people who would later become famous (Roy Cohn, Anthony Lewis, William Greene, and Si Newhouse), the school, Anthony Lewis subsequently wrote, "fostered . . . ignorance [about] politics and social and economic conditions." Lowenstein "[was not] quite respectable" to Lewis and his friends; he was too "Bohemian," too liberal, perhaps too esoteric. Although he ranked academically in the top 10 percent of the student body and came close two years in a row to winning election as class president (he lost by two votes both years), Lowenstein was different, perhaps the only person in the school with his particular interests and convictions. As editor of the school paper in 1944–45, he championed popular causes such as a coed "canteen" without adult chaperones and opposition to a curfew for juveniles. But he also continued his defense of the Spanish Republicans and other causes that set him apart. Indeed, so well known was he for his politics that one young woman who was asking him to a dance pleaded with him not to let political considerations determine his response.[32]

Most revealing of his thoughts during these years, perhaps, were a series of term papers that focused on the individual in history as hero or villain; and on how much difference an individual can make in history. Two of the papers dealt with Pericles and Caesar, as though each represented a possible answer to the puzzle. Lowenstein observed that Pericles was a democrat, not a dictator, who used his speeches to mobilize the masses and evoke trust, but never in a demagogic fashion. Pericles, he concluded, proved that "democracy does work." (His teacher responded, "But Democracy is not one man rule.") Caesar, by contrast, seemed to Lowenstein like Huey Long—a flawed character posing as a friend of the common man who subsequently betrayed the people's trust. The keys, it seemed, were individual character and whether the *leader* decided to make democracy work.[33]

Although on one level these papers represented a simple workaday response by a bright student to a series of random assignments, on another they suggested the beginnings of an exploration into how, or whether, an individual could conceive of a life committed to politics. The choices might be bipolar—democrat or dictator?—but the scenarios vibrated with real questions. Does the individual make a difference? Through what means, demagoguery or reason? Is there a raison d'être for courage in the face of inexorable fate? Above all, how does the individual find out who he is, and how does he chart his path to independence, especially if he feels himself different from all others?

THE FAMILY STRUGGLE—CONTINUED

If the last question was one that Lowenstein was exploring intellectually at Horace Mann, it was *the* issue central to the emotional struggle he was waging at home with his parents, especially with his father. Florence continued to dote on Al, lauding him to the sky one moment, nudging him to be more responsive and attentive to her the next. In a near parody of the stereotypical Jewish mother, she wrote him at camp how much she was

"looking forward to seeing our doctor, our farmer, our lawyer, our statesman, and our boy. *Such a boy!*" If Bert was to bring Gabriel fame in the
scientific world, she told her husband, Allard would do the same in politics. Yet Florence bemoaned Al's failure to share the details of his life at
camp with her. "You open your heart and feelings to everybody but us,"
she complained. "You seem to have shut yourself up away from us and I'm
annoyed and disturbed at a little boy who seems to want to draw away.
After all, your best friends are us. Remember that!" Constantly scolding
Allard for the "undertones" she detected in his phone calls when he was
away, she accused him of engaging in a calculated effort to hurt her feelings, all the while devoting his energies to his "causes," like rights for Negroes. After all, she wrote, "I'm a minority person too; maybe you ought to
concentrate on matters pertaining to persons whom you know best."[34]

Gabriel remained Allard's pivotal authority, engaged in what would be
for both a lifelong battle for control of his soul. On a daily basis, there
were the admonitions—"systematize your work, systematize your hours of
study . . . get out of the habit of procrastinating . . . keep your teeth clean,
scrub, soap and wash [your hands], keep your nails short, tie your laces."
It would be a mistake to underestimate the cumulative impact of this
drum roll. Whether over breakfast or through letters, Gabriel pounded
away at his children—and especially Allard—to conform totally to his almost tyrannical regimen of respectability and personal orderliness. Even
Allard's sojourn at camp was not for the purpose of having fun: he was to
become "the ideal boy that I had expected you to be."[35]

Yet these injunctions simply reflected how soaring and boundless were
Gabriel's hopes for his youngest son. The intensity of his passion to shape
and mold Allard's hour-to-hour behavior was a mirror of his hunger for
this young man to break all barriers and conquer the world. Gabriel had a
vision for Allard, a vision that in many ways projected the side of his own
personality that he had denied when he opted for the life of a businessman. Allard would be all the things that Doc had put behind him, and
Doc, through Allard, would finally fulfill his own deepest ambitions.[36]

In an extraordinary letter he wrote to Allard in the summer of 1943,
Gabriel conveyed these hopes. In the middle of a sound sleep, Gabriel
wrote, "a vision, à la Joan of Arc," had come to him. He was "in a marble
castle suspended from the stars," being served by four angels, three male
and one female. ("I know there are no female angels," he said, "but the vision was a vision, therefore we will assume that there are female angels.")
The first angel was a twenty-four-year-old man, "happy [and] cheerful,"

whose task was "to provide for the health" of the family. Second was a twenty-year-old, "quiet, logical . . . non-garrulous, loving and lovely," whose job was "to provide food and other necessities of life." The fourth angel was a twelve-year-old, "vibrant with health and joy," whose "function was to bring cheer . . . and happiness." But the *third* angel was different. "He really set an example for all the other angels." Fourteen years old, "he was interested in philosophy, logic, history, politics and all other matters of the spirit. Ah, what a pleasant angel he was. . . . He was the incarnation of intellectual angelility. . . . [His] function was to provide all the mental relaxation for the family." Indeed, angel number three was such a perfect model that "he spoke quietly and slowly . . . was neat in dress and appearance . . . his shirt never stuck out of his pants, and his shoe laces were always tied. . . . What a sight for the angels." But then, Gabriel wrote, "I awoke, damn it! . . . I saw heartaches, ugly reality . . . quarrels, arguments." Maybe, he concluded, his dream would come true some day. In the meantime, "I am hoping and expecting with impatience the return of the prodigal."[37]

With precision and poignancy, Gabriel had offered his own fantasy of a "Lowenstein dynasty." "That is exactly how he felt about each of them," his daughter-in-law Marie commented. Bert had ceased to occupy the premier niche in his father's dreams; in fact, he soon would shatter Gabriel's world by experiencing a series of mental breakdowns. Larry was indeed the "provider"—conventional, reliable, but also, in Gabriel's eyes, unexciting. He would soon join the restaurant business and be responsible for everyone's material comfort. Dorothy was the young athlete whose grace on the tennis court and golf course always delighted her father, the Lithuanian immigrant. But it was Allard who now carried the hopes and bore the weight of his father's personal agenda for rescue and redemption, who was "the incarnation of intellectual angelility."[38]

The young man fought back tenaciously. Allard resisted his father's insistence that he become "the ideal boy" and recoiled from the overpowering reach of the man who wanted to dictate his life. "When I spoke to you . . . on the way to the city on the day you left for camp," Gabriel wrote, "you shook your head and told me that you were not interested." He went on:

> No man but a fool would permit his ego to overpower him to that extent. I am as mad as hell and I mean to be mad for a long time. . . . This is a sermon or "lecture" if you please. I suppose you will throw it in the basket before you read it. The loss will be all yours. If you consider this letter a punishment, you shall have learned something of great importance. . . .

"He who loves his son punishes him." . . . Based upon this Biblical admonition, I did not love you in the past. I expect to acquire a tremendous love for you in my old age.

But Allard continued to resist. "Dad has some peculiar conceptions about me," he wrote his parents; "it is very discomforting and not at all healthy." On both counts, of course, he was right, far more than he perhaps knew. But that did not lessen the immediate dilemma of finding a way out.[39]

The very complexity of Gabriel's mixed messages compounded the problem, making it even more difficult for Allard to know how to respond. Each letter, whatever its surface rigidity and repetition, contained a subtext of humor and love. "Consider your brothers and sisters," Gabriel wrote in a letter admonishing Allard to be the "outstanding one" in the family; "you should have no difficulty in being a top man among those mediocrities." The sentence almost assumed that Al could see the smile on Gabriel's face, "your slavedriving and harassing father." But how did one discern the real message contained in such "playful" letters? Allard should be proud to be Gabriel's "black sheep," Doc once wrote:

> I prefer black sheep to gray ones for I always prefer strong colors to weak ones. I probably would have loved to have at least one of my children a green sheep, but no such luck, and so in the absence of green or purple sheep among my children, we will proudly accept black ones as long as they will not permit themselves to be colorless, gray or any other nondescript color. . . . I keep with me the strong hope that you will utilize . . . your intellectual capacities . . . in becoming the pride of our parents. . . . Try to live up to your reputation as your father's pet—a real black sheep.

But which text should one read? The praise for being colorful, or the insinuation of being less than worthy, a "black sheep?"[40]

In fact, Gabriel was desperately in love with his son. He criticized, he preached, he lectured, he tyrannized; but he reposed all the love and aspirations he had in the world in this third-born child. Sometimes he expressed this love with winsome humor. "Maybe you and I will still become good friends," he wrote. "I kind of like you, even though I would never have created you with as many faults if I had my way." And once, when Bert had suffered a breakdown, Gabriel put it directly. "I am guilty of neglect," he said, for not writing. He had been working so hard, day after day, "carrying a tremendous load . . . trying to establish [financial] security" in order to care for Bert. "I stay up nights trying to solve [Bert's problem]," he said, "but to no avail. Nobody ever to talk to, nobody even to confide in, nobody to take counsel with. The burden is mine, the agony is mine. The heartbreaking reality that I am confronted with frightens me, but I will continue to fight to try and save him no matter what the cost." By writing the letter, of course, Gabriel was saying that there *was* someone to talk to, someone to confide in—the only person he could turn to. Not Florence, not Larry, but Al. At the end, in an uneven scrawl, he reverted momentarily to form, enjoining Al not "to neglect, don't postpone . . . systematize your life, your time, your sleep." But then he concluded: "I love you, and I need you. . . . A silly letter, Love, Dad."[41]

At some level of his being, Allard must have understood how deep that love was. Most immediately, he intuited that he could survive the day-to-day regimen by playing up to his father's affection for him. When he came home from a trip, his brother Larry recalled, "[Dad] would become a piece of lettuce . . . I mean, he would write all these nasty letters, but when Al got near him, Al would touch him and say 'Poppy' . . . and he would just crumble at his feet." While Dorothy would lash out and confront her father, getting into endless screaming matches with him, "Al kind of scooted around him." Rather than pay the price of open combat, Al shied away. "He would just sit there," Dorothy commented, "[saying] 'yes, papa, yes papa' and then he would do exactly what he wanted to." Avoidance would defer a showdown until another day, buying him time to discover some other stratagem for keeping himself intact.[42]

For the most part, however, Allard was simply buffeted by the mixed messages and torn by the conflicting pressures. "His father was somebody he really loved and admired," Jenny Littlefield observed, "but on the other hand, [he was] someone whom he was afraid of at times . . . because he was [so] fierce and demanding." To Al's friends, the same impression came through. "What I saw," Sandy Friedman said, "was the intolerable, unbearable, Atlas world pressure on Allard. . . . Gabriel was a very remarkable man, but a very powerful . . . and exacting man . . . a fault-finding man, and a loving man, but a loving man who couldn't really [show] his love." What an impossible dilemma for a fourteen-year-old already tormented by doubts about his physical appearance, his Jewishness, and his social acceptability.[43]

As if all that were not enough, Lowenstein's fourteenth year also brought him face to face with a second secret that would haunt the rest of his days. Keenly aware already of his "difference" from others, Lowenstein discovered with the onset of puberty that he might have instincts his society viewed as deviant. "The urge I get when I see certain boys is getting out-of-control," he confided in his diary in 1943. Allard became aware of his sexual impulses at roughly the same time he discovered the truth about Augusta. Only this secret was even more taboo. "God, God, what will I do?" he exclaimed in his diary. At least he could share the secret about his mother with two other people. But there was no one—not even his best friend Sandy Friedman—whom he could tell about his "urges" toward boys. Friedman himself, already in the process of becoming aware of his own homosexuality, recalled it as a "source of tremendous shame . . . feeling like the pariah or outcast, Ishmael." Some part of Allard may have "sensed that aspect of himself," Friedman speculated. "I don't think Allard was ever comfortable with his body in those days . . . he was not comfortable 'in his own skin.'" But the very shame associated with homosexuality made voicing such thoughts unthinkable. It was a time in America when love between members of the same sex was treated as perverse, dirty, furtive, and evil—the very antithesis of those qualities Allard aspired to, being honorable, wholesome, clean, and aboveboard. Even to admit of such an interest was thus inconceivable, especially in a moralistic household where allegiance to noble causes was the order of the day.

As a result, Al kept this secret completely to himself. Resolving that "this can't go on," the tormented adolescent determined to take control of his unacceptable urges. He would act the role of the traditional heterosexual, play the dating game, and nurture romantic images of finding the right girl. In the meantime, he would find a constructive outlet for his other urges. "I can see only one solution," he wrote, "very good friendships." If he could translate his interest in boys into platonic relationships, the stigma of sexual perversion could be averted while his impulse for bonding was gratified. But how, he asked, could this be done? The search for an answer would occupy him from that moment forward.[44]

Meanwhile, in the face of all these pressures, Allard could only persevere in building his own distinctive world while continuing to "scoot around" his father. One way of doing this, as reflected in his diary entry, was simply to acquire as many friends as possible. Beginning a pattern that he would continue the rest of his life, Lowenstein wrote letters and postcards to virtually every person he met, asking them to list their favorite actors and actresses, compiling and comparing "Hit Parade" preferences, commenting on the latest Katharine Hepburn movie. Perhaps as much a way of making contact with people as anything else, his correspondence helped fill Lowenstein's life with activity and, together with his schoolwork and editing of the *Horace Mann Record*, kept him busy enough to leave little time for introspection.

Most of these friendships were casual, not intimate. Beginning a pattern that would became legendary in the 1950s and 1960s, Al would invite a friend to join him for dinner at Granson's, his father's restaurant; upon arrival, however, the friend would discover that ten other people had been invited as well. "Al had a tremendous desire to bring his friends together," his school friend Alice Gilbert remarked. But he also had an abiding fear of being alone with a person unless he felt sure of his or her interest in him. Hence, he preferred to make social contact with large numbers of people, inviting them to parties at his house, prodding them to write letters to keep up their end of the correspondence (he would most often write only postcards, making the exchange woefully unbalanced), and focusing on the common ground of popular culture (movies and records) as a meeting place.[45]

Another way Allard coped was through developing an alternative definition of reality. If New York and family meant Jewishness, anti-Semitism, insecurity, and conflict, there was another world, called America, where innocence reigned, good and evil were clear, and simplicity prevailed. "Allard had a myth," Sandy Friedman observed, "a kind of Hallmark card vision of America, of Saturday night dances and moonlight rides and holding hands and drinking Cokes." It was like a MacKinley Kantor valentine, Friedman said, everything perfect and right, with barefoot boys and hayrides and no Jews, no fights, no complexity. Al used to love to host MacKinley Kantor–style parties, Friedman said, "and we'd all be in saddle shoes and sweaters and doing the American hop." Ironically, in some ways the Goldbergs fit that myth—theirs was "conflict-free Jewishness"—but, so, too, did Katharine Hepburn movies and Broadway musicals. Whenever he was most in need of escape, Jenny remembered, Al would say, "Let's get back to the real world and go to the movies."[46]

The Vermont farm where Al went in the summers both to work as a volunteer and to take part in a teenage drama company had some of those traits. The people were simple, the relationships wholesome, the other teenagers full of innocence and idealism. Al's first romance was with one of his fellow campers, a girl named Robin Fau, and it revolved around a magical evening they spent listening to music and thrilling to their experience together during the playing of *their* song, "You'll Never Walk Alone." Like Lowenstein's alternative America, the Rodgers and Hammerstein music pointed to a purer, more noble set of values:

When you walk through a storm, hold your head up high,
And don't be afraid of the dark,
At the end of the storm, there's a golden sky,
And the sweet silver song of a lark.
Walk on through the wind, walk on through the rain
Though your dreams be tossed and blown,
Walk on, walk on with hope in your heart
And you'll never walk alone, You'll never walk alone.

What a glorious vision to escape to! What a stark and simple contrast to the painful complexity of New York.[47]

But Lowenstein's most fundamental response to his father's pressure was rebellion. How better to define a self distinct from the model being imposed by an authoritarian father than to develop and cling to a persona exactly the opposite. Thus, if Gabriel lectured his son to tie his laces, shine his shoes, "systematize" his time, and comb his hair, Al insisted on flouting his instructions at every step. He became legendary for wearing his shirttail outside his pants, he never tied his shoelaces, and he always wore a rumpled jacket. His trademark became the "vile, bilious-green plaid shirt" that he wore everywhere, usually with a brown jacket and blue serge pants, topped off with a red beanie. So notable was Al's dress that when his friend Jean Teller asked him to a formal party, she explicitly warned him not to wear his plaid shirt (though she said she would like to bid on it if it shrank). After a rare occasion on which he was somewhat conventionally clad, Sandy Friedman wrote in astonishment, "Dear boy . . . there was never a time in this life when you came anywhere near looking that presentable." As if to drive the point home, Allard would even come to the dinner table with old ice cream caked on his face and wearing a scrummy hat. While some friends explained these dress choices as a conscious effort to dissociate himself from the privilege and wealth of his family, his real motivation seemed much more transparent—an insistent determination to defy parental injunctions and declare his independence.[48]

Finally, there was Allard's lifelong rejection of his father's impulse to "systematize" his life. *Never* did Al appear on time. The clock seemed to symbolize all that was constraining, rigid, doctrinaire, and tyrannical about his father. Thus, it would not only be ignored; it would be kicked, throttled, and stomped upon. If there was one characteristic that ran through Al Lowenstein's entire life, it was his contempt for punctuality. The trait infuriated his friends. "When we were adolescents," Sandy

Friedman recalled, "over and over and over I would wait forty minutes, and then he'd come and I would just scream . . . [and it became clear] that either I accepted it or I wouldn't be friends with him." Countless others faced the same choice; most capitulated. Allard had succeeded in building his own sense of self, free, if only in part, of that projected by his father. He—and he alone—would be in control, whatever the cost to others.[49]

In the end, however, wars for control over a person's soul are not won or lost by skirmishes. During his early teenage years, Lowenstein had sought a way out, a path by which he could achieve independence and define his own identity within the vortex of a world shaped by his father and mother. Through friends, lifestyle, and his vision of an idealized America, he could begin to develop alternative routes that would enable him, for a while, to avoid dealing directly with his father. There was one question, however, that would brook no delay and whose ramifications bore on all the other conflicts between Al and his father. It posed directly the problem of control, and its resolution shaped Allard's future life course.

CHOOSING A COLLEGE

If he could have dictated his children's college choices, Gabriel Lowenstein would have sent them all to Columbia. He loved the institution, bestowing upon it all the devotion that one might expect from an immigrant who had come to intellectual maturity and career fulfillment through its good offices. Never did he cease lamenting his departure from the Columbia faculty. He still took his children to all the Columbia football and basketball games, followed the intellectual life of his colleagues through their professional journals, and yearned for the kind of continued linkage that would nourish and sustain his own identification with the college.

Although Gabriel had hoped that Bert would attend Columbia, he was at least mollified by his son's entrance into Harvard instead. After all, this was the giant of the Ivy League, and any man could be proud to have a son earn a degree from America's most distinguished university, especially in three years. Besides, there were Larry and Allard. Under Gabriel's prodding, Larry had applied to Columbia; with Gabriel's influence, he not only was admitted but also succeeded in getting a dormitory room, something not many New York City students were able to do. But after three days in residence, Larry decided he could not go through with it; turning his back on Columbia, he chose to attend Cornell instead. "[Dad] never recovered from my leaving," Larry later said, "[but] I just had to get away from New York. I don't think I was trying to get away from home . . . I really wasn't unhappy [there] . . . . I just think I wanted to get out of New York." And so the only one left was Allard, by then the repository of Gabriel's hopes and dreams.[50]

Although the record of Gabriel's exchanges with Allard during the academic year of 1944–45 is scanty, there is good reason to believe that the tension between them reached new heights as Allard's college decision date approached. For the most part, Al seems to have consciously ignored or avoided Gabriel. "You have refused to consult me," his father wrote Allard after the choice had been made. "You have made your mistakes. You might have made them even after consulting me, but at least you would have had the consolation that you could have blamed your father." With frustration and some bitterness, Gabriel berated Allard during his first year at college for "having benefited nothing from your experience of last year. . . . You cannot go through life the way you have tried to."[51]

But if Gabriel was intentionally ignored, he would not go unheard. During this year of decision, he mobilized Larry and Bert to be his surrogates. Having determined that Columbia was perhaps too much to hope for, he zeroed in on Harvard as the school of preference. Evidently Al had let it slip that he might choose Michigan, or Wisconsin, or some other midwestern school (in keeping, perhaps, with his Hallmark card vision of the heartland), and so Bert wrote him declaring that Harvard was "perhaps the only oasis of cosmopolitanism in all of the states." If Al was really "bent on meeting midwesterners," he said, "it might interest you to know that we have more Michiganders on the Harvard faculty than does Michigan." Only Harvard, Bert insisted, ranked with Oxford and Cambridge, and if Al would apply, Bert promised, as a faculty member of the medical school, to expedite his application. Chiming in three weeks later, Larry warned Al that he was "crazy to go anywhere but Harvard" and said he would "take it as a personal insult if you don't apply." Larry had only to add, perhaps unconsciously remembering his own experience, "and when you get in you had better go!" Later Larry would recall that he had no idea of even where Michigan was, and that Bert hated Harvard. The whole enterprise of the letters, Larry concluded, had to have been Gabriel's idea.[52]

Not only was a massive struggle going on, but it clearly intensified with time. In an extraordinary letter on the eve of Al's sixteenth birthday, Bert lambasted his youngest brother for the immaturity with which he had approached this decision. "The one thing that is certain to cause the most trouble," he wrote, "is just not to face the decision, and to run away. . . . You haven't sat down to think about it rationally for even the semblance of an hour." In Bert's mind, there was no question that only an Ivy League school made sense for Al. But Allard had not even developed the case for an alternative choice! Instead, whenever the issue was raised, he had responded "by breaking down and shouting, or by running into that bathroom . . . or by saying that 'you don't care what anybody says about it.'" Reflecting at least some sensitivity to Allard's perspective, Bert assured him that "none of the family would have the slightest desire to influence you away from a sound point of view that you have adopted after careful thought," but Allard had not even faced up to the question. "What do you think you are running away from?" Bert asked, "because whatever it is, you don't get away from it that way—it's only inside you."[53]

Bert, of course, had put his finger precisely on the problem. In the process of conveying Gabriel's anxiety over all the devices Al was using to avoid dealing with the college question, he had also identified Al's fundamental determination to escape, to fly away. Indeed, Al may even have heard Bert's question, "What do you think you are running away from?" and understood it. Both Jenny Littlefield and Sandy Friedman—the two people most likely to know—later commented that at the age of fifteen or sixteen, Al experienced a crisis and reached a decision to remake himself, to cease being "the brilliant little boy who was going to fight his way to the top and do what . . . his father wanted him to do," and instead to become a different kind of person "whose values were not as monetary." Like his film heroine Katharine Hepburn, he would *will* a change in his life and, with resolute determination, become a new person. "Al had a . . . fierce will," Jenny observed, and in the account he gave her of his childhood, this was the moment when he decided that, whatever the odds, he would make himself into something different—*positively* different. Other people were trying to change him into the image *they* had of what he should be. But as he wrote Sandy Friedman in June, "Only one thing I am sure of: either I've been right since my 'great divide'—right in the *essentials* as modified by time and experience . . . or else I am *wrong*. . . . I know my viewpoints [on how to dress, on college, on Zionism] are often against the tide my elders swim mentally in; but I am used to being against the tide, if I'm convinced my side is *right*."[54]

Yet if he were to find a way of answering the question, "What are you running away from?" he had also to face the question, "Where are you running to?" Notwithstanding his sense, both at the time and in retrospect, that this was a moment of crisis, Allard in all likelihood chose to respond to these questions primarily by indirection. He never clearly confronted his father over the choice of a college—or, for that matter, over any other issue. "It [was] a familial characteristic," Marie Lowenstein observed. "They [seemed to acquiesce] and then went and did what they wanted to do." So, too, in this instance. Procrastinating endlessly, Allard fussed over his applications to Harvard and Yale, finally submitting them—as if to please his father—but so late after the deadline had passed that he could not be accepted. The tactic was devious, but successful. In the meantime, he was sending off his applications elsewhere. And in April, he announced he would attend the University of North Carolina in Chapel Hill.[55]

The choice in some ways seemed bizarre. Why would a Jewish boy from the West Side of Manhattan go to a small southern town so "Christian" and traditional that its inhabitants (and the alumni of its university) called it "the southern side of heaven"? How could someone raised in a culture of sour cream and the *New York Times* find a home in a world of grits and the *Chapel Hill Weekly?* Where would a sophisticated intellectual devoted to the Broadway theater create a niche in a village with two cinemas? And how could a partisan of integration and the Spanish Republicans "fit in" at a school that had been racially segregated for its entire history?

To ask the questions, of course, was to find the answers. If Chapel Hill was not the geographical embodiment of Lowenstein's "Hallmark card vision of America," it came so close that only a stage set could have improved on it. From the Colonial Drugstore with its soda pop and stools to the Carolina Coffee Shop with its fresh baked biscuits and redeye gravy, this was *the* America of "Saturday night dances and moonlight rides and holding hands." And far from being a liability, North Carolina's Jim Crow culture was an attraction. Here, after all, "were all his beloved black people," commented Sandy Friedman, at a time (World War II was ending) when someone like Al Lowenstein could make a difference and help end that scourge of a social system. Chapel Hill was even—and perhaps especially—attractive because it was so un-Jewish. "That's one of the reasons we went there," recalled his sister, also a UNC student later. Al may have told Jenny that he never wanted to bob his nose or change his name, but, she said, "you have to assume that somewhere in the dark recesses of his soul there would have been a temptation to do that. . . . And look where he goes to college."

And so the choice was made. "He was going to live in a bigger world," Jenny Littlefield said, "and he was going to be accepted by a larger community." So he went to Chapel Hill, perhaps because it was as far away as one could get from New York in a one-day train ride, but basically because "it was totally opposite from [everything] he'd grown up with."[56]

CONCLUSION

The decision to go to Chapel Hill represented a fitting end to one part of Allard Lowenstein's life, even as it signified a brand new beginning for another part. There had been so many roles to perform, so much pressure on Allard to exhibit his own precocious talents so that his father—and stepmother—might be fulfilled. Now he had escaped, at least physically, from his need to "scoot around" the family. Not only had he run *to* a place that promised clarity and simplicity, but he had run *from* a place—and a father—that symbolized complexity and conflict. At some level, everyone understood that. As Dorothy reported to Al in a letter, whenever Gabriel was asked by a visitor where Al was, he replied: "Oh, that son of a bitch! Why he's at the University of North Carolina (said as if it was Sing Sing or something); that jerk, he's in *exile*" (italics added).[57]

But if going away to a school exactly opposite from what his father desired helped to solve one problem, it simply provided a new context for other abiding dilemmas in Al's life. There remained his terrible sense of inferiority, of being different, marginal, unlikable—perhaps at some level even unacceptable. In part, that related to the feeling of inadequacy he had about his body and appearance. "He didn't like himself physically," Jenny Littlefield recalled. "He always thought of himself as an ugly duckling . . . [and so] he'd seem awkward . . . he'd sort of stumble into a room. . . . [He had a sense of] perpetual discomfort . . . with himself." Lacking confidence in his own body, he also lacked confidence in his attractiveness to others, doubting whether they would value him; and so he sought security in numbers, in having many acquaintances, hoping for validation even while fearing rejection.

Yet, in a deeper sense, Lowenstein's feeling of vulnerability went back to fundamental issues of identity—who he was and where he had come from. At one level, that involved his real mother, her death, and the concerted effort to hide the truth about her. "You don't have to be a psychoanalyst to know *that's* important," Sandy Friedman noted. But there was also Allard's confusion and ambivalence over his Jewishness, his identification with the oppressed and the outsider on the one hand, and his desire to flee from anti-Semitism, push his nose back to a smaller size, and sing the Notre Dame fight song on the other. And all of his identity issues were linked to the most potentially explosive issue of all—his sexual identity. If being Jewish in a WASP culture full of prejudice was enough to make a person feel different and insecure, how much more excruciating would it be to fear that one had sexual impulses classified as impure and impermissible. How to deal with the hidden urges, the difference that was the most unacceptable, the secret that could not be shared even with one's best friend; where to find someone to trust, how to develop the capacity to believe in other people enough to confide in them, how to accept oneself as well as be accepted by others—these were his compelling questions.

It was not surprising, then, that Lowenstein devised his own fantasy life of a purer, more innocent America. The simplicity of a MacKinley Kantor valentine or a Rodgers and Hammerstein musical offered exactly the right antidote to the turgid, painful, and conflict-ridden life of his immediate family. Here too was another explanation for Lowenstein's politics: if the world was divided into heroes and villains, Fascists and Republicans, he could identify with the underdog and feel strength and confidence in himself precisely because of the justice of his cause. The cause enhanced him, even as he became more acceptable in his own eyes by identifying with it. With the Spanish Republicans, and with Rodgers and Hammerstein, Lowenstein found affirmation and clarity, while at home there seemed only fear and confusion.

Thus, it all came back in some ways to Gabriel. The central figure, *the* authority, the source of all intimidation and control, Gabriel was the one individual Allard could *not* go to in his moments of crisis because of fear and the instinctive sense that his father did not want to talk about issues that were taboo—or perhaps was even incapable of doing so. Yet this one man, so lovable on the one hand, so full of wit, intellectual acuity, and passion, was also the person who clearly depended so much on his youngest son that it was almost unbearable to imagine disappointing him. How was Allard to handle such fundamental emotions, such profound conflicts, especially when he knew from his experience with the secret of Augusta's death that Gabriel was unapproachable?

Al's response to that dilemma had always been avoidance. He "scooted around" Gabriel, finding ways to circumvent the immediate challenge, delaying the time of accountability, running to some other reality. As a youngster, Al would "tweak" his father on the cheek, turn his harsh demeanor into jello just by uttering a sweet "Papa," or use his wit and intellect to entertain and thus deflect. When tensions worsened, he relied more on direct escape—running to the bathroom or bedroom to avoid a confrontation, or, eventually, putting fourteen hours by train between home and college. From early on, his most reliable ploy was simply arranging his life so that he was never alone with his father. "I never thought that was an accident," Marie Lowenstein said. "He never came anywhere by himself . . . and in his own home . . . he would show up always surrounded by people. . . . That was part of his defense mechanism, of not having a one-on-one confrontation with his father."[58]

In the end, Lowenstein tried to create a new self that would be different and free of the old self he hoped to leave behind in New York. In some ways, that effort was connected to his choice of personal image—the untied laces, the shirttail outside the pants, the plaid shirt. "Those are all [elements of] some kind of eccentric image-making," Friedman said, "[by] someone who wants to represent himself very differently from the other members of the family and friends and society." But there was a method to Lowenstein's slovenliness as well. After all, Friedman noted, "if you were coming in—late—with the shoelaces untied and this armful of papers . . . it attracts a lot of [attention], it's exhibitionistic in some way . . . it's called 'making an entrance.'" Not only might such theatricality alleviate the danger of not being noticed or appreciated; being late and eccentrically dressed also ensured that the gathering would focus on the distinctive personality playing the part, and on the message he had to convey.[59]

In perhaps the greatest irony of all, acting out the unkempt, unconventional, disorderly role that was anathema to Gabriel might also have been Allard's surest means of sustaining that relationship and guaranteeing his father's persistent attention. If all relationships, especially pathological ones, depend on reciprocity, what better way for Allard to carry out his end of the dynamic tension with his father than through playing the part assigned him? Was there not some level at which both understood that? If the businessman in Gabriel, his conventional side, was represented in Larry, was not his intellectual, dramatic, and bohemian side represented in Allard? And what, after all, was the hidden message of Gabriel's portrayal of Larry as predictable and bland? And of Allard as a colorful sheep, even if a black one?[60]

Thus Allard Lowenstein began his college years in a new place, but with a family history that would powerfully shape the life he carved out for himself. Notwithstanding his self-doubts, he also came to Chapel Hill with a clear sense that he was someone special. His parents had told him that since he was old enough to understand words or intuit feelings. "You are very different," his stepmother wrote him when he was thirteen; "extraordinary is the word I would use." But the family was not alone. "You are you!" Sandy Friedman said in a letter written just after their high school graduation. "There is only one of you in our school—maybe a hundred you's in our generation. . . . Don't ever change yourself. . . . Even your lateness, your bad manners, your lack of poise, your sloppiness. . . . There aren't many people in the world like you . . . and we need everyone of your type we can get." There would be times, still another friend wrote, when Al would be tempted to compromise, or to abstain from engagement. She urged him to remember at such moments the words of William Lloyd Garrison: "I will be as harsh as Truth and as uncompromising as Justice. . . . I will not equivocate—I will not excuse—I will not retreat. . . . And I will be heard."[61]

It was a heavy mandate, but with a clear sense that it was his to carry out, Allard Lowenstein set off for Chapel Hill in June 1945.

2
Halcyon Days

It IS DOUBTFUL THAT THERE EXISTED ANYWHERE ELSE IN AMERICA IN THE summer of 1945 the peculiar combination of town and gown that gave the University of North Carolina (UNC) at Chapel Hill its special texture and atmosphere. The oldest public university in the nation, UNC was situated on a slight rise overlooking the town and residential neighborhoods. Its measured courtyards were distinguished by romantic landmarks such as the "Old Well," a dome-covered meeting place in the center of campus, and its tree-lined paths were broken on occasion by vine-laced arbors. The town merged with the campus as though the two were simply different parts of the same body. Fraternity houses, built in a Greek revival mode, lined Chapel Hill's downtown streets, and the community's many haberdashery and food establishments catered to student as well as older town trade. The symbiosis was reflected in the goings and comings of local inhabitants. President Frank Porter Graham's stately offical residence stood off-campus; two blocks down Franklin Steet, it was open to students and townspeople alike. Some professors, like E. J. Woodhouse, were famous for holding classes on the grass of the quad, within view of the town, or on the stools at the snack bar in Sutton's Drugstore. If you happened to be there in the spring when the dogwoods bloomed, you might easily be persuaded that this was, indeed, "the southern part of heaven."

Thus Allard Lowenstein chose wisely when he selected Chapel Hill as the place where he would—in his sister's words—"get out of that atmosphere [of ethnicity and big-city dirt] . . . and meet more normal, run of the mill Americans." The time was ideal. America had just celebrated victory in Europe and would soon do so in Japan. The war for democracy had focused new attention on the sores of racism and poverty, and the cold war had not yet begun. Tens of thousands of veterans prepared to go to college on the G.I. Bill, while countless others planned to use their government benefits to make a down payment on a first home. Some even talked of starting a national health insurance system. There was a sense of open frontiers, of new opportunities to right ancient wrongs and move toward a more just and humane society. Where better to act on such dreams than a small southern hamlet where liberal opposition to racism was sanctioned, where people were willing to talk seriously about ideas like world government, yet where the pace and quality of life seemed free of fractious squabbling and ethnic rivalry.[1]

It was here that Allard Lowenstein made his public debut in the political arena, addressing issues and taking stands that would persist through his entire career; it was here also that he experienced profound personal relationships whose patterns would recur, shaping his private life until his death. That the personal and political aspects of his life were so intermixed was only fitting, for through most of his days on the planet it was almost impossible to say where the political started and the personal ended—as if Lowenstein, like Chapel Hill and the university, could not draw boundary lines that separated one sphere of life from another.

THE POLITICS OF COLLEGE LIFE

The juxtaposition of personal relationships and political activism began on June 30, 1945, the day sixteen-year-old Allard Lowenstein arrived in Chapel Hill. "It was a warm, rather humid night," Jimmy Wallace and Douglass Hunt recalled, "and there was no air conditioning [in the dormitory]." With the door open, Hunt and Douglass "were discussing the grand affairs of campus politics." Hunt, twenty-one at the time, was the speaker of the student legislature. Wallace, slightly older, had run repeatedly as a candidate for the editorship of the campus paper and was a well-known and outspoken partisan on campus political issues. "It was 10:30 when a person, rather thin . . . came shuffling down the stairs, sort of kicking his

35

feet as he went," they said. With a clock in one hand, he went to get a drink of water, then stuck his head in the door to ask what time it was.

There ensued a four-hour conversation that none of the participants would ever forget. It covered racial bigotry in the South, Zionism, world government, and myriad other subjects. When the three parted, Wallace walked Hunt back to his room on Rosemary Steet, across downtown Chapel Hill. Pausing under a streetlight, Wallace said to Hunt, "You know, [that's] a very smart person, with a remarkable . . . understanding of a tremendous number of things." Hunt agreed; he had been struck particularly by how "extremely articulate . . . quick of mind, [and] nimble of tongue" Lowenstein was, "with a kind of wisdom in dealing with human beings, a kind of kingly view of them . . . much beyond [his] years."[2]

The three became fast friends, and their first conversation would prove to be a road map of the issues and concerns to which each would devote himself, not only at the university but throughout his life. "I find myself fondly thinking," Jimmy Wallace wrote four years later, "that there was always one central friendship, to which all the others were tributary, one compelling bond which lent coherence to all. . . . [It] was the beginning which so carefully . . . bestowed upon our relationship its mark," delivering an enduring "richness and timbre to our lives." With Hunt and Wallace as his anchors, Lowenstein could begin to explore the waters of UNC student politics. By virtue of his friendship with them, he had an authority and legitimacy almost inconceivable for one so young, and he could return to them for counsel whenever he was unsure of which direction to go in.[3]

Predictably, Lowenstein's first campus venture involved university policies on ethnicity. "Questions of race and injustice were very much on his mind," Douglass Hunt said, "and Al had a very keen sense . . . that if human beings didn't tackle problems like that, they didn't get tackled, and he had about as much of an obligation to do something about that as anybody else." Having come to UNC in large part to escape the stigma of being thought of as "a little Jewish boy from the West Side," Lowenstein was particularly sensitive to issues of anti-Semitism. "He was very interested in being accepted [as] . . . a regular fellow," one of his classmates noted. Given such a perspective, it is probably not surprising that Lowenstein immediately noticed that almost all Jews at UNC lived in the same cluster of dormitories. When he made this observation to Wallace and Hunt, they were dumbfounded and asked him for proof—so Allard Lowenstein walked around the dormitories copying from the doors the names of each room's occupants. In every case, it seemed, people with Jewish-sounding names were paired with each other.[4]

With that evidence, Wallace and Hunt proceeded to inform President Graham what was taking place in the liberal bastion of Chapel Hill. "The situation is disgraceful," Hunt wrote Graham, a "flouting" of all the principles for which Chapel Hill stood. Graham reaffirmed that university policy was to assign students to dorm space on a random basis; he sent the students to the university's business manager to confirm that fact while he perused the evidence they had presented. The manager agreed that there was no exclusionist policy but admitted that "like follows like," at which point—"almost by accident," according to Hunt and Wallace—Graham appeared. "Now Claude," he said to the business manager, "the policy of the university is . . . ," and as Hunt and Wallace reported, "with his gnarled little right hand, he [wrote] in the palm of his left hand . . . 'this will not happen anymore.'" And it did not.[5]

The issue of anti-Semitism proved pivotal as well to Lowenstein's abiding concern at Chapel Hill with revising the fraternity system. Every fraternity and sorority on campus, it turned out, practiced a policy of excluding Jews. Moreover, the fraternities largely controlled campus politics by their domination of student government. Seemingly no more liberal in their public approach to student political issues than they were in their private approach to "outsiders," the fraternities thus became a prime target for Lowenstein's political activism. Yet he sought reform, not abolition—unknowingly anticipating the position he would take in later years on countless other issues. "The structure of our present [fraternity] society," he later wrote, "is basically sound, although unhealthy practices have arisen within this structure; therefore, I say, get rid of the unhealthy practices but do not go around making foolish statements favoring abolition of the structure itself, for then undoubtedly some other structure will arise and the basic problem we are fighting will still be left unattacked."[6]

By September, Lowenstein was seeking to achieve his objectives through serving on a special "constitution committee" established to write a new charter that would govern all student activities at UNC. The only freshman involved in a group of high-powered seniors, Lowenstein soon dominated the proceedings, playing a key role in drafting the committee's final document, which had as its hidden agenda the goal of curtailing fraternity power over student government. Simultaneously, and representing nonfraternity concerns, he began the arduous process of creating a strong political alternative to contest the entrenched power of the fraternity status quo.

Lowenstein's reform stance on fraternities would frame his prominent role in student politics throughout his years at Chapel Hill. Few questions evoked a more powerful emotional response than that of preserving or assaulting the Greek system, in which political power was associated with a lifestyle of masculine domination and privilege. The issue encapsulated themes of elitism and racism. Perhaps predictably, the stance that Lowenstein adopted almost ensured his denunciation as an outsider intent on subverting and overthrowing established norms, even though in fact he wanted to clean up, not destroy, the fraternity system. Not for the last time, Lowenstein would find himself portrayed by conservatives as a radical for seeking reform, even as he would later be portrayed by radicals as a conservative for the same reason.

Without any question at all, the allegation of being a subversive would be hurled at Lowenstein when he expressed his commitment to end Jim Crow. Although Chapel Hill prided itself on having an atmosphere of racial tolerance and civility, in substance it was just as segregated as any other southern town. The political scientist V. O. Key hailed North Carolina as "an inspiring exception to southern racism," and Frank Porter Graham achieved national fame as an enlightened college administrator who defended the right of black people to attend meetings on white North Carolina college campuses. But blacks still had to "order out" if they wanted a soda at the Colonial Drugstore; the town's movie theaters had special days when blacks could see a film; and even the "benevolent" university paid its black service employees less than the minimum wage and terminated their services every few months so that they would not go on the personnel records as permanent state employees entitled to fringe benefits such as a medical plan, unemployment insurance, and a pension. Needless to say, no black students attended classes at UNC, nor was there a public forum in the state where blacks and whites could make common cause.[7]

In the aftermath of America's victory against racism in World War II, however, a growing number of students—Lowenstein prominent among them—determined that the time had come to reverse that policy. On his arrival in North Carolina, Lowenstein had intentionally sat in the Negro section of the segregated bus that carried him from Durham to Chapel Hill—to the horror of whites. Finding the right time and place to engage in further protest was always difficult, but when the North Carolina student state legislature convened early in December 1945, the occasion seemed to beg for action. The situation was ideal—a statewide meeting, theoretically of all student government associations, in the capitol building in Raleigh, with large numbers of returning veterans among the college student representatives.

With little advance planning, but with a keen eye for publicity and the symbolism of the moment, Lowenstein and his allies decided to explode a political bomb on the opening night of the convention by introducing a resolution to desegregate the student state legislature. The next day, media attention focused on the Raleigh statehouse as the debate ensued. Lowenstein made a powerful speech, arguing that North Carolina had the opportunity to lead the nation in beginning the final assault on America's oldest national shame. Others joined the fray. The delegate from Wake Forest University moved to table the resolution—a nondebatable motion—seeking, apparently, to kill the change in its tracks. But Douglass Hunt, another UNC delegate, voted *for* the Wake Forest resolution, shrewdly recognizing that as a "supporter" he could then, under parliamentary procedure, ask for a reconsideration of the motion, this time with debate on the substance permitted. (Reconsideration can only be asked for by the winning side, not the losing one). With that bit of political legerdemain accomplished, discussion on the resolution's merits could proceed.[8]

Hunt returned to the podium to reinforce Lowenstein's speech and lay out the political and philosophical groundwork for the resolution. Wallace then stood and, with the penchant for acerbic wit that would become his trademark, mockingly referred to the way the outside world viewed these student legislature meetings as "the children's hour" where young neophytes came to "play" at being statesmen and were tolerated in their "games" because they were so young and unimportant. But, Wallace continued, as he looked out at the "children," he could not help noticing how many of them wore veteran's pins in their lapels. If they had been old enough to die for democracy on the battlefield, he declared, should not these "children" be able, as well, to deliberate on the content and direction of the social order they had defended in uniform. Or must they, like blacks, wait thirty or forty years to "be admitted to these hallowed seats" and be treated as equal citizens. Some might urge delay, he concluded, or even threaten to punish the students by cutting off support for the universities. But if the choice came down to defending free speech or having appropriations cut, "then I say to hell with the appropriations." By a two-to-one margin, the desegregation resolution passed, and when the North Carolina secretary of state urged the students to reconsider and go more slowly, he was hooted down.[9]

Naturally, the student legislature's action prompted an outcry from more conservative citizens. With newspaper stories appearing in the *Washington Post* and elsewhere, North Carolina editorialists and politicians seized on the occasion to blame "agitators from out of state," accusing Wallace among others of being an interloper, and singling out New Yorkers for special condemnation. (Wallace was as native as they came.) "Everybody felt that surely the Communists had arrived and taken over," Wallace later noted. Lowenstein himself reveled in the response, suggesting to some of his New York friends that he might get kicked out of UNC because of his "work against intolerance." But in fact he had simply cemented further his reputation on campus as a principled foe of racialism and ethnic exclusion, in whatever form they might be manifested.[10]

DR. FRANK

Through all these activities, Lowenstein quickly developed ties with his first real political hero, Frank Porter Graham. "Dr. Frank," as he was fondly called on campus, had been trained as a historian, and then, after a few years of teaching at UNC, had risen rapidly through the ranks to become president. Universally revered by liberals both inside the state and out, he provided a model of enlightened white liberalism. A charter member of the Southern Conference on Human Welfare (SCHW) (see chapter 4), he had boldly identified himself with left-wing causes, including the uphill struggle of unions to organize textile and tobacco workers in North Carolina, and the right of dissident political organizations to enjoy free speech on the UNC campus. Each Sunday afternoon, Dr. Frank held an open house in his Franklin Street manse, engaging students in lengthy conversations about affairs of the state and world, then startling them by recalling with exactness their names and interests when they returned at some future time or when he saw them on the quad. Dr. Frank was a slight man, less than 5'5" tall, with hands that were tiny and covered with hair. But the shadow he cast across the campus and state was as large and expansive as his generous soul.

Lowenstein first came to Dr. Frank's attention during his campaign to end the clustering of Jewish students in UNC dormitories. Rapidly, they came to know each other better, at first through the Sunday open houses,

40

then through campus politics, finally through a personal relationship both deeper and wider than political sympathy alone might suggest. Clearly, the political bonds were important. When commentators attacked the UNC students who had led the fight to desegregate the student state legislature, Dr. Frank responded quietly that before any students were thrown out of the university, he would have to be disposed of first. "If the issue were drawn between the freedom of the students to speak their honest opinions," he said, "and the threat of a reduced appropriation as the price of such freedom . . . in all humanity we would take our steadfast stand . . . on the side of freedom and conscience." It was easy to worship such a man.[11]

But gradually, the relationship became more intimate. Al would drive Dr. Frank around town or to the train or airport when he went on trips. By December 1945—six months after Allard had arrived at UNC—his father was referring to Graham as "your old friend." The two saw each other more and more frequently, with Jimmy Wallace even asking Al to put in a good word for him "in your next daily visit to your second home." "You, dear Lancelot," he wrote Al, "have the ear of a very significant gentleman." To Allard, the older man was a role model and a mentor, "almost a saint," according to one person who had seen the relationship evolve. Others made the same observation. Al was so closely tied to the university president that one friend called him "junior grade Graham." Dr. Frank, in turn, grew to regard Al as his conscience, someone he valued for always giving the right advice. Underneath everything else was a relationship that was filial, almost paternalistic. Al once sent a telegram to Dr. Frank, signed, "from your wandering son." When Al turned twenty, it was Graham and his wife who threw him a surprise birthday party. "Here was a man," Jenny Littlefield said, "who . . . in Al's view . . . was so loving and kind," and who sanctioned a different way of living. Here, above all, was someone a young person could venerate without conflict and emulate without pressure. With Dr. Frank behind him, so many goals, personal as well as political, suddenly became possible.[12]

By the time Lowenstein had completed his first six months at UNC, he had achieved a visibility and prominence that were exceptional, especially for one so young. "His rise in [student politics] was meteoric," Wallace and Hunt observed. Lowenstein had been instrumental in generating Graham's intervention on dorm assignments for Jewish students; he had reinvigorated political debate; and above all, Hunt wrote, he had "stopped the process of atrophy in some of us. You were the catalyst that made the

41

[new student] party possible. You have held the constitution committee on the road . . . you changed the freshman class elections bill. You finally got around to infiltrating the [*Daily Tar Heel*] . . . . They all add up to the fact that you are a most amazing freshman."

When Al's brother Larry went to visit Chapel Hill in December, he was astonished at what he found. "It is unbelievable to hear what everybody down there thinks of him," he wrote his father. "I was called aside several times by some of the big shots down there and told all about him." So impressed was one female student that when she saw a piece written by Al, she imagined someone saying at some later date, "this note was dashed off while the statesman was forming those ideas for which he later became famous." Clearly, the sixteen-year-old had very quickly made a mark.[13]

PERSONALITY AND POLITICS

Lowenstein also cut a figure that amused his companions almost as much as it distinguished him from his peers. He wore "sort of catty-looking trousers," one friend commented, topped by a black-and-green plaid lumberjack shirt. His shoes always looked run-down, primarily because he tied the laces only once and thereafter forced his feet into the shoes until the backs were broken. Once in his freshman year he took a beautiful co-ed to a formal dance; she was dressed in a black lace dress, while he was "clad in chocolate brown pants and a blue jacket . . . and some inappropriate shirt." But the couple had a wonderful time "as they danced around . . . in the little back room at Danziger's Viennese Candy Kitchen back in the summer of 1945." Al may have chosen slovenliness in part because he was embarrassed by his parents' wealth and wished to not "be seen as a rich boy," but in the process he carved out an image that totally distinguished him from everyone else, thereby establishing even further his reputation as exceptional.[14]

Not all the events of that first year were fun or rewarding. Al had been assigned a room with two North Carolina boys who already were friends and felt hostile to a third person who was also an outsider. Some of his New York friends shared his discomfort, one writing that a northerner must feel alienated in Chapel Hill, "where any intellectual aspirations are seen as unfortunate." After his experience on the segregated bus, Al had written Sandy Friedman of his "shock and disappointment." "I don't think I've felt lower in ages," he said.[15]

But there were so many enjoyable things to do as well. With four or five friends, Al would go at lunchtime to the green courtyard beside the Presbyterian church, lie lazily in the sun, play 20 Questions, and sing popular songs. Where there was a piano, friends noted, Al would sit down and "assault as many keys simultaneously [as possible], ramping up and down the keyboard, playing popular songs and singing in a voice that you wouldn't have expected from his speaking voice." Sometimes at night, the group sat on the steps of Wilson Library, "singing to the moon. And break into three part harmony on 'Amazing Grace' or 'Hark the Sound.'" Those "were magnificent days," Hunt and Wallace observed. "They were halcyon [days]"—singing hymns on the quad, gathering at Danziger's for coffee and conversation ("a [Peter] Lorre, [Sidney] Greenstreet-ish place," Al called it), dancing, making plans to change the world.[16]

One of the instruments by which Al hoped to accomplish that goal was the National Conference of Students (NCS), a group that took on a distinctly "Lowenstein" coloration in the spring of 1946. The group had antecedents in the Conference of Southern Students that had formed the previous spring. State Department representatives had urged southern students to come together in representative assemblies and prepare to become involved in national and international postwar events. In response, the Conference of Southern Students had formed, and Douglass Hunt, shortly after Lowenstein met him, journeyed to San Francisco for the first United Nations conference as a delegate from the student association. Thereafter, the group continued to function, debating, for example, whether to send delegates to the first conference of the International Union of Students (IUS), a left-leaning group with strong ties to Moscow. Eventually, the southern group evolved into the National Conference of Students, and that group, by the late 1940s, was one of several that provided the foundation for the National Student Association (NSA) when it was started in 1947–48.[17]

In the spring of 1946, however, the NCS was an embryonic entity seeking self-definition and a constituency. Lowenstein, together with a band of cohorts at UNC, issued a call for student bodies throughout the country to send representatives to Chapel Hill in April to chart a new course of student activism. As much as anything else, Lowenstein's personal stationery delineated the group's approach: "WE DON'T GIVE A DAMN," the heading read, "FOR Jim Crow, the Bosses (political, of course), Franco, olives, radicalism . . . Fascism (in all its forms, red and black); HURRAH FOR, The Frankies, Graham and Roosevelt; Wendell [Wilkie] and Eleanor; K. Hepburn . . . Morse (Wayne and code), Nehru, Ickes . . . intermarriage . . .

[and] God (whoever He may be)." Supporters of the new group were expected to sign a pledge that more formally expressed the group's politics. "I believe that men should be treated as individuals and judged accordingly," it declared: "I can take no stock in selfish pride of race, color, or nationality. . . . I am opposed to discrimination, segregation, or any form of bigotry, as manifested in anti-Semitism, Jim Crowism—whether the object of the Jim Crow be Negro, immigrant, Mexican, Jew, Catholic, or Nisei— and in any concept of heightened racial, ethnic or religious nationalism." Few liberals could question the soaring rhetoric of the aspirations. But some would begin to wonder about the internal logic and politics of the statement's author.[18]

The first problem Lowenstein encountered with his student conference venture involved his insistence on equating Zionism with Jim Crowism. For generations, Jews from the Disapora had been seeking a state of their own in the biblical land of Israel. In the aftermath of the Holocaust, and with pivotal support from politicians in the West, the likelihood of that happening increased dramatically. But in Lowenstein's mind, the movement for a Jewish homeland in Palestine reflected "an unhealthy expression of race nationalism." Individualism and faith in personal freedom ranked highest in Lowenstein's political and life credo. Others might talk about categories of race, culture, nationality, or religion, but to him, Judaism belonged only to the last subset. Jews were individuals with a particular religious faith, he insisted, not a race or nation. If a person believed in abolishing segregation for blacks, the same person must believe in ending the separation of Jews. Integration was integration, whether the barriers to be broken down were between black and white or Jew and gentile. Indeed, as one Reform rabbi wrote him, the parallel was exact. "I can think of nothing that might have a more salutary effect upon the present muddled thinking of too many people in American life," he wrote, "than a forceful announcement of a truly non-sectarian group of college people dedicated to the proposition of integration in the American scene."[19]

Others were not so sure, however. Oppressed groups needed a place for refuge, one woman friend wrote Lowenstein. "What I can't understand is the fact that you go to the trouble to make it even harder for a suffering people by rounding up opposition to them. No matter whether Jew or non-Jew, would you hit a man when he's down?" Many Jews in Europe shared Lowenstein's ideas before 1934, she pointed out, and now they were dead. "Take yourself in hand, young man, and think it over!" So volatile was the response to Lowenstein's plan for opposing Zionism at the conference that a number of delegations threatened to pull out entirely. "You must be aware of what you're suggesting when you [recommend] 'intermarriage,'" Thelma Cohen wrote, describing the impending meeting as the "tension conference" (with the word conflict crossed out). When friends tried to persuade him that he was making an error, Lowenstein turned on them, accusing them of trying to sabotage a worthy goal. Eventually, he backed off, making condemnation of Zionism optional and secondary to opposing Jim Crow. But the imbroglio suggested a great deal about both Lowenstein's definition of individual freedom and his insistence on viewing his own politics as superior in righteousness to the politics of others.[20]

The debate over Zionism also reflected the profound conflict Lowenstein himself felt about being Jewish. On the one hand, he was deeply concerned about the likelihood of anti-Semitism exploding and spreading throughout the United States. On the other hand, he dreaded the day when, because of Jewish nationalism, he would be expected to root for Hank Greenberg because he was a Jew, not because Greenberg was an outfielder for his favorite team, the Cleveland Indians. In his own life, Lowenstein seemed torn. He had acted immediately to combat the anti-Semitism reflected in the assignment of Jews to the same dorms, and he had attacked fraternities in large part because of their policies of excluding Jews. Yet he also seemed desperately anxious to win acceptance from his non-Jewish classmates and went out of his way to hide his Jewish identity. "He called himself Lowen[*stine*] in those days," one friend recalled, because it sounded less Jewish than Lowen*steen.* And Al later told his best friend in the army that he had in fact gone to UNC to implement a decision "to take out of him any aspect of Jewishness that would keep other people from getting close to him."[21]

As one indication of his desire to escape identification as a Jew, Lowenstein made his religious base at Charley Jones's Presbyterian church. (Jones was a committed racial liberal.) A regular participant in Christian college groups at the Wesley Foundation or First Presbyterian, Lowenstein became fast friends with people like Nelle Morton of the Fellowship of Southern Churchmen, served as a delegate from Charley Jones's church to a conference at a Christian retreat center, and loved nothing better than to belt out old-fashioned hymns with his pals on campus. "I don't think I'll ever forget your leading off the singing . . . last Sunday night [at the Presbyterian church] before the [Christmas] holidays," one friend wrote. "I've never had such an experience through song." Perhaps most revealing, Lowenstein actually applied for admission to one of the fraternities that excluded Jews. "I remember very distinctly that he asked me to get him in," a friend said. "He wanted to be a member . . . ostensibly to break the Jewish barrier. It was a civil liberties thing. But I think there was . . . also another reason. . . . He wanted to be accepted into WASP circles. . . . Al really liked them . . . and [wanted] to be admired and accepted by them." Only when his friend told him that there was no chance that he would be admitted did Lowenstein desist. Thus the issue of Lowenstein's commitment to anti-Zionist individualism mirrored his own tortured struggle to deal with the meaning of his Jewishness as well as a concern with political principles of integration.[22]

The experience with the NCS also revealed another trait Lowenstein would have to deal with in his political life. The meeting itself was only a partial success: delegates had attended the conference from more than a dozen universities—and black colleges, including Howard, Shaw, and North Carolina College for Negroes, were substantially represented—but more than fifty colleges had been invited. And there was little follow-through; having poured his abundant energies into making the conference happen, Lowenstein seemed to abandon his mission once it was over. "Where are the minutes?" delegates repeatedly asked him. "The NCS has died above the Mason-Dixon line," one friend wrote, "because of the lack of interest and response [we have] gotten from Chapel Hill." In fact, Lowenstein had by then shifted his energies to other organizations; there was clearly a problem of consistency and dependability that he would have to overcome if he were to achieve the ambitious goals he set for himself and his causes.[23]

During much of this period, in fact, Lowenstein was unsure of which direction to go politically, reflecting in his own shifting interests the uncertainties of the entire postwar era. It was a time of enormous fluidity, with people searching for new points of reference. Those who had worshiped Roosevelt frequently found his successor, Harry Truman, to be short of vision as well as stature. Foreign policy debates roiled political party waters on every side; labor-management disputes resulted in a record number of strikes; and civil rights conflicts threatened to transform race relations. Like many Americans, Lowenstein tossed wildly about in search of his own position in these years. With some friends he shared a nostalgic longing for Roosevelt's liberalism. For a brief period in 1945, he apparently developed a "craze for 'mother Russia.'" Then, in 1946, he flirted with converting to the Republican party, and through much of 1947 and 1948, he developed a political infatuation with Harold Stassen, the progressive young Republican from Minnesota, and subsequently Dwight Eisenhower, the wartime general whom some liberal Democrats hoped to draft as a replacement for Truman. Throughout the entire period, Lowenstein also kept in close touch with the more radical wing of the liberal spectrum, those who advocated Henry Wallace for president because he had broken with Truman on the cold war and supported a political realignment of "progressives" against conservatives on behalf of "jobs, peace, and freedom."[24]

To an increasing degree, however, it became clear that Lowenstein would chart his course primarily according to the compass of anticommunism. The first sign of things to come involved, prophetically enough, student politics. Initially, Lowenstein had been a strong advocate of his friend Douglass Hunt going to the London organizing conference of the International Union of Students in the fall of 1945. The direction IUS would take remained unclear (the cold war did not officially begin until two years later), and Lowenstein felt that Hunt's voice would make a difference. Six months later, the issue arose again, this time over who would represent UNC at the Prague Congress of IUS in the spring of 1946. By this time, concerns over Moscow's influence in IUS had expanded, although Prague was not yet a Moscow satellite. The two candidates for delegate from UNC were Jimmy Wallace, a well-known anticommunist activist and Lowenstein friend, and Junius Scales, "a descendant of the former governor of North Carolina, blond-haired, blue-eyed and handsome," supported by the fraternities, but thought by some to harbor distinctly "leftist" political views. As the story goes, the selection committee was about to choose Scales by a one-vote margin when Lowenstein, characteristically late, rushed into the room carrying the proxy vote of a friend for Wallace. The chair then broke the tie in favor of Wallace, and Scales was defeated. A year later, Scales announced that since 1945 he had been the secretary of the Communist party in North Carolina.[25]

From that symbolic moment forward, Lowenstein was known, at least by people on the left, as an ardent anticommunist. To Scales, in particular, Lowenstein's position went beyond the bounds of reason. "I recall how arrogant and assertive . . . he was," Scales said. "You were a total villain in his eyes, there seemed to be no grays or anything." The next year the two clashed again at the Presbyterian church, where Scales had been asked to speak. The event stood out in Scales's memory because of the intensity of the conflict, and because of Lowenstein's rage when—at least in Scales's eyes—the Communist got the better of the debate. Yet eight years later, when Scales was on trial for advocating the violent overthrow of the U.S. government, Lowenstein, when approached by Scales's lawyers to testify, denied any recollection of the experience. Scales was incredulous. Lowenstein's anticommunism, he concluded, "seemed to be more than obsessive; it was damned near psychotic."[26]

Whatever the exaggerations in Scales's assessment, it was clear that a passionate anticommunism had joined an intense commitment to individualism as a pillar of Lowenstein's political faith. Nowhere was that more clear than in Lowenstein's stance toward Henry Wallace, the candidate of the Progressive Citizens of America for president in 1948. "That man has guts, and he's on the right side," one of Lowenstein's closest friends wrote him in 1948. "Here is someone you can agree with almost unequivocally and you—the great humanitarian, the champion of the underdog—talk about Stassen and Eisenhower." Yet Wallace was against the cold war, enjoyed support from Amerian Communists, and therefore was suspect. On most issues, including opposition to universal military training and support of civil rights, Lowenstein *did* agree with Wallace; but in the end, he apparently agreed more with his friend Jimmy Wallace, who called Henry Wallace "either a crypto-communist or a dupe." Thus, when Lowenstein presented his candidate for the 1948 presidential election in the *Daily Tar Heel*, it turned out to be Norman Thomas, the Socialist. Here was a man whose anticommunist credentials were as strong as his social democratic bona fides. Anyone who was for Wallace, Lowenstein charged, should "ask himself how good any President can be who by his platform and principles would be obliged to turn over posts in his Cabinet to the Communist Party." An old friend wrote to Lowenstein, imagining the response of student readers: "Goddam . . . I always thought he was *for* Wallace . . . Ha, ha, here's where he tells them off. Goddam reds around here—pretty good column."[27]

The third pillar of Lowenstein's political credo, of course, was his commitment to end racism. Already established before he came to Chapel Hill, his fierce hostility toward racial prejudice had animated his campaign to desegregate the student legislature. It appeared again a year later when Lowenstein introduced a bill at the student state legislature to abolish the poll tax, and then again when, as a member of the UNC debating society, he sponsored resolutions to desegregate the university. But his antiracism received critical reinforcement during the summer of 1947 when Lowenstein attended the Encampment for Citizenship (EFC), a six-week gathering at the Fieldston School in Riverdale, just outside of Manhattan.

Sponsored by the Ethical Culture Society, the Encampment represented a marvelous opportunity for young people of all backgrounds to come together, share their cultures, and determine the contribution they would make to their society. It was there that Al Lowenstein first met Eleanor Roosevelt, that he first came to know Lucille Kohn—an Ethical Culture teacher in her sixties who ran the Encampment and taught labor history—and that his intense commitment to convert people to the cause of racial brotherhood achieved new personal meaning through the campers he lived and worked with.

Students at the Encampment came from all over America, but by design, a large number were either black or Native American. They lived in bunk rooms at Fieldston, attended lectures and discussion groups during the day, went on field trips to museums, theaters, and political gatherings, and held endless "bull sessions" to solve the problems of the world. "[The environment was full of] high-minded liberalism," one camper observed, "democratic, and anti-fascist, and certainly anti-racist." The campers would go to the city to meet political and civil rights leaders; one time they went to Hyde Park for a picnic and talk with Mrs. Roosevelt. Henry Wallace came to lecture, Saul Padover, the editorial writer for the progressive newspaper PM, warned against the evils of class distinctions, and Henry David blasted the maldistribution of wealth under capitalism. Lucille Kohn, who had spent a lifetime in progressive causes such as feminism and international peace, presided over the whole affair with a gentle, persistent near saintliness that made her everyone's favorite. The purpose was to generate a sense of mission; the means to that end were discussions and cultural events designed to create political sensitivity. Students shared the experience of "sitting on rugs, listening to 'Talking Union' and Josh White," and making plans to change the world. Not surprisingly, the international bill of rights drawn up by the campers for presentation to Mrs. Roosevelt emphasized civil rights, the challenge to authoritarianism, and an end to peonage and poverty.[28]

Al was the charismatic center of the Encampment. A beehive of activity, he organized outings, prodded slowpokes who resisted a change in consciousness, and led the group sings. "Al was just in heaven," one camper said, "and he got very involved particularly with the Iowa farm boy types. . . . He was always running around talking to somebody. . . . [The whole thing] was very Lowensteinian in its way of operating . . . [reflecting the belief] that somehow you can get these people together and talk to them and they would become good people." Certainly many of them got the message. "I nearly started a race riot," one camper wrote him the first day after returning to Charlotte, "[and] last night I nearly parted company with a long time friend about labor. I keep telling myself to be pacifistic, conciliatory, Christian and understanding, but my blood pressure still rises." Another wrote of coming back to Iowa State to work for Negro rights, and a third ruminated about the responsibilities of a white liberal working in the South. "I can't just sit back and moan anymore," one typical camp friend wrote. "I want to DO something." Not surprisingly, at least one camper was convinced that Al Lowenstein would become president "of a new, truly democratic United States."[29]

Lowenstein's intense interest in black campers even resulted in a celebrated "dance-in" at a rich Jewish country club. One weekend, Allard arrived at his parents' home in Harrison with seven guests, one of them a young black woman. He then announced to his parents that after dinner, the group would attend a juniors dance at the Fenway, the exclusive club to which his parents belonged. Al's father took him aside, suggesting the dance was not a good idea. But Al responded, "I didn't invite [the Negro woman]. I invited Bob and Bob invited her; what am I going to say, that he can't invite her?" Dorothy Lowenstein and her brother Larry went off to the dance, and shortly thereafter, Larry said to Dorothy, "Al must be here." "Where is he?" she asked. "I haven't seen him," Larry replied, "but there's a colored girl here, so he must be here." Eventually the group was asked to leave and did. The next day, Al's father challenged anyone at the club who had any objections to debate him at the club pool. No one did. Meanwhile, the campers returned to Fieldston, delighted with their achievement.[30]

The Fenway episode conveyed a thousand messages. Al, of course, had broken at least two taboos—he brought not only a black to the club but "goys" as well. Gabriel, whatever he thought of the enterprise initially, would always stand by his son. Al had also, however, demonstrated once again a less attractive trait of being disingenuous—of calculating how to make something happen, even at the potential expense of one of the parties involved, while professing total innocence. "This was all orchestrated," his sister Dorothy said. "It was something that Al was very glad to have happen to see what the reactions were." That fact bothered at least some of the participants. "His plan [was] this is totally spontaneous, we're just going with our friends," one friend commented, "[but] I got worried . . . [that] we didn't want to take . . . this black woman out there and have her hurt ... [with] Al ... [being] just so innocent." In the end, no one was hurt—but the possibility had still been there.[31]

Yet the final impact of the Encampment was to deepen Lowenstein's personal and political commitment to fight racism. He alone, one of the black campers wrote, "was completely, genuinely, and sincerely interested in the effect which the Encampment had on the ideas and prejudices of the camp participants." "I have talked about you so often since I've been home," another black woman said, "[that] my mother is beginning to wonder if you were the only fellow at the camp." Others might make fun of an "integrated" experience and warn her never to forget that her face was black, but she had seen the possibility of a different world through the Encampment. Al had, too, and "after six weeks of Democracy," as one camper put it, he was going to push on in his own fight for racial justice.[32]

POLITICS AND COLLEGE—RUNNING FOR OFFICE

What was less clear were the means he would choose to realize his political goals. Ever since he had been a small boy, one friend recalled, "Al knew how to round up the troops ... he knew who his constituents were, and he had a great ledger ... in which he wrote down the names and addresses of everybody who was ever going to vote his way ... or [of anybody] he needed to be in touch with." The same pattern continued in college. Lowenstein's notebooks were full of notations on how different dormitories would vote, with political affiliations written next to the names of dorm residents.

But sensitivity to potential political allies did not necessarily translate into a course of action. Should he run for office himself, or manage the candidacy of others from behind the scenes? If he were a candidate, should he run to win, or simply stand up for principle and be a martyr to a cause? Where should he locate his energies? In the fraternity fight, the embryonic National Student Association, the *Daily Tar Heel,* or the Students for Democratic Action (a junior version of Americans for Democratic Action [ADA], formed in 1948)—or all at once? "If you [aren't going to] do everything in a haphazard way, and honestly have a master plan," one friend wrote, "it would be a good idea to let people know. . . . Then they wouldn't be so darn offended if six million new things pop up."[33]

Yet the abiding theme of Lowenstein's political life in college—and thereafter—was his inability to make these choices. Each year, he debated interminably over whether to run for student office and then, after waiting too long to make the decision, invariably discovered that he had lost by a narrow margin. Paralyzed beforehand, Lowenstein went around in circles trying to decide what to do; his friends, meanwhile, screamed at him to abandon his equivocation. "The odds are obvious," Jimmy Wallace wrote during one such episode,

> but have they not always been so[?] The situation has not been altered, in its significant outlines, since last year or the year before that. Nor will it be different on the morrow. Abdication produces [nothing]. . . .Don't hide your wares under a bushel even though there are no buyers when they are on display. . . . Morality is connected with freedom of choice. In the absence of this freedom there is no morality. Ergo, you are at the worst a hypocrite and at best a waster of time . . . if you do not provide some basis for principles to rest upon; and what better basis than the candidate himself? Give the bastards a choice and thereby retain a clear conscience when they suffer for taking the wrong one?[34]

More often than not, Lowenstein would *let* himself be convinced by such arguments, then decide *not* to campaign for his own cause, as if to do so might compromise the principles for which he stood (or perhaps bring victory?). Two years in a row, for example, he became a belated and allegedly reluctant candidate for student body vice-president, only to refuse to commit his energies to a full-scale effort on his own behalf. "The tragedy," one friend wrote, "is that this nomination above anything else was something you wanted." "I don't feel that it was unforgiveable of you not to campaign in your own behalf," Douglass Hunt noted, "but I am sorry you didn't if it would have helped. I wrote you beforehand that I thought you ought to run to win for a change."[35]

CONCLUSION

What did all this mean? How could one explain a series of actions that apparently defied reason and logic?

On one level, at least, Lowenstein's hesitancy and indecisiveness simply reflected his intellectual befuddlement. His mind was so brilliantly subtle that clarity easily became captive to complexity. Jimmy Wallace, recalling their first meeting, wrote Al in 1948 that "you were [then] in your circular period, with every argument well thought out, linked to each other, and gradually bending back upon themselves, leaving a great round zero." That process became a feature of Lowenstein's entire political life. Each layer of complexity opened on to another, immobilizing the thinker through the cumulative weight of the intricacies thus uncovered. In one brief rumination on the relationship between politics and thought, Lowenstein articulated his own definition of the problem. "When men stop to think," he wrote, "they get confused. . . . The less they think, the more they know. And *they* rule." While such reflections might be healthy for politicians to contemplate, they also suggest how paralyzing too much thought could be. Obviously, the capacity to leap ahead and think through the byzantine consequences of one's actions could prove helpful in a political context; but it also could lead to becoming enmeshed in an intellectual maze that became an end in itself, and to frenetic activity, intellectual or otherwise, taking the place of directed action. That certainly seemed to some to characterize Lowenstein, whom they accused of having too many irons in the fire, talking in riddles, and "popping in and out of" far too many causes.[36]

At another level, however, Lowenstein's contradictory behavior reflected an even deeper conflict. Should one act directly for one's cause or indirectly? Behind the scenes or out front? With candor or with deception? By forthright persuasion or manipulation? These were not easy questions to answer, but the intensity with which Lowenstein and his friends debated them suggested just how pivotal they were to his own sense of political self. Douglass Hunt posed the key question early in Lowenstein's UNC career. "It seems so very obvious to me," Hunt declared,

> that [whatever you can do through others] can never outweigh in value . . . the things you can directly do. . . . And if you put that first, it indicates to me how woefully you misjudge your own *raison d'être*. . . . You are a person of brilliant intellect, [and] a genius for dealing with the most diverse persons . . . who must make his own contribution in his own way to a world which cries aloud for help. For you to think that contribution can be made indirectly through any other person is wrong.

The same point was made by Al's father. "How do you think a man becomes president of the United States," he asked. "By saying no, by refusing to run? When a man has the necessary talent he must create the necessary opportunity and . . . take full advantage of it." Gabriel disapproved of "the idea of Al working in the back of political campaigns and getting people elected," his daughter Dorothy said. "He wanted his son to be acknowledged . . . [his] picture [to] be in the paper." Hence the pressure on

Lowenstein, from Hunt, Wallace, family members, and countless others, to seize the moment and actively pursue political office.[37]

Yet there was a side of Lowenstein that preferred orchestrating events from behind the stage. This was the Lowenstein who "managed to have a hand in directing almost every campus organization and at the same time considered himself a sleeper," as one college friend wrote. Operating out of sight, using his massive data base of political intelligence, plotting strategy for others to act out—this was the leadership of a behind-the-scenes strategist whose feints and ploys would entrap the enemy until the decisive blow for victory could be struck.

The problem was that this kind of political leadership all too often descended, even if only in appearance, into manipulation and deception. Trying to line up people behind the scenes to do his bidding was very Machiavellian, and no matter how lofty his pronouncements of principle, the issue of trickery was never far from the surface. "There was [always] something in Allard that was secretive," Sandy Friedman had said. But mystery and conspiracy engendered suspicion as well as curiosity. Hence, at least some people thought that Al was "too cloak and dagger . . . not predictable [enough], too much on the edge of things to make large bodies of people trust him." One student leader referred to him as the "Disraeli" of UNC politics, a person who looked like he stood for one thing but in fact represented another.[38]

Torn between direction and indirection, Lowenstein thus often waited until the last moment to decide what his own course would be. Even then, if he chose to be a direct candidate, he protected his earlier self-image as a reluctant standard-bearer by refusing to campaign. Moreover, he frequently arranged matters so that his other political instinct would be gratified as well; thus, when he finally ran for vice-president in 1949, he succeeded in getting his good friend Bill Mackie nominated for president. "My guess," one close friend of both men said, "is that Al was the planner, and the goader all along." In the end, Mackie's victory by a large majority and Lowenstein's loss by only a few votes might have been a perfect solution to the latter's inner conflict.[39]

But why would a person praised for his political skill prove to be so reluctant a candidate? The question went back to the problem of Lowenstein's hesitancy and indecisiveness—and identity. "It's always hard for me to realize," a student friend wrote in 1949, "that Al Lowenstein, of all people, doesn't know how to make up his mind." But then, almost accidentally, he discovered the answer. "I'm surprised over and over too *that you don't think you're fitted for anything.* Of all the people I know, you are the man that I have probably the most confidence in." There was the link. While others placed almost infinite faith in Lowenstein's ability, he himself was profoundly uncertain that he had anything worthwhile to offer—and afraid that if he did offer anything, it would be rejected. Consumed by the fear of being exposed as different, perhaps even deviant, he preferred to hold himself back.[40]

If Lowenstein had little faith in his own value, then understandably he would prefer to work behind the scenes where he could hide his light under a bushel rather than expose himself to public examination. That way, he could go about converting people to his causes and letting them carry the battle forward under his direction rather than take the risk of putting his own name forward and being confirmed—by a negative vote—in his own self-doubt. Just as logically, when he did decide to run, it made sense for him to wait until the last minute, then commit himself only because he was, in effect, drafted in service to a higher cause. Hence, he would be legitimized by the goal for which he was sacrificing himself; moreover, by not making his own personality or credentials the focus of the campaign, he could escape any sense of personal rejection were he defeated. Indeed, he would thereby become a martyr for a higher purpose.

This analysis makes comprehensible some of the anomalies of Lowenstein's life at Chapel Hill. What his father referred to as "your calamitous ideals of self-effacement" continually were at war with his will to control, direct, and manage. If he began from a position of self-doubt—whether about his appearance, ethnicity, or sexuality—it was necessary to receive constant reassurance that he was valued by others. Hence, Lowenstein would "test" his standing in the eyes of his compatriots. Once, after a political occasion in Raleigh with friends, he insisted that the group take a taxi back to Chapel Hill, thirty miles away, rather than wait for a bus. He had to study for an exam, he said, and needed to get back quickly. "To a New Yorker, used to taking a taxi to LaGuardia," one of the group said, "I suppose it was nothing, but to three North Carolinians, it was an extravagance beyond measure." So they lent Lowenstein the money, but he went alone. Later, Lowenstein told one of the friends involved that what he really had been looking for was some "moral support." "He made it something of a personal test of loyalty . . . and felt he had to be the best judge of what should be done," Douglass Hunt said. "There was a quality of that in Al . . . of [measuring] his friends early on for loyalty."[41]

The same test occurred everytime Lowenstein was late, since, in effect, he was demanding that the people waiting for him prove their devotion. It was administered again when he borrowed money—as he did frequently, often taking months to pay the money back. And in some ways the test was implicit in Lowenstein's proprietary expectation that he could make demands on people. "Al always used people," one friend said, "but they knew they were being used. . . . He was not embarrassed about asking people to do things for his convenience." If people responded, they confirmed his worth and he could carry on; if not, they were undeserving of his time. "Al was the kind of person people made concessions to," a classmate observed, "whether it was [lateness] or the fact that he was in and out of your life without much notice. . . . Those who knew him and liked him were willing to put up with some . . . irritations that they might not have endured with other people."[42]

Perhaps most important, however, his "self-effacement" and doubt helped explain his attitude toward winning and losing. If he selected only issues of the highest principle to take a stand on, he automatically enhanced his own worth in the process; in effect he was elevated in his own eyes and those of others by the nobility of the cause he espoused. And in the crazy world that said politics was "bad" but moral crusades were "good," he actually won when he lost. One acquaintance, not understanding this, addressed Al as "William Jennings Bryan," and asked, "How many elections can you lose?" But another friend, more comprehending, observed that "there was something in Al that when he lost, he won. . . . The issue was what kind of fight you put up." Allard's father took the same position. "Victory is won," he telegraphed Al after one defeat, "when a job is well done. . . . Results are often elusive and rarely based on desserts. There is joy in victory in fighting for a just cause. Win or lose, take cheer." Those close to Al knew that, on one level, he deeply wanted to win—for vindication of his worth, of his acceptability as a Jew by WASPS, of his principles. But they also understood the peculiar dynamic whereby something much more complicated was going on. Al himself had written Jimmy Wallace that when his friends won for a change, it was "a new political experience for me—to experience Defeat and Unhappiness in Victory—instead of Victory and Unhappiness in Defeat."[43]

In that sentence was embodied the classic, convoluted Lowenstein—only nineteen years old, yet totally enmeshed in the circular ironies and endless passageways of the political journey he was beginning. When you won, you lost; when you lost, you won. Either way, the important thing was to move on to "another campaign," continuing the quest for that elusive moment when—finally—things might come together.[44]

3
Friendship

At THE SAME TIME ALLARD LOWENSTEIN WAS CREATING A WHIRLWIND OF political activity at UNC, he was also working toward a clearer sense of who he was as a human being. With his family, he continued to grapple for some sense of autonomy, to struggle against the persistent efforts of his stepmother and father to control and dictate his life. But beyond the family claim, he confronted a sustained attempt by individual friends to engage him in committed relationships. Two of these stood out in particular, one with a man, the other with a woman. These were not his only friendships of importance during these years. Nor did either of them have a clear end or resolution. But each, in its own way, suggested patterns of interaction that would be repeated many times in Lowenstein's life and that spoke powerfully to the dilemmas of intimacy, sexuality, and ethnic identity that would follow him through his days. Each relationship also revealed, together with his ongoing family interactions, some of the dynamics that helped shape Lowenstein's public life.

THE FAMILY CLAIM

Although Al Lowenstein had moved as far from his family's reach as a full day's train ride could carry him, no act of physical distancing could forestall his parents' efforts to control him. One month after arriving in Chapel Hill, Al complained that his stepmother was going berserk with her constant intrusions into his life. Sandy Friedman, Al's closest friend through high school, jokingly wrote to ask whether Florence had yet sent him frozen chicken soup through the mail. But if Friedman had known the lengths to which she and Gabriel actually went to remain in command, he would have blanched.[1]

Gabriel Lowenstein played a dual role during Al's college years: on the one hand, he reached out for a more direct and fulfilling relationship; on the other hand, he maintained his characteristic sermonizing and admonitions. For example, on July 13, 1945, Gabriel wrote: "The topic of our sermon today is CCC vs. JJJ. Everybody likes a fellow who keeps cool, calm and collected, and nobody likes a fellow who is jerky, jumpy and jittery." In the midst of another typical lecture on keeping hands and teeth clean, Gabriel departed enough from his stern text to confess to Al, "I want to live through you your college career. If you think you know too much to consult me, then don't consult me, but tell me all." Words of encouragement accompanied repeated suggestions that Al transfer from UNC, and whenever the "college boy" sent a column he had written for the paper or some other evidence of his remarkable reputation at UNC, Doc became positively "chesty," boasting to all who would listen about his marvelous boy and what he was achieving. If electoral competition brought defeat, Doc was there with comfort—as well as with injunctions to speak more slowly. In a feeble effort to alter his son's character flaws, Doc sent him alarm clocks to wake up by. And when Al was feeling really low—as after his defeat for vice-president of the student body in 1949—his father bought him a new car, causing Lowenstein's playful classmates to name him a charter member of the Order of Abandoned Proletarians.[2]

It was Al's stepmother, however, who wielded the psychological whip. In his early months at UNC, Al received a minimum of one letter a day from Florence, occasionally as many as three or four—all of them nudging him to get proper exercise, dress well, eat good food, and above all, write home. Occasionally, she used positive reinforcement, as when she told him after he had come home for her birthday, "When I take pen in hand to write you, a feeling of love pervades my whole body. You are the man, the human being supreme." But more often, her letters were petulant, chiding, and wrathful.

"Have you ever seen me very angry?" she asked in one letter. "Well that must be the expression in my heart toward you. You know we haven't heard from you in seven days, 24 hours × 7. Are you ill? Or are you minus feeling for us? There is no excuse for this, even illness. You answer by phone the minute you get this letter. Don't quibble either!" In fact, Al was in the middle of the first meeting of the National Conference of Students when she wrote, but the letter suggested the kind of control she sought to exert. On one occasion she telegraphed him, "No letter in five days. Are you ill? Answer immediately," and then the very next day sent a follow-up: "Still no answer. Wire or phone immediately." In the fall of Al's first year, Florence urged him to come home during his break for a "calm, un-emotional (no recriminations)" discussion about his status and grades—he had flunked trigonometry and otherwise had mostly Cs—but given the general tenor of their correspondence, Allard had good reason to doubt her assurances. More to the point, perhaps, was her acknowledgment two weeks later, after he had *not* come home, that "we are jealous of every moment you spend elsewhere. . . . I think maybe this is the crux of all our disagreements."[3]

Florence's key instrument of control, however, was the threat that Gabriel would suffer were Al not to do his parents' bidding. In August 1945, Doc had suffered a heart attack. His recovery was slow, and in the ensuing years, his health could always be invoked as a concern whenever Florence thought it convenient. Al held his father's life in his hands, she wrote in October 1946, asking about his grades. "If they are not the best you can get, I'll have to keep them from Dad. . . . Marks that are not worthy of your ability will hurt Dad very much. . . . And you must promise me that in the future that won't happen. Dad's condition doesn't allow of any surprises." Not only was Florence holding up the specter of Gabriel's death as the ultimate punishment if Al were to perform poorly; she also was weaving a conspiratorial web between herself and her stepson, keeping them tied to each other by their fear of and love for the primary figure in their lives. Florence even recruited Larry to the effort. "Dad is not well again," he wrote Al early in 1947, "and to give him [these poor grades] will be murder. For God's sake, not for your own good, but for your father, try to make him happy by getting decent marks." Later, Marie Lowenstein commented that she "was stunned" by the family's behavior. "They laid such guilt on him," she said.[4]

The rapid deterioration of the family's relationship with Bert, the eldest son, served only to heighten the pressure. After fulfilling his father's hopes by excelling at medical school, Bert began to behave erratically. The first indication of trouble, at least to his parents, was his decision to marry Helen, a non-Jewish woman the family had never met—without telling them. "The only one to whom we are confiding our inner most thoughts is you," Florence wrote Al, making him a special participant in the ensuing melodrama. A week later, she confirmed Bert's elopement. "And that's how the most wonderful Daddy, with a weak heart, was informed of the marriage of his son. The Daddy who breathed and lived for his children. . . . What a slap in the face!" And lest the implicit message be missed, Florence added: "Don't do the same to a Daddy who forgives anything."[5]

Within a little more than a year, it became clear that Bert's problem went further than having married a woman his parents did not approve of. "Between you and me," Florence wrote Al, "Bert has a pathological disease, or you might call it, to be nice, a very, very exaggerated way of talking." In fact, Bert exhibited a variety of disturbing symptoms. He went on buying sprees for expensive medical equipment, failed to appear for appointments for days at a time, rarely collected bills from patients, rang up huge personal debts, and apparently made up fantastic stories to explain his way out of trouble. By early 1947, Doc had to go to Cleveland to rescue his oldest son from disaster and bring him back to New York. "Dad thinks Bert is sick and needs watching," Florence wrote Al, in the process giving Al her own opinion that "Bert was born gifted, but developed into a playboy" because he was not indoctrinated earlier with a feeling for others. After receiving all this news, Al composed one of his terse, newspaper headline–style diary entries: "Fear For Mental State of Brother Has Grown."[6]

Significantly, Florence insisted once again on linking Bert's situation with Al's. "You're not showing the proper spirit toward your . . . school [work], and particularly Dad," she told him. "You're not honoring the love, consideration and respect we have for you. Right now Dad loves you maybe more than any of the others, and you're not respecting it very much! Well, that's Bert all over again." By the spring of 1948, Bert had been institutionalized for psychiatric care, and it had become clearer than ever that Doc's hopes for realizing his own frustrated dreams were now totally dependent on Al's success. "Al had taken over where Bert—we hoped Bert would be," Larry said. "I was the one who was going to work and help him if necessary . . . but I was never going to amount to being famous or do anything major." That was Al's responsibility.[7]

Although she never said so explicitly, Florence Lowenstein repeatedly insinuated that the real cause of Bert's illness was his decision to marry a non-Jew. After the family learned that Bert and his wife Helen had taken their vows at a Catholic church, Florence wrote: "This is a death blow to every principle I hold. Dad makes no comment. . . . Your brother is a dope and no mistaking that. Ha ha. He wears a wedding ring, ha ha." In virtually every communication thereafter about Bert, Florence reiterated her hostility to Helen and her conviction that at the root of all other problems lay the original sin of marrying outside one's faith. Once when Helen came to visit the Lowensteins, she wore a cross on her necklace, a fact that led Florence to tell all her friends, "She did it just to scorn me, [as though] if I went to a Catholic house I would wear a star of David." Witnessing the event, Dorothy Lowenstein was disgusted. "Mother just won't give anyone a chance," she wrote Al, and "everything with her [friends] is Jewish or goy (however you spell it)."[8]

Nor did Florence fail to define the meaning of all this for Al. Always concerned that her stepson was not confiding enough in her, or that his "undertones" suggested distancing, she demanded to know whether his interests were engaged elsewhere. "Remember," she said, "if you want to love us and live with us, what you become interested in must also be the kind we love and live with." As if the message were somehow not clear, she elaborated on it two months later. "If you want to continue your close relationship with your family, friends and neighbors," she wrote, "*stay in your own back yard*. From the practical point of view [marrying outside your own kind] does not give the fullness of life you've been looking for. You are not only 1 step ahead of the fellow who marries outside, you are 3, 4, 5—way ahead. You start with the first essential, a common understanding and feeling. The most complete marriages are based on a common bond." Anticipating Al's probable response, she even set out her own defense: "I'm not narrow, but practical. I'm not medieval but knowing. I'm not anti-Semitic, but pro-happiness for Jew, Christian, Catholic and Protestant. . . . I am an American!"[9]

To all of this, Al responded with a combination of passive nonparticipation, finesse, intellectual defiance, and outright resistance. Nonparticipation proved to be his most consistent response, and from his parents' perspective, the most galling. Repeatedly, he avoided his parents' injunctions to return home for vacations and breaks, as though keeping a safe distance would somehow provide the insulation necessary for him to become his own person. Florence certainly understood the strategy. "You've been away so much," she wrote in 1947, "that we're beginning not to know you . . . . Come home, get reacquainted with us, learn your people . . . get angry and disgusted and love us at the same time. . . . All personalities, yours particularly, need an anchor, family-love and appreciation. Those who run amuck are those who think . . . that families don't count."[10]

Even when Al gave in to such family pressure, he did so in a manner that thoroughly circumvented at least his stepmother's intent. He almost always arrived home with an entourage of friends. Al's favorite idea of a good time, his brother recalled, was to come home during Passover with twenty goy companions. He left little time for intimate family talk—indeed, he seemed obsessed with avoiding it—and when he was not arranging something like the Fenway dance visit, he usually made a rushed introduction of his friends, grabbed a quick meal, and then beat a rapid retreat to the city for the theater. Hard as she might try ("Be specific," she wrote Al, "name definite dates and plan to keep them"), Florence could not pin him down to specific times when he would return *and stay* with family members.[11]

In the meantime, Al did everything he could in his college and intellectual life to defy his parents' control. Attending the Presbyterian church and frequenting the Catholic student center, he consciously selected Christian, not Jewish, social peers. With vigor and persistence, he carried on nearly a year-long fight against Zionism, writing lengthy papers comparing the establishment of an Israeli state to the kind of ghettoization of Jews as a race and nationality advocated by Goebbels. "Zionism," he wrote, "is unwise, undesirable, and evil . . . and keeping silent on Zionism . . . is equally unwise, undesirable, and evil, as well as cowardly."

As if his schoolwork were designed as a direct response to his stepmother's pronouncements, he insisted that the answer to religious nationalism was assimilation and, specifically, intermarriage. Opposition to Jewish-Gentile marriages, he wrote in a sociology term paper, reflected the insidious errors of Jewish nationalism—the idea that Jews were so inherently different from others that they could never be part of normal human intercourse. But adopting that attitude, he said, was to buy into anti-Semitism, to "accept prejudice as inevitable, and cloak it with respectability." No religion, he said, "ought to require . . . not marrying the one you love to perpetuate itself. We should not all rush out to our nearest convent . . . to find an appropriate person from some other group to marry, but neither should we approach the matter as if it were lecherous and diseased, and as if only traitors to something or other (heaven only knows what!) would contemplate such sinfulness." The record does not show whether Lowenstein ever sent a copy of his paper to his stepmother.[12]

As often as possible, Al engaged in direct opposition. Clearly, the family as a whole had decreed that Bert's wife Helen was a pariah, whether because of her religion, her association with Bert's deterioration, or what appears to have been her own covert hostility. Al's cousin Frances, for example, wrote that Helen was making "a laughing stock of the entire family as well as your brother through six states," taking all of Gabriel's largesse and then laughing at him behind his back. But from the very beginning, Allard defended her. "He only saw what he wanted to see," Marie Lowenstein said. "He wouldn't see the other side. . . . The moment [Helen] became an underdog, Al took up her cause." In fact, he went to visit Helen and Bert in South Carolina, corresponded with Helen for years after her divorce from Bert, and was viewed by her, from the beginning, as the only person in the family she could trust. If, as one of Al's closest friends said, "he felt estranged from his family" during these years, there was no better way for him to express that estrangement than through openly identifying himself as Helen's ally. Together with his affiliation with Christian student groups, his anti-Zionism, and the physical distance he attempted to place between himself and his family, this alignment with a clear family enemy came as close as one could get to an act of rebellion.[13]

Perhaps most important, Lowenstein gave himself a new and different identity by changing his body. Throughout his life, he had thought of himself as small and unpleasant to look at. He was "physically a kind of weakling," his friend Sandy Friedman said, "a little boy, and he . . . thought of himself as extremely homely." College friends had the same sense. Al told them about classmates beating him up at Horace Mann. "He really had a very bad self-image," one observed. Now, in the midst of his college career, he determined to change all that. Going on a systematic body-building campaign, he visited the gym daily, lifted weights, and sought, through sheer grit and determination, to create the kind of strong body that would at least earn physical respect. In effect, he became a different physical being, one with the eighteen-inch biceps that people would comment on thereafter. He also became a wrestler, beginning his lifetime reputation for challenging every jock he met to a wrestling match, and widened his circle of acquaintances beyond intellectuals and politicos to the "gym boys," who were a different breed entirely. Sandy Friedman compared Allard's conscious decision "to make himself into a muscular Adonis" with Teddy Roosevelt's body-building effort after he was treated as a weakling. It was a "triumph over neurosis," he said. Al's friend Mimi Massey saw the same process at work; "he wanted to be a normal boy," she said, and becoming a "muscle man" helped.[14]

Whether or not Lowenstein's decision to reconstruct his physical body was directly related to his growing determination to achieve independence from his family, the college years were clearly a time of significant new departures as he tried to define his personal and political identity. In that process, few things would be more pivotal than the personal relationships he developed, two of which, especially, helped delineate the patterns that would characterize his ongoing ties with women and men.

DOUGLASS HUNT

Through his college years, as well as before and after, Al Lowenstein was a person who disclosed very little of himself to others. Although he was one of the most gregarious individuals on campus, he focused on accumulating quantities of acquaintances rather than on only a few intense, one-on-one relationships. In one reflection of his underlying insecurity, he kept tallies of those he had contact with during the year, and he burst with pride when the ledger indicated the number was growing. "1949 Letter Totals Show Balance 234 to the Good," one diary headline read, "A Huge Gain". Lowenstein had sent out 484 missives and received back 718.[15]

Al's style of interaction reflected this overall approach. Typically, he expressed interest in someone, and drew that person out through prolonged inquiry, but he rarely volunteered much of his own inner thought. His diffidence infuriated his associates. "Are you allergic to yourself, or something?" one friend wrote. "You [almost never] in person and never in a letter say anything about yourself. What have you been doing? What are you thinking? . . . Are you happy or not, and why?" Alice Gilbert, someone Al had known since high school, expressed the same sentiment. "Your letters are magnificent," she told him, "except that they say absolutely nothing. By a careful reading of your letters, I know nothing about your life. . . . What you are thinking, doing, seeing is totally absent." Al never engaged in a dialogue, Sandy Friedman noted. "It was always a monologue," with Allard revealing little about himself.[16]

Any exception to that pattern, therefore, was remarkable, particularly if sustained over time. Even when—as in his friendship with Douglass Hunt—only one side of the relationship is clearly documented, much can be learned at least indirectly about Lowenstein himself and the various challenges and emotions he was experiencing.

Al had met Douglass Hunt that first night in Chapel Hill, when he joined Hunt and Jimmy Wallace for their epic four-hour conversation about the fate of the universe. They had formed their own triumvirate; each one's individual friends respected the preeminence of the ties already existing between the three. Yet, despite Wallace's own significant relationship with Lowenstein, it soon became clear that the Hunt-Lowenstein interaction possessed an intensity and singleness of purpose that made even Wallace's ties to the two seem secondary by comparison.[17]

On one level, Hunt and Lowenstein could not have appeared less likely to become intimate friends. Lowenstein was sloppy, fast-talking, Jewish, hilariously funny, and spontaneous; Hunt, by contrast, was fastidious, measured in speech, Anglican, and almost prematurely aloof, and dignified. "Douglass should have been born a female and spent life as a virgin schoolmarm," his Yale Law School roommate wrote. Elegant in both his prose and its presentation (Wallace referred to one letter as "addressed by the very feminine hand of Rev. Hunt"), Hunt stood in relation to Allard almost as a well-schooled teacher stands in relation to his pupils. "[He] was physically commanding . . . big, tall, impressive," a friend said. "[He had a] persona of being dignified, and his voice, which was God-given, [was] cultivated as if he had been to elocution lessons." To the still slight and somewhat frail Lowenstein, the larger, older, more commanding Hunt must have seemed a powerful figure, especially given his political prominence on campus as speaker of the student legislature. Yet within weeks, it would be the elder Hunt seeking out the younger Lowenstein, striving for a friendship that would be extraordinary in its closeness.[18]

Shortly after their first meeting, Hunt had gone to San Francisco as an official student observer of the opening United Nations session. When he returned, the two men started to see each other frequently. Lowenstein's willingness to trust Hunt was shown by his remarkable admission to the older man that he was only sixteen. Given Lowenstein's self-consciousness and the superimportance he imparted to revealing such vulnerablity, his sharing of the secret information amounted to a substantial declaration of faith. "He made me swear that I would not reveal that he was so young," Hunt said, "but a lot of traits that I remember in him at that time—his sort of clinging, in a way, to students a bit older than he . . . for support, I . . . think were attributable a bit to his extreme youth." Lowenstein also displayed his trust in Hunt by confiding that his true reason for asking Hunt and others to join him in the taxi ride back from Raleigh to Chapel Hill was to test their friendship. Hunt assured him, he said, that "if I had seen it in those terms at all, I would have given up a week's pay, because I think that much of you."[19]

The more the two shared, the more each came to see the other as special. Lowenstein revealed to Hunt that he had never had a best friend, at least in the sense of someone with whom he felt complete and mutual opennness. Hunt reciprocated with the same disclosure, commenting that most of his relationships were one-way, and that others wept on *his* shoulder, but not vice versa. Yet, he went on, "there is a different kind of best friend," someone with whom one could have a relationship like that found in the "classical friends of antiquity." "Sometimes," he wrote,

> friends achieve that intimacy of thought which enables them really to say what they mean to each other. Sometimes, each gets a glimpse of what's going on in the mind of the other. Sometimes, even though each dislikes what the other occasionally does, two friends develop a forbearance which has in it nothing smug, or proud . . . but which contains only sympathy, understanding and kindness. There is intellectual delight in such companionship—embracing as it does the noblest in both friends. And there is a warmth of heart and compassion of spirit which one encounters nowhere else in the whole world. If I were to dream of a best friend, it would be someone like that.

Although he did not say it in so many words, Hunt was describing what he quickly came to see as his relationship with Lowenstein. His own "eccentricities . . . and stupidities," he said, made his part in such a relationship difficult; Al, on the other hand, was "a rather wonderful and amazing person. Sometimes you scintillate, [other times you] exasperate. . . . [And] as for friends, you'll probably always be a better friend than anyone can be for you." But Hunt was clearly transported by the possibilities he saw for each of them.[20]

Like all friendships, this one, even when it was only two months old, was fraught with disagreements, conflicts, and, inevitably, pain. "Because I value you (what a pitiless, frail, inadequate word), hurting you is the furthest thing from my mind," Hunt wrote in early September. But difficulties there would be. Al, for example, thought Hunt should go to the London student conference to inaugurate the International Union of Students; Hunt demurred. Lowenstein, he said, had put him on a pedestal, made him an idol, expected too much of him, and hence magnified any conflict that then arose. "I have tried for a long time to be a 'surgeon' [in personal relationships]," Hunt wrote, meaning that he cut his ties with others before they got too close. "With most people I don't find it difficult. [But] two or three times in my life I've run into persons whose friendship I have *wanted* to value more than what I believed to be right. You are one of those persons." Thus, when Al took a position opposite to his own and expressed it with intensity, Hunt was profoundly disturbed. "I have let my relations to individual human beings rot," he wrote Al after the London conference imbroglio,

> [but] you [are] a godsend, because I [can] talk with you, because you *would* talk to me. . . . You brought home . . . the fact that I am dreadfully dependent on other people. . . . This past year I somehow have forgotten [that] and it is good to know it again. The world is a warm and wonderful place. . . . I not only like you, I'm proud of you, and I'm very grateful that I know you.

Then, in a statement that revealed the full depth of his commitment, Hunt concluded: "You see, in so many ways—and this hasn't happened to me in a long, long time—you are as I should like to be."[21]

The relationship continued to intensify, with long evening conversations intermixing political discourse and mutual self-discovery. By mid-October, their dispute over the London conference had given way to a far more searing and personal battle—Lowenstein's effort to come to grips with the issue of Zionism. The fervent discussions provoked powerful emotions in both men, setting off a series of personal exchanges that suggested just how embroiled each had become in the other's life. After one particularly volatile interchange in October, Hunt paced the streets, desperately trying to put his turbulent feelings in order. When he returned to his room, he penned a sonnet to Lowenstein, seeking somehow to convey through poetry the full measure of what he had not been able to express in person:

> Whenever I want most to speak my heart,
> And find my speech foreshortening my thought.
> When tongue has failed to do its puny part,
> And words leave love within the breast unwrought.
> A fated captive, doomed to silent life
> Though all its being cries aloud for tongue;
> When all else fails and I'm the slave of strife,
> I curse the joyless God who made me young.
> The while I mourn a creeping doubt assails
> My weary mind. "Perhaps," it chants, "he sees."
> But, wanting this too much, Love tries, and fails,
> To win back Hope—frail Hope, which ghostlike, flees
> Be swift to show my heart thy secret face,
> That love may fly its deadly prison place.

Boldly, with a daring totally out of keeping with his staid persona, Hunt had found the courage to state just how deep his feelings were.[22]

As might have been expected, much more needed to be said after the sonnet was received. Hunt expressed remorse that he had sent it, "[knowing] entirely too well your capacity for self-sacrifice and needless self-hurt where you feel you may have hurt another." He would desist, he wrote Al. "Will you understand, I wonder, that surgery is of the essence, that I will not rush in where I have no right to tread?" The focus of discussion returned, at least for the moment, to Zionism. Yet the real purpose of the renewed dialogue was different. "Your barriers [are] up again," Hunt told Lowenstein. There had been a distancing after he sent the sonnet, a breach that both had felt and that Hunt had tried to heal by bringing Wallace with him when he visited Lowenstein next. Al seemed not particularly bothered by the "barriers," but they were devastating to Hunt, who used the occasion of reopening the Zionism question to reopen as well the deeper, more personal issue. "How can I say what is on my mind?" he asked. "You won't hear it, and I can't say it."

Still, he had to try. Recalling his own words, that he was not only proud of Al but wanted to be like him, Hunt concluded that he had fallen victim to the temptation to idolize Al—hence his need to write the sonnet. Now he had to state his feelings directly. "I didn't want to tell you," he wrote:

> I had—and have—no right to say so much. [But] I had come to feel that you were the "best friend" I had been looking for. I had futilely hoped you might feel the same way, even though I knew deep down it wouldn't happen. . . . Let's leave it this way. I'll say no more; if you feel we can, and want to, let's keep open the avenues we have thus far opened. But apparently we'll have to let it go at that. We'll let it go at less if you say so.

Having bared his soul, Hunt reconciled himself to his fate. "I write this with more fear and with more affection than you know," he said. "But I must write it nonetheless." Then, in a handwritten postscript, "I hope you will answer it—and I'm afraid you will."[23]

Al did in fact respond, perhaps the only time he wrote Hunt directly that year. His letter evidently conveyed at least some assurances of mutual commitment and caring. The two men did not break off their friendship but rather continued and deepened it over the ensuing months. Hunt would bring Lowenstein the Sunday *New York Times* after finishing his stint working at a Durham radio station, and the two would chat as Lowenstein, sitting on his bed, leafed through the paper. They plotted strategy for the constitution committee, decided on who should run for which offices in the spring elections, and debated whether abolition or reform was the better strategy for dealing with the fraternities. When Lowenstein got sick before Christmas, Hunt visited him daily at the infirmary, taking his dirty clothes to the laundry, sending his telegrams, and making his bank deposits; Lowenstein's protestations notwithstanding, Hunt carried out all these tasks because he wanted to, and because it was the kind of thing a best friend did. The relationship was productive, warm, and lively, often shared with the coterie of friends who gathered at Danziger's to drink Viennese coffee, or on the green outside the Presbyterian church. The friendship was cherished by both.[24]

But the passage of time, if nothing else, would separate the two friends, especially given their age difference. That fact virtually crashed into Hunt's consciousness during the spring of 1946. "If I kept a record of terrifying emotional events," he wrote, "I would ... underscore that night [March 2] as one of the most disturbing I think I ever spent. . . . It was the first time I can ever recall being completely lonely while I was with you." Whenever there had been barriers between them in the past, Hunt said, he had always been confident that a good talk would make them go away. At the only other time of critical doubt (in the autumn, after the sonnet), Lowenstein had responded to Hunt's need. "I had to know—I could not wonder any longer," Hunt had confessed, and Al had made his own protestation of affection. "When I received your answer, I felt that all I felt about you was so far justified that I reproached myself for my foolish fantasies" and thereafter was daily grateful for "something which seemed to me too intimately wonderful to be wholly true." Al had been the "gift I did not deserve, and would not, in my wildest longing, have hoped to receive." But on March 2, the realization had suddenly struck, "quite blindingly and for the first time, that I would see you as I have seen you ... for perhaps another three months ... [and] that all this idyll was dying, going, fading," that each of them would get caught up in the vortex of his own life. It was that realization that had brought on the loneliness, "not the loneliness of not-having-found—the loneliness of imagination, [but] the loneliness of having-found-and-lost."

Suddenly perceiving the beginning of the end, everything took on a different light. "It was very hard to say good-bye to you the other night," Hunt wrote, because each moment had become irretrievable. And now he had to steel himself for the separation. "Understand me: I do not want to say it—I'm that selfish," but when the break came, "there must be no strings attached—there can be none, and withdrawal must be easy, painless, quick." In the meantime, the two would continue as they had been, seeking wherever possible not to erect barriers. "I shall try to remember," Hunt said, "that each moment I am with you may be—indeed, *is*—the last." Theirs was a special relationship. "It may be beyond the power of men to be friends," he wrote. "I half believed that until I came to know you. Emerson's evening of silence with Carlyle seemed so unreal and improbable that I held such an event to be an apocryphal occurrence and thought of it only in half-hope." But now that was no longer true, for he too had found such a relationship, "[and] I shall be grateful as long as I live—and, if I am conscious, after I die—for one Al Lowenstein." There remained only one last regret: "the fact . . . that someday you will find a person to whom you will be similarly indebted—I'm sorry I'm not that person." And so he had done what he had to do. "The worst and the best is said, and I shall mail this before I lose the courage."[25]

With acute accuracy, Hunt thus foretold the future of what would remain a pivotal relationship for both men. Their correspondence continued back and forth after Hunt joined the army and moved to Fort Belvoir in Virginia. At first, the two men also saw each other fairly frequently, then less so. Hunt detested the army, and his letters to Lowenstein took on a wan, homesick quality. At least once, he reflected again on what their year together had meant; he longed "for days that cannot come again" yet also faced candidly the realities that separation had created. "I could selfishly wish it to be otherwise," Hunt said, "but I do not think that any single person can (or should) ever come first with you. The *first* thing is what all the people who know you will demand of you: your loyal, unflagging devotion in terms of the . . . things in which you believe. . . . As for me, things are demanded of me too; but some other things I cannot help: for all the foreseeable future, you will come first with me in my thoughts, and in whatever I may be able . . . to do with and for you."[26]

In his own way, the "Rev. Hunt" had pronounced an appropriate benediction on a certain phase of his relationship with Lowenstein. Thereafter, it would be more difficult to lower the "barriers" or "clear the dust from the cabinets," as Hunt liked to say, when miles and divergent interests interfered. The correspondence became more snippy over the months, each friend riled at the other either for not writing (always Lowenstein's jibe, with every acquaintance) or for not placing the other at the top of his priority list. Yet there would always be that central friendship, at times shared with Jimmy Wallace, but in its closest moments confined to those two disparate and highly idiosyncratic characters. Hunt had experienced with Lowenstein a closeness, a "friendship between men," that he had not thought possible. It was the kind of friendship that thereafter Lowenstein would pursue repeatedly—albeit with ambivalence—in his struggle to find an answer to the problem of intimacy.

MIRIAM MASSEY

Al's relationships with women were different from his relationships with men. In some ways they were more regularized, in other ways less serious. Like many youngsters who have grown up in an affluent, urban environment, he lacked opportunities for casual contact with members of the opposite sex. Horace Mann was a boys' school; despite occasional "canteen" nights with a sister school or special dances, it was hard to develop a natural network of female friends. Al reached out for such contact more than his brothers had, but it was all "fairly formalized," according to Larry Lowenstein; large group dates were more common than couples going off by themselves. Al functioned well in that world; he wrote dozens of notes to female friends asking them for their personal "Hit Parades" and he played an active part in setting up and attending group events. But it was not until he went off to camp in Vermont that he experienced a typical teenage "crush," when the magic of a song and the inspiration of a special moment made a girl, Robin Fau, seem like the person he had been waiting for.[27]

Nevertheless, Al was more often the intimate good friend who lost out romantically than a Don Juan. Even in his relationship with Robin Fau, the dominant theme was the bittersweet one of love never quite grasped, with loyal friendship the consolation prize. "It's people like you that make this miserable old world worth living in," one of Robin's friends wrote Al after his relationship with her had fizzled; "don't you ever lose that wonderful something which makes you everyone's best friend and the swellest brother a person could ever ask for." The words of condolence were welcome, no doubt. But what kind of message was conveyed when, on the field of romance, one was described as a "swell brother?"[28]

In fact, Al seems to have given off mixed signals, on the one hand actively seeking out women companions, on the other hand retaining some distance to prevent intimate relationships. "The people with whom Al was involved tended generally not to be sexually active," one friend noted. "I mean [the men] would date, but I don't think they were on the make [like some of the fraternity brothers]." One of the women Lowenstein went out with commented on the difference between Al and some others who pursued her. "The situation is not the same as with you," she wrote. "You never gave any indication there was any sex involved." Many women were apparently drawn to Al. After all, his political prominence, idiosyncratic manners, and bohemian image had a certain appeal. "I just don't like guys who think of nothing but money and liquor," one coed from the Women's College of North Carolina in Greensboro wrote; "I like guys who want to go to Poland on cattle boats and start revolutions in Spain." But even then, something seemed lacking in the chemistry. "I now know why . . . from the Freudian point of view . . . you leave me vaguely irritated," wrote a close woman friend from New York. "It's because you are impervious to my feminine charm. You don't even *look* as though you *might possibly* want to whisper sweet nothings in my ear. It is bad for the vanity."[29]

It was against that backdrop of ambiguity that Miriam Massey first met Al in the fall of 1946. A year older than he was, she had transferred to UNC for her final two years of college. (First- and second-year women were not allowed at UNC). One day, she said, "[I saw Al] in a red and black checked shirt walking on the campus carrying some kind of shoes . . . over his shoulders." Someone introduced them, and they were off. "From the first he was talking about politics," she said. "Truth to tell, I didn't care a whole lot about student politics, but I probably would have cared about anything Al said to [care about]." She fell quickly in love, and he at least was interested. She was a Georgian—and therefore an excellent candidate for conversion to the Lowenstein gospel of racial liberalism—and a Gentile. "I would never have gotten as far as I did if I had been Jewish," she observed.

That summer, Mimi went with Al to the Encampment for Citizenship, and the two became a couple, at least in the eyes of others. "I remember always wishing I was seeing more of Al than I was [that summer]," she recalled, "but he was always out trying to meet somebody new [and convert] these boys from Iowa." Still, it was a glorious experience. Mimi was there when Al "integrated" the Jewish country club; she sat on the floor and sang Josh White songs with him during the evening get-togethers; and she rode off with him in his convertible at the end of the summer as their fellow campers serenaded them.[30]

By the fall of 1947, most people treated Al and Mimi like an "item." Fellow campers from EFC addressed letters to "Al and Mimi," friends asked whether "engagement [was] approaching," and classmates presumed that wherever one went, the other would follow. Mimi brought Al home to meet her family in Milledgeville, Georgia, and although she had a difficult time combating her relatives' anti-Semitism (one referred to "that Hebrew boy"), the visit generally went well; Mimi followed Al's lead and emphasized the "individual by individual" approach to overcoming ethnic slurs and stereotypes. Her friends might still think of Jews as "uncouth, noisy, brassy, dirty and pushy," but at least in her presence, they controlled their tongues. Douglass Hunt expressed his support—"You two appear to be friends as well as lovers," he wrote—but told Al, "Don't burn it out by pushing it too hard too soon." Other friends took the opposite approach, asking Al, "Why in heaven's name don't you fall in love with that wonderful girl?" Fearing the worst, Al's stepmother asked, "Am I to gather anything from [all these letters mentioning Mimi]? To be perfectly frank, she's probably too good for us." Then to make the point crystal clear, she added: "There *is* happiness in this world, and you can attain it if the foundation is well laid with common background, feelings and interests." Mimi herself, meanwhile, was only hoping that Florence Lowenstein was right; she addressed Al in most of her letters as "Dear Angel" and signed them, "Slavishly yours."[31]

Yet there had always been an imbalance in their relationship. She was much more in love with him than he was with her. She was ready for commitment; he feared it. She called him "Angel"; he called her "Dearie." "That was real ambiguous," she commented. "It always had a slight joking edge to it. . . . He just couldn't go too far, he couldn't trust anyone too much." Sometimes he would even call her a "hatpin," for deflating him in conversation. "It was better than 'castrating bitch,'" she said, "but that was the general idea." Al would deploy her to do political chores for him but at the same time never really trusted her to do them well. "[He] was sure that I could almost wreck anything," she observed, "left to my own devices." He would deputize her to tell someone to vote a certain way, only to chastise her later for not being subtle enough in her approach. He took her with him on political visits to Raleigh or Durham, but as often as not he left her to wait in the car while he—late as usual—went about his business.[32]

Although Mimi was intellectually precocious, she also wanted a romantic relationship. "She liked to play, she liked to do silly things, and she was very much a girl, very much a flirt," a mutual friend said; "[she was] able to turn off the intellectual stuff easily." She also had normal sexual interests and was quite good at conveying them to Al, sometimes in a teasing manner. Writing about dogs in heat, she once asked him, "How do they get back to back when one starts out on top?" As if to make fun of

Al's naïveté, she added, "This has to do with the mating of dogs." They did a lot of necking, she later recalled, "but I always had the feeling that Al was doing this for my sake, not his, that what Al really wanted to be doing was talking about politics or something." When they were interacting on his terms, it was fine; but when it came to hers, he pulled back. In a fundamental way, she understood that. Reading the biography of Eugene Debs at Al's suggestion one summer, she wrote: "I somehow feel very close to you now, closer than when in your arms. . . . [There] I felt more female than Miriam." As a friend and an intellectual with political interests, she could be close to him; as a sexual partner, she was more an impersonal object.[33]

By the summer of 1948, Mimi's sense of estrangement from Al had reached the point where she was willing to express it directly, with some sarcasm. Al had barely managed to make an appearance at her graduation, perhaps fearing more romantic pressure, and she was angry. "You see," she wrote, "my problem then, as it had been for some weeks before, was to adjust myself to the classification to which you had relegated me, i.e. a shapely piece of dead wood. I have, it seems to me, filled this role adequately with only an occasional revolt at which time I became a hat pin, a more active if less desirable version of dead wood." Al had given her a political conscience, she acknowledged, but that did not prevent him from viewing her as a member of the ignorant masses, inferior in judgment and perception. "Thus, when I said nothing after you had nobly said that 'it has been nice knowing you,' I guess I wanted to apologize for being a blob. . . . Of one thing I am sure. Once an intelligent, honest ineffectual blob, always an intelligent, honest, ineffectual blob. In a way I am sorry, because I hate to madden you and bore you like almost all your followers do in large doses." Clearly, Mimi had been burned by the imbalance of their relationship. She, and by implication hundreds like her, felt judged and condescended to by someone so bright, so alert, so hyperactive, and so commanding that virtually everyone else had to accept being caught in his wake, or have no relationship with him at all.[34]

Throughout the following year, Mimi ruminated on this dynamic, occasionally writing to Al about her own experience of now being free from his control. She had gone to Harvard for graduate study in social relations. Benny Johnson, one of Al's close friends from UNC, was also there in the same graduate program. Al remained in Chapel Hill, completing his final year. Although she found the intellectual smugness of Cambridge infuriating, Mimi also welcomed the laissez-faire atmosphere, especially, she wrote Al, "the fact that I have found it so convenient not to make value judgments, much less transfer said judgments to the unenlightened masses as was my Lowenstein-given role at Carolina." Geographical and psychological distance was obviously giving Mimi Massey a new sense of what had occurred, not only in her own relationship with Al but also in Al's relationship with the entire student community. "I am feeling this fall for the first time," she wrote him at Christmas, "a certain independence with regard to you. . . . I don't need you to hold me together any more." If she was not writing as often as he would like, therefore, it was because she needed to let this independence flower. "This should relieve you," she wrote, "[as] it certainly relieves me not to have my joys and sorrows so bound up with your life and chameleon-like attitudes. . . . And I suppose I reason that I can retain this hard-won freedom by not communicating." Here, then, was another portrait of Al at UNC, that of a person whose capacity to consume people made it extraordinarily difficult for them to find lives of their own, or to be equals with him.[35]

During the same months, Mimi and Benny were falling in love. Fellow students in the same department, they partied together, visited Scollay Square and Durgin Park, and gradually developed a deeper, more romantic relationship. Although Al had initially suggested that the two "get together" (largely, Mimi thought, to get her out of his own hair), both were close to Al and sensitive to his feelings about his (former?) girlfriend. In a humorous letter full of byplay, they tried to let Al know what was going on between them. In the months following, they repeatedly gave him similar clues. Benny wrote to say he was pinned to Mimi; Mimi wrote that she had taken Benny to meet her sister. Although she was still somewhat ambiguious, Mimi was signaling Al that she was far more interested in Benny than in remaining involved with Al.[36]

Yet at precisely that moment, Al began wooing Mimi again, bringing her into his confidence more than he had in over a year, and suggesting, by his decision to share his innermost thoughts with her, that he expected her to respond similarly, as though Benny did not exist. "I have missed you sorely for the past month," Al wrote Mimi in May. "I am confused and hopelessly indecisive." A week later, he told her about his plans for the graduation dance, saying, "I wish I were going . . . with you," and then he telegraphed her, begging her to set aside time during her visit to Chapel Hill at graduation time for them to be together.[37]

Graduation weekend turned into a disaster of missed signals and wounded feelings. Al had waited in Chapel Hill for Mimi to arrive before going to a party, but when Mimi and Benny reached Chapel Hill they were not interested. When they talked by phone, Al later wrote, Benny was "almost hostile [and] bored sounding," while Mimi acted "like a parrot." Al had "planned and when necessary plotted to arrange for [them] to be together," making no date one night ("despite a strained social situation") and fixing it so they could double-date the following night, only to have all his schemes disintegrate; Mimi went off to Georgia having exchanged barely a word with Al. Clearly, events had not gone as Al had hoped.[38]

Yet the imbroglio did trigger a barrage of letters, which are remarkable for what they reveal about Al's sense of self, and his willingness, under stress, to share at least some of his deepest conflicts and fears. Writing to Mimi while on a European graduation trip, Al declared that, "except maybe at the end of the Encampment, I never felt as close to you . . . as I did the last month before graduation." He had stated these sentiments repeatedly, had "poured forth my deepest thoughts," only to receive a cold shoulder from her. "You stopped confiding in me so completely that I had to glean tidbits about you from ex-roommates." Even more important, "you shrouded the Benny business so completely that I still have to infer and just plain guess what's what." Accusing her of running off without even saying goodbye, he concluded, "In any case I've never felt so great a gap between us, and it's only one month since I never felt closer to you. Why? . . . I love you dearly," signed "Allard."

Mimi's response fully engaged the emotion of Al's letter, while adding a degree of analysis of their relationship that rocked him back on his heels. She appreciated his tenderness and concern, Mimi said, but was appalled by his paranoia. "I would not have left Chapel Hill if I had thought I could have seen you," she wrote:

> But Al, I felt that you were determined to arrange things so that you couldn't possibly see me except in unsatisfactorily hurried and crowded snatches [which you would then] be noisily inconsolate about. . . . You wailed over the phone that it was impossible for us to get together, I [then] suggested ways in which we might, and you reject[ed] them, all the while being unhappy. *You have always done these things, and they somehow must enhance your security.* I do not pretend to understand the underlying motivation of your creation of and enjoyment of semi-dramatic mix-ups and misunderstandings. . . . For heaven's sake, stop being paranoid.

Whatever Massey's own responsibility for the distress of the weekend, her assessment of Al's role had clearly upped the ante in the struggle to figure out what had happened.

In response, Al gave a breathtaking view of his own self-image, as well as his perception of reality. Calling Mimi an "erstwhile moll" intent on explaining his entire existence as an exercise in paranoia, Lowenstein issued his own rhetorical blast. "One survives as a 'conciliator,'" he wrote, "and becomes known as 'the crisis averter' in school . . . when cometh a piercing announcement that one is a fiend for the drama, a lover of the absurd situations one has been loathing, a thriver on crisis—and goodness only knows what else. One cannot deny, one can only gasp." Massey's charges, he declared, were like "the final, oblique triumph of the opposition party on campus," accepting all his enemy's political assertions about him and turning them into a description of his personality.

It was she who was responsible for the disastrous weekend. "You must realize I was left to guess, up to and including the first phone conversation, if there was anything between [Benny] and you." As for the allegation of paranoia, "you must know what people suffer from who imagine other people don't *really* want to be with them, no matter how often the other people show that they do." Professing that he "had never loved you or needed you as much as I did then," Al concluded by saying how resentful he was of her charges of "duplicity," and how "stunned" he was "at the reception accorded perfectly normal overtures for a perfectly normal resumption of a very warm and wonderful relationship."[39]

Notwithstanding his protestations of normalcy, however, Al began to brood on the comments Mimi had made about his life and behavior. Perhaps as much as at any time thereafter, he engaged in serious introspection, seeking to understand his own unhappiness. "I'm realizing things about myself which it is hurting to do," he wrote Mimi after returning to the United States:

> The hardest new realization to own up to is also the hardest to state. There are in the world people who are always sought after, people who are sometimes sought after, a few people who like to be alone (a very few, really); and people who are always doing the seeking-after. This last is me. . . . It is depressing in a way to realize that in all the years I have been suggesting to people of all sizes and descriptions that we do things together, never (I omit political considerations and instances where 'favors' were sought) have the people who I most often ask and whose company I most enjoy — never has one of them sought *me* to do anything.

All these people might like him, Lowenstein granted ("and what's more they all vote for me"), but on a social plane, "whoosh." Moreover, not only did they now avoid initiating social contact, but they were rejecting his advances as well. "Thus, while I have never known more people on campus, have never had so many 'friends,' or such 'political strength'—I am now lonelier than I have been in years. . . . Every day in every way I get reminded fifty times. I must be a terribly dull person to have to spend more than an hour with, outside a meeting-place. . . . I guess I'm [just] a sweet kid with ideals and an automobile." Thus at the end of a new rhetorical courtship that could only have happened, in Mimi's view, because she was safely ensconced in another relationship, Al had plumbed the depths of his personal being, where he discovered, with Mimi's prodding, the courage to acknowledge his deepest doubts. One of the most well-known, popular, and powerful people on the UNC campus, Allard Lowenstein was not even sure that anyone liked or accepted him.[40]

CONCLUSION

In the end, it all seemed to fit together. Every day Al flitted from one cause to another, laughing and joking, politicking behind the scenes, making speeches, inspiring comrades—never still, always in motion, forever playing a critical role. "He was sort of what Alice Longworth Roosevelt said about her father, Teddy," one political ally said. "'He wanted to be the bride at every wedding, and the corpse at every funeral.'" As the center of attention in any group, he dominated his peers, striding over the political life of UNC like someone accustomed to being in command.[41]

Because of that pivotal role, Lowenstein exercised enormous influence. "Few friends have ever taught me as much as he has," a former roommate said. "Such are the people who move mountains." Yet there was a downside as well. "His great ego (in the finer sense) usually completely dominates everyone," the same friend wrote, with the result that it "often overshadows others who must themselves someday take hold and grow." Hence, he went on, the only way one could "breathe free and be your own, erring self" was to move away from Al.

Another way of saying the same thing was to recognize that Lowenstein thrived by feeding on people. He consumed their energies and adulation as well as dominated their activity. Control was thus essential to the process; as long as he was in charge and in motion, his impact was extraordinary. "It was utterly fantastic," the same friend observed, "the sway that boy had on people. When he moved, in space or in thought and action, he did not move alone, hundreds moved with him, first the closest satellites, the few close compatriots, then the outer satellites, his friends and workers, then the outer constellations, those who followed him. To watch him and see him work day by day was always a source of wonder to me . . . a mere mortal. . . . Lowenstein was able to move people with a power that is all but earthly."[42]

On the other hand, once people escaped that orbit, they recovered their own egos and no longer fed his. His security and dominance ceased because he no longer could be in charge of them. At that point, he became vulnerable and had to deal with the same insecurities all mortal beings suffer. Playing a critical role at the center of things thus became Lowenstein's way of avoiding having to deal with himself. Activity—especially the *group* activity he thrived on, the rash of political engagements and meetings—was a means of evading introspection and self-disclosure, on the one hand, and of achieving dominance on the other. He wrote letters that said nothing about himself because he did not wish to expose his weaknesses. "I don't know whether it's better to hear from you and realize that I am being told nothing," Douglass Hunt wrote during one of the low points of their relationship, "or not to hear from you and not have to overcome the illusion of knowledge."

Some friends saw through Lowenstein's elaborate evasions and even took the risk of confronting him. At one point in 1949, Al had asked a number of acquaintances what they thought of him. Most of the answers were predictably reinforcing, praising his character, nobility, and morals. "You simply couldn't be improved upon on that score," one longtime friend wrote. "But to get down to you,"

> although you are a very strong person . . . you seem to have an area of insecurity. What are you afraid of? . . . And what is it you're running away from within your own self. Actually, I've never seen anyone who is liked more than you . . . yet you don't seem to feel sure of this. . . . You seem to be searching for something. But you're directing that search everywhere but within yourself. Perhaps you don't want to go beneath the surface because you're afraid of what you'll find there.[43]

At least part of the answer lay in Al's discomfort with his Jewishness. He had gone to UNC, by all accounts, to escape a Jewish milieu, "to become a normal American." He wanted desperately to be a regular person, "so gentile, so white bread." "Don't stick to people with the same background," he had written in pencil on the back of an envelope. Everything Al did at UNC—his commitment to each individual being treated as an individual and not as part of a racial group, his denunciation of Zionism as race nationalism, his successful effort to break up the clustering of Jewish students in the same dorms—was designed to achieve that end. Al never dated a Jewish woman at UNC, had almost no Jewish friends, and went to the Presbyterian church. In another of his famous headline diary entries, he exulted in the fact that he had 150 friends, *"113 of them Protestant."*[44]

Yet he could not escape the issue of his Jewish identity, however hard he tried. It was there in the fraternities with their exclusionary policies; it was present in people's suspicion of him as "too cloak and dagger," "too much on the edge of things"; and it was part of the North Carolina environment. Charges of anti-Semitism, for example, were made against the history department at UNC. A professor had been denied tenure, primarily, some believed, because he was both a leftist and a Jew—a lethal combination. "Undeniably," Jimmy Wallace wrote, "the vast majority of the history faculty . . . is anti-semitic and anti-communist." Then there was the time Al went to the movies and saw a newsreel that featured the Ku Klux Klan in Georgia. When the audience applauded, Al found himself hissing. Then when Eleanor Roosevelt was shown denouncing the Grand Dragon and condemning intolerance, the audience booed and hissed. "I realized I was so tense," Al wrote, "I would have hit the hissers had any been near enough. For me this was all a very strange reaction. It's been eight or ten years — [since the Spanish Civil War] — since anything in a Newsreel had tensed me up so." Yet when he revealed his response to the people he was with, "they were rather inclined (I suspect) to regard it all as a sort of Jewish hypersensitivity. 'Good people' in Germany did exactly that until it was too late."[45]

Perhaps worst of all, the issue could not be erased from Al's private life. Mimi and Al talked about his Jewishness all the time. Her mother had "apoplexy" as the postmarks flew back and forth between Scarsdale and Milledgeville, and of course his stepmother made apoplexy look like a state of calm. One of Mimi's friends confided in her that all Jews were innately different. Another was willing to concede that Al was "the one great exception to the Jewish race. Your genes just got twisted somehow and you turned out to be a person instead of a Jew." A friend of Mimi's family told her mother that she had met Mimi's "little Jewish friend," and later, when Mimi appeared with someone else, she was told, "I'm glad to see your taste is improving, bringing a good Presbyterian down here instead of that Hebrew." No matter how hard she tried the "individual by individual or Lowenstein technique," Mimi wrote, the stereotypes remained.[46]

He might pronounce his name Lowen*stine* rather than Lowen*steen;* he could write endless numbers of term papers that supported intermarriage; he could even associate almost exclusively with Christians. But the Jewish label remained. In the opinion of many of his friends, it was the sole reason he lost almost every election he ran in at UNC. "He was just this strange, Jewish boy," Mimi Massey said, "who looked strange, and he really was so brilliant, [but] he just couldn't make it with the regular folks." It was what made the difference between the power he had as a political presence behind the scenes and his endemic failure as a candidate. (When Lowenstein lost the student body vice-presidency in 1949, the fraternity vote against him made the difference.) No matter how hard he sought to suppress or ignore it, the issue of his Jewishness persisted. "Once when he came to visit us," Benny Johnson recalled, "I said to him, 'Al, you look like a dry goods merchant,' [and] something in his eyes made me realize that I'd gone much too far. . . . That was an unintentionally anti-Semitic remark [that revealed in Al] a kind of ultimate hurtability."[47]

But the problem was not only Al's Jewishness. It was also his unresolved sexual identity. Although there is little direct evidence that speaks to this question, the indirect evidence is overwhelming. Al's relationships with women in these years seemed never to have sex as a primary energizing force. He danced, he courted, he double-dated, he "necked." Yet his relationships with most women appear to have been asexual. The one woman he did have a "necking" physical relationship with perceived their limited lovemaking as a favor he was doing to please her, not as something he wanted to do for himself. "He would rather have been talking politics," she said. When she was in his arms, she felt "female, not Miriam."

Al's closest relationships during these years were with men, and most notably, with Douglass Hunt. The two shared an intense camaraderie. Their closeness, at times, seemed to partake of at least the spiritual side of romantic love. In many ways, theirs was a courtship, a process of discovery in which affection was exchanged, inner thoughts shared, visions and dreams imagined together.

The most analagous kind of relationship historians are familiar with is that of the "female world of love and ritual" among middle- and upper-class women in late eighteenth- and nineteenth-century America. Women in such relationships, according to Carroll Smith-Rosenberg, confided their deepest secrets to each other, surrounded their interaction with terms of endearment, talked about the plateaus of understanding they were able to reach together, and frequently spent the night together, exchanging hugs and affectionate touches. These relationships, Smith-Rosenberg writes, were often far more intimate than the women's marriages. But they were not homosexual relationships; rather, they were homosocial—exchanges between people of the same sex that had erotic overtones but no actual sexual interaction.[48]

Anthony Rotundo has described parallel, though different patterns of interaction among some nineteenth-century men of the same class and background. The intimacy of same-sex relationships among men, Rotundo writes, also involved sharing innermost thoughts and exchanging terms of affection that late twentieth-century culture might see as erotic. Some of the men he studied also slept together, writing to each other of the closeness they felt as a result of the confidences they shared in the privacy of the bedroom. As with Smith-Rosenberg's females, Rotundo's males shared not only their most private hopes and emotions but also their concerns about the women they would eventually marry. The greatest difference between the two groups, according to Rotundo, was that for the men same-sex bonding was a youthful experience that they relinquished when, as adults, they found a marriage partner; by contrast, women were likely to continue their intimate relationships throughout their lives. Both scholars, however, present a portrait of same-sex interaction that featured expression of a "wide latitude of emotions and sexual feelings."[49]

These broad descriptions help to place in perspective Al Lowenstein's relationship with Douglass Hunt. It was primarily an intimacy of the spirit, one compared, by Hunt, to the soulful union of Emerson and Carlyle. It represented the marrying, as it were, of two minds equally dedicated to truth and transcendence. They were "best friends"—the kind of relationship Lowenstein had defined in his diary entry at age fourteen as the only acceptable solution to controlling his urges toward men.

Yet it would be a mistake to call the relationship sexual. Al had not yet come to a clear understanding of how to define or express his own sexuality. "There always is a great deal of masturbation in Allard's life," Sandy Friedman said, "[but] that was verboten." Homosexuality was something you hid, something that was dirty, something that you neither talked about nor acted upon. "We lived in a very different time," Friedman said. "[There were too many] inhibitions and too many ignorances [for Allard] to act on [any homosexual instincts]." Later in his life, those instincts would become more obvious and pressing, and also more discussable. But the 1940s was a time when society allocated no sanction or place for openly contemplating one's sexual preference. Instead, if there were conflicts or desires, they might find expression in relationships like those of nineteenth-century women and men, relationships homosocial, not homosexual.

Still, one can imagine the turbulence and anxiety of a young man like Allard Lowenstein as he sought to struggle with these issues. Was he Jewish or not Jewish? An individual or part of a race? A "normal" man, with "normal" sexual instincts, or "peculiar," with instincts that he could neither understand nor rationalize? How could he live, carve out a community, define a lifestyle, become a person at home with himself, publicly and privately, in the face of such tensions?

Politically, it was a time when the House Un-American Activities Committee (HUAC) had started to identify "queers" with subversives and to persecute anyone in government service who might be sexually "deviant," hence allegedly vulnerable to blackmail by a foreign foe. Nor were the opinions of psychiatrists and other "experts" on the family any more enlightened. Homosexuality was viewed as a sickness that should be cured, a behavior that could be renounced and corrected with proper psychiatric care. In most people's view, homosexuality was a perversion one chose to indulge—and hence could choose *not* to indulge—not an impulse that was natural, or a condition of birth. Anyone who felt sexual attraction toward members of their own sex, therefore, had no sanction and no place to go to talk about the issue or express confusion, doubt, or desire. In a very literal sense, such desires had to be kept in a closet and never let out lest one's whole world come crashing down.

One of the only solutions to this dilemma was to avoid intimacy, at least on an equal basis with another person, where you would have to share and make yourself as vulnerable as the other person. It was for that reason that Al had so many acquaintances, and for the most part, insisted on being with them in groups. It was also for that reason that when he did become involved in a one-on-one relationship—something he desperately craved but mortally feared as well—it was almost always one-sided. "Allard had a tremendous need or skill, or both," Sandy Friedman said, "[to be] the Confessor. . . . It was a need and a capability that enabled him to draw anyone into a fifteen-hour talk, overnight, where that person revealed his entire soul." But how much did Allard reveal? Usually nothing. "Allard shortchanged [people] in that exchange always . . . to a point where I felt

Allard didn't want to speak of himself personally." Revealing himself would be too painful for a Jew in a world full of goys, or for a sexually confused young man in a world full of straights.[50]

To most people, Al Lowenstein was a bon vivant, a self-possessed, confident, electric kind of personality who was on top of the world and the envy of all his compatriots. But a few saw his other side. One friend observed: "Keen of intellect, steady of purpose . . . he loves people in groups and greets everyone with outgoing affection. . . . In a crowd he laughs and clowns as if he never had a care or a heartache. But alone, or with some one person he reveals the strange and sad strain of melancholy that underlies the gaiety." It was that dimension of his personality that Miriam Massey and Douglass Hunt had some insight into. But it was also the dimension that impelled Al to run away from self-confrontation whenever he could. Fearful of sharing with others the turbulence of his self-doubts, he escaped by immersing himself in his public role, creating through his hyperactivity such a presence that few people would see behind the illusion to the gnawing anxiety he was afraid to confront. It was here that the personal and the political were most closely connected, because it was the *type* of activity Lowenstein wanted to be identified with that most clearly revealed his anxieties: aligning himself with principled causes and righteous figures, he rejected any allegation that he was a Machiavellian engaged in deception and chicanery. Thus did he deal with the feelings of marginality and inferiority he associated with his Jewishness and his sexuality. Lowenstein's political self-image had to be that of a crusader pledged to noble causes and the reign of righteousness. "The bad side of Allard" that Sandy Friedman talked about, "the double dealer . . . dirty politics . . . that backroom stuff . . . was inadmissable to his own image of himself." It had to be purged. It could not be acknowledged or accepted. By devoting himself to the purest goals and staying above the selfish battles, Lowenstein could retain his self-image as a knight in shining armor. "Al is from Heaven, as I have always known," Benny Johnson wrote in one acerbic dialogue. "Yes," Mimi added, "now this makes Al safely loved for his own immaculate virtues."[51]

Yet there was the occasional tear in this elaborately woven self-image. Sometimes candor and honesty intruded. "As I look at myself less than three weeks before graduation," Al wrote Mimi, "I cannot fail to be disappointed, worried and even a little horrified at what I see. . . . The confusion and indecision is not merely a reflection of having no notion of what comes next in my 'young life'; it is a reflection as well of some alarm at the course my personal development is taking." In her response, Mimi zeroed in on the problem. "You're just at the crisis that you knew would have to arrive sooner or later—that time when you'd have to *look at yourself instead of hiding yourself in activity.*" Whether Lowenstein could or would act on that insight became a theme that dominated the rest of his life.[52]

4

The NSA Years: The Apprenticeship of an Anti-Communist Liberal

Dᴜʀɪɴɢ ᴛʜᴇ ʏᴇᴀʀs ꜰᴏʟʟᴏᴡɪɴɢ ʜɪs ɢʀᴀᴅᴜᴀᴛɪᴏɴ ꜰʀᴏᴍ UNC, Aʟʟᴀʀᴅ Lowenstein pursued a kaleidoscope of activities, bewildering in their variety. He went to Washington to help Frank Porter Graham in the Senate, then quickly relocated to Madison, Wisconsin, to serve as president of the National Student Association. After that year, he finally enrolled at Yale Law School (having been admitted for the third time) and astounded everyone by securing a law degree while hardly ever appearing in class. A hitch in the army provided a hiatus between two terms as a student coordinator for Adlai Stevenson—in 1952 and 1956—followed in 1956–57 by a year-long job drumming up support for the United Nations on college campuses. By 1957, Lowenstein was ready to return to Chapel Hill, this time as a part-time graduate student and dormitory counselor. On the surface, it looked like the résumé of someone lacking focus and discipline, who bounced from one place to another, without direction or purpose.

Yet beneath the apparent aimlessness, a pattern was emerging. Although the colors and shapes of Lowenstein's activities altered with astonishing speed, the underlying method and rationale soon became clear— simply to stay in motion was a goal in its own right. Above all, each of Lowenstein's diverse activities reflected consistent themes: his political life would be guided by the twin poles of anticommunism on the one hand

86

and liberal engagement, especially regarding race, on the other; and the constituency that would provide the base for both his personal and political agenda would consist primarily of young people, usually from college campuses. For these reasons, the NSA experience proved the most decisive—and revealing—of all his involvements during this period.

FRANK PORTER GRAHAM

As he pursued political life, Al Lowenstein cultivated two kinds of relationships. One was with younger people, who became protégés and disciples. The other was with older people—usually much older people—who became mentors and exemplified the personal and political qualities that Lowenstein venerated and had not found in his complex relationship with his parents. Through association with these individuals and their values, Lowenstein could feel enhanced in his own self-image and ennobled in his political activism. The pantheon of his heroes included Eleanor Roosevelt, Norman Thomas, Lucille Kohn, and eventually a younger person, Robert Kennedy. But the first among equals was Frank Porter Graham, a man whose qualities best symbolized the virtues of all the others, and in whose honor Lowenstein would name his firstborn son.

In uncanny ways, Graham's life bore a striking resemblance to what Lowenstein's would become. Graham, too, was a blur of activity at college and conveyed no clear sense of what he wanted to do. After graduation, he experimented with law school, then with graduate school in history. A dynamic teacher, he inspired a large following of students at UNC by asking his classes to get involved on different sides of issues; like Lowenstein, he became president of the debating society. His forte, though, was being a dean, and then a university president, in which position he became famous for the number of students he knew—all by name. Slight of build, Graham decided to work out rigorously at the gym to increase his strength. He was very popular with his male colleagues but seemed less confident with women. Whenever his sexual urges became dangerously strong, he told a friend, he exercised to the point of exhaustion and then went to sleep. At the age of forty-five he married Marian Drane, a woman fourteen years his junior. Graham seemed careless, even indifferent, in his attitude toward money, but when it came to friends he paid attention. Frequently, he asked young students like Al Lowenstein to drive him to and from engagements so that they could spend time together.[1]

Throughout his years as a student, Lowenstein had become ever closer to Graham. Whether driving him to the airport on his many trips out of town on government assignments or dropping by the presidential manse on Franklin Street for late-night conversations, the two kindred spirits had ample opportunity to become closer. Douglass Hunt and Jimmy Wallace spoke of Lowenstein as "the keeper of [Graham's] conscience," and the two men together seemed to exemplify the meaning of moral politics. As if to sanctify the relationship, or at least remove a possible barrier to it, Doc Lowenstein idolized Graham also and wrote repeatedly of his desire for Al to go to work for Graham in Washington—if necessary, for no salary. It was a classic "conflict-free" choice.[2]

No issues were more central to national and southern politics in the late 1940s than anticommunism and civil rights, two questions on which Graham and Lowenstein were agreed. The cold war had begun in earnest by the time Graham was appointed to the U.S. Senate in 1949 to fill a vacancy caused by the death of Senator J. Melville Broughton. Equally important, the witch hunts of the House Un-American Activities Committee had proceeded apace. Harry Truman's Civil Rights Commission had also made its report—signed by commission member Frank Porter Graham—and a change in the South's age-old commitment to racial separatism seemed imminent. Almost all of Lowenstein's time on Graham's staff was taken up with defending Graham against vicious attacks on these two issues as he sought election to the Senate in his own right in 1950. In the process, Lowenstein's own positions on civil rights and anticommunism were honed in ways that would shape decisively his political activity from that point forward.

Frank Porter Graham's record on race relations was crystal clear. He believed in the teachings of Jesus of Nazareth, acted to ensure that all individuals were treated with dignity, and, as a member of Truman's Civil Rights Commission, agreed that a "separate but equal" social system was unworkable because segregation automatically "brands the Negro with the mark of inferiority." But Graham's solution—as forward-looking a proposal as most white liberals in the South could envision in the 1930s and 1940s—was voluntary desegregation through education and moral persuasion. Hence, he specifically dissented from the Truman Commission's proposal that the federal government use grants-in-aid and a Fair Employment Practices law (FEPC) to force desegregation. Graham approved federal aid to education but opposed federal control over the nature of that education, believing that states and localities should allocate the monies as they saw fit. In spirit, of course, Graham probably believed a lot more, as reflected in his support for imposed integration *after* the Supreme Court's 1954 ruling on *Brown* v. *Board of Education of Topeka*, and in his praise for sit-in demonstrators in 1960. But in the 1940s, he thought he had gone as far as he could go in support of civil rights without losing altogether his credibility with white voters. Testifying to the success he had in walking that tightrope was the confidence with which Governor Kerr Scott appointed Graham to the Senate. Presumably, North Carolina would accept a "saintly" liberal who refrained from overt interference with ancient social patterns.[3]

The key was the apparatus that defended states' rights and upheld "voluntary" action. A foundation stone for that apparatus was the right to filibuster in the U.S. Senate against any civil rights legislation—a right that could be terminated only if two-thirds of the Senate voted to end debate through "cloture." By the spring of 1950, FEPC legislation was once again before Congress for debate; southern senators were trying to talk the bill to death, while northern liberals were demanding cloture. Graham was confined by the flu to a sickbed in North Carolina. His aides, including Lowenstein, pleaded with him to ask his North Carolina colleague, Clyde Hoey, to announce that were he in attendance he would vote against cloture, thereby upholding states' rights and protecting himself against the charge that he was conspiring with northern liberals to force integration on the South. But Graham denied permission for such an announcement to be made. He had not heard the debate, he told Lowenstein and others; therefore, he could not know firsthand whether it should be terminated and hence could not declare himself to be on the side of his southern colleagues. "Perhaps," his biographer wrote, "he felt that such an act would be self-serving and that he later would find it hard to justify to himself. Perhaps, also, there had long been at the base of his character a touch of the desire for self-immolation." In any event, he chose not to defend himself against attack on one of the two issues that could end his Senate career.[4]

The other issue was the charge of being "soft on communism." In 1938, Graham had joined Eleanor Roosevelt, Clark Foreman, and a variety of other liberals to form the Southern Conference on Human Welfare, a group committed to racial and economic justice that included in its ranks at least some individuals who were Marxists. Graham became its first president. (When Eugene "Bull" Connor, the Birmingham, Alabama, police commissioner, attempted to enforce the segregation statutes at the first SCHW meeting by having the Negro delegates sit on one side and the whites on the other, Eleanor Roosevelt responded by placing her chair in the middle, half on one side, half on the other). Within two years, the Dies Committee (HUAC under Chairman Martin Dies) had denounced the SCHW as a "transmission belt" for the Communist party, and Graham as a fellow traveler who in addition to serving with the SCHW had also served on the board of the "University of Moscow summer school for training students in communism [*sic*]." Although Graham survived that initial attack, the allegations persisted and were repeated again when the HUAC described the SCHW in 1947 as "perhaps the most deviously camouflaged Communist-front organization [in America]." Two years later, the radio commentator Fulton Lewis, Jr., charged that the staff of the Atomic Energy Commission had recommended denying Graham security clearance because of his "known" association with Communists. "[If] Dr. Graham is not a communist or fellow-traveler," one southern congressman said, "he performs like one."[5]

Graham held his ground and rallied his defenders. "I propose not to run [away] because some groups shout Communist or Negrophile," he said to a friend. "Even more important than this is that we be open and candid with both friend and foe." Graham believed that exposing all political viewpoints to the light of day served as the best guarantee of preserving democracy and freedom. "I do not object to the members of any political party, Democrats, Republicans, Socialists, Communists, or what-not coming into an open democratic meeting so long as it is open and above board," he declared. The people could be trusted to make their own decisions. Al Lowenstein agreed and was furious at the time with a student colleague who accused Graham of "political myopia" for joining "so many Communist front groups." In response, Lowenstein denounced his associate as a "professional anti-communist loud mouth" seeking to "smear [Graham's] Christian-ethical behavior."[6]

By the late spring of 1950, however, Lowenstein and other Graham backers were desperately engaged in a last-ditch effort to save Dr. Frank from scurrilous assaults on both these issues. Although the governor had been supremely confident that North Carolinians would send Graham back to the Senate with a resounding endorsement, conservatives in the state had a different notion. Led by Willis Smith, the former head of the American Bar Association, they portrayed Graham as a leftist who had supported communist causes and as an integrationist in favor of race mixing. Sometimes the two issues were joined, as in one leaflet that listed Graham's alleged Communist-front activities at the top of the page and ran a picture of black soldiers dancing with white women at the bottom. By May, Graham's foes were headlining the charge that Graham had named a North Carolina black to the U.S. Military Academy at West Point. "No other Southern Senator or Congressman has ever appointed a Negro," the ad declared. (In fact, the candidate was an alternate who had scored third in a competitive examination.) Against these attacks, Lowenstein and others waged a valiant campaign, arguing that Graham had always opposed federal coercion on civil rights, stating the facts on the West Point cadet, and emphasizing testimonials to Graham's anticommunism. On the day of the primary, it seemed that they might even prevail. Graham won over 300,000 votes, only 11,000 short of a decisive majority, while his two opponents split the remainder. But just when it seemed the battle had been won, Willis Smith exercised his right to call for a runoff, and the bitterest, ugliest, most smear-ridden campaign of modern times was set in motion.[7]

This time, Smith and his allies accepted no bounds. Although the candidate himself refrained from the most gratuitous assaults, he freely denounced Graham as a Socialist and sanctioned mailings that accused Graham of being "up to his neck" in Communists. With a young newcomer named Jessie Helms helping with mailings and advertisements, the Smith campaign cropped photographs to suggest that Graham approved of race mixing, superimposed the face of Graham's wife, Marian, atop the body of a white woman dancing with a black man, and raised the specter of a bloc vote of Negroes sending Graham to the Senate to preside over the abolition of Jim Crow. "White People WAKE UP Before It is Too Late," one campaign pamphlet said, "You May Not Have Another Chance. Do you want Negroes working beside you, your wife and your daughters in your mills and factories? Negroes sleeping in the same hotels and rooming houses? . . . Frank Graham favors mingling of the races." As if to make matters even worse, the left wing mounted its own attack on Graham, accusing him of selling out labor and blacks, and of being a red-baiter and a militarist. To Lowenstein, the assault from the left seemed even more outrageous than that from the right.

By the time the runoff election arrived, Graham was constantly on the defensive. Mill hands and tobacco farmers whose rights he had advocated all his life now shunned him, turning away when he tried to shake their hands. No matter how many times Graham declared his patriotism or affirmed his faith in voluntary desegregation "through the teachings of Jesus," he could not reassert his own character or values as the primary focus of the campaign. Smith soared to victory by nearly 20,000 votes, almost all of his new votes coming from those counties with the highest black populations and the fewest black voters. Although Graham pledged to support the Democratic ticket and urged his followers to continue to work "for democracy without vulgarity, [and] differences without hate," there were some who would never forget the beating that those ideals suffered in North Carolina's 1950 senatorial primary. "I don't care what you say," Lowenstein told Graham, "no force on this earth could make me vote for that man. . . . There's one person in this room who won't vote a straight ticket." To which Marian Graham replied quietly, "[No,] there are two persons."[8]

In the end, Lowenstein had not lost his hero and mentor. Rather, he was confirmed in his faith in Graham, and also in the stances he had taken on the critical issues of civil rights and anticommunism. Ironically, rather than renounce out of hand the use of red-baiting by the right wing, Lowenstein seems to have become more conscious of the importance of keeping a distance from anything or anyone that might remotely be associated with communism. The critical lesson, it appeared, was never to be vulnerable to the charge of "fellow-traveling." Just as Lowenstein held Stalinists more responsible for the defeat of the Republicans in the Spanish civil war than the Fascists (because of the way they "played politics"), so he seems to have viewed the left with as much suspicion during the Graham campaign as the right because of the way leftists attacked Graham as a "tool" of capitalism. Lowenstein also gleaned from the campaign experience the value of being moderate on race relations; a politician should be at least sensitive to a conservative white constituency as well as to a morally deserving black constituency. Above all, though, Lowenstein learned from his mentor the importance of defending a moral agenda, one of principle and righteousness, where the cause itself was adequate reward, and where fighting for justice was more important than triumphing at the ballot box. For a twenty-one-year-old just out of college, that lesson powerfully reinforced his belief that, as often as not, winning meant losing, and defeat brought victory.

THE NATIONAL STUDENT ASSOCIATION

Just one month after Graham's defeat, Lowenstein journeyed to the National Student Association's annual congress where, for the third year in a row, he served as a delegate from UNC. The congresses were lengthy deliberative sessions: although leavened with a certain amount of frolicking and the exhilaration of meeting new friends, the meetings were also portentous with deep conversations and debates on the future of the universe by those convinced that they bore the responsibility for determining its fate. It was a heady experience, especially for someone like Al who believed with such intensity that history would be made by the young. How appropriate, then, that he should be chosen as the third president in NSA's history at the August 1950 meeting—and not through a close election he had to compete in to win, but through a genuine draft in which near consensus validated his leadership and affirmed his self-worth.

From the very beginning, the NSA had embodied a dual focus—a liberal agenda at home on behalf of academic freedom and civil rights, and active engagement with the international student community on behalf of American values. As early as 1945, the State Department had encouraged formation of the Conference of Southern Students so that it could send representatives to various international forums; the immediate impetus for the NSA itself came from lengthy shipboard discussions among twenty-five American students returning from the IUS world youth congress in Prague during the summer of 1946. Indirectly, at least, Lowenstein was involved in all of this. Douglass Hunt had been the first leader of the Conference of Southern Students; Lowenstein had urged Hunt, unsuccessfully, to attend a preliminary international meeting in London; Jimmy Wallace was UNC's delegate to the Prague meeting, chosen over Junius Scales by the tie vote Lowenstein had cast; and throughout the fall of 1946, Lowenstein had participated in conversations preliminary to the first NSA meeting in Chicago in December.[9]

Reflecting Lowenstein's own approach, the NSA came into existence in 1946 largely because of the need for a student organization to represent the United States in international meetings. World politics was always central to the agenda of such meetings, beginning with the Prague congress. Czechoslovakia had been selected as an appropriate place to create the new International Union of Students because it was a democratic republic in Central Europe, situated between the two emerging power blocs of East and West. Uppermost in many people's minds was the danger of a resurgent fascism, and the value of forging international ties between students based on a collective commitment to peace and democracy. Some members wanted the IUS to concentrate on practical problems of student rights and exchanges; others sought to create a centralized institution with power to impose its will on various national student bodies. The latter group seemed most often to voice a pro-Moscow line, and the former to speak more for West European constituencies. Yet so powerful was the anti-Fascist mystique of the congress that "whenever any question was raised that was likely to embarrass those in control of the nascent machinery, all they had to do was to cite the specter of Fascism to submerge the issue under a wave of emotion."[10]

The American students at Prague came from a variety of backgrounds. Some were Catholics, dogmatically opposed to the left; a few were sympathetic to Communist positions; most were neutral, waiting to see what happened but committed overall to the importance of forging unity on behalf of the idealistic goals espoused in the conference literature. One American, William Ellis, introduced a motion to shift ideological issues of how to fight fascism to the end of the agenda in order to focus initially on such issues as reconstructing libraries and developing exchange programs. Although that motion was defeated, it received strong support among students from those countries that within another year or two would be aligned solidly with the United States in the cold war. It was after talking about their own lack of consensus on the way back from Prague that the twenty-five American delegates decided to call a conference in December to form an American national student union.

When the student delegates met to create the NSA—first in Chicago, then in the summer of 1947 in Madison--the issue of how to deal with the IUS dominated their deliberations, as it would much of NSA's subsequent activity. Many American student leaders wanted to develop some links with IUS, both as a means of reaching out to groups in Eastern Europe and as a vehicle for trying to transcend the already visible cold war. The new organization insisted on being treated as the exclusive body representing U.S. students and on having autonomy from the IUS, reserving the right to issue minority reports on any questions where disagreement existed. Still, the NSA mandate was to seek affiliation and cooperation. In the meantime, the NSA also affirmed its strong commitment to equal rights in the United States, without regard to race or creed; defended academic freedom against the onslaught of anti-Communist crusaders seeking to impose loyalty oaths and political litmus tests on faculty and students; and pledged to fight all discriminatory charters in fraternities and sororities. The new group set up a student travel service, initiated exchange programs, and began efforts to reach out to students in developing countries. The organization's first president was a black, Ted Harris, and the meetings were thoroughly integrated by race.[11]

By the time the NSA met again for its 1948 congress, however, negotiations with the IUS had exploded. Two NSA representatives were abroad in the winter and spring of 1948, one of them posted as a delegate to the IUS executive committee. But then with sudden terror came the Czech coup of February 1948, the arrest and beating of students in the streets of Prague, the firing of professors who were called collaborators despite their fight against fascism, and the approval by IUS leaders of all these actions. "I refuse to be a partner to your dastardly non-action, your past omissions, or your future political machinations," the American delegate said in his letter of resignation from IUS. Gradually, other Western student associations withdrew their representatives as well. Although the NSA continued to send informal delegations to IUS meetings to protest past policies and seek future changes, it no longer made any effort to work out a basis for affiliation. The IUS itself adopted a "united front" kind of attitude, seeking reconciliation on the basis of anticolonialism and other common goals. But there was little positive response to its overtures from the United States, especially in light of the IUS's decision to expel Yugoslavia—a non-Stalinist Communist country—on ideological grounds. On the other hand, the NSA appeared reluctant to initiate a counterorganization that would provide a rallying point for non-Communist students and ratify the division of the world's students into two opposite camps. International activities remained a dominant focus for the NSA—the IUS consumed enormous amounts of time and energy at each congress—yet for the moment, the NSA was not inclined to become aggressively involved in the controversial political disputes of the cold war.[12]

It was against this backdrop that Lowenstein assumed the NSA presidency at the Ann Arbor congress of August 1950. To him, the NSA clearly represented the best of all worlds. It provided the opportunity at congresses for schmoozing over Coke and pound cake until the wee hours of the morning, trying to convert resistant delegates to his point of view. It offered the camaraderie of retreating with fellow staff members to places like Paisan's Grotto in Madison and listening to Mario Lanza sing "Be My Love." And it supplied a forum for exercising his political brilliance, reaching out to people, lining up votes, cultivating new members and supporters—all in the name of high ideals.

To his friends and admirers, Al never seemed more at home than in an NSA context. "It was good to see you in a serious—not grim—mood," Lucille Kohn wrote before the 1949 congress. "I don't think I ever have before. [I hope your meeting] is swinging into action—idealistic Wilkie-Hepburn action, of course, and that you young ones are going to take over and recreate the messy world we oldsters hand down to you." When Al was asked to be a national candidate in 1949, he debated over it but eventually declined—as usual. But when the call came again the next year, he was ready to go.[13]

In his presidential acceptance address, Lowenstein sounded themes that would reverberate through much of the rest of his life. Almost anticipating the SDS (Students for a Democratic Society) young people who would write the Port Huron statement twelve years later ("we are a generation bred in at least modest comfort . . . looking uncomfortably to the world we inherit"), he underlined the paradox of a society that displayed proficiency in smashing the atom but had not yet learned the meaning of progress in human relationships. "Modern civilization," he noted, was "replete with conveniences for many," yet it provided neither universal security nor the values "without which so many of the great strides that have been made . . . become amoral tools." The result was pervasive uncertainty and confusion. What was necessary above all, he suggested, was a purpose for technology, a vision for science, so that progress had an end that would guide and justify it. Referring to the Korean War that had just begun, he declared: "Perhaps we had to have our focus sharpened by tragedy . . . before we could adequately appreciate that it has been more than futile to continue deepening our technical know-how without learning to use it to help us live together." Now, he concluded, with every improvement to modern life placed in peril by the renewed threat of war, perhaps it would be possible not only "to learn to build better bridges and do better research, but . . . also learn to value varying viewpoints and to live with one another."

With an explosive energy that soon would be legendary, Lowenstein set out to convert American student bodies to his perspective, cajoling them to join NSA, exhorting them to become responsible citizens of the world. Elmer Brock, a fellow staff member, recalled all the comical moments: "Lowenstein planning a tour; mad dashes for Chicago; . . . the day we went on a treasure hunt and found several hundreds of dollars." Lowenstein himself described his presidency as a "vaudeville act, making one night stands hither and yon, descending on various unsuspecting and innocent groups, beleaguering them with the virtues of becoming—or staying—members of NSA." But then there were the rewards as well, especially the chance to win new souls to the cause, or discover another part of Hallmark card America—like the College of Idaho, "a land," Lowenstein wrote, "not buried beneath snowdrifts and belted by blizzards . . . but rather a spot well nigh as lovely as Chapel Hill, in a valley of warm sunlight and gentle breezes where the stranger on his arrival could find himself surrounded at once by friendly folk." For someone of Lowenstein's needs and desires, it was almost an idyllic life.[14]

A more serious agenda preoccupied the new president, however, and that was the goal of organizing the NSA to fight communism, albeit in a manner that would preserve civil liberties. The late 1940s had witnessed rampant disregard of due process and the Bill of Rights as HUAC called witnesses to testify about "fellow travelers and comm-symps" who at one time or another had endorsed Marx, supported the Soviet Union, or simply questioned America's own democratic practices. By 1950, Senator Joseph McCarthy of Wisconsin had joined the fray, armed with his fictive yet frightening lists of so-called Communists in the State Department. Professors were being asked to sign loyalty oaths, intellectuals were suspect if they even uttered a word of dissent, and students were being warned to be on the lookout for those who might be less than 100 percent patriots. Liberals faced a difficult dilemma. Some, like the historian Henry Steele Commager, took the position that the Bill of Rights was absolute and indivisible, hence that everyone—even avowed Communists in school systems or government—had the right to their individual political beliefs. Others felt that the Communist menace was both real and pernicious, that communism itself had to be fought at every turn, and that even as one tried to defend civil liberties one should do so clearly acknowledging how evil the left was, and the importance of destroying its influence.

Lowenstein took the second stance. The lesson he had learned from the Graham campaign was that critics on the left were as reckless and dangerous as hysterics on the right—hence the need to attack the former while defending oneself against the latter. He pursued the first tack in 1951 when he lashed out at leftists at the University of Chicago who were complaining that the editor of the school newspaper, the *Maroon*, had been dismissed in a political witch-hunt by the dean. Conflating those who were "of the left" with those who supported "the party line"—a dangerous leap to begin with—Lowenstein charged that the campus paper had long taken editorial positions "very near the party line," even on matters such as responsibility for the Korean War and the cold war. Such posturing, he wrote, was made possible by the undemocratic structure of university governance, in which student activities such as the school paper were not made accountable to larger student body opinion. When a new editor of the paper gave every indication of continuing past practices, Lowenstein said, "the student government, dominated by the active left whose voice is always heard whenever it is present, did nothing at all and *The Maroon* was well on its way to another year of prattling."

Finally, after the editor had attended a Communist youth festival in Berlin and identified himself as speaking for the paper, the dean dismissed him and suspended publication of the paper for a week until a new editor could be chosen in student body elections. Lowenstein defended the action, arguing that the editor had gone to Berlin not "just to observe and talk with the young folk of the rest of the world," but because he was "completely in sympathy, not with the democracy that gave him the freedom to be an editor and go to Germany, but with the Communism that made him feel so much at home from Gdynia to Berlin." The dean's actions, Lowenstein concluded, may have technically been in violation of the student bill of rights, but the editor had given ample provocation, and in any event, no evidence existed that the administration had as its intent "to censor the content of the press or cut off the free flow of information." It was an interesting formulation of how to proceed with defending civil liberties.[15]

The other tack, of course, was to denounce McCarthyite tactics whenever they were aimed at mainstream liberal groups free of any taint of Communist association. Thus, when one congressman launched an attack on the NSA and its Illinois chapter for being critical of the McCarran Act—legislation seeking to mandate 100 percent Americanism—Lowenstein issued a ringing defense of his colleagues. Ironically, though, in so doing he helped legitimize the issue of a Communist threat. What made the University of Illinois NSA chapter so valuable, he declared, was the "outstanding job" it had done "of defeating by democratic means the very left-wing elements on their campus" that the congressman was concerned about.

Thus, Lowenstein seemed to be saying, the threat itself was real. "Our campuses are among the strongest bastions of democracy. . . . It is therefore natural that Communists and other enemies of this ideal are to be found directing early and vigorous attacks against these bastions." But that made it even more important that when truly anti-Communist democrats defeated such assaults, they should be praised for resisting thought control, not attacked. In a clever kind of reverse red-baiting, Lowenstein then charged that those who made such attacks were playing into the hands of the Communists. After all, the Communist party had recently pilloried the NSA as a Fascist, warmongering organization. Hence, if the congressman also attacked the NSA, he would be giving aid and comfort to the enemy. "It is shocking," Lowenstein declared, "to find a Republican Congressman from Abraham Lincoln's home state, following the Communist party line so closely that he finds cause to rejoice in the possible weakening of [the NSA]."

Clearly, Lowenstein was ready to defend civil liberties against McCarthyism—but only when the people under attack passed his own litmus test of anticommunism. In effect, Lowenstein had his own ground rules: if you were in reality a Communist, civil liberty concerns were secondary; if on the other hand you were falsely accused of being a Communist, they became primary and even sacrosanct. Through such a formulation, Lowenstein recognized the legitimacy of anti-Communist politics as a dominant force even as he challenged the excesses of McCarthyism. Ironically, the very allegation that McCarthyite groups were playing into the hands of a Communist plot helped to confirm the importance of resisting that plot, thereby ensuring the central role anti-Communist concerns would play in American political discourse.[16]

The consuming focus of Lowenstein's politics as NSA president, however, was his determination to mount a powerful counterattack against the IUS. Indeed, a direct link existed between his commitment to defend academic freedom against McCarthy at home and his leadership against the machinations of communism in the international student movement. The hallmark of his presidency would be "striving to meet the grave menace to all that we hold dearest in its national and international manifestations." In that regard, the international battle was most important because of "its potential crucial impact on the outcome of the cold war." NSA representatives had tried without success in the summer of 1950 to persuade the IUS to modify its political devotion to the Moscow party line. Now, in the aftermath of that failure, Lowenstein was intent on developing a counterforce strategy. Although the NSA congress refused to support a new organization that would lead an anti-Communist crusade, it was willing to meet with other national student groups to forge practical plans of cooperation designed to facilitate student interaction across national boundaries. With that mandate in mind, plans were set in motion to convene an assembly of student groups from twenty-one different countries in Stockholm in December 1950.[17]

Whatever other people had in mind, Lowenstein viewed the Stockholm meeting as a forum for declaring ideological war on the Soviet Union. "New Strategies," his newspaper diary headlined; "Scandinavians' Christmas Parley To Be Utilized." Elaborating on his intentions, he told the *Raleigh News and Observer* that "students must assume the obligation of stopping communism in areas of the world where they alone can best reach out to other students with the truth about democracy." Communists were just "Nazis with promises," he declared, seeking to seduce students with their "siren song." Lowenstein even took his case to Secretary of State Dean Acheson. "The fate of the world" might well be at stake, he wrote Acheson. While the IUS was parroting the Soviet line and winning converts in colonized Africa and Asia, the West had been sitting idly by. It was urgent, he told Acheson, that the two meet to plan strategy "in order that we of the United States NSA will be able to fulfill our responsibility to the students at home and abroad." His letter concluded, "With all the confidence of the Student in his Master, and the Citizen in his Statesman, I await your reply."[18]

Although Lowenstein never met with Acheson, he stormed the International Student Conference (ISC) at Stockholm as though he were delivering a personal message from the author of the Truman Doctrine. Consistent with their announced agenda, the delegates spent most of their time talking about student travel and exchange, scholarships for teachers from underdeveloped nations, and technical cooperation—until Lowenstein rose to address the convention at one of its last sessions. Taking a leaf from his NSA presidential address, he declared that all the "practical" and "technical" improvements in the world mattered not at all unless attention were paid to the values and political framework that shaped world events. "It is about time," he said, "that we took stock and faced facts."

The overwhelming reality of student life in 1950, Lowenstein declared, was that "the world [was being] pushed to the brink of tragedy by the willful scheming of evil men bent on world domination for one nation." The sole purpose of the IUS, he went on, was "the furtherance of the will of these same evil men." Using distortions, lies, and propaganda, the IUS had tried to persuade the colonial world that it could "find freedom through the slavery of Soviet rule." Armed with "unscrupulous deceit and unflagging zeal," it had sought "to turn against freedom the very parts of the world where today freedom is most sought after." When challenged, the IUS pleaded, "Let us negotiate," but such negotiations "have been doomed to failure because we are [dealing] with students who are not free agents, as we are, but who are Soviet agents." If students of the Western world did not awaken and throw down the gauntlet of freedom in return, Lowenstein warned, not only would the "independence and fruitful growth of lands on three Continents of the earth" be at stake, "but the peace of the world may be in [peril] as well."

> What we face today is not primarily an obnoxious political ideology . . . nor an unruly Soviet nationalism. What we face . . . is the greatest menace to civilization, to the timeless truths preached by all religions . . . to the art, the literature, the games and the homes that have evolved over the centuries.

In the face of such a challenge, Lowenstein concluded, "techniques designed to effectuate increased student exchange or better travel programs" would mean nothing; only if "we prepare ourselves to compete ideologically" would technical know-how and scientific achievements make a difference. This, then, was the high purpose to which Western student bodies were called—not just the development of "practical" cooperation, but commitment to a new world crusade for freedom.[19]

Significantly, delegate response to Lowenstein's exhortation ranged from anger to disbelief. Immediately after he finished, speakers from Scotland and Canada disassociated themselves from his remarks. The next day, the conferees voted twelve-to-one (with two abstentions) to express formal regret that Lowenstein had injected a call for ideological confrontation into a meeting specifically convened to address a nonpolitical agenda. Delegates were especially distressed by Lowenstein's characterization of all future negotiations with IUS as fruitless, and by his call for a centralized counterorganization that would have as its primary purpose combatting IUS. The conference did agree to set up a special commission to reach out to students in Asia, Africa, and Latin America—one of Lowenstein's aims—but it clearly repudiated any suggestion that ideological *engagement* should become the raison d'être of any subsequent meetings.[20]

Nor did the contretemps cease when Lowenstein returned to the United States. Herbert Eisenberg, NSA's international vice-president, continued to oppose Lowenstein's call for a new, anti-IUS organization; an NSA executive committee meeting in February 1951 divided deeply over Lowenstein's plan, although it did accept responsibility for coordinating a mutual aid program for Southeast Asia; and critics, from within and without the United States, continued to attack Lowenstein's action in Stockholm. "What we missed in the entire conference," one Nigerian wrote, "was any mention whatsoever of . . . complete independence" for colonial peoples. Indeed, "the voice of the colonial students themselves was not even allowed to be heard." To this IUS supporter, the whole plan sounded like a "junior edition" of Truman's foreign policy. Arguing a somewhat different case, another student wondered why one ideologically determined political force was necessarily any better than another. "You cannot gather a group of men . . . or nations," he wrote Lowenstein, "around a philosophy that expresses itself only in opposition to another philosophy."

When the full NSA congress met the following summer, it apparently agreed with those who had reservations. "Lowenstein must be stopped!" one NSA-er wrote from abroad. "All the Europeans are opposed to him and his Stockholm speech." To at least some people, Lowenstein wanted too much control. "Always remember, Duchess," one staff member wrote him, "you can't have everyone for a friend." Thus, when the vote came, NSA delegates rejected by a narrow margin a motion to support a Western student union driven by the goal of fighting the IUS and communism. Alienating European students or students from developing nations seemed too great a chance to take.[21]

Yet with single-minded determination, Lowenstein persisted until he prevailed. As NSA president, he held the decisive advantage of being able to frame the issues through his public pronouncements. Hence, the official report about Stockholm and NSA's investigation of student conditions in Southeast Asia commenced by talking about the "ideological aggression" of the IUS, the challenge to "the students of the free world" to launch a counterattack, and the "turning point" at Stockholm when student delegates agreed on a program to promote technical assistance to undeveloped areas and "answer the distortions" of the ideological aggressor. The report on Southeast Asian students, meanwhile, underlined how effective IUS had been at selecting student leaders for indoctrination in Moscow, and how imperative it was for Western groups to respond with their own fellowship programs, student exchanges, and aid to counter IUS propaganda about Western imperialism in Vietnam and Indonesia. This was explicitly to be a Truman-style kind of outreach program: Asian student leaders would be brought to the United States to see and learn about the American way of life.[22]

Lowenstein himself continued to agitate on behalf of his plan. It was imperative, he told one sorority leader, to combat the "menace" of the international Communist conspiracy by supporting the NSA counterattack. The IUS, he said in another speech, was an "arm of the Cominform—Soviet dominated"; student leaders in the underdeveloped world held the key to the future, and in order to win their minds, students in the NSA had "to sharpen our thinking and draw our lines tighter." Educational leaders bore a special responsibility, Lowenstein wrote President James Conant of Harvard, if the Stockholm effort to win the war for the minds of students in colonialized countries was to be won. The State Department and Voice of America could help, but so would "attention and assistance from those who have the financial and other resources to help American students to do a real job of striking back." If the NSA had not yet determined to give formal backing to Lowenstein's grand scheme, it hardly seemed to make a difference as he waged his own campaign to win support for the crusade against communism.[23]

In some ways, internal staff relations at the NSA took on their own cold war character during these months. Erskine Childers, the previous international vice-president, had substantial support for his position that it was better to cooperate with the IUS on colonial student issues, especially in light of the history of Western imperialism. Herb Eisenberg, the current international vice-president, shared at least some of Childers's reservations and threatened to resign over the issue. Lowenstein himself, meanwhile, indulged that side of his personality that willingly engaged in intrigue and behind-the-scenes maneuvering in order to win. One means of implementing his strategy was to secure financing for the program to "win the hearts and minds" of the Southeast Asian students. Paul Pitner, an ally in this effort, wrote Lowenstein of his success in soliciting money from the Committee for a Free Asia, a group willing to fund seminar programs in Asia, the Middle East, and Japan, as well as support foreign student visits and the creation of an international information service. But the negotiations had to remain quiet. "The Committee," he wrote, "would not request a load of publicity for its contributions." Indeed, it might prefer to remain anonymous. As an offshoot of the Crusade for Freedom, the Committee for a Free Asia had already incurred a suspicious response from Erskine Childers and others. Yet it had abundant resources, evidently, and few places to spend them. Pitner assured Lowenstein that the operation was not McCarthy-inspired, but he also acknowledged the need to be careful about revealing its operations. "This cloak and dagger stuff may seem nuts," he said, "but I feel that I have to handle this matter that way [lest] this information . . . get into the hands of those who are not on our side."[24]

By the winter of 1951, Lowenstein's plans had begun to fall into place. Despite what one friend called "the hard feelings at the Congress this past summer," Lowenstein's candidate for NSA president—William Dentzer from Muskingum College in New Concord, Ohio—won election. A good "inside" man, he reduced personal tensions on the staff yet simultaneously led the NSA toward more open and definitive commitments to a new world student organization—the International Student Conference—that would fulfill Lowenstein's vision of an organized, fully funded, clearly focused student group reaching out to colonial countries with a strong anti-Communist message. A second world congress was held in Edinburgh in January 1952, and a third in Copenhagen a year later. When a tentative campaign of outreach to the west by the IUS foundered after Yugoslavian and West German delegates were banned from IUS membership, the way seemed clear to proceed with a fully developed organizational commitment by NSA to a counter–IUS organization.[25]

By early 1953, an infrastructure was in place that embodied Lowenstein's 1950 blueprint. An international information service was established that eventually would publish literature in five languages. Student exchange programs were put into place whereby the "best and the brightest" young people from developing countries could come to the United States for semesters of study, summer visitations, or professional training. U.S. students, in the meantime, would be sent to speak on behalf of American values and ideals at world youth congresses whenever they occurred. To make these American students more knowledgeable in foreign affairs, the NSA took to sponsoring each summer at Bryn Mawr College an international relations seminar, many graduates of which then assumed responsibilities as NSA "desk officers" for various regions of the world. It was a brilliant, well-run, highly successful international program that, in almost every sense, realized the aspirations Al Lowenstein had first articulated in 1950.

It was also an operation that from 1952 onward was totally subsidized by the Central Intelligence Agency (CIA). The NSA confirmed in February 1967 that the CIA had initiated its relationship with NSA during the presidency of William Dentzer. All during the Lowenstein presidency, financial troubles had plagued the association. The foreign travel service by which American students secured inexpensive charters to Europe had lost $20,000 in 1950–51, and telephone bills far exceeded budgetary allocations. Former officers worried that the entire enterprise would fall apart for lack of financing; some staffers predicted a slow and painful death for the organization without an infusion of funds. Clearly, Lowenstein's program for ambitious and aggressive outreach to foreign students would have no chance of success without outside help.[26]

Precisely in response to that financial concern, CIA funding began. "It would have been nonsense for there not to be . . . support to organizations like this," one CIA officer said. "If we hadn't done this, we would have just been run over by commie front organizations." As a result, the NSA was suddenly rich. The millionaire Walter Annenberg agreed to provide NSA rent-free facilities in Philadelphia, and relatively unknown foundations flooded the organization with grants. All had altruistic-sounding names—the Independence Foundation, the Foundation for Youth and Student Affairs, the Alexander Hamilton Fund, the Independent Research Institute. As many as fifteen different organizations served as conduits through which CIA monies flowed to the NSA to pay for international relations seminars, foreign students' visits to the United States, exchange fellowships, U.S. delegates' travel to youth festivals (usually IUS-sponored) in Vienna and Helsinki, and all the administrative expenses of the international relations operation both at home and abroad. Frequently, CIA subsidies were more than $500,000 per year, amounting to as much as 80 percent of the total NSA budget.[27]

The CIA's involvement had an insidious impact on the NSA. As the *New York Times* editorialized at the time of the revelations in 1967, "Intelligence services [do not] underwrite indigent good causes unless the beneficiary can be expected to pay off the debt, directly or indirectly." To be sure, only a few NSA officers each year were made "witting" about the relationship. These always included the vice-president for international affairs, and, almost always, the president. Yet these positions were where the focus and the power rested. Staffers wondered sometimes where the international vice presidents came from. They were not well known and seemed suddenly to appear out of thin air, but always with the "right" people supporting them. In fact, they had usually been recruited by the CIA. Presidents and other staffers who were to be made "witting" would be called to a small meeting by a "friend," who then left. A CIA representative—usually a former NSA person—then announced that he had some critical information to impart, but first the staffer would have to sign a pledge promising never to reveal the secret information, on pain of lengthy imprisonment. Ordinarily, the form was signed. Then the staffer was made "witting," with resignation or exposure ruled out of bounds by the previously signed document. In that fashion, one administration after another was co-opted into the CIA apparatus. No one ever knew who else was witting, though people who were knowledgeable watched to see who received phone messages from "Aunt Alice" and left the office to return calls from a pay phone. Most witting staffers assumed that their phones were tapped and that some surveillance was occurring as they went about their daily activities. All became superconscious of the difference between themselves and the "unwitting" staffers and carefully maintained their secret. By definition, the arrangement entailed conspiracy and manipulation—no matter how much former presidents and international vice-presidents swore that their independence was never compromised.

Perhaps the most pernicious part of the process was the way the CIA used apparently scholarly and aboveboard conferences to recruit operatives and shape the behavior of innocent students. Each year's international relations seminar, for example, had two purposes: first, to provide CIA recruiters the opportunity to observe and select those students most likely to be loyal and effective members of the Agency; second, to introduce all the students to a point of view and geopolitical framework that they could carry with them to international conferences where—whether witting or unwitting—they would then articulate positions partly shaped by the Agency. The international relations seminars became an ideal conduit for channeling a whole generation of bright young minds into Agency service, a superb vehicle by which the CIA could winnow out potential recruits from those it would be content simply to manipulate.[28]

Notwithstanding Lowenstein's intrigue with groups like the Committee on a Free Asia, there is no evidence that he was involved in starting the CIA connection with the NSA, or that he was aware of its development during the 1950s. William Dentzer, who was in charge of the entire NSA operation at the CIA during the 50s, flatly denies that Lowenstein ever knew of the relationship. Indeed, he insists, a conscious decision was made to exclude Lowenstein from the inner circle. Witting staff members, another NSA-er said, "saw Al as a loose cannon." He was a maverick, and no one knew whether he could be trusted to keep a secret. In fact, the very belligerence of his anticommunism made him less than ideal as an operative. He was too loud, too intent on holding forth.[29]

Yet it is beyond credibility that Lowenstein did not at least suspect the connection. Here was a person of consummate political brilliance who grasped, almost intuitively, the most complicated and convoluted political relationships. He clearly knew how desperate the NSA's financial condition had been when he was in charge, and he was in a far better position than most to understand how radically that condition had changed by the mid-1950s. Nor was he naive about such groups as the CIA. In his 1951 letter to James Conant speaking approvingly of State Department and

Voice of America interest in the NSA's activities, he noted that "there are [other] government agencies that might prove damaging to have too close a connection between our program and theirs." Furthermore, his own penciled notes about the NSA revelations discuss the aid given by a "mysterious agent" and recall how "later on things began to happen and made me wonder," including how the international relations seminars were conducted. Lowenstein himself was heavily involved with Algerian students brought to America with CIA funds, and he actively recruited people to attend various world youth festivals with promises that their travel would be paid for by one or another of the "foundations" through which the CIA funneled its support to NSA. In light of such circumstantial evidence, to assert that he had no awareness or suspicion of a CIA connection strains credulity.

In addition, there is more than circumstantial evidence that, by the 1960s at least, Lowenstein was witting. In handwritten notations at the time of the disclosures in 1967, Lowenstein declared:

> If the current sensation should result in any permanent damage to the Association, the result would be a serious misfortune for students in this country and throughout the world. . . . We state categorically [that] independence and integrity have never been compromised. . . . We never sought nor accepted funds on any basis from any group. . . . All funds [were] expended under the full control and independent judgment of responsible officials acting in accordance with the declarations of the NSA Congress. . . . [The] U.S. government never exerted financial pressure on association policies and such attempts would not have been tolerated.

That statement is based on a presumption of his knowledge about the connection, hence his denial that it ever entailed any interference or compromise of integrity. In fact, Lowenstein was enlisted by the CIA in 1967 to persuade the sitting NSA president *not* to confirm the connection, and in conversations throughout this period, he displayed firsthand knowledge and familiarity with CIA activities that suggested at least an awareness of the connection during the 1960s.[30]

The key point, however, is that the CIA-NSA connection would not have been conceivable in the first place without Lowenstein's indispensable work in initiating the anti-Communist crusade within the NSA. Whether and when he was witting are largely irrelevant questions. What matters is the fervor, vision, and conviction of a twenty-one-year-old student leader who seized the moment, introduced an agenda, transformed an international meeting, and then persisted in developing support for his program until it became the full-blown apparatus of an ISC, a coordinating secretariat, and an international exchange program—all with the purpose of defeating the "ideological aggressor" in an all-out competition. Obviously, there were others of similar viewpoint. But were there others of comparable talent and acuity? In the end, regardless of what he knew or when he knew it, the NSA's leadership in the cold war battle against world communism must be seen as one of Allard Lowenstein's most significant and lasting achievements.

CONCLUSION

A combination of personal dynamics and his own proclivity for the politics of youthful idealism made the NSA the metaphorical center of Lowenstein's life in the 1950s—and beyond. Where else could he have made such an impact? What other environment could have guaranteed a supply of ready young minds, anxious to be inspired, prepared to commit themselves in service to a noble cause championed by a charismatic crusader?

Although Lowenstein served as NSA president for only one year, he was a pivotal presence in the organization for more than a decade and a half after his term in office. At nearly every national congress, he would fly into town, begin an endless round of caucuses, deliver a passionate keynote address, and bask in the enthusiasm and hero worship that inevitably surrounded him. "I regret that we were unable to have a long chat at the NSA convention," another former president observed with some sarcasm, "but there always seemed to be intimate groups of 500 people with you at all times." The NSA provided an ideal location for Lowenstein to work his magic. In 1954, with the congress threatening to split acrimoniously over a resolution on the Supreme Court's *Brown* decision, Lowenstein closeted himself with delegates from all the key states for more than twelve hours and emerged with unanimous backing for a compromise statement that pledged support for immediate desegregation in every state's first-grade classes. In 1956, he gave a keynote address that regalvanized the association behind a commitment to end complacency in national politics. Each year thereafter, he helped focus the NSA's commitment to seek racial justice and fight world communism. More than any other figure in the organization's history, Lowenstein defined the NSA's mission and charted its direction.

As a result, Lowenstein received much of the adulation and validation he so deeply needed. "Along with hundreds of people in my generation," noted Michael Horowitz, a high official in the Reagan administration and former NSA associate of Lowenstein's, "[Al Lowenstein was] the extraordinary figure who [provided me] the voice and leadership for change . . . during the apathetic Eisenhower years." No matter where he later traveled, Horowitz said, "whenever there was a spark, whenever I felt a bond of kinship with someone, I would routinely ask, 'When was the last time you saw Al?'. . . He was really a link to an entire generation of . . . moral politics."

For such people, Lowenstein became a person "literally of mythic proportions." His speeches, one woman wrote him, were like poetry; his words created "an effect by themselves, something apart from what they connote with their literal meanings." After hearing one address, another young fan declared, "Tonight I shall go to sleep with renewed faith in our country's future. . . . I want really to tell you how happy I am that there are young people who even now are concerning themselves with the future; that there is a generation who accept the wonders of our country with humility and with a deep sense of responsibility." As long as Lowenstein received such support, how could he doubt the importance—or impact—of his leadership? "In our age," another NSA delegate said, "ideals seem to be passé or something. I'm glad that you had the courage to shoot a few of your ideals into the arm of NSA."[31]

During these years, virtually all of Al Lowenstein's many different activities—except for his army stint—revolved around the cultivation of young people that emerged as a primary concern from his NSA years. When he coordinated youth campaigns for Adlai Stevenson's presidential bids in 1952 and 1956, he simply activated in a new form his NSA network. As recruiter and publicist for the College Association of the United Nations in 1956–57, he did the same, looking up the same people, speaking on the same campuses, mobilizing the same battalions. Even when he went back to UNC to serve as a dormitory counselor and attend graduate school in history in 1957–58, his lifestyle never changed. Always, there was the round of speeches, the constant trips, the young people to be counseled, the converts to be made.

It was an extraordinary life, one that seemed to overflow with excitement and rewards. "So many young people on campuses," Gary Bellow observed, "found themselves attracted to someone who articulated what they saw about the world in ways that gave them some possibility for action. [And Lowenstein had such a] capacity to personalize political life, to make what each person did [seem] important and worth doing." Michael Horowitz agreed. Here was a man, he said, "who had this [incredible] capacity for intimacy when he was with you . . . who was tireless [and] would sleep three, four hours a night and just had plenty of time for all the people that wanted to talk to him on really quite an intense, intimate, one-to-one basis. . . . None of us sensed that we were part of some massive entourage."[32]

And so the NSA constituency became the means by which Al Lowenstein conducted his quest for friends and followers and satisfied his desire to lead crusades for moral renewal. To most who observed him, his choice appeared uniquely appropriate. No one else had "quite the demonic intensity, the 24 hour a day purposefulness" of this campus crusader, David Broder remarked thirty years after his first encounter with Lowenstein. But whether intentionally or not, Broder had struck upon Lowenstein's Achilles' heel in his use of the word *demonic:* For underneath all the activity Allard remained a person still caught by his own demons. Lowenstein had the genius and rhetorical skill to galvanize generations of American young people for a life of moral commitment and political reform; but did he have the ability to find personal happiness as well?[33]

5

Seeking a Place

LOWENSTEIN COULD NOT OFFICIALLY CONTINUE AS NSA PRESIDENT AFTER 1951 because of constitutional provisions mandating one term only. Thus, while in reality he continued to spend as much of his time as possible on student politics, he was compelled, for the record at least, to move on in his career. Three times his parents had encouraged him to apply to Yale Law School; friends and classmates had even volunteered to facilitate his law school applications and entry exams. Now, thrash as he might against the harness being fitted to him, he was unable to find any recourse but to acquiesce.

An abiding subtheme of these years—in law school and in the army stint that followed—was Lowenstein's quest for a lifestyle, friends, even perhaps a lifetime mate who would provide some answer to the unresolved dilemmas of his private life. Though experienced in different form, the problems he had encountered at UNC kept recurring. So, too, did his halting, idiosyncratic, and intense struggle to find some solutions. If in the end, the complexity and power of his conflicting drives made a simple way out impossible, the nature of his search revealed in new ways some of the reasons he felt so trapped.[1]

LAW SCHOOL AND THE ARMY

Lowenstein's real problem was that going to law school made little sense except as a way of fulfilling his parents' wishes. First, as his old roommate Harding Menzies wrote, Lowenstein was a charismatic leader able to inspire hundreds, even thousands, by the lilt of his rhetoric and the intensity of his political passion. "[He] is able to move people with a power that is all but earthly," Menzies wrote. "He would make a better preacher than a lawyer." In addition, the study of law was "irksome and dull." Even Douglass Hunt, who in many ways wished nothing more than to have Lowenstein join him at Yale, acknowledged his perplexity at the law school option. The first year was a "seemingly interminable grind"; "the humanity this law is supposed to serve . . . is bewildered by wierd legal gobbledeygook and is the frustrated victim of legalized injustice." The chief value of Yale lay in its ability to train the student to be something more than a lawyer. Why then should Al subject himself to three years of boredom in order to earn a professional degree he hoped never to use.[2]

Indeed, Lowenstein remained sufficiently unconvinced about a legal career that he went to extraordinary lengths to rationalize *not* going. In a classic attempt to "scoot around" his parents, he declared in a 1950 letter that he *must* join the army and go to Korea. "Simply stated," he wrote, "I cannot sit this war out. . . . I would not want to survive long in a communist world." It would be a betrayal of his principles to go to Yale Law School, he said. "I am a creature of conscience, and it has brought much that has been pleasant in my way to be such. If now it brings something which appears to be momentarily less pleasant, I would be foolish to try to abandon my most essential characteristic." How could Gabriel counter such an idealistic affirmation? And what a clever tack for Al to take in rationalizing his impulse to avoid law school. But then he was elected to the NSA presidency, received a draft deferment, and fought his anti-Communist wars in another forum.[3]

With few other options left in 1951, Lowenstein finally complied with his parents' wishes and went to Yale once his NSA term expired. Still, almost every letter and diary entry he wrote during his first year at law school suggested that he had been dragged kicking and screaming to an awful fate. "After One Month, A. L. Not Pleased With Self, Not Sure Law Is It," he announced in his journal. Nothing about the law per se seemed to please him (Hunt had been right), and like an addict hooked on constant highs, he craved a return to the crazy life of travel and exhortatory speechmaking. His friends—to whom he wrote even more frequently than usual—were genuinely concerned about his state of mind. "Do hang on," Mary Ellen Knight urged, "even without a student government or the prospect of one." With perspicacity, she and others recognized Lowenstein's hunger for student politics.[4]

In fact, Lowenstein quickly struck upon the only appropriate solution: continue his life of politicking and speechmaking, whenever possible, while *appearing* to study law. No sooner had he arrived at Yale than he left to fulfill NSA speaking engagements made long in advance. By midyear, the 1952 presidential campaign was well under way, and although Lowenstein temporarily had flirted with the idea of supporting Eisenhower, he now plunged headlong into the Stevenson effort, heading up the National Students for Stevenson operation. He participated in campus debates throughout the country, spoke at the National Press Club, and appeared on a network radio hookup—hardly a life of studious contemplation.[5]

Even when he was on campus, Lowenstein conveyed an image of hyperactivity that awed most of his fellow students. Since the Encampment in 1947, Lowenstein had developed a close bond with Eleanor Roosevelt. Now, back in the New England area, he saw much more of her, driving her to and from speaking engagements in the New York/Connecticut area and, in the process, boosting his own status on campus by sharing Mrs. R. with his friends. Once, when he arranged for her to speak at Yale, he crowded his favorite people into the car for the drive from Hartford to New Haven. His own political activity, meanwhile, became legendary. He invited friends to accompany him (which usually meant drive *for* him) on debates at various campuses and delighted in talking about his experiences with others. Whenever he was on the Yale campus, one classmate recalled, he was a social butterfly, "constantly rushing around, seeing people, introducing one person to another." He always took pains, through advance consultation with his women friends, to make sure that all the female law students (there were not that many) had dates for the law school dances so they would not feel left out, and whenever he arranged to go out for a Coke or a meal with somebody, he made sure "to include everyone in the immediate radius [of the conversation] in the invitation, and . . . that was born largely of his fear of hurting somebody." At Yale, as elsewhere, Lowenstein reached out for companionship, seeming to find security and happiness through including the largest number of people possible in his circle of activity.[6]

Before long, therefore, Lowenstein had become a notorious figure on campus, the peripatetic campaigner who was never there but always there simultaneously—in short, a magician. "How do you maintain the dual role of a world traveller and a student of law?" his UNC history professor Howard Beale asked. "You are never at Yale." Fellow students marveled at how easily he seemed to shed all the typical law school anxieties. "I was a plodder," one of his classmates remarked. "but there were a handful of people [like Al] who seemed to be . . . free spirits and to have the security of feeling that they'd get through it all without a huge amount of effort." Sometimes, in fact, Lowenstein was so notably absent that when he appeared it became an occasion for campuswide levity. "He would come through occasionally to pick up a few things [for his travels]," one friend recalled, "and one day he went to a class in the Yale Law School":

> Al had a habit of sending postcards to people all over the world, and on this day he was sitting in the back of the room . . . writing cards through the entire class and listening to the man at the front of the room. . . . [He] hadn't been in the law school very much that year [and] . . . at the end of the class he discovered that the man sitting next to him was the Professor whose class it was, and it was a guest lecturer [at the podium].

Such stories quickly became widespread; some of his friends dreamed up a special award for "Al Lowenstein—the student who graduated from Yale having attended the fewest classes." Even his family was bemused. "Congratulations," his stepmother wrote, "for having accomplished almost the impossible; that is, passing subjects that you know nothing about."[7]

By the end of his three years of law school, Lowenstein had succeeded in making the best of a bad situation. He survived classes for which he studied only during the period he referred to as his "mental novocaine" time—the last week before exams. He took a speed reading course (years before John Kennedy made them popular), increasing his comprehension from 171 to 480 words per minute. ("Your gains," his instructor said, "are amazing—especially considering your schedule conflicts which limited your attendance.") And he even managed to get three Excellent grades and eight Goods. In fact, Lowenstein ranked 85th out of a class of 203 after two years. In the meantime, he had largely maintained his distinctive lifestyle, continuing to serve as the center of activity, whether on or off campus. It may not have been a law school experience designed to make a good junior partner for Wall Street, but it clearly served the goal of not diluting, in any respect, the dramatic features of Allard Lowenstein's public personality.[8]

Even the U.S. Army failed to transform "Lowenschnitzel," as one of his buddies called him. If possible, Lowenstein detested the army even more than he did law school. Although he had professed an eagerness to "do his time" ever since the Korean War began, he did not enlist until November 1954, after he had secured his law degree. Some thought he joined for political reasons—to have a service record to point to in a campaign. But whatever the reason, he quickly discovered the inanity of army procedures, the hatefulness of drill sergeants, and the intellectual hypocrisy of commanding officers. At Forts Kilmer and Jackson, he was struck by the "deliberate, sadistic viciousness" of army basic training; after that experience, the "unpleasantness" of enduring imbecilic instructions as a company clerk seemed mild, though he could not help noting the dissonance that a thinking person felt in "watching middle-aged men in a state of almost constant obsequiousness, along with all the other appurtenances inherent in the more absurd military customs." "The waste, corruption and pointlessness that mar almost everything we do," Lowenstein wrote Sandy Friedman, "is unbelievable unless lived through." Obviously, this was not a place where the free and commandeering spirit of Allard Lowenstein could find much nurture. Humorously, Sandy Friedman imagined what it must be like, "marching double-file, stenographic books in righthand, into Clerk-Typist school, and wasting the taxpayers funds on: 'sgt. adlain stevneson is mu first ch oce for pediment.'"

Life became more interesting when Lowenstein was shipped to Germany to finish out his army stint. Almost immediately, he faced the shock of confronting a nation whose Nazi regime had killed six million Jews. When local citizens asked whether his name was German, he wanted to respond, "No, Jewish." Lowenstein sought out members of the small Jewish community that was left in Mannheim so that he could attend temple services with them. He was appalled by the "blithe assumption [among] most Germans that 'both sides did cruel things,' and 'war is awful' and therefore Germany really has nothing to feel [bad about]." After hearing so many Germans passionately describe how cruel the Allies had been in their bombing policies, Lowenstein concluded that "most of the natives here [only] think war is terrible when you lose it." By contrast, he fell in love with the British, marveling at how fortunate America had been "to have gained such rational, funny, calm, friendly people for our chief allies." He loved the candor, intelligence, and wit of British political campaigns, in which candidates actually discussed issues and scored—with biting sarcasm—intellectual points.[9]

Above all, though, being in Europe opened new stages on which the irrepressible Lowenstein personality could assert itself. Whenever possible,

Lowenstein cajoled passes from his commanding officers, walked the Philosopher's Path above Heidelberg, hiked the Swiss Alps from Interlaken, and visited cities like Berlin, Amsterdam, and Paris. He reunited with old friends like Mary Ellen Knight, made new ones, and impressed everyone with his connections and bravado. When Eleanor Roosevelt came to Europe, she called his headquarters and arranged for him to get a special pass to visit her in Paris (*everyone* heard about *that*), and when Grace Kelly married Prince Rainier in Monaco, Lowenstein was there. Never one to miss a chance to see a movie star, he journeyed to the tiny Mediterranean principality, recognized an old school friend who was a member of the wedding party, and, as he later *claimed,* sneaked into the church for the ceremony. Everyone back at the army camp, plus gossip columnists for American newspapers and the hundreds of people to whom Al sent postcards, all heard the dramatic and stunning news that Al Lowenstein had "crashed" Princess Grace's wedding. It was reported that Al and his GI friends rented top hats and tails and walked into the gala opera ballet at the Monte Carlo Casino unchallenged, and that they had met King Farouk and Ava Gardner.

The only thing that could match the energy Lowenstein brought to making the best of his situation was his desperation to get out. As restless as ever, Lowenstein plotted constantly to secure an early release and get back in political harness in time for the 1956 presidential campaign. Having pulled enough strings among deans and Democratic party friends to make even a Metternicht envious, he was finally discharged two months early and proceeded immediately to the Democratic convention; from there he went in late August to the NSA congress, at which he had agreed to give the plenary address. He was back in his element, unsure of what he would do next, but happy at least not to miss his favorite gatherings. He had survived the army, as he had law school, not so much by becoming part of the experience as by flying above it, adamant in his refusal to stifle his swirl of activity. As one of his army buddies later wrote him, "You are still a rare person in my memory. . . . As I said a long time ago . . . 'After you had gone, it seemed that our ranks had been depleted by more than one.'"[10]

PERSONAL TURMOIL

Through all this, Allard's personal anxieties persisted. Although on the family front conditions appeared to improve—largely because he had so successfully resisted his parents' efforts to control him—more pressing questions arose. In an age when early marriage was almost a badge of citizenship, what could he do about finding a mate? Who would be the "right" person, and how should he proceed when ease with women—especially comfort in expressing physical affection—had always proven so elusive? And what could he make of the fact that his closest relationships continued to be with men, particularly younger men, and were characterized by all the confusion that homoerotic instincts engendered? Above all, how could he find stability in personal relationships when the very hyperactivity he relied on to escape these personal dilemmas made such stability impossible to achieve? It was a personal agenda that seemed to heighten, not diminish, the unsettledness of Lowenstein's life.

In spite of improved relations with its youngest son, the Lowenstein family continued to generate enough conflict and turmoil to preoccupy most people. Gabriel suffered enormous financial losses due to business miscalculations, making everyone anxious about his health and state of mind. For a brief period at least, Al had reason to doubt the absolute economic security that had allowed him to do whatever he pleased with barely a second thought. While Florence insisted that he still come to them for money and *never* borrow from others (Al did so constantly, often without repaying), he now worried about his father and how he was coping with financial reversals, bad health, and ongoing problems with Bert. "I've been wondering for years how Dad has borne up so well under all this," Dorothy wrote him. "He must be made of iron."

Even the secret of Augusta had to be confronted—at least indirectly—when Grandpa Goldberg died and was buried next to his daughter. "I didn't know where to stand," Al noted on a scrap of paper, "with Grandma in her agony, or with Dad who looked white as a sheet and must have felt awfully tired and sad and sick on his first visit to his first wife's grave probably in 20 years; or with Mother who must have felt awfully alone and lonely with a . . . dozen or so sobbing relatives." Dorothy had some of the same reactions. "After all these years and all the hush-hush that has been practiced," she wrote Al, "it must have been mighty strange bringing it out in the open like that." Although Gabriel evidently made no comment on the issue, Dorothy was astonished at how many bizarre things went on in the Lowenstein household. "It just doesn't seem like anything that would happen in 'your' family," she observed, "though there are quite a few things in *our* family like that."[11]

Compared to earlier days, however, a reign of peace seemed to have descended on the Lowenstein clan. Florence nagged and nudged far less often; family letters were more newsy and less pressured; and Gabriel found it easier to express directly the devotion to Al that had so often been submerged beneath his tyrannical exhortations. Some of his letters were now signed, "with fervent love," and one he sent to Al in Germany was as poignant as the letter he had sent Al in the 1948 about his anguish over Bert. "There is a feeling of lonesomeness around here," he wrote, "and that is the time when one develops a feeling of 'bankenish' for those who are dear to him. I do not know whether it is German or only a Yiddish word, but it means a longing for somebody. So I decided to drop this letter to you. I too am counting the number of days left in the Army. . . . We all love you and long for your return." With such messages, the family dynamics could easily seem a little less fearsome.[12]

On the other hand, the pressure to marry—from peers and elders alike—became more intense with each passing year. In the 1940s and 1950s, *everyone* was expected to be "pinned," if not engaged, by the time they graduated from college. Hence, Mimi Massey's recollection that she would have given up everything to marry Al if he had only proposed, and the constant drumbeat of queries from Al's classmates, male and female alike: "Have you found the pretty woman yet?" "Have you had time in all your mad dashes . . . to become interested in some fair damsel long enough to latch on permanently?" "What is the current status of your romantic life?" It was as if the whole world's $64,000 question was, "When will Al get hitched?"[13]

A more sensitive and perceptive form of the inquiry came from a college friend in 1950. "Is love being kind to you," he asked, "or is it still in multiples and plurals? Are you happy?" Then, in a more existential mode, "What can I tell you about me? When I don't know about me myself? . . . I realize deep inside that when the hour comes—I shall be alone. And 'there' will be only a void. Life is that way." Whatever his internal confusion, Lowenstein knew that he did not want to be alone. He wanted to be a father, musing with friends about naming his firstborn after Frank Porter Graham—if only he could find a woman willing to cooperate. Yet he also resisted the idea of marriage; following a deeply ingrained pattern of approach-avoidance, he would come close, then flee. Some of his friends saw a romantic commitment as the way to solve all his "problems." "I pray that you will be able to make some definite . . . decisions about your future," Mary Kay Perkins wrote in 1952; "when you stop to think of it, I suppose what you really do need—and you seem to feel it too—is a truly fine, understanding, and helpful wife."

Yet Al's way of conceptualizing the issue was strange. He told his best army friend that "a wife had to be steadfastly loyal . . . and give him absolute freedom to be nothing but political most of the time." "To Al," the army friend said, "marriage was a business proposition. It was just one of those things you do and get out of the way with as little danger to your real mission in life as possible." Consistent with such a vision, Lowenstein decided that he was "in the market for a wife" and set himself a deadline of 1955 to acquire one. But as Mimi and Benny Johnson wrote him, "Nowadays, one does not seek wives via a market, so to speak, [a fact that] has escaped you," to which another woman friend added, "[Why did you] set a time bomb for your marriage? . . . Do you think you'll be more mature and readier by then?" In fact, Al's response to the pressures to marry—internal and external—suggested just how ill at ease he was with the whole notion of romance. If only one could approach the problem mechanically, make a decision and then set a deadline, perhaps the problem would resolve itself, perhaps it could simply be *willed* away.[14]

In reality, there were many marriage candidates in Al's life during the 1950s. At least some some of these women pursued him; with others, the interest seemed mutual, but then he would distance himself; and in one particular instance, he plunged ahead full speed, oblivious to the reality that little reciprocal interest existed on the other side. But certain patterns clearly emerged. Almost all the women he dated were non-Jews. Most came from upper-class WASP backgrounds. And each relationship exemplified an awkwardness and unease that would mark nearly all of Lowenstein's romantic interactions with women.

One of Lowenstein's first love interests of the decade was a fellow NSA staffer, Helen Jean Rogers, whom he met at NSA congresses and who later became an international representative for the NSA in Latin America. As had been the case with Mimi Massey, friends had them "paired off" almost immediately. The NSA secretary, Joan Long, wrote how exciting and romantic it was to see the two of them "sneaking off" together at the congress. In correspondence, the two were considered an "item"; Al's friends asked constantly how she was and what their plans were. She was clearly interested. "My darling," she wrote from Latin America, "I've . . . met one interesting man, but even with it all, I wish I could put my head on your shoulders and have your arms very tightly around me for just one minute."[15]

With Rogers as with Massey, however, Lowenstein seemed to pull back once he sensed a more lasting relationship was in the offing. She wrote from Brazil asking him to come meet her family in the Midwest at Christmas, or at least to see him in New York. His initial response was silence, followed by a casual letter saying he was going to Chapel Hill over the holidays. "I'm afraid I felt pretty hurt and terribly sad when I got your letter," she wrote. She thought they felt the same toward each other, but then she realized that "you never once said in a letter [even] that you missed me, or any of the similar things you might have been expected to say." That was unfortunate, she went on, because at some point, Al would have to be more forthcoming with his emotions if he were to find contentment with a woman he loved. One of the people Al had written to about his marriage dilemma was Lucille Kohn, his white-haired heroine from the Encampment, and she perhaps had the most acute insight. "As for your matrimonial problems," she answered, "I think if you have to ask advice you are not very eager."[16]

There were others as well, throughout the 1950s—Katherine "Kacky" White, who pursued Al, as Helen Jean Rogers had, this time from the Caribbean; Judy McMichael, who in a series of winsome letters engaged in a courtship during 1957; and Frances Suzman, a young woman from South Africa who played a pivotal role in Al's encounter with apartheid at the end of the 1950s. But perhaps the most emblematic relationship was the one in which Al himself seized the initiative and declared *his* intentions. Her name was Mary "Muffie" Grant, and she was a Smith College student who hailed from Connecticut.[17]

Although Al had met Muffie while he was still at Yale, their first encounter in Europe was of an entirely different dimension. "I want you to be the first to know," he exulted to Sandy Friedman, "it has happened, once and for all, no chasing elusive will-o-the-wisps . . . no doubts, no problems. . . . Except that she happens to be engaged to somebody else." But that was beside the point. "You will be amazed to hear—as I am amazed to realize—that I am confident, for some uncanny, inexplicable reason that it will work out. . . . She is wonderful, marvelous—in short she is *it*. The whole world looks just like the songs and movies said it would. . . . Love, love, love, love, love—a wonderful word." Perhaps it was significant that, despite Lowenstein's joy, "not a word was spoken, let alone anything being done about it," but from his perspective on reality— "just like the movies"—"there it was screaming louder all the time."[18]

The two had gotten together in Switzerland as part of a larger group of Americans. The women were on a year abroad program from Smith, the men either in the army or on their own "grand tour" of the continent. Almost all their activities were group oriented, whether hiking, dancing, or singing. The group had an enormous admiration for Al, Grant recalls, because of "his activity, his awareness of the injustices and wrongs in society that he was trying to help correct." Even in Europe, whenever he arrived somewhere, the phone would start ringing. "He was constantly agitating, restless, always thinking, and never wasting a moment of conversation—always projecting ahead." The two spent hardly any time alone—none, in fact, until one night Al invited her to dinner, just the two of them. She was experiencing some ambivalence about her engagement to Rob Redpath, also a member of the group, but had no hint of Allard's romantic interest in her. Suddenly, in the middle of their meal, he proposed that they marry. There had been no physical expression of affection in their relationship, and she had not given him even a smidgeon of evidence that she was interested in him as more than a friend. "It was [all so] premature," she said. "What I had thought was friendship, he had thought was something else. It was as if he had been thinking this way for a long time, and talking to other people about it, but I wasn't aware of it." Stunned, she had no idea of how to respond. Looking back later, she concluded that, "perhaps in his view, he was a person who fantasized things as being possible that [in reality] were not."[19]

Smith women, by tradition and socialization, were neither cruel nor ruthless in saying no to suitors, and Muffie Grant went out of her way to be gentle with Al. Although she never seriously considered his proposal, she responded with empathy to his needs and his anxieties.

> I have a marvelous time with you and feel I understand you pretty well, and yet it's unfair to keep you 'encouraged' and 'dangling.' . . . I feel a certain compassion for you that's hard to relate. . . . I can imagine how you feel, having made all the preliminary steps one can, being ready for marriage and feeling incomplete without it, wanting a home you can call your own and someone to share your ideas and hopes . . . and yet this is all meaningless unless you find the person you want to do it with, and for.

With some sadness, Muffie told Al that she could not be that person, and that it would be a form of torture for her to encourage his hopes. Yet her letter conveyed the extent to which she did care, and her understanding of how deeply he needed to hear another answer. "It was [so] painful for him to get too close to people," she later said, "because he was afraid of rejection. . . . He kind of wanted to get through this [proposal] thing quickly, because he was so afraid that it was not going to succeed." Even a fantasy could last only for a time.[20]

At another level, Muffie also had a profound insight into Al's existential anxieties, which were reflected in Marty Bennet's letter to him about being alone. "I don't know if you could ever say Al seemed happy," she observed. "He wasn't that kind of person. He had so many things he was charged up about. . . . I would describe him as somebody with an intense drive to accomplish a lot and never sit still." In that process, though, he craved a reinforcement that somehow was connected to his personal life. "I know how you feel about helping others," Muffie wrote him, "how so often you feel bitter, and can't feel 'wholehearted' about giving, because it just doesn't come. *One can't 'love' indefinitely without being loved in return. You can't give yourself to others and to helping them if someone isn't there to share it*" (italics added). Muffie even made the connection between fighting for Negro civil rights and finding a supportive companion. "All such ideals need a secure foundation," she said, "[and] it's difficult to help Negroes in the South when someone isn't answering your own needs." It was an acute observation that went to the heart of the connection between the personal and political in Lowenstein's life.[21]

But what were Al's needs? And with whom did he seek to satisfy them, particularly given the ambivalence and ambiguity of his romantic relationships with women?

For most of these years, as for much of the rest of his life, Al seemed above all to want intense relationships that reinforced his sense of being a worthwhile person, someone doing important and noble things. Ordinarily, these relationships were with men rather than women. Usually, they involved younger men in a dependent role who looked to Al for guidance, advice, and inspiration. "Acolyte" was the word that some used to describe these young men. Frequently, there was a subtext of sexuality implicit in these relationships, and where that was the case, the young man invariably was white, Anglo-Saxon Protestant, and often very handsome. Whether consciously or subconsciously, Al intentionally placed himself in situations where he would have maximum contact with such people. And though, in the end, these relationships proved no more lasting or complete during the 1950s than the ones he had with women, they provided a much more constant source of reinforcement and ultimately occupied a more central place in his emotional makeup. Al wanted marriage with a woman; he found solace and validation with young men.

The solicitude that characterized these relationships was already apparent at Chapel Hill, where, in addition to his intense early ties to Douglass Hunt, Al developed close bonds with other classmates as well. It was at Yale, however, that he developed most clearly his role as counselor-confidant to younger students. While in the law school, he secured a job as a residence adviser to undergraduates. Living in the dorms, he ran semiofficial "bull sessions" on politics and public affairs, was available for students to chat with at meals or in the evening, and wrote regular reports on how well his charges were doing in handling the pressures of student life. Precise, nuanced, and full of psychological insights, these reports revealed just how complex and observant Lowenstein was as he dealt with these young men.[22]

Inevitably, Lowenstein became an intimate companion of some of his students. With an unerring eye for people in trouble, Al could walk into a crowded room, one longtime associate recalled, and spot a young man in crisis almost instantly, responding—before the evening was over—with a long, soulful conversation that brought solace to the person in need and produced gratification for Lowenstein himself. It was this attentiveness that generated the devotion and loyalty that so many of "Al's boys" displayed. A man of great talent, warmth, and genius had taken the time to single them out and respond to what was on their minds. It may not have been a conversation between equals, and perhaps they felt embarrassed and abashed at their own sense of inadequacy. But these were special moments, with a special person.[23]

Gary Bellow, a young Jewish student, was one of these young men who felt that Lowenstein would listen to his problems. One morning at 3:00 A.M., deeply upset about a hazing procedure he had just been subjected to before joining a Yale club, he knocked on Al's window. Lowenstein pulled on some clothes, said, "Let's get something to eat," and talked with Bellow for three hours. Just a youngster, Bellow did not even know how to articulate his concerns, much less act on them, but Lowenstein drew him out, showed him how hazing was part of a larger social and political structure, related the experience back to McCarthyism, and inspired Bellow to take action against the whole process. "He opened up for me possibilities that I hadn't seen before," Bellow commented. "For me it was a step toward acting on my own beliefs that made a big difference to me." The two became fast friends. Lowenstein once called Bellow from Ohio to ask him to drive to North Carolina with him and subsequently urged him to go to the NSA meetings that drafted resolutions on complying with the *Brown* decision. Recalling their friendship years later, Bellow noted: "What's interesting [is] that there are hundreds of such stories, being told by people all over the country, [where Al] would, in some symbolic way, put on his clothes, go out for a cup of coffee, and talk in ways that made what happens to you make sense." Almost all these "Al stories," he observed humorously, occurred between 2:00 A.M. and 7:00 A.M., or in automobiles when the student was driving Al to the airport or a speaking engagement.[24]

Sometimes, however, the contact took on other overtones. Al became deeply involved with a number of students who had psychiatric problems, going so far as to correspond with therapists about their treatment and prognosis. On occasion, a student expressed concern about the intensity of the relationship and the problem of feeling inadequate in Al's presence, especially given the imbalance of power and control that existed. After leaving Yale in December 1954, one young man wrote of his sorrow "that we would not have a chance to talk again," and of his being "totally unable to say what I wanted to." As the year had passed and their conversations had become more frequent, he noted, "I felt myself becoming more dependent on you [and] I soon realized that this was not healthy." In particular, he had felt this way about discussing his relationship with a young woman. Still, he now wished they had talked more, and that he had filled out one additional course review: "Lowenstein's Humanity I—superb."[25]

Significantly, sexuality was a consistent theme of many of these talks and appeared in Lowenstein's other interests at Yale as well. In a term paper he wrote for a class on psychiatry and the law, Lowenstein and a classmate administered a questionnaire to Yale undergraduates about their sexual experiences. The cover sheet indicated that the survey was for a graduate thesis and was being administered at random. Among other things, the questionnaire asked where the students came from, whether they had gone to public or private schools, whether they had engaged in heterosexual or homosexual activity, what attitudes they held toward such activity, and whether or not it continued.

Two things are striking about the questionnaire. First, it was administered under false pretenses. The survey did not come from a graduate student, nor was it related to a dissertation. Moreover, internal evidence suggests that at least some of those who filled it out lived in Lowenstein's dorm and were recognizable by virtue of their answers. Some of these respondents were also interviewed. Second, Lowenstein himself appears to have spent an enormous amount of time correlating the data (there are extensive calculations and notes in his handwriting), focusing on the connections between type of school attended, religious background, and the actual practice of sexual intimacy. The whole questionnaire seemed designed to figure out the differences between attitude and actual behavior, and the relation of both to social and economomic background.[26]

Although the paper and survey, by themselves, might not be important historically, they become so considered alongside other evidence that Lowenstein frequently concentrated on issues related to sexuality when counseling his students. On at least three occasions reflected in the correspondence, students specifically referred to how important issues of sexual experience or anxiety were to their conversations with Lowenstein. This was clearly a question on which college students were both vulnerable and very much in need of advice. Hence, a sympathetic ear would be most welcome. It was also, however, an issue that, once exposed, could lead to other revelations and confidences—including fears about, or interest in, homosexuality, which Lowenstein needed desperately to examine in himself. Such conversations could thus provide him with the occasion to explore, tentatively, his own sexual needs and impulses, while retaining the superior and powerful role of adviser-confidant.[27]

Nowhere was this pattern better exemplified than in Al's relationship with David Lapham, a young student from New York whom Al became deeply attached to at Yale. Like others before and after him, Lapham stood in awe of Lowenstein and felt both incredulous that such an extraordinary person would deign to spend time with him and overwhelmed by the difficulty of measuring up under such unequal conditions. "Even now," he wrote, well after they had become good friends, "when I write these sentences I try to think what effect they will have on your mind." His letters were so unimaginative. "I can't let myself go and express my true feelings. I've been trying to tell you this . . . that I am really a weak person." Yet the two were very close. Lowenstein had confided in Lapham that he, too, was troubled, "not physically, but mentally." There was something very special in the bond between them. Occasionally, they had intentionally excluded others so that they could be together. "I don't think . . . our friendship . . . would be what it is now," Lapham wrote, "unless we had done those things together, and doing them meant shutting ourselves [off] from others."[28]

Among other things, they shared concerns about sexuality, concerns that Lapham wrote openly about when he was on a trip across the United States to see the country. "There's a boy up here who is terribly homesick and also mixed up sexually," Lapham told Lowenstein. "I keep wondering what you would say to him." Lapham was doing his best to help but was having trouble. "I don't know what to do," he confessed, "since it's unlike any problem you have told me about where you were able to talk to the boy and discuss the whole thing."[29]

In early September 1955, David Lapham was killed in an automobile accident while hitchhiking across Florida. Lowenstein was crushed. He poured out his emotions in letters to Lapham's family, to his own friends, and to some people he barely knew. Among others, he wrote to Adlai Stevenson and Eleanor Roosevelt and Frank Porter Graham, asking them to send letters of condolence to the Lapham family. In reality, he was asking them to console *him*. For weeks, he seemed preoccupied with his friend's death. David's father puzzled about the friendship. "I assumed you had a keen mind, liked politics, organizing people, etc," he wrote Al. "I was proud of Dave for liking you, but always wondered why you liked him." Partly, Al liked David for being willing to share so much with him; but the younger man had also given Al a chance to share something in return. It was what Muffie Grant was talking about when she wrote, "You can't give your life to others . . . if someone isn't there . . . to love you in return."[30]

Ironically, it was because of Dave Lapham that Al had the occasion to fall in love with Muffie. She was the former roommate and best friend of Carol Hardin, one of David's oldest friends from childhood, and the woman everyone believed he would have eventually married. Carol and Muffie were together in Geneva for their junior years when David was killed. Al wrote to Carol immediately and soon thereafter arranged to visit her; once again he was the confidant, offering solace and sharing grief. Carol was "terrifically grateful," Muffie wrote, "[because] you understood Dave so well and were such a 'guide' in many ways to him." Soon, it was Al's turn to declare his love for Muffie, their lives intertwined in a bizarre drama, with Dave Lapham the thread that held it all together.

CONCLUSION

In all of this, there were two things that were striking. The first had to do with Lowenstein's abiding sensitivity to ethnicity. With only a few exceptions, most of the young men he was most attracted to were from a common background. Ivy Leaguers, "preppies," sometimes "jocks," they were mostly non-Jews. "I don't know whether you could say [Al] wanted to disassociate himself from his past and his family," Muffie commented, "but the friends I know of were all very similar [in that they were] very different in background from Al." As early as the UNC years, the pattern had been clear. "Strangely enough," a Chapel Hill friend had written Al in 1951, "the first time I saw —, long before I knew that you knew him, he struck me as your type." Marcia Borie, a close friend Al had first met through NSA in 1951, made a similar observation. "I was never surprised . . . when he would show up with mostly white, Anglo-Saxon Protestant good-looking friends, the blond, blue-eyed, 6'3" [type]," she commented, "because everytime he made a friendship [with] one of these people, it was an inner acceptance." Al lacked self-esteem, and that lack was somehow connected to his ethnicity, to his habitual effort "to make a little pugnose." So "everytime a Gentile found him compelling or interesting or whatever . . . [that] meant a great deal."[31]

Conversely, nothing could inflame him more than feeling rejected by WASPS. Any such rejection confirmed his deepest feelings of inferiority and his worst fears of being viewed as worthless. When Muffie Grant refused his marriage proposal, for example, Lowenstein wrote a letter to a friend suffused with self-hatred and bitter ethnic commentary. "[Muffie] will marry her fenceman in due course," he said sarcastically, "and I will probably be asked to usher since they admire and love me so much." In a mood of self-abnegation that also dripped with venom, Lowenstein observed that "only someone as pigheadead as I . . . could conceivably have not realized . . . that if one is going to hang around with the grape-juice-by-the-pool-while-the-dogs-bark-set, Yale sets the styles and it's time to fall-to or move out. All I want is a job teaching in a town of 20,000 in Miss. or central Florida. . . . I'll marry the first homely old maid who promises to breed properly and keep the bathtub clean." Although Lowenstein would not—could not—remain long in such a mood, the very depth of his momentary animus toward the WASP upper class (those who will "always be elected Captain of the team and Queen of the Maypole") disclosed just how much ethnicity played a role in his own self-definition, and how much he needed the validation of non-Jews to feel good about himself.[32]

Equally important was the extent to which men—as much or more than women—provided the focus for his efforts to find emotional gratification. Lowenstein liked women. He wanted to be married and raise a family. But he often was uncomfortable with women, not knowing how to act, how to initiate physical contact, how to court and seduce. With men it was easier, especially with younger men who saw him as a hero, who welcomed his interest, who responded to his solicitous outreach, who hungered, in their own way, for someone who would listen to their confessions about sexual ambivalence and anxiety. In effect, Al Lowenstein constructed his life so that those encounters could happen. He was torn about his own sexuality.

Already, he had developed a pattern, when traveling with a male companion, of finding accommodations where there was only one bed. "Sure did enjoy your company," one friend wrote. "I must say, however, (to you) that I would have slept better in a bed by myself." Others had the same experience. "I found myself with the wrestler's left arm over my torso," a UNC associate said, "and I was awake for the rest of the night." In the army, Lowenstein later told a friend, he had at least some homosexual experience. In all likelihood, he had not resolved his ambivalence about his sexuality during these years, or about how overt he should be in expressing his more hidden desires. But if anything at all was clear, it was the degree to which sexuality and concern about intimacy constituted an ongoing theme of his life, one that would not go away, and yet one that, by virtue of the secrecy and deceptiveness involved in it, could not easily be addressed openly.[33]

Lowenstein thus seemed caught in a vicious cycle of his own making. He wanted a wife yet appeared unable to proceed in a way likely to produce that alternative. He craved intimacy with men but ran away from confronting all the inner conflicts and secret desires that lasting intimacy of that kind might involve. Instead, he became someone devoted to causes and to movements on behalf of those causes—as though sheer activity provided the best means of escaping his problems and enhancing his self-image. If self-sacrifice on behalf of righteous goals did nothing else, it validated the "good" side of Lowenstein's ego and, with some luck, even provided the opportunity—however fleetingly—to explore the less clear and less straightforward aspects of his personal needs.

In the end, of course, choices had to be made and priorities established. Writing to Lowenstein about the perennial problem of finding a lifetime mate, his NSA colleague Joan Long hit the nail on the head. "Do you love the person enough to place them first [ahead of your own activities]?" If not, she wrote with prophetic insight, "then you haven't learned to love." There was the rub. Friends might be persuaded to go along with Lowenstein's hyperactivity. "But what about someone whom you would want to marry?" Marriage, she pointed out, "involves sacrifice from the minute you say 'I will' . . . and *you* wouldn't be willing to make the sacrifices involved if your partner failed to evidence his willingness to do the same. I don't think it's enough to *say* that you're in love. You have to prove it. Without action to back it up, words become empty phrases and mean very little."

The key, then, was the meaning of love, and the choices it entailed. Douglass Hunt, Mimi Massey, and Helen Jean Rogers understood that Al had not reached the point of being able to make those choices. Muffie Grant came to the same conclusion. "We look at life and at relationships and at each other too differently to ever merge spontaneously in any lasting way," she wrote Al. Instead, she recognized "what different levels we live on, what varied emotions and ideas move us, [and] what divergent ends and means we strive for." Unless Al were willing to alter his priorities and make the choices that a commitment to love required, he seemed condemned to a lifestyle that frustrated his need for intimacy, even as it constantly reminded him of how great that need was.[34]

For the moment, Al found partial gratification through his role as a mentor and counselor. Interestingly enough, Lowenstein coined the phrase "Father-Confessor" to describe that role. With wonderful precision, the term evokes the texture of the part he played: Lowenstein, the kindly, sensitive figure to whom one could tell all, no matter how revelatory the details; Lowenstein, the mentor with the wisdom and compassion to respond accordingly, thereby imparting grace and inspiring devotion. Yet it was also a role that generated pain and frustration. As Muffie Grant wrote, "I know . . . how so often you feel bitter . . . about helping others . . . and can't feel 'wholehearted' about giving because . . . you can't give your life to others . . . if someone isn't there to love you in return." The very nature of the father-confessor role precluded its being a source of permanent gratification: because, by definition, it was an *unequal* relationship whose very structure prevented the kind of commitment that is made by autonomous figures capable of *choosing* love. A father-confessor could have "acolytes," or "boys," but not lovers who stood on the same footing. To find such a lover, Al needed to be able to share intimacy with someone as an equal, not as a dependent person in trouble.

Such equality, however, presumed a foundation of self-love and self-worth, and that was precisely what Al lacked because of his feelings of "difference" and inferiority. The friend to whom Lowenstein had written so bitterly about his father-confessor role suddenly realized that Al never understood he was "actually more fair-haired than a large part of your fair-haired contemporaries." No matter how abundant the evidence of his popularity and power, he could not feel good about himself. "Al had the most compelling personality, the most witty, genuinely . . . humorous personality [you could imagine] on the one hand," Marcia Borie said, "[but] he also lacked confidence . . . [and] had an inferiority complex . . . [and so] he surrounded himself [with] pretty people who were more attractive than himself, almost as if that beauty could rub off on him."[35]

Thus, in the end, the trap came full circle. Because Al's insecurity about his own worth made it impossible for him to interact with others on an equal basis, he had to structure relationships where his need for intimacy could be met through his role as counselor-confidant. To break out of that cycle would require addressing all the conflicts and instincts he found most unsettling; and since taking that path was unacceptable, Al plunged ahead, becoming ever more hyperactive, "always on the move," as Muffie said, "never able to stay very long anywhere with anyone," except, perhaps in his father-confessor role. But even with the rewards that the role brought, satisfaction was temporary; it would always be necessary to move on again, ever fearful of rejection, ever committed to escape. "Do you ever get sick and tired of running all the time?" Norma Nelson asked him. The answer was both yes and no. In the deepest part of his being, Al was desperately sick of running all the time. But whether consciously or unconsciously, he decided he had no other choice.[36]

6

The South Africa Years

Having determined that young people would be his principal constituency, Allard Lowenstein devoted most of the rest of his life to identifying political issues that would rally them to his side. He always had a "project," both in the immediate sense of a new goal to be achieved—such as racial equality in Mississippi or peace in Vietnam—and in the existential sense of reaching beyond the present moment to find some future task that would provide, at least in anticipation, greater fulfillment than could be found in the here and now.

When the quest for new projects became too frustrating, Lowenstein's fantasy of settling down came to the fore. At times, this took the form of searching desperately for an idyllic small-town newspaper he could edit in a middle American hamlet full of white steepled churches. Or it appeared in his on-again, off-again pursuit of the perfect marriage partner, the woman who could offer a haven from turmoil. Ironically but appropriately, this passion to find a wife became, if anything, even stronger as the pace of his activity intensified. Although ultimately there was a fatal incompatibility between seeking the stability of marriage and his quest for an endless supply of new causes and followers, a kind of meaning emerged from the process: perhaps finding a home would provide the strength to replenish his impulse to stay in motion.[1]

All of these tensions and issues became clearer after the NSA had provided the métier for Lowenstein's political life. From 1957 to 1962, he pursued what at times seemed a chaotic array of projects, but one of them would transform his life and help change history. Al's trip to South Africa—and the United Nations testimony and book manuscript that followed—embodied the message that he never stopped preaching: intervention by one person in a situation of moral crisis can make a critical difference. If anything, his South African venture provided the model of personal efficacy that would justify his subsequent activities in Mississippi and Vietnam. Unfortunately, during these same years, Lowenstein also experienced the frustration of losing one of the few women he ever deeply loved, one more indication that a causal link existed between his need to stay in motion and his inability to find peace within.

THE JOURNEY TO SOUTH AFRICA

Lowenstein's interest in Africa flowed naturally from his concentration during the NSA years on winning over developing nations to western-style democracy and the cause of anticommunism. After organizing campuses for the College Association of the United Nations in 1956–57, Lowenstein had briefly returned to UNC for a year of graduate study in history and a job as a dormitory counselor. But despite his love for Chapel Hill and his fondness for academia, he remained restless. As always, travel provided one outlet for his energies, and in the summer of 1958, Lowenstein set off on a journey to twenty cities in seventeen countries, from the Soviet Union to the Middle East to Africa. Armed with a series of questions about student life in Africa and Asia from the NSA's international vice-president, Lowenstein circulated widely among university groups, focusing especially on Rhodesia and South Africa. He met supporters of the African National Congress (ANC) in Port Elizabeth, held discussions with Alan Paton, the antiapartheid novelist, and encountered some of the representatives in South Africa's Parliament who opposed the racial polarization in their country. Lowenstein also joined forces with members of the South African student association who were preparing to engage in mass protests against the government's decision to close the University of Capetown to nonwhite students.[2]

On the basis of that experience, Lowenstein secured a job—with the help of Frank Porter Graham—as a foreign policy specialist on the staff of Senator Hubert Humphrey from Minnesota. Lowenstein's most important role was to guide Humphrey on issues relating to the Third World, especially Africa. When the American Committee on Africa urged Humphrey in 1959 to make a major speech on Africa Freedom Day, April 15, Humphrey welcomed the opportunity, telling Lowenstein, "Keep on top of this [South African issue]. I want my statement to be good and I want something original." Rising to the challenge, Lowenstein crafted a superb speech laced with quotes from scholars like Melville Herskovitz celebrating the triumphs and survivals of Africa's past, noting that the continent's nadir coincided with the advent of colonialism and the slave trade, and focusing on the universalist theme that "no man is good enough to rule another without his consent." Showing the parallel between the American revolution and African nationalism, Lowenstein wrote that the tradition of America fighting against master races, whether in World War II or now, was part of the task of freedom. "It means that we are against the enslavement of one people by another—in Eastern Europe, in China, or in Africa." Above all, he told Humphrey, it was crucial not to talk down to Africa or try to impose western values on the continent. Although Lowenstein himself was not above using cold war rhetoric to bolster his points, he emphasized to Humphrey the importance of viewing Africa not in a cold war frame of reference but from the point of view of mutual respect and reciprocity. Both the speech and the advice were cogent expressions of a sensitive foreign policy observer who deserved to play a significant role in world events.[3]

By the late spring of 1959, however, Lowenstein was no longer sure that Humphrey's staff was the place to play that role. The office was disorganized (hardly an unusual state of affairs for Lowenstein), but more troublesome were the rivalries for Humphrey's attention and, in the end, the inadequate recognition, especially for someone who may well have believed that he knew more than his boss and was better qualified to have a voice at the tables of power. "I have no desire to sit there and listen to the Senator spout the words that I wrote," Lowenstein once penciled on a memo pad. Why stay in a staff position and write speeches about Africa if one could actually go there and attempt to alter the awful conditions in which people lived?[4]

The circumstances of Lowenstein's return to South Africa went back to an impromptu encounter he had during his first visit there in the summer of 1958. Speaking at the nonwhite Fort Hare University College, Lowenstein had been attacking apartheid while arguing that the American people, however problematic the racism in their own country, could not be held accountable for it. Indeed, Lowenstein said, since Americans were ignorant of South Africa's policies, they could not possibly be blamed for them.

At that point, an African in the audience stood up to speak. "You say your people don't see that they are responsible for the things that are done to the black man in South Africa," the African declared. "Well, I come from a place for which your country and the United Nations are directly responsible, and there things are so much worse that I must come *here* [to South Africa] to get a breath of fresh air." The African was Jariretundu Kozonguizi; his native land was South-West Africa (now Namibia). Ever since World War I, his country had been living under an international mandate created by the Versailles Treaty to deal with former colonies of Germany. Great Britain had ceded responsibility for the territory to the Union of South Africa, and now South-West Africa, still theoretically under the ultimate supervision of the United Nations, lived under a system of oppression and exploitation even worse than that which prevailed in South Africa. Lowenstein was stunned by Kozonguizi's story, and the two men stayed up until dawn discussing the anomaly of a nation being protected by a world organization dedicated to human rights but exemplifying in the most glaring ways the suppression of all those rights.[5]

Within weeks of his return to the United States, Lowenstein's interest was piqued again, this time by meeting Father Michael Scott, an Anglican priest who had gone to South-West Africa in 1947 at the request of African chiefs to investigate the conditions of their people and to speak on their behalf at the United Nations. Two years later, Scott had been banned from the territory. No African representatives were allowed by South Africa to leave South-West Africa or to communicate with the United Nations. In effect, with Scott's expulsion, South-West Africa became a nonentity. Father Scott's protestations represented the only reminder to anyone of this suffering people who were in crying need of help.

Upon meeting Scott, Lowenstein was overwhelmed by both the power of his personality and the urgency of his cause. "Nothing I had heard . . . had prepared me for the remarkable impact of the man," Lowenstein later wrote. "There was a great strength and simplicity to what he said that evoked the deference of diplomats and touched that which makes men want to cheer and weep at once. He was somehow both blunt and gentle, a lean pacifist lion full of a restraining patience and an urgent impatience, as if the two go hand in hand." Exerting the full power of his personality, Scott implored Lowenstein to go to South-West Africa as a "disinterested" observer and to bring back to the United Nations documentation about the real conditions there so that the conscience of the world might be awakened. His own cries had lost their relevance, Scott said, because his information had become dated. Yet if new information could be produced, the world might once again be prepared to puncture the complacency with which the South African regime dismissed all complaints about its governance of South-West Africa. The journey might well be dangerous, Scott acknowledged, and it certainly would involve subterfuge and intrigue. But whatever the odds, the outcome would be extraordinary if the mission were successful.[6]

Lowenstein was interested first because of the need to intervene on behalf of black Africans. But he also wished to go back to South Africa because he believed he had the ability to save white Africans as well, to persuade them that there was a better path, a more gentle and humane future. "I have found [here] some of the most generous and wonderful people I have ever met," he told one group of white South Africans. "I have felt more at home with you than at any other place outside my own country; this has become, in some magic way, my country too." And precisely for that reason, he believed he could persuade these friends to reverse the "mad racial policies" they were pursuing, lest they "be pushed into the sea." Thus, even as he determined to fight apartheid, he also aspired to become the figure who would help whites in South Africa transcend their racism and find ultimate reconciliation with blacks.[7]

To make all this happen, however, Lowenstein needed a plan of action, compatriots to undertake the journey with him, and financial support. The first two prerequisites were interrelated. Any plan to gather data from South-West Africa that was announced in advance would quickly have been derailed by the South African authorities who issued visas of entry and controlled travel to the mandated territories. Hence, the journey had to be covert, its true purpose disguised behind a cover story that any reasonable South African official would accept. Lowenstein already had a letter of invitation from Dan Verwoerd, the son of South Africa's prime minister, whom he had met on his previous trip at a student government conference. But beyond that, he needed associates who would buttress and make more credible an innocent explanation for the journey.[8]

Lowenstein cast a wide net seeking volunteers to join him. The demands were great, and the search proved difficult, but in the end he settled on two young people who were ideal for the occasion. One was Sherman Bull, an Ivy League student from a distinguished Connecticut family; with his scientific background, he was able to piece together a reasonable story that he and his friends were interested in various forms of wildlife in South-West Africa that were not observable anyplace else. "South-West Africa is the home of the aardvark," Bull could argue, and he wished to pursue scientific research on the subject. Bull even recorded a series of strange animal sounds at the beginning of the tape on their recorder so that if authorities started to play it, they would find evidence confirming the cover story. The second travel companion was Emory Bundy, a University of Washington student who lacked Bull's scientific credentials but made up in innocent enthusiasm what he lacked in technical qualifications.[9]

The story of Lowenstein's relationship with Bundy illuminates the interpersonal dynamics on the trip, as well as the process by which Lowenstein attracted disciples throughout his life. The two had first met in 1957 when Lowenstein spoke at the University of Washington, where Bundy was student body president. With Bundy as with so many others, Lowenstein ignited a spark of intense personal devotion and loyalty. Lowenstein would come into a large gathering, already a legendary figure because of his frenetic travel schedule and "star" quality, and then, despite being surrounded by scores of other people, he would zero in on a particular person as though that person alone mattered in the entire world. The individual himself might feel small, meaningless, and inexperienced, especially in contrast to the worldliness Lowenstein displayed. But it was precisely "this sense of being paid attention to by somebody with an extraordinary set of connections and talent" that made Bundy and hundreds like him immediate converts.[10]

Within weeks after their first meeting, Bundy and Lowenstein had begun to deepen the bond that existed between them. "Almost daily I wish that you were here so that I could ask your advice on various problems," Bundy wrote. "As it is, I often feel that I'm not being as effective as I could be—and my spirits drop. Right now I'm on fire, burning to swing into the job." Lowenstein, in turn, suggested that they meet in New York and drive together to visit Chapel Hill before going to the NSA annual congress. The auto trip was "classic Lowenstein," Bundy recalled. "You couldn't really go by a crossroads without him at least making a phone call." Lowenstein visited everyone he knew, from his black commanding officer in the army to former classmates at UNC. "The conversations never ended," Bundy said, and more often than not, he fell asleep in a living room chair while Al carried on.[11]

It was not surprising, then, that Lowenstein turned to Bundy when he was recruiting traveling companions for the South African trip—precisely because of his youthful enthusiasm and devotion. Although Lowenstein subsequently singled out Bull's mechanical skills and the adventurous spirit of both men as the reasons for their selection, Bundy never took those claims seriously. "If there was anything sensible about our going," he said, "it was none of the . . . reasons we had ever been told . . . but [the fact] that we were damn good cover . . . precisely because we were as young and innocent and WASPish as we were." Had the mission consisted of three people like Lowenstein—"older, and more sophisticated and possibly Jewish"—questions might have been raised. But Bull and Bundy "were the sort of sporting and athletic young Americans that South Africans would most take to." Preppy-looking, blue-eyed, and rugged, "we would kind of breeze into [a place with an] . . . innocent, reassuring image." Neither companion had any illusions of being anything but helpers who "ran errands." The primary reason for going was to be with Al.[12]

All that then remained was to find the money for the trip. Lowenstein and Father Scott approached various foundations for travel support. Lowenstein went to Dorothy Schiff, publisher of the *New York Post*, for help. But the need to obscure the real purpose of the trip made fund-raising difficult, and in the end, most of their money came from private sources. Speculating about Lowenstein's possible connections with the CIA, some observers have cited the substantial expense of the South African trip as one indication that Lowenstein must have been on the government's payroll. But other evidence raises doubts about such allegations. Not only have CIA operatives themselves offered plausible reasons for denying any connection between the CIA and Lowenstein, but the financial situation of the three travelers does not fit well into a CIA scenario. Bundy had to borrow money for the trip, and his check for the airfare bounced. Bull was independently wealthy. And Lowenstein continued to receive most of his money from his father, who paid for all his phone bills and much of his travel. Furthermore, the stupidities committed by the trio once they were in South Africa made their mission seem more like a parody of a spy story than a credible CIA venture.[13]

Nevertheless, intrigue marked the entire journey, threatening at any moment to explode their mission into an international scandal. Capturing some of the flavor of the venture, Perrin Henderson, a former Lowenstein travel companion, wrote that he only wished he could be there "as valet to

U.S. undercover agent no. 1001." "What are you doing?" he asked. "Do you carry a gun?" Secrecy was pervasive. Just before the trio left, a *New York Times* reporter had been arrested and deported for trying to talk to Africans in South-West Africa. Scott and Kozonguizi were convinced that the mission would not last more than a day before its real purpose was unearthed. Telephones were tapped in the places the Americans stayed; surveillance by government authorities seemed to be everywhere; and notwithstanding the innocent appearance of Bull and Bundy, Lowenstein was already known as a foe of the government, based on his speeches the previous year. He was staying at the Johannesburg home of Helen Suzman, a leading white dissident and member of the South African Parliament, and was afraid to tell even her of his real purpose. "He was moving in and out of different worlds," Suzman's daughter Frances said, "and not everybody knew all the areas that he was encroaching in." He did finally take them into his confidence, but fearful that he might get them into trouble by his activities, he proposed to move out. They quickly reassured him that they shared his goals and would do whatever they could to help. Bundy had taken some precautions against discovery, writing all the secret information they carried about their mission in tiny script on the back of a travel map that he then hid inside a pair of trousers he wore under his outer pants. But in a city where the secret police were reputed to be everywhere, it was difficult to believe they would not soon be exposed.[14]

Almost immediately, they dramatically increased their vulnerability by becoming involved in the celebrated case of Hans Beukes, a South-West African who was seized by authorities just as he was about to depart for university training in Norway. No African had ever been allowed to leave South-West Africa to attend a university, but Beukes had won a scholarship and been given a visa. "I was always so careful," he said, "I did nothing they could object to—*nothing*." Nevertheless, his passport had been taken, allegedly because he carried Communist propaganda—a book by Adlai Stevenson. Lowenstein met him the day after his case became a cause célèbre, urging him to cable the United Nations to protest against his treatment since the United Nations bore legal responsibility for South-West Africa. The next time they met, a few days later, not only had Beukes fired off the cable, but he had also decided to escape from South Africa illegally and go in person to the United Nations to register his complaint. Furthermore, he expected Lowenstein and his compatriots to arrange and participate in his flight to freedom. The Americans recognized how crazy and dangerous the scheme was. "I kept thinking," Bundy said, "[that] the point of all this [was to go to] South-West Africa . . . and the time and the risk of doing [this] seemed a tremendous diversion over what we had come to do." Yet Beukes insisted, and since he was even more at peril than the Americans if they were caught, Lowenstein and his friends saw no choice but to help. "[It was] a foolhardy thing to do," Bundy said, but to do nothing seemed even more unacceptable.[15]

What then ensued was a comedy of errors. "[We were] like the Keystone Cops," Bundy recalled, "because we were so naive about what we were doing, we were frightened by the implications of it, [and] we had no guidance in how [to do] this sort of thing." The day of the escape had begun in helter-skelter fashion. Sherman called Lowenstein at the Suzmans' and asked, over the tapped phone, "Are we taking Hans out today?" Lowenstein quickly said, "Oh, you mean to the zoo?" to which Sherman replied, "No, no, I mean out of the. . . " while Al shouted, "I know what you mean!" Then Sherman and Hans could not find each other; after they did, the two drove up to the large, all-white tennis party that Lowenstein and Bundy were attending, creating a huge spectacle. "So far in the day," Bundy noted, "we had done almost everything possible to telegraph what we were trying to do and to draw attention to ourselves."

No one had even given any thought to what would occur at the border crossing between South Africa and Bechuanaland, the British protectorate that was their destination. Initially, they thought of swimming the Limpopo River, which constituted the boundary, but then someone remembered hearing that there were crocodiles in the stream. Eventually, they decided to fold Beukes up, "accordion-like," in the small well behind the backseat of their Volkswagen Beetle and cover him with papers and blankets. But even that solution occurred to them only after they had experienced the stares of policemen and white citizens in the towns they drove through, their audience aghast at seeing three white men and an African traveling together. Beukes by then was a familiar figure to newspaper readers, and his face was potentially recognizable by countless authorities. They continued their journey through desolate countryside in the dark of night, with car trouble threatening to terminate the entire adventure. In the end, the border crossing was the easiest step, and by dawn, Beukes had left South Africa forever and was now free to pursue the arduous journey to Norway and U.N. headquarters in New York. But it had been an escape notable as much for the amateur recklessness of the American "spies" as for the collective daring of the enterprise.[16]

Unfortunately for the Americans, the harrowing, spine-tingling quality of the Beukes flight into exile was fully matched by the rest of their mission. At each step they narrowly evaded discovery. Their car was broken into and robbed by the security police; every document but those that were most directly incriminating were captured by South African intelligence officers. Extensions of their visas—made necessary by the delay caused by the Beukes affair—were initially denied. And there was a feeling of being under constant surveillance.

Yet the Americans persisted and, with an extraordinary mixture of good luck and determination, succeeded in recording on tape and in writing virtually every piece of evidence Michael Scott had ever hoped they could retrieve. Having delivered Beukes to Bechuanaland and survived the break-in of their car, they finally set off by road for South-West Africa. As they drove lonely long hours through the desolate Kalahari Desert, they entertained themselves by singing spirituals and folk songs, desperately hoping that when they arrived at their destination someone would know who they were and trust them enough to take them to the African leaders who would be their witnesses for the United Nations. Always there was the problem of being detected by white authorities or turned in by the African spies the whites had hired. Walking past hovels on dusty paths at their first stop, Lowenstein felt everyone's eyes on him, even though no one would meet his glance, and experienced "the shame of being white where white men have so comported themselves that terror is their trademark to nonwhites."

Frantically seeking out the meeting place where he might find his contact, Lowenstein thought to himself: "It's not the laws or even the poverty that are the worst thing; the worst thing is the terror . . . to exist at the whim of a race of people each of whom represents danger; so that soon the eyes are always clouded, the stomach always tense, the emotion always fear." Finally, Lowenstein found the place he wanted, only to discover the same suspicion and wariness conveyed in the eyes of the people on the streets. "Many men denounce things they serve," one African told him after Lowenstein had tried to indicate that the purpose of his visit was to combat South African oppression. But eventually the man was convinced, contact was made, and the process of discovering the truth about South-West Africa could begin.[17]

That truth was even more horrendous than anyone had told them before they set out. A young man could not visit his dying mother thirty miles away because it took three days to get the necessary travel permits. A person who became ill and unable to work could be arrested because he had

Gabriel "Doc" Lowenstein was the most important figure in Allard's life. Imposing and sometimes dictatorial, he nevertheless cared passionately for his youngest son, seeking to live through him and find the personal fulfillment he felt he had been denied in his own career.

His stepmother, Florence, treated Allard as if he were her natural child, doting on him. Here, she hugs Allard and his sister, Dorothy, born after Gabriel and Florence had been married a year.

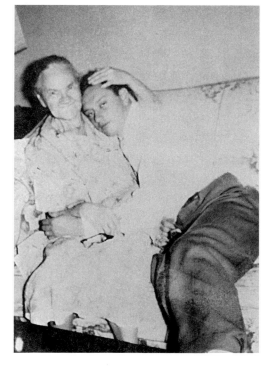

Despite the dark secret of Augusta's death, Allard remained devoted to his Goldberg relatives from the "old country." Here, he is being embraced by his grandmother Goldberg. In the Goldberg family, he found a warmth and ease frequently absent in his own home.

Florence treated Allard as someone "special," frequently dressing him up to show him off to friends and relatives.

Florence wrote often about Allard's eyes, his "limpid pools," clear in this bicycle scene.

By the beginning of World War II, the Lowenstein family had moved from Manhattan's Upper West Side to this elegant home in suburban Westchester County. Dorothy and Allard had a special playroom in the house where they engaged in mock World War II battles.

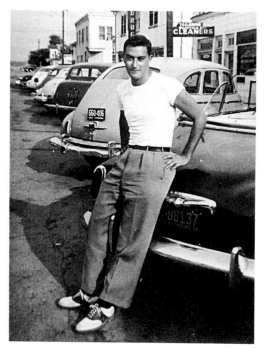

Allard chose to go to college at the University of North Carolina, defying his father's wish that he attend an Ivy League school. He fell in love with Chapel Hill, where he quickly became a prominent personality. Here, he is shown on downtown Franklin Street.

Allard loved to sing and play the piano with friends. At Chapel Hill, he found a community of people who remained a central part of his life long after college.

While at Chapel Hill, Allard attended the Encampment for Citizenship, an annual gathering of young people from divergent cultures, united by their commitment to progressive ideals.

He also became devoted to three of the heroes and heroines of his life—Eleanor Roosevelt, Frank Porter Graham, and Norman Thomas. Here, he is shown with "Dr. Frank."

Lowenstein met Eleanor Roosevelt first when he attended the Encampment for Citizenship. Subsequently, they became devoted friends.

One of the things Lowenstein did at Chapel Hill was to remake his physical appearance through bodybuilding, thereby overcoming his self-image as weak and fragile. Here, wearing his Yale Law School t-shirt, he displays the results.

During his year as National Student Association president as well as in law school and after, Lowenstein became notorious for his peripatetic travel, newspapers and books frequently overflowing from his bags.

Risking arrest and deportation, in 1959 Lowenstein and his friends, Sherman Bull and Emory Bundy, undertook a fact-finding mission to highlight the impoverishment and neglect suffered by South West Africa (now Namibia). They brought back photographs like this to document their findings.

not received permission from his employer to stay at home. A husband might work four months to save the money to take a train to visit his wife and children, then be forbidden to get on the train. One tribesman who came to seek work in a city was fined ten pounds—over three months' wages—for lacking the necessary papers. Not a single African in the entire territory had been able to get more than an eleventh-grade education, and in 1959, there were only 367 who had gone beyond the fifth grade. In the Windhoek location, the government provided one toilet for every 150 people, and 12 showers for a population of 20,000. Above all, Lowenstein later wrote, there was "the vast, brooding despair that sits silently everywhere when ten thousand inevitable tomorrows loom worse than ten thousand grim yesterdays, when there is never the hope of getting ahead of today so that tomorrow can be better, or even so that the tomorrow of the children can be better." And then the afterthought: "How do you understand such a despair when you have experienced none of the yesterdays and will presently escape even the anticipation of the tomorrows?"

As much as anything else, the testimony of two African leaders crystallized the dismaying reality that Lowenstein and his friends found in South-West Africa. The first was the Reverend Markus Kooper, minister of the African Methodist Episcopal Church that served the Rooie Nasie tribe in the village of Hoachanas, homeland to the Rooie Nasie people since before 1700. The tribe had been ordered by the government to relocate 150 miles away in a barren, desolate place called Itzawisis. The people refused to give up their ancestral land, and they were led in that fight by their pastor. One Sunday the police came and tossed Kooper and his family into a truck, carting them away to Itzawisis, presuming that his banishment would break the will of the people. But it had only deepened their rage.

Lowenstein and his friends finally located Kooper after a circuitous trip designed to avoid all white eyes. The area was even worse than they had been told. "For some time," Lowenstein wrote, "we drove along what might have been the surface of the moon, for all the living things that broke the expanse of brownness separated from the scorching sky only by waves of heat that tormented the interloper with memories of iced drinks and blue swimming places." Finally, they came to a hut "made of sticks in the ground bound together by canvas . . . [with] a dog and some scrawny chickens" the only life visible in the dusty yard. Such was Markus Kooper's exile. Quickly, they plotted to meet Kooper far enough away to elude the local spies, then they were off on a new adventure, a fourteen-hour drive back to Hoachanas, with Kooper, another secret cargo, hidden the same way that they hid Beukes during his escape.[18]

Throughout the trip, Kooper testified about the fate of his people under the South African mandate. The tribe's land was being stolen, he said, in return for a plot of ground where not a single drop of water existed. The government had given no education or protection to the people, only sadness. When the group reached Hoachanas, Emory Bundy recalled, "we found greenness, palm trees, and a beautiful spring of clear water." It was this land that the government wished to give to whites, while consigning the Rooie Nasie to an arid wilderness. Almost prophetically, the group arrived just as the Sunday morning church service was to begin. The people "threw their arms around our necks," Bundy said, "and cried openly. They had written and prayed so long for deliverance, and we were the first sign of help."

That afternoon, the Americans recorded further testimony. "We were made to see our blood run down on the ground," one man said, as he told of his pregnant wife being beaten by police until she miscarried. At one point, a tribal leader went on for what seemed an eternity, carried away in a florid explosion of words while the Americans anxiously awaited a translation. Befuddled, Kooper struggled for the right words, then simply condensed the plea into the plaintive cry, "Help! UNO [United Nations Organization]! Help!"

Then the Americans experienced their ultimate moment of grace when they met Hosea Kutako, the chief who spoke for almost 90 percent of the people in South-West Africa. A devoted Christian, the chief had led the opposition to South African oppression ever since World War II. Almost ninety years old, he refused to be intimidated or overwhelmed by the odds against his people's struggle. "We stepped in and were awed by [his] presence," Bundy testified. "His skin was deeply wrinkled; he was tall, powerful and very black." With magisterial dignity, he recounted the story of his people: German colonists and soldiers had killed all but 15,000 of his 85,000 tribesmen, and the South African government had stolen their dwelling place. "We are just like animals who have nowhere to live," he said. For hours, the Americans listened and recorded, then at a signal that the police were coming, impatiently denounced the authorities. To which Chief Kutako responded, "God has sent his Son to die so that all men might live as brothers. We must oppose the cruelty and injustice of the South African government; but don't hate." With those words as their farewell, the Americans departed to Windhoek. After hours of searching, they finally found the contact person who would take their tapes and evidence out of South Africa. Their journey now almost over, they prepared to return to Johannesburg.[19]

All that remained was to say goodbye to friends and comrades, return joyfully home, and present the evidence they had compiled to the United Nations. But as with everything else on this trip, nothing in the last part of their mission came easy. Always apparently just one step behind, the South African authorities haunted every move the Americans made. While much of the most critical material had already been smuggled out of the country, Lowenstein and Bundy carried some important tapes and notes in the bottom of a laundry bag, the top portion filled—appropriately enough—with Afrikaaner propaganda. Bundy and Lowenstein sailed through customs but then were warned by friends, "You're being followed." Suddenly, just as they were crossing the tarmac for the BOAC plane, Special Branch officers raced up to them and demanded that they empty their bags. Seizing on the Afrikaaner propaganda, Lowenstein berated the officers for questioning what they were carrying. But knowing the Special Branch was about to hit paydirt, he set up a terrific fuss, calling the crew of the airplane to his side and indignantly accusing the officers of seeking to delay an international flight. When a stewardess stepped in and chastised the officers, they subsided and Lowenstein boarded the flight. "It's all right now," the stewardess said. "You're on British territory."[20]

When Lowenstein and his cohorts returned to the United States, they embarked on a whirlwind tour to maximize the impact of their findings. At the NSA annual congress, Lowenstein recounted the sensational adventures he had been through, pleading with the delegates to raise funds to bring Hans Beukes to America and carry forward the fight against apartheid. Back at the United Nations, meanwhile, Lowenstein, Michael Scott, and others prepared to bring their case before Committee Four, the oversight body for mandated territories. Eric Lowe, the South African foreign minister, attempted to dismiss the group in advance, claiming that Lowenstein and his friends were international Communist conspirators and agents provocateurs planning all along to subvert the peace and promote rebellion. Next to such a portrait, however, Lowenstein and his preppy young friends seemed dramatically nonthreatening. "You have to imagine the scene," Bull said, "when Al, Emory, and I appear . . . in front of this huge group, looking very young, very bewildered, rather ill at ease. Emory happened to have his wife's knitting bag that she thrust under his

143

arm at the last minute, so he arrived with the knitting needles sticking out, and there was an audible ripple of laughter throughout the delegates. . . . So I think our testimony had some instant credibility."

As the hearings unfolded, South Africa looked worse and worse, the young Americans and Hans Beukes better and better. It turned out that the only evidence the South Africans could produce about the secret purposes of the trip had come from the luggage stolen from the Lowenstein car, proof that the Special Branch had committed the theft. At each step, the case against South Africa became more compelling. Lowenstein talked about his concern with racism in America, thereby refuting the charge that he was ignoring his own country's ills to concentrate on someone else's; at the same time, growing police violence against blacks in South-West Africa reinforced their claims before Committee Four that something desperately needed to be done.

As Lowenstein, Bundy, and Bull spoke and appeared on national network television like "The Dave Garroway Show," the pressure grew to act. In the end, not only was the South African government embarrassed in front of the world, but Committee Four authorized an appeal to the International Court of Justice on whether South Africa's mandate over South-West Africa should continue. In a remarkable series of events, something *had* happened to shift, however briefly, the course of world events. "You have come along out of nowhere, it seems," one of Lowenstein's friends working at the United Nations said, "and all of a sudden, the world—including Africa—is a better place to live in."[21]

All in all, the South African venture had been a Lowenstein tour de force. Full of harrowing escapes and thrilling encounters with the forces of evil, it provided precisely the experience of living on the cutting edge of history that he so craved. The adventure had included the conspiracy of plotting with sympathetic white South Africans, the danger of smuggling black Africans into situations that were flagrantly provocative to those in power, and the tense thrill of confronting as an individual the whole structure of racism and oppression. There had even been romance, a brief, almost magical flirtation with Francie Suzman, whom Lowenstein later described as a "Mata Hari" who coyly prodded the truth from him about his mission as they danced by moonlight at a white South African club. "We had been present at a very epic set of events," Emory Bundy later said, "a great and life-shaping experience." More to the point from Lowenstein's point of view was the fact that "these were events that Al had set in motion."

In that sense, the South African adventure represented the quintessential Lowenstein fantasy come to life. He had been the central actor in making something happen that would have seemed inconceivable to anyone else. Moreover, he had summoned all his skills and used them for the purest purpose possible—to help those least able to help themselves. One side of Lowenstein's liberalism always focused on the responsibility of the elite to rescue and *do good for* those who could not act on their own behalf. In such an effort, the role of the charismatic savior achieved its purest form, distinct from any collective effort or movement. The South African journey, Emory Bundy observed, epitomized "the breadth of [Al's] vision and the kind of commitment he had. . . . South-West Africa [was] symptomatic, because you [can't] think of anybody more remote and more helpless and more in need of a champion. . . . But the fact that there was this need was what he responded to, and it was almost that the degree of powerlessness of a people was the thing that mostly brought out his desire to help."[22]

It was a key insight into a complicated man. Allard Lowenstein was never happier than when he could act in an apparently selfless way to rescue those who were helpless, especially when he could indulge in "cloak and dagger" intrigue in the process without having to feel guilty about it. No other activity was more consistent with his most cherished self-image, and how much more preferable it was to writing speeches for someone else to give! South Africa had indeed provided a moment of triumph. But could it be repeated? And could its rewards be found in a normal—or even abnormal—career?

TRYING TO FIND A NICHE

The dilemma plagued Lowenstein in the period immediately following the South Africa venture. He seemed little prepared for the journeys down from the peaks of such "mountaintop" experiences, suffering periodic bouts of depression, confusion, and ambivalence when the never-ending quest for new activities and projects failed to produce satisfying results. The months between Lowenstein's U.N. testimony in 1959 and the fall of 1961 were a particularly painful example of such confusion. Although in the end, this period produced a major book on South Africa—Lowenstein's *only* sustained effort at a different kind of "intellectual" project—and a powerful emotional attachment to one of the two women he deeply loved in his life, it was a time that ultimately said more about the pitfalls of his hyperactivity than about its rewards.

The most important immediate decision Lowenstein had to make was whether to become a candidate for political office. For months he had toyed with the idea of running for Congress in Manhattan as one of the "reform" Democrats who were trying, on a variety of levels, to unseat and destroy the Tammany Hall machine led by Carmine DeSapio. The world of New York Democratic politics was so arcane and byzantine that one almost required a degree in political psycholinguistics to understand it. In the 1940s, progressive Democrats had split into two factions, the American Labor party—more clearly leftist—and the Liberal party. In the meantime, the regular party machinery remained in the hands of the "bosses." The reform Democrats were the latest variant of generally left-of-center groups that had been seeking to end the tyranny of the bosses, introduce more democratic procedures into precinct and neighborhood party clubs, and support city, state, and federal policies that were strongly New Deal-ish. Backed on a state level by people like Eleanor Roosevelt and Senator Herbert Lehman, the local reformers were seeking to build an infrastructure of grass-roots participation that would allow the mobilization of voters and activists to take arbitrary power away from a few patronage-wielding traditionalists. Although the movement had been started a few years earlier, 1960 would be the first year it mounted candidacies across the city for city council, state assembly, and Congress. And Lowenstein was one of the leading lights being considered for nomination.

The problem was that other people wanted to run as well, and although the reformers eschewed such retrograde methods as arm twisting, they could play as well as anyone the game of behind the scenes manipulation. The basic question facing Lowenstein was whether he wanted to play that game as well, and with what measure of seriousness. His primary adversary for the congressional designation was James Scheuer, a well-known local activist who had spent more time in reform activities than Lowenstein had—since Lowenstein had been off on various missions across the world and otherwise away from Manhattan. The reformers wanted to make their selections at least seven months before the Democratic primary in order to have time to make their case with the voters and energize the troops. Hence, in the fall of 1959, Lowenstein was asking virtually everyone for advice.[23]

In a manner completely consistent with his past record of political performance, Lowenstein eventually chose to withdraw from the congressional contest on the principle of sacrificing himself for the larger cause. Playing with the idea until the very last second, he clearly wanted—in one part of himself—to run. But higher-ups in the reform movement—including Lehman and Roosevelt—quietly let it be known that someone among the candidates should give in. Lowenstein was not being drafted to run as the only person who could carry the reform banner, and as Nathan Straus, one of the reform power brokers, later wrote him, there were few greater errors a man in public life could make than to try to go too far too soon. "You have a brilliant mind," he observed, "and you are young. Those are both inestimable assets." And so Lowenstein passed up his first opportunity to run for national office, persuaded evidently that his greatest contribution would be to serve the larger cause of reform unity. Ironically, Scheuer ultimately ran in another district, and William Fitts Ryan was nominated for the Manhattan seat, but by then, Lowenstein had already made his choice.[24]

Still left was the problem of finding a career that met Lowenstein's political as well as personal needs. Although he had spent much of the fall and winter crisscrossing the country to lecture about South Africa, public speaking did not constitute a permanent job. He might have cast his lot with one of the candidates seeking the Democratic presidential nomination in 1960, but none of them particularly excited him. Although Frank Porter Graham urged him to go back with Humphrey and study international law on the side, Lowenstein had already expressed his "grave misgivings" about a Humphrey presidency. John Kennedy, in turn, seemed too cold and aloof, and many New Yorkers—Lowenstein included—considered his record insufficiently liberal. It was not surprising that Lowenstein, following Mrs. Roosevelt's lead, ended up belatedly supporting an Adlai Stevenson draft. Although Lowenstein was only an alternate delegate to the Democratic convention, he persuaded James Nash and John Wilson, friends from Seattle, to give him a floor pass. In a wirephoto sent across the country, Lowenstein could be seen raising a Stevenson banner in the midst of the New York delegation during the "draft Stevenson" floor demonstration.[25]

As the Kennedy presidential campaign unfolded, Lowenstein's political position remained marginal and tenuous. He used his continuing contact with Douglass Hunt, now plugged into the Democratic party apparatus, to announce his "availability" for campaign chores. Other friends interceded with Kennedy associate Harris Wofford to volunteer Lowenstein's assistance. But the Kennedys were not known for welcoming with open arms latecomers to the bandwagon; moreover, as late as the end of September, Lowenstein had still been writing essays that were seen by some, at least, as anti-Kennedy. In the meantime, Lowenstein reverted to his custom of

sending out a flurry of requests for help in finding *some* gainful employment, including inquiries to people who might know of a newspaper he
could edit or publish. In desperation, he actually opened a law office in
New York for a month. Clearly, he was troubled by his inability to find the
right project, and was on the verge of real depression. "I wish you
wouldn't take such a dim view of AKL," Lucille Kohn wrote him after one
phone conversation during which she had been particularly bothered by
his tone of voice, "for he is one of the most remarkable people I know. I
realize you can't make a living by taking care of all of humanity, but that
God of yours should pay you a big salary for taking care of his unfinished
business."[26]

Alas, nothing developed, and during the late fall and early winter of
1961, Lowenstein became ever more troubled. He thought he deserved a
position of importance in the new Kennedy administration, yet he was
damned if he would lower himself to asking for it directly. When a U.S.
Information Agency (USIA) official wrote Lowenstein saying the White
House had forwarded his résumé for employment consideration, he responded archly, saying he was mystified by the reference to his "offer to
be of service." On the other hand, he recognized that his tardiness in joining the ranks of Kennedy supporters was the reason for his dilemma. So
he was angry at himself, furious at the insult to his pride when the
Kennedys left him out, and humiliated by the number of times people
asked him what he was going to do in the new administration, "Unless
someone launches a campaign on your behalf," Douglass Hunt wrote,
"nothing will happen. Moreover, nothing you'd want to have happen would
be likely even then."[27]

What made the rejection even worse was that it came in the midst of an
even more unsettling enterprise—trying, for the first time, to write a book.
After he withdrew from consideration for the reform Democratic congressional candidacy, and with other job possibilities not panning out, Al became increasingly fascinated by the proposal that he describe his South
African venture for a larger audience. As Emory Bundy pointed out, "[Al]
was the greatest storyteller I have ever known . . . unmatched [in] his ability in a profound and entertaining way to [describe what happened]." If
well done, such a book could become a best-seller; it would also offer the
chance to merge politics and morality in a genre over which he could retain complete control. Thus, even as he awaited the hoped-for summons
from the Kennedy administration, Lowenstein signed with Macmillan to
write the story of his adventures in South Africa.[28]

But how did someone like Al Lowenstein construct a 300-page manuscript? What tone should he use? What points should he make? Who else
should be involved? Above all, how did someone whose life consisted of
nonstop activity, usually with constantly changing companions, settle
down to the lonely task of sitting month by month to write a book manuscript, which required sustained, concentrated, and isolated effort?

The first dilemma was how to cast the book. Initially, Lowenstein seems
to have thought of it as a semiautobiographical work, a "light and witty
volume classified as 'general travel,'" one friend wrote, rather than a portentous tome on issues of statecraft. Lowenstein sent letters to numerous
friends inviting them to send "anecdotes" that might add flair to the book
and illustrate the famous Lowenstein character. But then it became clear
that the book had a far more serious potential. Lowenstein, however brief
his experience in South Africa, possessed insights about the entire sub-
continent of Africa that desperately needed to be understood by the
broader public; a dramatic narrative of his visit could, if properly presented, make a significant difference both at home and abroad.[29]

Then came the problem of authorship—how and where to write a book.
Somehow, Lowenstein understood that he had to get away from New York
to write, and so, in January 1961, he journeyed to Florida. Living out of a
motel in Sarasota and surviving on a diet of frankfurters and beans at the
drugstore lunch counter, he tried to get started. But old habits—and de-
pendencies—were hard to break, and almost desperately, he reached out
to friends for help. Curtis Gans, a new friend from UNC, accompanied him
on the trip south, Sherman Bull came down soon after, and by March, Al
was pleading with Emory Bundy to join him. (Bundy had no money, as
well as a wife and young child to support, so his response was a tortured
plea that Al think seriously about how important his presence was. Eventually, Bundy went.) Lowenstein even proposed that a New York friend,
Ethel Grossman, write a number of the chapters for him, receiving a portion of the royalties in return. Grossman was already transcribing a good
part of the book from dictated recordings that Lowenstein sent from
Florida. In the end, she did only a small part of the writing herself, but
more than anyone else, she helped shape the book in her multiple roles as
critic, secretary, and editor.[30]

Worst of all, perhaps, was the anxiety associated with functioning in an
unfamiliar world and bearing the lonely responsibility for the final product. Lowenstein's relationship with his editor at Macmillan, Peter Ritner,
was stormy, with few moments of calm. At one point, Ritner accused

Lowenstein of trying to go over his head at Macmillan and of being more difficult to deal with than all his other sixty-five authors combined. There may well have been truth in the charge. Al's father wanted to supplant Macmillan's promotional campaign with a full-page ad in the *New York Times Book Review;* Ethel Grossman was an emotional wreck much of the time; and once the manuscript was completed, Lowenstein insisted on making so many last-minute changes that Ritner threw up his hands in disgust. Al himself, whose inexperience in writing books made him fearful of failure, was frequently despondent over his progress.[31]

The persistence of these problems made the final product all the more remarkable. *Brutal Mandate* is a superb book. Although it never received the large trade audience Lowenstein had hoped for, the book was a critical success and helped cement his reputation as a commentator on the South African scene. With a foreword by Eleanor Roosevelt that highlighted the "courage, good judgment, coolness and persistence [under pressure]" of Lowenstein and his companions, the book brilliantly accomplished its mission of interweaving the dramatic events of the trip with analysis of the structural barriers imposed by the system of apartheid and the international mandate system. Well-paced, clearly written, and often eloquent, the book succeeded in entertaining readers through its narrative of the Buekes escape, the Kooper reunion with his congregation, and the clandestine interview with Chief Kutako, while never losing sight of the larger, more intractable geopolitical problems that framed those adventures.[32]

Above all, *Brutal Mandate* reflected, in its best moments, a degree of sensitivity to African nationalism and the dangers of white paternalism that remains, decades later, a testament to how politically precocious Lowenstein could be. He understood the fundamental horror of being "always at the mercy of someone else"; he perceived the black African "common denominator of unvarying mute misery—a misery compounded of poverty and fear until there seemed no way to filter out the one from the other"; and he realized the supreme importance of acknowledging the need for Africans to control their own movement, of supporting fully a policy of sanctions against South Africa, and finally, of accepting *all* the consequences of a "one man, one vote" definition of democracy, notwithstanding the squeamishness of "liberal" white South Africans about all this. Lowenstein would not always display such sensitivity on these issues, but for that time, and in the context of existing international race relations, his view testified to a political intelligence of the highest order.

Thus, despite the trials that accompanied his nearly two year quest for a new career direction, Lowenstein had once more apparently prevailed. Writing *Brutal Mandate* had been an arduous ordeal in an arena where Lowenstein was a stranger; writing did not entail organizing students, giving speeches, or setting travel records. He had passed a kind of test, even in the midst of his frustration over not being able to "settle down" in politics or receive the recognition from the Kennedy administration that he wanted. Yet he was not satisfied. However much others might admire his achievement, it did not bring with it the acclaim or appointments to high office that he craved. Once more—in his own eyes—he had fallen short. And to make matters worse, in the midst of this he experienced a period of turmoil in his personal life that put in doubt whether he would ever be able to combine the settledness of married life with the continued desire to stay in motion.

THE STORY OF TWO WOMEN

With all his friends, and throughout his correspondence, Lowenstein talked repeatedly about getting married. Whatever his conflicted impulses about sexuality, his desire to have children and be in a family was a constant. "[Remember] the conversations we used to have about what we'd like to do," one friend wrote. "It included settling down in a nice small town with a nice little woman to raise kids, etc." The vision seemed part and parcel of Lowenstein's Hallmark card view of America—home as a simple place, a "haven in a heartless world," as Christopher Lasch has called it, the anchor that might somehow provide a mooring for Lowenstein's otherwise uncontrolled perambulations.[33]

Yet the marriage predicament remained intractable. To start with, his stepmother harped constantly on the need for him to marry a "nice Jewish girl," someone comely and of "your own kind" who could be an attentive housekeeper and mother and would "fit in." Lowenstein's ambivalence about all things Jewish underlay his almost allergic reaction to that advice, and with rare exceptions, he avoided romantic relationships with anyone who was not Christian.

Still, there were plenty of these. As a spokesman for numerous noble causes, Lowenstein encountered hundreds of people who were electrified by his words and inspired by his political leadership. "You . . . are moving a heck of a lot of people," a college classmate wrote at the end of the 1950s, "[and] snowing all the girls along the way. One Queens girl said if she could just touch you she wouldn't wash her hand for a week."

Notwithstanding his shyness, Lowenstein understood at some level the erotic subtext of much political activity; he almost always had at least one young woman following him around hoping to kindle in him the same ardent response that he had generated in her.[34]

Yet Lowenstein's track record in these relationships was abysmal, almost predictably so given the patterns that recurred over time. As long as he was the pursuer, his passion flamed, and he wrote repeatedly to friends about finally having found the right woman. But when the woman returned his interest, or even worse, initiated the pursuit, his passion abated or disappeared and the relationship ended. Over and over—from Mimi Massey on—women pledged their love to Allard, hoping against hope that he would respond, only to find that he would do anything to evade the commitment they sought. In one typical exchange, a young woman named Sarah assured Al that she was being "loyal, loyal, loyal" because she could think of no one but him, "an angel and real, not just a dream." But then, as soon as it started, the relationship was over. More than a few women developed a sense that no matter "how wonderful you are . . . you seem to have a block against marriage in general."[35]

Some, indeed, recognized a profound flaw in the Lowenstein approach to life and love. In one of his quixotic infatuations, Lowenstein proposed to Beth Brod, a young woman he met. He predicted that the relationship might not work out but asked her to at least consider a life together. Her response took up the theme of Joan Long's letter five years earlier: love involves choice. Their brief time together, Beth wrote, had "portend[ed] a certain kind of life, a life of frustration and incompleteness." She pointed out that in fact Al had already decided against the kind of commitment that was involved in marriage, and that choice, she told him, would prove fatal to all his hopes for such a relationship. "No matter how inspired we are," she wrote him, "or what great things we look to do for others, the picture isn't quite complete if our personal relationships must be sacrificed to it." She told him this, not for herself, but "simply because some day there will be someone else who loves you and may feel that she needs you (sometimes as much as your friends)." In that instance, Lowenstein would have to decide whether he wished to give himself over to his "bigger hopes" or make a different kind of choice—one that would put family and marriage first. Otherwise, she predicted, his commitment to all the causes in the world could easily "be turned into a selfish indulgence."[36]

It was against this background of trenchant advice that Lowenstein entered into two of the most volatile and important relationships of his life.

The first of the two women he truly seems to have loved was Barbara Boggs, the beautiful and brilliant daughter of Congressman Hale Boggs of Louisiana, one of the most powerful men in Congress. Barbara Boggs represented all that Lowenstein ever hoped to find in a romantic union. The other relationship was with his secretary, friend, and confidant, Ethel Grossman. Pathetically in love with Al, deeply dependent, and emotionally in dire need, Grossman desired Lowenstein almost as much as he desired Barbara Boggs. As the two relationships evolved, each revealed the dangers and possibilities of a life plagued by lack of intimacy and honest communication.

Al met Barbara Boggs in August 1960 at the annual NSA congress. She was a delegate from her school, Manhattanville College of the Sacred Heart. Immediately, they hit it off. He told her, as she later heard him tell countless others, that she "was one of the ten funniest people in America." She was charmed. Although she claimed to be "totally oblivious to any [romantic] thoughts," at the end of the congress Al gave her a big hug and said, "We could have had a lovely life together."

Within a few weeks of the NSA congress, Al had committed himself to a whirlwind courtship. "It was irresistible in many ways," she noted, "a combination of the [1960 presidential] campaign, and the 'Holy Trinity,' that is, Norman Thomas, Eleanor Roosevelt, and Frank Porter Graham sort of dropping in and out of a young woman's life." Al introduced her to Oliver Tambo of the African National Congress and to folksinger Miriam Makeba, who was also heavily involved in the antiapartheid struggle. It was a heady experience, and notwithstanding the benefits of having grown up in her own famous family, she was impressed.

What made the relationship so striking was how different the two were in so many ways. Barely twenty-one years old, Barbara Boggs was ten years younger than Lowenstein. She was an ardent Roman Catholic, worshiped her family, and identified strongly with her New Orleans roots. On the other hand, it seemed to be precisely those differences that most attracted Lowenstein to her. Stunningly beautiful, her blonde, blue-eyed appearance fulfilled all his fantasies of meeting and marrying someone totally the opposite of the "comely" Jewish matron his stepmother wanted for him. Even Barbara's religion, which quickly became the primary topic of conversation and disagreement between them, seemed to be part of her appeal. Indeed, it seemed to contribute to the romance of the situation. "We felt that there was one of those Tristan and Isolde type of swords between us, namely, my Catholicism," she recalled. "I suppose it was [like]

153

safe sex . . . you could sort of flirt with the notion of getting married and all the rest of it, and think . . . 'but for the sword, the dear old sword there, we could have a lovely life together.'"

As the fall of 1960 turned into the spring and summer of 1961, however, fantasy began to turn toward reality. Barbara met—and began to be part of—Al's family, as well as his far-flung network of friends. Neither set of parents was thrilled by the relationship. The Westchester wedding of Al's sister Dorothy was a terrifying ordeal for Barbara as Florence Lowenstein held her hand and cried hysterically because Dorothy was marrying a non-Jew. Al's reception by the Boggs family was less visibly hostile, but there were still problems. Barbara's mother was skeptical of the relationship for religious reasons; her father was doubtful because, as she said, "he just didn't see any stability and any life for me . . . [and] thought I was caught up in a hopeless romanticism about a life of good works through someone else." Still, all signs indicated an approaching engagement. Although the relationship became increasingly long-distance after Al went to Florida to write *Brutal Mandate*, Barbara talked at length to Ethel Grossman—with whom she had become friends—about wedding dates, family problems, and birth control. Al was pressing for an early wedding, and Barbara was still excited about the impending union.[37]

By early June, however, she felt compelled to address the religious issue. Al might make fun of her concerns and tell "his acolytes" that, once away from her family, Barbara would be less firm in her Catholicism. But in fact she took it so seriously that she wrote him a twenty-page memo, pleading with him to take seriously the concerns she previously had "never been able to get past the lump in my throat when talking to you."

Barbara began by declaring eloquently how much Al had changed her life. "Among other things," she wrote, "you gave me the courage to love. . . . I've always had the feeling that if anyone really got to know me, he or she would hate me. Along with this feeling comes the lack of ability to express one's deepest feelings, especially to loved ones, and the belief it's better to keep things as they are rather than to risk anything by revealing anything deeper." But Al had taught her the meaning of unconditional love. "I always felt . . . that you would love me no matter what. And also I loved *you* despite the consequences. Which helped me to be much more open with a great many people about very many things I was thinking." Similarly, Al had made her see what it meant to envision the brotherhood of mankind—not just among Westerners but among Africans and Asians as well. Through all this, he had helped provide the "love and grace" that had enabled her—and them—to grow.

Which made all the more important his recognition of how primary was her Roman Catholic faith, especially as it related to "those blessed, non-existent children [we might have] who would look like Bernard Shaw." Al had told her that he "could understand why a superstitious Polish peasant [would] insist that his children be raised Catholic." But why theirs? In her answer, Barbara wrote a brilliant theological treatise on exactly how and why faith—to a believer—must transcend all other concerns. Christianity, she pointed out, is more than a set of ethical do's and don'ts. Rather, it involves a belief in God become man through the gift of his son, Jesus Christ. "Action follows upon belief," she said, and "belief in Christ is most fully contained in the Catholic church." Hence her children would have to be baptized and trained in the Catholic faith because the sacrament of baptism represented "the 'putting off' of the 'old man' of sin and its wages, and the putting on of the 'new man' who lives not by himself alone, but in Christ." Since baptism was central to the faith, she argued, "I could not deprive my children of it." Even if later they were to reject that faith of their own free will, she—as a believer herself—bore the responsibility to at least start them in the direction of her faith.

She understood that a life with him would provide "optimum conditions" for living the effects of her faith. "But effects are only important to me because of their source [and] without a true source, the effects are meaningless." Locating the source of his own beliefs, she said, would give him more confidence about them. She acknowledged the power of her own background—"the time I was elected, at age 8 to be 'little Virgin Mary'; ... the inscription of my father in my missal at my confirmation ('to my sweet lovely daughter, Barbara, who I know always will love God and keep the faith'); the sweet treble of the little boy in the choir singing 'et incarnatus est' on the Sunday after that dreadful Saturday night with you during the Thanksgiving holidays." But she insisted that this was a faith she had chosen and could not forsake, even if clinging to it meant they could never marry. In that case, she concluded, "I have no doubt that in the 'appointed time' I will be bouncing little Catholic babies on my knee—and as far as your children are concerned, you wait and see—I'll subvert them by enrolling them in perpetual novenas ... from the moment they're born."[38]

Interestingly enough, Lowenstein responded to Barbara's impassioned plea by showing a new sensitivity to her religious concerns. Stunned by the apparently irrevocable end to their marriage plans that her letter signified, he backtracked and sought a compromise. She, too, retreated from the precipice, regretting how much their discussions had gotten mired "in that silly conversation about that mythical first communion day of that mythical child." Having not seen him for a week, she wrote that "it seems like a lifetime I'm so lonesome for you." Still, she stuck to her guns. If she married him without his signature on a pledge to raise their children in the church, she said, she could no longer receive the sacraments. On the other hand, "*if* we could work out a private agreement (as you said some couples do) in which I would honorably regard that my children were being raised Catholics while at the same time *your* own conscience regarding your own rights and duties in this matter were not being violated, would you ever sign the promise?" If he could—thereby preserving her right to practice her faith—then once again the marriage issue would be open for discussion.[39]

For the moment, that formulation seemed to put the engagement back on track. Al would sign the pledge, but with "mental reservations"; then, when the children reached the age of fourteen, they would be free to choose their own form of religious expression. Al's stepmother continued to prod. "Get a lovely Jewish girl to marry," she wrote him. "I saw a doll, elegant, intelligent, plays the piano . . . has four children, not yet 30 years old. . . . Pick that kind! I'd love it." And even his father, who liked Barbara enormously, hoped he would find someone else.

But in the end, Al saw the wisdom of compromising one principle for the sake of the larger objective. As Ethel Grossman advised him:

> They would still be your children and greatly influenced by you; to marry anyone else, loving Barbara as you do, would be to live a lie, and your marriage would be a farce; not to marry at all, to live out your life alone and unfulfilled as I do, is to make a mockery of life which no amount of devotion to good causes or attention from the opposite sex can ever compensate. Of the three choices, I think a partial surrender of one principle is preferable to the others.

Al agreed, joyfully writing all his friends that he would be married within a year.[40]

But that was only the beginning. Having removed the insurmountable obstacle that gave their fantasy life free play, Barbara and Al now had to face other problems. "Once the sword of Tristan was no longer there,"

Barbara observed, "the other kinds of more natural differences began to emerge." One of Al's main characteristics, of course, was his peripatetic lifestyle, and above all, his failure to settle down and find a career. Already opposed to the marriage in principle, Hale Boggs, Barbara's father, zeroed in on the issue. "Mama says that the reason that he worries so much about a career," Barbara wrote, "is that his father jumped around from one thing to another without a sense of direction or inner stability, and this produced a great feeling of insecurity in the children. I think it is easier to forgive him his abruptness when you know this."

But in fact Barbara shared her father's concern. As early as her twenty-page theological treatise, she had asked Al to decide on his life's priorities. "You have done an immeasurable amount for your fellow human beings," she wrote, "but life is selective—it works in such a way that after a while in order to make any contribution at all you have to do it through choosing one vocation and sticking to it." Al had told her he would never do this until he settled down to "wife and babies." But she disagreed. "A man has an obligation to become vocationally selective despite his marital status (or lack thereof). . . . I think it [is] imperative for yourself and for the world to which you contribute so much that you get quickly to this 'settling' process."

These issues gnawed at the relationship during the months Al and Barbara were engaged. Barbara had started the fall of 1961 touring the country in a kind of Catholic domestic peace corps, then in the winter had moved to Washington, D.C., to work in the White House. Al was on the West Coast. They saw each other only periodically, and often Al postponed his trips to Washington because of other commitments. Moreover, when he did come to town, he often had such a long agenda that the two had little time together. In classic Lowenstein style, he would show up at the White House gate for a dinner engagement with Barbara—and then twenty-five other people would appear, with the White House guard continually calling her office to say, "Miss Boggs, there's another person here who says he's supposed to be going out to dinner with you tonight." While Barbara welcomed the scintillation of such an entertaining cast of characters, she also wrote Al that "I'd love to be with you *alone* for a while."[41]

Perhaps inevitably with these other unresolved issues, the religious question resurfaced. A friend of Lowenstein's wrote that he was planning a similar interfaith marriage, and that the church was demanding that he fill out a complicated questionnaire about his religious beliefs. The letter reactivated all of Lowenstein's anxieties, which in turn caused Barbara to wonder whether she had understood Al's "compromise" correctly in the first place. From that point forward, the situation deteriorated—notwithstanding poignant and heartfelt expressions of affection—until in the middle of August 1962, three weeks before the wedding was to take place, it was announced that the engagement had been called off. Barbara's mother had already bought the linen, and a silver pattern had been chosen, but neither Barbara nor Al had the will to make the wedding happen.[42]

It seems likely that Al and Barbara each chose to use the religious question as a way of getting out of a marriage neither could envision. Al recognized that, however much he loved Barbara, he was not yet ready to sacrifice his lifestyle and his friendships to the demands of a family life that would pressure him into a traditional career pattern, no matter how "liberal" Barbara might be. For her, the converse was true. "It became very evident to me," she noted, "that Al was never going to settle down and be there for the bad times as well as the good, with the little ones. . . . He [would be] off saving the world while I was changing the diapers. . . . If I wanted to be a nun and lead a self-sacrificial life like that, I mean [why not] skip the middle man. . . . It's very difficult to lead the kind of life that Al led, very much the life of a missionary priest, and have a wife and children." Thus, the religious issue covered the larger one: Al's refusal to define his priorities so that family came first. "I mean," she said, "it would be nice to have him there for the baptism, but it would be nicer to have him there for endless 2:00 A.M. feedings."

Ultimately, then, Barbara Boggs chose to affirm her own selfhood rather than have it consumed by Lowenstein's all-enveloping energy. In breaking off the engagement, she wrote, it was not that she was "up against some external structure [like the church]"; rather, she was up against herself. Thus, at least in retrospect, she recognized that the twenty-page memo on theology "was really a defense of the selfhood of Barbara Boggs at that point." She may have been defending the institutions that had shaped her life, "but in doing so, to my way of thinking, I came down on my own side as well," preserving and protecting what otherwise would have been obliterated by the Lowenstein lifestyle. The issues in 1962 were the same ones he had encountered in 1948 with Mimi Massey—and would encounter every time in the future he was forced to choose between making a commitment to one person and staying in motion. Once again, for the moment, staying in motion had won out.[43]

The emotional roller coaster of the Barbara Boggs affair contained a subtext, the parallel unfolding of a very different kind of relationship that

Al had with Ethel Grossman. "There was the ultimate left-out person in society," Barbara Boggs commented, "that Al tried to make feel good about herself." If Al's relationship with Boggs illuminates one way he interacted with others, the relationship with Ethel Grossman is no less revealing. Al invited "parasitic, masochistic" relationships with people who were close to him, Curtis Gans observed, and Ethel epitomized that dynamic. "Slavishly devoted, passionately in love with him [and totally dependent], there were as many delusions in that relationship," Gans said, "as Allard had about politics."[44]

Ethel Grossman met Al in the fall of 1959 when he had come back from South Africa and was contemplating a run for Congress. A political secretary who worked for numerous employers—including Senator Herbert Lehman, Julius Edelstein of the Leatherworkers' Union, and the United Nations—Ethel had very low self-esteem, experienced great difficulty in holding onto a job, and found her primary satisfaction in cleaving to people who had needs she could help meet. Overweight, highly emotional, and in her midthirties, she seemed constantly on the verge of a nervous breakdown. "I [knew] how to recognize people on the edge," Barbara Boggs said, and Ethel was on the edge. "Looked at in [one] way," Boggs recalled, "Al used her, but God, no more so than I've seen people use much more attractive people. . . . She didn't have anything else to do, really."[45]

Ethel developed her attachment to Al both through offering excellent political feedback and doing all his chores. She helped organize his Christmas card list, ordered presents for his friends, clipped the *Times* and the *Post* for him, typed his correspondence, reviewed and helped select textbooks he could use when he was teaching, and transcribed every word of *Brutal Mandate*. Her apartment was his second home, where he sent out-of-town guests for lodging or convened late night meetings of friends and advisers. During most of this time, she performed these services out of love and devotion, earning her income from the various secretarial jobs she was able to find for brief periods. Although Al insisted she take 20 percent of his advance and royalties from *Brutal Mandate* ($2,000 was the figure most often bandied about), the value of her contribution to his work was in fact incalculable.[46]

Nor was Lowenstein always an easy boss. When an African visitor came to town, Al expected Ethel to put him up, create a schedule for him overnight, and coordinate his entertainment. Rarely was he available for counsel. "Last week," she wrote, "in a rare moment of inspiration, I figured out that if I really *had* to see you, the only way to arrange it would be to add my apartment to your list of Kaffee Klatsches for the evening—and to forget to invite either guests or candidates." And frequently he overwhelmed her with tasks to complete. His handwriting was obscure, he refused to write on every other line as she requested, and his interlinear corrections were indecipherable. Moreover, he would peremptorily criticize her for a gift she had chosen on his behalf, or for selecting the wrong letterhead for his stationery. If he were going to get 80 percent of the profits from his book, she observed, he had better assume 80 percent of the responsibility. "As a boss, you are required to look after an employee; as a senior partner, you automatically assume the responsibilities of the junior partner."

On the other hand, Al could be one of the most caring, compassionate, and sensitive people alive. He paid attention to Ethel's political advice, he asked her to try her hand at writing part of the South African book (she did), he introduced Ethel to all his dearest friends, and he made her part of his ongoing community. "I think it's wonderful the way your friends and family have opened up their hearts to me," she wrote. "They're all so wonderful. It's just as though the phrase, 'I'm a friend of Al's' has replaced 'open sesame' as an international password." Al's father offered to send her on vacation for a week and pay all her expenses; and Al himself flattered her by suggesting that he might dedicate *Brutal Mandate* to her.[47]

One of the chores she masochistically assigned herself was to befriend the one woman in the world she would have most liked to replace. Early on in his relationship with Barbara, Al introduced the two women. Quickly, Ethel became Barbara's confidant, as if hearing from Barbara about *her* love problems could provide surrogate satisfaction of Ethel's needs. Knowing that Al would respond with gratitude if Ethel shared these conversations with him, and that he would react with complete hostility to any negative comments, Ethel made a cottage industry out of nurturing the two lovers in their relationship. In the midst of the first religious crisis, for example, Ethel wrote Al: "I think now that you do need Barbara and that she could make you happy as no one else could, and since your happiness is very important to me, I hope that you will reconsider and marry her." On the other hand, when she could, Ethel also insinuated a different angle of vision, suggesting that since Barbara "was convent-trained to be a dutiful daughter," she might well be unable to resist her parents' opposition to the marriage. Sometimes, she even let her true voice speak, albeit while empathizing with his pain. "When I heard the disappointment in your voice last night," she wrote, "I wished with all my heart that I could turn into BB long enough to relieve your worry and anxiety. Perhaps it would be more truthful to say that I wished I could turn into BB. . . . More than anything in the world, I want you to have happiness in marriage, but since this depends firstly on your choice of a partner, and secondly on how much effort you put into making the marriage work, there's not much anyone else can do except hope that you make the right choice." With those words, Ethel was almost saying what she really meant.[48]

As Al must have known, Ethel believed passionately that *she* was "the right partner" for him, the "one who will understand you and who will be proud to share you with the world." From the very beginning, her dependency and devotion were obvious. "Thank you for the steak. Thank you for the baked potato. Thank you for putting up with me," she wrote early in 1960. "Thank you for noticing the haircut. . . . You're still wonderful— and I still worship you." She boasted to him when she had lost weight, expressed gratitude when he put up with her "bitchiness," and declared herself to "be content to be allowed to go on trying to please you and take care of you." She even offered to pay for his suits so he could be better dressed. Frequently tormented by deep depressions, Ethel was totally dependent on Al's support and affection for retaining her sanity, and when that support was not forthcoming, she threatened to go over the edge. "You know, in the last couple of years I've done an awful lot of lying and covering up for you," she wrote. "None of it was pleasant, some of it was necessary, all of it was discomfiting. But I did it because you wanted it done and there was no one else to do it, and mainly because I could never refuse you anything. Because we had that sort of relationship." But she expected him to reciprocate if she were in trouble and needed help, and when she discovered that he would not—at least as she saw it—she disintegrated. "Do I have to be on the U.N agenda [to get your attention]?" she asked.[49]

But the full pathology of the relationship was not revealed until Barbara broke off her engagement with Al. Three days after the wedding was to have taken place, Ethel wrote him saying that she too was breaking off their relationship. "Only you," she said, "would have told a woman with my problem to see a psychiatrist." In fact, she had seen one, and he had both predicted the dissolution of the Boggs-Lowenstein engagement, and counseled Ethel to enter the fray and compete for Al's affections openly. Yet she disregarded his advice; because Al had shown so little sensitivity to her, she was afraid "of being hurt again." "Needless to say," she wrote,

"I am not going to do tonight what I told you I was thinking of doing [and] . . . if and when I do it, you need not worry that you will be involved in any way. I told you it would look like an accident." But while promising not to take her own life, she was going to leave *his*.

Then, having prepared the way by trying to activate his guilt, she got to the point. "You said last night there was nothing you could do to help me," she noted. But in fact there were many ways. "If you really wanted to salvage my future and give me something to live for," she said, "you could marry me for ll or l2 months so that I'd have a baby born in wedlock," then they could get a Mexican divorce. Or they could go through the marriage ceremony and stay formally married long enough to institute adoption proceedings. Either way, he could at least do *something* to help. Otherwise, it was over between them. "It's ironic and tragic and quite unintentional," she claimed, "that this separation should come so close to the other. But otherwise there is no connection and no pattern: Barbara is giving you up because she doesn't love you enough to accept your values and your way of life—I am giving you up because you don't love me enough to let me share the same things, and because I love you too much to hang around and be a sister to you when my feelings are so unsisterly." Some part of the truth was finally on the table, however bizarre and perverse its formulation.[50]

In the end, of course, Ethel would not—could not—go through with her threat to leave Al. Two weeks later, she was writing that she had no control over her own life and thus had no right to try either commiting suicide or getting out of his life. "Even if I do get hurt," she said, "I don't ever want to go out of your life." Indeed, she now claimed that her whole life had followed a predestined pattern, from meeting Al to seeing him lose—for the moment—his chance for Congress, to meeting Barbara, to seeing their relationship collapse. "I do not know of any other person whose life is so controlled," she said, by patterns that worked so strangely. It may have been the first time—but tragically, not the last—that Al Lowenstein encountered paranoid schizophrenia.[51]

CONCLUSION

The years from 1958 to 1962 were full of excitement, achievement, pain, and turbulence for Al Lowenstein. They included the longest sustained relationship he had had with a woman since Miriam Massey, an electrifying trip to the world's most racist country, and the totally uncharacteristic experience of staying put long enough to write a book. And yet there were recurrent themes. First was the issue of "settling down"; second was choosing whether to marry, whom to marry, and with what consequences; third was deciding whether some people mattered more than others; and fourth—uniting all the others—was the issue of accountability. When and how would Allard Lowenstein take responsibility for his own life and actions?

Now more than thirty years old, the questions from family, friends, and acquaintances about Al's "plans" became ever more nagging and bothersome. At some level, Lowenstein felt like a failure for not having made a choice. Yet he seemed desperately to want to avoid deciding. Even the career ideas that he had already entertained turned out to be more fantasies than real possibilities. Running the small-town newspaper was clearly the best example: as a single editor and publisher, he could have achieved his dream of being both at rest and in control. But neither a newspaper job nor a prep school teaching position seemed especially appropriate—except that the latter would have kept him in close contact with the young. Clearly, political work was more consistent with both his abilities and his desires. Yet Lowenstein never considered settling down in one place long enough to build a political base from which to run for office. Instead he wanted to jet around the world and have a political career come to him, to "call" him to a mission that he could not refuse because he had been drafted for it—all the while kept financially solvent by his father's wealth.

The first set of choices—or unchoices—seemed to determine the second. Marriage—like the small-town newspaper—was part of his American dream. It was something he wanted—as evidenced by the number of times he proposed to women. But he also wished to avoid the responsibilities marriage entailed. While seeking to be a "normal" man, with an attractive wife (almost always non-Jewish) and children, he also hoped to live an "abnormal" life of quixotic adventure—and he was unwilling to face the contradictions of those desires. As Beth Brod had written him, "No matter how inspired we are or what great things we look for, the picture isn't quite complete if our personal relationships must be sacrificed to it." In its own way, the marriage question simply crystallized the larger issue of whether some relationships had priority over others and deserved nurturing. Implicit in such a choice to nurture a relationship was a willingness to take the risk of intimacy and of truth-telling, of sharing enough of oneself and one's frailties that a bond of lasting trust would emerge. Lowenstein was brilliant in his ability to establish intense rapport with individuals, but he was far less able to sustain that rapport, especially if it required recognizing some people as more important to him than others.

Lowenstein's inability to define his priorities was especially acute in his interactions with women. He had always felt a sense of inadequacy in approaching the opposite sex. One Smith friend (Jewish) who knew Al for years pondered this. "You are the kind of person," she wrote, "that others don't feel neutral about: you either like AKL a great deal, or you dislike him a great deal. . . . And if you're a woman (this is another thing I'm not sure you ever knew about me) then liking and disliking moves into the realm of loving and hating. I confess that I was a victim of the former emotion. . . . [But] you never did relate to me as a woman and I was too scared and neurotic to ever be a woman with you." Then she took a leap and tried to get at the heart of the problem. "Sometimes I think," she wrote, "and I realize more and more that this is closest to the truth—that we represent to each other a very deep threat: a threat of communicating with a man/woman on an intimate mature level." It was the intimacy that Lowenstein so desperately needed but found so inherently threatening. Intimacy required recognizing not only that one person was more important than another, but that time alone together was necessary—not bringing twenty-five friends to dinner with one's fiancée. [52]

Instead, he wanted it all: a wife, but not settling down; a chance to make history, but not a career; a series of intense relationships, but not sustained intimacy; everybody's love, but no prioritizing of relationships. Al wanted to please everyone. He considered dedicating *Brutal Mandate* to half a dozen people—telling each one of his idea—then failed to dedicate it to anyone, lest someone's feelings be hurt. All his life, people like Miriam Massey, Mary Ellen Knight, and numerous others (almost all women) had been telling him that he could not have a thousand "best friends," and that closeness entailed making choices. But Al refused to listen, because he was afraid to choose.

Underlying all these issues was his rejection of the notion that he should be accountable—that he was responsible for making decisions about his life and identity. Thus, when it came to running for office—either in college or in the reform movement—he hoped to be drafted so that he would not have to put his qualifications on the line. He went to South Africa because he was "called" to the task by Father Scott. Even with *Brutal Mandate*, he sought to evade decisions. "You seem to have been quite reluctant to assume any responsibility in connection with the book," Ethel Grossman complained, "and even more reluctant to delegate any of it." His indecisiveness traced a vicious circle: his unwillingness to settle on a career was directly connected to being unable to put himself on the line in a political race, make a decision about marriage, or accept responsibility for his personal habits. All entailed a level of self-knowledge that Al had not yet reached. "He didn't want peers, he didn't want close friends, he didn't want to share doubts and insecurities," one observer said. "He didn't want to be equal with anyone."[53]

And so Lowenstein made the decision to stay in motion. "He had appointments to make, he had people to see, and he had the next destination [to reach]," a South African friend said, "and no sort of private involvement could interfere with these." That was the way Al chose to see it as he set off on a new adventure in the early 1960s with Stanford University and the civil rights movement. Once again he was ready to try the mountaintop.[54]

7

Stanford and Civil Rights: 1961–1963

Whatever else Allard Lowenstein accomplished in his life, he will always be associated with the student activism of the 1960s. A peripatetic Pied Piper, followed by legions of young disciples, he moved from campus to campus provoking students to think anew about the injustices of their society, urging them to "make a difference," and providing countless examples of actions they might undertake to move America closer to the perfection to which it aspired. Most could only stand in awe of the energy, charisma, and brilliance of this political troubadour, but thousands—even tens of thousands—were moved to act in ways that helped transform the nation as well as reshape, dramatically, their own lives.

Although the Lowenstein army had numerous battalions, none proved more pivotal than the students he recruited at Stanford while serving as assistant dean of men and lecturer in political science. He was employed there less than a year, but the impact of his presence grew through a generation as the people whose lives he touched—and the causes they embraced—altered, in ways no one could have foreseen, both Lowenstein's life and the political history of the country. Stanford joined Yale and UNC as a home base for Lowenstein's distinctive brand of youth-oriented politics. In the year he lived there, and during countless visits back, the campus took on a magic and a charm for him that at times even exceeded the magnetic pull of Chapel Hill. In the relationships he established there, he tested both the limits and the possibilities of his lifestyle—one premised on intense interactions with the young, who, by virtue of their drive for independence, almost inevitably broke free of his mentorship and struck out, often in great pain, on their own.

Perhaps appropriately, Stanford also became a central setting for one of Lowenstein's most critical ventures into national politics, the mobilization of white volunteers to join the civil rights struggle in Mississippi. No episode would reveal more about the tensions and drives that animated Lowenstein's political style, nor would any offer greater clues to the values embodied in his philosophy of liberal activism. As Lowenstein mobilized, guided, and eventually became alienated from the "best and the brightest" white students he enlisted to serve in the civil rights trenches of Mississippi, he became a virtual one-man spotlight, illuminating the structural forces that determined America's racial politics during perhaps the most volatile decade of the century. These years were more than just the most critical in Al Lowenstein's personal journey—they were also pivotal for a generation, and for a way of life.

STANFORD

Probably no decade in recent memory has been the subject of such vicious caricature as the 1950s. Portrayed in satirical novels as the era of "gray flannel conformity" and "split-level traps," the 1950s are associated with McCarthyite repression, mindless consumerism, and political thoughtlessness. In reality, life was far more interesting than the stereotype: citizens struggled to build better and more creative public schools, develop community institutions that would offer an anchor against a tide of mobility, and find intellectual and spiritual answers to the problems posed by the threat of nuclear annihilation. Yet if there was one prestigious campus in America that seemed to embody all the conformist restraints associated with the 1950s it was Stanford—literally the kernel of truth that gave credibility to Malvina Reynold's song about children born in "ticky-tacky" houses going to the university so that they could learn to do more of just the same.

Invoking the terms of the Leland Stanford bequest as a rationale, Stanford officials vigorously pursued an in loco parentis policy that sought to ensure the complete regimentation of student life. Any coed social function had to be registered with college authorities. Women were permitted to enter only the downstairs "social area" of men's residences except for special open houses. Any overnight social function required that two adult guest couples be present as chaperones, at least one of them married. All liquor was banned from campus. Worst of all from an intellectual point of view, no political speakers were allowed on campus, nor was any religious activity tolerated. In effect, one student recalled, "such subjects were considered to be dangerous and divisive and [therefore] could not be discussed." Enforcing all this was an administration with hidebound attitudes. The dean in charge of the whole university was "one of the old guard," an inside critic said, "very concerned about students and their [potential] movements. . . . They were pros at . . . put[ting] the lid on students . . . and really ran the organization. The old boys' network. They were back in the eighteenth century as far as I was concerned."[1]

The situation was even worse for students not pledged to a fraternity or eating club, institutions that, for the most part, controlled Stanford social life. Elitist, proud, and self-important, these private associations boasted of greater "freedom" to drink, carouse, and independently carry on their own social agenda. But the male students who either were not accepted by the "frats" or chose not to apply were assigned arbitrarily to residence halls like Stern and Wilbur, which were regarded as "the pits" by most other students. "It was really the bottom of the ladder" to have to live in those dorms, one university official said. The women on campus had chosen to abolish sororities after World War II, but the men had retained the Greek and eating-club systems, with all the invidious consequences for nonparticipants. Stern Hall became a "turkey house," one campus veteran declared, "[and] there was [little] self-esteem among the kids who lived there." Even residence officials recognized the problem. The psychological atmosphere was "oppressive," one dean wrote; students were second-class citizens. "It is impossible to build an effective house program in the resulting atmosphere of rejection."[2]

Blasting holes in this system became, in effect, the mission assigned to Allard Lowenstein by his old friend Bill Craig, the dean of students at Stanford, in the fall of 1961. The two had met in 1950 at Washington State University when Lowenstein was on an NSA recruiting trip. Looking out the window of his house one day, Craig, who was a dean at the university, saw a college student "lying on the lawn . . . in animated conversation" with his two young sons; as Lowenstein and Craig became friends over the ensuing years, that scene, in Craig's eyes, encapsulated Lowenstein's effectiveness. "He was remarkable with young people," Craig observed.

"He excited them [and] they responded to him, they read and they wrote and they acted. It was marvelous."

Now, after coping for five years at Stanford with the intransigence of the fraternity system, he struck on a solution to his problems. One day, friends remembered, "[Craig] just lit up and said, 'I've got a guy I'm going to bring in . . . and put in the middle of [Stern Hall] and let him figure out what to do.'" Having completed *Brutal Mandate* and given up, for the moment, a political career, Lowenstein responded positively, "captured by the notion that things were happening [here]." Although Craig had to struggle to get approval (his bosses had to be assured by UNC deans that Lowenstein was not dangerous) and pull strings with a conservative political science department to secure Lowenstein a part-time academic appointment (they were dubious about his credentials), the position finally came through. Once more back in his element among the young, Al Lowenstein prepared to "blast away."[3]

Not too surprisingly, Lowenstein hit the road running. In his orientation address to the students at Stern, he took a leaf from John F. Kennedy and urged them to ask not what Stanford could do for them, but what they—during their time at the university—could do for the larger community. Each person, he insisted, could "count for a great deal," whether seeking to improve the environment at Stanford or acting to end apartheid in South Africa. When the evaluations came in from students on the orientation speeches, Lowenstein received a score of 63, the president a 28. It had been a good start.[4]

If Lowenstein's largest task was to make Stern Hall a formidable competitor with the fraternities when rushing season arrived, he understood that he first had to erase the stigma associated with living there. Since fraternities emphasized exclusiveness and party life, Lowenstein believed Stern should be able to offer at least equal advantages. Each living unit within Stern, he argued, should have its own identity, like an eating club. Going out on a limb, he encouraged students to have liquor at their parties, as long as they were careful; to have fires in the fireplaces, which had never been used; to paint their own rooms whatever color they pleased; and even to bring women in (but to act properly toward them). Before, one administrator remembered, "the lobbies had been empty tombs." Now they became social gathering places with jukeboxes, a stereo, a radio, and a hi-fi, even live music. Lowenstein's philosophy was, "If they can do [it at the fraternities], we can do it here."[5]

More important in the long run, though, was building a following so that the values and lifestyle represented by the "new" Stern Hall would achieve popularity and legitimacy. In that process, Lowenstein's personal cult became indistinguishable from—and indispensable to—the larger goal. His method was hyperactivity and nonstop motion. "I don't know how he ever slept," Craig recalled. "[He] was constantly talking all day and all night . . . with students coming in, groups, meetings, discussing issues. . . . When he was there, things happened. People would congregate, and the first thing you'd know they'd be talking about the things that he thought were important. . . . It was a process that just went on and on." Most deans worked a nine-to-five day, one of Lowenstein's colleagues said. But "he kept very, very different hours. . . . Al's real working hours were 8:00 P.M. to 3:00 A.M."[6]

Lowenstein's personal mannerisms seemed to embody the different values he advocated. Stanford "was a very ruling-class kind of Protestant place," one student observed; and suddenly, here was a New York Jew setting out to shake the foundations. "He always looked like an unmade bed," another student commented, "his tie over here and his shirt all over, and his hair was always kind of off this way . . . and he was running at such fast speed . . . just zipping in and out and stirring up concern all along the way." He was not only anti-"establishment," he *looked* anti-"establishment"; as a result, students "saw him as a romantic figure." "I remember walking with Al into his room," still another student said, "into stacks of papers that were six feet high that he could reach into . . . and pull out the exact document he wanted. . . . We would walk with him and talk with him and eat with him, as well as listen to him. . . . He was a very powerful personality drawing people into his life."[7]

And he knew so many important people. When the phone rang, it might be Norman Thomas or Eleanor Roosevelt, and "the kids hung around all the time to be in on the action. I mean you never knew who would be on the phone, and what he was going to have to do. And it was exciting." So when Al told them to speak up for themselves or to challenge the administration, the students listened and felt empowered. After all, one student said, this was a person who was a great teacher, who talked prophetically about injustice, and "who had put his life on the line" in South Africa. "Al had the charismatic kind of magnetism" that commanded attention, another student noted, "[and] who could charm [and] . . . just talk the pants off of anyone." Therefore, when he said, "If you don't like the rules, see if you can't get the rules changed," the students responded. They may have already been prepared to be activists, but now they had an inspiration, a guru, a leader.[8]

Lowenstein was not, however, simply reaching out indiscriminately; his apparently nonstop activity was governed by a careful method. Quickly, he learned who were the most important students on campus. Many were "sponsors"—specifically appointed student leaders for individual living units. The twenty-four sponsors were the campus elite, chosen for their talent and character. "They were really campus heroes," recalled one student, people respected by their peers and elders alike as "natural" leaders. "The most powerful combination you could have had on campus," one sponsor said, "was the head sponsor and the student body president working together." It was that kind of combination Lowenstein set out to cultivate.[9]

The Lowenstein followers fell into three groups. The first consisted of those passionately devoted to him and consumed by the desire to serve. These students were often what one friend called "rough gems in whom he saw a lot of potential, people who may not have had a great deal of self-confidence at the time, but who were so taken by Al's interest in them that they became true believers." Among that group was a young man from Oregon named Dennis Sweeney, destined to become a student leader. The second group consisted of those already acknowledged to be major figures. Usually self-confident and mature, they were drawn to Al but maintained a greater distance and independence than did the "true believers." This group included Fred Goff, a missionary's son known for his devotion to social justice, and John Steinbruner, a sponsor with strong international interests. The final group was made up of people who moved in and out of Al's orbit but chose not to become engaged emotionally as "groupies," usually because of a natural cynicism or detachment. These were potential allies to be courted, not disciples to be deployed at will. Among them was Skip Martin, a future journalist.

Intuitively, Lowenstein understood the differences among these students, as well as the advantage to be gained from forging them into a coalition to serve his—and the university's—larger end. From the start, it was clear that Lowenstein's underlying agenda was political: to transform Stern Hall, then the campus at large, and eventually American society. Gradually, the connection between these goals became clear. Where you lived on campus, Lowenstein emphasized, represented a "political" choice. By carefully identifying student leaders who would support his point of view, Al was able to make "independent" residence houses a positive option for students. "[That year] marked the watershed of a movement away from fraternities," Skip Martin said. "Previously they attracted people who would become the student leaders. . . . Beginning with that year . . . that all changed for some time to come." But eventually, other issues came up. "Initially, it was a kind of internal thing," according to Martin, "football jocks versus people who [were] more interested in academic topics." Within a relatively brief time, however, the issues broadened to include coed living, then the civil rights movement, and eventually the protest against the Vietnam War.[10]

Clearly, Lowenstein represented a serious threat to the Stanford status quo. "He turned me into a liberal within a few weeks of arriving on campus," one student said, an observation that could have been repeated a hundredfold. Rarely had a single person developed a mass following so quickly. "I think I [even] remember what he smelled like," another woman student remarked. "I remember that he wore his blue bomber jacket." And he had a tremendous hold on his students. "He spoke with such passion and such conviction," a Stanford alumna remembered. "He was so brilliant, you were almost entranced." In just one year, a student body president observed, "he got these kids . . . to renounce fraternities and their shallow values and . . . to democratize the living system." Nor did he seem to have exhausted his potential. "Almost to a person," a fellow dean commented, "people saw Al as . . . a larger-than-life figure, so that he had about him a group of people [who were] not just students interested in his cause [but] really admirers, who were caught up in a special spirit and ethic." This was the Dean Lowenstein who told students that "almost anything can be done in the University by organized student pressure"; the authorities could only imagine what such a "larger-than-life" figure might set in motion were he to stay.[11]

Largely to avoid that possibility, they set out to discourage Lowenstein's return the following year. A state of near civil war developed between the residence hall business manager and Lowenstein. Calling Stern Hall "a pigpen," the manager constantly complained to Lowenstein about each of the latter's efforts to liberalize living conditions. On one occasion, Lowenstein's assistant wrote, the manager "found an icebox, two empty cans of beer, and a half bottle of wine" in a graduate senior's room and threatened to bring in the top university administration "to view the atrocity." The business office turned down a request for university funds to buy a jukebox, accused Stern Hall students of painting their walls *three times,* and sent out memos denouncing the "deplorable housekeeping conditions" in the dorm, including "indiscriminate throwing of cigarette butts." The drumbeat of charges began to seem like systematic harassment. Bill Craig was forced on the defensive and constantly had to come to the aid of his young associate. Finally, he resorted to full-scale sarcasm. "Now hear this," he wrote in a memo from Admiral Craig to Captain Lowenstein, "lay to and scrub down fore and aft, all hands police the barracks—stand by for inspection, hup two, three." On one level, of course, Lowenstein thrived under the business office's pressure, viewing it as dramatic confirmation of how small-minded and petty all such bureaucracies were, and of how liberated and righteous, by contrast, his own approach to such matters was. But such antagonism could not help but erode Lowenstein's staying power; his simplest plans for residence hall reforms were frustrated, suggesting a larger policy of intimidation and surveillance designed to subvert his assigned mission.[12]

Indeed, behind the bureaucratic nitpicking lay a much larger anxiety about Lowenstein's impact on the hierarchical structures of Stanford. Those officials dedicated to the status quo could not help but see him as a "flaming radical" who, in the words of one student, was "using [his] undue influence over students" to promote a political agenda that bordered on revolution. Some even called him a Communist. And, in truth, this "whirlwind" activist was stirring things up, coming, in one friend's words, "into a previously unpoliticized place . . . and using [an assistant dean's role] as a soapbox . . . dealing with young impressionable people . . . [and] turning them around," whether the issue was fraternities, challenging the administration, or advocating that Stanford rejoin the "radical" NSA, from which it had earlier disaffiliated. As a "barely contained youth agitator," Lowenstein profoundly offended people like J. Wallace Sterling, the Stanford president, for whom propriety was a cardinal rule, including above all dressing in a certain way and behaving with respect toward authority. To such a person, Lowenstein, a New York Jew with his shirttail hanging out and a penchant for breaking rules and "stirring the kids up," constituted almost a mortal threat, someone who would have to be removed from the campus if his insidious challenge to decorum was to be contained.[13]

Unfortunately for Lowenstein, one of the people most sympathetic to the administration's perspective was James T. Watkins IV, the most powerful member of the political science department. The campus adviser to the interfraternity system, Watkins prided himself on being the most popular professor at Stanford; he was also suspected by some to be responsible for the good grades football players got in political science. Always dubious of Lowenstein's politics, Watkins had every reason to be particularly threatened by this Pied Piper who appeared to be taking away his reputation as the students' leading hero. In the opinion of John Cahill, one student who spoke with Watkins about Lowenstein, the senior political scientist believed Al was part of "a devilish plot to put control of the university in the hands of students" and bring "crumbling [down] around him [his] world of fraternities, aristocratic pull, and social prestige." Some Stanfordites speculated that Watkins was anti-Semitic as well.[14]

Thus, when Lowenstein sought appointment to a tenure-track position in political science as a condition for his remaining at Stanford, it was almost a foregone conclusion that he would be turned down. Not only did he not have a Ph.D.—the primary prerequisite for teaching at a place like Stanford—but he also had deliberately set out to undermine all that the department's leading member stood for. Many observers believed that Lowenstein could not have been unaware of the trap he was setting for himself. Consciously or unconsciously, he seemed to be asking to be released. "He unwittingly gave [the administration] a perfect out," one of his student friends said. "They didn't particularly want a student agitator . . . and they also didn't want to have student demonstrations on their hands. And this was the perfect out. *They* weren't asking him to leave. He was leaving on his own because [of] the political science department." Lowenstein later would seem never to have recovered from what he perceived as Stanford's rejection of him; he talked about it for the rest of his life. Yet he had set it up. The same year, Bill Craig, his main sponsor, also decided to leave. In the latest of what by now had become a staccato series of one-year jobs, Lowenstein had come, had seen, had conquered, and then had departed. The Stanford administration believed all its problems were solved. But Lowenstein's departure served only to accentuate, not diminish, his continuing influence.[15]

In fact, the Lowenstein presence appeared to become more tangible day by day, despite his absence. The students he had mobilized to so many different causes wrote letters to the newspaper protesting his departure. But more than that, they used their involvement in such issues as South Africa and fraternities to begin new organizations and carry over to the next class of students the networks he had begun. A significant portion of the Stanford sponsors for 1962, 1963, and 1964 had received the Lowenstein message and carried it forward. Every student body president for the next five years could be counted as a Lowenstein follower. And the growing involvement of Stanford students in activities related to civil rights, Africa, and the peace movement reflected an agenda of concerns that had first been planted and nourished during Lowenstein's one year on campus.

The election of Armin Rosencranz as student body president for 1962–63 highlighted the direction of things to come. A graduate student, Jew, and all-around iconoclast, Rosencranz appealed to all the same constituencies that Lowenstein had. He ran on the slogan, "Send a man to do a boy's job: elect charmin' Armin," then proceeded to swamp six fraternity look alikes. "The whole thing was a spoof," he later said. Yet many of the people who flocked to his side were former Lowensteinites—committed to social action and a value system different from that of the frats. The group became Rosencranz's "kitchen cabinet" and eventually gave themselves the acronym GRIP—the Group with Real Inside Power. It was, Rosencranz remarked, "a spoof carried through."[16]

Meeting in Rosencranz's house in the hills outside Palo Alto, the former Lowenstein protégés plotted strategy with their new leader. The house itself was a former saloon and brothel with thirty-six rooms, most of them just large enough for a bed. There, the wit of the original campaign was revitalized as students talked about how to disguise references to Lowenstein in meetings with the administration. His pseudonym became "Joe Blatz," and when students wished to allude to him in "enemy territory," they might comment, "Well, Joe Blatz says so and so." But the more serious agenda soon became obvious when the new student regime began to articulate its program.

Rosencranz's inaugural address to the new freshman class in the fall of 1962 left some Stanford administrators wondering if Lowenstein had ever really left. Calling for a "new fearlessness" on the part of the student body "to speak out and take stands on things which they deem unjust," Rosencranz challenged the young to organize collectively and disdain petty differences of status. His administration, he declared, was committed to its own "Four Freedoms" (à la Franklin Roosevelt in World War II): the freedom of students to participate in setting university policy; complete academic freedom "for anybody who has anything to say that is worth hearing," including radicals and atheists; the freedom of students to govern their own nonacademic lives (read social regulations); and the freedom "to emerge from the lethargy and the apathy that binds our generation." "We are too fat and too lazy," Rosencranz continued.

We have slept on our rights. But we are a sleeping giant . . . and we must awake and empathize with students all over the world who are being imprisoned and tortured for passively resisting government authority. . . . We can't fight [injustice] with a drink in one hand and a deck of cards in the other. Accordingly, I urge you to tear down the walls which surround you. . . . The people of the world are looking to America, even to us at Stanford, to redeem them from poverty and from intellectual bondage. This is the task of the students at a great university.

Suddenly "charmin' Armin" had delivered a body blow to the Stanford administration's smug self-assurance. Not only had the new era of student activism not ended; it had barely begun.[17]

Within the next few years, the news from Stanford was full of student activities dear to Lowenstein's heart. Demonstrators conducted a vigil near the president's house to protest the administration's decision to put up fallout-shelter signs all over campus in the wake of an escalation of the cold war. New regulations were issued reforming fraternity rushing procedures. The student body passed a constitution for the first time, a step Lowenstein always saw as crucial to student self-government. Social regulations became more sensible; and coeducational living appeared on the university's agenda for the first time. Speakers like James Baldwin highlighted the degree to which the Stanford student body had become engaged in the larger struggles that Rosencranz had emphasized, and committees to deal with local civil rights issues as well as conditions in South-West Africa were formed. Appropriately, when Bud Wedin, another Lowenstein ally, was elected as Rosencranz's successor, the inner circle toasted GRIP and Lowenstein for making it all possible. As one student wrote Lowenstein in the fall, Stanford was a very different place in 1962 than it had been in 1961, "and I can only ascribe this change to the Lowenstein catalyst."[18]

As if to tighten the screws further on his old bosses, Lowenstein returned periodically to campus, addressing enthusiastic throngs in the role of conquering hero and urging students on in their new activism. On one visit in January 1963 to talk about Africa and Spain, Lowenstein's student hosts were so worried about the administration's paranoid response that they warned him to say nothing controversial. His presence alone, they suggested, would be enough to redouble student energies and make administrators apoplectic. On each of these trips, Lowenstein re-created the hyperactivity of his year on campus, rushing from one meeting to another, staying up half the night with ten or fifteen new recruits, saving two or three hours in the early morning or on the drive back to the airport to spend with the "special" people who were his favorites. It was almost as if a two- or three-day visit distilled the Lowenstein mystique and magnified the larger-than-life memory he left behind, rekindling the devotion that others used as their inspiration for action, and that Lowenstein himself fed upon.[19]

In one such typical visit, Al joined his closest supporters for a weekend retreat at Big Sur. There, the group discussed the issues of most concern across the world as well as at Stanford, focusing more and more on the centrality of civil rights. With Al teaching the students Negro spirituals like "Amazing Grace" and movement songs like "Oh, Freedom!" the meeting took on a special quality: the people there—Fred Goff, Dennis Sweeney, Ilene Strelitz, Nancy Steffen, and others—were preparing themselves for a new stage of activity. It was almost as though the group had formed its own kind of fraternity, one of the participants recalled, solidifying bonds that would be crucial to the new struggles that lay ahead. The Lowenstein impact would not go away. As the Brookings Institution's John Steinbruner recalled thirty years later, "When I went to Stanford in 1959 . . . it was very, very conservative and insular and isolated from the world. . . . [But by 1963] the university [had] just totally transformed itself. . . . And Al was probably the single most important figure in that transition . . . the impetus behind it all."[20]

CIVIL RIGHTS

The issue that would eventually catapult Lowenstein back to visible leadership among Stanford students was the civil rights struggle in Mississippi. Ever since he was a child, Lowenstein had been absorbed by the issue of racial injustice—at first through his correspondence and conversations with Rex Freeman, the family chauffeur, then through his active involvement in the battle at UNC to end Jim Crow in North Carolina, and at NSA to support desegregation nationwide. His South Africa venture reflected the same commitment. Now, with the student-led civil rights movement spreading like wildfire throughout the South, a whole new generation of young black students—with some white support—were dramatizing insistently the evil of segregation, imprinting on the nation's consciousness the moral urgency of eliminating this scourge. The struggle contained precisely those elements that evoked Lowenstein's instinct to become centrally engaged: those who mobilized the battalions to topple racism could claim, with justification, to have helped "make the difference" on America's most fundamental moral dilemma.

From the beginning of the sit-ins at five and dime stores in North Carolina, Lowenstein identified himself as a champion of "the movement." In

a vintage Lowenstein performance at a student conference, he so moved
Vassar students in his description of the brutality rained on the heads of
black demonstrators in the South that hundreds organized to picket Wool-
worth's in Poughkeepsie in a sympathy march. Lowenstein, in turn, received the credit (or blame) in the New York press for having inspired the
action. At other campuses as well, he began to focus on the problem of
race relations in America. Urged by student leader Casey Hayden and
others at the University of Texas to enlist Eleanor Roosevelt's aid in a
local Austin effort to desegregate a theater showing *Sunrise at
Campobello*—a movie about FDR—he responded with alacrity, as did
Mrs. Roosevelt. Soon it became clear that, on predominantly white campuses especially, Lowenstein was a charismatic point man for the movement, someone who could use his talents for energizing students to en-
large and lead the ranks of white civil rights demonstrators.[21]

Lowenstein's civil rights activity deepened considerably when he returned to North Carolina in the fall of 1962 as assistant professor of social
studies at North Carolina State University. In terms of its status and professional rewards, NC State was one of the least satisfying of Lowenstein's
brief job assignments during the 1960s. Dubbed a "cow college" by
Chapel Hill wits, NC State primarily trained engineers and agricultural
scientists. Its student body was almost totally local; with very few humanities majors, it offered a paucity of the "natural recruits" Lowenstein had
found in such large numbers at Stanford. Nevertheless, he plunged into
his assignment, teaching a section of the departmentwide course on civilization and science, as well as more specialized classes on the affluent
society and the challenge of the 1960s vis-à-vis the cold war and the
world order. He often seemed to be preparing his lectures as he raced to
class, and his syllabi were covered with handwritten notes on reading assignments that he had probably just completed himself. But, as usual, he
was a stunning success in the classroom, mesmerizing his students on
subjects as diverse as Albert Camus and Aldous Huxley, new Israeli educational techniques, Paul Tillich's theology, and how the ideas of existen-
tialism summoned the young to "responsible social action."[22]

By the spring of 1963, Lowenstein's involvement in the civil rights
issue had become a cause célèbre in North Carolina, and a signal to students elsewhere that Lowenstein was ready to assume a bold leadership
role akin to that he had taken with the South-West Africa question a few
years earlier. Shrewdly, Lowenstein used his connections to national and
international leaders to highlight the absurdity of segregation. Inviting

Angie Brooks, Liberia's U.N. Ambassador, to Raleigh for a lecture, Lowenstein arranged for an integrated group to go to the Sir Walter Raleigh Hotel for dinner, knowing in advance that they would be turned away. The same group then went to a large, well-patronized cafeteria where, once again, they were denied service. Lowenstein, of course, knew exactly what he was doing. Brooks was a friend from the days of his South African testimony at the United Nations. She had also attended Shaw, a black college in Raleigh, and so was very familiar with local customs. Disingenuously, Lowenstein denied that the incident had been staged. But the results were exactly what he intended—headlines across the state, humiliation and embarrassment for North Carolina's "liberal" governor, Terry Sanford, and a shot in the arm to the local civil rights movement. How better to underline the stupidity of Jim Crow.

Within days, the episode had escalated. Hundreds of blacks doubled the ranks of the Raleigh civil rights movement, insisting on admission to local restaurants and theaters. Two Negroes were arrested for trying to eat at the cafeteria in the state legislature, and more than 500 demonstrators drowned out a performance of the North Carolina Symphony at the governor's mansion with their singing of freedom songs. As the movement intensified, local officials were forced to respond. The merchants' association urged desegregation; the governor and other officials entered negotiations with movement leaders; and by the end of June, eating and theater facilities had been opened to blacks.

Clearly, a civil rights struggle of significant proportions already existed in Raleigh, as elsewhere in North Carolina. Indeed, during the same weeks, thousands of black demonstrators (and some whites) had been jailed in Greensboro, Durham, Chapel Hill, and Charlotte. Thus, Lowenstein, in one sense, simply "dropped in" on a movement that was already cresting. Yet in North Carolina, as at Stanford and countless other sites, Lowenstein was given credit by many observers for what happened. Jessie Helms, the owner of the area's leading television station, editorially lambasted Lowenstein (and Brooks) for staging a provocative incident as part of a "subterfuge" designed to precipitate unrest and bitterness. "Is it only an accident," Helms asked on television, "that [Lowenstein] has the appearance of one dedicated primarily to agitation and promotion of strife?" Others demanded that Lowenstein be fired from his teaching post at a public university. By a simple daring tactic, Al Lowenstein had made himself the focal point of controversy, while simultaneously advancing dramatically a cause he cared about passionately.[23]

THE MISSISSIPPI FREEDOM VOTE

All that, though, was only prelude to what would come in Mississippi. Lowenstein first went there in July 1963 after Medgar Evers, the National Association for the Advancement of Colored People (NAACP) leader, was gunned down in the driveway of his home because he so unflinchingly refused to be intimidated by whites desperate to stop the movement he was building. On many subsequent occasions, Lowenstein commented that he had been "called to" Mississippi to provide help. It is not clear who called him, but Ed King, a white Tougaloo chaplain and movement activist, suggests that it may have been Aaron Henry, a black Clarksdale pharmacist and an old Lowenstein friend from NSA days in the 1950s. William Higgs, the only white lawyer in the state willing to take civil rights cases (there were only three black lawyers), had been run out of Mississippi, and the movement desperately needed legal assistance. Hence, Lowenstein went to Jackson, initially intending to stay just a few days.[24]

By Lowenstein's account, that initial visit was a turning point in his own life, and for the movement. Mississippi was a state so immersed in the evil of racism that nothing short of total commitment—and daring new ideas—could rescue the situation. "People were being beaten and arrested and terrorized," he recalled two years later, "and nobody seemed to know or care." Lowenstein had expected to find Mississippi to be similar to North Carolina, "but after . . . I spent a little time [there] . . . I realized the difference—I think it is Marx who once said that 'if the degree of difference gets big enough, the spark jumps the gap and you get a difference in principle'—. . . Well Mississippi was different in principle from the rest of the South. . . . It was as if the Constitution of the United States had been repealed in Mississippi and didn't exist." There was no rule of law, no First Amendment, no security against murder or arson. It was as bad as—maybe worse than—South Africa.

Lowenstein's assessment was based in large part on conversations he had during his visit, primarily with white friends who were active in, or sympathetic to, the civil rights movement. "We were at a point in 1963 where we didn't know what to do," Ed King noted in recalling his first conversation with Lowenstein. "Medgar had been dead about three weeks . . . the movement had been smashed by illegal mass arrests, tying us up in court; massive violence, very heavy fines . . . the U.S. government working to stop direct action . . . and lots of dissension within the black community." In Leflore County, all political protest had been suppressed; a Coahoma County injunction against the NAACP had brought activity there to a halt; and in Jackson the terrorism of murder prevailed. Ever since the summer of 1961, workers from the Student Nonviolent Coordinating Committee (SNCC) had been struggling to register voters and mobilize a mass movement, but the repression had been overwhelming. "We needed something new," King observed, "or we needed to quit." Although a number of black activists had a different viewpoint—many saw the repression as just one more test during the ongoing, and successful, process of movement building—everyone would have agreed that on July 4, 1963, when Al Lowenstein arrived in Mississippi, white resistance had the upper hand.[25]

Lowenstein himself saw the situation in its worst light. "When I first got [there]," he told one student audience, "everything was finished. The whites had won. There were a few SNCC kids holding out . . . but the people literally had no hope." In reality, that was not true. SNCC had field offices throughout the state; campaigns in Greenwood and McComb had already mobilized considerable grassroots insurgency; and SNCC workers were intent on continuing the struggle, filled with determination as well as hope. But Lowenstein insisted on emphasizing the bleak side. Given the predicament of black Mississippians, he reasoned, adding one more lawyer to defend arrested demonstrators was a futile gesture, especially in a legal system in which even federal appeals court judges referred to blacks as "chimpanzees." What was needed instead was the kind of bold action that would highlight, glaringly and dramatically, the systemic ways in which Mississippi was "different in principle" from the rest of America, and why that difference required national attention and intervention. "We had to shake people on the outside out of thinking that Mississippi was just another state," Lowenstein said.

Searching for an answer, Lowenstein was struck by the analogy of South Africa. "I remembered," he said, "[that] the Africans who could not vote [on election day] had called a day of mourning in South Africa . . . and the day of mourning touched the conscience of the people who [had] never understood that Africans cared." In Mississippi, unlike South Africa, the government said in theory that blacks *could* vote, then set out to deprive them of that right, claiming in the process that blacks *chose* not to vote and were indifferent to politics. Instead of a day of mourning, then, Lowenstein asked, "why not a day of voting?" SNCC, of course, had been bringing blacks to register for years but had suffered only brutality and incarceration. "So we decided, or I decided," Lowenstein said, "that [it] didn't make sense to try to do that. . . . [But] there was no reason why people couldn't vote without going through all that rigamorole, that they could vote where they *could* vote instead of trying to vote where they couldn't. And that was the genesis of the idea of the Freedom Ballot."

In the past, Mississippi blacks—with SNCC support—had run candidates for congressional seats, using those candidacies to mobilize black political support. Under a nineteenth-century law, people eligible to vote who were not on the registration list could cast their ballots and then have them challenged. In this way, blacks could go to the polls, even though their votes would not be counted. Now the idea was to have statewide, black-nominated candidates for governor and lieutenant governor, and to have black citizens cast their ballots, not at the official election sites where they would be subject to arrest or harassment, but at churches, clubs, and schools in their own communities. In that way, the whole world would see that blacks wanted to vote and would do so if allowed. In a single stroke, the structure of hypocrisy on which white Mississippi had built its political system of racial exclusion would be demolished.[26]

As Lowenstein later recounted the story, he took his idea to Bob Moses, the field leader for the SNCC forces in Mississippi, and Charles Evers, brother of the slain Medgar and an important figure in his own right. Moses was already a legend in Mississippi. Quiet, gentle, and devoted to the ideal of developing a community of love as well as strength in the movement, he practiced leadership by listening to people and transformed impotence into empowerment by letting people arrive at their own decisions. Evers was the more traditional and older leader. Both seemed enthusiastic about the Freedom Vote, as it came to be called, if Lowenstein would raise money and recruit outside resources. The North Carolina professor, officially on a one-semester leave of absence, readily agreed. A convention of Mississippi blacks nominated Aaron Henry, a black Clarksdale pharmacist and an old Lowenstein friend, for governor, and Ed King, the white Tougaloo chaplain and a new Lowenstein friend, for lieutenant governor. Hoping with that ticket to attract more than 50,000 black voters, Lowenstein proceeded, in coalition with his black allies, to secure the help he had promised. He became chairman of the Aaron Henry for Governor Advisory Committee, embarked on a fund-raising and media blitz to promote the Freedom Vote, and activated the Lowenstein network of student followers that he had been developing over the previous decade.[27]*

* It should be noted that Moses and others have a different recollection of this chronology; they emphasize that the idea of the Freedom Vote emerged through a collective process. That difference of opinion will be dealt with at length in the conclusion to chapter 8.

Lowenstein decided early on that the size of his own contribution to this venture would hinge on his ability to recruit students to come to Mississippi to help. He had already brought Dennis Sweeney, his protégé and a Stanford student leader, back to Mississippi in the late summer. Now, with Sweeney as a confidant and lieutenant, he returned to Stanford to encourage other students to commit either their financial resources or their persons to the Freedom Vote campaign. There was a kind of "mystical" quality about Lowenstein, one student recalled, linked to his image as someone "speaking fast, making friends . . . gathering commitment." Young people at Stanford were still "terribly naive about the political process," she noted, "[and] there was a belief that if people did the right thing, then that would really have an impact. That was great stuff to hear. It was straightforward and one of the most powerful things you can imagine, as other people looked around and said, 'Yes, that really does make sense. It's what my father said. It's what we were told.'" With such motivated and idealistic students, Lowenstein could work miracles. "He made you feel like you weren't doing enough and you weren't caring enough," another student said, "[and he was] living on such an intense and lofty level . . . [caring] for these downtrodden people . . . putting his life on the line." Lowenstein insisted that one person could change the world, and in the atmosphere of budding confidence and optimism in the early 1960s, that message generated an extraordinary response because there were so many ready to hear it.[28]

Lowenstein also returned to his old haunts at Yale. With contacts like the chaplain, William Sloane Coffin, as well as student friends made during various visits to give speeches on campus, Lowenstein quickly established the same kind of support network he had built at Stanford. Lowenstein had paired up with Dennis Sweeney to make his appeals at Stanford; at Yale, he brought in Robert Moses and Marian Wright, a black law student. Warning the Yale students of the danger of racial tensions and segregation, Moses declared: "We must have a different response, one of Negroes and whites working together. Otherwise, the pentup bitterness of the long subjugated Negro will be vented in a mass racial uprising. It is this we fear most. We must convince both races that it is not a racial battle of black versus white, but one of both races cooperating in the struggle for social justice." Conveying a dose of reality about racial divisions already brewing within as well as outside the movement, Moses and Wright nevertheless exhorted the Yale students to join the struggle. "We can see the subtle bigotry beneath the veneer of liberalism," Wright said, "and so we wonder whom we can really trust as a friend." It was up to the Yale students, she suggested, to show how they could be trusted.[29]

On both campuses, the response was immediate. Sweeney left Stanford with a carload of students, including Fred Goff and other sponsors, on October 7, with additional carloads planned. The Stanford newspaper—edited by Ilene Strelitz, one of Lowenstein's most fervent admirers and allies—published almost daily stories about the venture, urging students to respond with money if nothing else. At Yale, meanwhile, fifty students signed up to journey to Mississippi to prepare for the early November election. In response to Lowenstein's specific request for writers and photographers, their ranks included the editor of the student newspaper and campus leaders like Steve Bingham, Joe Lieberman (both also with the *Yale Daily News*), Jon Else, and Bruce Payne, all of whom would later achieve broader fame. As had been true throughout his years of campus organizing, Lowenstein was convinced that if "the best and brightest" students from the American "establishment" would make a commitment to show that the "system" of American democracy worked, they could provide the energy, the publicity, and the talent to end inequality and rally the forces of social justice. Never before had there been a more dramatic scenario for testing that proposition, or a more enthusiastic response by Lowenstein's constituency.[30]

As if to confirm Lowenstein's instincts, the state of Mississippi responded with hysteria toward both the Freedom Vote and the white students. An "unbelievable atmosphere" surrounded the election, Lowenstein declared. "For some reason the white authorities panicked, even though the Freedom Election had no standing. Just the fact that Negroes were participating in the process of voting was apparently too much to face. Anywhere you went in Mississippi during the campaign, you could not arrive safely at your destination if the police didn't want you to." Lowenstein talked with humor and biting sarcasm about his own experiences that month. One night in Clarksdale, he and Steve Bingham were driving around in search of the place they were to stay. The first time they were stopped by police, it was for going through a stop sign that did not exist. The second time, they were crossing the street on foot from their car to the Alcazar Hotel when they were arrested for loitering and violating the curfew. Booked at the Tullahoma County jail, Lowenstein experienced the customary fear generated by police talking about cattle prods and speculating about whether the prisoners should be allowed to live until morning. And so Lowenstein identified himself as a lawyer and demanded to make a phone call. When miraculously his wish was granted, he quickly calculated how to make the biggest impact. In the middle of the night, with the police still in the same room, he placed a collect call to Franklin D. Roosevelt III—spelling out the name slowly. Although Roosevelt was barely awake, Lowenstein acted as though he were intensely engaged, telling him, "No, don't call President Kennedy tonight, wait until tomorrow." The story, of course, became richer in the telling, but evidently it had its effect: from that point on, the prisoners were treated in a model fashion.[31]

The student volunteers recruited by Lowenstein were far less fortunate. Each day new episodes of violence and intimidation were reported, some of them coming perilously close to murder. Ivanhoe Donaldson, a black student, was stopped by a policeman who pointed a gun at his head and said, "I'm going to kill me a nigger." Bruce Payne and two other civil rights workers were forced from their car in Fort Gibson and beaten by four men, then followed all the way from Natchez. On another occasion, Payne was chased by a pursuing car that fired three shots into his vehicle before he finally escaped. Nicholas Bosanquet, a Cambridge University graduate holding a distinguished fellowship at Yale, was arrested with a black classmate for attempting to attend a Jackson Philharmonic concert. Stanford students had similar experiences, creating the very real sense that the campaign was continually subject to the arbitrary exercise of terrorism. It was an experience that black Mississippians had been living with all their lives, but it stunned students from Yale and Stanford, who were accustomed to lives of privilege and security.[32]

Still, the repression had a salutary impact nationally: it focused more and more attention on the Freedom Vote and generated an ever greater response. In the face of daily front-page stories phoned in directly by Lowenstein and Sweeney, Stanford students collected over $5,000 to send to their colleagues in Mississippi. Yale reacted with similar excitement; students phoned and wrote their parents, their congressmen, and their hometown papers in outrage over what was happening to their friends. Frank Porter Graham wired that he would provide bond money to the full extent of his savings in order to get students out of jail; Norman Thomas flew south for a day of campaigning for Aaron Henry; and the news coverage increased dramatically, with *Newsweek*, the *New York Times*, and other major publications devoting special stories to the Freedom Vote.[33]

In the end, it all paid off. Between November 2 and 4, more than 85,000 black Mississippians cast Freedom Ballots at their churches, lodges, and community associations, blowing away the myth of their indifference. The presence of white volunteers in the state had helped generate a national attention to Mississippi that had never existed before, largely for the racist reason that the victims of past brutality there had been black, not white. But the results were dramatic. The editor of the *Stanford Daily* was correct when she later wrote that, "in retrospect, it seems clear that the Aaron Henry Campaign was the turning point of the Mississippi Movement—the one tactic that, after long years of failure, finally showed the way for success." And Lowenstein had helped make it happen. "Without him," Bob Moses declared, "it never would have come off as it did."[34]

Perhaps most important, the Freedom Vote campaign led eventually to plans for Freedom Summer, the project that would bring over 1,000 white volunteers to Mississippi for the summer of 1964. The presence of the Stanford and Yale students in October and November had shown what outside help could do. "If we could get the [students] to answer the telephone, deal with the press, and run the mimeograph," Ed King said, "that left the black SNCC males [free] to go out into the plantations [and] . . . into totally new counties . . . and left the black SNCC women . . . to go into the safer churches." Furthermore, the white students automatically brought national news attention to the state, since so many of them came from famous and powerful families. Thus as soon as the Freedom Vote campaign had ended, discussions began about how and whether to extend its approach—on an even more massive scale—to the following summer.[35]

Clearly, Lowenstein had a powerful impact in Mississippi. But his involvement also generated a series of questions about white-black relations inside the movement—above all, about who would exercise control—that eventually produced a schism within Mississippi and fragmentation of the movement as a whole. In the fall of 1963, these tensions remained, for the most part, beneath the surface. By the late spring and summer of 1964, they would explode into national disputes that spoke to core issues of what equality was all about, how social movements should be constituted, and what the word *self-determination* really meant. At the center of all these disputes, once again, was Allard Lowenstein.

8

Mississippi Freedom Summer

IN MANY WAYS, THE VERY IDEA OF IMPORTING WHITE VOLUNTEERS FROM elite colleges to help in Mississippi was fraught with peril. They might be adept at writing press releases, handling the media, or doing typing and mimeograph work, thereby freeing blacks in SNCC to go out into the field. But the very ease with which Yale and Stanford students did these tasks raised issues of status and class. The whites were privileged and *accustomed* to wielding power and influence. "It was hard to establish a tone appropriate to the task," one black staff member said, "with a bunch of Yalies running around in their Triumph [sports cars]." Moreover, movement people pointed out, as much as the volunteers were needed, "there was some fear and a little bit of resentment . . . [when people] in the offices, who weren't doing the dangerous stuff in the field, began to make decisions." One Yale student wrote that, "after we all left Jackson, [apparently] . . . a certain reaction against the Yale people set in . . . resentment at the way in which [we] had come and gone." Local people knew the subtleties and the ins and outs of county differences. The volunteers might be good at getting national coverage, but they had no grasp of—and sometimes no patience with—SNCC's concern with events in Copiah or Jefferson counties.[1]

Not surprisingly, Lowenstein was identified as a source of these tensions. He had spearheaded the student blitzkrieg; he had been the one who expressed impatience at SNCC's inefficiency and slowness; and it was Lowenstein who allegedly had ordered some SNCC workers to go into Yazoo at a time when SNCC knew that area to be a minefield that they should stay away from at all costs. Lowenstein had anticipated these tensions and had tried to prepare the students to be sensitive to them. But despite his good intentions, he himself could not avoid them. When he told some black SNCC staffers that he and two other whites had taken refuge from the police by going into an all-night hamburger joint, the SNCC members were outraged, since SNCC had a rule about never patronizing Jim Crow facilities. Bob Moses cooled them down by pointing out that blacks could escape by disappearing into the Negro community, and that their white allies should have the same opportunity. But the nerve endings were clearly there, and it would not take much to irritate them.[2]

Still, the positive impact of the Freedom Vote seemed sufficiently powerful to justify pursuing plans for an even more ambitious project—bringing as many as 1,000 white volunteers to the state for Freedom Summer in 1964. If slightly less than 100 such students had brought the national news media to the state for the Freedom Vote, how much more attention would be gained by multiplying the number tenfold. Although the idea was tabled at the initial SNCC staff meeting because of concern over what might happen if so many whites came in, Bob Moses was for the plan and eventually won the reluctant support of his fellow staff members. Moses all along had mediated between SNCC and Lowenstein (while Ed King served the same role between Lowenstein and Moses). Although Jim Forman, the executive secretary of SNCC, had disliked Lowenstein ever since an NSA meeting in the 1950s in which Lowenstein had steamrollered a leftist faction, Moses believed it was wrong for any personal or political grievance to obstruct the long-range best interests of the movement. Despite the tensions, Moses wrote Lowenstein in late 1963, "I think we should be able to work well together after we are around each other a day or so—and the combination will be good." Even when respected SNCC field leaders like Lawrence Guyot went to Moses and said, "Why are you dealing with this guy? . . . This is contrary to everything we operate by," Moses persisted, believing that Lowenstein was indispensable to the effort to recruit northern students, and that the students, in turn, were essential to the movement's success in Mississippi.[3]

Lowenstein himself, meanwhile, was chomping at the bit to implement the plans for Freedom Summer. He pressed people like Marian Wright to get a firm okay from SNCC so that he could begin recruiting; he set in motion once again his campus publicity network; and he began to enlist lieutenants at key colleges to serve as local organizers—Barney Frank at Harvard, Jim Scott and Bruce Payne at Yale, Dennis Sweeney at Stanford, and people at countless smaller colleges where he went to give talks and urge students to apply to join the Freedom Summer volunteers, now talked about as potentially 2,000 in number.[4]

PROBLEMS

As early as January 1964, however, Lowenstein began to send out signals that he was having his own problems with the Freedom Summer project. Frustrated by SNCC's decision-making process (which he viewed as cumbersome) and the lack of clarity about who was in charge of what, he confided in friends that he was dubious about the direction the project was taking. "I hope that . . . summer plans are looking less smoggy," one student associate wrote him after Lowenstein met with Ella Baker, a brilliant and radical senior movement leader from New York, and Bob Moses. Although he continued to recruit for the project, Lowenstein's skepticism persisted, finally prompting Moses to plead with him for support. The situation was desperate, Moses wrote:

> We are being deluged: there have been five killings . . . in the last three months . . . three whippings, scattered shootings, a hundred eighty cross burnings. If you pull out it won't reduce any tensions absolutely, it will merely be an exchange of one set for another. You know that nothing political and significant can be done without public tension—it stands to reason they won't be done without private ones also. You not only have to stay—*you must* . . . come to the March . . . meeting. . . . We are just beginning to open up the pandora of inter–civil rights organization tensions. You have got to help us iron them out. If we lose dialogue, then we will be lost.

Clearly, Moses remained committed to working out his problems with Lowenstein and continued to perceive Lowenstein as critical to the success of the Freedom Summer project.[5]

At least part of Lowenstein's problem with the planning process involved the interorganizational tensions that Moses alluded to. Lowenstein's closest ties in Mississippi were to the NAACP—people like Aaron

Henry, Charles Evers, and R. L. T. Smith, the older black political leader. Although all the civil rights groups were members of the Council of Federated Organizations (COFO), SNCC clearly predominated, and SNCC supporters were deeply at odds with the NAACP, which was older, more traditional, and more middle-class in orientation. Increasingly, SNCC's experience with poverty, terrorism, and the federal government's failure to provide *any* of the protection it promised voter registration workers had generated greater radicalism in the SNCC ranks. Symbolized by the overalls that SNCC workers wore as a movement uniform, the organization's identification with the black proletariat—and with a poor people's critique of power and wealth—proved problematic for the NAACP and for Lowenstein, who always seemed curious about tensions between the two groups during his trips to Mississippi.[6]

But the basic issue for Lowenstein was SNCC's political inclusiveness, and in particular its willingness to welcome the support of people with a leftist past. As early as December 1963, Lowenstein had begun to raise questions about the role in the movement of the National Lawyers' Guild and the Southern Conference Educational Fund (SCEF). Each group had figured prominently in the McCarthy era, being cited by McCarthy followers and anti-Communist liberals as "fellow-traveling" organizations full of "Communist sympathizers." According to liberals, like the labor lawyer Joseph Rauh, who cut their teeth on the faction-ridden left politics of the 1930s, the Lawyers' Guild represented the "last bastion" of the Communist line and supported "every Russian move." SCEF, led by Anne and Carl Braden, had a similar reputation among many anti-Communist liberals, notwithstanding its persistent and heroic stance in support of desegregation and labor rights.

From SNCC's point of view, these were organizations full of decent people who were volunteering their services at a critical time. Whatever their past political allegiances, they were ready in the here and now to provide help that was desperately needed. "SNCC was an open organization," John Lewis, its former chairman, observed. "It was sort of 'Who so ever will, let him come.'" William Kunstler of the Lawyers' Guild had sent his daughter to Tougaloo, a black college, in 1962 and had himself helped defend people arrested in the Freedom Rides. The Guild's Arthur Kinoy had for years distinguished himself by taking civil rights cases. Joni Rabinowitz, another child of a Guild member, was one of the first whites to volunteer for SNCC's southwest Georgia project. And SCEF had provided bond money for jailed demonstrators in Mississippi when the NAACP backed away from doing so. Clearly, people in these groups cared deeply about the struggle and performed valiantly. Moreover, SNCC workers noted, when they volunteered their services, they agreed to take orders, not give them. In a period when the Mississippi movement anticipated hundreds—perhaps thousands—of arrests during Freedom Summer, it seemed the height of folly to refuse the Lawyers' Guild's offer of legal help, especially when there were almost no lawyers on the ground in Mississippi, and when the NAACP was hanging back.[7]

Lowenstein, on the other hand, shared Rauh's view of members of the Old Left and was deeply suspicious of their motivation. Reflecting the anticommunism of his NSA presidency, he perceived any efforts by "progressive" groups to join a liberal coalition as the first step toward infiltration and takeover. To like-minded Socialists, especially Lowenstein friends such as Norman Thomas and Michael Harrington, SCEF and the Lawyers' Guild symbolized the threat of Stalinism. "You cannot expect liberals in this country to support the civil rights movement," Lowenstein had told Ed King, "when you are using people who don't really believe in freedom." Despite his reputation on campuses as a "flaming radical," Lowenstein, as one close student friend observed, was in fact "a very mainstream kind of person. . . . Inside this certain framework . . . he moved people in very progressive [directions, but] at some point you had to do it Al's way."[8]

In spite of his doubts about the Freedom Summer project, Lowenstein continued to scour the country picking lieutenants to coordinate the volunteers. His diary—written in headline form to emulate his beloved *New York Times*—suggested, however, the depth of his concern. "'Wrong' Decisions and 'Wrong' Group Making Them Combine to End 'Deep' Commitment: Problem Rises of Who To Tell How Much. Campus Center Leaders in Mixed Role. Obligation to Keep Them Informed Called 'Great' But Particularly on Question of 'Infiltration' Dilemma is Acute and Has Not Been Solved." Almost paralyzed by his confusion over what was actually happening, and deeply concerned with the specter of "reds" taking over and using "his" project, Lowenstein faced the approaching summer with what amounted to schizophrenic ambivalence: only his total support could make the project work, he thought; yet what if, all along, he were a tool in someone else's plot?[9]

Lowenstein acted out his ambivalence throughout the spring, oscillating between inspirational public speeches on behalf of Freedom Summer and lengthy phone calls interrogating COFO staff members. "There was just a lot of tension there," Moses noted, "because Al was out doing his own recruiting . . . and SNCC was getting geared up on its own." SNCC members resented Lowenstein's asking "Why is this being done, etc.?" Moreover, SNCC had its own questions about Lowenstein's style. Not only did some SNCC people believe that Lowenstein was red-baiting them (Lawrence Guyot claimed he was going around saying "there were Maoists in SNCC, there was no concern about structure, no concern about order . . . they were being influenced by the left"), but in addition, they worried about the recklessness of Lowenstein's recruiting practices, fearful that he was encouraging, in Ilene Strelitz's words, "a casual invasion of whomever felt so inclined into the state of Mississippi," while showing little appreciation of the need for disciplined training and preparation. Dorothy Zellner, in charge of SNCC recruiting in the Boston area, was furious that Lowenstein wanted to do his own recruiting without following SNCC procedures. "Lowenstein was up here . . . several times," she wrote Mendy Samstein, "and left . . . without having contacted a single person I knew or me." Zellner concluded that Lowenstein "was one of these types who [want] to be like the Lone Ranger. . . . Between you and me, something about him does not grab me." SNCC workers, meanwhile, were getting tired of receiving checks made out to Al Lowenstein, as though *he* were the movement and not them. Thus suspicions mounted even as misunderstandings intensified.[10]

By the end of April, Lowenstein had decided to break with the Freedom Summer project. A letter Emory Bundy wrote to his brother John, an applicant for the project, listed his reasons: SNCC's failure to cooperate with the NAACP and CORE (Congress of Racial Equality); SNCC's willingness to use attorneys from the Lawyers' Guild, "a communist infiltrated organization"; and the SNCC decision-making process. "He said he wouldn't mind abiding by democratically decided and discussed decisions that he disagreed with," Bundy wrote, "but he both disagrees with what they are deciding and their method of arriving at decisions." The Guild issue was key, though, according to Bundy, and SNCC's argument that it could not afford to turn down help from anybody "outrages Al since they have so bullheadedly refused student help. At any rate, that topped it off and Al isn't going." Having used Bundy to describe his feelings, Al then added a footnote in his own hand. "Basically," he said, "[this is] accurate but very unknown and very private. I have not disassociated myself in any public way and don't want to do so, or to hurt the project in any way, so please keep this all strictly to yourself."[11]

In reality, of course, there was no way that Lowenstein's decision could remain private or not hurt the project. Although he seemed to want to have it both ways—being a loyalist in public and a skeptic in private—he was already perceived, accurately, as trying to sow doubts about the entire enterprise. Ilene Strelitz and Dennis Sweeney invited Moses to Stanford in early May because word was out that Lowenstein had changed his position and that Stanford's continued support of the project was questionable. "He called key people," Moses commented, "so I'm summoned out to Stanford because Al has broken . . . and they are considering abandoning the project." In the aftermath of the "summit" conference, Strelitz assured Moses that Al was still critical to the project's success and that "he alone could have brought recruiting [so far]. . . . He has been a wonderful influence in garnering only those people who have clear talents to lend to the project, and by his very words, philosophy and commitment, has been a one-man self-selection process. . . . The main division between you and Al is one of miles, not of concepts or approach."[12]

But in fact it was precisely concepts that were at stake. Almost simultaneously with Strelitz's letter, Lowenstein publicly criticized the movement's tactics in a speech at Stanford. "Recently," he said in a newspaper interview, "I've had some deeply disturbing disagreements with some of the leaders I've worked with. . . . It's important to assess whether what one's doing is getting toward one's goal or not. . . . The problem is one of increasing frustration, leading to increasing alleged militancy, leading to reaction, at the very moment when progress seemed possible." Although Lowenstein's comments did not refer specifically to Mississippi, Moses was the target of his remarks, particularly Moses's endorsement of more aggressive acts of civil disobedience. "We are not far from violence," Lowenstein declared: "Imminent is a breakdown in communication because of the inability of people of good will to act. . . . Civil disobedience doesn't contribute to what we are trying to achieve." Meanwhile, Lowenstein convened a meeting of about thirty students at the apartment of a friend, John Rosenberg, to denounce Kunstler and the Lawyers' Guild and to set forth his own dissociation from the Freedom Summer campaign. According to one Stanford student leader, Lowenstein charged that Bob Moses was being "run by Peking," and even envisioned a joint press conference by Yale, Stanford, and Harvard students announcing their withdrawal from the project.[13]

For a brief period, confusion still reigned, largely because of Lowenstein's desire to have it both ways. After talking with Robert Moses, Marian Wright pleaded with Lowenstein to reconsider, also using the rationale that "somebody misunderstood somebody." "There's little hope in getting the organizational taint out of the summer project," she admitted, referring to the National Lawyers' Guild controversy, "but . . . that is one of the realities we are going to have to learn to live with. The important thing is not to let SNCC's seeming intransigence spoil whatever potential that does exist for the summer." Lowenstein himself seemed to want SNCC to woo him back; he urged Ed King—behind the scenes—to intercede with Moses to get him appointed to an important position in the Freedom Summer ranks, thereby allowing him to come back on board without losing face. But by that time, King observed, "there were . . . enough SNCC people who were angry or afraid of Al that it would be very awkward to find that kind of spot for him . . . unless [he] was just going to be an obscure volunteer in some place."[14]

Instead, Lowenstein retained his distance. Word continued to spread of his disaffection, frightening students who had responded to his enthusiastic recruiting calls. "I have recently heard that you have dropped out of the project," one North Carolinian wrote. "Since it was your discussion which was instrumental in acquainting me with COFO, I would be interested in knowing why you have done this . . . [because I] do not want to be a pawn in any activity which is aimed primarily at creating publicity." Others wrote with similar concerns. But Lowenstein could not resolve his ambivalence, and as the summer volunteers were gathering in Oxford, Ohio, for their orientation and training, he departed on a trip to Europe.[15]

Inevitably, the turnabout created consternation and confusion among Lowenstein's most ardent followers. Some felt manipulated. Nancy Steffen, for example, believed that Lowenstein had used his friendship with her to persuade her to present his point of view in her columns for the *Stanford Daily*, making her "his spokesperson [against Moses] without saying I was being his spokesperson." Others felt deeply the stress of divided loyalties, none more so than Ilene Strelitz. Desperately trying to reconcile Moses and Lowenstein, she was moving to the left politically while retaining strong positive feelings for Lowenstein. Hence, even as she was driven crazy by Al's circuitous syllogisms on the Freedom Summer project, she let herself be used as a vehicle for "annoying [COFO people] with all kinds of questions" and sought to win his favor by saying she would "appear with a sign saying, 'Some of my best friends are power hungry white liberals'" when Moses arrived. Strelitz's pain was almost palpable as she tried to work her way out of the dilemma. She believed in

Al and empathized with "the feeling you must have as so many people lean on you for so many things"; yet she desperately begged him to do whatever he could to help the Mississippi Freedom Democratic Party (MFDP) because "without you there would not have been a summer project."[16]

Others, however, felt simply abandoned and betrayed. Lowenstein's simple message that one person could make a difference had motivated many whites to go to Mississippi. His idealistic faith in democracy had sanctioned their activism. And then he renounced what he had been so deeply involved in creating. Friends and followers were stunned. After Michael Schwerner, Andrew Goodman, and James Chaney, two white volunteers and a black Mississippian, disappeared in Philadelphia, Mississippi, the second week of June, Norman Thomas cabled Lowenstein in Rome: "Developments [in] COFO seem to some parents and me to make your return imperative since you recruited students." Nicholas Bosanquet, the English student from Yale whom Lowenstein had recruited for the Freedom Vote campaign in October, pleaded with Lowenstein to come to Mt. Olive to help out, assuring him that the local SNCC field secretary supported the idea. And when Al did not come, Bosanquet wrote one final letter: "Al—why aren't you here? Your work was crucial in making all this possible. . . . Drop everything and come back. . . . Leave Spain and Southwest Africa—you can't do anything there but exhaust yourself and add to the stream of paper in the world. This is your country. . . . Those ideals which you helped to sow in so many minds are about to reach a supreme test of action. Mississippi needs you this summer." Many felt the same anger and despair. They had been enlisted in this crusade for human dignity because Al Lowenstein had argued how pure, selfless, and idealistic it was; then he pulled out, claiming that the project now involved some impure, Machiavellian plot. "Students in the 1960s . . . were very gripped with the ideas that they were committed to," one Stanford alumnus recalled, "and they thought Al was, too. And when they saw him shift, they were annoyed, upset, perplexed. . . . They began thinking it was hypocrisy." Lowenstein had found them; now he was losing them.[17]

Still, Lowenstein persisted in his ambivalence toward SNCC and the Mississippi project through the end of the summer. On the one hand, he sought to work his behind-the-scenes magic to contain SNCC's influence at the August NSA congress, plotting with NSA leaders to invite anti-SNCC spokesmen like Bayard Rustin to address the conference, making sure that NAACP and CORE representatives had a significant role, and ensuring participation by whites from the Freedom Summer project. "I do not think this strategy should look openly [like] we are trying to gang up on SNCC," one NSA student wrote Lowenstein, "but they should be neutralized as best as they can."[18]

On the other hand, Lowenstein went out of his way to adopt a rhetorical posture similar to SNCC's in his presentation before a national workshop on race and religion in early August. When blacks stalled traffic on New York bridges during the 1964 World's Fair, or engaged in other disruptive acts of civil disobedience, it was too easy for whites to denounce the "stall-ins" as extremist, he declared. Yet, "if you are not sharing in the bounty and goodness of so much material progress in American life, then disrupting it becomes more and more your weapon. . . . No one has yet figured out a way of making people dissatisfied with a pleasant existence without unhinging it." The real stall-in, Lowenstein said, was among white Americans who asked blacks to continue to wait for equality. The removal of legal barriers was a step, but until the gap was closed between white and black incomes, the goal of racial justice remained a distant dream. "So when you hear all this talk about pressing too far, too fast [alongside] complaints about all these outsiders invading Mississippi, you know that no one is pressing anything too far, too fast. It's too slow, too late." For someone who three months earlier had denounced SNCC's endorsement of the stall-ins as misplaced militancy, the August speech represented a significant gesture of reconciliation.[19]

ATLANTIC CITY

The real test, though, came at the Democratic National Convention in Atlantic City, where COFO hoped to win support for replacing the all-white, pro-Goldwater Mississippi party delegation with an integrated delegation representing the Mississippi Freedom Democratic party. All along, one of the purposes of Freedom Summer (and the Freedom Vote campaign) had been to lay the groundwork for a challenge to the Mississippi congressional delegation in January 1965—at which time, if the congressional elections could be shown to have been unfair, then under House rules those chosen in such elections could be turned back. Part of the preparation for that challenge involved collecting affidavits that blacks had been excluded from the electoral process. When it became clear that the same body of evidence could be used to mount a case against the existing rules for delegate selection, the MFDP challenge at Atlantic City became an

objective in its own right. Joseph Rauh, counsel for the United Automobile Workers (UAW), had agreed to represent the MFDP before the credentials committee; an integrated, broad-based delegation had been chosen to go to Atlantic City on behalf of the MFDP; and a compelling case of
intimidation and exclusion had been prepared for presentation. The
MFDP delegates had good reason to believe there would be enough supportive votes to at least bring the issue to the floor for the entire convention to decide.

The MFDP battle was fought over issues of power and control. As the
MFDP delegates soon discovered, Lyndon Johnson did not want *his* convention disrupted by any controversy, particularly one that might alienate
southern whites and limit his drive for a record electoral mandate. To prevent such disruption, Johnson assigned Hubert Humphrey to devise an
acceptable compromise that would keep the issue off the floor; by most
accounts, Johnson made the successful implementation of that compromise the condition for Humphrey's selection as his vice-presidential running mate. So intent was Johnson on getting his wishes that when Mrs.
Fannie Lou Hamer, one of the MFDP's most eloquent witnesses, mesmerized a national TV audience with her testimony about being beaten for
trying to register to vote, Johnson preempted her by holding a sudden
news conference to announce the end of a railroad strike.

The process by which Johnson was eventually successful remains, in
some crucial details, unclear. Rauh had presented his witnesses on Saturday. On Sunday, Congressman Al Ullman, representing the administration's forces, proposed to grant two seats out of forty to the MFDP delegation. At that point, Rauh remained confident that he had the votes to
force a floor fight, which in all likelihood would have resulted in an
MFDP victory of some kind. A committee was set up under the leadership of delegate Walter Mondale, Attorney General of Minnesota and a
Humphrey confidant, to report on Ullman's proposal. That night, in the
suite of Martin Luther King, Jr., Rauh talked to delegates in the living
room. In the bedroom, a smaller meeting was held, allegedly attended by
Bob Moses, Martin Luther King, Jr., and Allard Lowenstein, who had re-
joined the Mississippi forces and was lobbying effectively among delegates on behalf of the MFDP. The next morning, another meeting took
place in Humphrey's suite to discuss the compromise. Lowenstein was
present again, to Rauh's great surprise; "that secret room" took eight
badges to get to, and Lowenstein had not been involved in most MFDP
strategy discussions.

The next day, the UAW chief Walter Reuther called Rauh to describe the latest version of the compromise—two delegates, plus a loyalty oath for future conventions. Reuther urged acceptance of the deal. "This is an order," Reuther said. "You can't give me an order," Rauh responded, pointing out that he was not working on UAW business. In the meantime, the Johnson people picked off Rauh's votes on the credentials committee; one woman was told that if she supported the MFDP, her husband would not get the judgeship he wanted, and a Canal Zone delegate was told that he would lose his job if he did not switch sides. When the credentials committee met that afternoon, the vote fell four votes short of the minimum necessary for Rauh to bring the issue to the convention floor, and the two-vote compromise was accepted, with reporters receiving the erroneous impression that the vote had been unanimous. Furious, Bob Moses ran out of his room upon hearing the news. MFDP delegates felt betrayed, sold out, and abandoned—especially by their liberal allies. Through two days of meetings, they debated what to do about the compromise. Eventually, they rejected it—overwhelmingly. Speaking for the delegation, Fannie Lou Hamer said, contemptuously, "We didn't come all this way for no two votes."[20]

Lowenstein's role in all of this is unclear. In subsequent conversations he had with Ed King and Joe Rauh, he claimed that the two-vote compromise had been discussed the first night in Martin Luther King's bedroom, and that Moses declared, "If that's the best we can do, so be it." Moses denies having said that and recalls that Lowenstein was present only at one large meeting with Humphrey. The other related evidence is equally opaque. Nancy Adams, a close personal friend of Lowenstein's, wrote Al, "What was beautiful was seeing your plan emerge with all its symmetry. Damn shame it didn't come off as you urged; that, dear, is a long, long story." Finally, there is the testimony of Michael Harrington, who was present at a February 1965 meeting with Ella Baker, Bayard Rustin, and James Forman at which Lowenstein berated the group for scapegoating him on the MFDP issue and claimed that *everyone* had been in on the compromise. According to Harrington, those present offered no rebuttal.[21]

What is unmistakably clear, however, is that Lowenstein was *perceived*, particularly by SNCC supporters, as part and parcel of what they considered a "sell-out" to the white liberal establishment. Al himself "wanted to be the convention strategy," Ed King commented. Lowenstein was deeply hostile to Ella Baker, the person in charge of MFDP activities in Washington; he linked her directly to SCEF and the Lawyers' Guild and sought to replace her with Bayard Rustin. Al wanted to be the facilitator who would bring all the sides together, Ed King noted, and although he lobbied effectively for the MFDP position, he really favored the NAACP people in the delegation like Charles Evers and Aaron Henry, who were much more likely to "go along." When Aaron Henry urged acceptance of the compromise and entered the convention hall with delegate's credentials, he was seen as acting in a manner consistent with Lowenstein's politics; although Lowenstein himself disagreed with parts of the compromise—notably, the provision that allowed the Democratic National Committee to name the MFDP delegates rather than let the MFDP choose them itself—he publicly supported the settlement.[22]

Most important of all, though, was the sense that the "deal" was consistent with the kind of behind-the-scenes maneuvers that Lowenstein was now identified with in the minds of many students and SNCC members. "Al was a political animal . . . more than a political activist," John Lewis commented. "[Through his travels and sophistication] he had information. . . . I think people within SNCC . . . had a certain amount of distrust of people . . . [associated] with the so-called 'establishment.' There were people who thought that Al had tried to engineer . . . the compromise." A Stanford student shared the same sense:

> There was lots of backroom horse trading [at Atlantic City]. Al was politically involved. *Operative* is a word that you would use now. He was a guy who . . . was willing to engage in negotiation in a way that didn't make sense to a lot of people . . . younger than Al. I think it was at that point that people began to feel that things weren't entirely genuine, that Al kept a very complex agenda, that despite his amazing gregariousness and engaging manner, that the pattern of activity that he was involved in wasn't really known to anybody. It was difficult for people to contend with.

Certainly, that was the response of students like Dennis Sweeney, whose disillusionment became profound.[23]

We will never know all of what transpired in Atlantic City. In all likelihood, Lowenstein did not initiate the proposal that emerged from the credentials committee. Like his friend Joe Rauh, he probably was more a victim than a perpetrator of "the deal." But whatever the actual truth, the *impression* arose, based on months of tension about the Freedom Summer project, that this was precisely the kind of compromise Lowenstein might have engineered. Therefore, whether he was responsible or not did not matter to many people; it was a question now of underlying values and ideology. As Bob Moses observed, "Atlantic City . . . marks a watershed . . . the [official] end of the consensus on which the movement in Mississippi grew, which was the voter registration work." New rules would prevail after 1964—and new alignments.[24]

As if to confirm that fact, Lowenstein moved more clearly than he ever had before to isolate SNCC. Throughout the spring of 1964, according to Ed King, Al had been toying with the idea of creating a new leadership structure for the Mississippi movement. One person he mentioned as a possible "czar" under the new structure was William Sloane Coffin, the white chaplain at Yale; another was Bayard Rustin. (Coffin was never approached with the suggestion.) The idea, King said, was to make Mississippi susceptible to national influence and simultaneously to "wipe out SNCC."

Now Lowenstein elaborated his plan, presenting to an autumn New York meeting of civil rights and religious groups a blueprint for a new national decision-making structure. The local concerns of people in Mississippi had to give way to "national considerations," one Lowenstein ally told the meeting. Striking the same chord, an NAACP representative declared: "I have been listening to people from Mississippi for seventeen years; I don't want to listen to Steptoe [a black grass-roots leader]. We need a high level meeting so that we can cut away the underbrush. . . . [In Mississippi] we would have to meet with every Tom, Dick and Harry." Understandably, the SNCC representative at the meeting felt like an outlaw. "It is unreal," he said, "as far as Mississippi is concerned, for an ad hoc group to meet in New York and determine what should go on."[25]

At the same time, Lowenstein solidified his ties with Aaron Henry and other more mainstream politicians both in and outside of Mississippi. During the fall of 1964, Lowenstein wrote speeches for Hubert Humphrey, dug up negative information about the activities of the Republican vice-presidential candidate, William Miller, as a strikebreaker, and began his close association with Robert Kennedy in New York. But he also supported Charles Evers and Aaron Henry in their effort to control the Freedom Democrats in Mississippi and sought—both directly and indirectly—to persuade people like Ed King of the wisdom of his position.[26]

Perhaps most reflective of Lowenstein's personal views were the comments of a former student, Kris Kleinbauer, whom he sent to Mississippi to report back to him. (Deeply in love with him, she was more likely than not to tell him things in her letters that reinforced his preexisting beliefs, thereby winning his approval.) "Things are as bad if not worse than you think," she wrote in December. "The stifling of dissent . . . is incredible."

Even the "young, eager, wealthy New Haven types," she said, were mouthing the SNCC party line. The "movement" was spoken of in reverential terms, an effort was growing to oust Henry, and "no one wants to believe that they are being used. . . . Moses spent a day charming [Ed and Jeanette King] . . . and now they're back to where they were when I got here." Lowenstein had been right, she implied, about the cleverness of the famed SNCC method of seeking consensus, and "now I understand why they're able to persuade people that their records are fair (if the real critics are excluded). . . . I don't know what you, or anyone, does next. . . . [These characters are convinced that] they are the people." Reflecting Lowenstein's own disaffection, Kleinbauer's letters suggested that relations between liberals and SNCC had reached a state of near civil war.[27]

The most painful break of all, perhaps, came with former students who had been won over to SNCC's point of view and now found themselves thoroughly alienated from their mentor. Lowenstein had asked the students to believe in the system, to work to secure the vote, and once it was secured, to use established electoral processes as a means of achieving further change. Now Bob Moses was saying that "the best way to keep a man a slave is to give him a vote and call him free," and Dennis Sweeney was declaring, "Does voting make a man free? . . . Clearly it doesn't." Lowenstein defended the results of the Democratic convention. "Far from being a 'betrayal' or a 'defeat,'" he argued in 1965, "Atlantic City was one of the greatest proofs of the vitality of American democracy—when the President of the United States, at the height of his power, was forced—by the aroused conscience of the nation—to move, to compromise." Yet to SNCC, the compromise had been a sellout, ending up with two delegates—named by someone else—instead of the forty the MFDP deserved and might have had were it not for opportunistic wheeling-dealing by power brokers. What Atlantic City really signified, Dennis Sweeney commented, "[is that] democratic politics isn't all it's cracked up to be." Like a geological fault line, the divisions between Lowenstein and SNCC—and many of the whites he had recruited to SNCC—had widened to the point where reconciliation and reunion were impossible.[28]

REFLECTIONS

"More is going to be revealed about Al by looking at Mississippi than anything else he was involved in," Ed King once observed. Although King may have overstated the case, his fundamental insight was on target. From start to finish—his inspirational outreach to students, his passionate commitment to democratic reform "within the system," his bold and visionary strategy, and the alienation and bitter disillusionment—the story of white students and the civil rights struggle in Mississippi is a paradigm of Allard Lowenstein's political life. Few episodes more effectively crystallized the values that guided his activities, the style he used, his attitudes toward decision-making and power, or the dynamics that explained people's responses to him.

The first source of tension between Lowenstein and SNCC proved symptomatic of all the rest—namely, the controversy over who conceived the idea for the Freedom Vote, and then for Freedom Summer. Fifteen years after the fact, Lowenstein told a Mississipi audience that "*I* decided" not to have people go back to the regular polling places to try to vote, but instead to have them cast their ballots at sites within the black community; "*that,*" he said, "was the genesis of the idea of the Freedom Ballot." Repeatedly during the intervening years, as well as at the time, Lowenstein claimed authorship of the idea with students and other friends. He even wrote in pencil on the back of a 1963 press release on the Freedom Vote that "the whole thing started in my bedroom." Lowenstein's understanding of the entire process was reflected in an interview he gave to the *Stanford Daily* in 1965: "When I first got to Mississippi," he said, "everything was finished. The whites had won." Thus, one could infer that Lowenstein had rescued a dying movement and turned it around with his idea for the Freedom Vote, and then Freedom Summer.[29]

SNCC staff members, however, had a very different version. They had already run candidates in congressional contests who had no chance to win. Through the legal research of Timothy Jenkins, *they* had found an old statute that allowed people who were not registered to cast ballots and challenge the existing voting lists. Moreover, they were already committed to a "mock" election of some sort in the fall of 1963. Thus, the foundation had already been prepared for the Freedom Vote campaign, with only the details of implementation to be worked out. Clearly, these details were critical, and Lowenstein was responsible for many of them. Still, the groundwork had been laid and SNCC's own ideas existed parallel to those of Lowenstein.

More to the point, SNCC resented anyone trying, or needing, to take credit single-handedly for any idea. "I have no real recollection how the concept of the Freedom Vote was generated," Robert Moses observed, "but . . . one of the things about the movement, particularly in Mississippi, was that no one was really concerned with whose idea this or that was. . . . So the idea that it was important to record who first had such and such an idea is itself sort of foreign to the whole culture of the Movement as it developed." In short, claiming a "patent" to an idea was antithetical to the organic and collective nature of the movement itself. "Who you want to give credit to . . . really wasn't a question anybody ever [discussed]," Moses said.[30]

In all likelihood, the truth lay somewhere in between. As Ed King subsequently observed, "Al deserved more credit than SNCC gave him and less credit than he took." In King's view, Lowenstein was the primary source for the specifics of the Freedom Vote campaign. He had been to South Africa, he saw the analogy to Mississippi, and he understood the dramatic publicity potential of mobilizing 80,000 black ballots and importing white students. But he was not the initial, the prime, or the sole source of the idea; so much had gone before—the candidacies of Bill Higgs in 1960 and R. L. T. Smith in 1962, and the research of the SNCC staff into all the legal issues. "SNCC [was] right," King said; "these kinds of moves preceded Al's idea to move . . . to something beyond running for Congress. . . . [But Al never] understood how ready we were. . . . I don't think he ever grasped that, and he resented SNCC's feeling that he wasn't the absolute father creator. And then when SNCC criticized him, his resentment got stronger . . . and the tension just got worse . . . and by the end of the '64 summer, it could never have been bridged anywhere." In retrospect at least, the question of how an idea originated seems of far less importance than what happened to the idea; yet the controversy highlighted all the other issues that more profoundly separated Lowenstein from SNCC.[31]

Among other things, the Freedom Vote discussion reflected a dramatically different conception of how decision-making should take place. SNCC developed a community-based style of organizing that was premised on the idea that every person had the right to participate in setting and implementing policy. SNCC field workers received $10 a week, lived with sharecroppers and laborers, and sought to become one with the communities they served. It was all well and good to have "experts," Ivanhoe Donaldson observed, but SNCC's goal "was to allow people to grow and develop in their own way." That meant not *telling* them what to do, but having them decide for themselves. Many whites in the movement shared that sensibility. "When we got into the movement," Casey Hayden, a white SNCC worker from Texas, noted, "we dropped all our socially defined . . . roles . . . everybody's in their work shirts and we're all doing one thing." Wearing overalls was part of that process; listening carefully to someone with poor diction and no education was another. In part, the whole idea was romantic—this was the "beloved community" that Bob Moses talked about, where everyone shared equally their concern for and commitment to each other, united by a bond of Christian love. But it was also the real world, at least for many black Mississippians.[32]

Lowenstein was unaccustomed to such a modus operandi. Fast-paced, quick-moving, darting from place to place, he liked to size up situations, make plans, get people started, and then move on. He had little patience for interminable meetings, none for inefficiency and delay. In Lowenstein's eyes, it was possible for people with sophistication and knowledge to analyze a situation, design a plan, and give orders for its implementation. He believed in experts and was confident enough in his own political intelligence to know that few people could match him in strategic insight. His lightning trip to Mississippi in July 1963 encapsulated much of his method. Quickly grasping the urgency of the crisis, he made the creative leap to the South Africa analogy, brainstormed the idea for a Freedom Vote (perhaps ignoring or overlooking what had already been done in that direction), then set out on his own—consulting little with others—to recruit the elite college students to put the plan into effect.

This difference in approach reflected an ongoing tension within Lowenstein himself over which kind of liberalism he would espouse. On the one hand, he obviously felt comfortable with an elitist, top-down attitude toward social reform: the "best and the brightest" should act on behalf of the poor and disenfranchised; they had a moral obligation to preserve and protect American ideals. On the other hand, Lowenstein occasionally embraced a more populist liberalism; he did understand the importance of empowerment for groups of people, and the critical need for those at the bottom to decide for themselves what was good or bad about their society. His appreciation for the Republican fighters in the Spanish civil war and for the freedom struggle of the African National Congress testified to his ability to empathize with this more radical and collective form of liberalism.

In effect, the Mississippi experience placed in bold relief the tension between these two approaches to liberalism with Lowenstein in this instance coming down decisively on the side of the more conservative, individualist, and elitist interpretation of the term. "Here we were talking about 'Every man a leader,'" Lawrence Guyot said, "and they were talking about 'Every man must be led.'" When Al came up with a brilliant idea, Ed King noted,

> he could not understand why a group of SNCC leaders in the room couldn't decide right then and there that's what SNCC would do. . . . [But] people said we've got to talk about it. . . . The people who are suffering, the people on the bottom have something to say . . . not as a lawyer, not as an expert economist, but they do know what they need. And this was very hard for Al to take. . . . [He] wanted . . . his own version of democratic centralism, where the leaders know what is right for the people, and then can decide it. And the people will be told and will follow.[33]

To be sure, on one level, Lowenstein understood the importance of respecting local wishes. "Never give advice as long as an outsider," he jotted in pencil on one Freedom Summer brochure, "never tell people to undergo what you won't have to." But at another level, he could not tolerate the gap between his way of operating and SNCC's. He was result-oriented; the SNCC staff cared more about process. He focused on Washington and legislation. They cared more about grass-roots pride and self-esteem. He wanted answers to questions, preferably ten minutes ago. They had to consult. He was the one who was recruiting the student volunteers and felt he should be in charge of their activities. SNCC insisted that all decisions be made by people on the ground and in the community. "Basically, I think Al thought it was ludicrous for staff to run [things]," Moses said. "My . . . idea was that people who ran the risks needed to be in control of the decisions, [but Al thought there should] be some board and then the staff works for the board and the board makes the policy decisions." One model elevated hierarchy and decisiveness; the other promoted egalitarianism and tolerated ambiguity. Clearly, Al preferred the former, and in the end he was driven to propose a virtual takeover of local Mississippi decision-making by the national directorate in New York. His concern with structure had some merit and might have served as a healthy counterpoint to SNCC's commitment to "participatory democracy." But in an atmosphere increasingly charged by ideological and racial tensions, the two positions became polarized, with reconciliation impossible.[34]

Nowhere was this conflict more pronounced than on the question of whether the National Lawyers' Guild and SCEF should be welcomed into COFO's ranks. Here, Lowenstein believed, a command decision was needed. With their subversive pasts (according to him), these groups, once given a toehold, would take over the movement and destroy its credibility. Any organization worth its salt, he believed, should act decisively to remove such a potential cancer with surgical precision. A profound anti-Communist, he was convinced that the Lawyers' Guild was a party-line institution that, by definition, should be excluded from any freedom movement. As one of his students observed, "Liberals are as ideological as anyone else. It's not just the left-wing sects that have their litmus tests," and for Lowenstein, any hint of Communist affiliation constituted such a litmus test.[35]

But SNCC had a different perspective. Not only did it welcome all support, whatever its source, but it also refused to be crippled by someone else's inherited political baggage. "There was an effort continually not to let the bad . . . relations from the past really interfere with the work we were doing," Moses remarked. "We did not let Forman's feelings about Al prevent us from working with [him] . . . [and we had the] same point of view about the National Lawyers' Guild people. . . . [We just didn't want] bad leftover feelings from the past being foisted on us." Many SNCC supporters seriously doubted the allegations about the Lawyers' Guild's subversive activities and attitudes. But even had they shared Lowenstein's perception about the Guild's past, they would still have disagreed with him. As Lawrence Guyot observed, "When [Al] looked at a situation, and we looked at it, we were looking at the same fact pattern from a totally different frame of reference." SNCC's approach was inclusive and nonjudgmental, Lowenstein's exclusive and punitive. Indeed, there were some SNCC supporters—white as well as black—who were convinced that Lowenstein was using the issue primarily "as a means of attempting to get rid of rivals."[36]

All these issues came down to the question of control—whose movement was this, and who would determine its direction? In his role as a uniter of two generations of liberals, Al was accustomed to entering a situation as the charismatic hero who inspired young undergraduates with his energy, his eloquence, and his idealism. With a devoted army ready to follow him, *he* was in control, and young students were prepared to do his bidding. But SNCC was different. "We weren't dazzled," Ed King commented. "SNCC felt they could pick and choose ideas from anywhere, be it [from] Lowenstein, the Lawyers' Guild, or Ghandi. . . . Al would not have impressed SNCC the way he would have impressed a group at NSA." Hence, SNCC never was ready to automatically accept Lowenstein's leadership; indeed, SNCC staff members were deeply suspicious of anyone who presumed such authority. And that response was both unsettling and unfamiliar to Lowenstein. "Al was not comfortable with the idea . . . that you had this little . . . group of people that no one knows down in Mississippi who are sort of calling the shots on him." He wanted to give the orders, not take them.[37]

Perhaps appropriately, the issue of control became a metaphor around which almost all the internal disputes of the movement revolved. Thus, Lowenstein fought vigorously against the Lawyers' Guild and SCEF because he insisted that if they were welcomed into the movement, they would soon take it over and shape it to their own ends. But to Moses, that argument was full of irony "because, in trying to keep them out, you're trying to do what *you* say *they* want to do. I mean, you're [saying], 'They're going to come in and tell us who we can associate with'—that's why you don't want them in. [But] you're doing that right now." Moreover, the assumption that one could dictate such terms seemed inherently paternalistic. "We're our own people," Moses pointed out, "and are able to figure out who we want to associate with . . . [and] you don't really credit us with being able to do that, [as if] we are somehow people that need to be protected and you are the people to protect us." So the issue of who would control the movement reflected volatile themes of race and class as well as organizational style.[38]

Political values and ideology were also pivotal. More than anything else, Lowenstein believed passionately in the workability of American democracy. His politics were those of a liberal reformer who believed that change could be achieved *within* the existing political system by using the values of that system to remedy its inadequacies. The system itself was sound, and one could achieve tangible progress only by staying inside it. SNCC, on the other hand, threatened to burst out of the system and call into question the values and rules undergirding it. Its grass-roots emphasis, insistence on collective decision-making, and identification with the poor raised the specter of a revolutionary movement that would wage war on the existing structure of authority, as well as the values it represented. "[Al had an] intuition that SNCC was a radical force . . . that he could [not] control, influence, understand and predict," Ed King observed, "and that might quickly drift to the left." Hence, "he wanted to head off people before they reached alienation from the system."[39]

In part, of course, that political perspective simply represented his own experience. Al had grown up in a liberal Democratic tradition, believing in the programs of the New Deal, the reality of a Communist conspiracy, and the possibility of achieving reform—including racial equality—through the existing electoral process. It was an ideology that presumed a certain level of comfort and confidence. Casey Hayden had her own explanation for what made people liberal or radical. "It all depended on what [they] saw when they woke up in the morning," she said. "Al's in a nice apartment, he looks out the window, there's Central Park. And Stokely [Carmichael] wakes up in Greenwood [Mississippi] and looks out, and there's a lot of hungry people. . . . Once people have had certain life experiences, they're radicalized. If they haven't, they aren't. . . . Al just never got there. . . . It was almost like he walked around with this building around him . . . that Central Park West building." Al, of course, had his own version of that scenario. As he saw it, a group of Old Left people had combined with New Left allies to use the romantic vision of participatory democracy as a facade behind which to promote irresponsible left-wing elitism. The romanticization of participatory democracy would simply serve as a facade behind which a calculating cadre of revolutionaries plotted to seize power.[40]

In the end, not surprisingly, the issue of control proved decisive to Lowenstein's break with the Mississippi movement. In his view, he had created the idea that had rescued that movement from oblivion and had then mobilized the white foot soldiers who generated the publicity and national outrage that made success possible in Mississippi. He had carried the torch of liberal activism successfully to the next generation. Yet neither his authorship nor his authority had been acknowledged. Despite his insistent efforts to clarify who was in charge, he had been denied access to the inner circle and his politically shrewd warnings about "leftist" infiltration had been snubbed and ignored. By the spring and summer of 1964, he decided that there was no way he could continue to support a project that he had conceived (by his lights) if he were not allowed to determine the ground rules and to feel comfortable with its organizational structure. Thus, he broke with Freedom Summer, he left in the lurch many who had joined the project at his urging, and eventually, he waged his own miniwar to deprive SNCC of political and financial support, even going so far as to stop a New York foundation from funding a SNCC-based newspaper project. The irony was that it was evidently all right for students to challenge authority and rebel against the "establishment" if Lowenstein was leading the charge—as at Stanford—but verboten if he was expected to be one of the foot soldiers instead.[41]

Tragically, because Lowenstein saw his political beliefs as a direct extension of his person, he perceived anyone who disagreed with him as a personal as well as political antagonist. If he was single-handedly responsible for "saving" the Mississippi movement and devising the Freedom Vote and Freedom Summer, anyone who doubted his role or questioned his authority over those ventures took on the character of an enemy. "I learned the word 'betrayal' from Al," Armin Rosencranz noted. "It was one of his favorite words. Betrayal. Treachery. These are words that he used as easily as [Coca-Cola]." "If you had any doubts," Skip Martin said, "you were somehow the enemy . . . helping to cause splits and what not."[42]

Indeed, if anyone not for you was against you, then it became very easy to see the world in terms of plots and schemes and to retaliate. "[Al] was a conspiratist," Geoff Cowan, a friend and civil rights worker, said, "[and] he would be mean about people. . . . If you were against him, you were part of some conspiracy, and the conspiracy generally had no good origin." Much of Al's anticommunism, in fact, was connected to this view of "evil forces" out there scheming to defeat his moral ideas. As one student later noted, "The whole split, when he felt people were being disloyal to him . . . was all wrapped up in the cold war business."[43]

Such a personalized definition of right and wrong, however, made it excruciatingly painful for students who had been devoted Lowenstein followers and now found themselves asked to pass the test of personal loyalty. "There was a lot of moral absolutism going around," Nancy Steffen observed, and a lot of anguish for those who could not in good conscience agree with Al 100 percent. Throughout his career as a student organizer, Al had used surrogate leaders who were tied intensely to him by their veneration for his insight and wisdom. But when these students went off and experienced their own version of reality, whether in Mississippi or elsewhere, they inevitably developed different ideas. To Lowenstein, that was impermissible. "It was so difficult to have legitimate differences [with him]," Skip Martin said, "and if you got into one of those arguments, you were in danger of having a break. Al would decide you were the enemy." So a follower either was totally subservient to Lowenstein or eventually became alienated; he seemed to allow no middle ground.

By the end of 1964, many of the students Lowenstein had inspired at Stanford had experienced the pain of these expectations. Dennis Sweeney had been a devoted follower of Lowenstein, who cared deeply for his young protégé. But Sweeney had become radicalized by his SNCC experience, and in a reciprocal dance of torture and agony, the two came to see each other as symbols of what had gone wrong in the civil rights movement. For Sweeney, Lowenstein was "the enemy" of SNCC and a liberal apologist for the "white power structure"; for Lowenstein, Sweeney illustrated how SNCC had turned "his" people against him and plotted to undermine his leadership. Ilene Strelitz and Nancy Steffen had similar experiences. Both were in love with Lowenstein, almost worshiping him. But they, too, were developing doubts about his political stance and were tormented by the impossibility of defining political positions for themselves that allowed them to continue their personal relationships with Lowenstein while preserving their own integrity.[44]

Almost self-destructively, therefore, Allard Lowenstein had set in motion a process by which he "lost" those he had "found." Wrapped up in his own vision of how to save America, he insisted on making *his* program the sole basis for collective action. Conceivably, a different posture by Lowenstein might have resulted in a greater likelihood that black/white and liberal/radical tensions could have been ameliorated. Had Lowenstein remained inside the SNCC-led coalition, he might have been able to bring his political wisdom to bear as part of the larger give and take of movement politics, with constructive results for everyone. Yet that was not to be. Tragically, the same genius that allowed Lowenstein to inspire a generation of students to work on behalf of racial justice also constituted the hubris that drove him to want to control their activism, instead of joining their ranks as part of a larger collective process. In a prophetic letter from Mississippi, Sam Beard, another Lowenstein protégé, penetrated to the core of what had happened. "You deserve a round of applause . . . as one of the architects of change," he wrote. Like the mythical hero in Albert Camus's *Myth of Sisyphus* (1942), Lowenstein had pried the boulder "off its precarious perch" and begun the struggle for reform. But in taking the responsibility for that beginning, Lowenstein must also "ride [the boulder], follow it, [and] maybe be crushed by it."

If, in the end, Lowenstein *was* crushed, it was because he did not heed Beard's next line. "The forces you unleash are larger than something you can individually control and keep in balance." It was a lesson that Lowenstein would not easily learn.[45]

9

The Personal *Side* of the Political

At the heart of the dynamic between Allard Lowenstein and his student followers was a phenomenon emphasized by feminist historians and activists in the 1970s—the political is personal, and the personal is political. How we behave in our public lives inevitably reflects values, attitudes, and experiences embedded in our private lives, and vice versa. Far from being compartmentalized, then, our personal and political activities, rooted in common emotions and motivations, constantly overlap, informing each other, and drawing from the same reservoirs of belief and ideology, need and desire.

More than most public figures, Allard Lowenstein vividly illustrated this link. His mode of recruitment for political activity was a deeply personal appeal to potential supporters that highlighted the individual bond uniting leader and follower. As observer after observer noted, Lowenstein's style of political activism was not "collegial" but rather based on a one-to-one appeal—hence the vocabulary of individual betrayal that came to characterize political disagreements between Lowenstein and his former supporters, and the bitterness and anguish that accompanied the process of separation. It was almost as though the political arena were a public stage for acting out a personal psychodrama, with many of Lowenstein's public activities reflecting an agenda rooted in his private struggles.[1]

For that reason, those caught up in the vortex of Lowenstein's life frequently pondered the more subterranean influences that seemed to shape his behavior. This was especially true for those who suddenly found themselves outside the chosen circle of believers. Like children disillusioned by a fallen hero, they sought to understand what had happened to disrupt the idealistic journey toward reform that they had started with Allard Lowenstein just a few short years—or months—before. And as they pursued that question, at least some discovered in their mutual reflections a complexity and ambivalence in Lowenstein's private life that seemed to correlate with—and explain—what they found most problematic in his public life.

MAKING THE PERSONAL THE BASIS FOR THE POLITICAL

In many ways, Lowenstein's extraordinary appeal to the young rested upon his own sense of inferiority and unacceptability. His constant references to himself as "an ugly duckling" bespoke a larger perception of himself as someone not worthy of anyone's attention. Even as an acknowledged politician in the 1960s and 1970s, according to Jennifer Littlefield, he would initiate phone conversations by announcing his name with a question mark in his tone, as if no one would recognize him or want to talk with him. Self-consciously, other friends pointed out, he would denigrate his physical appearance, commenting on his big nose, his poor eyesight, his inability even to choose matching socks. "There was a part of him that always felt terribly shy and awkward and unself-confident," Littlefield noted; ironically, he was supremely certain about the correctness of his political views and analysis, while feeling totally inadequate about his personal acceptability.[2]

With very few exceptions, Lowenstein sought his validation not from his own peers but from either the very young or the very old. In part, that was because of the simplicity of such relationships. "[A kind of] uncritical affection . . . was possible for him with both naive young people and older people," the former *Stanford Daily* editor Nancy Steffen noted. With Frank Porter Graham or Eleanor Roosevelt or Norman Thomas, he could experience a purity of devotion that bypassed the more engaged and conflicted involvement of same-age relationships. Something similar happened in his relationships with the young. "When you are seventeen or eighteen . . . or into your early twenties," one close Lowenstein associate remarked, "there's a lot of real doubt as to whether you measure up.

[You're vulnerable,] and if a person as accomplished and bright as Al . . .
was interested in you . . . then you became attached to him." The result
was something like simple hero-worship.[3]

Perhaps not surprisingly, Lowenstein also sought out people with the
qualities he thought he lacked. Thus, as Kris Kleinbauer noted, the most
likely objects of Al's attention "[were] the best looking and the smartest."
These people did not have "thick glasses" or big noses but were handsome, well dressed, apparently secure, and more often than not white
Anglo-Saxon Protestants—precisely those most likely to be found at NSA
congresses, Stanford, Yale, and the other schools where Lowenstein taught
during these years. Given his own sense of unworthiness, Lowenstein cultivated such people by magnifying the qualities that made them so attractive in the first place. "He always elevated you to a level of importance
that you really shouldn't be at," one of his more acerbic critics observed,
"[and] people loved that." Barbara Boggs was always introduced as the
"funniest person in the world"; Greg Craig and his roommate, Rich Hammond, were presented to Norman Thomas as the "two leaders of the Harvard revolution." It was a heady experience. "There was such a magnetic
quality about Al," the reporter Steve Roberts recalled, "and I think it was
partly because he made younger people feel so important . . . he made
them feel they were involved in something bigger than themselves."[4]

Yet the very nature of the recruitment process proved destructive to
long-term intimacy, not least because expectations for the relationship so
rapidly faded in the light of everyday reality. "You may have been introduced and talked about as one of the rare few," a former Stanford student,
Patti Hagen, observed, "but then you weren't . . . treated that way." Instead, young followers were demoted to making phone calls to "advance"
Lowenstein's next visit, inventing excuses for his tardiness, or even lying
on his behalf so that someone would think he was detained by an urgent
meeting when in fact he was having a shave. "One of the things that made
Al so appealing," the California politician Gary Hart said, was his ability
to convey "the sense that you were someone who was terribly important in
his life . . . but it also ended up disillusioning people, because . . . you've
been told by this man, 'You're one of my closest friends' . . . [and then
you discover] there are so many other people . . . waiting in line" who
have the same impression. The gap between expectation and reality could
be shattering.[5]

Worst of all, the imbalance of the relationship often generated a feeling
of inferiority and inadequacy in the followers that, in its own way, repli-

cated the sense of inferiority that had fueled Lowenstein's quest for the relationship in the first place. Most of these young people felt awed by Lowenstein—not just by the pace of his life but by his brilliance, his articulateness, his range of associates, his commanding presence. How could an eighteen-year-old *not* feel inferior? "I am unconvinced (but glad) that you feel I deserve all those kind words," Kris Kleinbauer wrote Al, "because whenever I am around you I always feel hopelessly inadequate. You are unbelievably good . . . witty, intelligent . . . and fun . . . but it always overwhelms me and I can never think of anything to say." Even the best and brightest of his followers succumbed. "The hopes for one's leadership from Al were always beyond what you felt you were able to perform," Greg Craig noted. "You always fell short. . . . He would identify you as a critically important . . . historic figure. . . . Then you do your bit, and [there's this awful] sense of disappointment."[6]

The devastating impact of the "reverse" inferiority complex fell full force on Rich Hammond, another Lowenstein protégé. Hammond had been president of his class at Exeter four years in a row, captained the Harvard soccer team, and was first marshall of his graduating class. Apolitical through his early college years, Hammond first became fascinated by Lowenstein during the summer of 1966. After a series of conversations about Africa, civil rights, and the peace movement, Lowenstein asked Hammond if he wanted to "do the rounds" with him in New York City. Although not aware in advance that this would mean twenty-hour days of driving Lowenstein to various appointments with politicos, African exiles, and writer friends, Hammond responded with alacrity. "He made a very big deal about who I was," Hammond recalled, once introducing him to Hubert Humphrey as the man who "runs Harvard." The two also shared deeply personal moments, once staying up until dawn on a Central Park West bench when Lowenstein told Hammond of his hope that they might be "best friends."

Later that summer, the two went on an auto trip from Washington, D.C., to Chapel Hill, then to Nag's Head. (It was a trip Lowenstein took often with young friends.) As the journey unfolded, so did Hammond's "growing awareness and self-consciousness about the disparity of my own talents, knowledge, [and] intellectual capabilities, and Al's." Feeling unable to hold up his end of conversations or to even move in the same circles as Lowenstein, Hammond "felt very insecure and . . . unequal to the task of being in Al's world." Once, finding himself on the wrong side of an interstate highway, he even began to fantasize about his responsibility for get ting Al killed in an accident, when he was "such an important resource to mankind." Mortified at his inadequacy, he became almost paralyzed by the imbalance in the relationship. "I was suddenly so aware of this gap. . . . Some of it had to do with a sense that the only role that there was for me in this relationship was to run around and make phone calls and be the driver [and] I couldn't even drive the car straight." But above all there was the difference between the equality that seemed implicit in the notion of being "best friends" and the pervasive inequality that then emerged. "I was so emotional about it that I couldn't talk. I just started to try to talk and I broke down." The ride back to Washington was a silent one, Al angry at Hammond's emotional state, Hammond unable to express himself.

Later, Hammond put in a letter his feelings about the three-hour silence. "I was tired of your patronage," Hammond wrote Al, and he resented Al's hyperbolic praise of even his most pedestrian political observations. Conversely, he found unnecessary Al's constant taunts about whipping his butt in wrestling. "Did I spend all my time at the beach trying to goad you into a race along the shore?" he asked. But above all, Hammond was bothered by the feeling that "you don't really have time for the kind of friendship we talked about one night in front of your place in New York." Hammond could neither keep up with nor fit into Al's world; nor could he be "your close friend, the way I once naively envisioned it." Like countless other Lowenstein supporters, he would look forward to brief visits, occasional postcards, and perhaps even participation in a campaign.

> I'll accept the fact that you'll be late to every meeting and then spend half the time away making phone calls, and I'll shake my head and laugh and say, "Good old Al." . . . But I don't see how I can be much else, Al. I've never really been skilled at a close relationship entirely on the other person's terms. I mean I'm not good at having my head patted all the time. . . . I'm not good at being constantly complimented or criticized according to the chance depth of a naive observation. All of these things I can do as just an acquaintance, or as an employee. But as a close friend—uh, uh. It's just not for me, if for no other reason than that my ego's a trifle more demanding.[7]

Hammond's experience encapsulated the complexity and self-destructiveness of the Lowenstein protégé relationship. One did, in fact, become an acolyte—to serve but not question, to respond but not challenge, to share intimacy but not receive it back. There were rewards. "Somehow you were loved and strengthened by his advice and counsel," his close friend Bruce Payne observed. But then there was the downside. "You always stayed something of a child . . . he always knew about your weaknesses and problems [and] there was some way in which he wouldn't allow you to grow . . . [but had] to keep people in their place as his minions." There was the rub. For how could you be a best friend if you were not allowed to think of yourself—or to act—as an equal?

In the end, therefore, political disagreements became issues of betrayal because, for Lowenstein, the political could not be separated from the personal. To disagree was to assert oneself and presume some measure of autonomy. Yet since most of Lowenstein's political recruiting was based on making people his acolytes, protégés, or disciples—all terms used interchangeably by Al's young friends—autonomy was a logical impossibility. Indeed, such roles permitted no challenge or dissent. "For all his openness and talk of the democratic process," the young Harold Ickes noted, "[Al] was, in my view . . . a democratic centralist . . . who had to control the agenda . . . in both personal and political relationships." Precisely because "everything he did revolved around him," former Stanford student Jim Haas observed, "he never gave people the [possibility] of creating something that wasn't totally dependent upon him."[8]

Sustaining a long-term relationship with Lowenstein thus became almost impossible. "You had to keep it in perspective at all times," Greg Craig noted. "It was like a moth near the flame. If you didn't keep your own independence and your own judgment intact . . . your relationship would die because you'd go into the flame. . . . But [on the other hand] you always had to give enough so that [Al] would be there for you. . . . It was a delicate balance." Despite enormous tension and strain, Craig succeeded in holding onto the relationship. "I think I am the only person who did it for [so] long," he said. But even he could continue only by periodically distancing himself from Al. "It was a question of whether I was going to allow myself to be drawn into the flame again." Then, with additional reflection, came Craig's final assessment: "It was not [really] distancing, it was . . . self-preservation."[9]

SEXUALITY

For a significant number of young men during these years, the anxiety over how to relate to Allard Lowenstein was compounded by concern that his personal interest might include the desire for some kind of homosexual attachment as well. In an era characterized by ignorance, prejudice, fear, and hysteria about same-sex relationships, it was not surprising that these young people responded with apprehension and confusion about Lowenstein's intentions. In reality, Lowenstein himself appears to have been as confused as anybody. Nevertheless, it became ever more apparent in the early 1960s that the need to express physical affection toward other men was an abiding quest for Al Lowenstein—and a problem that both exemplified and nourished his larger search for intimacy and identity.

Going back to his high school diary entry, Lowenstein had always evinced a powerful interest in close same-sex relationships. The intensity of his relationships with other men—and the difficulty of his relationships with women—became a prominent feature of his life. Issues of sexual attraction between men comprised a familiar topic of conversation for Lowenstein in the 1940s and 1950s. One close male friend from college wrote Lowenstein repeatedly about the friend's occasional infatuation with young men students, implying that he and Lowenstein had talked about this in the past. During the 1950s, as we have seen, Lowenstein devoted one of his lengthier papers at Yale Law School to sexual practices among the young—including homosexual practices; and as a counselor at Yale, he had numerous conversations with students that revolved around questions of sexual identity. Lowenstein alluded to at least one homosexual experience he had while in the army, and a letter from a navy friend suggested that a conversation about issues of homosexuality had occurred between them. "My honesty and health have never really been questioned by the Navy," the friend wrote. "From this I think you will get an idea why I was discharged. Would like you to keep this letter [to] yourself."[10]

Whatever Lowenstein's actual sexual experience prior to the 1960s, his contact with attractive male students at various universities during that decade intensified his pursuit of physical relationships with young men. At Stanford, as elsewhere, Lowenstein was selective in choosing those to whom he made advances. Ordinarily, they were attractive, preppy young men who were sensitive, reflective, and open about their own doubts and anxieties. Almost all were "straight"—confused perhaps about their sexuality, but still oriented, for the moment at least, to the heterosexual world. Lowenstein appeared to have a sixth sense about who might be approachable. For some, there was never even a hint that he might be interested in more than conversation; others uneasily deflected his advances and, for a long time, never talked about the experience with anyone. But by the late 1960s, enough of Lowenstein's Stanford associates had tentatively

217

broached the topic to each other that it became clear they all had participated in a common Lowenstein ritual—one that involved a substantial number of the "best and brightest" young men he met there.[11]

The scenario was almost always the same, albeit with some important variations. Frequently, a long automobile trip was involved, with an overnight stay at a motel. Lowenstein would go to the desk clerk and return saying that the only available room had just one bed. Or the place would be his stepmother's New York apartment, where, again, one sleeping possibility was a double bed. "A number of us had the same experience," a former Stanford student recalled. "Somehow, a situation would arise . . . [where] you'd be spending the night with Al. . . . Through physical contact . . . it was clear that Al wanted more than simply spending the night in the same bed . . . [the way] one would spend the night with your brothers in a Boy Scout tent."[12]

Sometimes a verbal initiative preceded any effort at physical contact. After indicating that they would be sleeping in the same bed, Al told one Stanford associate "that the highest form of personal relationship, as in Greek times . . . was between two men, and that he was interested in pursuing that with me. I said I just couldn't handle that," and nothing further happened. Even when explicit discussion about same-sex relationships did not precede sleeping in the same bed, however, there usually had been intense conversation about critical life issues that created a context of intimacy for the physical advances that followed. In almost all these cases, Lowenstein's desires seemed limited to being held tight and to hugging the other man back—itself a rather ambiguous expression of need. Thus, while one might fear he was the object of a homosexual advance, "what [the encounter really] did was raise lots of questions."[13]

Confusion and consternation became the normative responses to Lowenstein's actions—responses that gradually came to be talked about by a number of good friends who had shared similar experiences with Al. At a time when even the mention of same-sex encounters was culturally impermissible, it took a special kind of confidant to evoke, on a one-to-one basis, such revelations. Armin Rosencranz, the graduate student who was elected student body president after Lowenstein's departure from Stanford, was ideally situated to be that confidant. Worldly-wise and older than most of Lowenstein's student friends, yet often in contact with them because of their prominence as campus leaders, he naturally engaged in numerous conversations about Al. After a while, his familiarity with the basic story became such that when a former student approached him nervously to express concern about a furtive experience with Al, Rosencranz could reply, "Surely you're not anxious about having shared a bed with Lowenstein. . . . [And] it was like a weight was lifted from their shoulders. They would say, 'Oh, God' and . . . be absolutely delighted to learn that . . . several others, indeed everyone else practically that was in that age group . . . had shared the same experience."[14]

Nevertheless, anxiety was inevitable. "[Al] wanted to [make these advances]," another friend noted, and "[they came] at a time in one's life when you are most . . . vulnerable . . . and out there experimenting." Al may not have consciously exploited the young, but he certainly planted seeds of doubt. For one young friend, in particular, Lowenstein's approaches were a "deep, dark secret" until one day a fellow student tentatively asked, "How do you deal with Al at night," and as with the Rosencranz group, it was a liberating question. "I said, 'You mean you too?'. . . I mean it was for me. . . like $50,000 worth of psychotherapy. . . because suddenly there was somebody I could share this with."[15]

By the late 1960s, others had joined the network of the "cognoscenti." Nancy Steffen learned from David Harris that Al had wanted to "cuddle with him." Other observers noted "that particular quirk [about Al, his] . . . repressed sexual attraction for blossoming WASP-y men." More people began to comment on Al's love of wrestling, and his choice of wrestling partners. "Al just got a lot of his joy of living out of having these really eager young guys around him in close contact," a former Stanford colleague remarked. "[One could] see [the wrestling] as a physical side to the bonding that was taking place, because people would say, well there were certain guys who were chosen for that activity."[16]

In Rosencranz's view, Lowenstein's behavior seemed "unconventional . . . at the outer edge of acceptable behavior," but still acceptable. It was all "midway," he later said, "sort of [an] unfulfilled, unrealized, sublimated kind of homosexuality. . . . You talk long into the night about the person's most intimate secrets. You try to reveal some of your intimate thoughts, although he never gave as much as he took in these kind of exchanges. . . . And he got off on that." Clearly, trying to define a "place" for such same-sex relationships had become a preoccupation for Lowenstein at Stanford and afterward; but what that meant for his overall existence remained murky. In Rosencranz's words, Lowenstein was living on "the borderline," seemingly unsure just where his own boundaries should be.[17]

All these strands of uncertainty came together most clearly in the summer of 1965, when Allard Lowenstein became director of the Encampment for Citizenship (EFC) at the Fieldston school in Riverdale, New York. This "progressive" summer camp for future American leaders had already decisively shaped Lowenstein's life when he was a camper there in 1947. Now without a permanent job, and in the aftermath of Freedom Summer in 1964, he was hired—with the substantial help of his good friends Franklin Delano Roosevelt III, and Lucille Kohn—to run the Encampment for 1965.

"It was," Nancy Steffen later said, in classic understatement, "a very Allard-centered group." Many of his best friends from Harvard, Yale, and Stanford were in attendance, including Steffen, Kris Kleinbauer, John Steinbruner, David Harris, John Kavanaugh, Bruce Payne, Greg Craig, and Barney Frank. Bringing together students of diverse backgrounds and interests, the EFC sought to generate conversation about *all* the pressing issues confronting America. Kenneth Keniston was there to talk about the "youth crisis"; Robert Moses, Ed King, and Aaron Henry discussed Mississippi and civil rights; Paul Goodman lectured on "the authentic and inauthentic"; Donald Rumsfeld updated the young people on modern Republicanism; and William Sloane Coffin, the Yale chaplain, talked about contemporary ethical issues. Three of the candidates in New York's mayoralty campaign appeared (most of the campers were inveigled into doing volunteer work for the reform Democrat, William Fitts Ryan), as did two out of three members of the Lowenstein "holy trinity"—Frank Porter Graham and Norman Thomas (Eleanor Roosevelt had died).

There was a quintessential debate between Barney Frank, a Harvard graduate student and later a congressman from Massachusetts, and Tom Hayden, leader of the Students for a Democratic Society. The issue was whether to work inside the established political system, or attack it. Frank functioned as Lowenstein's surrogate, Hayden represented all those who were angry at the "system" after Freedom Summer. Hayden refused to stand in front of the campers and debate Frank face to face, insisting on sitting among the campers on the ground. "I told him," Frank later recalled, "that he was such a 'grass root,' I didn't know whether to debate him or water him." It was that kind of summer.[18]

The Encampment was a political psychodrama that brought into head-on conflict all the contentious forces and questions that Lowenstein had been struggling with over the past half-dozen years. Virtually all the significant actors from his life were in attendance, as either speakers or conferees. Frenetic bull sessions occurred on every conceivable topic—from "the new sexuality" to revolution in Africa. Bill Buckley showed up, but so, too did the militant black organizer Milton Galamison and peace devotees David McReynolds, A. J. Muste, and Dorothy Day. It was a "who's who" gathering of the infamous and provocative, all orchestrated under the benign directorship of "Saint Allard." Lowenstein's slogan for the summer, "Hang loose," meant "a way to live which avoids troublesome commitments" to one camper, but to most it simply signified "no rules, anything goes, and if something can go wrong, it will." Bruce Payne, the Yale Ph.D. candidate who was a political theorist and Mississippi veteran, "was like a pig in shit teaching Plato's *Republic*"; David Harris, about to become Stanford's student body president, romanticized about how Al helped him "untie the Gordian knot" that was in his stomach; and most campers luxuriated in an environment where, as one student wrote, "the issues are hot and the people are cool."[19]

But it was also an atmosphere suffused with the personal and sexual tensions that were such a part of Lowenstein's political life. "It was a very, very intense experience," one Lowenstein confidant remembered. "Some people were having incredibly important sexual relationships. There were older men pursuing younger men . . . lots of drugs . . . and polarization every day." Al was in his element, seeking out new friends, leaving others still wondering what it was all about. "I opened up so much at the Encampment I felt almost naked," one student wrote. But another noted that, "although you seemingly bared your personality to me last week-end, there are lots of questions I still have." And a third—a woman—described Al as someone "who has a tragic view of life . . . has only been in love with one girl . . . [and is] sometimes troubled and uncertain." Indeed, so concerned was this student that she worried about Al's falling apart.[20]

Most prominent in the emotional undergrowth, though, were strains over various same-sex relationships. Bruce Payne had brought with him a young man who was his current love interest. A student from California got involved with these two in a complicated triangle that later expanded to include a student from Duke and another from Stanford. It was like "bathing in a steam bath," one person said. "It was so intense and so hot and the passions and emotions were so high. . . . And there were 100 people who all had this very intense and special relationship with Al." Although Lowenstein was occasionally bothered by what Payne called "the more theatrical side" of the sexual interaction, he was also deeply involved, counseling people with sexual problems, getting embroiled in various relationships, and becoming the object—or subject—of some. Writing from California, "Harry" described to Al how, during the bus trip home, "I continually thought of you and —. I love you both so much and both of you are 1500 miles away by my own choice. Perhaps that is what insanity is." Then, in another letter, "I miss you very much. Each day I come closer to quitting school and going to Tunis with you masquerading as a piece of luggage."[21]

In an extraordinary way, then, the Encampment for Citizenship magnified the various currents crisscrossing Lowenstein's life. Conflict, polarization, and intensity were the words of the day, counterposed against metaphors like nakedness, baring one's soul, and emotional "steam baths." Significantly, as much as any gathering in Lowenstein's life, this one was his creation—"Allard-centered," as Nancy Steffen said—so that virtually everything that happened represented a theme that he viewed as pivotal. If the 1965 Encampment had been set up as a stage on which to play out all the psychological tensions of Al Lowenstein's life—both political and personal—it could not have more perfectly scripted. Thus, it was no accident that the months before and after the Encampment witnessed the onset of at least two running conversations about Al's sexuality, and ultimately, a turning point in his thoughts about politics as well.

The first conversation was with Bruce Payne. Lowenstein first met Payne through NSA and then came to know him better during his many trips back to New Haven to recruit for the Freedom Vote and Freedom Summer. Acutely sensitive to Payne's self-doubts, Lowenstein—almost alone—intuited when Payne was about to have a breakdown and alerted William Sloane Coffin and others at Yale to Payne's quandary. During 1964–65, the two became ever closer, and they began at that time a series of conversations, which continued until Lowenstein's death, about issues of sexual identity.

Critical to those discussions was the fact that Payne was initially confused about his own sexual preferences. Deeply attracted to men, especially those who were handsome and apparently heterosexual, Payne worried about whether it made sense to live a homosexual life, especially since he dated women and had enjoyed some stable, rewarding heterosexual relationships. When Payne shared these concerns, Lowenstein responded sympathetically, urging Payne to meet Sanford Friedman and his partner so that he could know people in a long-term homosexual relationship. Although initially the two talked mostly about Payne's life, Lowenstein gradually shared some of his own concerns about the same questions. After one of these discussions, the two went to bed together. Lowenstein's arm fell over Payne as he was going to sleep, and although Payne was not especially attracted to Lowenstein sexually, he remembers that "it was real nice to be hugged by him . . . [to] feel close to him, and [to] wake up still somehow nestled against him . . . thinking, 'Gee, this is unusual but terrific.'"

During one conversation in 1965, Lowenstein opened up more. Although he was not homosexual, he told Payne, "he had a lot of friends who said he ought to be." When Payne spoke of being more attracted to men than to women, Lowenstein responded very personally, saying that "these things were hard to sort out [but] that having touching relationships with guys, being able to be physically close . . . sleeping with a man in the same bed . . . [all this] was really nice . . . and the wrestling was a great satisfaction." Yet Lowenstein did not see himself as a homosexual, saying that "his sexual relationships had always been with women." Whenever the subject turned to his own sexuality, Payne recalled, Lowenstein would "shrug his shoulders," as though he could not figure it out. "Maybe Freud was right," Lowenstein had told Payne, "that we're all bisexual." But, he added, "my guess is that there are a lot of differences out there." The truth, Payne concluded, was that Lowenstein "thought he was different from other folks and that he didn't know quite what to make of himself." On the other hand, Payne also sensed that many of Al's friends did indeed have interests that could be interpreted as homosexual.[22]

The second conversation also began in 1965, once again under circumstances of intense intimacy and sharing. Al took the position then—"which I subsequently believed was a rationalization," his second friend said—"that the culture and society that we live in does not understand the need for males to be intimate and immediately ascribes to male intimacy homosexuality, when in fact males need to be as intimate with males . . . as with females, and they want to express it physically as well. So we create ways to do it that are not overt. We wrestle, we roughhouse, we do all that, but in fact, males like to hug as much as anybody else." Through such arguments, this friend concluded, Al created the justification "to sleep in the same bed and to embrace and hug and have physical intimacy, although it was not naked, not kissing, not the classic sort of homosexual behavior."

What bothered this particular friend was that Al seemed to give physical intimacy a central place. "I found my relationship impossible to carry on with," he said, "because [it] was something that he found to be so important. . . . I didn't object . . . to having physical contact with him. It was just that this was something that he wanted more than I did. . . . And I said, 'I'm just not there anymore for that kind of stuff' . . . [but] you couldn't cool out with him on that." On the basis of his own experience, this friend concluded that if Al really thought that "all he was doing [was fighting the cultural barriers that prohibited men from expressing affection to each other], he was very deceiving of himself." Even more, this friend found it an "ugly discovery" that WASPs were the only friends Lowenstein physically approached, even though he had many friendships with Jews as well. So much for the argument that he was seeking just a natural expression of intimacy among *all* males.[23]

There remained the issue of how open Lowenstein was ready to be about his feelings. To this second friend, as to Bruce Payne, Lowenstein implicitly denied that he was homosexual. "He would say," the friend observed, "that he had a range of experiences that sometimes included greater physical intimacy." Once, when a former student protégé tried to talk to Lowenstein about their former "homosexual encounters" of sleeping together and hugging, Lowenstein allegedly retorted, "Homosexuality? How could you possibly characterize this as homosexuality? . . . Homosexuality is oral or anal relations between men. Have we done anything like that?" And when another protégé, who had "come out" invited Lowenstein to "resume where we left off," Lowenstein did not respond— as though he were not interested in intimacy with an avowedly gay person.[24]

In the confused world of sexual terminology, therefore, Lowenstein was not easy to locate. Clearly, his behavior had a sexual dimension in the sense that he reached out for some physical and erotic contact with other men. But it may not have been homosexual in a "classic" definitional sense. His interactions with men did include orgasm—at least sometimes—but not necessarily through fondling or genital contact. When Bruce Payne once observed, "I'm not sure [Al has] ever had what I would call a real sexual relationship with a man," a friend retorted, "Of course he has. Lots of them." But on balance, the evidence suggests continuing confusion and befuddlement, and over issues so basic that Lowenstein's tortured uncertainty about his sexual identity may have carried over into other aspects of his life as well.[25]

In this context, it is important to recall again the ambience surrounding homosexuality during the 1950s and 1960s. Although there had been some increase in societal awareness of homosexual behavior during World War II, the issue was still verboten. The Kinsey studies showed that at least 10 percent of all adult men and women were practicing homosexuals, but the popular culture still had no terms of respect or recognition for this minority. Instead homosexuals were objects of derision, and "queers" were often grouped with "commies" and "pinkoes," often in the same McCarthyite sentence. Even the human rights organizations that were formed to protect homosexuals—the Mattachine Society for men, the Daughters of Bilitis for women—were so dedicated to propriety and legalism that they never demanded public acknowledgment and affirmation of homosexuality as a lifestyle. Indeed, the Mattachine Society functioned as a collection of self-contained cells so that male homosexuals ran only a limited risk of being "exposed." Suspected homosexuals were run out of the State Department; careers were ruined if one did not look "straight"; and teenagers grew up knowing there was no more venomous epithet than to call someone a "fairy" or "lesbo."[26]

Within such an atmosphere, a young person with mixed sexual desires lived in constant terror. Al's oldest friend, Sanford Friedman, recalled his homosexuality as "a source of tremendous shame" while a young man. Other friends of Al's testified to the excruciating pain of growing up in a homophobic culture. "You lived in constant and perpetual fear," David Mixner, an antiwar activist who came out in the 1970s, observed: "There [were] no . . . positive role models. Society, at every turn, including the most progressive people . . . reinforced the image that you were a sick, terrible, perverted child molester. The only homosexuals you saw on the media were those who were serial killers or child molesters." In that context, Mixner noted, you were "always afraid of being exposed or being discovered. . . . You would try to leave . . . a trail that no one could track you on. . . . If you moved fast enough, if you changed people quick enough, they couldn't catch you." Hence, one's impulse was to dart and escape, to have "quick and intense intimacy with people . . . quick hits, letting people think they're seeing the most intimate side of you . . . and then quickly moving on. . . . Because if you're found out, it's not trouble; you were *destroyed.* I mean destroyed, family, career, friends—everything gone . . . forever."[27]

In light of Lowenstein's inevitable awareness of such pressures, it becomes easier to understand the stress of his emotional struggle, and his constant impulse to move on. He could not have participated in any of the struggles he cared about, Mixner observed, if people thought he was homosexual. "His whole life would have been dramatically changed. I think he knew that. . . . [I] sat in more meetings as a closet homosexual during that period, with vicious, ugly, derogatory things said regarding faggots and dykes [being] sick and abnormal . . . perverted. . . . I know he heard them, too." Yet hearing the contempt would simply reinforce the instinct to hide, to dissemble, to not confront or work through and resolve the tension but instead to move on, rationalize, and simply keep wondering, Who am I? Why am I different?[28]

Given such a dynamic, it is also easy to understand why so many of Lowenstein's young followers, already caught up in the dilemma of whether to go into the "flame" or remain outside it, came to see Lowenstein's sexual agenda as a reason to suspect his motives. If one had been wooed to become a "best friend" as well as a political ally and then had experienced feelings of inadequacy and rejection, it was not difficult to conclude that perhaps you were being used, manipulated, even mistreated, by someone whose secret agenda might be selfish and sexual rather than altruistic. At the very least, one would be uneasy. As one Stanford protégé noted, "The experience of . . . the veiled advance, together with what seemed to be cryptic political agendas . . . just made [us] wonder what was going on after all. . . . Was this a conspiracy . . . was [Al] never candid with the people he was dealing with as friends and as confidants?" Al's enemies had always attacked him as a manipulator; now here, in the most private areas of life, there seemed some confirmation of the allegation that he was not facing or telling the truth.[29]

For some people, the physical side of the relationship with Al Lowenstein was one more expression of a wonderful bond. "Growing [always] involves some pain and awkwardness," one protégé wrote, "as it did that night . . . [when] feeling suddenly well[ed] up; with less good people it would never have come, without my upbringing it needn't have been sad—but as it was, it was good, and neither you nor I deserved to feel any guilt. What a good friend you are, and were that night."[30]

But there was damage done as well. So many of Lowenstein's young friends were vulnerable, unformed, and susceptible to being caught up in something they would later regret. One person had to forsake a career in a high government agency because he could not bring himself to answer a question during his security check about his relationship with Allard Lowenstein. Others took years to work through their sense of guilt and ambivalence over what Armin Rosencranz correctly described as "just hugging Al" in bed, but which the individuals themselves clearly felt was illicit activity—especially in the homophobic environment of the early 1960s. And there was always the way that the "physical thing" complicated everything else. "I was just exploding with excitement about being turned on to politics and meeting so many fantastic people through Al," one friend said, "[but] at the same time [the physical contact with him] was difficult for me." Life would have been easier without it.

The ultimate damage, though, was to Lowenstein himself. Al often said, one of his closest associates observed, that "there's nothing more tragic than unrequited love. . . . [He had this] desire to be intimate with people . . . who would be best friends . . . [to find] the relationship that works . . . [so he could] then stop traveling." What Lowenstein failed to realize was that traveling itself was part of the problem, and that he could never find the relationship he craved until he stopped running long enough to decide who he was.[31]

FAMILY, MARRIAGE, AND CAREER

Even as Lowenstein's personal and political conflicts—how to operate inside the system, how to define one's sexual identity—reached a crescendo in the mid-1960s, so too did other strains over finances, choosing a career, and relations with his parents. More than at any time since the 1940s, Lowenstein seemed at odds with his family. Their concern about his lifestyle and inability to choose a career coincided with an economic decline in the family fortunes. Amid this travail, Doc Lowenstein suffered a recurrence of his heart ailment and died, resurrecting all of Al's anxieties about satisfying his father's wishes. In the meantime, Lowenstein faced other reversals in his professional life and in his ongoing quest for a bride. Together with all the emotional turmoil connected with Mississippi, the Encampment, and his relationships with his protégés, these events precipitated a crisis that compelled Lowenstein to make some hard choices.

Gabriel Lowenstein had been delighted when his son went off to Stanford. Having provided the financial wherewithal to get Al through the ordeal of writing *Brutal Mandate,* he could now take justifiable pride in his son, the author, being a teacher and administrator at one of the nation's leading universities. Perhaps because of his father's happiness, Al may not have told him about the tenuous academic connection he had with the Stanford political science department, or about President J. Wallace Sterling's disapproval of his role in inspiring student activism. In any event, Al's "dismissal" from Stanford came as a great shock to Gabriel. "[Al's] father was so sad," a fellow administrator at Stanford observed. "I had a conversation with him . . . and he asked me why did the people at Stanford not like Al. It always hurt him. . . . He wanted Al to be an academic and that appointment . . . meant an enormous amount to [him]. . . . He was so . . . disappointed that Al wasn't a professor of politics."[32]

Al's departure from Stanford, of course, reopened all the tensions associated with Gabriel's desire that he settle down. "Please understand me," he wrote Al in 1963, "I do not disagree with your decisions, [nor do I] want to make any attempt to influence your thinking." Yet it was time for Al to "think in terms of permanence" and financial stability. Gabriel had just lost one of his restaurants. "As long as I am around and as long as I'm able," he declared,

> it'll be my pleasure to help out. But who knows and when. . . . If you spend a lot of money by going to distant lands because of an inner urge to be of help to deserving people—it is good, ideally, but can you afford at your age to be devoid of means of taking care of yourself—particularly in case of an emergency or should you find it possible to get married. I told you before that your decision is mine too after you make it, but I feel that you will not accept in good grace my expression of opinions which may be different from yours. . . . There is no difference fundamentally between your thinking and mine. I understand your difficulties and I sympathize with them. Don't worry. Be happy.

Clearly, Gabriel had not found it easy to write this letter. Delicately, and with abiding love, he was raising issues that concerned him profoundly. And whatever Al's resistance, he had to know that now, more than ever, these issues were real. Whether he appreciated fully the devotion out of which his father had written, he could not fail to understand the nature of the problem.[33]

Far more irritating was the reappearance of carping letters from his stepmother. Allard never let them know what he was doing, Florence complained, and seemed "not of the family." Furthermore, his room continued to be cluttered and dirty, full of disintegrating newspapers and magazines "that have no bearing on your life." She told him to put his rubbish outside his room at 10:00 A.M. and 5:00 P.M. daily, warning that "any other mother would have made short work of . . . your room [by now]." Most distressingly, she wrote, "I feel my bed has been used. I asked you not to at any time." If he were "anybody else's son," she concluded, "Dad would tell the world about this in a most *derogatory* way." Whatever his sins, this thirty-five-year-old man was being infantilized by his stepmother. Presumably, Al had erected buffers long before to deflect this type of message. But together with his father's far more legitimate concerns about his life choices, the parental injunctions to "grow up" had to take their toll.[34]

How great a toll would become clearer after Doc's death from a heart attack in March 1965. Doc knew he was ill, as reflected in his reference to his own death in his 1963 letter to Al. His secretary urged Al to write more often, since Doc was not well and always asked whether there was any mail from Al. When Al received the phone call informing him of his father's death, he was at Berkeley seeking to mediate the controversy over the Free Speech Movement there. Without telling anyone about the call, he went onstage and delivered a speech to a packed auditorium, then returned to New York.

Gabriel Lowenstein was the most important person in Al's life. Despite his ritual exhortations to Al to comb his hair, shine his shoes, and get a job, Gabriel loved Al more than anyone else in the world; even his harshest letters conveyed adoration as well as chastisement. Al's friends knew about his father's love. Many of them had spent endless hours with Gabriel at Granson's Restaurant while they all waited for Al to appear. "His conversation was mostly about you," Elise Lapham wrote: "He had such pride in you and such understanding. . . . It worried him that you were giving so much of yourself for others and taking so little . . . . but I have the feeling he was the same sort of person." Another friend recounted how Doc regaled his guests with stories of all the wonderful people who knew his "brilliant son . . . [and] he seemed to have trouble deciding whether he was most proud that there were so many people of stature that knew you and praised you, or [so many of] the little people, the students and the unknowns. . . . 'Now don't tell Al I said that,' he would say, as he insisted that you had little idea of what a wonderful creation he found you to be."[35]

Yet Al could never believe such stories. "He felt his father had never been proud of him," recalled Nancy Steffen, who was with him at the time of Doc's death. "His father had wanted him to settle down in a straight job and not live out of the back of Granson's and carry his belongings around in a paper bag . . . which is what Allard was still doing then." The only unconditional love he had experienced was from the old Jewish women in his life, Gary Bellow observed—Aunt Ruthie, Grandma Goldberg, Lucille Kohn. But from his father, he had felt only "conditional love . . . the problem of achievement tied to love."[36]

Most poignant, perhaps, was a letter from Marcia Borie, one of Al's oldest friends, whose own parents had died tragically when they were very young. "I know that on several occasions," she wrote, "you have opened your heart and expressed sorrow at what you felt was your father's disappointment in you. In the fact that outwardly all the brilliance you possessed was not fully utilized for YOUR own good. I know that deep down you hoped one day to write that great book, or play, or movie, or do something so publicly spectacular as to make your father truly proud of you." Borie pleaded with him not to let these feelings of guilt take possession of him. "I am living proof of how a life can be ruined when it is lived in the past and not the future," she declared. "Never forget that you are your father—part of him is in you. Every good and noble deed you ever did was one done with your father always a part of that deed. . . . [So] if ever . . . you sink into . . . feelings of remorse, remember the greatest tribute to your father's memory is your LIFE." With Doc now gone, what would that life be? How should it be lived? With whom? And devoted to what purpose?[37]

Unfortunately, just when these questions became most salient, Al was as mired in confusion about his future as at any other time in his life. His basic integrity was being called into question, not just by disaffected students who had been radicalized in Mississippi but by powerful members of the "establishment" who were suggesting that he was deceitful and perhaps even fraudulent in how he presented himself. During the spring of 1965, Lowenstein had arranged to be an educational consultant with the Ford Foundation, his assignment being to explore sources of student unrest and make recommendations on university governance. That appointment was sabotaged by Stanford's president, J. Wallace Sterling, who told Ford Foundation officials that Lowenstein was "an agitator and a liar." Sterling even questioned whether Lowenstein had really occupied the position of writer in-residence at Yale the previous semester. In the ensuing flurry of correspondence, Al's consultancy at Ford was terminated—on the lame grounds that "educational policy" was no longer a top priority for the foundation. And although Richard Sewall, master of Ezra Stiles College at Yale, came to Al's defense, indicating that he had been a "guest of the Master" and had spoken at the college as a writer-in-residence, some doubts about Al clearly remained in the minds of people outside of New Haven.[38]

The bottom line, of course, was that Lowenstein's character had been called into question by important people whose approbation was essential for both his self-image and the effectiveness of his work. In retrospect, it seems clear that the whole episode amounted to a vendetta by Sterling and other high-level Stanford administrators against the man who had done so much to call their own authority into question. For them, it was payback time. Yet others took the charges seriously. Moreover, the deeper issue was how Lowenstein presented himself to the world: how much basis was there for the suspicion some people had that he was a Machiavellian who manipulated facts and people for his own secretive ends? For someone whose self-image *required* that he be seen as noble, righteous, and selfless, such questioning, by important people, could be shattering, casting doubt on whether he could continue to carry on the same type of life he had in the past. It could also only redouble any anxieties he had about what would happen if these same important people discovered—and talked about—his ambivalent sexual instincts.

Another source of consternation to Lowenstein was his ongoing inability to find a marriage partner. Three women Al knew at Stanford were in love with him, and each fell victim to the acolyte "syndrome" of thinking herself totally inadequate for the relationship. Nancy Steffen and Ilene Strelitz both served as editors of the *Stanford Daily* and made the pages of the paper an extension of Al's voice whenever he wished, especially during the civil rights battles of 1963–64. Conflicted in her feelings about Lowenstein's role in Mississippi yet devoted to him as well, Strelitz was torn apart and did not know how to proceed. Nancy Steffen, her close friend and successor as *Daily* editor, had a similar crush on Al. But unlike Strelitz, she talked openly with him about it, thus making it less emotionally traumatic.[39]

Kris Kleinbauer shared the same sense of devotion and inadequacy but for a brief period was actually engaged to Lowenstein. One of those who became active in African and civil rights issues because of Al, she served as his eyes and ears in late 1964 when she visited Mississippi and sent back various reports critical of SNCC. Although by December of that year they were talking about marriage, Kleinbauer was dismayed by their relationship. "Why is it always so hard to write letters to you?" she asked. "I feel positively inarticulate even on paper, and you no doubt remember me in person. So things come out mixed up and incoherent and you get impatient and then I don't know what to say, which is where we are now, isn't it." Doomed from the beginning, the engagement was mercifully brief, yet Kleinbauer too was "fixated" on Lowenstein and urged him not to give up on their relationship. "It will be worth the hell," she wrote. "I don't know if I love you, but I love [you] too much to end it now at the beginning."[40]

During the same period, Al also developed a romantic relationship with

Nancy Adams, a secretarial colleague at NC State. A beautiful woman who was also a millionaire, Adams took care of all of Lowenstein's errands, shared an important part of his life in North Carolina, and wrote endearing, affectionate letters when he was away. In the midst of verbally blasting a male friend for failing to rendezvous with him in Europe, Lowenstein declared: "Each back to his cocoon. I've been sharing mine with a doll called Nancy. Not too much communicating but lots of love. It's no substitute, but it substitutes." In fact, Adams and Lowenstein slept together—but Adams found the relationship strangely unsatisfying because, she told a friend, at their most intimate moments, Al would look at his watch and say he had to leave for an appointment. In every visible way, Nancy Adams fit Lowenstein's ideal: she was a rich, beautiful WASP. But clearly, he found something missing—not enough "communicating"—and anyway, the relationship was only a "substitute," so he did not propose.[41]

Now, with his father's death, Lowenstein was determined to resolve the question of family and career. Throughout 1964, he had been torn between his desire to remain active in politics, and the pull he felt toward writing as a full-time career. Friends noted how depressed Al was during the spring and summer of 1964. In the midst of all the conflict roiling around him in Mississippi, Al seemed without direction in his personal life as well. To one of his friends he wrote that he had decided to forsake politics for writing and teaching. "There is a limit for all of us," his friend wrote back in response to Al's complaint about being besieged by problems, "some point where giving more to others and to causes would so seriously deplete our reserves that we then have nothing of value for any of those who have come to depend on us. The worst part of that is the cycle of despair and doubt that begins."[42]

Gabriel's death precipitated an immediate urge to break out of that cycle. Talking with him at Berkeley right after he received word of his father's passing, Nancy Steffen remembers Al saying, "Now I'll have to do it. Now I'll have to decide." "For a long time," Steffen commented, "[Al] had been a political person without a portfolio . . . but that was very different from what he was going to do now." In her reading of the situation, the Encampment summer was a time "of deciding and gearing himself for what he did shortly thereafter." Significantly, this was the summer of the "steambath of emotions," the intense sexual byplay, the lengthy personal conversations in which Lowenstein began to discuss, if haltingly, his bewilderment about his sexuality. It was also the summer when he started to come to grips with the meaning of his father's death for his occupational life. "The 'shoulds' and 'oughts' were coming down on him very heavy," Steffen observed. "He'd never made anything of his life in those very traditional terms [his father cared about]." Thus, this also became the summer when Allard Lowenstein decided to "run for office, to get married, and to establish a family."[43]

JENNY, MARRIAGE, AND POLITICS

Jennifer Lyman was a Boston Brahmin reared in what she herself described as a "rigid upper-class family [from] Beacon Hill." Her parents were divorced when she was three. Her mother moved to New York and subsequently remarried several times. Jenny lived with her straitlaced father until she went away to college at Barnard when she was seventeen. From her lighthearted mother, she absorbed a streak of rebelliousness and playfulness; these traits modified her otherwise aristocratic demeanor with a mischievous touch that conveyed warmth and good humor. Despite her father's rock-ribbed Goldwater Republicanism, she yearned for a broader, more exciting political perspective. At Barnard, she went to Nigeria with Crossroads Africa, then after graduating took a job as a secretary for the American Committee on Africa.

Jenny met Al through Sam Beard, a mutual friend she was dating who was also involved with Al's political activities in the reform Democratic movement in Manhattan. Soon she was volunteering her time as Al's secretary, knowing he could not afford to pay her. Al took Jenny with him to meet Lucille Kohn, one of the cherished older people in his life, and she was immediately taken by the warmth and tenderness of the relationship between the octogenarian and the disheveled political activist. Al was very shy, she noted, and on their first date they went to the movies—with Lucille. "It was not the date of one's dreams," she wryly observed, but "that's how the romance got started"—movies on a Saturday night, often with someone else, a quick meal grabbed on the run, conversations in the car while "making the rounds." But it was enough to intrigue Jenny. "This was the best person I'd ever met," she said.[44]

For his part, Al was smitten—and overwhelmed. "He was just glowing about [Jenny]," Nancy Steffen remarked. Once, after watching her "work" a political gathering, Al turned to Steffen and said, "Isn't she wonderful?" Others agreed. "She [was] the best of all . . . of us, close and distant friends," Bruce Payne said. "What Al had to offer to everybody, but particularly to his men friends in those kinds of intimate ways . . . there was all of that with Jenny. . . . She had an enormous amount to give, which she gave richly and freely. . . . She just carried delight with her, [and] . . . it seemed to me . . . a really complete relationship." It was the total person also that impressed Harold Ickes, another of Al's political associates. "I liked her instantaneously," he said, "her wit, the grace with which she handled herself . . . her lack of bullshit." When Al was with her, Payne recalled, "[he] was a different Al, and it was even better. It was wonderful to see him then."[45]

In fact, Jenny was so perfect that the relationship reactivated all of Al's self-doubts. "I remember Al talking about himself and Jenny," Rich Hammond said, "and how disbelieving he was. . . . Al had this sense of himself as not being worthy [what with his glasses and nose and all] . . . so when he found himself in love with . . . such a remarkable woman . . . who is a Boston Brahmin, for God's sake . . . [the] symbolism must have been overwhelming. . . . Al [tried] to come to grips with what it meant that he was going to be married to this woman, [and] he was really struggling with that, struggling to feel equal in the relationship." It was the old phenomenon of low self-esteem and ethnic inadequacy, focused this time on his prospective bride rather than a protégé. His self-doubt was perhaps also a way of dealing with deeper doubts about marriage. Driving with Nancy Steffen to Indiana in the summer of 1966, Al broke the news of his engagement but also confessed his anxiety about the fifteen year age gap between Jenny and him and about people's perception that he was robbing the cradle. Despite his awe at the miracle of this relationship, he felt the same ambivalence and avoidance that had surfaced whenever marriage became too close a reality in the past.[46]

Jenny also had profound doubts. "I remember really wondering whether I ought to marry someone that I didn't know," she said. "I mean, I thought he was wonderful, but that was different from feeling that I really knew him." So many of their "dates" were with other people; rarely was there a chance to be alone, let alone to share very much physical affection. Jenny's mother used to kid her about the nature of their courtship. "So where is he taking you tonight," she would ask, "the Orange Room at Nedick's?" Nor was Jenny unaware of Al's complex feelings. Once she asked Bruce Payne to explain why Al sometimes seemed cold and distant. They did not see each other all that much anyway, and when they did he would be remote. Payne's response was, "Al wants to marry you, and he doesn't think it's a good idea for you. He's trying to show you how bad it might be. . . . He's testing you." For the moment, Payne's explanation seemed to make sense to Jenny, perhaps even suggesting a degree of maturity as Al sought to make clear how difficult things might be; and so she put aside her concerns. But Payne later thought, "My God, what have I done? Should anybody marry Al?"[47]

But her doubts did not go away permanently. When Jenny spent time in Mississippi during the summer of 1966 working on a civil rights project (largely because Al thought she should have that experience), they rushed back to the fore. Al came down to visit, Jenny noted, "[but] we had no time alone. There were millions of people he had to meet with." When Jenny tried to tell Al that they were not really ready for marriage, he brushed aside her concerns, saying, "Well, we'll just have to carve out more time." Jenny shared her concerns with more and more people—"she was very scared about marrying him," said one friend she visited—but the more she considered postponing the wedding, the more overpowering became Al's determination to proceed. "I greatly regret being as young as I was when I knew Al," Jenny later said. "There were a lot of questions that I didn't ask, that I didn't push further. . . . He was such a complicated and guarded person in [so] many ways."

But perhaps because she was so young—and Al was so overpowering—Jenny decided to go ahead with the wedding. "I had an awful lot of conflicts about my own upbringing and was terribly young and unformed," she recalled. Still trying to resolve the family strains between her "stalwart, WASP-y Bostonian father" and her "freewheeling" mother, she did not feel a great deal of security and certainty in her life. "I was just trying to figure out who I was and where I fit into the world," she observed, "and along came Al." Flattered that he would pick someone like her—"I was no great shakes," she said—she decided to set aside her doubts on the grounds that, "in the end . . . marrying him would be a way of getting to know him, and it seemed like a worthwhile thing to do. . . . I was a pretty young, naive, not-sure-of-where-I-was-going kid . . . [and] I suppose to some extent [Al] was a solution. I was not especially liberated, you know. I wasn't going to find my own career. I didn't know what I was going to do." In the meantime, there were all the good things, "the slapstick comedy routines" when the two were together, how "at ease [Al] . . . was with Jenny . . . and gleeful." Perhaps the leap of faith made sense for both of them.[48]

Appropriately, the wedding itself commemorated all the tensions and conflicts implicit in the joining of two such extraordinary families. "You needed a Tom Wolfe to do justice to [it]," Harold Ickes observed. Consistent with the abiding importance of the religious issue, two clergymen were asked to preside, the Reverend William Sloane Coffin, who had been Al's ally through so many social crusades, and a Reform Jewish rabbi from New York. In fitting acknowledgment of the roots of Jenny's family, the ceremony took place at the Vale, a 200-year-old estate in Waltham, Massachusetts, that had been given by the Lymans to the National Historic Trust and ordinarily was open to the public for $2 tours illustrating how the "aristocracy" used to live. A prenuptial reception was held in the Beacon Hill home of Jenny's Republican father. "Now tell me, Reverend," one of Jenny's relatives asked Bill Coffin, indicating Jenny and Al's friends, "who are all these people?" Coffin responded, "These are the people you've spent most of your life voting against," then pointed to a conversation group consisting of Norman Thomas, Frank Porter Graham, and Franklin D. Roosevelt III. It was that kind of gathering.[49]

On the eve of the wedding, Al evidently experienced another "dark night of the soul" when he relived all the anxieties he had ever entertained about getting married. "It was one of the loneliest times of [my] life," Al told Rich Hammond later. Al had expected Rich and his other "best friends" to be there for him. "I . . . remember his saying," Hammond recalled, "that he really needed me at that time . . . that he walked around Cambridge all night in the cold weather [of late November] . . . and he . . . professed to have been very hurt and angry" that no one was there for him to confide in. In fact, most of his friends were at the wedding—though not Hammond—and the conversation is significant primarily for what it says about Al's retrospective consciousness of his despair and anxiety about taking such a critical turn in his life.[50]

The next day, however, all doubts seemed forgotten. Although Al insisted that Greg Craig stop the car so they could have a Drake's cake and a Coke on the way to the Vale—thereby making them fifteen minutes late—it was still probably the earliest Al had ever appeared anywhere for a social engagement. He and Jenny had plotted with Jenny's mother to print up an additional 500 "contraband" invitations beyond the 200 planned by Jenny's father so that more of Al's friends could be invited. Many came, and "the wedding was a whole comic scene itself," Bruce Payne recalls, "random troops of Lowenstein nephews wandering up the aisle, Jenny's stiff and formal father trying to be nice, but not succeeding." It was just a "crazy coming together of forces from opposite ends of the earth," Susan Goodwillie said, "sort of goofy and wacky." To Harold Ickes, it was like a Broadway burlesque. "Talk about a clash of cultures," he said. "You had . . . the hustling, bustling Jews from New York and their crowd . . . [then] the Boston patricians. . . . The New Yorkers would have their plates filled high with food, [while the Brahmins had] their austere plates. . . . It was just phenomenal . . . standing there watching . . . Allard, of course, flitting around like a butterfly . . . and Jenny, gracious to everyone, all combined with her cool, acerbic wit." The experience required not only a Tom Wolfe but a Woody Allen as well.[51]

Thus the moment Lowenstein had contemplated for years had finally come. Jenny knew by then that theirs would not be an idyllic or relaxed life together. All the experience of the previous spring, summer, and fall had confirmed the problems of not knowing each other very well and not having a great deal of time alone together. As she later noted, "Al was not good at . . . sustained intimacy. . . . There was not a lot of hanging out. I think it took a while for us to really get to know each other." In subconscious fulfillment of one of Al's other family fantasies, Jenny immediately became pregnant, having accidentally mailed her birth control pills to the rabbi in New York in the same envelope with the wedding certificate. Hence, they would not be alone for long.[52]

Whatever the remaining anxieties, Allard had made one of the biggest choices of his life. At the end of two years of turbulent and sometimes frantic immersion in a series of personal crises, he had defined at least one direction he would pursue for the future. Still torn by all the conflicts he had been grappling with, he had nevertheless made a fateful decision that, henceforth, there would be other family members who would be implicated and shaped by his struggles. For the moment, at least, he seemed happy with the decision and appreciative of all he had gained. "What I don't know," he wrote Jenny eighteen months after their wedding, "is how I ever did anything without you . . . and since it seems impossible that I ever did or could, in some strange way it seems like you've always been there, and that's how I made it through till you finally came." Al Lowenstein had found a blessing. "I didn't know anyone could ever love anyone the way I love you," he wrote, "least of all me, and I hope one day to be able to give you a millionth of the joy and strength that you give me every moment."[53]

CONCLUSION

There may have been other periods of Al Lowenstein's life when the currents underlying his deepest anxieties came together in an equally powerful way. But the years from 1964 to 1966 are distinctive, if for no other reason than that they highlight how the personal and the political were intertwined in his life. How he recruited for his political causes emerged directly from his sense of inferiority. The one-on-one intensity with which he compensated for that inferiority, however, almost guaranteed that his sense of inadequacy would be replicated in reverse in the "acolytes" he wooed as "best friends," then treated as aides. In his personal connections, as in his political behavior, being in control was the only way to ward off insecurity. Politically as well as personally, challenge could not be tolerated, dissent was not acceptable, and loyalty was the criterion for love. That the people who rebelled against such treatment in the political arena were often the same people who could no longer stand to be consumed personally by the Lowenstein flame dramatizes just how impossible it was to separate the one from the other in Lowenstein's life.

When all of this was suffused with tensions over sexuality, the situation became—for some at least—almost unbearable. There was something integrally and inescapably erotic about the intensity with which Lowenstein reached out to the young. Not only did he need their devotion to overcome his feelings of inadequacy, but he also needed a physical expression of their intimacy to fill the deepest void in his life. The fact that these relationships occurred almost exclusively with handsome, young, WASP males only highlighted the depth of his need and its fundamental connection to his feelings of inadequacy about being Jewish. Most tragic of all was that Lowenstein's approach to these relationships of discipleship—whether sexual or otherwise—literally guaranteed his inability to find fulfillment in them. The imbalance of power and need with which he burdened his "best friends" destroyed the possibility of treating them as equals—the only basis on which such relationships could have been sustained and fulfilling.

One of his friends, Clinton Deveaux, observed that ultimately Lowenstein's quest for affection and fulfillment was traceable to his own feeling of having been "abandoned." Abandoned by whom? "By his mother. And his father taking on a stepmother that no one accepted, that isolated him from his father. . . . That's how he got to be so needy." That was why, Deveaux continued, Al connected so "quickly and fully with blacks [and other oppressed people]," as well as why he reached out so intensely to younger people—they offered the comfort and devotion that might overcome the feeling of abandonment.[54]

In the end, Gabriel Lowenstein remained pivotal to Al's story. He was the authority who could not be satisfied, the patriarch who refused to talk about his dead wife, the symbol of all the hidden secrets; yet he was also a figure of love, the individual Al so much wanted to satisfy and make proud, the one person Al needed most to communicate with. For, ultimately, was not Gabriel the reason for Al's abandonment? Hence, was he not the only person who could fill the void and make it right again?

Now Gabriel was gone, and with his death, at least some of the conflicts and confusions that had been festering suddenly came to resolution. "Now, I'll have to do it," Al told his friends. Nor were the two issues of career and marriage unrelated. If you were to be a politician, you had to appear "normal." How better to be normal than to have a wife and children? How better to display direction and purpose than to pursue a political career with that family by your side?

Ironically, even as Al Lowenstein considered these options, another side of his imagination was playing out, with an eerie degree of self-analysis, the dynamics that might control his fate. "Angus" was a screenplay and novel that Al worked on periodically during 1964–65.[55] Never published or dramatized, "Angus" speaks to many of the deepest themes of his personal and political life. He told many of his friends that it was about Dennis Sweeney. In reality, it seems to have been about himself. Angus was the district attorney of a medium-sized southern city. He was married to a beautiful southern woman, the daughter of a U.S. senator. A decent person, Angus wanted to "do right" by the Negroes in his community as the civil rights revolt began. Yet he also wanted to control the pace and direction of the movement, to "go slow" and make change happen peaceably. He was all the more encouraged in this opinion by his father-in-law's conviction that, if he acted shrewdly, he could be elected the state's next governor.

Eventually, however, Angus became convinced that he must take sides in the racial revolt. Moderate white people had lost credibility, he now knew, and the veneer of moderate progressivism had been shattered. Putting his own political aspirations and marriage on the line, he appeared at a black civil rights rally, announced his conversion to the doctrine of immediate and far-reaching racial change, and prepared to launch his own one-man white political campaign for the principles of justice and honor, no matter what the cost.

In the midst of all this, Angus went for a drive to visit his parents on their wedding anniversary. On the way, he picked up a hitchhiker. While Angus was paying for gas at a roadside store, the hitchhiker stole the car, ramming it into a tree miles away. Angus's political opponents, however, chose to tamper with the story of the theft in order to destroy Angus once and for all. To do this, they planted stories in the local press claiming that Angus had made a homosexual advance to the young man, who had fled in the car because it was the only means of escaping Angus's perverse assault.

A few pages later, with his political career now ruined, Angus ventured once more into the black neighborhood of town. A race riot broke out. Angus desperately tried to mediate, one last time putting himself on the line to do the only honorable thing he could in a crisis growing out of control. But events outpaced his effort to control them, and in the course of a final lunge to stop the fighting, Angus fell dead, the victim of a bullet fired by a racist police officer.

Lowenstein was not an introspective man. Indeed, as one of his closest friends observed, "he appeared *deceptively open* because he was [so] fundamentally defended." "Angus," however, reveals some of Lowenstein's inner reflections about the forces competing for control of his life. Perhaps most important, it offers Lowenstein's view of his own role in politics. In a world where ethical issues are paramount, one cannot compromise. The only honorable course is to set oneself against the world, in righteous defense of the highest principles. For to lose is to win. Yet even then, tragedy is inevitable. Someone will seize an issue like homosexuality to destroy one's credibility; and in any event, the ultimate price of devotion to principle is martyrdom.[56]

By the end of 1966, Allard Lowenstein had made some decisive choices. He was going to marry the wonderful woman he was in love with, and he had chosen politics as his career. But as "Angus" reveals, there remained a subterranean dialogue that was not yet complete. How it would end became the story of the rest of his life.

10
The Political *Side* of the Personal

IF THE CIVIL RIGHTS MOVEMENT REPRESENTED THE MOST IMPORTANT DOMES-
tic protest of the 1960s, the war in Vietnam soon became the focus for an
equally profound and powerful social movement calling into question
American foreign policy. Like the civil rights movement, the antiwar
struggle started with the assumption that government policies could be
changed if only enough well-intentioned, decent people raised their
voices in protest. But as in the civil rights movement, those pursuing a
moderate, reformist path soon had to grapple with the issue of whether the
source of injustice and oppression might not be the underlying values and
institutions of American society itself. Both movements did more to shape
the structure and character of political activism in the 1960s than any
other events of the post–World War II era.

Significantly, Allard Lowenstein played a pivotal role in each movement. He recruited thousands of people to both the fight for racial equality
and the struggle to bring an end to the war, and he served as the lightning
rod for the factions that battled for control of both movements over the divisive issue of liberal versus radical politics. Like an Atlas bestriding the
universe, Lowenstein sought to take unto himself the conflicting forces
struggling to define the fate of political activism and to control the outcome through the sheer force of his will.

From 1965 to 1968, Lowenstein continued to display his trademark behaviors—delay in making decisions, diversion of energies in numerous
directions, and occasional uncertainty over staying power and tactics. He
not only ran for Congress twice and led the "dump Johnson" movement;
he also devoted significant amounts of time to events in the Dominican
Republic, Spain, and South Africa and became embroiled in the NSA-
CIA debate. Still, a coherence to Lowenstein's activities appeared during
these years, signaling a change in his life. The emergence of the public
politician, together with his marriage to Jennifer Lyman, suggested just
how much Lowenstein had set about recasting his life in the aftermath of
his father's death. With the Vietnam War providing a framework for the
wide range of activities he would engage in, he was approaching the pin-
nacle of his public life and authority.

The Race for Congress

If ever there was a congressional district that encapsulated all the internecine squabbles of the liberal-left in America, it was the nineteenth
congressional district in Manhattan. Running south from Ninety-sixth
Street down the West Side, the district encompassed the entire Greenwich
Village area, then hooked back up the East Side to take in Chinatown and
the old Jewish neighborhoods around Delancey Street. Shaped like a sax-
ophone, the district was characterized by anything but mellifluous harmony, at least in its politics. Originally the home base of the Tammany
chieftain Carmine DeSapio, it now was the heart of reform Democratic territory; legions of left-leaning, intellectually oriented partisans could be
galvanized in a second, especially around issues of peace, Israeli foreign
policy, or American civil rights. For more than a decade, the area had
been represented by Leonard Farbstein, a colorless, workaday machine
Democrat whose specialties were constituent services, defense of Israel,
and resolutions commemorating the "captive nations" of Eastern Europe.
Since 1962, however, the reformers had been challenging Farbstein's reelection bids. Energized by William Fitts Ryan's victory on the Upper
West Side in 1960, they were determined to topple this last bastion of
Tammany strength, and each year they came closer. William Haddad lost
the 1964 primary by fewer than 4,000 votes. The 1966 reform designation, therefore, became a prize worth competing for.

By the late fall of 1965, the field was already crowded with reform aspi-
rants. Ted Weiss, a Hungarian-born "scrapper," had worked his way up

the ladder of education and politics. Elected to New York's city council in a multicandidate race in 1961, he was known for his advocacy of civil rights, school integration, rent control, and—most important—creation of a civilian review board that would serve as a barrier to police brutality. Associated from the beginning with the reform movement, Weiss was a clear favorite because of his ideological convictions, his political courage, and his service in the ranks. His chief competitor was Peter Straus, the millionaire owner of one of New York's leading radio stations. Straus was extremely well connected to the liberal political establishment, possessed enough money to run an effective race against Farbstein, and was sufficiently moderate to garner votes from those who remained somewhat aloof from the ideological wars of the West Side. The third candidate was Justin Feldman, a well-respected lawyer whose primary strength lay in his reputation as a hard worker during the political battles of 1964. By November, the field seemed complete, with Weiss and Straus the two front-runners.[1]

Then Al Lowenstein parachuted in. Never one to decide early on a course of action, Lowenstein characteristically waited until late November, the last possible moment, to jump in. "[Al's] a rescuer, right?" his friend Gary Bellow observed, "so that [by] delaying things . . . he would come in with the [answer]. . . . His best skill [was] to allow a crisis to start to emerge, and [then] to turn it around."

Although the reform race was not a "crisis," one could argue that the contest was stalemated between two very different political types, and that a newcomer who fell between the two might well be able to "rescue" the situation. In any event, the district was an eminently sensible place to run. Lowenstein lived there; he knew most of the reform club members, even though he had been away for most of the preceding five years; and he had the charismatic ability to electrify a constituency looking for new and inspired leadership.[2]

Almost immediately, Lowenstein became a dominant figure in the race. He was surrounded by bright, dynamic young people destined to become major political figures in their own right—Barney Frank, who helped to coordinate volunteers; Harold Ickes, later a major figure in the Eugene McCarthy and Bill Clinton presidential candidacies; and Sam Beard, a teacher in New York who subsequently ran for U.S. senator in Delaware. Ronnie Eldridge, a district leader in one of the reform clubs, ran the campaign brilliantly. Jack Newfield and Paul Cowan, journalists for the *Village Voice*, provided a press outlet for Lowenstein's views, as did Steve Roberts, a close friend who wrote for the *New York Times*. Then there was the candidate himself. Tie askew, his remarks laced with biting but brilliant humor, boyish and lovable, Lowenstein made the rounds of all the clubs, attended hundreds of kaffeeklatsches, and charmed his way into the hearts of those he met. As one Village reformer observed, Lowenstein "captured the imagination of more people than was expected because he turned out to be [such an] able, articulate, thinking candidate."[3]

In the end, the contest revolved less around issues than around ideology and political personality. Each of the candidates vigorously opposed the Vietnam War, making the campaign one of the first in the country in which hostility to America's involvement in Southeast Asia was the centerpiece of political discussion. Despite minor differences, all the candidates also advocated greater attention to civil rights, the war on poverty, defense of Israel, and urban renewal. Indeed, so similar were the four that Harold Ickes once asked Lowenstein what there was to distinguish between them—a query that brought a blistering, nonappreciative reply. Ultimately, though, that was the key question, and with the passage of time, the query increasingly focused on Weiss and Lowenstein, the two candidates whose views about the war, activism, and social change were most similar, yet whose backgrounds and ideological leanings were significantly different.[4]

Not surprisingly, Lowenstein's greatest strength in the campaign was his record of struggle—and achievement—on behalf of oppressed peoples everywhere in the world, from the anti-Fascists in Franco Spain to the black Africans of South Africa and the Negroes of Mississippi. "There is hardly a worthwhile issue which has not summoned up his militancy and devotion," the democratic socialist leader Michael Harrington wrote in the *New York Herald Tribune*. Lowenstein was a "man for all seasons," his good friend James Wechsler echoed in the *New York Post*. "Often he seemed a one-man movement in Mississippi. . . . [and] his name is known and valued in far more places than those of many celebrated figures." So impressive was his list of credentials, a *New Yorker* reporter wrote, that "we were beginning to suspect that Lowenstein must have doubles planted in trouble spots around the world, poised for action whenever the need arose." Lowenstein's literature seized on these "qualifications of intellect, spirit and background," featuring endorsements from Norman Thomas, Joseph Rauh, Aaron Henry, and Ed King, as well as kind words from Roy Wilkins, Eleanor Roosevelt, Frank Porter Graham, Martin Luther King, Jr., and the former bishop of Johannesburg. It was an all-star cast for an all-world candidate.[5]

Yet Lowenstein's strongest advantage proved also to be his Achilles' heel. For many people, Al Lowenstein had spent too much time galloping around the world and not enough time tending the difficult but enduring issues right in his own backyard. "Listen," Jack Newfield's father used to say, "your friend Lowenstein thinks he can flush every toilet in the world. Tell him *his* toilet is right here on the West Side. Tell him he should stay here in the nineteenth [congressional district]." In contrast with Lowenstein, Ted Weiss had dug in his heels locally, distinguishing himself with courageous stands on homosexual rights, a civilian review board, and school desegregation. He had "paid his dues" where it mattered, the *West Side News* said, instead of becoming a "political dilettante" who left reform politics in the early 1960s to "concentrate on greener sociological pastures" in South Africa and Mississippi. As Barney Frank stated the problem, "Okay, you're Mr. Worldwide, but we want someone who's local. Teddy has been . . . working hard within the district, and you've been out all over the world."[6]

The second issue, directly related to the first, involved the ideological baggage Lowenstein carried with him because of his "worldwide" activities. While many people deeply admired Lowenstein for his work in Spain and South Africa and Mississippi, others were all too ready to believe that there was something suspect about his far-flung travels and interventions. A full year before the revelations about the NSA's connections to the CIA, rumors circulated through the West Side about Lowenstein's alleged links to the CIA. Nor was the reform movement that far removed from the internecine struggles of civil rights activists in Mississippi. Few areas of the country were as invested in the Freedom Vote and Freedom Summer. New York liberals provided substantial financial aid to SNCC, including $100-a-plate dinners addressed by James Forman; the lynching victims Mickey Schwerner and Andrew Goodman both came from a West Side school; and politicos in the reform clubs kept fully abreast of divisions within the movement over the Mississippi Freedom Democratic party. Thus, Lowenstein touched deep ideological chords on the West Side when he attacked the National Lawyers' Guild and appeared to red-bait SNCC. "There were people that hated him," Ronnie Eldridge noted. Al would accuse the Lawyers' Guild of being Communist, Jack Newfield said, and his detractors would accuse him of working for the CIA, both sides "play[ing] out the cartoon of the cold war." In this context, it is not surprising that Lowenstein won the endorsement of Joe Rauh, Aaron Henry, and Ed King, and that Weiss received the backing of SNCC members Fannie Lou

Hamer and Julian Bond. In the ideological left-of-center test tube of West Side Manhattan, Allard Lowenstein appeared a little bit less "pure" than Ted Weiss, particularly given Weiss's record on police brutality and gay rights.[7]

As it turned out, such distinctions made a difference. Given the difficult choice between the flashy, peripatetic Lowenstein, with his record of leaping into trouble spots around the globe, and the tenacious, dedicated Weiss, with his reputation for dogged persistence on local issues, at least some reformers seem to have felt that they *owed* Weiss their first vote. Although Al was "sharper, politically, theoretically, [and] intellectually" than Weiss, one reform leader said, "there was a solidity about Ted." The nature of the balloting process by club members, moreover, made such a judgment critical. On the night of the designation vote, each member of a reform Democratic club was to cast a preferential ballot, listing in order the four candidates. As might have been expected given the overall similarity of their viewpoints, Weiss and Lowenstein drew on a similar constituency, so that reformers voting for Weiss first would likely choose Lowenstein second, and vice versa. Whichever of the two survived to the final cut would in all likelihood inherit the majority of the other's second-place votes.[8]

That is exactly what happened. Drawing on a substantially different body of supporters from those backing Weiss or Lowenstein, Straus led the first ballot with 681 first-place votes. Weiss and Lowenstein ran almost neck and neck 100 votes behind. When Feldman was dropped, his votes were split almost equally between the other three, leaving Straus still in the lead with 736, and only 13 votes separating second-place Weiss, at 650, from third-place Lowenstein with 637. When Lowenstein then was cut, however, two-thirds of his votes went to Weiss, giving the city councilman a 40-vote victory over Straus. Although most newspapers reported the close contest as between Weiss and Straus, in fact the critical choice had been between Lowenstein and Weiss. Perhaps nowhere else except in the rarefied atmosphere of the West Side of Manhattan could hairline differences of ideology and style play so critical a role.[9]

In the end, Lowenstein had run a superb race. As he lined up his fellow candidates for a chorus line "unity kick" at the end of the vote counting, he could take justifiable pride in the enthusiasm of his campaign team, their skill at reaching out to virtually every potential voter, and his own genius at orchestrating his national—and international—battalions of supporters. Once again, as in college, he had waged the good fight on issues of principle, in the process mobilizing a band of devoted followers who would never forget their introduction to politics, not least because of the bittersweet taste of feeling morally victorious even though politically defeated.

The larger question, though, was what Lowenstein would learn from this first venture into the congressional arena. As most people at the time recognized, he might easily have won the campaign had he announced his candidacy earlier or committed himself to working harder *inside* the district, making the nineteenth "his toilet," as Jack Newfield's father said. Significantly, his own brother Larry, who almost never uttered a word critical of Allard, this time laid the issue on the line. Regretting how little time he was able to spend with Al alone (when that did happen, Larry wrote, "you seem very condescending and disinterested"), he felt compelled to resort to a letter. "What you want from life is in your hands," he told Al. "However, I doubt that you are keeping faith with those who are close to you." If Al wanted to go off and write, so be it.

> But let us not repeat the same errors—and they were errors . . . since a little vision would have given you the twelve votes [you lacked] quite easily. . . . Nobody can guarantee what will happen two years from now. But if you had thought ahead two years ago, 12 more votes would have been yours. There can be no excuse [in the future] except immature thinking. . . . We believe that Al Lowenstein belongs in Congress. You've convinced us of that in the 19th. And if it isn't in 1966, why then let it be in 1968 from the 19th. [But] if you are not willing to be a little bit calculating, you are not deserving of what you ask of others by taking on this task. . . . If you had not put all of Gabriel's thoughts away as poppycock, you would now be running an active race in the 19th. . . . [The] question is simple. Is there a good reason for Al Lowenstein to be in Congress? If so . . . do what can be done about it. If not, then get out of the picture. . . . Write? Teach? Congress? Causes? It's your life, Al.

The challenge could hardly have been clearer. Lowenstein had made a start on his father's advice by finally running for Congress. Yet he had done so in a way that hindered rather than helped his eventual chances of electoral victory and that recalled all the indecisiveness of his student political campaigns at UNC. He could now learn the lesson of that experience by digging in—as Ted Weiss had done—and preparing the groundwork for a rerun in 1968 should Weiss lose. Larry Lowenstein, at least, was certain that by being a "little bit calculating," Al could easily reach his goal, in a congressional district almost tailor-made for his politics. The question was, would he do so? Or, would he, as Larry wondered, continue "drifting . . . [like] our policy in Southeast Asia."[10]

FIGHTING THE PRESIDENT—STAGE 1

The reference to Southeast Asia was only appropriate given how much time and energy Lowenstein devoted over the ensuing seven years to the war in Vietnam. Like all the candidates in the nineteenth congressional district, Lowenstein criticized the war as a primary tenet of his campaign strategy. Yet he became the only one of the four to make political opposition to the war—and the president—the raison d'être of his life. Distinctively qualified by virtue of his far-flung network to reach out for help across the land, he possessed the exact combination of attributes necessary to generate a comprehensive national base from which to fight the president. He was ardently anti-Communist and therefore could not be smeared as a left-wing kook (though some tried); he operated sufficiently inside the political system to have credibility with mainstream politicians; and he worked far enough out "on the edge" of social insurgency to deserve an audience among those contemplating outright dissent against U.S. foreign policy. Joined to the charismatic enthusiasm Lowenstein was able to generate almost everywhere he went, these attributes help to explain why he became the indispensable pivot of the "dump Johnson" political movement.

The precursor to much of Lowenstein's subsequent antiwar activity came in the fall of 1965, when he agreed to become a principal organizer for ARFEP (Americans for Reappraisal of Far Eastern Policy). Begun at Yale under the leadership of William Sloane Coffin, ARFEP was a classic early antiwar group. Since assailing America's Vietnam policy outright seemed too radical and premature, the organization tried to generate debate about the whole sorry state of U.S. foreign policy in the Far East, beginning with the government's refusal to recognize or deal with the People's Republic of China. It was clearly a group that provided an outlet for "establishment" dissent, featuring on its board of directors such notables as Norman Thomas, John Fairbanks, the noted Asian scholar, and Roger Baldwin, the distinguished founder of the American Civil Liberties Union (ACLU).[11]

At the same time, ARFEP also made a bold move into the future by defining its principle constituency as students on college campuses. By the end of October 1965, more than thirty colleges and universities had been lined up on a closed-circuit hookup from Union Theological Seminary for a simultaneous rally in protest against America's Far Eastern policy. Addressed by Lowenstein, Coffin, and Thomas, the rally won national news coverage and seemed a sign of things to come. It also proved the central importance of Al Lowenstein. When he was an active organizer, ARFEP grew. Lowenstein would send word out over his grapevine that he was coming, students would gather, he would make an inspiring speech, and then fifteen or twenty would stay behind to be assigned specific tasks before Al went off to a wrestling match and his next engagement. "As long as Al was doing it," Coffin said, "it was fabulous because he was the one everybody could relate to." But when Norman Thomas urged him to commit to the organization for a year, Lowenstein declined, entering the Manhattan congressional race instead. "That was pretty much the end of it," Coffin said, "because there wasn't enough student structure." Nevertheless, the ARFEP initiative provided an important model for what was to come.[12]

By the time the National Student Association met in Champaign-Urbana, Illinois, in August 1966, a vibrant antiwar movement had clearly developed throughout America. Lyndon Johnson had begun a multifaceted escalation of the war in early 1965, with extensive bombing raids of North Vietnam. American combat troops arrived by the tens of thousands, allegedly to protect air bases, but they were soon involved in search and-destroy missions against the enemy. Casualties mounted, and more and more young Americans realized that they too might end up in the quagmire of Vietnam's jungles and rice paddies.

As the number of American troops in Vietnam climbed, so, too, did the number of students engaged in protests against the war. There had been teach-ins on most university campuses designed to persuade administration spokesmen that Washington's Vietnam policy had no intellectual credibility; political campaigns were under way making the Vietnam War a major issue of contention; and groups like Students for a Democratic Society, founded in 1962 with the moderate objective of perfecting and humanizing American society, were moving quickly to a far more radical critique of the war as an embodiment of the oppressive qualities of American capitalism. Many moderates had high hopes for the teach-ins. Yet, for the most part, they had not worked, except as catalysts to alienation after administration leaders like McGeorge Bundy and Walt Rostow condescendingly rejected criticism of the war. Perhaps conceived in naïveté by those who had hoped that foreign policy could be altered via intelligent debate and reason, the teach-ins nevertheless left a huge vacuum. Now it seemed that the vacuum might be filled by people advocating much more militant resistance to the war.

It was in this context that a major debate began to rage. On the one side were liberals who sought to work within the political system to bring about reforms in government policy; on the other side were radicals who wanted to organize outside the "establishment" to bring about far-reaching structural change in American values and institutions. Lowenstein occasionally displayed sympathy for the more radical insurgents. He appreciated the depth of their anger, the purity of their conviction, and the idealism of their goals for transforming America. But as in the civil rights movement, he found it more consistent with his own political past and principles to work on the inside rather than join a mass movement seeking revolution from the outside. One more time, he sought to be the critical individual who would bridge the gap between generations of liberals by giving direction to the moral sensibilities of the young.

Those were the issues that framed discussions about the war at the 1966 NSA congress. There ensued a confrontation between the radical antiwar caucus at NSA, headed by the Stanford student body president David Harris, and the liberal-moderate caucus led by followers of Al Lowenstein. In a debate that would soon be famous, Harris denounced the war in absolutist terms; he suggested that those who did not resist were acting like "good Germans," and, by implication, sanctioned protesters who marched on draft boards and assaulted ROTC buildings. There was no hope in turning the administration around by working through the system or using peaceful petitions, Harris declared. The time had come to lie down in front of troop trains and engage in massive civil disobedience.

Lowenstein, by contrast, insisted that the system could work if people only gave it a chance. "[You have] to grab it and make it respond," he said. It was all well and good to denounce the war with moral indignation, but that would not end the fighting. "If you want to [do that]," Greg Craig recalled hearing Lowenstein say, "you have to be pragmatic and realistic. . . . David Harris lying down in front of a troop train is not going to end the war, but if you get 100 student body presidents to lie down . . . [that] might make a difference." The key, Lowenstein emphasized, was to reach out to the nonconverted to build the broadest base possible, thereby making the antiwar movement "reflect the mainstream of American students," even those who might otherwise call themselves conservatives.[13]

As a direct consequence of that debate, Lowenstein and Greg Craig and their allies developed the concept of drafting a letter to Lyndon Johnson on behalf of student body presidents throughout the country. Going back to the notion of 100 campus leaders lying down in front of troop trains, Lowenstein now proposed that 100 signatures be gathered for the letter to LBJ, representing all the major campuses in America. At a meeting of more than 200 NSA delegates, Lowenstein mesmerized the group with images of how potent such an appeal would be as a means of building the base that could actually have an impact on ending the war, instead of just excoriating it with self-righteous words. When the NSA congress finally confronted the choice between David Harris' denunciation of the war and Greg Craig's call for a broad-based letter of inquiry and concern, the Craig option triumphed, with even David Harris agreeing to give the process a chance. The bottom line, as the UNC student body president Bob Powell observed, was "who is most effective in protesting the conduct of the war, liberals or radicals." On that issue, he told his campus, the NSA had decided that "responsible action could be more effective than using the rhetoric of the New Left."[14]

With the NSA resolution as a mandate, Lowenstein set out to draft a final version of the letter to the president, aided by a group of student body presidents from Northeast campuses. Along with some other student leaders, Greg Craig from Harvard, Steve Cohen from Amherst, and Clint Deveaux from the State University of New York at Buffalo gathered periodically at Lowenstein's New York apartment to rework the language. Throughout, the emphasis was on making it possible for the largest number of people to sign the letter. Although some of the campus presidents had taken part in teach-ins, "for the most part," Clint Deveaux noted, "we were not associated with the antiwar movement. We were too middle of the road, and this letter was not an anti-Vietnam letter, it was much more a series of questions."[15]

In fact, the letter was a model of reasoned discourse. Seeking to "encourage a frank discussion" of the war, the students expressed concern about the "increasing confusion [surrounding] both our basic purpose and our tactics," as well as "increasing fear that the course now being pursued may lead us irrevocably into a major land war in Asia—a war which many feel could not be won without recourse to nuclear weapons." As loyal Americans "devoted to the Constitution, to the democratic process, and to law and order," the students modestly urged an extension of the truce announced for the New Year's holiday and renewed consideration of whether the Vietnam War was consistent with America's vital interests. A masterpiece of decorum, the letter received front-page coverage the next week in the *New York Times*.[16]

If Lowenstein's plan had been to convince as many people as possible to oppose the Johnson administration on his terms, the strategy was working perfectly. Within days after the publicity surrounding the letter, administration officials telephoned student leaders to schedule a meeting of the campus presidents with Secretary of State Dean Rusk. Carefully preparing for the encounter, Lowenstein and thirty-nine student body leaders met at Dunbarton College of the Sacred Heart to rehearse their moderate and pragmatic approach. Dean Rusk did his part by appearing completely intransigent in the face of their questions. What would happen, a former Goldwater supporter from Michigan State asked, if both sides kept escalating until the United States finally dropped nuclear bombs. Rusk took a long drag on his cigarette and coolly replied, "Well, somebody's going to get hurt." The room was silent. "You could have heard a pin drop," one person said. "We just looked at each other around the table and said, 'My God, the secretary of state of the United States is crazy. This guy has lost it.'" That day, Greg Craig recalled, Rusk "transformed the makeup of the antiwar movement with a single stroke. It was no longer SDS and Port Huron people and Tom Hayden and those folks. It became a mainstream student movement. . . . that went straight into the 'dump Johnson' movement." All these student body presidents, fraternity leaders, and team captains suddenly felt that no one in power could really defend the country's Vietnam policy. It was the exact moment, Colgate's Rick Weidman said later, that he turned irrevocably against the war. Within weeks, more than 200 student body presidents signed a new letter to Rusk. Al Lowenstein's mainstream political movement was rolling.[17]

In essence, Lowenstein had achieved two major objectives with the letter strategy. First, he had won critical backing among student leaders for the notion that the antiwar movement should be political and liberal in nature rather than moralistic and radical. The goal, he agreed, was to end the war, but the means to that goal must be consistent with maximizing the appeal of the antiwar effort to middle-of-the-road Americans. Bombastic language and confrontational tactics only alienated the majority; persuasion was the key to success. Thus, the radical left had to be—and was—contained.

Second, he structured the organization of his forces in such a way that he could remain in charge. If the administration altered its policy in response to the student protests—as at times he hoped it might—his approach would be recognized as having made the difference. If, on the other hand, the administration refused to listen to the voice of reason, he would have all the more basis for bringing additional mainstream people—who would now see how obstinate the government was—into the next phase of his political scheme. Whichever the case, his political approach would prevail with his constituency of moderate leftists, while those who favored polarization and confrontation remained on the fringe.

It was a key moment that distilled most of the critical issues dividing liberals from radicals. The New Left believed that America's institutions were fundamentally flawed, that change within the system was impossible, and that in the face of a brutal war that sometimes seemed genocidal, the only response was to refuse to participate and to use "whatever means necessary" to stop the killing. According to this viewpoint, Greg Craig observed, Lowenstein was indistinguishable "from the Hubert Humphreys of the world, working for the LBJs of the world, [who] were manipulating the Aaron Henrys of the world—[all as part of] a massive conspiracy to destroy, or at least subvert, the revolution." Lowenstein, on the other hand, saw those who would "hate America rather than [work to] save it" as the ultimate threat. In his view, the Democratic party was, and should be, "an instrument of salvation rather than of oppression"; if only people would enter the political process and work to turn things around, the system would respond and peace would come. "You don't indict an institution," Rick Weidman said, "you change its behavior." Thus, as William Sloane Coffin pointed out, the greatest difference between Lowenstein and his radical critics was that they condemned the entire political process and said "a pox on your [entire] society," while he remained a "prophet who stands clearly within the tradition and says, 'The tradition is being corrupted, [let us restore the tradition].'"[18]

In the end, few differences were more profound, or more significant for the politics of the Vietnam era. As 1967 unfolded, the basic tension between the two points of view would constitute a major subtext of the anti-war movement. For the moment, however, Lowenstein remained in charge, his ability to marshal support for his mainstream approach a signal tribute to his political skill.

THE CIA REVISITED

Even as the tensions between radicals and liberals played out, the revelation that CIA money had provided the basic financing for the National Student Association since the early 1950s exploded on the scene. Although in theory the exposé had little to do with Lowenstein's efforts to forge a political antiwar coalition within NSA, in reality it fueled a whole series of questions implicit in the radical-liberal split. What did it mean to work "within the system"? How close did one have to get to those in power before becoming co-opted by them? Where was the boundary between being complicit in covert intelligence activities and operating, independently, at the outer edges of these activities? And could one escape responsibility for the consequences of such activities, even if one was not "witting"? In short, the simple issue of Al Lowenstein's awareness—or nonawareness—of the CIA-NSA connection could easily become a surgical probe into all the implications of working as a liberal activist inside, rather than outside, the prevailing structure of power and values.

As discussed in chapter 4, the formal link between the Agency and the NSA began in 1952, after Lowenstein's presidency. Later, he acknowledged having been offered money from an "unknown source" in connection with his Stockholm trip in 1950, but he turned down the funding because of suspicion about its origins. Although most of the international student agencies he was instrumental in creating subsequently received funding from the CIA, there is no basis for thinking that in the 1950s Lowenstein was aware of that fact. As he told reporters in 1967, "To imply a CIA connection indiscriminately to those who . . . opposed and worked against Stalinist dominated organizations is a very dangerous and fruitless game." The CIA official responsible for handling the NSA link has insisted that Lowenstein was always kept "out of the loop" because he was a maverick who could not be trusted. That person's successor in the 1960s—Robert Kiley—has confirmed that, as a matter of policy, Lowenstein was intentionally excluded from all channels of information about CIA-NSA cooperation.[19]

At some time in the 1960s, however, it appears that Lowenstein developed suspicions about the NSA-CIA link. Given his political shrewdness and intelligence, it would be inconceivable that he would not have done so. In 1964, for example, when an NSA international vice-president won Arab-bloc backing for a position in the rival, Communist-backed International Union of Students, Lowenstein turned to Greg Craig and said, "I tell you, I think there was a deal here, and there were more people involved in it than just [the NSA officer] and the Arabs." According to NSA officials, Lowenstein became aware of the NSA-CIA connection well before its public revelation. He participated in a meeting with a CIA official and the NSA president Phillip Sherburne, trying to persuade Sherburne not to corroborate the NSA-CIA relationship, and later he confirmed that he was asked by both sides to help "facilitate" the subsequent disengagement of NSA from the CIA. According to Rick Stearn, NSA's international vice-president in 1966–67 (and a "witting" individual), Lowenstein exhibited in those discussions a fairly comprehensive knowledge of CIA activities—more than one would expect from a total newcomer to the story.

Thus, while there is persuasive evidence that Lowenstein lacked any formal awareness of the relationship in the early days, there is also abundant indirect testimony that he became knowledgeable sometime in the 1960s.[20]

Much more difficult to explain is Lowenstein's lengthy history of involvement with groups and activities that subsequently were shown to have CIA connections—links that a person of Lowenstein's sophistication might well have suspected. Throughout the 1950s and 1960s, for example, he regularly directed students to the NSA's international relations seminar at Bryn Mawr. Dubbed the "CIA camp" by one participant, the seminar became a primary recruiting ground for the Agency, with many of the seminar's graduates later becoming international vice-presidents of NSA—who were always witting—and direct CIA employees. There was sufficient gossip around the NSA about the seminar that Lowenstein must have heard some reference to its sponsorship; moreover, in keeping in contact with those he had recommended, he should have seen the pattern in their subsequent careers.

Lowenstein also served as a primary recruiter of students to attend world youth festivals sponsored by the Moscow-dominated International Union of Students. Particularly for the Helsinki festival in 1962 and the planned Algiers festival in 1965, Lowenstein sent students to the Independent Research Service, where, he assured them, they could find funding for their trip. It would not have been unnatural to ask where the Independent Research Service secured its funding, and why he was so certain that money would be made available to "his" recruits. Similarly, he was deeply involved in the NSA's Algerian program. When Ben Bella, the Algerian leader, came to America shortly after his country won independence, he specifically acknowledged the CIA's assistance to Algerian students. Whatever the exact nature of Lowenstein's awareness of CIA activities, therefore, his contact with CIA-connected operations was by no means distant and removed.[21]

The murky nature of these associations was perhaps best exemplified by Lowenstein's involvement in the elections held in the Dominican Republic during the late spring of 1966. Juan Bosch, a democratic Socialist, had been overthrown by a military junta in 1963, at least in part because the United States had not followed through on its pledges of support after the detested Trujillo regime had given way to democratic rule. Two years later, in April 1965, the Constitutionalists—supporting Bosch—started their own revolution. Based in the army, they had achieved virtual control over the country when J. Tarpley Bennett, the American ambassador—with no evidence at all to support him—claimed that Communists were about to seize power and that American lives were in danger. Lyndon Johnson sent in the Marines, victory was snatched away from the Constitutionalists, and a right-wing government remained in charge. Ever since his overthrow, Bosch had lived in exile in Puerto Rico, continuing to work for the restoration of independence and democracy in his country. By early 1966, he had been persuaded by American officials to return to the Dominican Republic to participate in free elections in which, once and for all, his support could be fairly tested.

It was at this point that Lowenstein entered the picture. The Constitutionalist army forces were being terrorized by the right wing in the military; Bosch was holed up in his rural home, threatened with assassination if he dared to campaign openly among the Dominican people. Bosch was prepared to drop out of the election and acknowledge that, once again, democratic reform had been snuffed out in his native land. In response, Norman Thomas created the Committee on Fair Elections in the Dominican Republic. With his prestige as an international Socialist leader, Thomas hoped to persuade Bosch to remain in the contest and, as part of the inducement for him to do so, proposed sending an observer team from the United States to guarantee the fairness of the election process. The committee included Thomas, Bayard Rustin of the A. Philip Randolph Foundation, Victor Reuther, head of the international division of the United Auto Workers, and Allard Lowenstein. In fact, Lowenstein was the chief organizer of the venture. He was as close to Thomas as anyone, a confidant of Reuther and Rustin, and the person whose energy, ability, and sophistication made him the ideal coordinator for the task.[22]

On his first trip to the Dominican Republic, Lowenstein found Bosch alienated, cynical, and resigned to defeat. Even if he won the election, Bosch told Lowenstein, a military coup would occur as soon as he called back from exile any of his Constitutionalist officers. "I have lost all my faith in America," the former president told Lowenstein. "Never again will I have confidence in the possibility of a political understanding with Americans. Privately, yes. Politically, no." Feeling deceived at being persuaded to return to a country where he was virtually under house arrest because of the military's terrorism, Bosch concluded that the whole free election process was meaningless. "The problem is with . . . U.S. policy," he repeated. "I will be trapped by that."

To a large extent, Lowenstein agreed with Bosch's assessment. Outraged by U.S. intervention in the Dominican Republic in 1965 and the persistent failure to exert leverage on the right-wing government, Lowenstein told a Stanford audience that "American action in the Dominican Republic represents a desire to oppose social change in the name of stability. Stability means a freezing of the status quo in which 80 percent of the people are starving." Nevertheless, Lowenstein joined Thomas in imploring Bosch to remain a candidate and participate in the election process. Even though he understood that Bosch's failure to campaign would tarnish his credibility and substantially erode his potential base of support, he cajoled Bosch into the paradoxical stance of agreeing to sanction, by his participation, an electoral process that he already had dismissed as hopeless because of "U.S. policy."[23]

How the CIA fits into this scenario is complicated and somewhat speculative. Presumably, CIA operatives had been involved in the initial overthrow of Bosch (as of Rafael Trujillo) and would be supportive of a right-wing regime. Yet such a presumption does not necessarily preclude the involvement of Agency officials as advocates on Bosch's behalf—or at least, as supporters of an electoral process that would appear to be fair and would sanction the existing regime. Especially in the 1940s and 1950s, the CIA often provided a welcome refuge for progressive, social democratic forces, which found the Agency a more hospitable environment than a State Department paralyzed by the fear of McCarthyism. Many CIA-funded activities were on the liberal side of the political spectrum, including the NSA. Another such progressive recipient of CIA support was the Institute of International Labor Research, a New York–based group headed by Norman Thomas and financed by the Kaplan Foundation, the same CIA conduit that provided funds for the NSA. Although Thomas himself was presumably not aware of the CIA connection, he had

once applied to Allen Dulles, the head of the CIA, for support for a magazine project he was involved with. Most of the Labor Institute's monies
went to international labor projects. Among Thomas's associates in those
projects were many individuals who subsequently became associated with
the Committee on Free Elections in the Dominican Republic, including a
Rumanian exile named Sacha Volman.[24]

When the committee was first established, Lowenstein recruited Fred
Goff, a former protégé from Stanford, to serve as its primary staff aide. The
son of Protestant missionaries in Latin America, Goff was one of Lowenstein's favorite people—bright, sensitive, and politically engaged. Lowenstein had earlier urged Goff to attend the NSA international relations seminar and had tried to get him placed in excellent job positions. His flu-
ency in Spanish as well as his knowledge of the area made Goff the ideal
person for the job. The task of the committee, Lowenstein told Goff, was to
ensure fair elections, and if the elections were fair, Bosch would win.
Goff's role was to be the liaison, to set up appointments with various officials, and to serve as Lowenstein's aide de camp when he was in the Dominican Republic.

Goff's suspicions about the committee began when Lowenstein gave
him a list of three people to contact. The first turned out to be a Bay of
Pigs veteran who had been a trainer at the institute in Puerto Rico where
Bosch taught. The second was a former FBI employee. And the third was
Sacha Volman, who met Goff at Bosch's sister's house in Puerto Rico and
asked him if he knew where the CIA office was in the U.S. embassy in
Santiago. Volman then started to draw a map, only to pause—as if discovering he was not talking to the person he thought he was—and say, "Forget I ever talked with you about that." Volman had been the secretary-
treasurer of Thomas's Labor Institute—the person who actually ran the institute—and thus was the one individual in that organization most likely
to be witting about the CIA. And although in 1966 Goff did not know
about Volman's background, his conversation with the Rumanian led him
to wonder whose instructions he was operating under.[25]

Goff's suspicions about the committee's activities came to a head at the
end of its work in the Dominican Republic. About seventy observers were
on hand for the election, but most had flown in for just the last two days of
the campaign. On election day itself, Goff drove Lowenstein to meet Ambassador Ellsworth Bunker, the primary U.S. policymaker on the scene.
When he emerged from the conversation, Lowenstein told Goff, "Boy, I
just made an agreement." If Bosch won the balloting, according to Lowen-

258

stein, Bunker would use his influence to get that result accepted. On the other hand, if Bosch's opponent, Juan Balaguer, were victorious, Lowenstein promised Bunker that he would use all his influence to have the elections declared fair. There was only one problem: Lowenstein told Goff he could not tell his fellow committee members about the agreement because it was too volatile and confidential. That same day, Bosch informed Lowenstein of his serious concern about the violence and fraud occurring at the polling places. In response, various committee members agreed that no one would make any public statements until all the returns were in and the irregularities had been investigated.

That same day, Lowenstein and Norman Thomas flew back to New York from the Dominican Republic. At the airport, Norman Thomas issued a statement saying that the elections had been fair, and that if Balaguer were the winner, his victory should be recognized. Subsequently, Lowenstein and Thomas reaffirmed that conclusion. In a conversation with Bosch's wife, Lowenstein acknowledged that votes had been stolen and soldiers had intimidated people at the polling places. Nevertheless, the important thing, he insisted, was to "fight for the integrity of the process," because once free elections were legitimized as a means of making political decisions, reform could take place through normal procedures. In short, *this* election may not have been completely fair, but it was more critical to secure acceptance for the *idea* of elections than to make an issue of the irregularities that had just occurred.

Needless to say, not everyone agreed. Many of the committee members felt betrayed that Lowenstein and Thomas had broken their word and issued a judgment prior to consultation and complete evaluation of the results. The Puerto Rican members of the committee, in fact, wrote a dissenting report, arguing that violence, fraud, and military intimidation in the countryside had been so widespread as to invalidate the election. Nevertheless, it was the Lowenstein-Thomas assessment that carried the day in American political circles. From Fred Goff's point of view, that assessment rested primarily on Lowenstein's shoulders. Norman Thomas was in his eighties, nearly deaf, and quite infirm; in most cases, he did what Al wanted him to do and rarely acted against Al's advice. Thomas's statement bore a remarkable similarity to the agreement that Lowenstein had just made with Bunker, though the other committee members did not know that. The end result, for Goff at least, was reinforcement of Bosch's belief that U.S. policy would never allow his resumption of the presidency. The incident also left a permanent question in Goff's mind about Lowenstein's ultimate motivation, and particularly about his sense of the relation between means and ends.[26]

The larger issue posed by the Dominican experience is not Lowenstein's conscious complicity in a CIA-influenced political operation. There is no visible evidence of such complicity. Rather, it is the question of how closely one cooperates with those whose motives one might have reason to suspect—what political agenda does such cooperation ultimately serve? It is difficult not to agree with the journalist Ruth Sherif's judgment that, rather than report on the situation in the Dominican Republic, the committee on Free Elections "ended up . . . smoothing over and covering up the real event." That, in turn, raises the question of what the committee's own political interests were. There, the answer seems equally clear: to legitimize an electoral process. Yet when that process occurred within a structure completely biased toward victory for the conservative Balaguer forces, the actual conduct of the voting process itself became far less significant. Military officers loyal to Bosch had been exiled; the army, by most reports, intimidated pro-Bosch activists; and the candidate himself was afraid to campaign because of assassination threats. Moreover, the United States had staked much of its prestige on an electoral victory for Balaguer.

Focusing only on the voting process therefore became almost a charade, providing the illusion of legitimacy for a result largely predetermined by other factors. Yet Lowenstein persisted in viewing that process as key to the possibility of any future reform. Indeed, he feared that any condemnation of fraud would simply provoke violence by angry Bosch supporters and lead to renewed civil war. In that context, reinforcing the electoral process might well make sense. Still, if the primary consequence was to provide cover for a rigged political agenda, how could one avoid responsibility for helping those who did the rigging? Within days, the U.S. Information Agency was quoting Thomas's statement to support its own assertion that the election results had been fair. As Ruth Sherif observed, "For all the good will of the liberals who worked in the Dominican Republic, the Dominican people had to bear the brunt of their experiments."[27]

To some extent, the same issue of cooperation, rather than conscious complicity, was at stake in the NSA. Technically, the former NSA president Greg Gallo pointed out, the CIA never tried to interfere in the NSA's domestic political agenda. Yet the Agency helped determine who the officers would be who generated that agenda, thus exercising all the control they presumably needed in advance. Although Lowenstein was not aware of this process during most of the NSA's history, he clearly had reason by the mid-1960s to suspect a collaboration. Yet he continued to work closely with groups, like the Independent Research Service, that were part of the NSA-CIA connection.

Lowenstein claimed throughout that he knew nothing about this connection and had never been part of a CIA operation. As his wife Jenny said, "He would have to have been the greatest actor in the free world" if he had known, because he was so shocked by the revelations. In the aftermath of the disclosures in early 1967, Lowenstein defended himself—for the most part successfully—from those who charged he was part of a CIA conspiracy. But ultimately, the more pivotal issue was how close one came to such CIA activities by defending so vigorously the system itself and the importance of staying within it to work for social and political reform. On the basis of Lowenstein's experience with the NSA in the 1960s and with the Dominican Republic in 1966, the line between his maintaining an independent political viewpoint and becoming co-opted on behalf of someone else's political agenda seemed very thin. Treading that line, and deciding how totally he should commit to working inside the electoral process instead of outside it, would continue as preoccupying themes through all of Lowenstein's activities.[28]

11
"Dump Johnson"

Iғ HIS RATIONALIZATION OF THE ELECTION OF JUAN BALAGUER ILLUSTRATED the cautious, conservative side of Allard Lowenstein's political activism, deciding to remove Lyndon Johnson from the presidency through electoral politics exhibited exactly the opposite characteristics. Stunning in its tactical boldness and outrageous in its assumptions about the vulnerability of those in power, the "dump Johnson" campaign was the effort of a few reformers, propelled by conscience, to marshal enough political power to achieve, in essence, a peaceful coup d'état. Never before had so vast a venture been attempted in so short a time. Rarely, if ever, had political activists reposed more faith in the capacity of a democratic process to turn its leaders and policies upside down. In 1967 and 1968, Allard Lowenstein put himself at the head of an insurgent movement that pledged to accomplish radical ends through reformist means. The degree to which that effort was a success testified dramatically to the genius and political passion of Allard Lowenstein and represented the apex of his political influence. The degree to which that success led him to believe that he and his ideas were invincible represented the start of his political downfall.

DEVELOPING A STRATEGY

Despite the national brouhaha over the CIA revelations in February 1967, Lowenstein and a growing cadre of student supporters persisted in building a base for political opposition to the war. David Hawk had met Lowenstein when the latter was recruiting for the student body presidents' letter. Although interested in a variety of options, including draft resistance, Hawk was immediately impressed by Lowenstein's approach. "He had what other people . . . in the antiwar movement did not, which was a sense of political strategy," Hawk declared. "There were a lot of activists who didn't see beyond the semiannual mobilizations. But Allard was not only extremely articulate about how they're lying to you . . . he [also] had an idea of how to stop it." And so Hawk signed on. Starting in February, he and Clint Deveaux, soon joined by Sam Brown, opened a closet-sized office at Union Theological Seminary to coordinate opposition to the war. Using a long-distance WATS line and appealing to affluent peace liberals for donations, the Union Seminary operation was the first in a series of logistical outposts that provided the coordination for the burgeoning antiwar effort.[1]

Lowenstein himself, meanwhile, was searching for a viable battle plan to sustain and nourish his political alternative to radical confrontation with the government. The Rusk meeting seemed to leave little hope that a change would come from inside the administration, an impression only deepened by additional one-on-one meetings Lowenstein had with Vice-President Hubert Humphrey and presidential adviser Walt Rostow. The Rostow visit, in particular, was "very depressing," Lowenstein said; it "[highlighted] all the worst little blindnesses of the administration." In light of all these developments, Lowenstein and Curtis Gans, his colleague from Americans for Democratic Action (ADA), a liberal anti–Communist group, concluded that Lyndon Johnson himself was the Achilles' heel of the Democratic party and set out to explore various options for mobilizing opposition to the president.[2]

There were a number of possibilities. Many antiwar activists hoped that Martin Luther King, Jr., and Dr. Benjamin Spock, the legendary antiwar pediatrician, might be persuaded to run together on a third-party presidential ticket. Other ideas included running slates of peace delegates in the presidential primaries, initiating a "Vote No" strategy in the Wisconsin presidential primary (where "none of the above" was a ballot possibility), and working with congressional antiwar forces to develop a legislative base from which to attack LBJ. King's position was especially important. Far more open to the radical alternative than Lowenstein, he nevertheless viewed Lowenstein—one of only two whites on the Southern Christian Leadership Conference (SCLC) board—as a key adviser. Thus, although King agreed to address the April 1967 mobilization rally against the war—a gesture to radicals—he insisted that Norman Thomas introduce him, that mobilization leaders reach out to peace liberals like the historian Henry Steele Commager, and that Lowenstein play a major role in drafting his speech. Furthermore, Lowenstein was to be the contact person for setting up sessions with the peace liberals.[3]

At a critical meeting in the early spring of 1967, these options were narrowed considerably. Gathering at Granson's, Andrew Young, Curtis Gans, Jimmy Wechsler, and Norman Thomas discussed strategy. King would not be a candidate under any circumstances, Andrew Young declared. Others suggested using ADA as a base for opposing Johnson—an idea that eventually led to Wechsler introducing a resolution at an ADA board meeting threatening withdrawal of liberal support from Johnson if his war policy did not change.[4]

By May, Lowenstein had a different idea. He started broaching the nucleus of his emerging strategy to friends. "It is now clear what must be done," Lowenstein told Greg Craig and Barney Frank at a meeting in Cambridge. "Dump Johnson. We can do it. No one wants him out there and all that we have to do is have someone say it. Like, 'The emperor has no clothes.' There's a movement within the party that is dying for leadership." Later in the summer—after returning from a trip to Africa—Lowenstein talked about this idea with his Union Seminary crew, David Hawk, Steve Cohen, and Clint Deveaux.

In both cases, the first response was astonishment. "I've never had any questions about [Al's] political judgment in the past," Barney Frank told Greg Craig, "[but] I think he's crazy. The idea of upsetting a sitting president with the power of Lyndon Johnson. . . . Crazy." The first reaction of the New York contingent was to ask what kind of mushrooms Al had been eating in Africa. But Lowenstein persisted. The idea might sound brazen and bizarre when first set forth, he agreed; but his friends should think about the logical sequence. The public was changing its opinion on the war and had no enthusiasm for LBJ; all people needed was an outlet for their grievances. Momentum would develop, Johnson would plummet further in popularity, suddenly a candidate would emerge who "will get on the bandwagon that we've built," and voila! Johnson would fall. The idea suddenly sounded plausible, especially to those who were captured by the conviction and energy of the person presenting it.[5]

Any such national campaign needed a base, however, and the next question was where to find it. Two logical possibilities were ADA and SANE. Lowenstein had been elected to the ADA board in May 1966. A year later, in response to Wechsler's resolution, ADA went on record as willing to support a peace candidate from either party if Johnson did not change his policy, and John Kenneth Galbraith, an ardent antiwar foe, was chosen ADA president. But there was dissension within ADA as well. Lowenstein was elected vice-president of the organization in May by a vote of 16–15, a margin that reflected, according to one board member, "substantial pique that a young man without national reputation" should be trying to impose his will on the ADA. Indeed, a substantial backlash set in against the Wechsler resolution, especially from labor mainstays like Gus Tyler, who feared that ADA was being turned into a one-issue organization. By July, Joseph Rauh—one of ADA's most powerful leaders— was rejecting the idea of a "dump Johnson" movement, declaring that "no responsible people inside the Democratic Party will allow their names to be connected with . . . so helpless a drive." Instead, he argued, ADA should devote all its energies to developing support for a peace plank in the Democratic platform, thereby showing the true strength of antiwar sentiment while avoiding "the ugliness of just being against someone." SANE, the peace organization committed to abolishing nuclear weapons, was more clearly ready to support an anti-LBJ movement. But its base was more narrow, and the organization was torn by an internecine dispute over how and whether it should align itself with more radical peace groups, like Women Strike for Peace and the National Mobilization to End the War. Clearly, neither ADA nor SANE would be adequate for the crusade Lowenstein envisioned.[6]

Not surprisingly, Lowenstein then returned to the place from which he had first launched his political alternative to radical protest—the NSA. Mainstream students had provided the base for the Lowenstein-inspired student body letter to LBJ. Nothing in Johnson's response since then had done anything but swell the ranks of those willing to protest the war. Why not mobilize these students, then, as the vanguard for carrying the "dump Johnson" movement forward into the Democratic party and the primary states. Thus when the NSA met for its annual Congress in August 1967, two headlines emerged: the student delegates had decided to sever their ties with CIA-supported international organizations; and they determined to organize an "alternative candidates task force" that would pave the way for unseating Lyndon Johnson. "This congress," Lowenstein told the delegates at College Park, Maryland, "can be a launching pad for a decision to make 1968 the year when students help change a society almost everyone agrees is headed for destruction." If older Americans in the ADA and

SANE would not harness their energies behind a "dump Johnson" effort, the cream of America's youth would show them the way.[7]

Ironically, the attractiveness of Lowenstein's "dump Johnson" strategy was heightened by the dissension and disarray among radicals who met later that summer at the National Conference for New Politics (NCNP) convention. More than 3,000 delegates gathered in Chicago, representing a variety of antiwar, Black Power, and community action groups. Most appeared committed to a total overhaul of American society, rejecting the feasibility of working for change through existing institutions. Almost immediately, however, their deliberations were taken over by fractious infighting. A black caucus demanded unconditional acceptance of a thirteen point ultimatum requiring 50 percent black representation on all committees (later expanded to require 50 percent voting power throughout the convention), support for all wars of national liberation, condemnation of Zionist imperialism, and creation of "white civilizing committees" to extirpate "the savage and beastlike character that runs rampant through America." In what seemed to many a paroxysm of guilt, the overwhelmingly white delegates accepted the black caucus's demands. But then the convention devoted most of its energies to discussing how to create a revolution and barely mentioned the 1968 election or presidential politics. Thus the "new politics," especially as conveyed by the mass media, seemed to boil down to two essentials: a willingness to embrace inflammatory rhetoric as long as the source of the rhetoric was black; and an insistence that "politics," at least as conventionally defined, was beneath radical contempt—a tool of the establishment that should be abandoned as irrelevant.[8]

From the point of view of Lowenstein and his allies, the NCNP's activities simply confirmed the legitimacy of their own effort, while removing one source of possible competition for the loyalties of those who still wanted to make a political fight against the president. "The third party had died with the New Politics," David Hawk noted. "The chance of denying the army the manpower to fight [through draft resistance] . . . was equally impossible." The counterculture's assertion that revolution would come "when you could fuck in the streets" was a disaster. "So Allard's stuff—even as implausible as it sounded—still made more sense than [anything else around]." Suddenly, Lowenstein's contention that mainstream college students could provide the organizational infrastructure for unseating the president became not only credible but, for many antiwar activists, the only ball game in town.[9]

SEEKING A CANDIDATE

At just this critical juncture, other political voices began to provide reinforcement. Writing in the *New Yorker* under the pseudonym Bailey Laird,
Richard Goodwin, a speech writer for Robert Kennedy and a former aide
to John Kennedy, cleverly dissected the conventional wisdom that an incumbent president could not be unseated. "The rules [of politics]," Goodwin wrote, "are only a summary of what's happened before. The trick is in
trying to see what's going to happen next." According to the "rules," John
Kennedy could never have been elected because "he was too young and a
Catholic." But Kennedy chose to ignore the rules and create his own new
reality. So, too, with the 1968 election, Goodwin reasoned. "People just
don't like [Johnson]," he pointed out. "You can go around the country and
you just don't meet anyone who's enthusiastic about [him]. . . . People
tend to vote against someone rather than for someone, and I think they
could really turn on the President." Thus, Goodwin concluded, "this nomination is really up for grabs. . . . People are looking for a fresh face . . . a
man who really stands for something. . . . I think someone like that would
find help . . . in the most unexpected places."

Allard Lowenstein could hardly have asked for a more ringing endorsement of both his own political assessment and his plan of action. He
had maneuvered much of the student leadership of the country into a position of supporting his mainstream political approach to the war. Now he
had escalated that campaign to an explicit assault on the president himself. The challenge he faced was to use his student base as a foundation
from which to build buttresses of support to other segments of the party.
Goodwin had written that "once in a while you have to take a big chance.
Knowing when that time has come is what separates the great ones from
the others. [But] I tell you, the big prize is hanging right up there ready to
be grabbed." Lowenstein had decided that *this* was the time to turn fantasy into reality and reach for the prize.[10]

He coordinated a remarkable team effort. Forces in the field were deployed far beyond what anyone could imagine, based on the number of
people involved, and the results were literally stunning. There were three
centers of operation. David Hawk, Sam Brown, and Clint Deveaux continued to work from their postage-stamp office at Union Theological Seminary, coordinating student activities throughout the country, making contact with campuses where Al might speak, and lining up potential canvassers for primary campaigns. Harold Ickes dropped out of law school to

spend up to twenty hours a day as "dispatch central," his New York studio apartment serving as the headquarters for scheduling "dump Johnson" activities. "I would literally work as the sun moved," he recalled, "from the East Coast to the West Coast. Al would call in and give me names of people I should follow up with, whom I should call, introduce myself to, etc. There was just this bewildering array of people that I kept in touch with." Pivotal to the whole operation, of course, were Lowenstein himself and his coworker Curtis Gans, who resigned from his ADA job to devote all his time to the "dump Johnson" project he had helped to create. Gans in Washington and Lowenstein in New York would target key constituencies to visit, orchestrate their travel schedules, pool their political contacts and resources, then hit the road in a political assault pattern that might well have made Jim Farley or Larry O'Brien feel outclassed.[11]

The scenario became routine. Collecting lists of names and phone numbers of all the "friendlies" they could identify from sources like ADA, Women Strike for Peace, and antiwar advertisements, Gans and Lowenstein would schedule a series of meetings in a local area. Lowenstein was teaching constitutional law at City College every Tuesday and Thursday, so he made East Coast trips after class on Tuesday and on Wednesday, then headed west from Thursday night through Monday. "I never missed a class," he boasted. Gans's role was to "advance" the joint mission, meeting with local politicos, scouting the territory for potential allies as well as minefields, and setting up speaking locations and private meetings for Lowenstein. A few days later, Lowenstein would parachute in for his part of the tandem operation, while Gans moved on to prepare the next landing site. Lowenstein would meet privately with important political figures, give a public address about the "dump Johnson" campaign in a community setting, then sometimes speak to a university group. Always the message was the same: this campaign was a mainstream effort of concerned Democrats; its purpose was to save the country and the party, not destroy them; the nation was full of people convinced that Johnson's Vietnam policy was disastrous, and working together, these people could make a difference and turn the country in a new direction. As reassuring as it was bold, the Lowenstein message hammered home the theme that concerted political action—within the party—was the highest form of Democratic loyalty, and the only way to save the country.[12]

Almost magically, the pieces started to fall into place. Right after the NSA meeting in August 1967, Lowenstein flew to California, where he enlisted the support of Gerald Hill of the California Democratic Council, along with a $1,000 donation from the council to help defray his travel expenses. Shortly thereafter, $5,000 was collected from an East Coast antiwar source. The actor Robert Vaughn helped establish a group called Dissenting Democrats for antiwar activists who were outside the Democratic party structure. By early September, the "dump Johnson" forces took the first giant step toward credibility *within* the party structure when Donald Peterson, the Democratic party chairman of the tenth congressional district in Wisconsin, signed on, soon to be joined by Alpha Smaby, a widely respected legislator from Hubert Humphrey's home state of Minnesota. Newspaper stories proliferated as the campaign took on a life of its own. "Al seemed to be at every airport, every college campus, every state," Harold Ickes said. "It was just amazing where you would get calls from."[13]

By the end of October, the "dump Johnson" movement had achieved a momentum that even hardened politicians could no longer ignore. The state party chairman in Michigan—a critical Democratic stronghold—embraced the campaign, as did the "young Democrat" organizations in Iowa, Michigan, and Wisconsin. Affiliate organizations multiplied, from the Coalition for a Democratic Alternative (CDA) to the Conference of Concerned Democrats ("concerned demagogues," Ickes called them) and Concerned Democrats of America. In a devastating blow to traditional Democrats, the liberal *New Republic* endorsed the campaign in a front-page editorial—"We don't know whether Lyndon Johnson can be denied. . . . We do know the attempt must be made"—and public opinion polls showed a growing groundswell of support for an alternative to Johnson, accompanied by a near free-fall decline in Johnson's public standing. It was as if everything Lowenstein had predicted in August were a carefully drawn blueprint for what was happening in October and November.[14]

All that was missing was a candidate. From the beginning, Lowenstein had argued—undoubtedly with greater self-assurance than he felt—that once his coalition of forces had proven the depth and breadth of political alienation in the land, a candidate would "jump on the bandwagon." Furthermore, he insisted that such a demonstration had to come from "responsible, broadly based" groups within the party who could not be dismissed as marginal—thus providing another persuasive argument for excluding the "crazies." "These [potential candidates] cannot be expected to undertake so gruelling a contest [as an assault on the president]," he wrote, "unless they can be shown that it will not be an act of political hari-kari." But now that demonstration had been made and it was time to deliver on the final promise, without which the entire "dump Johnson" edifice might crumble.[15]

Throughout the campaign, it had been clear that Lowenstein's ideal candidate was Robert Kennedy. The two had initially been wary of each other when Kennedy ran for the U.S. Senate from New York in 1964, but rapidly they became closer, especially after Kennedy enlisted Lowenstein's aid in drafting his antiapartheid speech at the University of Capetown in South Africa in February 1966. "He and Bobby [developed] a tremendous affection for each other," Jack Newfield commented. When Lowenstein found himself on the same plane Kennedy was taking to California in the spring of 1967, therefore, he took the opportunity to brief Kennedy on his plans. Student-manned organizations would drive Johnson from the presidential race during the primaries, he told the senator, and the nomination would then be wide open. Although he did not ask Kennedy to become a candidate at that point, he nevertheless hoped to plant a seed that would grow. Kennedy responded with interest but contented himself primarily with speculating about other potential candidates, especially General James Gavin, a prominent military hero who had turned against the war. Lowenstein viewed Kennedy's response overall as "very friendly."

In their next meeting, the issue was broached more directly. At Hickory Hill, Kennedy's house in McLean, Virginia, after the ADA's board meeting in September 1967, Lowenstein and Jack Newfield engaged in a three-hour debate with Arthur Schlesinger, Jr., and James Loeb on the merits of Kennedy entering the race. "Argue it out," Kennedy told them, and while Schlesinger and Loeb defended the tactic of supporting a peace plank, Lowenstein and Newfield—with Lowenstein doing most of the talking—insisted that Johnson was going to fall and that Kennedy had a moral and political responsibility to step in. "Al was eloquent," Newfield said; he pulled out all the stops. At different points, Kennedy made remarks suggesting his fundamental agreement with Lowenstein. "When was the last time millions of people rallied behind a plank?" Kennedy asked Schlesinger. He also agreed that Johnson was vulnerable. "I think Al may be right," he said. "I think Johnson might quit the night before the convention opens. I think he is a coward." But Kennedy also told Lowenstein and Newfield that he saw no politically convincing argument for jumping in. Mayor Richard Daley of Chicago and other politicos were giving him no encouragement. Furthermore, any action Kennedy took would be seen

as "splitting the party" out of personal spite toward LBJ. As Newfield later
wrote, Kennedy's gut instincts were all for going in. But he could not bring
himself to make the leap. "You understand, of course, that there are those
of us who think the honor and direction of the country are at stake,"
Lowenstein told Kennedy as he left. "We're going to do it without you, and
that's too bad, because you could have become president of the United
States." It was a poignant moment, two politicians in quest of redemptive
meaning in their public lives exchanging bittersweet comments on the
larger struggle of conscience that engulfed them both.[16]

In the meantime, Lowenstein took Kennedy's advice and approached a
series of other potential candidates. General Gavin was interested but, in
Lowenstein's view, completely naive, and more important, he indicated
that he would run as a Republican if he ran at all. George McGovern also
responded positively to the idea and was seen by some as the best overall
candidate because he understood the need for far-reaching reform in the
political system. But McGovern was deeply concerned about the impact a
presidential candidacy would have on his chances for reelection to the
Senate from conservative South Dakota. When Lowenstein went to Sioux
Falls, he discovered a mood substantially different from that of the rest of
the country. "The picture of [South Dakota] unravelling" under the impact
of the war just was not present, Lowenstein concluded. For McGovern to
run for both president and the Senate, therefore, would create a problem
of "two vocabularies, two emotional tones"—a prospect that seemed to
confirm McGovern's doubts.[17]

That left the one name that was on everyone's list, Eugene McCarthy.
The senior senator from Minnesota, McCarthy had once been a close ally
of Lyndon Johnson. His eloquent nomination speech for Adlai Stevenson
at the 1960 Democratic convention was widely viewed as a last-ditch effort to block the Kennedy juggernaut and buy time for Johnson. In 1964,
moreover, LBJ had publicly toyed with the idea of McCarthy as his vice-
presidential choice (going to Humphrey only at the last minute). On the
other hand, McCarthy had become a powerful voice against the war. His
daughter Mary served as a persuasive intermediary for the "dump Johnson" forces, having been deeply impressed by Lowenstein's NSA speech
in August. From talking to Mary, it seemed clear to Lowenstein that Mc-
Carthy was more ready to make a positive decision than anyone else.

Pressed especially by Gans, Lowenstein finally agreed to initiate a formal approach to the Minnesota senator. A man of deep Catholic morality
but appropriately moderate demeanor, McCarthy in many ways was the

ideal torchbearer. He would scare no one with his gray hair, his gray suit, and his dignified appeal for people to "speak out if you agree . . . there is no justification for continuing this war." But he could also inspire audiences with the simplicity of his moral commitment. "There comes a time," he said repeatedly, "when an honorable man simply has to raise the flag." Now, when Lowenstein and Gans went to him, McCarthy appeared ready to raise his—and to carry the banner for the "dump Johnson" movement.

On a three-day trip through the Northeast to test the political winds, the response was overwhelmingly positive. At a hastily massed rally in Cambridge, hand-lettered signs proclaimed, "The war is obscene, we want Eugene." In response, McCarthy told the crowds, "Vietnam is part of a much larger question, which is, is America going to police the planet?" The crowd went wild. Political supporters of the "dump Johnson" effort began to believe in it. "A month back," observed Gerald Hill, "I would have said our effort was an attempt to modify Johnson's policies by giving him a scare. Now it is becoming a real attempt to beat him." Having already scheduled a national Conference of Concerned Democrats in Chicago for December on the presumption a candidate would have emerged by then, Lowenstein and Gans were now confident that they had their man. "There are some things that are just so wrong that you have to take a stand," McCarthy said as he left Boston, "no matter what." Eleven months after the student body presidents' letter to LBJ, six months after first articulating the idea of "dumping Johnson" to Greg Craig and Barney Frank, and four months after the NSA convention at College Park, the final piece of Lowenstein's "impossible" plan had fallen into place. A candidate had emerged "to jump on the bandwagon."[18]

CONCLUSION

No matter what political observers or historians think about Allard Lowenstein's style and effectiveness, his success in putting together a mainstream Democratic effort to defeat a sitting president was one of the most remarkable political achievements of contemporary American history. With unerring singleness of purpose, Lowenstein identified his objective, created a brilliant strategy, and mobilized an elite battalion of supporters to achieve his goal.

At the root of Lowenstein's success was his passionate preoccupation with showing that protest could triumph within the system. Countless thousands of other opponents of the war believed that the political process was so contaminated by militaristic values and materialism that only a struggle to change the soul of America and destroy capitalism could bring about the kind of change that was necessary. But whatever sympathy Lowenstein occasionally showed for the genuine alienation and idealism of these antiwar critics, he refused to play in their ball game and, in the way he defined their tactics, made sure they would not be accepted in his. Lowenstein denounced the "hate philosophy" he identified with the New Left and dismissed the inflammatory rhetoric that first decried the "system" and then tried to trash it. "Al [not only] didn't have much use for [the hard left]," Greg Craig noted, "[he had] some contempt for [them]."

To isolate and defeat the left, however, Lowenstein had to show that the politics of the center could work in addressing grievances identified by the left and shared by liberals. Thus, he had to reach out to the mainstream and simultaneously move it leftward, cultivating a heightened consciousness among "moderates" about the dimension of the problems that existed. It was like an upward spiral: you appealed to people's traditional values as the basis for mobilizing them, then kept them activated and working inside the system, initially as a way to prevent the left from triumphing, but ultimately as the only means of defeating the warhawks on the right. In everything Lowenstein did, Greg Craig noted, "there was an ongoing assumption that he defined the limits of the [permissible] left, wherever he was. Beyond that [there'd] be dragons." Thus, Lowenstein made his program the definition of acceptable dissent, galvanizing support precisely because the effort was to make democracy work, not destroy it. As one student supporter said, "Al [gave] me a way to do what I believed, and honor where I came from at the same time. . . . There was no way I was going to go against the system altogether, because I knew what it had done for my family. And here was an opportunity to take the tools of the system and make it work for what I believed in. I always believed that was what he wanted to do."[19]

At every stage, Lowenstein devised ways of proceeding that reinforced such instincts. The student body presidents' letter offered a rallying point for people who were conservative as well as liberal, but it also provided a process of education and socialization through which students could develop the potential for moving on to the next, bolder step. At each way station, moreover, Al emphasized what united people behind a common cause and how their collective commitment could be turned to practical effect. "Al's greatest contribution," the journalist David Halberstam said, "was in making people feel they were not alone. He once told me, 'You know, the students think they're the only ones who are angry, and the middle-class women in the suburbs think they're the only ones who don't like the war' . . . and what Al did was [make] those people feel they were not alone. He was the ultimate moralist-activist . . . and he could touch in you and evoke in you those things that you believed in when you were very young."[20]

There were some who believed Lowenstein took too much credit for the "dump Johnson" movement. "If the author supplies the idea and the architect the blueprint," Curtis Gans said, "he was neither the author nor the architect" of the campaign. Clearly, countless individuals were involved, some—like Gans—more important than others. Still, Lowenstein was the source, the inspiration, and the genius that made it all happen. "Al had the ability of taking very complex issues," Harold Ickes said, "and redefining them so that people who were not that sophisticated . . . really understood them in a very profound way." He could translate the most byzantine political strategy into terms that others could immediately identify with. Others provided the mechanical skill, Greg Craig pointed out, but Lowenstein had the creativity to make the impossible seem doable. "He was articulate as hell . . . he knew a bunch of reporters, [and] he was eminently quotable," Craig observed, thus becoming the critical pivot around which the movement turned.[21]

Because of his talents, Lowenstein may have been the only person who could have achieved the triumph of 1967. Acknowledged as a member of mainstream, anti-Communist America, he could articulate his position without automatically incurring dismissal as a "crazy." Yet, as a perennial student leader and reformer, he could reach out to the angry young and get their attention. Combined with an extraordinary political intelligence, these qualifications placed him in the unique position of being able to chart, direct, and then put into place a plan to show that the American democratic system would work, and that people who cared could make a difference. In the meantime, he made a series of choices for his own life that seemed to ensure a career of sufficient public importance to satisfy even the high standards of his father. During that period, David Halberstam observed, "[Al] became more focused, tougher of mind, tougher of spirit. . . . It was probably the strongest and most coherent part of his life."[22]

It appeared that Lowenstein had arrived at a turning point. Despite continued questions about his recruitment methods and his involvement in the behind-the-scenes machinations of those in power, he had defined an agenda of reform that seemed likely to alter the structure of American politics. What had begun as "a classic Don Quixote manuever that no one believed in except himself" was now on the verge of victory. The fall of 1967, *Newsweek* observed, had been "one of the most histrionic autumns America has ever known . . . a season of blustery rhetoric and even stormier deeds." Into that autumn, Allard Lowenstein had brought a vision of change. "He said that . . . we're going to organize the students of this country and go in and do the work that the political hacks normally do," Amherst student body president Steven Cohen said, "[and he said] the students of this country are going to bring it back to sanity . . . and the most marvelous thing . . . is that he really predicted [what was going to happen]. And then he said . . . 'It will be the biggest news story of 1968.'"[23]

With astonishing insight, Allard Lowenstein had prophesied—then helped bring to reality—a program of political protest that promised to redeem the faith of Americans in peaceful change through democratic processes. In the parlance of the day, he had delivered a "heavy" message and done so with style, brilliance, and panache. What was not yet clear was whether 1968 would bring the fulfillment of the promise he had made.

12
1968: Year of Triumph, Year of Tragedy

ONLY RARELY IN U.S HISTORY HAVE ISSUES FATEFUL TO THE NATION'S DIrection come to a crisis at the same time as a presidential election; such a benchmark year had not occurred in more than a century, until 1968. As the war in Vietnam reached a crescendo of destruction, the antiwar movement in the United States hurtled toward its own climax, and discord between supporters and opponents of the war threatened to erupt into open violence. Racial tensions festered, student alienation from the "establishment" reached new levels of intensity, and the rhetoric of revolution became almost commonplace. Politics quickly reflected this emotional fervor, with virtually every month bringing some dramatic episode that mirrored the deep passions dividing the country—the Tet offensive in January, Eugene McCarthy's near upset of Lyndon Johnson in the New Hampshire primary, Robert Kennedy's entry into the presidential race, LBJ's sudden withdrawal from the presidential competition in late March, the horrible assassinations of Martin Luther King, Jr., and Robert Kennedy, and the bizarre guerrilla theater of the Chicago Democratic convention in August. It was a year when hyperbole seemed understatement.

For all these reasons, 1968 also represented a crisis for postwar liberalism in America. Ever since the late 1940s, American politics had largely been shaped by those who believed in simultaneously fighting

276

communism abroad and seeking incremental reform at home. One of the domestic effects of the cold war was that any position too far left of center became suspect; those who advocated fundamental changes in America's social and economic structure were dismissed as "fellow-travelers" or "comm-symps." Liberals, on the other hand, were acceptable because they endorsed the organic health and stability of capitalism, believed that any lingering problems of injustice could be solved through remedial legislation, and looked to economic growth as the ultimate means of creating a "good" society. Change would thus occur by working within existing economic and political processes; to call these processes into question violated the rules. Now, in 1968, the student revolution, antiwar radicalism, and the insurgency of Black Power were challenging the very assumptions under which the liberal consensus operated.

In all of this, Allard Lowenstein was a singularly important figure. Having largely shaped and inspired the liberal "dump Johnson" movement, Lowenstein now saw it come to fruition. He had pushed the boundaries of the system as far as they would go, in the process achieving a victory that few had believed possible a year earlier. Yet in the midst of triumph, he struggled to retain a central role in determining what that victory might mean. Torn between his public commitment to Eugene McCarthy and his private devotion to Robert Kennedy, Lowenstein illuminated—on a personal level—the tensions fragmenting the entire liberal community. At the same time, his effort to walk a tightrope between the two candidates revived all the questions people had entertained about him—especially his capacity for dissembling. When he chose to run for a congressional seat as a means of solving his ambivalence about the party's presidential choices, he was seeking a new platform from which to operate. In many ways, Lowenstein's victory in that congressional race was the high point of his life, bringing the political and personal vindication that his father had so yearned for, and inspiring a quest for validation through the electoral process that would last until the end of his life. In an even more fundamental way, that congressional contest, together with all the national political adventures that accompanied it, testified to the distinctive contribution that Lowenstein brought to politics—a compelling, quixotic, passionate belief that he had been given a special "mission" to save liberal democracy.

THE MCCARTHY MISCONNECTION

As with so many dramatic episodes of 1968, the first public manifestation of trouble in the relationship between Eugene McCarthy and Allard Lowenstein took place in the city of Chicago.

Although Eugene McCarthy would never have become a candidate for the presidency without Allard Lowenstein, their political personalities were totally opposite. "It was almost an oxymoron for them to be in the same place at the same time," the New York political activist Sara Kovner observed. For some, the difference seemed mostly one of presentation. "Allard's passion and style just didn't mesh with McCarthy's laid-back, lackadaisical [approach]," observed the McCarthy coordinator Sam Brown. One man was frenetic, a nonstop blur known for racing the clock to squeeze twenty-seven hours of activity into a twenty-four-hour day; the other read poetry, broke up campaign days by visiting movie theaters and ballparks, and refused to pay attention to media deadlines or politicians' concerns. "McCarthy was very whimsical," William Sloane Coffin said, "[and] his attitude toward power was much too ambivalent." While Lowenstein could hardly wait to plot the next move in the chess game of deposing Lyndon Johnson, Eugene McCarthy preferred "wandering around with [the poet] Robert Lowell."[1]

Under normal circumstances, such differences might have been less noticeable, but Allard Lowenstein emblazoned them in neon lights by the way he introduced McCarthy at the national conference of Concerned Democrats in Chicago in December 1967. Already there had been some disagreement about who should have the honor of presenting McCarthy. Lowenstein claimed he was asked but at first demurred; others said Lowenstein insisted on the role, overriding those who favored Gerald Hill of California or Donald Peterson of Wisconsin. Whatever the case, when the convention opened, Lowenstein rose to address the throngs whose presence he had helped to make possible.

On the one hand, his task was simple—quickly, cleanly, and directly to prepare the way for the delegates to meet their chosen standard-bearer. In this scenario, as *Newsweek* portrayed it, Lowenstein was John the Baptist, and McCarthy the Anointed One. Yet in another sense, this was Lowenstein's moment of glory. He had sown the seeds for the political antiwar movement, he had cultivated them, and now before him, he saw the harvest that had come forth from these months of toil. Why not be uplifted and transported by such a dramatic setting?[2]

Whether by design or spontaneous eruption, Lowenstein delivered one of the most impassioned, vivid, and inspiring speeches of his political life. With a rhetorical power that many in the audience had already experienced in the months of mobilization preceding Chicago, he rang the chimes on each of the major antiwar themes, growing more powerful and emotional with each wave of applause and response. "We were there because Al had brought us there," Clint Deveaux said. "He had asked an awful lot of kids to . . . abandon the craziness and fringe stuff and jump into electoral politics [and] . . . he was responding [to] these people whom he had asked to do something different from where they were headed." If, in his heart of hearts, Lowenstein believed that *he* was the one who had made this happen, why not make everyone aware of that fact by rising to a new level of inspiration? "Al rabble-roused [that night]," his former wife Jennifer recalled. "Absolute 100 percent demagoguery, and nobody did it better. He was wonderful."[3]

McCarthy, on the other hand, was furious. Gary Hart, Lowenstein's right-hand man, was near McCarthy as the "introduction" unfolded. "It was one of Al's greatest speeches," Hart said, but McCarthy was "visibly pissed." Harold Ickes stood next to Jerry Eller, a longtime McCarthy confidant from Minnesota, and watched him become "almost incensed by what was going on." Indeed, as Al rolled into "high gear," Ickes recalled, politicos everywhere were "getting very, very antsy about what he was doing, why he was doing it, and where he was going." Curtis Gans described Lowenstein's speech as a "forty-minute emotional harangue in which he mentioned the name of McCarthy exactly once." By the time McCarthy reached the podium, the main event was clearly over. As if determined to *not* play Lowenstein's game, the new presidential candidate gave one of the driest, least passionate, most detached talks of his long campaign. "Bobby Kennedy at his best, or King at his best, might have come on and kept up the momentum," Jack Newfield observed, but McCarthy could not compete. Al had given a "knock-your-socks-off introduction," the California politician Howard Berman later said, "and then a diffident, low-key McCarthy came out. It was almost embarrassing." Nor was the contrast lost on the general public. Reporters throughout the country commented on McCarthy's lackluster performance, and conference participants wrote Lowenstein asking why the "dynamism and general fired-up attitude" of his speech could not have been transfused into McCarthy.[4]

There were numerous explanations for Lowenstein's behavior. The most benign was that he had simply gotten carried away with the emotion of the moment. A second, related view concerned Lowenstein's misgivings about McCarthy. Although the Minnesota senator had always been on Lowenstein's list of possible candidates, he had never ranked high, perhaps because of his previous involvement with Johnson, his low ADA rating (62 percent), and his preference for abstractions. Now, Harold Ickes said, "the Rubicon was there, and once [Al] got up and spoke, there was probably no way of turning back, [so] . . . there was this inherent ambivalence in him." Finally, there were some who believed that Lowenstein intentionally created a situation that would embarrass McCarthy while promoting himself. "Al was confused about who was running for president," Curtis Gans said.[5]

Lowenstein himself insisted on the total innocence of his speech. By his account, he had agreed to talk until McCarthy arrived. Completely unaware that McCarthy was in the hall, he continued as he had been instructed until suddenly somebody came running up, "maybe Curtis Gans, looking absolutely deathly, [saying] McCarthy had been in the hall for a while and was in a rage." To Lowenstein, that seemed "odd." "No one has to think my speeches are any good," he later said, "[and] it didn't bother me if he didn't, so as soon as I had word that he was in the hall, I stopped, literally in midsentence, and he was introduced." The whole affair, moreover, left Lowenstein "feeling queasy." McCarthy had virtually ignored an overflow audience in another hall, not even stopping to say hello, and he had intentionally offended Ted Kennedy by announcing he would be a candidate in the Massachusetts primary without first informing the Massachusetts senator. To Lowenstein, it was McCarthy, not himself, who had acted in a bizarre fashion.[6]

Yet there was something else going on. Until that moment, Lowenstein had occupied center stage of the "dump Johnson" movement. He was the glue that held it together, the "walking Rolodex" that comprised its data bank, the charismatic presence who galvanized the foot soldiers into action. Now, he faced a choice. By some accounts, Lowenstein wanted to retain at least a portion of center stage—and a large measure of control over the movement—by becoming McCarthy's campaign manager. Yet he undoubtedly sensed how difficult it would be to work with McCarthy—a man whose ego was at least as large as Lowenstein's, yet whose pace and political style were so different. The last thing in the world Lowenstein could be was a foot soldier under someone else's command. "He knew his own talent to the degree . . . that he believed that only he was right," Rich Hammond observed. "He was completely incapable of delegating things, because nobody could do things quite the way he wanted." But neither would he take someone else's orders.[7]

In such a dilemma, perhaps the only way to force a resolution was to act out the crisis, even if that acting out were accomplished without conscious design. By giving the kind of speech he did at Chicago, Lowenstein not only highlighted the part he had played in the "dump Johnson" movement; he also threw down the gauntlet regarding any role he would play in the McCarthy campaign. Given his doubts about McCarthy, he was making it clear that he would define his own style and behavior and never modify his political persona; given his fundamental political intelligence, moreover, he also undoubtedly understood that such behavior would effectively guarantee that he would never play a significant role in the McCarthy campaign. Lowenstein never acknowledged this mental process. But events throughout the next year seemed to confirm the intentionality with which he pursued his posture of ambivalence toward McCarthy.

By the end of December, in any event, it had become clear that Eugene McCarthy would not permit Allard Lowenstein to compete with him for primacy in the presidential campaign. Never even considering Lowenstein for a major managerial role, McCarthy turned first to his Minnesota chieftains for help, and then when they proved reluctant, he put Blair Clark, a wealthy Democrat, in charge. "The only person who was politically savvy and emotionally stable [in the campaign] was Abigail [McCarthy, his wife]," Curtis Gans later said. Eschewing campaign appearances and more often than not playing the recluse, McCarthy seemed by early January as much a millstone as the lifesaver he had been one month earlier. Jack Newfield, who had sung McCarthy's praises in late November, now wrote: "Let the unhappy, brutal truth come out. Eugene McCarthy's campaign is a disaster. It has been run as if King Constantine was the manager. McCarthy's speeches are dull, vague, and without either balls or poetry. He is lazy and vain. . . . McCarthy earned my vote just by announcing. But he doesn't deserve anything anymore."[8]

Newfield's despair about McCarthy was shared by many, including Lowenstein. More than ever convinced that he had been right in his suspicions, Lowenstein frequently worried out loud about the fate of the campaign, serving as a magnet for many who came to see Lowensteinian tactics as a vehicle for resuscitating the antiwar struggle. The problem was that by his own actions, Lowenstein had cut himself off from the inner circle of the campaign, thus creating a self-perpetuating vicious cycle. Removed for the most part from day-to-day campaign activities in New

Hampshire, he had the freedom—and Olympian detachment—to condemn the incompetence of the McCarthy operation and go to Sam Brown and Curtis Gans with a series of demands on how McCarthy should alter his campaign. Yet his exclusion from the campaign elite meant he would be either ignored or viewed with hostile suspicion. The wonderful irony was that Lowenstein could be *right* in his analysis but not responsible, because of his situation, for acting on his insight.[9]

Nevertheless, the McCarthy campaign *was* revitalized, largely owing to the Tet offensive and an extraordinary decline in the credibility and popularity of the Johnson administration. As U.S. army troops came under attack in Vietnam, student battalions of McCarthy supporters ("Be clean for Gene") invaded New Hampshire. Lowenstein himself spent little time there, but hundreds of the young people who did traced their presence directly to his exhortations. Knowing little of the estrangement that had occurred between Lowenstein and McCarthy, they thought of both men as heroes. They canvassed each voter three times, sent out campaign literature, made follow-up phone calls, and in general fulfilled perfectly Lowenstein's vision of students transforming the political system by working from within. What they were not aware of was just how systematically their two heroes were undercutting each other even in the moment of triumph. On primary night, Lowenstein wondered aloud how the McCarthy campaign could survive a candidate who refused to work hard, and McCarthy greeted Lowenstein in his hotel suite by staying in his chair and saying, "Oh Al, where have you been." Significantly, when the hundreds of campaign workers gathered at the Dunphey Hotel for their victory celebration, the candidate recited a long list of people to whom he was indebted—without even mentioning the name of Allard Lowenstein.[10]

THE KENNEDY LINK

At the heart of Eugene McCarthy's intense dislike of Lowenstein was the latter's deep and transparent devotion to Robert Kennedy. Lowenstein and Kennedy were not natural political partners. Lowenstein had never been particularly enamored of John Kennedy. More an Adlai Stevenson/Eleanor Roosevelt Democrat, he might ordinarily have shared the skepticism that they had displayed toward the hard-nosed realpolitik of the Kennedy family—best exemplified by Robert, a former Joe McCarthy staff member who was legendary in the early 1960s for being his brother's hatchet man. But in the eyes of many observers, Robert Kennedy had undergone a profound change in the years since his brother's assassination—a change marked by a new compassion toward the powerless, a greater commitment to the nation's poor as well as to the disenfranchised masses of the developing world, and a keener sense of moral criticism about American foreign policy ventures, especially Vietnam. After Kennedy's election as a U.S. senator from New York in 1964, he became better acquainted with Lowenstein, and gradually that acquaintance turned to something more—deep respect and affection between two men who, though each struggled with his own inner torments, shared a Camus-like commitment to engaging the world, perhaps even hoping to transform it.

Particularly in light of that bond, it was appropriate that the more intimate part of their political relationship began when Kennedy reached out to Lowenstein for help in preparing for his 1966 visit to South Africa. One of a series of international trips that dramatically brought home to Kennedy a sense of the revolutionary forces at work in the world, his journey to South Africa carried with it a special burden: how to strike exactly the right note about the evil of apartheid in talking with black or mixed audiences. Adam Walinsky and Richard Goodwin, two brilliant speech writers, had worked on the draft of a major address to students at the University of Capetown, but Kennedy was still dissatisfied with it and sought Lowenstein's advice, reaching him at the airport as he was about to leave the country for the Dominican Republic.

Lowenstein postponed his trip at Kennedy's request and returned to New York, where he started poring over the speech draft. It was not strong enough, he told Kennedy; when dealing with apartheid, one had to sound the clearest of notes and rise rhetorically to the magnitude and horror of the evil being confronted. Setting to work with Kennedy and the other writers, Lowenstein then helped craft what most observers feel was the most eloquent speech Kennedy ever gave. The cruelty of the world, he told his South African audience, would never be changed "by those who cling to a present which is already dying." Rather, a revolution was afoot, Kennedy declared, "and it is young people who must take the lead." Some might say that no single person could make a difference, but "each of us can work to change a small portion of events and in the total of those acts will be written the history of this generation. . . . Each time a man stands up for an ideal, or acts to improve the lot of others . . . he sends forth a tiny ripple of hope, and crossing each other from a million different centers of energy and daring, those ripples build a current that can sweep down the mightiest walls of oppression and resistance." Although there is no way to establish definitively the authorship of any segment of a speech, it is widely believed that Lowenstein wrote this part of Kennedy's Capetown address. The words are a perfect distillation of Lowenstein's philosophy, as well as Kennedy's, and bespeak the union of two extraordinary political personalities sharing a common vision.[11]

From that point forward, the friendship ripened. Lowenstein once accompanied Kennedy on a visit to a veterans' hospital to see wounded soldiers returned from Vietnam. At each bedside, Kennedy stopped to spend long minutes in conversation; later Lowenstein told his wife how moved he had been as they left the building, Kennedy speechless and crying. It was because of such shared experiences that Lowenstein went to Kennedy first to ask him to run as the alternative to Lyndon Johnson. Kennedy demurred, repeatedly, arguing that his candidacy would be dismissed as a personal vendetta against Johnson and would destroy the party. And so Lowenstein had gone to McCarthy. Yet the bond remained. "I think Bobby admired Al," Jack Newfield said. "I think he always wanted to run, and I think Al touched him everytime he appealed to him to run." Indeed, some of Al's closest associates were convinced that the entire convention operation at Chicago in December was really aimed at Bobby. "In his heart of hearts," Harold Ickes observed, "[Al] felt that if he could show enough political support around the country, especially in some critical states, that he would have one more [chance] at Bobby."[12]

Subsequently, Lowenstein insisted that he had never asked Robert Kennedy to run after McCarthy had announced his candidacy. His public position was that he was committed to Eugene McCarthy's nomination from late November 1967 until the end of the Democratic convention in August 1968. Though literally true, such claims were disingenuous, belied at every turn by Lowenstein's behavior and, sotto voce, by his words. Lowenstein's protestations of loyalty to McCarthy may have satisfied, in some Jesuitical fashion, his need to be intellectually consistent; but to others, the effort to be for one candidate verbally and for another emotionally seemed like wanting to have your cake and eat it, too—dissembling at best, mischievous and manipulative at worst. Arguably, Lowenstein felt caught in a trap from which he could not in good conscience escape. But it was a trap he seemed in some ways to have created and to be reveling in. Why? some people began to ask.

Despite his protestations, Lowenstein had in fact been deeply engaged in Kennedy's struggle to resolve the presidency issue during the three months after the Chicago Concerned Democrats convention. As Jack Newfield wrote at the time, Kennedy was "torn about what to do." The "Bad Bobby," caricatured in Jules Feiffer's cartoons, reflected "the cold, cynical political manager with an instinct for arithmetic majorities" who said there was no guarantee of victory, and therefore no reason to run. But there was a "Good Bobby," too, "the Kennedy who emotionally told the girls at Marymount College . . . that America is doing to the Vietnamese what the Germans did to the Jews . . . the Kennedy who can read Camus and suddenly discover he no longer believes in capital punishment." If Kennedy refused to run, Newfield concluded, "the best side of his character will die. . . . It will die every time a stranger quotes his own words back to him on the value of courage as a human quality." Lowenstein persisted in his appeals to the "Good Bobby" after McCarthy's declaration of candidacy, at least in part because he, too, was divided, his heart still committed to Kennedy.[13]

These appeals took place, however, in a manner designed to allow Lowenstein to remain on his tightrope, to maintain, in his head at least, a delicate balance between the two roles he was playing. Commenting in retrospect on the first two months of the election year, Lowenstein acknowledged his growing disillusionment with McCarthy. "[His] behavior was so odd [then]," Lowenstein said, "that a very serious 'dump McCarthy' movement began among [his own] people" over issues like scheduling and commitment to campaign time. On the other hand, Lowenstein claimed, his own view "was still very profoundly colored by my gratitude to McCarthy . . . a greater gratitude than I'd ever felt in politics to anybody." Indeed, his gratitude was so great that, as Lowenstein explained, it was inconceivable that he should go directly to McCarthy with his complaints. Having thus defined the political terrain, Lowenstein insisted he could leave McCarthy's ranks only if the situation altered dramatically, that is, if McCarthy either clearly repudiated his central positions or refused to do what was necessary to make his campaign credible. "I felt it was duplicitous to go to Kennedy [under these circumstances] and urge him to run," Lowenstein said.[14]

The reality, however, was more complicated. For throughout this period, Lowenstein held conversations with Kennedy. Theoretically "off the calendar"—not part of Kennedy's public schedule—these discussions provided a vehicle (perhaps even an ethically justifiable vehicle, given Lowenstein's intellectual construction of the meetings) for Lowenstein to persist in his dual role. "I didn't feel I had the right to persuade Kennedy," he said, "so the limit of what I thought I could do was when

Kennedy asked me what I felt was happening, I could tell him that he was throwing away the presidency, which I think he was . . . [but] because I didn't feel I could urge Kennedy . . . and because Kennedy still needed to be urged and pressured, there was between us what amounted to a standstill." Yet the political truth was that Lowenstein continued to lobby Kennedy to run via such informational conversations. Even the veneer of being pro-McCarthy was abandoned after Kennedy told a group of reporters in January that he would not run except in "unforeseeable circumstances." "*I* am an unforeseeable circumstance," Lowenstein declared the next time he saw Kennedy.[15]

Within days of the New Hampshire primary, Lowenstein's continuing involvement with Kennedy became still clearer. Despite constant pressure from staff members like Jeff Greenfield and Adam Walinsky and JFK aides such as Arthur Schlesinger, Jr., Kennedy had continued to say no to a presidential race, always falling back on the rationale that it would divide the party and be seen as an act of personal animosity toward Johnson. After McCarthy's strong showing in New Hampshire, those arguments no longer seemed to hold any weight. The party was already divided; the voters had turned on LBJ. Furthermore, the prospect of victory now appeared credible. Thus, even though most of his advisers told him how "ruthless" and opportunistic it would look for him to now leap into the race, Kennedy's own instinct to run—so long tethered by his conservative side—rushed to the fore. "I've decided to take your advice," Kennedy told Lowenstein in a phone conversation. "You SOB," Lowenstein remembered replying, "don't come around to me [now] with your six months' late [decision]"—to which Kennedy responded, with mocking, Kennedy-style humor, "Oh, don't say that. That's what everybody else is saying. You can say something original." And then, when Lowenstein hesitated, Kennedy teased, "[That's okay,] you can keep me off your calendar," thereby reversing the pattern by which Lowenstein had stayed off of Kennedy's calendar during the preceding six months.[16]

The Friday night after the New Hampshire primary, Arthur Schlesinger, Jr., William Vanden Heuvel, and U.N. Ambassador Arthur Goldberg flew down to Washington for a meeting at Kennedy's house in McLean, Virginia. A previously scheduled party was already under way, but Kennedy quickly excused himself to meet with Walinsky, Greenfield, Schlesinger, and a "mystery guest," Allard Lowenstein, who had agreed to fly down the same day. A draft statement was already in the works; according to Lowenstein, he announced that he should leave because he was supporting McCarthy. But Kennedy reassured Lowenstein that "we are all after the same objective, so stay and eat and let's talk about it." With that minimal encouragement, Lowenstein pitched in. "I argued very hard about what ought not to be in the statement and what ought to be in the statement," he said, "and the tone of the [final] statement was very much along the ideas that I'd argued for." The earlier versions had been dismissive toward McCarthy, Lowenstein observed, and few people there "understood the depth of feeling on the issues, and therefore the depth of gratitude to McCarthy that he made the fight when Kennedy wouldn't." Although, according to Lowenstein, "a lot of Kennedy people . . . couldn't understand why anyone for McCarthy was allowed to sit there," he felt he was helping to prevent egregious errors by Kennedy aides who had no sensitivity to the McCarthy forces.[17]

In addition, Lowenstein pursued his own role as a possible unifying force who could mediate between the two camps. He had already spoken to friends in the McCarthy camp about the possibility of the two candidates agreeing to split up the remaining primaries so that only one antiwar candidate would compete against LBJ (that discussion took place two weeks before Johnson withdrew)—until the California primary in June, when they would go head to head. Richard Goodwin—another individual with ties to both candidates—agreed, and that night Edward Kennedy flew to Wisconsin with Curtis Gans, Goodwin, and Blair Clark to secure McCarthy's acquiescence. Lowenstein, meanwhile, stayed overnight at Hickory Hill and was present in the wee hours of the morning when Ted Kennedy returned with the news that McCarthy had rejected the proposal out of hand. "*Your* friend isn't interested in *your* plan," Kennedy allegedly told Lowenstein. In fact, McCarthy was furious about—even contemptuous of—Kennedy's candidacy. "I could have used a little help [back in December]," he remarked acidly. "I walked alone. They were afraid to come down onto the playing field. They stayed on the hill and lit bonfires and danced in the moonlight."[18]

Nevertheless, Lowenstein sought desperately to keep alive the idea of an eventual reunification of the antiwar forces. *Someone* had to be in the position to create a synthesis out of the polarities that threatened to consume the "dump Johnson" enterprise, and in Lowenstein's view, he was the ideal person for the task. Still convinced that he had done nothing to betray McCarthy, he saw his mission as interpreting to each side the more positive qualities of the other so that tolerance would be nurtured, the larger goal would be kept in sight, and the way would be prepared for eventual coalition around the winner of the California primary. Preaching that gospel, Lowenstein went to the New York convention of the Coalition for a Democratic Alternative, a McCarthy group, then to California to the Calfornia Democratic Council (CDC), telling both "what a calamity it would be if the ["dump Johnson"] movement was now poisoned and there were hate between people who agreed on the issues." "Bobby Kennedy is not the enemy," he proclaimed.

Yet within a week, it was clear that such a message had no home in this springtime of vitriol. The view of the "McCarthy claque," Lowenstein later observed, "and I don't know what else you can call them . . . was that this [approach] was an unacceptable heresy. . . . During that period, it became clear that McCarthy entertained . . . an obsessive hatred of Kennedy." On the other side, Kennedy campaign people had an imperious impulse to ride roughshod over McCarthy supporters, as though they were amateurs playing a game where only professionals belonged. Lowenstein himself became an immediate political casualty. Steven Smith, Kennedy's brother-in-law and major political adviser, wanted Al to run for the U.S. Senate seat from New York; so, too, did a number of McCarthy people involved in the CDA convention. The nomination to run against Senator Jacob Javits could have been his if coalition were possible. But Lowenstein refused to run as the candidate of any group that would attack Kennedy, and so the possibility was lost even as it came close enough to almost grasp. There seemed to be no place, at the moment at least, for someone who wanted to work the miracle of bringing unity out of division.[19]

Still, Lowenstein was determined to stay on the tightrope. At the victory celebration after the Wisconsin primary, Richard Goodwin had posed the decisive question. "You and I can make McCarthy president if we stay with him," Goodwin told Lowenstein. "The question is, do we want Eugene McCarthy to be our next president." Every fiber of Lowenstein's being seemed to strain to say no; yet, he could not bring himself to break officially with McCarthy, as Goodwin did. "While I would stay loyal to McCarthy," he reasoned, "my view of what was important in American politics . . . could [not] justify working night and day for McCarthy over Kennedy." He would make an occasional speech, respond when (or if) asked for advice, "but that was the limit of what I owed out of loyalty." More important, "that degree of involvement would make possible my retaining sufficient credentials . . . to go to either group . . . and try to get them to help the other one, whoever survived the primaries. . . . *Within my formula*, it would therefore have been proper to have worked for Kennedy at some point" (italics added). As Sara Kovner noted, "Al always wanted to be at the center of things, which may be one reason why . . . when there were two contending factions, he would be working with both of them. . . . To put a positive face on it, [he could say,] 'I can bring these two groups together and maybe get things to work out.'"[20]

But clearly some others, especially in the McCarthy camp, viewed Lowenstein's efforts as mischievous conniving with nothing but personal aggrandizement as a goal. Lowenstein might profess his loyalty to McCarthy and his devotion to the cause he had helped bring to life, but a large number of McCarthy supporters saw him as a traitor. Many of Al's followers, Harold Ickes noted, were idealists who

> had heard him thump the tub on behalf of McCarthy as the savior of the nation. . . . [Now for Al], who professed purity of motives, to be suddenly seen in the Kennedy camp . . . [generated] enormous ambivalence. . . . Why is our hero, the [purest] of us all, who started this effort, now not only associating with the bosses, but with a person who didn't have the fortitude to stand up when the wind was cold? So my sense is that . . . people's eyes were opened to Al . . . and a number of people just became very disillusioned with him at that point.[21]

Most bothersome perhaps was the aura of cleverness surrounding Lowenstein's actions. It was all too much like sophistry, Sam Brown observed. A lawyer might say in a sex case, "I don't think there was actual penetration, therefore I don't think it was rape. Okay, fine. That's not the definition we were looking for here. Allard was certainly seen as being close to Bobby." Moreover, he talked openly and repeatedly about that closeness. Even those basically on Lowenstein's side found the machinations a bit much. "How daft of us to have confused the Lowenstein motive with altruism," the *New York Times* correspondent Terry Smith wrote in a letter. "Obviously it is all part of a grand plan. Only one question remains: did you use McCarthy for President stationery in drafting Bobby's announcement?"[22]

In all of this, Lowenstein wanted—and needed—to see his own actions as morally unimpeachable. With a tortured logic reminiscent of his most elaborate intellectual disputes at Chapel Hill, he convinced himself that he could still be loyal to McCarthy even while helping to draft Kennedy's statement of candidacy. And so he persisted in his stance, hoping that the two sides would eventually come together under his leadership. In the meantime, he would seek escape from the national arena of contention by running a congressional campaign that brought together Kennedy and Mc-Carthy forces in precisely the kind of coalition he hoped to reinvigorate after the California primary. That coalition, he fondly believed, would be headed by his friend and hero, Robert Kennedy, someone who understood what Lowenstein was about. "For Al," Kennedy had written on a scrap of paper one night after Lowenstein had decided again not to break with Mc-Carthy, "who knew the lesson of Emerson and taught it to the rest of us: 'They did not yet see, and thousands of young men as hopeful, now crowding to the barriers of their careers, did not yet see if a single man plant himself on his convictions and then abide, the huge world will come round to him.' From his friend, Bob Kennedy." With understanding like that, perhaps it was worthwhile to continue walking the tightrope, hoping that somehow a miracle might happen.[23]

THE FIFTH CONGRESSIONAL DISTRICT

Even before it became clear that the Kennedy-McCarthy animosity would not abate, Lowenstein had been giving thought to his own political fortunes. Still with no career, Lowenstein could not go on forever as the itinerant director of various crusades for freedom. While lecture fees and dividends from the family restaurants ensured him an income of $12,000–15,000 a year (equivalent to $50,000 in 1990 dollars), his life needed solidity. Frank Graham Lowenstein had been born in August 1967, on the eve of the "dump Johnson" campaign, and a second child was on the way. The 1966 congressional race in Manhattan suggested that, consistent with his father's wishes, public office would be Lowenstein's profession of choice, and many believed that starting a family would "make it easier to settle down and aim for the 1968 nomination [in the nineteenth] now that Weiss has lost."

In fact, the reform designation for the nineteenth congressional district would have been Lowenstein's for the asking. As his brother Larry pointed out shortly after the 1966 loss, Al had only to make the commitment to set down roots in the 19th to ensure support. Having missed out by only twelve votes in 1966, he would have soared to victory and, in all likelihood, defeated the incumbent Leonard Farbstein to obtain a "safe" seat in Congress for as long as he wished. For that reason, his friends in the reform movement urged him to make the appropriate gestures to convince the "doubting Thomases" of his sincerity. "It would serve you and your cause to establish some base of operations in New York," one local politician wrote, "and to dissipate the image . . . that you are more at home away from home." Still another friend urged him to run for district leader "to quell a great many questions in peoples' minds about your commitment to the district."[24]

Despite his new determination to build a political career, Lowenstein ignored such advice, refusing to accept the constraints of a "conventional" political plan. How could he jet from campus to campus, building a "dump Johnson" movement, if he got bogged down in neighborhood concerns? What would happen to his individuality were he to trim his sails to meet someone else's expectations? If an ideal opportunity such as the U.S. Senate nomination became possible, so be it. But if that did not work out, something else would come along. With the "hang loose" approach that came to characterize his entire occupational history, Lowenstein seemed to prefer waiting for lightning to strike.

Such was the context in which Lowenstein decided in the spring of 1968 to run for the Democratic nomination for Congress in the fifth congressional district of Long Island. Ted Weiss had again laid claim to the reform designation in the nineteenth. Lowenstein contemplated running on Manhattan's East Side but was discouraged from doing so because Ed Koch, another city councilman who had served his time as a district leader, was a candidate, and that race threatened to become a rerun of the contest in the nineteenth in 1966. In the meantime, Lowenstein had started to do a great deal of speaking at Long Island forums run by peace Democrats. Thus, when Jenny opened a telegram one day inviting him to be a candidate in the fifth congressional district, Lowenstein was thrilled. "What a great idea," he told her on the phone, "it will get me out of all this [national controversy]." Although Jenny worried about moving to the suburbs, predicting that "I'll be stuck out there with the kids and you'll be traveling around," Al reassured her. "You forgot one important thing," he said, "and that's how much I love you." So she found a house, packed their bags, and got ready to move. "Al was too big a figure to be [a lieutenant] in anyone's campaign," she later said. "[The fifth congressional district] was a perfect answer because he would be his own man."[25]

As with most Lowenstein political "drafts," of course, the substance was more complicated than the appearance. Notwithstanding his "hang loose" demeanor, Lowenstein had carefully been exploring the options, including Long Island, prior to the invitation. Al used to talk all the time about "the grass roots," Harold Ickes noted. "He insisted on there being this showing of support . . . [but] it was Al's seeds and watering cans. . . .

He went to great lengths to try to create the facade of political support and would never concede he was doing it." Whatever the dimensions of a "genuine draft," Lowenstein almost always sculpted its contours.[26]

Still, he remained powerfully ambivalent even about an invitation he wanted. Nowhere was this better reflected than in his use of time, a near perfect barometer of Lowenstein's deepest conflicts and anxieties. A special meeting had been set up with Long Island McCarthy supporters, who would issue the invitation. "It was all sort of programmed," his aide Gary Hart said, "all of these people were coming together . . . to pass judgment on Al." Determined to reach Long Island on schedule, Hart got Al out of the city by 6:30, giving them an hour to reach the meeting. But as soon as they had left Manhattan, Lowenstein said, "We're going to see Norman Thomas." Thomas was now in a nursing home, and Lowenstein visited him regularly. The affection between the two was reciprocal and obvious; decorating Thomas's wall was a "Lowenstein for Congress" poster. Nevertheless, visiting him was "impossible," Hart responded. "He's up on [the North Shore]. This meeting is in the South Shore. If you go to see Norman Thomas, we're going to be an hour and a half late." But Lowenstein insisted. Three hours later, they arrived at the South Shore meeting, "Al sort of [running] up the driveway as the very last person was leaving. They were so mad, [and] he had to work very hard to get all those people back on board. To me it was suicidal . . . a death wish."[27]

In spite of such faux pas, the invitation eventually was tendered and accepted. The fifth congressional district was a complex of thirty middle-class suburbs, twenty-five miles long, running from Queens out to Oyster Bay. Catholics (43 percent) and Protestants (23 percent) predominated; nearly 70 percent of the Catholics and Protestants were Republican, with Jews (34 percent) providing most of the Democratic votes. Democrats had never won the district until the Johnson landslide of 1964, when Herbert Tenzer was elected. But a narrow reelection in 1966—he won by only 2,246 votes out of the 177,616 that were cast—plus strong family pressures, persuaded Tenzer not to seek a third term. That left selection of a successor to either the party regulars, led by the county leader Jack English, or the peace-oriented New Democratic Coalition (NDC), described by one observer as "moralists who prided themselves on their lack of pragmatism." When the NDC nominated Lowenstein, the regulars retorted by choosing Albert Vorspan, a progressive, antiwar Jewish leader, with the expectation that Lowenstein would then withdraw. Instead he remained, moved into the district on April 2, and commenced campaigning.[28]

The decision surprised many Lowenstein allies, not least because of the circumstances. Although the fifth congressional district had been Democratic for two terms, the Republicans had an advantage among registered voters, and most observers anticipated a swing back to the Republican column in 1968. In addition, the string of bedroom communities did not seem a natural home for Lowenstein. "It was never a good fit as a district," his friend Steve Roberts noted. "I remember it as sort of a bleak scene, with all these . . . shuttered summer bungalows. . . . [Al] was a city person." But most important, his primary opponent was an ADA liberal whose views on every issue were virtually identical to his own. Director of the Union of American Hebrew Organizations, the umbrella group of Reform Jews, Albert Vorspan had devoted his life to liberal causes. He led the fight to integrate the community of Five Towns, participated in the antiwar activities of Concerned Democrats, and presumably would have been acceptable to the NDC people had Lowenstein not already said yes to their call. Indeed, it now seems clear that both sides expected the other to drop out within the first forty-eight hours to support a unity peace candidate. But the hour was late, Lowenstein had nowhere else to go, and residual tensions between the "regulars" and the "moralists" made communications poor. By the first few days of April, angry words had already been exchanged, and the die was cast.[29]

In a primary campaign, relatively few voters cast ballots—only 30 percent of those who had voted for Tenzer in 1966 voted in the 1968 primary—and those who do tend to be more politicized, hence more responsive to issues of ideology and principle. On that score, Lowenstein probably benefited from the comparatively minor discrepancies between his positions and Vorspan's, especially with a peace constituency inside the Democratic party. The two most critical conflicts the two candidates had were almost litmus tests of antiwar "purity." When asked whether he would vote in Congress for military appropriations that would support the Vietnam War, Vorspan responded that he would have to wait and see the bill, and what kind of appropriations were involved. Lowenstein simply said no, insisting that any money for the war in Vietnam just reinforced a stupid and immoral policy. Along the same lines, Vorspan claimed that he could support any of the Democratic candidates for president—Humphrey, Kennedy, or McCarthy. Lowenstein pledged that he would back only Kennedy or McCarthy and would *not* support Humphrey unless his position on the war changed dramatically. While Lowenstein undoubtedly lost some votes with his "hard" positions, he also distinguished himself from the regulars through his clarity.

Equally symptomatic of his "new politics" were the hundreds of students who flocked to the fifth congressional district to toil for the hero who had introduced them to "working within the system." Many were veterans of the McCarthy campaign who were fed up with McCarthy's erratic behavior and failure to speak to urban and black issues. "A number of us sort of camp[ed] in [Al's] campaign as a way of getting out of the Kennedy-McCarthy split," Clint Deveaux noted. Others poured in from Stanford, the NSA, and NC State. There were the student body presidents from the "dump Johnson" movement—Rick Weidman from Colgate, Marge Sklancar from Mundelein, Greg Craig from Harvard; a legion of other protégés, such as Rich Hammond, Gary Bellow, Kris Kleinbauer, Nancy Steffen, and Paul Offner; and countless new recruits excited by the prospect of being involved in an electoral effort to turn around America's Vietnam policy. "You were thrust into things you were reading about in the newspaper," one volunteer remarked, "Lowenstein was charismatic . . . and you were fighting the good fight. . . . That was an extraordinary experience for virtually anyone." As Fred Millhiser observed, Lowenstein never promised anything "other than that you'll have a place to live and you won't starve." But for these young staffers, that was enough. Sleeping in the Lowenstein basement and living room and in "friendly" houses in the district, the Lowenstein student army represented perhaps the most distinctive aspect of his campaign.[30]

The students also made possible extensive outreach and canvassing—in many ways the strongest asset of the campaign. Storefronts were set up in each of the bedroom towns in the district, and these local headquarters became the departure point from which volunteers tramped through neighborhoods making personal contact with voters and distributing reams of literature. Such decentralization also helped to compensate for the chaos of the central campaign office. Never one to delegate authority, Lowenstein appointed, then discharged, a series of twenty-two- and twenty-three-year-old campaign coordinators, all of whom, Rich Hammond pointed out, were "in that terrible position of being in charge of a campaign that Al [wanted] to run himself." Campaign aides could neither challenge nor control their candidate. "Trying to hang onto Al was like trying to hang onto the wind," Rick Weidman said; moreover, Fred Millhiser added in classic understatement, "Al didn't have a good grasp of linear time." No matter how clever staffers tried to be in making up false schedules designed to get Lowenstein to a place on time, he would confound them and find some way to be late. And God forbid that a letter or campaign flier should leave the office without his direct approval. Thus, in some ways the campaign avoided complete paralysis only because the storefronts could operate on occasion with some degree of autonomy.[31]

Not surprisingly, the major liability Lowenstein had to contend with was his status as a carpetbagger who had shown up at the last minute to oppose a distinguished local resident with views similar to his own. "It seemed almost an outrage that [Lowenstein] would run in a district which [had] an anti-war candidate," Herbert Kramer, a "regular" Democrat and former county office holder, commented, "when there were so many CD's in Metropolitan New York where Johnson-Humphrey candidates . . . were running." Almost immediately, Vorspan seized on the issue, one of his brochures declaring: "In the name of Senator McCarthy's purity, we are asked to lend our prestige to a young opportunist who has shopped the country for a place to win a Congressional seat . . . and who has not been part of the fight for justice and peace in this district at anytime." In tones reminiscent of the Weiss-Lowenstein battle two years earlier, defenders of the "local" candidate insisted that the true test was a track record of involvement in the community. "A national figure must be weighed in only one way," Vorspan declared in a debate with Lowenstein. "What does he do in his own backyard?"[32]

Lowenstein's initial responses ranged from silly claims lacking in credibility to righteous indignation. At first, he insisted that he had long been planning to move to Long Island to raise his family—what Vorspan called his "dying to live in Woodmere all his life" explanation. "I am not a district shopper or hopper," he declared, saying he had turned down the designation to run in the seventeenth congressional district on Manhattan's East Side. But in light of the record, that line was not persuasive. Stronger was Lowenstein's insistence that the real issue was effectiveness in opposing the war. "If I were a power-hungry politician," he emphasized, "I wouldn't have spent nine months of my life traveling this country to find a man who would stand up against President Johnson." With the power of experience behind him, Lowenstein argued that he was running because two years earlier there had been no one in Congress who would stand up to LBJ. "There must be one person in the House who can be trusted in the event the war goes on," he said. "There must be one person who will stand alone."

That line made sense, even to those who began as doubters. When one Long Island voter was invited to a kaffeeklatsch for Lowenstein, she said, "You know what's wrong with this country? They really ought to develop local people to grow and to ultimately represent their district. Why do we always have to import people from New York?" But Gary Hart persuaded her to come and listen. "That was the end," she said. "I was absolutely captivated." Given the opportunity to present his views in person, Lowenstein could convert the world—even picking up support at American Legion meetings where he demonstrated the courage to debate the issues. "He really believed that everyone could understand if you took the time to tell them what was right, [and] what was important," Mimi Perr declared.[33]

Thus, the most effective tactic for Lowenstein to use against the carpetbagger issue was celebrating and magnifying his national importance, making it an asset rather than a liability. The *New York Times* reporter David Halberstam came to a kaffeeklatsch emphasizing that he had no voting address. "I'm always on the move . . . but I want representation. Put Al in Congress for me." *Newsweek* wrote about Al driving his campaign workers crazy by canceling local appearances in order to respond to national emergencies. But that was a plus as well, because other stories would highlight Lowenstein's visibility—flying to Atlanta to be with Coretta Scott King after her husband's assassination, plugging McCarthy at a Madison Square Garden rally, meeting in an emergency session to deal with problems associated with the Poor People's march on Washington. "It was a schizophrenic existence," Gary Hart said, "[going] from these international and national issues to a [local] kaffeeklatsch." But that was the difference between the candidates. Vorspan was a distinguished liberal who "was really, in a sense, entitled to have that seat. But here was this genius, this star, who was not only committed to the same principles but was able, unlike almost everyone else, to do something about it . . . and we had the chance to elect this great man." If Lowenstein's own sense was that the whole country was his constituency, so be it. Racing from airport to rally, trying to "work it all in, to do it in twenty hours . . . where no one else could even begin to imagine how to do it," all that provided the magic, the intensity, and the romance—as well as the frustration—that made the Lowenstein candidacy appealing.[34]

It was precisely this national prominence that gave such poignancy and political power to Lowenstein's final involvement with Robert Kennedy. Throughout April and May, Lowenstein had bided his time on the presidential race. He spoke at the Madison Square Garden rally for McCarthy and kept in touch with friends in the Kennedy camp, but mostly he just waited for the situation to ripen. All along he had predicted that California would be the turning point. "By the end of the voting [there] and in South

Dakota," he later said, "it was clear that, if we were going to be faithful to the goal of stopping Johnson, Humphrey and the war . . . it would have to be Kennedy that [we] rallied to." At last, the critical piece of Lowenstein's grand strategy for reuniting the peace coalition was about to fall into place.[35]

The Kennedy forces were thinking along the same lines. Whatever their initial hopes for a quick collapse of the McCarthy candidacy, they had long since gained a new appreciation for the tenacity and devotion of his followers. Perhaps for that reason, Robert Kennedy had not pushed harder for a switch in Lowenstein's loyalties, knowing that there would come a time when Lowenstein could play an even more critical role. On June 4, primary day in California, that time seemed to have come. Earlier that day, Steve Smith told Ronnie Eldridge in New York: "We've got to find out where Al's going to be tonight, because . . . if we win, we've got to begin to get the Kennedy people and the McCarthy people together, [and] I'd like to start with Lowenstein."[36]

As the evening wore on, the pattern anticipated by Smith and hoped for by Lowenstein began to unfold. Kennedy swept to an early lead. Lowenstein then received a phone call from John Kenneth Galbraith, who, according to Gary Hart, said, "Bobby wants to talk to you. He feels that you're the person who can help broker this with McCarthy and . . . bring the two sides together." Kennedy told his staff in Los Angeles, including the historian Arthur Schlesinger, Jr., that he had to get free of McCarthy and that Galbraith and Lowenstein were the keys. Later that night, Ronnie Eldridge called Lowenstein to repeat the message that Kennedy was going to phone him about reuniting the McCarthy and Kennedy forces; while they were speaking, an operator interrupted to say Senator Kennedy was on the line. It turned out to be Richard Goodwin, calling on Kennedy's behalf, to say they would be getting back to him after the victory statement. The next phone call was from Skip Martin, an old Lowenstein student friend from Stanford who was working the UPI wire at Dow Jones that night. "Al," he said, "Kennedy's been shot." As Lowenstein later retraced his euphoria that evening over how all his dreams seemed about to come true, he commented, "That period, of course, lasted about an hour and a half."[37]

The next morning, Lowenstein boarded the first flight for Los Angeles. It was the only time, Gary Hart remarked, when "[Al] was truly despairing, with tears, very upset. He didn't know what to do." Lowenstein later told friends he had been in Kennedy's hospital room and spent time with the family. When Kennedy died, Lowenstein flew back to New York on the plane that carried the body. After attending the funeral, he accompanied the family and casket on the special funeral train to Washington, holding conversations there about the future, and especially about New York's political situation. He then returned to campaign on Long Island, with barely a week left before primary day.[38]

Perhaps understandably, that was also a week when a martyred Robert Kennedy played a critical role in bringing victory to Al Lowenstein. Almost immediately, a rich folklore started to develop about the relationship between Kennedy and Lowenstein. As the stories now had it, Kennedy had come out of his shower before going downstairs on primary night and said, "Now we can go help Al." On the plane back from Los Angeles, Lowenstein reportedly asked Kennedy's widow Ethel what he could do to help, to which she responded, "Go back and win." Lowenstein canvassers called voters telling them that Kennedy had especially wanted Al to win, while advertisements linked the two campaigns directly. "Spring was a time of hope for all Americans," one ad said. "Some have been prompted [by recent tragedies] to question . . . whether the hope of this past spring was only a flickering and passing light. But this work, this hope cannot be in vain." The advertisement closed by asking support for Lowenstein, "the man who was instrumental in bringing this renewed hope to Americans."[39]

As the campaign rushed to a conclusion, Lowenstein even had a taste of the coalition he had so yearned to bring to reality. Mary McCarthy and Richard Goodwin both appeared at a Lowenstein rally. Telegrams came in from Kennedy staffers like Jeff Greenfield and Arthur Schlesinger. From the point of view of Al Vorspan, Lowenstein had "wrapped himself in the Kennedy mantle to such a point that it was almost ghoulish—it was like he was carrying the [banner] of the fallen warrior." Even more to the point, however, was the observation of Herbert Kramer, a wise politician of long standing in the community. What Kennedy's death had done, he pointed out, was to allow Lowenstein to lay claim to the mantle of *both* Kennedy and McCarthy. How could people not be impressed by Lowenstein's entourage of Kennedy and McCarthy confidants, and by all the national magazines and syndicated columnists writing constantly about Lowenstein, particularly about his intimacy with RFK. By election day, Vorspan did not have a chance. With a *New York Times* editorial endorsement in hand, Lowenstein scored a smashing victory, defeating Vorspan 14,881 to 10,908. At least for a moment, Lowenstein could feel a sense of triumph amid the overwhelming presence of tragedy.[40]

Later there would be controversy over Lowenstein's use of the Kennedy mystique. At least some observers close to the scene claimed that Lowenstein fabricated the "new" version of the Kennedy phone call, and then urged people in the Kennedy camp to say that the senator was calling not to find a way of uniting the Kennedy and McCarthy camps but specifically because he wanted so much to "help Al in his primary." According to some reports, Lowenstein had forced himself on the Kennedy funeral train, made up the Ethel Kennedy airplane story, and consciously set out to exploit Kennedy's death.[41]

But there is a thin line between genuine sentiment and sentimentality, between authentic mourning and "ghoulish" manipulation of death. There was never a figure in public life—not Eleanor Roosevelt, Frank Porter Graham, Norman Thomas—whom Allard Lowenstein loved more than Robert Kennedy, nor a person who more deeply affected his vision of what could and should happen in America. Thus, Lowenstein may have gone to excessive lengths to link himself to Robert Kennedy not to be selfishly manipulative but out of a profound need to create and cement a bond. Manipulation was there, but so, too, was devotion. The ironies of Lowenstein's victory were multiple. Once again, loss and triumph were inextricably connected, with sadness and tears accompanying joy. Connected too, as they had been all along, were principled advocacy and manipulation. Lowenstein clearly understood the one, even if he had not yet faced up to the other.

THE LAST STRUGGLE FOR COALITION

It quickly became clear that, tragedy or no tragedy, immediate steps were required to rescue the long-term project of preventing the nomination of a Democratic presidential candidate who supported the Vietnam War. With the leading antiwar candidate now removed from the scene, some means had to be devised to rally the larger antiwar constituency and provide a base from which to block the automatic selection of Hubert Humphrey as the party's nominee. To that end, Lowenstein took the lead—even before his own primary victory—in forging a coalition of antiwar forces that would come together almost immediately in a national convention to serve as such a rallying point.

With characteristic political astuteness, Lowenstein understood the need for keeping such a coalition independent of any particular candidacy. The abrasiveness of the Kennedy-McCarthy battles had left volatile personal animosities that would not heal in years, let alone a week. "The McCarthy people felt they hadn't succeeded because Bobby entered," Clint Deveaux observed. "The Kennedy people felt they hadn't succeeded because Bobby got killed. Now both [felt] locked out of the process." Blacks and Mexican-Americans in particular were deeply aggrieved by what they considered to be McCarthy's callous indifference to their issues. Yet they had to be part of any larger left-liberal constituency. Essentially, Lowenstein said, "what was necessary was to have a place where [people] could go, either a halfway house if they were going to end up with McCarthy, or a tent where they could at least unite against Humphrey." Thus, it became imperative to focus the spotlight on larger, nonpersonal issues that people from various backgrounds could unite behind without reopening old partisan wounds. How better to do that than to return to the "dump Johnson" model Lowenstein had created a year earlier—only now change it to a "stop Humphrey" movement, or even more broadly, a "coalition for an open convention"? That way, everyone could put aside their grievances against individual candidates, refocus on the larger objective, and at least keep alive the possibility of the grand peace coalition Lowenstein had envisioned all along, but especially after the California primary.[42]

With a boldness that seems stunning in retrospect, Lowenstein announced five days after his primary victory a July 1 meeting in Chicago of the National Coalition for an Open Convention. Emptying his campaign offices, Lowenstein sent staffers scurrying across the country to make logistical arrangements and recruit support from politicians. Twenty-two-year-olds called on mayors and governors; a national office was set up in Chicago; hotel accommodations for hundreds were arranged. In the meantime, national columnists highlighted the parallels to "dump Johnson" and Lowenstein's pivotal role in both. "He will go about it the same way as before," Flora Lewis wrote, "a convention, an organization, and then a frenzy of effort to show that there is wide popular backing for the drive . . . [which] the professionals will shrug off . . . as hopeless motion." Compared to the delegate counts and "hard facts of politics," Lewis said, it might sound fantastic. "Yet it comes out as calm, cool reason." After all, people had said "dump Johnson" was impossible, too.[43]

Almost miraculously, the Chicago meeting materialized, garnering headlines across the country and in Europe. More than 1,000 participants gathered (at first, only 200 had been expected), from 37 states. They included 75 delegates to the Democratic convention in August, scores of student leaders, substantial numbers of blacks and Mexican-Americans, and a significant representation of McCarthy and Kennedy supporters who seemed ready to work together on issues like a peace plank at the Democratic convention and credentials challenges. "So far," Lowenstein warned party regulars, "the democratic process has not worked. Either some changes are going to be brought about, or . . . everyone [will see] over national TV that [the party is] running a railroad." Before their meeting in Chicago, Lowenstein observed, "we were psychologically back where we were in October [1967]. Thinking that we've lost and can't do it. The difference is, now we know we represent the majority." Clearly, there were differences at the meeting. Kennedy people resisted and resented efforts to convert them into McCarthy supporters. There was also controversy over a resolution declaring that under no circumstances would people ever support Humphrey (Lowenstein left the chair's position to speak against it) or a new political party. ("If we get to that bridge, I'll jump off it," Lowenstein said.) But on balance, the meeting achieved its purpose. "We will fan out from here all over the country and we will make it impossible for Hubert Humphrey to become president of this country," Lowenstein declared. With national newspaper coverage and appearances lined up on major TV news shows as immediate dividends, Lowenstein could afford to feel confident. "[We will] figure out how to do the impossible tomorrow," he said.[44]

While the analogies to the "dump Johnson" movement often seemed stretched, one common ingredient was the desperate necessity, at some point, to find a candidate. In the period between the Coalition meeting in early July and the actual Democratic convention in August, Lowenstein and his staff worked on numerous ideas: bringing hundreds of thousands of young people to Chicago to demonstrate their opposition to the war and to Humphrey; holding a huge rally at Soldiers Field to dramatize on national TV the extent of dissatisfaction with the existing process; and mobilizing support among the delegates for a peace plank. Nevertheless, Lowenstein knew better than most that none of that activity would stop the nomination of Hubert Humphrey without a viable alternative to take his place.[45]

That dilemma, in effect, re-created the intellectual tightrope Lowenstein had walked ever since Eugene McCarthy became an announced candidate. As Flora Lewis noted in her column on the coalition, "Eugene McCarthy is [Lowenstein's] candidate, but not his purpose." While he personally remained pledged to support McCarthy, he repeatedly indicated that no individual candidacy would be advocated at the Chicago meeting in July. Even that stance clouded the increasingly evident reality that Lowenstein felt completely alienated from McCarthy and believed his candidacy to be dead. Nevertheless, Lowenstein sought to maintain the charade, entering into another byzantine process of self-rationalization, or as he put it, "a complicated series of decisions, political and moral . . . about what was the right thing to do." As the summer moved on, Lowenstein said, "it was clear . . . that [McCarthy] didn't want to be nominated. And that presented a new moral dilemma. If the man doesn't want to be nominated, are you being dishonest and deceptive to pretend that he does—to work people . . . hard . . . and ask for their money, when, in fact, it was impossible for it to bring any result?" Yet Lowenstein concluded that he had to remain formally loyal to McCarthy, lest McCarthy's supporters decide to leave "the canopy" he had constructed to shelter the coalition. In Lowenstein's eyes, "It was the height of loyalty to McCarthy to do [this], but . . . the higher loyalty . . . would be served only by being prepared. . . to go to somebody [else] . . . if McCarthy could not make it." In short, Lowenstein felt intellectually justified in actively seeking an alternative, even as he still appeared on the rolls as a McCarthy supporter.[46]

Indeed, behind the scenes, relations between McCarthy and Lowenstein were deteriorating rapidly. Lowenstein had cleared the Chicago meeting with McCarthy in advance; he later recalled that McCarthy had thought it "a very good idea." He had then asked McCarthy about his schedule on the days of the coalition meeting, only to discover that McCarthy would be in Chicago at the same time. "There was an awkwardness at that point," Lowenstein noted, and though he informally invited McCarthy to speak, he never followed through with a formal invitation, reasoning that McCarthy would understand why having a candidate in attendance would be counterproductive. Lowenstein did see McCarthy in his hotel right after the conference, and everything seemed all right. But Lowenstein then made a bizarre leap, psychologically and intellectually: he concluded, that he was the one who "was obviously being snubbed," because he was not invited to address McCarthy's rally that evening, an act, he said, "that obviously was designed to make me feel that I was not [wanted]." In a clear act of projection, Lowenstein had attributed to McCarthy the "snub" when in fact it had been he who had withdrawn the invitation to McCarthy.[47]

In reality, Lowenstein had begun to explore what came to seem the only way his dream of a unified political movement against the war could occur—the drafting of Edward Kennedy as the Democratic nominee for president. "It was always couched in the rhetoric, 'McCarthy can't do it,'" Harold Ickes noted, "and now that the real hero has been assassinated, we've got to find an alternative," but in Ickes's judgment, and that of others, it was clear that the open convention movement was a stalking horse for a Kennedy candidacy. Lowenstein himself observed that by late July, "it was impossible to take seriously the notion that McCarthy was going to emerge as the candidate." He had failed to condemn the brutal Soviet invasion of Czechoslovakia, was refusing to give media interviews, and in general seemed intent on "turning off" any potential supporters. Even before those developments, however, Lowenstein had begun to think about a Ted Kennedy draft.[48]

By the time the Democrats met in Chicago, the tantalizing straw in the wind seemed to have become a tangible possibility. McCarthy was more than ever removed from the process, and he had ordered his student followers to stay away (wisely, in light of what happened on the streets), thereby confounding Lowenstein's plans for massive protests against Humphrey by peaceful students. In addition, growing numbers of McCarthy delegates were indicating a willingness to consider an alternative. Meanwhile, Lowenstein's private communications with Kennedy in July had given him enough encouragement to proceed with a "draft Kennedy" program. Political intimates of the Kennedy clan were in town, apparently authorized to act in his behalf. Humphrey's standing in the public opinion polls was only 29 percent in a race against Nixon. The circumstances were right to move forward; any other alternative—such as nominating Humphrey—seemed to be political suicide. "This is what everybody wanted," Lowenstein said later. "It's difficult to have a draft if people don't want it, but when everybody wants it, there's not much planning or skill [required]."[49]

The key then became Kennedy's cooperation. Party chieftains, governors, congressmen, and senators were all checking delegate lists, preparing to go into action. But Ted Kennedy himself seemed deeply ambivalent. "If he had known the mood of the convention," Lowenstein said, "his doubt that there was a genuine draft would have been answered. But he didn't know the mood of the convention [because] he wasn't there." Steve Smith had been deputized to be his representative, but even Smith was not at the convention itself. Both Smith and Kennedy, moreover, were deeply concerned about Mayor Richard Daley, who wanted to play the role of kingmaker. Kennedy seemed unwilling to proceed without prior commitments that both Daley and McCarthy were amenable to a presidential draft—especially given the suspicion that what Daley really wanted was to get Kennedy sufficiently out front to then draft him as Humphrey's vice-presidential candidate.

In addition, there was the intangible personal issue in a Kennedy draft. When Lowenstein saw the black Mississippi political leader Charles Evers and told him, "We're going to save the convention [by nominating Kennedy]," Evers replied, "Uh, uh, you're not going to do it to that family a third time." The specter of another assassination hovered over the entire "draft Kennedy" scenario, making it all the more difficult to proceed without an explicit okay from Kennedy himself or Steve Smith. Yet Smith's reading of the situation had made him reluctant, and by the third day of the convention, Kennedy himself issued his second disclaimer of interest. Lowenstein still believed that the very introduction of Kennedy's name from the floor would "set off so spontaneous an eruption of enthusiasm that it wouldn't be necessary to have the big shots [like Daley and McCarthy]." But did he have the right to act on that belief, given Kennedy's reticence?[50]

As Lowenstein reconstructed it, the entire possibility of rescuing the convention and drafting Kennedy rested ultimately on Lowenstein's own shoulders. "That was the most traumatic and difficult decision of the whole campaign for me," he observed, "because it finally boiled down [to the fact] that if I didn't do it, no one would do it." Even with Kennedy's reluctance and all the concerns about another assassination, Lowenstein claimed that he would have proceeded to make the Kennedy nomination if only McCarthy had released him from his commitment to being a McCarthy delegate. But despite sending two emissaries to seek the release and numerous rumors that McCarthy would free all his delegates, Lowenstein insisted that he never received permission to proceed, either publicly or privately. "In that event," he told people, "there's nothing further I can do." Thus the Kennedy possibility evaporated even as it seemed within direct grasp. "If politics is a trapeze," Lowenstein observed later, "you could say the Kennedy nomination was missed, literally, by a gymnastic second."[51]

A year earlier, almost to the day, Lowenstein had galvanized the National Student Association congress with his vision of a "dump Johnson" campaign. As the critical player in that movement, he had brought it from a utopian vision to a practical reality. Profoundly committed to the goal of preserving the democratic process, he made his entire appeal contingent upon persuading people to reform the system from within. Hence his denunciation of SDS tactics and those radicals who insisted that the problems of America were so deep that the entire society had to be transformed.[52] To a remarkable degree, Lowenstein had come to see the preservation and reform of the democratic system as a goal he was uniquely suited—even "called"—to achieve, as though saving the country amounted to a mission that he, and perhaps he alone, could make possible. If someone were to reunite the Kennedy and McCarthy forces, he would be the one to do it. For Ted Kennedy to be drafted, Lowenstein had to be the one to make it happen. And maybe he was right. But in Chicago, the correct path proved too elusive.[53]

Now the last hope for a united coalition behind a peace candidacy was shattered. All that was left was for Lowenstein to seek in his own congressional race the victory that had eluded him on the national scene.

TRIUMPH ON LONG ISLAND

Having spent most of his summer organizing the National Coalition for an Open Convention, Lowenstein entered a very different political world when he went back to Long Beach to wage his general election campaign for Congress. Naturally, some of the issues were the same—the war in Vietnam, student rebelliousness, who should be president. But there was also a series of new concerns—jet noise at Kennedy Airport, pollution of Long Island waters—that now demanded equal attention, with a quite separate agenda of political priorities.

To begin with, the general election introduced a political spectrum dramatically different from that of the primary. There, Lowenstein's "purist" stance on the war proved advantageous because the target constituency was a relatively small, highly politicized group of liberals. Now, however, the voting public was enlarged eightfold; Republicans possessed a numerical advantage; and even optimists understood that Lowenstein would have to run far ahead of the Democratic national and state tickets to win. In short, by contrast with the primary, his major task now was to woo moderate and conservative votes even while holding on to his liberal base.[54]

Lowenstein was aided mightily, however, by the circumstances surrounding the selection of his opponent, Mason Hampton. A member of the Conservative party (a breakaway party, independent of the Republicans) who had secured the endorsement of the Republican machine in a backroom deal, Hampton had faced a strong primary challenge from a Republican rebel who appeared to be in no mood to bury the hatchet after his defeat. Although a former chairman of the Rockefeller-Javits reelection committee in Nassau County, Hampton had resigned from the Republican party in 1962, declaring that "the controlling forces within Republicanism have . . . diluted, ignored, compromised and abandoned the principles upon which I understand the party to be predicated." Such rhetorical denunciations did not sit well with many mainstream Republicans, notwithstanding the deal by which the Republican county chairman Joseph Margiotta had traded Republican endorsement of Hampton for Conservative party endorsement of other Republicans running for state and county office.

Moreover, much of Hampton's claim to fame rested on positions not acceptable to all mainstream Republicans. He achieved notoriety primarily by leading the fight against court-ordered school integration in the community of Malverne. As spokesman for Taxpayers and Parents, a group opposed to forced busing, Hampton undoubtedly earned the loyalty of constituents concerned primarily with that issue. But most Long Island Republicans were Javits-type voters more accustomed to casting their ballots for middle-of-the-road candidates than right-wing ideologues. Hampton's candidacy presented Lowenstein with a golden chance to cultivate these Republican moderates.[55]

With considerable skill, Lowenstein seized the opportunity. Emphasizing his positions on local issues like jet noise, pollution, and the wetlands, Lowenstein took his case to Republican strongholds. "Over and over again," one campaign worker said, "we'd see him go into audiences like American Legions . . . where these people obviously wouldn't agree with him on anything. Yet he was able to engage them in a civil dialogue . . . and he got a lot of votes that way." While Lowenstein would not moderate his antiwar views to please an audience, he welcomed the chance to engage people with a different point of view and showed respect for their positions. "In some ways," a campaign aide said, "[Al] was more effective with people he disagreed with from the right than he was with people . . . on the left, who were essentially unlikely to be persuaded by the fact that somebody had a sense of humor and was reasonable."[56]

Following through on these strengths, Lowenstein created a Republican beachhead in his political base. Friends like Bill Craig, who had brought him to Stanford and was a lifelong Republican, came to Long Island to help coordinate a campaign section specifically geared to Republican voters. Rod Boggs, son of a local Republican family, returned from

Africa in time to devote six weeks to Republican kaffeeklatsches. George Miller, the campaign manager for Hampton's Republican primary opponent, declared his support for Lowenstein early in the general election campaign, as did the head of the Republican club in Freeport. These were people, Boggs noted, "who could not tolerate what was happening with [their] party from the Hampton wing . . . [and who also] respected Al's integrity and his intelligence." Cleverly appealing to such divisions in the party, Lowenstein issued a political broadside declaring, "There is no Republican in this election." By late October, the local weeklies were carrying ads headlined "Republicans for Lowenstein"; the ads bore the signatures of more than 1,000 self-professed Republicans who were going to vote for Lowenstein.[57]

In the meantime, Lowenstein relied heavily on the one-to-one canvassing that had paid off so handsomely in the primary. Each weekend between 200 and 500 student volunteers from Yale, Cornell, Harvard, Smith—even from as far away as Notre Dame—descended on Rockville Center and surrounding communities. Going out into local neighborhoods, they became temporary Long Islanders, endearing themselves to many as examples of the youthful idealism so inextricably linked to Lowenstein's political image. (Not by accident, the Notre Dame students went into the most conservative Irish Catholic neighborhoods, as if to vouchsafe that this liberal Jew was really okay.) It was an experience most would never forget, an opportunity to make a difference, as Lowenstein had said, and more often than not, a chance to have a good time as well. Sometimes, one campaign coordinator said, "it became one big mixer."[58]

Nor was Lowenstein's youth army limited to college-age students. Hundreds of fifteen- and sixteen-year-olds were turned on to politics via the Lowenstein campaign, bitten by the bug of public service and engagement that would remain with many of them the rest of their lives. "They swarm through Lowenstein's campaign headquarters," one reporter wrote, "fluttering like moths, answering telephones, licking envelope flaps, typing . . . telling their parents, 'But you have to vote for Lowenstein.'. . . Their motto is 'Teenie Power.'" Fired by the excitement of working for someone who was a national celebrity, the teenagers added a compelling dimension to Lowenstein's candidacy.[59]

The campaign, in turn, was calibrated to maximize the number of enthusiastic Lowenstein supporters. "Al's theory about [running]," Jenny said, was, "Move them up a notch. . . . If you find somebody who's neutral, see if you can get them to vote. If you've got a voter, turn them into a worker. If you've got a worker, turn them into a contributor. . . . If you've got a Republican that you've turned around . . . see if he won't give money and be a Republican for Lowenstein." And a lot of them did, partly because they found [Al] fascinating. This larger-than-life character had come into their lives . . . [and] sort of blasted them with this giant light.

No matter how disorganized the overall campaign coordination was—and chaos remained a problem—at least the "move them up a notch" approach provided an ever expanding pool of energy and enthusiasm to fuel the effort.[60]

Jenny herself added enormously to Lowenstein's appeal. A tireless campaigner, she attended kaffeeklatsches he could not make, served as an "advance" speaker the countless times he was late, organized shopping center rallies, and entertained nonstop the students and campaign volunteers who regularly descended on the small family house at 163 Lindell Boulevard. There was rarely a night when Al did not show up for dinner with ten or twelve people in tow—often unannounced—and Jenny, with her neighbor Sue Andrews and others, somehow stretched the Hamburger Helper and noodles to serve them all. Described by one older campaign worker as looking a "little like a Jewish nun," Jenny marshaled all of her WASP graciousness and good manners to make people feel welcome. A campaign poster showing Al and Jenny walking down the boardwalk holding little Frankie's hands conveyed the simple but powerful message that here was an enormously attractive young family ready and able to handle anything.[61]

Lowenstein himself turned out to be somewhat inept in the day-to-day role of campaign glad-hander. Brilliant in a debate format, and inspiring in small group gatherings where he could articulate his views, Lowenstein became almost a nebbish when it came to meeting voters at railroad stations, factory gates, or shopping centers. All of his insecurity came to the fore, Jenny said, when he was called upon to plunge into crowds and greet strangers. "The only way I can do it," he used to tell her, "is to be on automatic pilot." The only voters he was comfortable with up close, his friend Gary Bellow noted, were older Jewish women. "He was hysterical," Bellow said. "He was the Jewish son. And he played that role and he loved it." Like his Aunt Ruthie, these women "were funny . . . and they made him feel loved and wanted." But at a suburban shopping mall it was a different story. "Where is the candidate," one reporter asked. "He stands to the side trying to avoid any meetings, his curly-cue strand of hair flapping in the breeze . . . his checkered shirt half-tucked in. . . . He doesn't look or act like a candidate. . . . He is a bewildered figure seeking to avoid the expectations of the traditional ways of election, an outcast in a middle-class suburb."[62]

Lowenstein also retained the annoying habit of trying to control every detail of his campaign. Although he had wisely gone out and recruited Herbert Kramer, who had been a Vorspan supporter, to be his new campaign chairman, Lowenstein still insisted on calling all the shots. For instance, he terrorized campaign workers by totally rewriting a brochure that had already gone through five layers of approval and was overdue at the printers. His schedule remained chaotic, and his demands seemed to increase exponentially as the campaign wore on. "Al really needed a . . . complete support system around him," Rick Weidman noted, and at times, he placed campaign workers in demeaning roles.[63]

Lowenstein's biggest problem, though, was holding together his coalition of NDC peace Democrats, moderate Republicans, and regular Democrats who viewed with suspicion and hostility his maverick politics. On the one side, the NDC constituency was adamant that Lowenstein do nothing to compromise his purity on the peace issue. As the political organizer Arnold Miller observed, although they were his base, "they were a little bit more left sometimes than he wanted to be," and they became furious with him for endorsing regular Democrats for state assembly and county offices. The regulars, on the other hand, insisted on the old-fashioned virtues of party loyalty and patriotism, threatening to sit on their hands on election day if Lowenstein did not come around. Labor unions, in particular, withheld their support because of Lowenstein's reputation for attacking the party.[64]

The heart of the question was whether Lowenstein would endorse Hubert Humphrey for president. At every debate during the campaign, Mason Hampton spotlighted the issue immediately, declaring there was one thing he and Lowenstein agreed upon completely, which was that Hubert Humphrey should never be the president. Put on the defensive, Lowenstein had no way to respond that did not alienate a significant part of his constituency. Yet he knew that he would have to make a choice eventually, and that his decision would critically affect his election chances. Initially, therefore, he took Herbert Kramer's advice and moved gingerly to defuse Hampton's allegation, saying he *would* vote, and his ballot would not be cast for either George Wallace or Richard Nixon. By most accounts, Lowenstein knew that at some point he needed to endorse

Humphrey explicitly and was hoping against hope that something would happen in the Humphrey campaign to make that endorsement more palatable. Lanny Davis, a youthful aide close to both men, had set up an earlier private session in which Humphrey tearfully begged Lowenstein for support, promising to meet with any group of antiwar activists, at any time, to address their concerns. But the meeting came too close to the Chicago convention for Lowenstein to respond. When Humphrey began, however, to distance himself from the Johnson administration position on the war in his Salt Lake City address at the end of October, and Johnson declared a bombing halt soon thereafter, Lowenstein felt able to proceed with an embrace of the party's standard-bearer.

The remaining problem was to break the news to his young staff members. Many had been through nine months of struggle, with Lowenstein as their hero and moral champion. "They had pictured Allard as a 'God' who had no human weaknesses," Herbert Kramer noted. Now this exemplar of purity was going to sell out and endorse the man who just four months earlier he had vowed never to support. For some of the more hardened staff members, the decision seemed a foregone conclusion. But others were convinced that their hero would never let them down. Calling a midnight staff meeting, Lowenstein conveyed the impression, one volunteer said, that the staff would have "a major influence on what he was going to do, and that it was some kind of democratic process." But in reality, the meeting was held primarily to provide a forum for catharsis; Lowenstein listened to the students' concerns and told them he knew how and why they felt as they did. If anyone wished to quit, he said, he would understand. But they must also know that, henceforth, no one associated with his campaign could say anything publicly that was critical of Humphrey or the decision to support him.[65]

In all likelihood, Lowenstein's decision ensured his election. The bombing halt and Humphrey's change of position meant an immediate shift toward Humphrey in the Long Island presidential polls. In October, Humphrey had stood at 33 percent, and a Lowenstein victory would have required that he run 50 percent ahead of the ticket—a virtual impossibility. By the end of October, Humphrey had moved up to 45 percent, and Lowenstein's endorsement was making it possible for disaffected mainstream Democrats to return to the flock and vote a straight party ticket. Peace Democrats had nowhere else to go, and in any event, Lowenstein's track record on the war was better than anyone else's, regardless of his support for Humphrey.

Mason Hampton, in the meantime, seemed intent on running a Thomas

Dewey campaign. Evidently convinced by an Oliver Quayle poll in late October showing that he was at least ten points ahead of Lowenstein, he sat back complacently and thought he would coast to victory. The Vietnam War was not an issue, he insisted, since he supported the president— which also meant he had no place to go when Johnson announced his bombing halt. Besides law and order, the only other major issue Hampton raised was the ludicrous charge that Lowenstein was vice-president of an organization (the ADA) that supported the legalization of marijuana. If, by that allegation, Hampton expected to associate Lowenstein in the public mind with a drug-crazed counterculture, the presence of 1,000 clean and well-tailored college students canvassing for Lowenstein each weekend provided a powerful antidote.

The odds still seemed against Lowenstein, but energy and the thrust of world events worked on his side. On election day, notwithstanding the chaos of the campaign, the tensions in his coalition, and the numerical superiority of the Republicans, Lowenstein finished ten points ahead of Hubert Humphrey and squeaked to victory by a margin of 2,600 votes. For the second time in a year, he experienced the joy and triumph of electoral victory. "How Professor Lowenstein would have relished his son being a winner!" Marcia Borie exclaimed. It was a moment to savor.[66]

CONCLUSION

In each generation there may come, once or twice, a time when the world reaches a turning point, when opposed forces race toward each other on a collision course, and when those blessed or cursed with the fate of being participants tremble before the pace and enormity of the choices being made. The year 1968—the time of Vietnam, the Tet offensive, the assassinations, the toppling of a presidency—was such a moment. "It was a passionate year, a benchmark year in American life," David Halberstam observed. "Everything was pulling [apart]." Only a few individuals were at the center, according to Halberstam. Bobby Kennedy was there. Martin Luther King, Jr., was there. And Al Lowenstein was there.[67]

Among the reasons Lowenstein belongs in that company is that it would be difficult to imagine a "dump Johnson" movement without him—or a McCarthy presidential bid, or Kennedy's entry into the race, or the open convention movement, or maybe even the events of Chicago at the end of August. Obviously, countless individuals shaped the histories of these events, some of which, arguably, would have happened anyway. Yet at virtually every critical juncture, Allard Lowenstein was not only there, he was also pivotal to what happened. In some ways, then, for Lowenstein—as for a generation—1968 was not just a single year but the culmination of a lifetime, a measure of what had been and what was to come.

It was certainly a year that highlighted the tortured complexity of Lowenstein's political persona. His words were always so clear. "I think this country faces the very serious possibility of falling apart if it continues on its present course," he said. The future of the democratic process hung in the balance, and only if right-thinking men and women joined together to end the war would there be a world worth living for. Tens of thousands responded to this pure and simple message. It was a way to save liberalism and American society at the same time, the one a means of protecting the other. And Allard Lowenstein would show the way.

Yet on another level, his presentation was so complicated—gratitude and praise for McCarthy on the one hand, behind-the-scenes carping at his incompetence on the other; publicly professing to be keeping hands off any effort to persuade Robert Kennedy to run, then privately being intimately engaged in drafting his announcement of candidacy; striving for the high principle of a truly "open convention" in order to build a united antiwar front, yet having the real agenda of promoting a "draft Ted Kennedy" movement. What troubled some people was not that politicians should not, or did not act this way all the time; rather, it was that Lowenstein appeared so unwilling to acknowledge his multiple roles and engaged in endless intellectual rationalizations to persuade others—and himself—that he was not really inconsistent, and that it was all part of a principled struggle to serve a higher cause.

Somehow, this complexity all went back to Lowenstein's perennial problem with his own self-worth—his inability to feel *right* about asserting himself. "[Al] was ambivalent about his own ambition," Gary Bellow remarked. "He had a view of the world in which people who were ambitious couldn't be in it." Wanting something for himself—like power, or fame—was unacceptable, almost "dirty." So instead, "the cause" became a substitute for self-assertion. "He never got this [quite] sorted out," Bellow commented, "[and] that's why he tended to create . . . fight[s] of darkness against light. He needed some way of understanding what he was doing. The only way he could win was to have that as his model." If the cause were noble and transcendent—literally a crusade of right against wrong—*then* ambition was permissible, because it was not a self-aggrandizing pursuit of power, but rather service on behalf of a higher goal.[68]

Although a similar process operated throughout Lowenstein's life, 1968 magnified and heightened the pattern, as it magnified and heightened so much else of American political culture. In fact, 1968 was a year of triumph for Lowenstein because in a manner that had never happened before and would never be repeated again, his distinctive political personality coincided with the mood and demands of the time. It was a year that required an overriding political leader who could define issues in terms of good and evil, light and darkness—a time when countless people needed a voice to tell them how urgent it was to commit themselves to working within the system to "save" democracy. It was a time when—however contorted Lowenstein's own definition of ambition—a person who had an impulse to turn the country around and save a way of life could almost succeed.

It was also a time when liberalism was able to survive, if only by the slimmest of threads. Despite pressures so extreme that there seemed on occasion no way that the country could avoid internal warfare, enough people had retained a commitment to established processes of politics to maintain the liberal tradition. Nixon may have been elected, but no one could deny that the liberal antiwar movement had irrevocably altered public opinion about the war, in the process unseating the president most identified with its prosecution.

And Allard Lowenstein was at the center of it all. "We have our country back," the Texas author Ronnie Dugger wrote Lowenstein after Johnson announced he would not run again, "and you are one reason we do." "Life looks good," a student protégé wrote from England in April, "because the ability of good people to reverse the course of events in the face of impossible odds is once again confirmed." You have "saved the world," still another said. David Halberstam telegraphed: "Once more you have made it a little bit easier to care about this country. Cheers." In a season of losses and disappointments, Lowenstein had kept alive the flame of hope for ultimate victory. "Many of us here [have] never won anything before," one celebrant at Lowenstein's primary triumph noted, "and no one but you could have accomplished this feat. All by yourself, you breathed new life into the democratic political process and made people want to do things they never believed they could do."[69]

In a profound sense, then, 1968 represented the redemption and fulfillment of Allard Lowenstein's political mission in life. Lowenstein was "a Renaissance man of the liberal movement," the *Washington Post* said, "one of the [people] . . . who has truly influenced events." Rising to prominence at precisely the moment his vision was most relevant, he played a role that no one else could have played, thereby realizing his highest personal hopes for the historical moment. "At a time when generational politics was very important," Rick Tuttle observed, "he was a massive figure. . . . Al was [the man] for [his] generation."[70]

The tragedy was that the person he cared most about in politics was no longer there to serve as his friend, leader, and ally. Lowenstein could take solace from the fact that Robert Kennedy had given him the only memento from that extraordinary year that really mattered to him—the quote from Emerson—and that the Kennedy family continued to be deeply devoted to his political fortunes. ("Next to the presidency," one friend said, "Steve Smith was most interested in [Al's race] on election night.") But the fact remained that the only person who might have satisfied Lowenstein's ultimate ambition for that political year was now dead, and his own desperate effort to create a substitute solution in the form of nominating Bobby's brother had foundered, with Richard Nixon being elected to the presidency instead.[71]

For Lowenstein, therefore, the mixture of triumph and tragedy was individual as well as political. The victories and defeats in his own life mirrored those of the country at large. Both would stay with him, shaping directly much of what he would attempt in the next decade. But if 1968 had indeed been a turning point, what would be the consequences? Could Allard Lowenstein's faith in liberal activism survive in a world still being ripped apart by ideological, racial, and generational conflict? And could Lowenstein sustain the triumphant role that he had created for himself during this year of decision?

13

Being a Congressman

THE SCENARIO WAS IN MANY WAYS ANOMALOUS. THE COUNTRY'S MOST PERI-patetic political agitator was joining an institution whose first rule was to stay put and do your homework. A man whose reputation was that of a maverick willing to take on the president of the United States now entered a body dedicated to hierarchy and deference toward one's elders. How would the House of Representatives contain Allard Lowenstein? More to the point, how could Allard Lowenstein remain a devoted individualist and be accepted in an environment dedicated to the collective etiquette of "getting along by going along"?

Not surprisingly, Lowenstein found a way. Long attracted by the prospect of winning the legitimacy conferred by membership in the congressional club, Lowenstein leaped to the challenge with the enthusiasm and commitment of a young cub. "He just exuded happiness . . . in those years," Jenny said. "[Congress] . . . took all that energy and gave it a place to go." Certainly there were problems. Chaos did not suddenly turn into order. The tension between rebelling against a government while fighting for acceptance within it continued to be as acute and unresolvable as ever. But to a remarkable degree, continuity rather than change marked Lowenstein's journey into this new role. He persisted in the balancing act of seeking change through incremental reform, all the while trying to sell his

315

own agenda as mainstream politics. At the same time, he continued to reach out to those who disagreed with him—especially on the right—hoping to bring them on board. That he succeeded at all in this endeavor testified powerfully to his passion, talent, and political skill. But his ultimate failure spoke with equal force to the difficulty, if not impossibility, of reconciling opposites.

Unfortunately, it was the "opposites" that controlled American political culture during the last two years of the 1960s. Lowenstein struggled desperately to preserve and protect his own definition of the liberal tradition—that common ground where people who shared certain assumptions about political discourse and reform could meet and find agreement. But even as he tried, centrifugal forces were pulling the society apart, undermining and eventually destroying the common ground Lowenstein held so dear. No matter how brilliant his efforts, Lowenstein could not prevail with his vision of working within the system to turn America around. In 1970, the man and his message went down to defeat—partly because of the manipulation and intransigence of his enemies, partly because of the flaws inherent in his own personality and politics, which, by 1970, had become indistinguishable. And that, too, was part of the problem.

THE CONGRESSIONAL SETTING

Lowenstein claimed never to have even contemplated what it would be like to sit in Congress. Finding himself there, he told a *New York Post* reporter, "had something of an Alice in Wonderland quality about it—something amazing, because it was unexpected, and because I felt this great awe for the electoral process." Consistent with that awe—and perhaps expressing how he conceived his new role—Lowenstein recounted an anxiety dream that he had just before being sworn in. He imagined that he was coming back from a trip abroad, only to discover that the House had convened already. A roll call was taking place on whether to continue the House Un-American Activities Committee. Rushing down the aisle to cast what would be the tie-breaking vote against HUAC, Lowenstein heard the Speaker intone, "But you weren't here in time to be sworn in, Mr. Lowenstein." It may not have been Alice in Wonderland, but it came close.[1]

In reality, Lowenstein entered Congress with two very different visions. On the one hand, Jennifer Littlefield noted, he saw Congress as a place "where you could completely be your own person and do anything that you wanted to do." In this vision, Congress offered a forum from which to convert people and "shed light" on issues and problems that otherwise might be ignored. Al saw being in Congress, Littlefield said, as a means of providing "constituent services for the Western hemisphere." The world would be his district, peace and justice in the universe his goals. His other vision, by contrast, was much more pedestrian. Many people had been reluctant to support Al in the first place, one politico wrote him, "because they felt you would not give enough of your time to local Nassau County affairs." Gary Bellow, one of Lowenstein's most trusted friends, shared such concerns, fearing that they would be "exacerbated by your tendency to overcommit yourself [and] by your focus on national issues. . . . I worry that you won't pay enough attention to those concerns and [will] erode the base on which you stand." Even before going to Washington, then, Lowenstein was challenged to reconcile being a spokesman for the world and an advocate for Long Island suburbanites, to combine the autonomy of speaking for the world's oppressed, anywhere and everywhere, with the captivity of being a local "pol."[2]

Nothing that happened when Lowenstein arrived at the Capitol made it easy to resolve the conflict. Although he had requested assignment to the House Armed Services Committee, the Democratic leadership decided he was needed more on the Agriculture Committee and assigned him to subcommittees on oil, seeds, and rice, and livestock and grains. Needless to say, there were no farms in Lowenstein's district. The leadership's committee choices for him seemed to convey the clear message that this freshman in particular had better not make any waves. (His constituents responded by sending him a gold pitchfork, and Lowenstein told reporters that he had been given the assignment in order to represent a roadside farm stand in Malverne.) The House orientation session, meanwhile, seemed to corroborate all of Lowenstein's worst fears about the troglodyte priorities of his peers. The first lesson congressmen had to learn, he was told, was how to get reelected. The second was how to conform most rapidly to the system of hierarchy and seniority. The experience, Lowenstein said, made him realize that "Congress is like Calcutta—nothing prepares you for it."[3]

By the time he had completed his first weeks in office, Lowenstein was convinced more than ever that reform of congressional procedures was imperative. Most of the criteria by which people judged the quality of their representatives, Lowenstein told a *New Yorker* reporter, were a charade. Roll calls served simply as a way of securing a quorum, not measuring a representative's vote. (In fact, votes on key amendments were not recorded). Theoretically, the *Congressional Record* provided written documentation of what was said and done on the House floor, but in reality, it was a catchall for statements drafted by congressional staff members to make it appear as though representatives were speaking out on major issues. Even the act of cosponsoring bills was meaningless, since it usually indicated only a willingness by one member of Congress to grant a political favor to another. Worst of all, people in Congress were taught to use the "frank"—their free mailing privileges—not to inform or educate their constituents but to disseminate political propaganda designed to ensure their reelection. The cumulative effect, Lowenstein concluded, was demeaning to morale and self-respect; House members were taught to deflect their energies into meaningless activities rather than tackle real problems, all the while reinforcing an insidious seniority system that rewarded age rather than talent. The leadership process, he told one audience in northern Virginia, was determined by a "system of advanced geriatrics, where you sit and wait to see who lasts the longest."[4]

Clearly, Lowenstein needed to find some way to make his mark, despite such institutional obstacles. Even though the liberal Democratic Study Group disappointed him when it refused to consider procedural reform at its first meeting, he sensed a growing desire on the part of younger members—Republicans as well as Democrats—to secure a larger voice in House counsels and cut away some of the antiquated rules of Congress. Beginning a two-year campaign to ensure that members were accountable for their actions, he reached out for allies on both sides of the aisle willing to defend the right of constituents to know how their representatives voted. At the same time, he set himself a standard that he hoped would keep him from falling victim to the charade. "My first rule," he told the reporter Flora Lewis, "is that if I don't do more . . . about the things I care about . . . by being there . . . than I would if I weren't there, then I shouldn't be [in Congress]. That rule will make a lot of decisions much easier."[5]

Lowenstein's basic strategy in all of this was to follow a two-track approach: he would go along with the existing House hierarchy as he functioned *within* the institution, but he would excoriate the system *outside* of Congress and demand its replacement. Notwithstanding his rhetoric, for example, he reached out to those who most personified the seniority system and won their approbation. No one came in for more public ridicule in Lowenstein's speeches about the "geriatric system" than L. Mendel Rivers—or "Old Man Rivers," as Lowenstein called him—the head of the Armed Services Committee and a chief beneficiary of a "safe" South Carolina district. Yet on the floor, Lowenstein became a favorite of Rivers, telling him he had relatives in Rivers's district, then joking about Rivers's response that, "yes, some of our best citizens in Charleston are Jews." At one point, Rivers came up to Lowenstein to complain that Ed Koch, another New Yorker, was coming into his district to make trouble. But "I've been there, too," working for civil rights, Lowenstein said. No, Rivers replied, "you deserve to be down there 'cause those are things that you've been doing for years and they're important to you. I understand that. But that man Koch, I just can't understand what *he's* doin' down there."[6]

Despite his anger at being assigned to the Agriculture Committee, Lowenstein accepted the position with grace rather than defy the leadership, as his fellow freshman Shirley Chisholm, a black congresswoman from Brooklyn, did when she did not like her assignments. He went to meetings, built rapport with his colleagues, and worked inside the committee on issues such as nutrition. "You're not a bit like they told me," House Majority Leader Carl Albert reportedly told Lowenstein. "You're not a long hair and bearded type at all." Moreover, Lowenstein used his favorite House perk, the gymnasium, as a haunt for developing friendships with people of a very different political bent. Republicans, not Democrats, were his closest friends—Pete McCloskey, Donald Rumsfeld, Don Riegle. He was always reaching out to the other side. "Al had a faculty . . . for reminding people who differed," his colleague Andy Jacobs said, "that they need not fear one another, and therefore they need not hate one another."[7]

Through such behavior, Lowenstein made friends far beyond what an observer familiar only with his rhetoric might imagine. On one occasion early in his tenure, Lowenstein took the floor during a bitter debate on military appropriations for Vietnam. The verbal exchanges had become heated and personal, and friends had advised Lowenstein not to speak. But he rose to say what a privilege it was to be a member of the House and be able to engage in free debate, and how much everyone there should celebrate the fact that they could disagree. The chamber quieted, according to witnesses, as Lowenstein evoked and articulated some of the bonds that brought the representatives together, whatever their opinions. It was because of this ability, one reporter noted, that "Lowenstein is both the darling and devil of this Congress. . . . He has been impertinent without antagonizing, daring without offending."[8]

To a large degree, Lowenstein used the same approach of welcoming debate and reaching out to the opposition back in his home district. Almost as soon as he was elected, Lowenstein scheduled a five-day series of town meetings in different communities to learn what his constituents were most worried about. Shortly thereafter, he announced his plan to hold congressional forums every two weeks in various communities within the district, each one designed to inform people about critical issues, while stimulating dialogue. "[Al] understood the role of the political person as teacher," one political adviser noted. Costing between $1,300 and $1,500 each, the forums brought up to 1000 constituents to daylong seminars and debates on issues as diverse as Jewish-black relations (featuring Shirley Chisholm), antiballistic missiles, jet noise, the environment, funding education programs, and law enforcement problems. Moreover, he consciously sought to spotlight Republican viewpoints, bringing in such prominent conservatives as William Buckley, Congressman Sylvio Conte, and assorted Nixon administration officials. "It's important at this time in our history for people to have opportunities to express and hear different points of view about things that bother them," he said.[9]

Lowenstein also brought to his Long Island district the same talent he had displayed in Washington for bridging political differences in his personal relationships. "Despite his opposition to the war," Rod Boggs observed, "he had the ability . . . to go off and visit a bereaved family and communicate with utter sincerity his real sadness and appreciation for the loss of these people." Lowenstein often visited the bedsides of hospitalized Vietnam veterans, or the homes of families who had lost a loved one in the war; when he could not make such visits, his wife Jenny went in his stead. For most antiwar leaders, such actions would be difficult to imagine, said Boggs, who worked in Lowenstein's district office in Long Island. "But in his case, it was a natural part of his style and . . . personality." Lowenstein displayed a similar breadth of interest, though in a more politically calculated way, when he invited the editors of conservative Long Island weeklies to have dinner with his forum guests. Here, too, the theme was to set aside political alliances when it came to personal relationships—understanding that doing so had political consequences.[10]

Lowenstein could successfully carry out his dual agenda of being a principled reformer and popular pragmatist only by putting together an excellent staff—a process that highlighted how distinctive Lowenstein's time in Congress would prove to be. First, he continued his campaign custom of acting as though he were his own best staffperson and no one else had the competence to do the right thing. Second, and by contrast, he insisted that staff members be available to him at all hours of the day and night to do his bidding. And third, by virtue of both his demands and his insistence on being in charge, he made life almost impossible for those who worked for him. The miracle was that Lowenstein nevertheless marshaled one of the most energetic, devoted, and talented groups of assistants on the Hill.

Chaos was the leitmotif of the Lowenstein congressional office. Ideally, one assistant said, a political staff should be "the tugboat moving the mother ship around to the right ports and the right locations." But such a definition presumed that the "mother ship" could be located, then controlled. Early on, Lowenstein decided not to rent an apartment in Washington, choosing instead to camp out with friends or sleep on his office couch—despite House rules prohibiting such a practice. Half the time, Lowenstein's staff had no idea where he was staying, even when he was in town (a rarity in itself some weeks, given his travel schedule). On the other hand, Lowenstein *always* wanted to know where his staff was. "It was funny and crazy and wild," Fred Millhiser commented. "You never knew when you'd get a call at 3:00 in the morning." In self-defense, staff members worked out a code, refusing to answer the phone after midnight unless the right signal was given, because otherwise Al would persist until he reached somebody, usually to ask that person to come get him at some location where he'd been dropped off, "or some [other] craziness."

Nor were his antics limited to late night. The staff would be struggling to catch up with an overload early in the morning, Millhiser recalled, when suddenly Al would call from Union Station where he went regularly for a shave and a haircut, demanding to be picked up. "There were three of us in the office," Millhiser noted. "The phones were going bananas . . . and he'd call and say . . . . 'It's just a disaster. . . . The only way for this all to work is if you come and get me.'" Finally, one day an aide took a cab to Union Station, and when Lowenstein, as usual, handed the aide a pile of papers and said he had to make a phone call, the aide said, "The cab is waiting." "A cab? A cab?" Lowenstein exclaimed incredulously, "I could have taken a cab." "I know," said the aide. And Lowenstein never called for the Union Station shuttle again.[11]

Lowenstein quickly became a figure of popular folklore in Washington. Once, when offered a ride home from a party by the NBC correspondent John Chancellor, Lowenstein admitted he had no place to stay, so Chancellor took him to his own house for the night. *Look* magazine called him "the most rumpled Congressman"; in fact, said his friend Marcia Borie, Lowenstein wore his sloppy appearance like a "badge of honor. . . . [He] never came off a plane with the suitcase zippered; it was always half-flying open, with three copies of the *New York Times* [bursting out]." When a member of his staff on Long Island visited the office in Washington, she discovered a file drawer in one of the offices stuffed with his laundry. "Why couldn't he wear a clean jacket," a friend wondered, "so somebody could focus on what [he was] saying rather than the lunch on [his] lapel?" If the year were 1989 rather than 1969, another staff assistant said, "you'd think he was some kind of street person walking around with his bag . . . always with his shirt out. You never expect a member of Congress to look like that."[12]

Still, working for Lowenstein was a constant adrenalin high. There were always "dozens of balls in the air," Rod Boggs said. So great was the amount of work to be completed that Lowenstein hired two shifts of staff members, one to handle the days, the other the nights. Since there were more people on payroll than was legally permitted, individuals took turns going off the books temporarily. As many as twenty interns added to the chaos in the summer, many of them working on ad hoc projects with little supervision. "You just couldn't move," one staff worker said. "You [can't] imagine how limited our time was to do all these things." On the other hand, the excitement was much greater than in most congressional offices. There was always a crisis somewhere, and Lowenstein was involved in so many politically volatile battles that a normal day in his office was like an extraordinary day in anyone else's.[13]

The greatest difficulty was trying to get the routine chores done, particularly given Lowenstein's penchant for signing off on everything. Thousands of pieces of mail piled up when he was away on lengthy foreign trips; some of it was never answered, according to his first administrative assistant, Emory Bundy, "because getting things through the office and past Al was an absolute nightmare." Even when form letters were prepared, Lowenstein would find some fault as he flipped through the stacks, throwing up his hands and proclaiming, "I can't trust anybody, nothing is to go out of here unless I personally see it." Written statements were a particular source of stress. Falling into the congressional pattern, Lowenstein's staff spent hours "revising and extending" remarks for insertion into the *Congressional Record*. But "it was a council of despair," Emory Bundy observed, "because he would never like it." A compulsive stylist, Lowenstein worked and reworked every paragraph, keeping both his own staff and that of the *Congressional Record* well past the *Record's* 2:00 A.M. deadline. In the meantime, aides would be trying to place phone calls to everyone Lowenstein needed to talk to, as often as not calling when they knew the other party would not be there, since a completed call would have extended their own day further. "Sometimes," his scheduling secretary, Susan Tannenbaum, said, "you just want[ed] to wring his neck."[14]

Because Lowenstein proved so difficult to deal with as an administrator, it took longer than usual for the staff to cohere. Lowenstein asked almost nobody from his campaign to join him in Washington. "We were really shocked," Rick Weidman commented. "Part of it . . . was that everybody either had or thought they had an intense personal relationship with Al, [so] who the hell could [he] have picked. . . . [Washington] was a different place and a different ballgame." Ironically, Lowenstein's first choice to be his administrative assistant was someone he had never met— Jack Watson, later the White House chief of staff under Jimmy Carter, whom Lowenstein called on Thanksgiving Day to arrange to interview. When Watson declined, Lowenstein turned to one of his oldest friends, Emory Bundy, who was then teaching political science at Oberlin College. Despite some apprehension—"working with you," Bundy wrote, "would be exhilarating, worthwhile, tiring . . . [and] could be frustrating"— Bundy took the job. But Lowenstein never gave Bundy control over issues and other staff appointments, and he soon found that working for Al "was a nightmare." Bundy left after six months and was replaced by John Curtis, a Washingtonian with more administrative experience and greater savvy about the Hill. Other early staff members resigned as well, but by the end of the summer of 1969, a team was in place, ready to at least try to cope with Lowenstein's demands and expectations. Mostly young, enthusiastic, and dedicated, they were willing to put up with Lowenstein's lateness, unreliability, and eccentricity in return for the reward of being involved in the most important battles of the day.[15]

Critical to their ability to survive was a marvelous sense of humor. Not only did they have their own telephone signals and subterranean plots to sabotage Lowenstein's designs on their free time, they also had the capacity to make fun of themselves and him. "Hon. Millard K. Loinsteen," their 1970 birthday greeting to him began, "menny gud wishes," and, "PS, this has been proofed and approved by our new writer." John Curtis produced a skit about the "Dump Al Movement"; in it, Al decides to leave on forty-five minutes' notice for a trip to Tierra del Fuego, and the staff scrambles to discover where the country is, and how to get notice of the trip into the *Congressional Record*. They even wrote a folk song, sung to the tune of "Charley on the M.T.A.," that included the chorus, "Will we ever see

Al?/No, we'll never see Al,/And our letters will all go amiss," and a concluding verse,

> Al's wife goes down to LaGuardia Airport,
> Every day at a quarter past two,
> And through the shuttle window,
> She throws a bologna sandwich,
> As the jet goes noisily through.

With that kind of spirit, one could tolerate the frustrations and appreciate the upbeat side of the experience. "It was a period of probably as intense excitement as you could [think about]," Roger Poole, Lowenstein's legislative assistant, said. "It's hard to imagine there was anything [controversial] going on . . . that didn't either originate in, or have major participation [from] our office."[16]

With all his idiosyncratic foibles, Lowenstein was thus well grounded for the assault he intended to make on Washington. Even if he insisted on approving every word that passed the threshold of his office, he had succeeded in molding a talented staff that could adapt to his demands and eccentricities. This team, in turn, was well prepared to help him carve out a niche where he could be both an agitator for reform and a hale fellow well met. Lowenstein had begun the process of rebelling against the anachronistic rules of the House while cultivating the anachronistic personalities therein, and of building an agenda of liberal achievement in his district while seeking coalitions with conservative antagonists. In all of this, his goal was to redefine the mainstream and then occupy it. The problem was whether he could find the center in an age of rapidly accelerating polarization.

LOCATING THE MAINSTREAM

Finding the center proved particularly difficult during the administration of Richard Nixon. Elected on the slogan of "Bringing us together," Nixon ostensibly sought the same goal of mainstream support for reform and ending the war as Lowenstein did. Yet Nixon intended to reach his objective not by cultivating those who disagreed with him but by pursuing a politics of polarization designed to turn the "silent majority" against his foes. Lowenstein, by contrast, specialized in reaching out to the opposition. Using such an approach, he sought to create "floating alliances": people who would normally disagree with him on most issues could nevertheless feel comfortable joining him to fight certain problems, such as jet noise. The question was whether even someone of Lowenstein's talent could achieve that objective when Richard Nixon was president and the war in Vietnam remained the single most important national issue.[17]

Even before he was sworn in, Lowenstein made it clear that international issues would be his primary concern. He had retained a strong interest in Africa, and carried significant weight both in Africa itself and in American foreign policy circles concerned with Africa. Before taking office he embarked on a dangerous mission to find a political and humanitarian solution to Nigeria's war with Biafra. Greg Craig accompanied him and left a letter behind that said if they were killed, the Biafran government should not be held above suspicion. "We'll have no warning," Lowenstein had told Craig.

But Vietnam remained the most difficult problem. Initially at least, Lowenstein felt he had no choice but to give Nixon's policies on the war a chance. Both men had been elected on the pledge to bring the war to an end, and in the beginning, Nixon appeared to be moving in the right direction, proposing a plan for an all-volunteer army that would eliminate the draft (an idea Lowenstein applauded) and proposing to withdraw American troops as the Vietnamese took on greater responsibility for the fighting. In a speech on the House floor, Lowenstein announced that while he preferred Senator George Aiken's plan to simply declare victory in Vietnam and get out, "Vietnamization is as close to that announcement as we are likely to get, so let's support it. The President is committed to getting us out. I wish he would do it faster, but all right. We're getting out." According to Lowenstein, Nixon had assured him that withdrawal would occur within six months. In another sign of his more accommodationist strategy, Lowenstein used the same speech to attack liberals who were unwilling to separate themselves from the left "lest they seem to be Red-baiting."[18]

On the other hand, Lowenstein needed to pay attention to the antiwar movement, which had provided such a strong foundation for his candidacy and which he had represented for so long. Consistent with his campaign promises, Lowenstein voted against military appropriations for the war in Vietnam, acting in concert with a large delegation of New York representatives. In addition, he offered his support to more than 250 student leaders—Lowenstein's old coalition of student body presidents and newspaper editors—who opposed the wartime draft and signed a petition declaring they would not serve if called as long as the war continued. These were the "elected representatives of a whole generation of college students," Lowenstein declared.[19]

By the summer, the antiwar student movement intensified its pressure even as it became clearer that Nixon's pledge to end the war was hollow. Embarking on a late summer tour that took him to Moscow, Prague, and Bangkok as well as Vietnam, Lowenstein laid the groundwork for initiating a new political assault on Nixon's Vietnam policy. In concert with Republicans Donald Riegle and Pete McCloskey, Lowenstein called a press conference on September 23 to declare a new national campaign, comparable to the "dump Johnson" venture, to rally opinion against the war. The national media treated Lowenstein's declaration as a major political event signaling the beginning of active opposition to the president's policies. Nixon's honeymoon was over, and Lowenstein, in the eyes of most journalists, was the tribune leading the opposition.[20]

But Lowenstein was also careful, for the most part, to present his antiwar position within the context of profound empathy for the American soldiers fighting in Vietnam. Amid pictures showing him dressed in battle fatigues, sunglasses, and a baseball cap, Lowenstein was quoted as praising America's military commanders for their graciousness to him and remarking on the plight of the troops. "People have no conception," Lowenstein said, "of the degree to which American troops do the most difficult things with courage. . . . They live for weeks in 120 degree heat. . . . They have no sanitation facilities; they slog through the mud. It's not just the deaths and the wounds, it's the misery. . . . If we were back in the days of Hitler, there would be justification for this kind of personal sacrifice. It isn't justified today." Brilliantly and effectively, Lowenstein thus used identification with the GI as the basis for critiquing U.S. policy on Vietnam—especially by contrast with World War II. As one veteran whom Lowenstein befriended observed, "[Al] viewed the vets not as the ones that were responsible [for the war] but as the ultimate victims of a bogus policy." That kind of perspective made it a lot easier for people who thought they were *for* the war to at least listen and respond to Lowenstein's arguments.[21]

Lowenstein's credibility was further enhanced by the testimony of two of his most devoted protégés, who had gone to serve in Vietnam. He could share with audiences their graphic accounts of the horror there as evidence of why Americans should be concerned. Jay Jacobson, a student friend from UNC, vividly depicted the dehumanization that occurred among the troops he led into a Vietnamese hamlet. "After herding all the people out of the village," he wrote, "we would burn the houses, destroy food, kill the pigs and chickens. I began to wonder if we were American fighting men or some sort of bandit gang." Then, after taking fire and incurring some casualties, "the burning of the houses increased. One day a patrol went out and seeing movement to their flank opened up. She was six, maybe seven; although alive when the patrol brought her in, she died shortly after. . . . To move all day long being sniped at, unable to make contact, seemingly fighting women and children, all this is most frustrating. I wonder how it is our country can let this war go on."[22]

Rick Weidman was another close Lowenstein companion. Formerly the student body president at Colgate, Weidman reluctantly joined the group writing the student body presidents' letter to LBJ in 1967, then became more and more convinced that the war was wrong. Initially, he signed the "If drafted, I will not serve" petition and prepared to be arrested when he was called for induction at Whitehall in New York City. But when his father, a Marine veteran, broke down and wept the night he saw his son in jail, Weidman reversed himself and joined the Marines on the condition that he could be a medic. Lowenstein counseled Weidman throughout his ordeal, an example, Rich Hammond said, of "the depths of commitment" Al generated.

Weidman also wrote Lowenstein from Vietnam. The news had said casualties were light that day, he said. But not for D Company: two were killed outright, two more critically wounded, and six torn up. One victim, he wrote, had both legs and his scrotum blown away; another had his leg severed below the knee. Desperately, the medics had tried to save them. After loading the wounded and dead on the helicopter, "you pour hydrogen peroxide on the bloodstains on the floor [but] the stains never disappear completely. . . . Time for chow. But I don't go. . . . I only wish some of those people back home who run around saying 'support our boys in Vietnam' [could know this]. . . . When do we end this madness, Al? American guys dying for nothing." Lowenstein received the letter on his way to a speech at an antiwar rally. It became his text for the evening, providing one more reason for conservatives as well as liberals to rethink what the war was about.[23]

But whatever the press said, Lowenstein was not the leader of the entire antiwar movement. With perspectives and a sense of empowerment quite independent of Lowenstein and Congress, other movements were demanding change in administration policies on the war. Their rhetoric and approach were substantially different from Lowenstein's; based largely on campuses and in big cities, they were tired of being co-opted by "liberals," angry at the timidity of "established" reformers, and convinced that the time had come to confront directly the persistent refusal of most politicians to alter their positions. Although some reporters had interpreted Lowenstein's public denunciation of Nixon's policies after his return from Vietnam as the beginning of a new phase of the antiwar movement, Lowenstein in fact was trying to catch up with antiwar activists who had already gone far beyond him and were pressuring him from the left. It was in Lowenstein's responses to the Vietnam Moratorium Committee and the New Mobilization Committee that the full complexity of his quest for a political middle ground became manifest.

In many respects, the Moratorium Committee emerged as a direct outgrowth of the college-based "dump Johnson" movement. After Sam Brown and David Hawk completed their stints with the McCarthy and other antiwar campaigns, they pondered what to do next to sustain their antiwar activism. Brown was teaching a seminar at Harvard's Kennedy Institute of Government on how to devise a series of activities that might force an end to the war in Vietnam. Jerry Grossman, a Massachusetts peace activist who helped run the seminar, was thinking along the same lines. Initially, Brown and Grossman focused on the idea of a national strike, one day at a time, to demonstrate dissatisfaction with the administration's policy, but a strike seemed too radical a notion and could easily be construed as an invitation to shut down universities. Anxious to avoid being tarred with the "student radical" brush, they instead struck on the idea of having people throughout the country declare a moratorium on all activity—one day the first month, two days the second, three days the third, and so on, until the war ended. Brown and Hawk, soon to be joined by Marge Sklencar and David Mixner, consciously set out to enlist student body presidents and "reliable" leaders and avoided giving leadership posts to radicals. The summer and fall of 1969 were the days when the Weathermen faction of SDS was threatening to bring "days of rage" to the entire country through disruptive acts. The Moratorium Committee wanted none of that, seeking instead a form of powerful but nonviolent action that would seize people's attention without alienating them. Another group, the New Mobilization Committee, also planned massive demonstrations in the fall of 1969, but the "New Mobe" was more inclusive; it welcomed participation by Communists, radical student groups, and all antiwar elements, even if they carried the banner of the Viet Cong.[24]

Because all of the Moratorium organizers had worked closely with Lowenstein, they went to him in the late spring of 1969 to discuss their idea. His response was enthusiastic but carried a twist. "What you really need to do," Lowenstein told Brown and Hawk, "is [have] a march from Arlington Cemetery to the Washington Memorial on the Fourth of July, led by an honor guard and people with [American] flags." Moreover, Lowenstein said, the march could be organized from his office—Brown and Hawk could join his staff. Almost immediately, they demurred. "That's an interesting idea, Al," Brown recalls saying, "and you can get up to twelve people who want to do that. [But] this is not the moment." In addition, Hawk noted, Al was just a freshman congressman; while they wanted his support, they knew that their potential audience included many older politicians "who would not want to follow Al. . . . I mean it's okay for people like us to . . . go with the Pied Piper, but senior congressmen won't do that. . . . You weren't going to get elected officials mobilizing behind a first-term congressman. We knew enough about how Washington worked on the Hill to know that it wouldn't work [his] way." Thus, Lowenstein's immediate instinct to incorporate a modified moratorium idea into his own political plan was rejected by those who once had been his protégés.[25]

In response, Lowenstein proceeded gradually to distance himself from the Moratorium, deciding only at the very last minute to offer his support. First, he worked hard to get his own idea for a July 4 march off the ground. Rounding up the "usual and customary suspects"—Greg Craig, Clint Deveaux, Dennis Riordan, and other student body presidents from prestigious colleges—Al sought to put together a coalition committed to ending polarization. They sent out letters seeking support for their venture and expressing their concern about both "the growing polarization in our society . . . and the increasing incidences of violence at American universities." (It should be noted that the Columbia University "revolution" of May 1968 had already happened and Harvard was about to experience its own radical insurgency.) The student presidents proposed holding a vigil at the Lincoln Memorial and then marching to the Tomb of the Unknown Soldier to hear eulogies to the "victims of senseless violence in Vietnam." Although the plan never came to fruition, Lowenstein's ideas offered the maximum possibility, Greg Craig noted, for controlling sectarian radicals. "The question was, would there be Viet Cong flags allowed? . . . Would the Weathermen participate? Who would speak? Would violence be denounced? Was it going to be a mainstream thing or was it going to be . . . anybody comes? . . . Al had a very strong feeling that if you ran this right, it ought to be controlled . . . you should make it mothers and kids, PTA members for peace, [that kind] of thing."

While the Moratorium organizers were willing to discourage Viet Cong flags and embrace nonviolence, they resented Lowenstein's order of priorities and his threatening stance. By insisting that the Moratorium Committee denounce the violence of the Viet Cong and of U.S. student radicals *before* condemning U.S. policy, Hawk and Brown felt, Lowenstein would divide the antiwar movement. "Our bottom line," David Mixner said, "was, 'We're not going to equate broken windows with the war in Vietnam.'" Rick Saslaw, a youthful follower of Lowenstein's, had this interpretation of what was going on between Lowenstein and the others: "Allard felt that he had earned his stripes as leader of the peace movement and these people were saying, 'Fuck you, this one's ours.'" All the other issues were symbolic, Saslaw said. "It was just a clash of three cocks in a fenced-in area." Perhaps, but it was also a question of who would dictate policy. "[Al told us] we had to disavow this and disavow that," Mixner noted. "You're either going to do this, or you're going to be out of business. . . . It was an ultimatum." Yet that was precisely the attitude most likely to infuriate the Moratorium organizers, giving the split a generational as well as a political cast. With Lowenstein and Sam Brown in particular, it was almost a "father and son" division. By the mid-1960s, Brown noted, "most people had generationally forgotten" the sectarian conflicts on the left over communism during the postwar years. But Al had not, and he seemed intent on resurrecting them in his own guerrilla war with the Moratorium leaders.[26]

When Brown and his colleagues proved unwilling to meet Lowenstein's conditions, he proceeded to undermine their efforts with other members of Congress. "You always got the sense with Allard," Brown said, "that once the break took place, the waters got poisoned fairly broadly." Mixner, the Moratorium Committee's congressional liaison, quickly heard that Lowenstein "started bad-mouthing us in Congress, [making it] . . . clear that he was going to play tough ball with us . . . saying we were going to support violent actions. . . . It was a very clear combination of what I would call violence and red-baiting. . . . If we weren't going to play his game, he would make sure that we didn't play any game at all."

To Brown, it was a painful, disillusioning process. "The bitterness I felt," he commented, "was probably the bitterness of the Mississippi Summer people in '64. Here's the guy who made politics live for me, whom I'd admired for so many years . . . [and] when I wanted to go off on my own . . . he immediately took off with other members of Congress about us like he took off about other people whom he regarded as having betrayed him. I mean it was his zeal—we were the enemy, we were the Stalinists. . . . It was . . . stunning." Jack Newfield felt the same way. "It was déjà vu for me," he said. "The Moratorium was clearly liberal, moderate, and Sam Brown was an apple pie, American kind of guy. . . . [Al] thought that he was always the absolute frontier of legitimate liberalism . . . [and] had a hard time imagining anything legitimately to his left."[27]

By the end of September, Lowenstein—just back from his Vietnam trip—was ready to heal the wounds and endorse the Moratorium. From his point of view, the critiques he had offered eventually persuaded Moratorium organizers to moderate their policies, exclude violence, and become mainstream. Without Lowenstein's critiques, Greg Craig and Clint Deveaux contended, the Moratorium would never have become so politically sensitive. Mixner and his colleagues, on the other hand, contended that they knew all along what they were doing, and that Lowenstein's change of heart was due mostly to their success in going around him and securing endorsements from people like Riegle, McCloskey, and New York congressmen Richard Ottinger and Ogden Reid, making Lowenstein's objections "a moot issue, quickly." Whatever the case, Lowenstein now jumped on the bandwagon and was portrayed by many in the press as the primary initiator of the Moratorium. Massive participation in the Moratorium, Lowenstein told a Harvard audience, "is the only choice open to those who oppose [both] the war *and* the radicals who use violence against it."

On October 15, more than 200,000 demonstrators gathered in Washington while hundreds of thousands joined other rallies throughout the country. Lowenstein spoke at six eastern colleges, including Brown, Princeton (where he was heckled by SDS activists), Villanova, and Yale. To his colleague Andy Jacobs, the day represented a culmination of Lowenstein's influence and talents. "It was beautiful," he said. "There were no VC flags. There was no violence. There was no denunciation of Lyndon Johnson, a human being. The only public demonstration was an endless and silent stream of people with . . . lighted candles past the White House one night." Riding with a reporter in a helicopter, Lowenstein acted as though he had totally devoted himself to the day. With 200 Villanova students flashing the peace sign upon his departure, Lowenstein commented: "God, they're such an incredibly beautiful generation. If we let them turn sour on us, we deserve everything we get." The Moratorium's organizers agreed on the results of their efforts. "[It] was wildly successful," David Hawk said. "We accomplished the first time in October what we thought it would take to December or January to build to." But what both Lowenstein and the Moratorium organizers knew was that the appearance of unity and enthusiasm barely disguised the reality of deep and bitter political divisions—divisions that would grow, not diminish, with time.[28]

In fact, the dispute over the Moratorium served in many ways as a dress rehearsal for the far more pronounced conflicts over the New Mobilization Committee's plans for massive rallies around the country on November 15. Unlike the Moratorium Committee, the New Mobe consciously enlisted radical groups on its steering committee, including the American Communist party, the Young Socialist League, and the DuBois Clubs. Many New Mobe supporters exhibited contempt for those who wished to work within the system, and initial plans for the New Mobe rallies sought to bar any "capitalist" politicians from speaking. Given its ideological politics, David Hawk noted, the New Mobe had far more difficulty controlling the "crazies." Its meetings witnessed endless debates, such as whether it was more fitting to have a Puerto Rican high school student from New Jersey address a mass rally or a prominent antiwar politician like George Mc-Govern. Commenting on these tensions, the political columnist Mary Mc-Grory noted that "doves who supported the October 15th Moratorium smell death in the radical endorsement of the [November] march," given the determination of some New Mobe members to lead an assault on the Justice Department and sanction inflammatory rhetoric.[29]

In light of that situation, it was not surprising that Lowenstein was bitterly critical of New Mobe plans. "There's a small group of people who want to gain control of the movement," he said, "to place it in the hands of a far-out minority. . . . They're really not interested in winning over the undecided people in the middle." In fact, many movement activists *were* fed up with official temporizing and wanted to draw a line in the sand and ask, "Which side are you on?" Fearful that such attitudes would play into the hands of those who wished to portray the peace movement as Communist-inspired, Lowenstein and other congressmen initially dissociated themselves from the New Mobe rally, saying they would neither serve as speakers nor appear on rally platforms.[30]

On the other hand, the average citizen—or peace activist—was oblivious to such arcane distinctions between the different groups. As Sam Brown indicated, the mobilization was "by definition a locally-oriented and quite broad-based [group] in which the acts of a few crazies will get washed away in a sea of reasonable and moderate people." Despite the significant differences visible to insiders between the two groups, there seemed to be a direct tie between the October 15 Moratorium rallies and the November 15 New Mobe marches. Moratorium leaders decided to cooperate as much as possible with the New Mobe in order to continue the momentum developed in the earlier demonstrations.

The Nixon administration's politics, meanwhile, placed antiwar moderates like Lowenstein in a scissors hold. Having learned from the October demonstrations how powerful a peaceful display of antiwar sentiment could be, Nixon and his aides now went on the attack, lumping all antiwar activists into the category of violence-seeking revolutionaries who wished to occupy Washington and physically attack the seat of government. In a speech to the nation on November 3, less than two weeks before the march, Nixon sought to rally public support by elaborating further his plans for Vietnamizing the war, while appealing to the "silent majority" to join him in turning back "lawless radicals" who would threaten the nation's lifeline. Spiro Agnew quickly followed with his own blistering attack on "effete" liberals, who, he claimed, promoted permissiveness toward the young in order to destroy the moral fiber of the country. In conjunction with Agnew's efforts, Nixon's speech signaled a new determination to use the politics of polarization to paint all antiwar supporters into a corner. "He either drives us into bed with the Communists and anarchists and destroys us," Lowenstein said, "or he counts us with his majority on the war." Nixon raised the ante even higher by having the Justice Department turn down a New Mobe request for a permit to march down Pennsylvania Avenue, making the issue for liberals one of civil liberties as well as antiwar strategy.

Faced with such tactics, Lowenstein and his allies desperately sought a middle ground from which they could support the march without embracing its rhetoric or the potential disruptiveness they feared. Doing nothing would play into Nixon's hands. So, too, would supporting the march, but at least that action would be consistent with the antiwar position they had taken in the past. Thus, Lowenstein, who had earlier called a meeting to find some way of opposing the New Mobe rally, now found himself forced by Nixon's speech into reversing position and endorsing the march. Acknowledging "very basic disagreements" with some groups on the New Mode steering committee, and anticipating grave discomfort with much of the rhetoric that would be used, Lowenstein nevertheless declared he would participate, and he was reassured by Coretta Scott King and William Sloane Coffin—New Mobe honorary cochairs—that the demonstrations would be peaceful.

Lowenstein's rationale was compelling. "If we suspend these activities because of the danger of extremists disrupting them," he told a press conference, "we turn the country over to the extremists. It seems to me that the most irresponsible action a person can take at a time of grave national crisis is to opt for silence and leave the arena to the people who are not committed to the preservation of the country's basic fabric." Trying to hold the middle and still retain an active voice, Lowenstein had determined to go with the insurgents rather than stay neutral or join the other side. (If he had adopted the same approach to the Moratorium in its initial stages or to the Mississippi Freedom Summer project five years earlier, it might have made a significant difference to both movements.) Lowenstein had made an honorable and intelligent choice, even if Nixon's political machinations left him little room for maneuver.[31]

Very quickly, however, Lowenstein reverted to his earlier state of war with radical peace activists. In the end, Senators Charles Goodell and George McGovern were invited to speak at the Washington rally, and a large bloc of liberal congressional leaders joined them. But Lowenstein, who had become anathema to the left, was shafted: having accepted an invitation to speak to the San Francisco New Mobe rally, he was disinvited at the last minute because he was an "establishment" liberal. In reality, he had done as much to prompt the clash as the New Mobe people, taunting them with charges of intolerance just as they "screeched and yelled and howled" him down when he attempted to preach the importance of a mainstream coalition. Indeed, he relished the notion, as he told the *Nassau* (Long Island) *Herald,* that "I was cancelled out by the San Francisco Mobe the same day I was asked not to speak at Malverne because my views were too extreme. . . . I don't know if either group is happy to discover this thing they have in common." What they had in common, of course, was defining the spectrum so that Lowenstein could occupy the middle.[32]

Carving out that middle-of-the-road niche vis-à-vis the New Left and the government "establishment" became Lowenstein's primary preoccupation. In typical debater's fashion, he sought to define his antagonists as equally reprehensible, thereby saving for himself the role of responsible "moderate." The Nixon administration, spearheaded by Spiro Agnew, represented one extreme, characterizing all dissent as unpatriotic, effeminate, and immoral. The New Left, a group of purist lunatics who wanted to impose their political "saliva test" on everyone, represented the other extreme. "You might call them the Agnews of the peace movement," Lowenstein said. That allowed him to defend the fortress of sanity and stability, the only real hope the country had for survival, because, "if we win, they lose. If we succeed, they have no constituency. The only way that extreme groups on the edges can get control of anything substantial in this country is if we can't—in Edward Kennedy's phrase—end wars and right wrongs." Hence, all those who wished to save America should rally behind people like Lowenstein, who spoke for the mainstream and had the answers to rescue the country from extremism. Lowenstein had settled on a strategy that was consistent with his own values and the only course likely to make possible his political survival.[33]

Lowenstein elaborated on the theme of mainstream reform with minor variations, wherever he went, but particularly on campuses. Ever interested in reinforcing his image as a defender of the young, he told Harvard students in a 1969 Class Day address that anyone who voted in Congress for military appropriations for Vietnam was "voting to send kids off to die." The young, he declared repeatedly, had the right to say no to being drafted. On the other hand, he denounced those who disrupted classes or stoned university buildings to express their anger. "Beating up professors in the name of social justice is something I don't buy," he declared. "This country does not belong to burners and haters, nor to those who disrupt free speech by shouting people down or shutting them up."[34]

On many occasions, Lowenstein almost baited the left, waiting for them to respond with fury so that he could take the "high road." Those who attacked college buildings, he declared, "were goons." "I don't like deans being pushed around . . . [or] rocks being thrown," he told an interviewer. "When someone can explain to me what makes it possible to justify burning down a building at Stanford in the name of stopping the war in Vietnam . . . then I will be willing to discuss whether those tactics are in fact justifiable." By selectively magnifying the most outrageous acts of the left, Lowenstein accentuated his own case; he also provoked the left to equally distorted expressions of anger. Thus, Tom Hayden called Lowenstein a "professional, CIA-oriented politician," and SDS members at Grinnell College in Iowa dumped garbage on the platform where he was speaking when Lowenstein attempted to criticize the SDS leader Bernadine Dohrn. As Sam Brown noted, "The left really grew to dislike Allard intensely. . . . He became a sort of nemesis."[35]

Such polarization fit Lowenstein's game plan perfectly, however, since it allowed him to portray his position as a "golden mean." When a Stony Brook student yelled, "Why should we listen to you, you politician,"

Lowenstein responded, "What is your alternative? Would you blow things up? Let me tell you that violence would bring more violence, and I am against violence. *I won't tolerate it from Ronald Reagan or SDS.*" As long as those extremes defined the options and controlled the political energy, Lowenstein said, disaster and repression threatened. "The middle, the vast disaffected student majority, must re-emerge and reassert itself. . . . The struggle now is over what happens to that vast middle group."

Lowenstein clearly saw his own approach as the only viable answer. "He always worked well when he had enemies," his close friend Steve Morgan said, "and he always felt more comfortable when he was sand-wiched between anger on the left and anger on the right." Was he a radi-cal? a friendly reporter asked after he had been elected "man of the year" by Notre Dame students. No, Lowenstein responded, "the position I take and believe is right [is] the position the mainstream would have taken and would have implemented had we been able to elect a president without the assassinations of 1968." Upholding the tradition of mainstream ac-tivism pioneered by Martin Luther King, Jr., and Robert Kennedy, Lowen-stein offered a course that eschewed the self-destructiveness of the two extremes. "The choice . . . is a very basic one," he declared, "to rail against [a problem] and do nothing, because still larger problems will lie ahead, or to cope with each thing in turn . . . because having done the smaller, the larger will seem easier."[36]

With all his soul, Lowenstein believed that the second path was not only the more honorable and wise but also the only way to avoid repres-sion and violence. That was the theme of "dump Johnson," and it was the text Lowenstein preached with increasing urgency as polarization in-creased in the Nixon-Agnew years. After the National Guard murder of peacefully demonstrating students at Ohio's Kent State University in the spring of 1970, the attorney William Kunstler raised a clenched fist and told a college audience to "bring this country to a halt and make it return to what it was supposed to be in 1776." Lowenstein, by contrast, said to a group of students: "When we look at the alternatives to our system, I do not find them attractive. We must abhor random violence. What is needed now in this country is for everyone who cares about our form of govern-ment to throw themselves into the effort to make the system work."[37]

In such a volatile time, Lowenstein appreciated how difficult it was to sell his approach. By choice, but also by historical circumstance, he was literally caught in the middle. Lowenstein understood that, as he put it, "our failure to bring change is what has created the climate for extreme action." Students were rioting, he told Congress, because adults had failed them. "The disorder comes not from Russian-supported revolutionaries, but from our children, brought up to respect law and order and nonviolence." Lowenstein also told students that he understood their impatience with him. "My life spans a longer time [than yours]," he said. "I have comparisons to make. You have seen only recent leadership and therefore perhaps are not able to compare and see the promise that has been and could be."[38]

Still, he clung to his rationale for holding on to the center, as he defined it. "If we can stop the war and . . . racial injustice and pull this country into programs that make life better for people," Lowenstein declared, "there is no place left then for [those who say] the country is inherently sick and so immobile that it cannot change its problems through constitutional means." Nor would there be any support for repression of radicalism from the right. There was only one way out, Lowenstein insisted. It was his way—a mainstream way. And however tortured the difficulty of holding to that path, he would persist. His political and personal life depended on it.[39]

Of course, if Lowenstein were going to win over that great "middle" mass whose allegiance he and Nixon were both competing for, he had to build ties to them on other issues besides the war and student revolts on campus. It was for that reason that Lowenstein spent so much time prodding the Federal Aviation Administration (FAA) to reduce jet noise at Kennedy Airport and became a champion of safety on the Long Island Railroad, of increased federal measures to protect local wetlands, and of improved conditions at his district's Veterans Administration (VA) hospitals, where so many wounded Vietnam veterans came back for care and rehabilitation. The biweekly forums, to which prominent Republicans were always invited, contributed to his image as an engaged and open-minded congressman—and incidentally led to the creation of his floating alliances with conservatives on issues of importance to the district. Lowenstein supported welfare reform measures in Congress, the shift of national resources to nondefense areas, and such popular legislation as reduced airfares for senior citizens and young people. He also injected himself—courageously—into the racial conflicts at local high schools, where parents and students were threatening to engage in outright racial warfare.

Lowenstein especially excelled at using his maverick image, often with sharp humor, to spotlight congressional policies that were inane or might seem so to his constituents. Thus, he used his position on the Agriculture Committee to sponsor an amendment that would limit all individual farm subsidies to $10,000 (it was defeated thirty-three to one), pointing out that Senator James Eastland of Mississippi received $129,000 each year from the government for not planting his crops while poor black children in the same county received only $6 a month for food, clothing, and housing. Arguing for an end to four American airbases in Spain, he said the only reason they existed—except to subsidize Franco to the tune of $2.5 billion—was to prevent Spain from being "attacked by hordes of Algerians that might swim the Mediterranean . . . to get to Spain." The Long Island press was full of his exploits, from pictures and comments about his trips to Vietnam to stories describing the arrest of a Lowenstein aide during their visit to Prague.[40]

In all these ways, Lowenstein strove tirelessly to create an identity among his constituents as a congressional leader who could serve their local needs and simultaneously rise above the crowd as a passionate but reasoned advocate for reconciliation and reform. Whatever the publicity he received for his antiwar stances, an equal or greater number of news stories recounted his being pilloried by the left, and attention to his exploits on behalf of constituents dominated the Long Island weekly press. "It was amazing how he was able to bring people around," one younger follower commented, "not necessarily to his point of view, but to less concern that he was somehow unpatriotic [and to] an understanding that he was [genuine] and honest." His goal was not to preach to the converted but to gain an audience among the uncommitted and the hostile. "It is the people who are honestly convinced that somehow they should support the war, that the blacks and poor represent a terrible threat to the middle class, it is those people I'd rather work on," Lowenstein declared.[41]

In that mission, Lowenstein succeeded far more than he failed. Republicans came so often to his forums that the Nassau County GOP leader Joseph Margiotta issued an edict that doing so was an act of disloyalty to the party. Lowenstein's colleagues in Congress—including Republicans and members of the "geriatric set" like L. Mendel Rivers—said good things about him. He even succeeded in enacting his pet reform—making sure that representatives' votes on amendments and bills were individually recorded. This Long Island congressman still appeared on national news shows—even on Johnny Carson's "Tonight Show" when it was being hosted by his friend Buck Henry. And in an age of inflammatory rhetoric from the Spiro Agnews on the one hand and the Abbie Hoffmans on the other, Lowenstein somehow managed to cast himself as someone who could speak to and for the critics while remaining ardently loyal to established processes of law. As the columnist Charles McDowell wrote in the conservative *Richmond Times-Dispatch,* Lowenstein was sui generis, a "moderate radical. . . . He marches with militants for peace and civil rights. But he urges the young and the black not only to avoid violence but to speak out against it." The essence of Lowenstein-style politics was to be "unusual, but within the system." If the young Long Island congressman could only convince his constituents that this was "the mainstream," he might even survive and prosper.[42]

THE REPUBLICAN CHALLENGE

Enough opposition political leaders were persuaded that Lowenstein had achieved his goal that they resorted to extraordinary measures to prevent him from being reelected. Throughout his term, Lowenstein had been bitterly attacked by Joseph Margiotta. Lowenstein was a "VietCongressman," Margiotta charged, a House member whose views ran totally counter to those of his constituents. Rather than deceive the people with fraudulent representation, he should resign his seat. Margiotta felt guilty perhaps for having gone along with the nomination of the Conservative party candidate Mason Hampton in the 1968 election—a decision that by all accounts helped Lowenstein's cause enormously. Most people had expected the Republicans to win in 1968, ending the brief hiatus of Democratic rule prompted by the LBJ landslide in 1964. But although Nixon had swept the district, Lowenstein prevailed, and his victory humiliated Margiotta. Now Lowenstein's energetic tenure as fifth district representative raised the specter of the seat remaining Democratic—an intolerable possibility to the Republican chieftain.

Clearly, Lowenstein would not be hounded from office by demands that he resign. But why not make it impossible for him to be reelected by taking advantage of the reapportionment the Republican-controlled legislature was about to undertake? As early as October 1969, rumors started to circulate about Margiotta's plan. By January 1970, the *New York Times* had confirmed the specifics. No district in the state would be changed more than the fifth. "It was drawn in such a manner," one of Lowenstein's congressional colleagues commented, "that nobody on earth on the Democratic ticket could win."[43]

The gerrymander was as crude as it was effective. In the 1968 election,

Lowenstein's greatest source of strength had been the Five Towns area. Predominantly Democratic, Jewish, and liberal in attitude toward the war, Five Towns had provided Lowenstein with an overwhelming majority— nearly twice his final margin of victory. The first step of the reapportionment plan was therefore to cut Five Towns completely out of the district. The second step was to put in its place the two communities of Massapequa and Massapequa Park. Overwhelmingly Catholic, Italian, and Irish, the Massapequa area was prowar and profoundly conservative on the social issues of race and sex. The move cut the Jewish vote alone by more than one-third, and most experts calculated that a Republican should win in the new congressional district by more than 20,000 votes. As the *Merrick Life* observed, "It is the right and duty of the Republicans to try to unseat the incumbent, but do they think they could not do it in open battle?"[44]

Never one to accept defeat passively, Lowenstein contemplated several different responses. He could acknowledge the power of the gerrymander and seek election in another congressional district more hospitable to his views; he could take on an even larger battle and run for the U.S. Senate; or he could accept the challenge, throw down his gauntlet, and with "The Impossible Dream" from *The Man of La Mancha* playing again in the background, seek to win the fifth congressional district, no matter what the odds. But before he made his choice, he was determined at least to embarrass Margiotta and play a trick of his own.

Ever since Margiotta had started to demand that Lowenstein resign his seat because he was not "representing" the district, Lowenstein had been furious. Margiotta was calling into question his integrity as an officeholder. Now, Lowenstein decided to turn the tables on Margiotta, in the process exposing the hypocrisy of the gerrymandering gambit. Going before the voters both on television and in the print press, Lowenstein said, "Let the voters decide whether I represent them." He would agree to resign from his seat immediately if Governor Nelson Rockefeller would then call a special election within 60 days to choose a new congressman. That way, the voters could determine the validity of Margiotta's charge, and the special election could serve as a referendum on how the fifth congressional district felt about the war in Vietnam. "If [the Republicans] do not endorse [a special election]," Lowenstein said, "I have to assume they either want the District to have no representation over the next ten months, or that they accept the fact that I do represent my District."[45]

Shrewdly—perhaps too shrewdly—Lowenstein thus put his enemies on the defensive. Calling Margiotta and his allies a bunch of "mini-Agnews trying to intimidate people into silence," Lowenstein sought to use the electoral system to rekindle debate and prevent the Republicans from taking away the power of the vote by gerrymandering. Knowing he was likely to win a special election—it would take place within the old district, not the new one—he could enhance his own position even as he focused dramatic new attention on voter sentiment about the war. It was a ploy no SDS member would ever have contemplated. But it was also too clever by half. Rockefeller dismissed Lowenstein's suggestion as "playing political games," and probably most voters saw it as a trick also. Lowenstein had tried to raise the ante and in the process drew further attention to the ignominious redistricting plan. But it was victory in a skirmish, not a main battle.[46]

Lowenstein then contemplated seriously running for the U.S. Senate. Two years earlier, he was almost the nominee of New York's peace Democrats against Jacob Javits. He had the statewide name recognition, at least among active Democrats. Although money was always a problem in a New York statewide race, Lowenstein's leadership in the "dump Johnson" struggle would undoubtedly have opened many coffers from out of state. The national media speculated about his possible candidacy, along with those of Richard Ottinger, Ted Sorenson, and Paul O'Dwyer, a New York City politician. But in the end, Lowenstein failed to make the move that most of his associates thought he should and would make. Charles Goodell, the Republican who had taken Robert Kennedy's seat, was a close friend who had aligned himself with Lowenstein on numerous issues, including the Vietnam War. The Democratic contenders were also friends, especially Ottinger. To plunge in would have required being decisive and taking the risk of further muddying an already ambiguous situation. Still, the option remained alive until the evening of April 13, when the Nassau County Democrats met in convention.[47]

That night, in by now predictable fashion, Lowenstein confounded all the experts and announced he would run for reelection, despite the odds. Since the reapportionment months before, friends had been invoking the highest moral arguments for taking on the challenge. The Senate already had antiwar voices like Harold Hughes and Frank Church and George McGovern, one man noted, but the House had no one with the charisma or principle to rally the antiwar forces. Susan Andrews, Lowenstein's neighbor and friend, wrote to offer her support. "It's not hero worship," she said, "and it's not because you came into the 5th and swept us off our feet and ran for Congress and won. . . . Most of all, [it's] because you are gentle and good, and you, Al, more than anyone else in the country today, care about the people—in the deepest sense."

And so, in the washroom of the Garden City Hotel, as he later recounted it, Lowenstein decided to run, to test whether his enemies could silence "a voice for peace, social justice, progress and human decency." "In terms of duty, responsibility, and honor I have only one choice," he declared, "so let the word go forth from this Convention that we are about to take on an impossible District for the right principles." One more time, Lowenstein would fight for noble ideals in a battle it seemed barely possible to win. According to press reports, you could have heard a pin drop in the hall, and many people were in tears. Wiping his own eyes after a meeting with students, Lowenstein told a reporter: "It's the kids that make it so hard. . . . I have to keep faith with them, I can't cop out."[48]

Having learned from the 1968 campaign the importance of running a viable candidate, the Republicans nominated a popular and well-known challenger, the state senator Norman Lent. Three times, Lent had emerged victorious in a predominantly Democratic district composed largely of Jews and Catholics. While Nixon had lost in Lent's senatorial area in 1968 by 17,000 votes, Lent had triumphed by 25,000. A Rockefeller-style Republican, Lent served his constituency well. Even on controversial issues, his stands seemed to balance liberal and conservative positions. He had introduced a bill in the state legislature in support of a constitutional amendment to ban busing to achieve racial balance, but he also had voted in support of a liberalized abortion law. Most dangerous of all, his former senatorial district contained 76 percent of the constituents who made up the fifth congressional district. In short, the Republicans had chosen a person who seemed to possess all the advantages Hampton had lacked, and none of the liabilities.[49]

Lowenstein's only hope was to hold on to his core support while persuading substantial numbers of new voters and old opponents to support his reelection. At the very least, he had to increase his margin of victory in the part of the fifth that remained constant from 1968, and in the new parts of the district, he needed to hold Lent's margin of victory to a minimum. Notwithstanding all that Lowenstein had done to portray himself as a moderate, that image would be difficult to maintain against a candidate who also had a middle-of-the-road image, and who had been reelected so often.

To make sure that Lowenstein's self-definition was not accepted, Lent's strategy from the beginning was to paint him as a far-out extremist. Instead of speaking for the mainstream, Lent charged, Lowenstein personified all the radical dangers that threatened to destroy America. In a litany repeated in every debate and in all his campaign literature, Lent called Lowenstein a "darling of the New Left," the "chief apologist for the Black Panthers," a "VietCongressman" who "echoe[d] the voice of Hanoi," and a coward who "crawled from under a rock" to vote against military appropriations for America's fighting men. By Lent's account, Lowenstein had done nothing but betray the constituents of Long Island. Not only had he "prolonged the war, encouraged disrespect for law and order, criticized our nation, downgraded our Presidents, and . . . not [supported] the men who are fighting in Vietnam," but he had also voted against legislation designed to control pornography, stop crime, and limit campus unrest.

Both in tone and content, the Lent campaign smacked suspiciously of the political strategy emanating from the Nixon-Agnew White House in 1970. Behind the scenes, reporters noted, Nixon's old hatchet man Murray Chotiner was orchestrating the Lent strategy, using the same smear techniques that had worked so effectively for Nixon in the 1940s against Jerry Voorhees and Helen Gahagan Douglas. Associated primarily with the rhetorical excesses of Spiro Agnew, the smear tactic was to tar one's opponent with so many charges of extremism that the opponent had no time or opportunity to reclaim his own voice and define the issues on his own terms. Indeed, the more outrageous the allegations, the less likely it was that the opponent could get off the defensive. Hence, Lowenstein was guilty of "inciting students to riot," and he was an "inflamer of youth, an encourager of draft-card burners," an extremist guilty of "coddling the leaders of violent confrontation on campus . . . the single most polarizing force in Congress . . . a supporter of the smut peddlers and dope pushers." The words were so similar to Agnew's in 1970—"coddling," "smut peddlers," "inciting students to riot"—that the allegations of control from Washington made sense, especially given that Lowenstein was the only congressman in the company of eleven senators singled out in a White House–sponsored ad as responsible for aiding the enemy.[50]

Occasionally, Lent's attacks turned into ugly personal assaults on Lowenstein and his family. "People either loved [Al] or hated him," Jenny Littlefield said. "There was nothing in between." One night, she was spat at during a rally, the assailant snarling, "You get away from me. I wouldn't vote for your husband if he was the last human being on earth." On another occasion, Al and Jenny were heckled and shoved at a Fourth of July celebration sponsored by a local fire department. Jenny was pregnant with their third child at the time, but her appearance seemed to make no difference. Lent "really appealed to the unthinking impulse that pervaded so much of the country at that point," a young volunteer observed. People would throw tomatoes at the candidate's wife, then greet Lowenstein himself "with this enormous blood-chilling 'Boo!'" after Lent had accused him of supporting Hanoi at the expense of American soldiers. "That [campaign] was probably one of the most wrenching experiences that anyone could go through," Jenny said, "because the rage about the war was so powerful, [as was] the hatred for Al."[51]

Though sickened by Lent's allegations, Lowenstein also recognized the opportunity to expose the Republican tactics for the demagoguery they were and to turn Lent's inflammatory rhetoric into an argument for his own moderation. Thus, he insisted in one radio debate, "we must reclaim this country, not abandon it to extremists who would polarize us." Situating himself in the middle, between Spiro Agnew and SDS radicals, Lowenstein accused Lent and his supporters of using loaded language to inflame passions and justify repression by violence. "I'd like to see," he said, "which of the great problems of this country—inflation, war, taxation, the collapse of the cities, poverty, hunger—have anything to do with the Hippies, the Yippies, the complainers and the protestors." Lent and his supporters were simply promoting illusory issues to deflect attention from the real ones, creating "mini-Agnews" everywhere, "smearing people that don't agree with them," and trying to polarize all the good people in the middle against each other. It was time for Lent to say where he stood on the real issues, Lowenstein argued, and stop polluting the campaign with reckless rhetoric.[52]

Local columnists and editorial page writers, meanwhile, underlined Lowenstein's allegations about Lent's attacks. "This is one of the dirtiest political contests in Long Island history," one reporter declared in an early October column. The *Long Island Press* denounced Lent's tactics as a "shocking display of falsehood and innuendo . . . a crude attempt to capitalize on the voters' fears through illegitimate means . . . political pollution created by unsubstantiated and distorted charges." *Newsday* called Lent "demagogic, dishonest and altogether shameful," and one of its columnists commented on Lent's unobserved departure from a debate: "It may be that he slipped quietly out through an open sewer." "The very best and the very worst that is American," the same writer noted, "will clash this fall in Massapequa and Oceanside."[53]

But Lowenstein was not content simply to lay out the contrast between his style and Lent's for the voters to contemplate. Instead, he insisted on taking his beliefs to the heart of enemy territory, displaying by his courage and combativeness that he was not a fringe figure begging to be caricatured. Attending a "Support Our Boys in Vietnam" dance, Lowenstein told skeptics in his campaign, "We have an obligation to convince these people, not . . . spit on them." When his opponents tried to call him unpatriotic, Lowenstein declared that the American flag was his as much as theirs and handed out flag pins to reinforce his identification with the nation's symbol. He welcomed the opportunity to speak at American Legion halls and often convinced people there that inflation, taxation, and the war were connected, providing grounds for people of all persuasions to criticize Nixon's Vietnam policies. "I can understand the position of those who feel that we should win the war or get out," he declared, but now the time had come to work together. "He would absolutely, stubbornly . . . go and try to win votes in the worst communities," Jenny Littlefield noted. "We sent the best and the brightest in to [Massapequa] to win. . . . He was absolutely determined to . . . try to be accepted by people that were the least inclined to accept him." And sometimes it worked. At the Oceanside VFW hall, one volunteer recalled, Lowenstein was booed when he rose to speak, but quietly, and then with increasing eloquence, he explained why he thought America's policy in Vietnam was wrong. "Something then happened that was entirely cinematic," the volunteer said. "It was right out of *To Kill a Mockingbird*. The entire audience just rose . . . [and as] Lowenstin walked through . . . the people I had seen booing and screaming 45 minutes earlier just sort of stepped aside and watched him. . . . I was awash with emotion."[54]

Lowenstein also used Republican endorsements to puncture the stereotype Lent was attempting to pin on him. No support meant more to Lowenstein than that offered by William Buckley, the founder and publisher of the conservative *National Review* and host of the controversial television program "Firing Line." As much as any American, Buckley symbolized the conservatism associated with Barry Goldwater and Young Americans for Freedom. His brother James, in fact, was the Conservative party's candidate for U.S. Senator in New York. Yet Buckley admired Lowenstein deeply. "I think Al is as accomplished a polemicist as I have come across," Buckley told *TV Guide* in 1970. "He knows his position well

[and] he desires ardently its advancement." Lowenstein had appeared on "Firing Line" numerous times, and the two clearly enjoyed sparring with each other intellectually. Endorsing Lowenstein, Buckley later said, "was an act of self-indulgence, [but] . . . since the Democrats were in control of the House no matter what, I thought they would benefit from somebody with his powers of penetration and his general idealism." The Buckley endorsement flew in the face of Lent's charge that Lowenstein was a "darling of the New Left," a foe of law and order and the most polarizing force in Congress.[55]

So, too, did the surprising support that came from two former New York police commissioners who were prominently identified with Nelson Rockefeller. Far from being an enemy of law and order, Lowenstein, according to Vincent Broderick and Francis Adams, "has counseled our young people to have patience and faith in the American system of government. He has [advised] them against violence, against drugs, and against dropping out. . . . He is as honest and has as much integrity as any man in American politics." Similar encomiums came from Republican congressional friends of Lowenstein. Donald Riegle of Michigan offered his support, and Pete McCloskey of California declared that Lowenstein was one of the members of Congress making "the greatest contributions to national welfare" in 1970. Appearing in full-page ads paid for by "Republicans and Independents for Lowenstein," such statements suggested the degree to which Lowenstein had wooed successfully people on the other side of the political aisle and vividly contradicted Lent's effort to paint him as a member of the lunatic fringe.[56]

Lowenstein also received significant boosts from entertainment and sports stars willing to campaign on his behalf. The actors Robert Vaughn, George Segal, Tony Randall, Jon Voigt, and Paul Newman appeared at Lowenstein campaign rallies, and the New York Knicks star Bill Bradley joined the baseball pitcher Jim Bouton and the fighter José Torres in lending their luster to his candidacy. So impressed was Lent that he charged Lowenstein with being "idolized by the Hollywood–New York jet set." Meanwhile, as many as 1,000 clean-cut students showed up each weekend to canvass the voters. "Their motivation was common," one of the students wrote, "a spontaneity defying category. They believed in a man and through him, wanted very desperately to believe in a political system. . . . There was some intangible feeling about a man who could say, 'Don't quit—work with me and together we can make the system work.'. . . The effect was exhilarating." Eating spaghetti suppers prepared in huge tureens by Jenny and her friends, the students shared an enthusiasm, an innocence, perhaps even a naïveté that added one more contradiction to Lent's portrayal of Lowenstein as a far-out agitator.[57]

On the other hand, Lowenstein ran his campaign in a manner that often seemed to minimize these pluses. As always, he refused to hire a campaign manager who could exercise real control and whose orders would be obeyed—especially by the candidate. Continuing to act as though he alone knew when and how to do everything, Lowenstein once again wrote and rewrote all the campaign literature, frequently getting it out so late that it was useless; he repeatedly confounded his schedulers; and he refused to take criticism. As one young worker wrote in his letter of resignation from the campaign, Al had no right to ask people from all over the country to sacrifice on his behalf if he insisted on surrounding himself with yes-men, never appeared on time anywhere, and failed even to wear decent clothes. One staff member—Arnie Miller—possessed both the political smarts and the autonomy to wage an effective campaign, and he was the only person, one longtime aide said, who would stand up to Al. But Lowenstein was unwilling to repose trust in anyone else or respect another politician's judgment as equal to his own.

Hence, the campaign was always digging out from disaster. What hurt Lowenstein most, his old associate Ham Richardson said, was "the impracticality of the way he ran [things]." Instead of meeting a prospective financial donor ready to give $10,000 to the campaign, he would go off to visit Lucille Kohn in New York. Those who put boundless energy into the big events were burned the worst. On one infamous evening, called the "Night of the Stars," campaign workers had scheduled a series of benefits throughout the district featuring George Segal, Robert Vaughn, the comedian Buck Henry, and the former governor of New York, Averill Harriman. At each venue, the starting time was staggered, giving the performers in Act 1 time to race to their next destination. The performance required pinpoint timing; each rally was to end with an oratorical flourish from Al. The problem was that Lowenstein had agreed to do a B'nai B'rith speech, outside the district, and refused to change or cancel it. "It was a logistical nightmare," Rich Hammond said. Trying to hold together the Massapequa performance, Hammond was finally reduced to leading a hootenanny with a friend. By the time Lowenstein finally showed, the audience had practically disappeared. "It was . . . mortifying," Hammond said, "it was just so ridiculous. . . . The whole thing had been put together so well . . . [and in the end] it was just a fiasco." Unfortunately, the "Night of the Stars" chaos was as much the rule as the exception.[58]

Other things went wrong as well, at least from the point of view of political consistency. Back in May, Lowenstein had voted against appropriations for the F-14 fighter plane; he was one of only 21 representatives to do so. On its face, the vote represented an act of courage, fulfilling one more time the pledge Lowenstein had made two years earlier to vote against military appropriations that would assist the war in Vietnam. The problem was that the F-14 was made at Grumman Aircraft on Long Island; thousands of Grumman workers resided in Lowenstein's district. Under growing pressure from local politicos who viewed his vote as suicidal, Lowenstein reconsidered, lamely arguing that his initial vote had been premised on the poor performance of the aircraft. Now, he said, he had spoken with F-14 pilots who had persuaded him the plane was a good investment—hence, he would change his vote when the final package came before the House. If Lowenstein had offered that rationale for a positive vote the first time, he might have gotten away with it, and if he had held to his convictions and voted no the second time, he could at least have argued that he was motivated by principle. But he shifted for what clearly seemed to be political expediency, thereby completely contradicting his image and losing votes on both sides of the issue.[59]

People on the left were also angry at Lowenstein for apparently seeking out encounters in which he came off as stridently antiradical. Especially bothersome was an episode at Stony Brook, the state university campus farther out on Long Island. Lowenstein wangled an invitation to the campus in late October, knowing that he would be heckled and abused by SDS members. Making sure that photographers and reporters were present, he then lambasted the students as reckless and irresponsible anarchists. When SDS supporters threw eggs and pelted him with water bombs, Lowenstein used the pictures and stories of the episode in a brochure to prove he was "responsible and centrist," not a "coddler" of radicals or a "darling of the New Left."

In one sense, it was brilliant politics. His encounter with SDS dramatized the message he had been trying to convey for two years. "America is not in any sense a Fascist country," he told the students. But in another sense, the episode was deeply troubling. "It just didn't feel right to me," Rich Hammond said. "There were people [in the campaign] who were in fact SDS-ers who had put aside the whole SDS critique . . . to come and work with him. . . . It just felt a little bit over the line of being too cute. It's one thing to marshal all your best arguments . . . and it's another one to start drawing lines between yourself and people with whom you've stood in the same lines fighting certain issues." It was all part of Lowenstein's larger problem of trying to be too many things to too many people, Arnie Miller said. "People respect you for what you are, if you are what you are and you say what you are. If you try to be something different, to the degree that you stretch it, it loses its political value." For some, the Stony Brook episode was stretching it.[60]

Trying to be too many things to too many people, and getting ensnarled in the contradictions—that was Lowenstein's major problem as the campaign wore down. Lowenstein wanted to be savior to the world—to have the universe as his constituency, as Jenny said—but what did that aspiration mean for the factory workers at Grumman, or the commuters on the Long Island Railroad? "He was out fucking around in Biafra," one staff aide said, "when he should [have] been right here in Lynbrook . . . how the hell does he expect to get reelected?" Lent was wrong in suggesting that Lowenstein spent most of his time junketing around the globe at government expense. In fact, he paid for his own tickets. But he did travel more than any other freshman congressman, and as one staff member said, "I think a lot of his constituents thought that was a mistake for somebody who was a young congressman." Thus, Lent's basic suggestion was accurate even if his actual statement was false; as Ham Richardson said, "[Lowenstein] was a national figure . . . interested in national issues. While I'm sure he tried to service his constituency, that wasn't his prime interest."[61]

Moreover, Al could not have it both ways. He could not be the keynote speaker on 50 campuses, encourage stories about blacks in Mississippi being his "extra" district ("Al runs a sort of shuttle between Mississippi and Washington," one news report said), and celebrate his fame as an international figure and still expect people to believe he cared most about Long Island—*even if he did.* He could not easily get away with defending the right of students to resist the draft and denying that he supported draft dodgers—even if both positions were true. And he could not attack Lent for calling him the chief defender of the Black Panthers and still continue to say, as he told an interviewer for *Look* magazine, that Panther rage was "the inevitable result of what's been done to them by the police [such as the murder of the Panther leader Fred Hampton]." In all such discussions, Lowenstein may have literally been on solid ground: he defended some student protesters while railing at others, and he criticized Panther tactics while seeking to make their anger more understandable. But the result was too much "noise," too many apparently contradictory signals emanating from a candidate who refused to be quiet and insisted instead on being a headline regardless of what he was doing. Eventually, the conflicting messages took their toll.[62]

The most painful example of such mixed messages was the question of whether the White House staff member Donald Rumsfeld supported Lowenstein. As a Republican congressman, Rumsfeld had been one of Lowenstein's closest friends on the Hill. The two men wrestled together in the House gym, debated political philosophy well into the night, and defended each other when the other was attacked. Lowenstein often stayed with the Rumsfelds in Washington. Lanny Davis, a young Lowenstein supporter, recalls Al taking him to Rumsfeld's house at 2:00 A.M. when Lowenstein was in Congress and telling him that Rumsfeld was one of his best friends. Indeed, in 1968, the Rumsfelds had sent Lowenstein a warm telegram wishing him luck in his campaign against Hampton, and Rumsfeld stood beside him on the victory platform when the election was over.

It was perhaps natural, then, that when Lent started to smear Lowenstein with charges of inciting students to riot and polarizing the Congress, Lowenstein should turn to Rumsfeld for support. In response, Rumsfeld consented to be interviewed by a Long Island paper; he affirmed Lowenstein's patriotism, denied that Lowenstein had ever advocated violence, and insisted that Lowenstein was "a man who has always advocated working within the political system to resolve issues." The "top White House aide" even defended Lowenstein for criticizing Nixon's Vietnam policy, declaring that there was nothing subversive or unpatriotic about having done so. All in all, Rumsfeld's comments rendered a body blow to Lent's allegations about Lowenstein's politics. Reacting to Rumsfeld's words, Lowenstein told the newspaper: "This only proves once again that men of moderation can and should work together."

The problem was that one week before the election, fliers appeared in every mailbox in the district featuring a letter from Rumsfeld endorsing Lent and headlined, "Lowenstein Debunked Again." Rumsfeld later explained to reporters that Nixon was supporting Lent, and that he was Nixon's assistant. "That's when you cease to be an independent operator." In reality, Lowenstein's use of Rumsfeld to deliver a supportive message had created such a backlash at the White House that Nixon demanded his pound of flesh. As Jenny Littlefield bemoaned, "We turned [Rumsfeld] into a figure in the district by saying he would not endorse, and then he turned us into a liar. . . . " The Rumsfeld episode was hurtful personally as well as politically. Yet it was just one more example of what happened when everything became blown out of proportion.[63]

Lowenstein's reelection could perhaps have been salvaged by the judgment of an impartial source that Lent had exceeded the bounds of fairness by his scurrilous charges. Such an opportunity arose when Lent himself went before the Fair Campaign Practices Committee in New York to accuse the Lowenstein campaign of fabricating some of the Republican names on his list of Republican and independent supporters. In response, the Lowenstein campaign asked the committee to censure Lent for two last minute advertisements, one of which showed Soviet tanks in Red Square under the caption: "What keeps them in Red Square Moscow, not Times Square New York?" The ad then went on to say, "If Allard Lowenstein's vote had prevailed in Congress, the United States would be without an Army, Navy and Air Force," and concluded with the plea, "If you've had enough of the Congressman from Cloud Nine and you want to curb smut peddlers, elect Norman Lent."

As a quintessential example of the meanness and distortion of the Lent campaign, the ad should have elicited a condemnation from the committee. Had Lowenstein been able to hand out a brochure during election week with "Fair Campaign Practices Committee Convicts Lent of Outrages" emblazoned on it, Arnie Miller observed, it might have turned the election around. Supposedly, a majority of the committee was prepared to issue such an indictment. But inexplicably, the Lowenstein team decided to agree to a negotiated settlement of the conflicting allegations, and each campaign withdrew its charges.[64]

The final question was whether Lowenstein could persuade enough Republican and independent voters that he was the moderate in the campaign and Lent the extremist. Statistically, the Republicans had a margin of 23,000 among registered voters, and at least some of them had to vote for Lowenstein if he were to have a chance. Clearly, he had made a dent in his opponent's strength with his endorsements from William Buckley and other Republicans, his willingness to go into the "lion's den" of VFW and American Legion halls, and his well-publicized condemnation of student radicalism at Stony Brook. One local Republican weekly came out with a twin endorsement of James Buckley, the Conservative, for the U.S. Senate, and Allard Lowenstein for the House seat, leading to a rash of Buckley-Lowenstein bumper stickers. Lowenstein himself insisted that the election was really a referendum on whether one could work through the system for change. "If what people do peaceably has no result," he said, "if we can't win elections where there is a clear choice, the polarization will increase because more people will turn fanatical." The fifth congressional district election, his columnist friend James Wechsler said, was "a test case for Agnewism . . . [and] the direction of the country—whether we will seek solutions or scapegoats."[65]

Certainly, Lowenstein had succeeded in making his case to the media. *Newsday* applauded Lowenstein for dampening campus radicalism, grappling effectively with local issues, and continuing to make the district proud with his national contributions. "He is a builder of bridges between generations, between ideologies, between classes," the paper editorialized. "During his two years in Congress, he has been more than a lawmaker; he has been a peacemaker." The *Long Island Press* agreed. "Not only is Senator Lent stooping to means similar to those used by the extremists he is supposed to be fighting," the paper said, "he is trying to achieve their main end—to destroy the moderate liberal who offers reasonable alternatives to the naysayers of the Right and the bomb-throwers of the Left." Lowenstein himself could not have written anything closer to his own specifications.[66]

But in the end, even ringing endorsements of Lowenstein as the quintessential "moderate liberal" could not save the day. No matter how hard he tried, Lowenstein could not finesse all the antagonistic forces ranged against him. He succeeded in outpolling Lent's turnout on the Republican line by 5,000 votes. But then there were the Conservatives; James Buckley received 46 percent of the total vote, and despite Lowenstein's desperate effort to generate support for a Buckley-Lowenstein combination, Lent received more than enough Conservative votes to make up for his deficit elsewhere. Lowenstein ended up losing by an 8,000 vote margin. Had he not improved on his 1968 showing, his margin of defeat would have been 25,000. But the demographics of the gerrymander, compounded by Lent's persistence in defining Lowenstein as an extremist, could not be overcome.[67]

Perhaps appropriately in light of what transpired, Lowenstein took solace in how close he had come, and in how valiantly his team had fought. "[It] was just an amazing accomplishment," Jenny said, "to almost hold that seat against the forces of dirty tricks." On election day, a *Newsday* columnist wrote, Lowenstein toured his storefront offices, "at 40 years [moving] effortlessly across the generation gap to extract from the thousands of college and high school students who have worked for him a measure of love, devotion, and hard work that is denied to all but the most gifted parents. He got because he gave so much, and of the very same things." Now they all gathered—5,000 strong—to hear his concession speech in a crowded ballroom. "He had been such an inspiration," one young volunteer commented, "moving through this thing with gentleness, with humor . . . and with absolute steadfastness." We would have won, Lowenstein told the crowd, if only the young people there could have voted. The loss, he said, was not a defeat, simply a warning—that the next time they would have to try harder. "In a lot of ways," the young volunteer said, "this was the triumph of gentleness over thuggery." Once again Allard Lowenstein had risen above the occasion at hand to proclaim moral victory in the face of political defeat, all the while sowing seeds of hope for the future.[68]

CONCLUSION

The two years Al served on Capitol Hill "[represented] a culmination of that which he most wanted," Jenny Littlefield observed. "He was a child who so deeply believed in government, and in benign and good leaders, and if you believe in that, maybe you believe that you, too, can be one." That certainly constituted a good part of Al Lowenstein's experience in Congress. He could "do his thing"—seek to rescue Biafra from starvation, Vietnam from corruption, and America from polarization, in short, be a good liberal activist—all the while wearing the mantle of legitimacy conferred by being a member of the U.S. House of Representatives. He would prove that the system could work, that people of reason and moderation could find mutually acceptable and just solutions, and that there was a basis for Americans—especially the young—to trust and believe in the democratic process. To achieve these goals, he would even cross lines and make covenants with conservatives, become friends with the opposition.

To a remarkable extent, Lowenstein achieved that goal during his two years in the House. He won the respect and affection of his colleagues on both sides of the aisle. As one Republican told him, "It's a disgrace that you weren't re-elected." While on the Hill, Lowenstein had raised the level of discourse and conduct among his peers. "The real loss," Democratic Congressman Jerome Waldie wrote him, "is to your colleagues who will be deprived of one of the few inspirations that are present in the House so far as ideals and conduct are concerned. Those of us who are not

possessed of the depths of conscience and integrity that you unconsciously exhibit all the time have been shored up in our convictions by
your example."[69]

Notwithstanding the institutional obstacles that surrounded him,
Lowenstein had also retained and enlarged his identity as a leader of the
young—especially on the war. "When I think of how to describe what you
have done for me," one student leader wrote, "I think of the word prophet.
. . . You can see the possibilities . . . you can see our potential . . . and
pull out the best we have. In moments of self-doubt and despair . . . you
give such hope." Always, Lowenstein's message was the same—how to
pursue the cause of justice and peace by leading from within, working to
make the system respond to reason, petition, and legitimate protest. Al's
true genius, Congressman Thomas Downey declared, was "being able to
explain to people the importance of the system . . . despite the tremendous
cynicism on campus . . . while at the same time tackling it head-on." You
had to be on college campuses where students were ready to trash book-
stores and assault buildings, Downey said, to appreciate what it meant for
Lowenstein to suddenly appear and say, "Look, let's make sure that the
revolution comes in a way that we want it to come . . . through the ballot,
and organizing dissent." That was Lowenstein's greatest gift, Downey said.
"If you stand up for [principles], if you are the tree that stands against the
wind . . . [others] will see that you can convince people by example."[70]

Lowenstein took as his special responsibility the mission to speak for
the young and their idealism, hence his intense preoccupation with their
thoughts and passions. He was extraordinarily eloquent in their defense.
"It was very cold in the dark," he declared about the antiwar march in November 1969,

> but there was no break in the line of people guarding candles, singing
> quietly, passing the great national shrines of America and on to the great
> centers of political power. What a beautiful generation we have pro-
> duced—what vibrant, good, gentle people. I kept wondering if any coun-
> try could be so stupid, so self-righteous and closed, to throw all this
> away. I decided that if we were that stupid and self-righteous and closed,
> we would deserve what we'd get; and to end up that way by default would
> be the most unacceptable thing of all.

It was precisely to avoid that defeat by default that Lowenstein made so
much of his own determination to stand like a tree "against the wind," and
to persuade the new generation to stay within the system.

Yet such an approach had problems. First of all, it flew in the face of a determination by Richard Nixon to divide the country, to polarize citizens, and to drive the young into either the arms of angry radicals or the ranks of law-and-order enthusiasts. Reconciliation and commitment to the process of orderly political involvement were not the likely results when an administration declared that the deaths at Kent State were the logical outcome of violence by protesters. Partly in response to such statements, a vigorous and dedicated minority of young Americans was beginning to give up on the system entirely. Over and over again, they had taken the word of moderates that if they obeyed the rules and made their case with reason, they would be heeded. But it had not been so. The teach-ins were ignored. Peaceful marches too often were met with violence. The government officials they were told to trust treated them with contempt and condescension. Many thus became convinced that it was not just a few leaders or policies that were flawed, but the entire culture, its values and its institutions. This was not an easy time, then, for Lowenstein to sustain the people's faith in mainstream liberal reform.

The problem was compounded, however, when Lowenstein began to make himself the test of the politics he espoused. Politicians frequently present themselves as embodying the principles they stand for, but Lowenstein carried this tendency to an extreme. The candidate thus became the cause, the person the definition of right and wrong. In this campaign more than most, the rhetoric of waging a holy war made some sense. But there was also a temptation to present everything in personal terms. Too often, one Lowenstein aide said, "it was all ego."[71]

That was the dynamic that made his reelection campaign both a soaring moral crusade and a deeply problematic test of faith in the system. For if this was to be an ultimate test of the principle of working inside rather than outside the established political process and Lowenstein was the sole embodiment of that principle, how could one not be totally disillusioned and radicalized by the result? The situation was a set-up for disaster, especially given the gerrymander and all the other obstacles against which Lowenstein was contending. It was the Dominican Republic all over again. "When the rules themselves embrace corruption," one student wrote, "when moral considerations of the means by which a candidate wins are dismissed as irrelevant and 'unproductive and not pragmatic'—when a system prostitutes the ideals upon which its own claims to legitimacy are founded, then the basis of that system and the direction it has taken can—perhaps must—be called into question." Lowenstein had made the system the issue, and the system had failed. "The children's crusade is lost," a Notre Dame student commented. "Hatred burns in the eyes beneath the tears. We have worked in the system and see where it has gotten us. Disappointment and defiance make comfortable bedfellows."[72]

Yet that was precisely the response Lowenstein could not afford to entertain. Although he had created the preconditions for disillusionment by making his personal situation the measure of the larger principle, he could not accept, for his own life and politics, the logical consequence of his election experience. Instead, he insisted on confronting the despair and transforming it into renewed hope, all the while taking upon himself the even larger personal responsibility of continuing to represent the system against all radical critics. Even as his followers fell into despondency and disaffection, the Notre Dame student commented, "Al . . . again transformed the enraged, dejected mass. . . . Where there is agony there is hope. Hope that we can win in the future." Indeed, defeat was transformed into victory precisely because the cause was so noble, the battle itself so redemptive.

To those who saw the man as the embodiment of the principle, it was still possible to say that the crusade remained alive. Expressing the gratitude shared by many, 16-year-old Randee Flug told a postelection gathering what the campaign had meant. "I . . . worked for Al," she said,

> because we saw a person who cared about what we cared about. . . . Maybe we were disappointed in losing the election, but not disillusioned in Al . . . because in Al Lowenstein, we saw a man who above all else honestly cared about other people. That's the kind of winning that can't be counted in votes. . . . After the Kent [State] and Cambodia incidents, I was very disgusted. . . . I saw a system that was so immense, so bureaucratic, so inhuman that I said forget it. . . . [Then] I heard Al Lowenstein speaking. He talked about fighting and not simply failing because we haven't tried hard enough. . . . Well, I still look at our system as a giant, inhuman machine, but he's given me a new hope, and watching Al has given me a new spirit to fight. For that, I'd like to say thank you Al.

With such spirit among his followers, Allard Lowenstein could believe in staying on to fight another day. "They can gerrymander a district," he told the same audience, "but they can't gerrymander a country."[73]

And so Lowenstein vowed to continue his lifetime commitment to making the system work, despite defeat and disappointment. But how long could that continue, with the stakes becoming ever higher? A critical stage in the evolution of Allard Lowenstein had ended. "The time he was in Congress was a beautiful time," Marcia Borie said. He achieved much of what he had hoped to do. "But it was over too quickly, and he then spent the rest of his life trying to get it back." How Al Lowenstein went about that process would say much about his political perspective, his personal agenda, and the intersection of each with the other.[74]

14

One Last Chance

Ever since he was a small boy plotting on his wall map the progress of the Republicans and the Fascists in the Spanish civil war, Allard Lowenstein had approached public life with the understanding that there were forces of good and evil competing for dominance in the world. Even when he resorted to behind-the-scenes manipulation to achieve his goals, he called upon a superstructure of ideals to justify his behavior and sustain an overarching sense of moral purpose. Although the triumph of good was by no means a foregone conclusion, as the Spanish civil war showed, in the end, he believed, justice would prevail. On the basis of these convictions, Lowenstein had recruited a generation of young people to assault the bastions of American racism and to protest an immoral war. Nothing confirmed his faith in the democratic process more than Lyndon Johnson's decision not to seek reelection in 1968. Indeed, it was a triumph so extraordinary that it represented the political equivalent of scaling Mt. Kilimanjaro.

Yet now Lowenstein's worldview seemed fragile and at risk. Doubt and despair had overtaken many of his supporters. His hero, Robert Kennedy, had been assassinated. Lowenstein's own electoral base had been taken away by a gerrymander. And in an election in which youth had been omnipresent and moral issues crystal clear, the political process had apparently failed. Lowenstein had made himself the personification of the values he espoused, and he had been rejected by the voters. Richard Nixon was in the White House, and the Vietnam War raged on.

For someone less personally invested in the legitimacy of the system and the efficacy of working within it, such setbacks might have provided the occasion for at least a momentary retreat for reflection. To Lowenstein, however, they constituted a mortal assault; everything he believed in and had built his identity around had been called into question. Far from leading him to a retreat, then, this crisis of faith propelled Lowenstein to redouble his commitment. He would *prove* that youth could transform American politics. He would take on in personal combat the embodiment of political corruption and lassitude—an absentee congressman from Brooklyn named John Rooney. He would, in his own words, give the system "one last chance" to prove itself. The gamble could hardly have been greater. At stake, quite literally, was a political philosophy that had now become synonymous with an individual human being—himself.

RECLAIMING AMERICA

When Lowenstein addressed the election rally on Long Island the evening of his loss to Norman Lent, he both explained his defeat and inspired the crowd with one critical assertion: if you could have voted, he told the thousands of young people present, we would have won. In that singular assessment lay the kernel of hope that shaped the next eighteen months of Lowenstein's life. With the twenty-sixth amendment lowering the voting age to eighteen about to be ratified, millions of citizens would be eligible to vote for the first time. If they could be registered and mobilized into a progressive political force, their ballots could end the war, throw Nixon from office, and transform frustration into efficacy. Through a new youth crusade, one columnist wrote in December 1970, Lowenstein was once again going to "organize the church militant" and repeat his triumph of just two years earlier. "Does Richard Nixon, one wonders, stir uncomfortably yet?" the columnist asked. "Doubtless not, but he will quiver soon enough. Lyndon Johnson could testify to that."[1]

Lowenstein's incipient new youth movement rested on a series of statistical realities and political calculations. Nearly twenty-five million Americans between the ages of seventeen and twenty-three would be eligible to vote in 1972 who had not been able to vote in 1968. Richard Nixon had won election that year by a national plurality of only 510,000, barely 2 percent of the total of potential new voters. According to Gallup Poll data, young people were slightly more liberal than the rest of the population and were expected to register Democratic by a two-to-one margin. If only half the potential new voters went to the polls, the results—based on such projections—could be astonishing. In five critical states that Nixon carried in 1968—California, Illinois, Missouri, New Jersey, and Ohio—the number of eligible new voters vastly exceeded his margin of victory. Assuming the poll data were correct, it seemed clear that the youth vote could transform American politics. Similar predictions had been made before. Fifty years earlier, when the nineteenth amendment was passed, many Americans had also anticipated dramatic results, believing that most women would cast their ballots on behalf of a particular point of view. But many women did not register immediately, and those who did divided their votes between the parties. Still, in 1972 the political potential of the new youth constituency seemed almost palpable.[2]

The key question was how to motivate the young so that their potential electoral impact could be realized. Here, Lowenstein brought to bear his own distinctive and impassioned political analysis. In the aftermath of 1968, young people had become increasingly alienated. Radicals attributed this to the intransigence of the system, and urged the young to move from alienation to revolution. Lowenstein, however, offered a different interpretation. "Students are frustrated not because they exerted no influence," he told a Harvard newspaper in late 1969, "but because they almost succeeded, because the consummation of their success was taken away by an act of murder." According to this analysis, in three months in 1968 students had "changed . . . the political equation . . . more profoundly than it had been in any period ten times that length in the past." The system had worked. Only Robert Kennedy's assassination had prevented their efforts from coming to fruition.[3]

Now the youth crusade to register new voters provided an opportunity to complete that insurgency. In Lowenstein's mind, the voter registration effort of 1971 thus became a "national Mississippi project" that, with the transformative impact of the Freedom Vote of 1963, would demonstrate to "young people opposed to the war [that] they have [a] choice, [an] alternative to the radicals taking over." In this way, the morally pure task of cleansing the system by working within it, an effort that had begun in 1968, could be completed. Moreover, the effort would be led by Republicans and Democrats alike, in a nonpartisan acknowledgment of how transcendent and idealistic this crusade of young people really was.[4]

360

As his own base for the voter registration venture, Lowenstein used his new position as national chairman of Americans for Democratic Action, the liberal anti-Communist group formed in 1947 by Eleanor Roosevelt and others to fight the "left-wing" challenge of Henry Wallace's Progressive party. Lowenstein had triumphed in a divided election of the ADA board, committed to revitalizing ADA and making it the vehicle, in James Wechsler's words, for "a new beginning in U.S. progressive politics . . . [with] an infusion of younger, untired blood and . . . more dramatic leadership." Somewhat dubious about becoming identified with what many viewed as a tired and far too predictable organization, Lowenstein nevertheless accepted the job because it gave him a platform, a title, and a structure from which to operate. Within weeks of his appointment in 1971, he had secured staff positions for his young allies in the voter registration drive and embarked on a campaign to use the ADA for his own purposes, regardless of its stodgy reputation. "It was mostly a rip-off on [Al's] part," one student staff member said at the time. But it was also possible to see the move, in Wechsler's terms, as "the moment for a fresh start for an independent political movement" at a time of political crisis.[5]

The overall operation, however, remained explicitly nonpartisan. As his chief lieutenant, Lowenstein chose Nick Littlefield, a young Wall Street lawyer who was Republican by birth and upbringing and had worked actively in the campaigns of the Rhode Island Republican John Chafee. Littlefield's task was to raise money, organize voter registration rallies in key states, recruit and dispatch student interns to various locales during the summer of 1971 (college students received $50 per week, graduate students $75), and keep track—without secretarial help—of all other voter registration activities. Pete McCloskey and Don Riegle, two GOP congressmen who shared Lowenstein's convictions, provided a Republican anchor for the project (McCloskey in fact had pledged to challenge Nixon in the primaries unless he changed his war policy); Lowenstein lined up a stable of Democratic presidential hopefuls to hold down the Democratic side, including George McGovern, Edmund Muskie, amd Birch Bayh. To reinforce the campaign's appeal to young people, John Denver, Peter Yarrow (of Peter, Paul, and Mary), and the antiwar balladeer Phil Ochs agreed to sing at registration rallies. Once registered, young people would rescue the political system and both end the war and remove Nixon from office. The plan made sense; it even seemed doable.[6]

Before long, the entire nation was taking note of the youth registration venture. Although there were other such efforts besides Lowenstein's, his garnered the most attention. *Newsweek* did a cover story, *Look* and *Life* each had major features, the nationally syndicated columnists David Broder and Jules Witcover wrote about it, and Lowenstein appeared on "Meet the Press." At the kick-off rally in Providence, Rhode Island, Edmund Muskie, at that time the leading Democratic presidential candidate, headed the cast of platform speakers. Clearly, this voter registration effort had captured a significant place on the American political landscape—it was large enough to make presidential front-runners take the chance of appearing at rallies suffused with antiwar rhetoric, and mainstream enough to attract the attention of the nation's journalistic gatekeepers.[7]

To a remarkable degree, this spotlight on the youth crusade bespoke the power of Allard Lowenstein's commitment to the idea. Intensely preoccupied with redeeming his vision of America (and his role within it), Lowenstein had seized on his most prized constituency as the key. Bella Abzug, the New York congresswoman and a frequent ally (as well as foe) of Lowenstein, captured some of the flavor of his mission in her diary. When he came into her hotel room at 2:00 A.M., after a meeting, she wrote,

> you should have seen him. He [had] this wild gleam in his eye, this urgent excitement in his voice, as he started to talk about how in this presidential election, we're going to inherit the political power structure. He was unbelievable, . . . a very motivated guy with a touch of madness. It's a fascinating thing, but he thinks he's a Messiah. He's a believer, largely in himself, which is the key to being a believer in others.

A *Newsweek* reporter conveyed the same sense of Lowenstein's larger-than-life impact. "[He] projects himself into national orbit," the reporter wrote, "achiev[ing] a rate of spin that defies the norms of human metabolism, and gradually, through a combination of personal magnetism and gravitational tug, sets tides flowing across the political map." This was obviously no routine political operation.[8]

But it took Lowenstein himself to express the sheer immensity of the task he had taken on. "What we're going to do is nominate and elect a president," he told a Minneapolis rally. "Why should we only play tactical maneuvers as if we're a tiny minority sitting along the fringes? That's not us. . . . We are the mainstream of the country. . . . We are going to win the Presidency. . . . This country is going to move in the direction it wanted to go in before the murder of Robert Kennedy. And we're finally going to get there." Lowenstein made the message even clearer in a speech to his old Long Island congressional district. "The long winter is at last coming to an

end," he declared. "We are many things and all kinds of people, but we
are alien neither to this land nor its constitution. On the contrary, *we are
the heart of the land.* So we are here today to tell the government that the
people have found their way. That we march henceforth not to 'Taps' but to
'Reveille' and that soon America will march not to war but to stop war."
The rhetoric pulsed with power and intensity. Fringe, no! Alien, no! Minority, no! Majority, yes! Mainstream, yes! Heart of the land, yes! "The
people have found their way." Led by youth, marching to "Reveille,"
under the direction of Allard Lowenstein, they would "reclaim America as
a nation which once again trusts its Presidents and whose 18 year olds
need not choose between exile and jail. We shall prevail."[9]

Perhaps appropriately, Lowenstein was simultaneously writing a
book—entitled "Reclaiming America"—that would articulate in greater
detail the kind of nation he hoped to find on the other side of his youth
crusade. Commissioned by Saturday Review Press for election year distri-
bution and written in association with Robert Anson, a well-known political journalist, the book was to be a road map showing America how to finish the journey so tragically interrupted by the assassinations of Martin
Luther King, Jr., and Robert Kennedy. The book was never published.
Lowenstein wrote on scraps of paper while riding in the car, dictated long
sections of chapters, and occasionally sat up late at night in bed with a
yellow pad. But he lacked the discipline to meet the deadlines set by his
publisher. Ever a perfectionist, he used to say that writing a page of prose
for publication was like "shitting grapefruits." Nevertheless, the unfinished manuscript, written with considerable nuance and depth, offers a
glimpse of the dynamics that informed Lowenstein's dedication to the
youth crusade as the penultimate moment in American history.[10]

Almost an intellectual autobiography, "Reclaiming America" begins by
returning to the tragedies of 1968. That year had started, Lowenstein recalled, with an organizing effort against the war and Lyndon Johnson
"[that] was very much like a blacksmith standing in front of a nearly dead
fire. There was a spark in there somewhere. All that had to be done was to
keep fanning and fanning until it caught." But then the flame ignited,
democracy took on new life, and there were "simply people . . . making
their minds up that nothing was impossible." At that moment the bullets
were fired that took Robert Kennedy's life, in the process taking away
people's hope as well. "It would not have been necessary to write this
book if Robert Kennedy were alive," Lowenstein said. "Had he lived . . .
people would not be arguing about whether the system works. Instead, we

would be reclaiming America, as he used to put it. . . . That is why the death of Robert Kennedy is the only one I can recall that seems to grow worse as time passes. No one fills the leadership vacuum, but the stakes continue to rise."[11]

Among those stakes was a surge of despair and cynicism at the very moment when the need for an all-out effort to turn the nation around was greatest. Lowenstein tried to identify with that despair. He recalled the moment in 1965 when he discovered, after hearing Lyndon Johnson talk about Communists firing on the U.S. ambassador in the Dominican Republic, that there had been no shooting at the embassy at all. "At that point for me," he wrote, "something happened. Belief fled." In similar fashion, he argued, belief had fled for the generation that came of age in 1968. They had toppled a president, yet nothing had changed, leaving them feeling deceived and betrayed. "It was Hannah Arendt," Lowenstein pointed out, "who once said that what drives people from being 'engagé to enragé' is the sense that words have lost their meaning, and that nothing one does is consummated, because there is always some way in which it can be distorted."

It had been Sirhan Sirhan's bullets that had distorted the meaning of 1968, turning victory into defeat, hope into despair, and belief into cynicism. The result was disillusionment and depression for a whole generation, especially for young people, "the most dedicated, the most concerned, the most generous" of recent history, who now had given up hope. "In terms of their own political experience," Lowenstein wrote, "leaders lying is all they've ever known. What they know of change is that when someone attempts it, *they* will get rid of him. Assassination has become almost an assumption. . . . [And] if all great men are destined to be shot, only the fool goes on hoping." Everything thus became its opposite, creating a world where "bombing is called peace, where the rich are paid not to grow food while the poor go hungry, where we send men to the moon, but not from Manhattan to Queens." What could be done?

To answer the question, Lowenstein went back to his own life experience for strength and inspiration. He had transformed his physical and spiritual being during adolescence by willing himself to become a new person. *Will* was the key. It was what the historian Barbara Tuchman had said "made things happen." Individuals had it; nations had it. "There are circumstances that can modify it or nullify it," Tuchman had observed, "but its presence is essential, and its absence fatal." The will to fan the embers into flame had made 1968 possible, and the situation in 1971,

Lowenstein said, was just like 1968—"only the names have changed, the story is the same." The difference, if any, was that this year was even more critical because as "the need for an all-out effort [for change] grows . . . the willingness to make that effort dwindles." Americans could either put together the greatest political coalition for change since the New Deal or sink further into hopeless political despair. "Before we all head for the trees," Lowenstein concluded, "let us pause that final moment, *and give it that one last chance*. America, and ourselves, deserve no less than that."

Once he had defined the struggle in such grandiloquent terms, Lowenstein was almost forced, of course, to describe the options with equal hyperbole. No one came in for greater scorn than radicals who insisted that the system itself was sick and that no short-term band-aids could alter the fundamental truth that revolution was the only answer to injustice. In a chapter of his book entitled "A Letter to the American Left," Lowenstein threw down the gauntlet. "First, some disclaimers. The police are not Fascist pigs. America is not a racist, imperialist society. Lyndon Johnson is not John Kennedy. Hate is not love. And no, I am not an agent of the CIA." By its rhetoric and distortions, Lowenstein argued, the left sought to remove human agency and attribute everything to conspiracy. "What is accident the Left regards as plot. What is chance, the Left sees as inevitable." Not only did such views totally invalidate such efforts as the civil rights and peace movements, but they also resulted in a rewriting of history—Korea became Vietnam, FDR part of a procapitalist Wall Street conspiracy, and every congressman a war criminal.

Even more disturbing were the activities endorsed by the left. "Slashing tires, blowing up toilets, burning buildings, and shouting down speakers," Lowenstein declared, only "distract attention from the issue of the war to the issue of the tactics used to stop it. When the battle is thus joined, peace will always be the loser." By rejecting reform as a meaningless palliative, Lowenstein insisted, the left risked converging with and reinforcing the right, which argued that nothing was wrong in the first place. "The biggest loser in all this . . . is change. Those in the Left who don't know that, either have no acquaintance with reality or haven't dug deep enough into dogma. It was Lenin, not Lowenstein, who said, 'Revolutions are not built on defeats.'"

By so defining the issues, Lowenstein distorted much of what the New Left was actually about. Although there had been reckless moments when New Left activists had started fires, ransacked files, and made inexcusable personal attacks on people, the larger movement was far more serious and disciplined. Dedicated to a collective process of organizing people to transform their society and create a new government and economy, movement activists spent most of their time seeking ideological clarity and fashioning tactics that could most effectively defeat their enemies. Still, Lowenstein disregarded most of these less dramatic New Left activities.[12]

Instead, in the face of what he regarded as the left's bankrupt and self-defeating invitation to resignation, Lowenstein returned to where he had begun—a ringing reaffirmation of liberal activism as the only way to rescue despair and redeem democracy. To be sure, the students who demonstrated peacefully within constitutional channels against Johnson's Vietnam policy had not ended the war. "But we have saved lives." FDR may not have devised an alternative to capitalism, but he helped prevent total hunger. "The choice then is a very basic one," Lowenstein declared: revolution, which was bound to fail, or reform, which at least had a chance. If the nation chose the latter path, it had one last opportunity to complete the insurgencies begun in 1968, to restore belief in the system—"government's most precious commodity"—and to unleash a coalition that could bring about the greatest social breakthroughs since the 1930s. "Three thousand kids [demonstrating] *outside* the hall in Chicago didn't stop Hubert Humphrey from being nominated [in 1968]," Lowenstein wrote. "Three hundred kids *inside* will this time." It was a huge promissory note, carrying a heavy penalty if unpaid.

The realities of organizing such a campaign, unfortunately, made it nearly impossible to achieve success. In practice, the voter registration venture involved only a few national staffers flying into a rally location one or two weeks in advance and being responsible for getting 20,000–30,000 people to a splashy event. Sometimes local interns were already at work, but frequently, their ideas were different from those of the national office; tensions were inevitable. In Austin, for example, some student groups were uncomfortable with the partisan "dump Nixon" purpose of the Lowenstein enterprise. Lowenstein responded with an emotional speech declaring that the movement had always been dedicated to ending the war. "Texas is part of the United States," he asserted. "You don't need a visa to get in here. It's time you people recognized that." To which a local woman responded: "If you want to come down here and run down this great state and make fun of us, you can just take your organizers and your money and get the hell out of Texas."[13]

There were other problems as well. Both the Austin and Pittsburgh offices were mysteriously burglarized; only mailing lists and local contact sheets were stolen. Los Angeles officials suddenly canceled a lease for use of the Cow Palace; and in Indianapolis, authorities reneged on a permit that had been promised, a $50,000 bond was demanded, and state police announced on the radio that hitchhikers coming to the rally might be subject to arrest. Lowenstein frequently reached out to associates who were experienced political operatives to fly into a rally site five days early and rescue the operation. "It's a disaster there," he told these friends more than once. "You've got to go help." Confusion over speakers and entertainers and conflict with local arrangements committees frequently kept organizers biting their nails up to the last minute.[14]

Given such obstacles, what remained most impressive was how successful much of the voter registration campaign was. More often than not, the Lowenstein network functioned well, notwithstanding its reputation and that of its leader for inefficiency, lateness, and last-minute improvisation. The kick-off rally in Providence drew nearly 20,000 people and, despite Edmund Muskie's anger at being supplanted by Birch Bayh at the last minute as the lead speaker, generated massive publicity. When Lowenstein and Pete McCloskey walked the beaches of Santa Monica in early July to sign up prospective youthful voters (they recruited 4,000), *Time* magazine wrote up their expedition. From Pittsburgh to Manhasset to Minneapolis, tens of thousands of young people trooped to meetings to sing with Peter Yarrow and be inspired by the rhetoric of a Lowenstein team that included John Lindsay, Don Riegle, Pete McCloskey, and George McGovern. On the basis of publicity alone, the youth crusade achieved enormous success, raising expectations throughout the country that Lowenstein's vision of a new progressive political coalition might well come to fruition.[15]

Overall, however, the results of the voter registration drive fell short of the hopes Lowenstein had generated. At too many rally sites, the procedures for registering people failed to corral more than a small percentage of the audience, and follow-up was inadequate. *Newsweek* estimated that, by October, barely 10–20 percent of those newly eligible to register had done so. Instead, the "pall of political apathy" seemed to be spreading. Part of the problem was the difficulty of developing a base against Nixon within his own party, notwithstanding the efforts of people like Riegle and McCloskey. Johnson—and Democrats—had been an easier target in 1968. In addition, Nixon's decision to end the draft, as well as the continued policy of withdrawing troops from Vietnam, made it far more difficult to bring the war issue home to the young. "As soon as the draft ended,"

Lowenstein's ally Steve Morgan said, "you could see the balloon burst on the campuses." But perhaps most important, Lowenstein had oversold his vision to such a degree that the chasm between promise and reality was unbridgeable. His intense need to reclaim America was compelling as a plan and made eminent sense as a political program. But he would have to find some other vehicle than registering young voters to make it credible and real.[16]

TAKING ON THE MACHINE

Regardless of what happened with his "dump Nixon" drive, Lowenstein knew he had to make his own personal choice about the 1972 elections. By now committed to the proposition that he could best achieve his own goals through elective office, the questions to be answered quickly reduced to two: which office, and where. Since there was no U.S. Senate race in 1972, Congress seemed the logical answer to the first question, but deciding on which district was not so simple. He could run again in the fifth district on Long Island, but there were tensions within the party there (he had lost an ill-conceived last-minute challenge to become head of the Nassau County Democratic organization in 1971). Also, the prospects of overcoming in 1972 a gerrymander that he had not been able to surmount as an incumbent in 1970 were less than bright. Manhattan was always possible, but there were no seats available there. That made Brooklyn the likeliest option.

Two Brooklyn seats were open to challenge, and both were held by old-line machine politicians who fit perfectly Lowenstein's characterization of the House as a "gerontocracy." The first was that of Emmanuel Cellar, the chair of the House Judiciary Committee, now in his eighties. Cellar had befriended Lowenstein during the latter's single term; a traditional liberal with a progressive voting record, he nevertheless seemed a likely target for a reform candidate. The second was the fourteenth district seat held by John Rooney. Having served twenty-eight years in the House, Rooney was a genuine Neanderthal from a reform perspective. Known on the Hill as J. Edgar Hoover's protector and chief ally, he had supported Lyndon Johnson and the Vietnam War and had remained aloof from most of the social crusades of the 1960s. That made the choice easier. As Jennifer Littlefield noted, "Rooney was a worthy opponent . . . a pretty horrible creature [who] had a stranglehold on his district. . . . [That seat] seemed to have a lot of the elements that were necessary."[17]

Lowenstein's next problem was how to make the move from suburban Long Island to polyglot Brooklyn. He had endorsed Peter Eikenberry's reform challenge to Rooney two years earlier and so had some contact with the district. But that was not enough. As Art Kaminsky, a youthful Lowenstein campaign aide, observed, "[Al's] favorite [fantasy] was, you can't do anything politically unless the local people want you. Of course, *you* create the local people wanting you." Quickly, then, Lowenstein recruited his friends in the district, including his old Yale Law School classmate Ann Feldman, to generate a draft "calling" him to the district. Various reform clubs were already interviewing candidates, and Lowenstein made a powerful positive impression when he was invited to speak. "They were delighted to have him, [of course]," Ann Feldman observed, "But it was his idea."[18]

As much as any congressional district in America, the fourteenth was a montage of clashing colors, languages, and interests. Although a number of public housing developments peopled by Puerto Ricans and blacks had been removed by redistricting since Eikenberry's 1970 challenge, in 1972 the district still was 21 percent African-American and 17 percent Puerto Rican, most of whom were located in the poor neighborhoods of Fort Greene (predominantly black), Bushwick (partly Italian, partly Puerto Rican), and Spanish Williamsburg. But that was just the beginning. Also included in the fourteenth's boundaries were the nouveau riche neighborhoods of Brooklyn Heights and Cobble Hill, the Italian working-class district of Carroll Gardens, Polish Greenpoint, and the Hasidic community of Jewish Williamsburg. More than one-quarter of the population required some form of public assistance, yet West Side Manhattan types were gentrifying Brooklyn Heights, buying and remodeling handsome brownstones.[19]

In the face of such balkanization, Lowenstein's fundamental dilemma was identifying where *he* belonged. "The problem with this district," Ann Feldman observed, "[was] that we had no reason to be here, we had no roots, we had nobody here [who] was really deeply involved." Thus, Lowenstein confronted a series of choices. He could concentrate his energies on those parts of the district that historically had been most friendly to insurgent challenge and/or most ignored by Rooney—neighborhoods such as Brooklyn Heights, Bushwick, Spanish Williamsburg, and Fort Greene. By following that course, he would maximize his appeal to a pre-existing anti-Rooney constituency. Or he could mount a campaign based on building bridges between ethnic communities and developing support for a new kind of progressive politics that would address urgent urban and social issues while rejecting the hierarchical, boss-based regimes of the past. As if the choice were not difficult enough, it was compounded by the fourteenth congressional district's low voter turnout rate—the lowest in the entire country. With 460,000 residents, only 29,000 people had voted in previous primaries.[20]

Local reformers had already engaged some of these issues, and Lowenstein's campaign needed to follow their lead wherever possible. One strategy, for example, was to have Lowenstein run at the top of a slate of local candidates supported by clubs that had endorsed his candidacy. Thus, he sought alliances with Mike Pesci, a reform candidate from Italian Carroll Gardens who was running for the state assembly, and Carol Bellamy, the West Brooklyn Independent Democrats' candidate for the state senate. Somewhat more difficult was the issue of what to do with nonwhite areas where the potential anti-Rooney sentiment was high but little meaningful contact had been made with community leaders. In such areas, Lowenstein had little choice but to work with nominal leaders, spending what one friend called "obscene amounts of money" in the hope that doing so would create a financial underpinning for deeper and more sustained ties to these communities. He also hoped that the local unions—the Longshoremen's Union led by Anthony Scotto, and the National Maritime Union headed by Joseph Curran—would follow through on their initial indication that they would remain neutral.

Predictably, perhaps instinctively by now, Lowenstein found the hardest decision the easiest to make. Of course he would go full sail into the blue-collar, white ethnic, and Hasidic Jewish areas of the district. What Al craved most, Jenny observed, was the challenge of convincing people opposed to his point of view. "He would insist on going into these most wretched, horrible redoubts in the district . . . and on throwing his top guns into those areas. . . . But that was what he was all about, 'I can convince people. I can talk to them and they'll understand.'" What made the Brooklyn campaign so special and meaningful to him, one close aide said, was how "viscerally and internally" he identified with the oppressed neighborhoods of the fourteenth congressional district, and how much he thrived on boldly striving to create dialogue between Poles and blacks and the Hasidic Jews of Williamsburg. Because "once that kind of chemistry [began] to unfold . . . the whole landscape of New York City politics [would be] transformed." After all, what was the point of undertaking any less than the largest challenge?[21]

With a campaign strategy in hand, Lowenstein proceeded to line up his troops. Nick Littlefield, who had coordinated the ADA voter registration drive, was named campaign director and given responsibility for raising money, recruiting staff, and implementing a plan to go into all sections of the district. Arnie Miller helped negotiate with those people Littlefield called "the crazies" across the district; he and, subsequently, Art Kaminsky, an experienced operative in the Lindsay and McGovern presidential campaigns, bore primary responsibility for coordinating the campaign among blacks and Puerto Ricans. Meanwhile, the call went out once again, just as it had in 1966, 1968, and 1970, to Lowenstein protégés and campus volunteers throughout the country to give one more spring and summer of their time for the cause of a new kind of politics.[22]

Before tackling anything else, Lowenstein faced the knotty dilemma of establishing his credibility in an area where he had never lived. Once before he had been saddled with the "carpetbagger" label. Now he had to endure the embarrassment not only of moving belatedly from a Long Island suburb into an inner-city area but also of not getting there soon enough even to register to vote. Making fun of both Lowenstein's non-Brooklyn origins and his politics, Rooney described him as "Mr. Low-Esteem . . . one of those liberal boids . . . who flies from Manhattan to run in Long Beach and then, when the voters reject him there, flies to Brooklyn to run against me." Mocking Lowenstein's record as a one-term congressman—Lowenstein's major achievement, Rooney claimed, was bringing cockroaches into the House cloakroom by dropping crumbs while he munched sandwiches and talked on the phone—Rooney boasted of his own ability to "deliver" to the fourteenth by having created more than 11,000 jobs and kept open the Brooklyn navy yard and army base. While Rooney had helped "thousands of the little people," according to his literature, Lowenstein could not boast of "a single law on the books." Furthermore, Rooney declared, Lowenstein had done nothing to obtain funds for his Long Island district—"Nothing, nada, niet, nicht, niente bupkis"—while voting against aid for Israel seven times, and against orphanages in Poland. "Lowenstein wouldn't know about our problems and needs," his literature concluded. "All he did for our district is move in with his carpetbag and about 800 strangers like himself, from all over the country, trying to fool us into giving him our vote."[23]

Lowenstein retorted by trying to turn the tables, claiming that he had spent more time in the fourteenth in thirty days than Rooney had in thirty years. Lowenstein charged that, despite his boast of community service,

Rooney had displayed nothing but contempt for Brooklynites; in fourteen terms, he had never opened a district office for constituent services. As if to highlight his own attentiveness Lowenstein made it his first priority to open storefronts in eighteen different neighborhoods in the district, each one staffed by a combination of student volunteers and community residents whose task was to follow up on citizen needs and complaints, doing the "case work" that Lowenstein claimed Rooney had so totally ignored during his entire career. Clearly designed for multiple purposes, the storefronts both established Lowenstein's presence in each community and served as a base for canvassing and local campaign organization. More than 100,000 shopping bags with LOWENSTEIN in huge letters on the side were distributed throughout the district. Jenny trooped through hundreds of tenements giving out the bags and introducing herself, helping in one more way to make the Lowenstein name a byword in the district.

And as if these efforts were not enough to establish his presence, the campaign called on the increasingly familiar Lowenstein stable of Hollywood stars and nationally prominent figures to give it added luster. Dustin Hoffman and Marlo Thomas circulated through busy shopping areas, Coretta Scott King, Congressman Ron Dellums, and Aaron Henry canvassed African-Americans in Fort Greene; Herman Badillo, José Torres, and Geraldo Rivera visited Puerto Rican areas; and Robert Kennedy's daughter Kathleen spoke at a rally. Between the visibility of the storefronts, the shopping bags, and the celebrities canvassing for Lowenstein, it was difficult not to be aware that a significant new political figure had established a presence in Brooklyn.[24]

The real struggle, however, was the day-to-day effort to mobilize an apathetic voting populace living in a hundred different neighborhoods. Rooney agreed to appear in only one debate, so television and news accounts of direct candidate encounters would not determine the election results. Literature and shopping bags might enhance "name recognition," but knowing a name and caring enough to vote were two different things. Unlike the Long Island suburbs in 1968, the fourteenth district would not be galvanized by the war in Vietnam; that issue was not going to attract thousands of voters. Rather, the name of the game was hard core ethnic and machine politics—who had the ammunition and soldiers to win the battle of the streets and tenements.

The contest produced a mixed bag of results. On the minus side, the unions quickly retreated from their vows of neutrality (or even possible Lowenstein support). Under intense pressure from Brooklyn boss Meade

Esposito, they lined up solidly behind Rooney, thereby providing him with a potentially huge bloc of votes. Nor was Lowenstein's campaign staff necessarily able to help. Despite his abundant talents, Nick Littlefield was a WASP New Englander. "[He] was so new to all of this stuff," Arnie Miller noted, "and so irrelevant to Brooklyn neighborhood politics." Whatever his intentions, Littlefield had little experience in dealing with ethnic clubs and leaders. The conflicts between headquarters and the neighborhood storefronts, while natural, sometimes reached crisis proportions. On the other hand, Lowenstein's campaign attempted to work closely with the local reform clubs. Wherever possible, the top of the ticket was anchored to an alliance with community politicians. To the extent the alliance worked and the storefronts delivered on their promise of community services, it might still be possible for Lowenstein and his staff to overcome the disability of being perceived as outsiders.[25]

On one level, Lowenstein seemed ideally suited and committed to this kind of politics. "Al galvanized the minority community and the Hispanic community to an extent that no minority person did before," Willie Vargas, a local activist, observed. "He gave us this shot of adrenaline. . . . After you keep getting beaten down all the time, Al provided some hope." A "quick study," Lowenstein helped unify ethnically divided neighborhoods, mediate disputes, and identify with local issues and candidates. Eileen Dugan, a leader of Independent Neighborhood Democrats, especially appreciated Lowenstein's willingness to work through local structures and attempt to give neighborhood leaders a substantial voice in the storefronts.[26]

Yet a subtext of resentment and alienation sometimes surfaced as well. Local reformers in a Puerto Rican area found a piece of Lowenstein literature insensitive and uninformed, even if written in Spanish, and refused to circulate it. An Italian-language brochure used the wrong verb tense and talked about the local candidate Mike Pesci as if he were dead. One Italian-American reformer saw Lowenstein as imperious. "He thinks he knows everything. He doesn't want to listen to us, and we can't trust him." Although Lowenstein was urged to focus on local issues and avoid talking about the war at kaffeeklatches in Italian neighborhoods, Eileen Dugan noted, "I swear to God, he'd be there for maybe ten minutes and start in about sorties over Vietnam." Trust, usually grounded in familiarity, was the key to ethnic politics. "Maybe [neighborhood leaders and] candidates didn't trust Al," one Lowenstein staffer said, "maybe they felt like they were being left out. You've got to remember he had not been in active duty very long, and he had to establish a track record very quickly with them." Surprisingly, he evidently did succeed to some extent—but was it enough?[27]

The role of volunteers in the campaign best symbolized this complex of issues—trust, being an outsider, finding a place in the community. As in all his crusades in the past, Lowenstein turned primarily to the young, his core constituency, and depended on them to bear his message and convey his passion for change and reform. But the Vietnam War was no longer the single overriding issue. Nor was this district populated by suburbanites who had—or aspired to have—college-age children like Lowenstein's idealistic young canvassers. What did it say about Lowenstein that his campaign fortunes ultimately hinged on having hundreds of other "liberal boids" fly in from campuses across the country? And if these young people represented the "new politics," what was the basis for their connection to the "old politics"?

The young people came from 30 states and just as many colleges and universities. More than 300 in number, they had been recruited either by Lowenstein in one of his many appearances on college campuses or by members of his network. The license plates on the cars parked around campaign headquarters at 383 Pearl Street gave a very cosmopolitan air to that part of Brooklyn. One night, Lowenstein introduced Carlos de Zayas, a Spanish friend and ally in the anti-Franco struggle who had come to the United States for a visit; from across the room came a whoop from an older Brooklynite who had served with the Abraham Lincoln Brigade during the Spanish civil war. On another occasion, a young volunteer stood to introduce himself. When he told the audience that he in fact lived in the district, the volunteers rose and gave him a standing ovation. The most important fact about the college volunteers, Ann Feldman recalled later, was that none was an Italian, Hispanic, black, or Hasidic Jew.[28]

The impact of the young volunteers was enormous. When they arrived, they may not have known where one ethnic neighborhood started and another ended. But they found out quickly and, in the process, experienced transformations in their own lives. "It is incredible to me," one volunteer wrote, "that I could have gone into Bushwick—the land of 'broken people and broken dreams'—where Bill and I broke up two gun fights and confronted a Puerto Rican gang, and where I saw poverty to a degree unknown to most people and frustration beyond belief, and yet where I have seen hope and potential." Campaign workers and neighborhood people came together, he declared, amid "a sense of community, love and understanding that is [ordinarily] so missing in that area." Debbie Wise, a volunteer from Oberlin, described a similar experience, extolling "the lasting rewards of working with a warm, closely knit community like Spanish Williamsburg for common causes which inspired so much dedicated effort." From the perspective of these students, the volunteer-run storefront operations had created bonds of community solidarity and commitment that promised a new day for Brooklyn.[29]

Yet the student perspective was not always shared by the locals. "Your fervent followers, the young college crowd," one woman wrote Lowenstein, "were strangers who swarmed the streets . . . looking very determined and busy, but *out of place*. . . . They didn't have a particularly friendly nor interested attitude toward the man in the streets. They could have slowed down, looked around, and mingled more, but they all seemed to be rushing around." The *Village Voice*'s Ken Sobol—who would come under bitter attack by Lowenstein supporters for his views of the campaign—noted that the volunteers simply "usurped what should have been the functions of local people and predictably balled everything up." Even devoted Lowenstein protégés saw problems. Too many of the volunteers were naive and inefficient, Ronald Tabak observed, and "almost all came from middle and upper class families ill-equipped to handle the emotions and life of the ghetto." The sincerity, dedication, and idealism of the volunteers inevitably won over many of the people with whom they had daily contact. But would that impact extend to strangers who saw them only on the street or through hurried canvassing interactions in doorways?[30]

As the June primary approached, it was anyone's guess whether the Lowenstein campaign's pluses would outweigh its minuses. The candidate had moved into the district, taking an apartment in the Fort Greene section. That decision had the positive effect of signaling blacks and Puerto Ricans—potentially very anti-Rooney—that Lowenstein cared enough about them to move into a predominantly black neighborhood. Yet on the negative side, the message given to Polish Greenpoint and Hasidic Williamsburg was that the candidate already pilloried as an outsider by Rooney chose to move in with African-Americans, the ultimate outsiders from a white ethnic point of view. In pursuit of his commitment to penetrate every neighborhood of the district, Lowenstein poured campaign resources into Hasidic Williamsburg. In doing so, however, he took the huge risk of alienating those people in Spanish Williamsburg and Bushwick who viewed the Hasidic community as their worst enemies. In the midst of such dynamics, Rooney himself became largely irrelevant. Having defined Lowenstein as an elitist outsider, he could absent himself and leave campaign matters to his precinct captains, the white ethnic chieftains who had been his allies through the years and who constituted the Brooklyn Democratic machine.

As it turned out, that was sufficient. Lowenstein turned up the heat on Rooney higher than it had ever been turned up before. He mobilized hundreds of volunteers and inspirited local reform organizations beyond any prior experience. With almost ferocious energy and intensity, he made his name and the change he symbolized known in each block of the district. By nearly everyone's account, he actually had put together enough pluses by primary day to outweigh the minuses. The crusade to create a new politics in Brooklyn, in New York, and in the country seemed on the verge of triumph. Except for one truth. "I don't think the Lowenstein people ever understood," a reporter mused, "that many of the regulars in one way or another depend on the machine for their *livelihoods*. Politics to them isn't a clash of principles, it's a battle for survival. They can't go anywhere else. You've got to beat them on their terms or not at all." What Lowenstein was about to learn was that "their terms" did not include handing victory to a liberal from outside the neighborhood.[31]

The first sign of things to come appeared shortly after the polls opened on June 20. Election board rules specified one voting machine for every 800 voters. At Cadman Place, a high-rise apartment that served as the polling place for one of the precincts where Lowenstein had the strongest support, only two machines had been installed instead of the four needed, and almost immediately, long lines formed. Many voters eventually got tired and left, but at the urging of Lowenstein poll watchers, many stayed. The last voter left Cadman Place at 2:30 A.M., almost five hours after voting was supposed to have ended. Elsewhere voters arrived at their usual polling place only to be told that, at the last minute, it had been moved— often as far as eight or nine blocks away. In one case, the new voting location for a pro-Lowenstein Puerto Rican neighborhood was an Italian social club with a sign outside saying "Members only." Countless voting cards were apparently "lost"; people who wished to pursue their right to vote were sent to election board judges downtown, to stand in another long line (except for one group of Hasidic Jews who received blank court orders allowing them to vote). Out of a total of thirty-eight hours of voting time lost due to machine breakdown, thirty-three occurred in districts favoring Lowenstein. "It was like suddenly being smacked in the face with powers against which you had no way of doing anything," Jenny noted. So much time and passion had gone into this struggle for a new kind of politics, one Lowenstein worker observed; but "our voters . . . [were] beaten by the *political* machine before they could even reach the *voting* machine." When it was over, Rooney had won by an 890-vote margin.[32]

Lowenstein was outraged. "He was like a madman," Eileen Dugan recalled; he shouted over and over again, "We've been cheated!" Tearful and shattered, the volunteers, who had worked so hard, experienced the sense of being betrayed and robbed, many of them for the first time. They, like Lowenstein, had believed in the system, had played by its rules, and now they had been shafted, their devotion thrown in their faces by the "old politics" they had striven so mightily to overcome. Always at his inspirational best in defeat, Al insisted that his supporters recognize how much they had won. Mike Pesci had been elected the state assembly candidate, Carol Bellamy the nominee for state senate. The reform movement had triumphed, not suffered defeat. And he, Allard Lowenstein, was part of that triumph. He had been robbed of a victory he had fairly won, but that venal act would not go unchallenged. The fight was not over.[33]

In retrospect, Lowenstein's decision to sue for a new election was one of the most momentous he ever made. Although later he and his closest associates claimed near unanimous backing for the court action from the Brooklyn reform movement, the evidence suggests that there was in fact widespread opposition. First of all, Pesci and Bellamy had won their races and Elizabeth Holtzman had defeated Emmanuel Cellar in the other Brooklyn congressional primary—all by narrow margins. A court victory for Lowenstein could logically mean that all these victories would be thrown out as well. Second, some people did not see the irregularities as that unusual. Rather than fraud, Carol Bellamy said, the election simply showed again the "total confusion, total incompetency, total stupidity . . . [of] the board of elections. . . . [It] was less venal and more just the inherent nature of New York City . . . elections." Third, and perhaps most important, large numbers of Lowenstein supporters knew a rerun would be disastrous. "Don't go after a special election," Eileen Dugan told Lowenstein. "You'll lose that even bigger. Leave [it] as having come so close, and come back and fight another day. Live among us, build up your career, and then you'll go back to Congress." For insurgents, election reruns were almost impossible to win. Other candidates like Bellamy and Pesci would not be on the ballot to draw votes, and the machine had a built-in advantage because of its organization. Significantly, the two major reform clubs that had invited Lowenstein to run in the first place bitterly disagreed with his decision to seek a new election.[34]

Why, then, did Lowenstein insist on challenging the election results in court? Surely, his own sense of grievance and outrage played a major role, especially when shared by a devoted youth following who looked to him to reflect and express their feelings of moral indignation. After all, how could he continue to be their knight in shining armor if he capitulated to corruption and, by accepting fraud, became an accomplice in evil? Yet, in reality, it was his own sense of being right that he most needed to defend and justify. His moral identity and commitment to the political system were at stake. He demanded—indeed, desperately needed—validation for that identity.[35]

And so the court challenge unfolded. Nominally mounted by a legal team headed by Robert Kennedy's former aide Adam Walinsky, the strategy and footwork were coordinated by a brilliant young lawyer named Harvey Lippman, who had been a Lowenstein disciple since meeting him at City College in the late 1960s. Directing a crew of student volunteers who stayed on through the summer, Lippman gathered hundreds of affidavits from voters who had been denied the ballot, searched through thousands of voter cards, and documented every instance of bias on the part of election officials. The trial judge was Charles Rubin, once the personal lawyer for Brooklyn boss Meade Esposito. Rubin told Lippman, "Look kid, there's no way you're going to win this case, but I'm not going to hurt you. I'm going to let you put on all the evidence you want." Those words were music to Lippman's ears. Not only could he develop his case fully, but he also would have a trial record on which to appeal. When Rubin predictably ruled against Lowenstein, Lippman noted, he "wrote such a bad opinion that it would easily be overturned." In fact, the appellate court unanimously reversed his decision on September 5, and seven days later, the court of appeals in Albany, by a three-to-two margin, ordered a new election. There had been 1,920 irregularities, the court held, making it impossible to determine who had fairly won the June primary. That night, Lowenstein's close friend Steve Morgan recalled, a feeling of exhilaration spread throughout the entire campaign staff. After nearly three months, justice had been done.[36]

In anticipation, Lowenstein sought to regather his scattered forces. Throughout the summer, the campaign flew in some volunteers who had gone home. Now the call went out to college students getting ready to return to their campuses. The court of appeals had set the new election date for September 19, leaving barely a week to mount a full-scale campaign. Lowenstein might have asked for a further delay but reasoned that a postponement would help Rooney by giving him time to crank up his machine. Once again, a parade of sports stars and celebrities descended on the district. Peter Yarrow came to sing. The popular baseball star Jim Bouton walked the streets. Jenny gave out more shopping bags. Rooney in turn distributed a leaflet headlined, "Don't Be Misled by a Tricky Outsider Who Was Rejected By His Own Constituents." A pamphlet printed in Yiddish accused Lowenstein of living in the Fort Greene area with enemies of the Jewish people. Just to make sure that all bases were covered, another pamphlet distributed in Polish and Italian areas urged voters to support Rooney, the Christian candidate.[37]

Election day confirmed the good sense of every Lowenstein supporter who had advised him not seek a rerun. A *Village Voice* reporter had written in June, "If [Lowenstein] does get the special election . . . all it will mean is an infinitely worse beating. Many of the local reformers will refuse to participate. . . . He'll be on his own against the regulars, and there's no way he can even come close." The reporter was right. Tony Scotto turned out the longshoremen as though there was a union convention. Busloads of Hasidim descended on the polls, while the Polish vote increased by 2,000. "The Brooklyn Democratic machine can turn its vote on like a faucet," the *New Yorker*'s commentator wrote, "but Mr. Lowenstein's margin would have had to come from black and Puerto Rican neighborhoods where only a huge job of organization can bring large numbers of people to the polls." Lowenstein had tried hard, even resorting to some of the machine's own tricks. Art Kaminsky spent $3,000 on fried chicken and special payments to black "leaders," seeking to attract Fort Greene voters. It all backfired. The chicken disappeared, but the votes never materialized.[38]

Lowenstein was crushed by this second defeat. One week earlier, he and his supporters were ecstatic in the belief that their cause had been upheld. Now it lay in tatters. "Al was very sad," Ann Feldman recalled. "It [had been] a very exciting occasion with all these people preparing for this great big reelection. He [gave me this look], and I knew what that meant. . . . It meant that he wasn't going to make it, and he knew that before it ever started." When Lowenstein took the platform that night, neither the inspiration nor the exhortation were there. "The speech that Allard delivered . . . was not at all like what I was used to," Ronald Tabak observed. "He was tired and visibly shaken."[39]

On the other side of town, meanwhile, the Rooney troops gathered for a celebration. With a margin of 3,000 votes, no one could contend that this election had been stolen (though Lowenstein and a few associates still made that claim). "We're beatin' him six ways to Sunday," a Rooney aide said. "Lowenstein won't know what hit him." Rooney himself had been upstairs collecting returns from his ward captains. Then, the reporter Pete Hamill wrote, surrounded by Hasidim, longshoremen, and his lieutenants, he headed into a crowd that was "packed with people from the neighborhood, women whose dresses weren't too chic, the guys with zipper jackets . . . who worked on the docks." Thirty more years, they chanted. Rooney moved to the speaker's rostrum flashing the V sign. Hamill concluded: "There were no students from other states, no Congressmen from California, no big spenders, or people using politics for therapy. Before him were the regular Democrats, and they had turned it on, perhaps for the last time."[40]

Despite its sarcasm, Hamill's column hit at least one nail on the head. Lowenstein's people, his staff, volunteers, and campaign workers, were indeed different from those who lived in the district. "It seems to me," Ken Sobol wrote in the *Village Voice,* "that there will probably never be a clearer case of the doctrinaire liberal's insensitivity to 'the people' than the Lowenstein campaign. It . . . never . . . occurred to them that the political traditions in the Italian, Polish, and Hasidic communities . . . might be different from those on the West Side of Manhattan." To reach these ethnic communities, one had to establish a personal relationship of credibility and trust. That was achieved by becoming part of the community, not by attacking as corrupt, old-fashioned, and unacceptable the personalized politics that for so long had prevailed in the community. Whatever the breakthrough experiences with poverty and ethnicity that some volunteers had, many in the neighborhoods saw their presence simply as an invasion by people with alien class, educational, and ethnic backgrounds. "The media [were] so busy pitting the people against the machine [and] the poor against the powerful," Sobol wrote, "that they never noticed that those terms [didn't] quite apply in a district [where] only the white liberals have any money and probably a majority of 'the people' still support the machine."[41]

Significantly, many of Lowenstein's closest allies and friends shared this assessment of the campaign. Notwithstanding her own intense involvement of Lowenstein's behalf, Ann Feldman observed that most people in the district saw the campaign as "total opportunism, except for those whose only issue was the war." Even blacks and Hispanics perceived Lowenstein as a carpetbegger, an impression that Feldman believed Lowenstein had reinforced by giving money to "expedient" black politicians. Pesci and Bellamy, the other reformers in the race, had run campaigns based on their roots in the local neighborhoods—roots that Lowenstein lacked. When Al came in with his volunteers, Ron Tabak observed, "many of the locals secretly resented the intrusion, deliberately excluding Al from their campaign efforts and in some cases working against him." Instead of going door to door and emphasizing local issues, Lowenstein had come in and attempted to define the election as a national referendum about the new politics. "Most of us," Steve Morgan noted, "thought that he was going out of his way to be confrontational and antagonistic."[42]

With few exceptions, politicians both friendly and hostile to Lowenstein agreed that the election could have been won—even with massive irregularities—had Lowenstein pursued another strategy. His campaign was well funded—$225,000 to Rooney's $73,000. If Lowenstein had concentrated his ample monetary and human resources on those areas already predisposed to his kind of candidacy, he could have developed a sophisticated voter turnout operation that would have become visible only on primary night and, potentially at least, would have left Rooney at the starting gate. Because the white liberal, black, and Puerto Rican areas were not Rooney's to begin with, he would not even necessarily have been aware of the full strength Lowenstein was marshaling. Conversely, by ignoring Rooney's districts in the white ethnic areas, Lowenstein might have lulled the Brooklyn machine into relative complacency.

Instead, Lowenstein chose the exact opposite strategy. Everytime he brought Geraldo Rivera into Spanish Williamsburg or Ron Dellums into Fort Greene, he headlined the extent to which an ethnic war was under way. When he poured volunteers into Hasidic Williamsburg rather than concentrate them in areas friendly to his candidacy, he rubbed salt in a wound. Everytime an affluent white college volunteer canvassed a Polish longshoreman's family in Greenpoint, that visit represented a foreign invasion as much as an offering of help and community service. As Ronald Tabak later wrote, "Lowenstein's constant presence in the white ethnic communities succeeded only in serving as a reminder of an upcoming election where they would vote against him." Every drumroll of the Lowenstein operation in those areas was like a wake-up call to the machine, with the result that the white ethnic vote for Rooney actually increased in 1972. Lowenstein was even brash (and stupid) enough to attack directly Meade Esposito, the Brooklyn boss who was not even that much of a fan of Rooney.[43]

As symbol, champion, and practitioner par excellence of the new politics, Lowenstein had always enjoyed a reputation for being a political wizard. His old friend Barney Frank called him "the best strategist and one of the best technicians around." Another longtime Lowenstein aide compared him to a chess player who sees eight or nine or ten moves ahead while the people all around him see only three or four moves ahead; when Al was able to "play the game," he said, "move the pieces . . . develop the logic of the situation, the results that were achieved speak for themselves." After all, was this not the person who had run the National Student Association for years, helped organize the Mississippi Freedom Vote, and led the movement to depose a sitting president?[44]

Yet the Brooklyn election experience fundamentally undermined that image of political brilliance and strategic efficacy. From the point of view of pragmatic politics, it could be argued that every decision Lowenstein made in the race was wrong. He listened to almost no one. "If you challenged a decision that he had made," one of his protégés observed, "he never felt he could trust you again." Friends learned to be indirect and oblique when raising alternative points of view. It was perhaps for that reason that Lowenstein went through so many advisers and campaign coordinators during the Brooklyn race, and that he never chose a manager who had the authority and standing to confront him directly with an opposing opinion. Despite Lowenstein's reputation, his friend Howard Berman, a California congressman, commented,

> [he] didn't know politics in a certain sense. . . . He was so into the grand message. [He believed] that personal magnetism was what got you elected . . . but in a district of 500,000 people, it's impossible for everybody to know your personal magnetism. And some people would be put off and scared by it [anyway]. . . . Al needed somebody to do the kinds of things that are just sort of pedestrian vote-getting. . . . Instead, [he] requir[ed] that an absolute majority of all the voting district [feel] personally that he [was] God's gift to the world."[45]

As much as in any other campaign of his life, Lowenstein made such a purist appeal the crux of his congressional race in Brooklyn. He would not accommodate the political realities of the status quo; instead, one campaign worker wrote, "[he] directly challenged the [entire] local power structure and value system." Because what was at stake was not a momentary political contest, but an ultimate principle. At issue was the idealism of converting all voters, regardless of their ethnic origins, to reform within the system—hence the compulsion to take the battle to Williamsburg and Greenpoint, to carry on a crusade, no matter how unlikely its success. Hence also Lowenstein's determination to be vindicated. "He was tormented by the fact that he thought he should have won," Eileen Dugan said.[46]

Inevitably, Lowenstein himself became the cause, and the cause in turn became one he could not give up no matter how impossible the quest or counterproductive and self-defeating the consequences. Thus the final scene from the Brooklyn campaign. Because he had been chosen as the Liberal party's nominee for Congress as well, Lowenstein's name would remain on the ballot in November unless he chose to withdraw. What should he do? Lowenstein asked his friends. With near unanimity, they advised him to pull out, recognizing the absurdity of the situation. But if he dropped out, Lowenstein told Jenny and Andrew Roffe, a campaign aide, he would be "letting the community down and destroying everything that had been developed as to grass-roots involvement." Only if there was an incontrovertible excuse to withdraw could he pursue that course. At which point, Roffe wrote, Jenny turned to him and "broke the tension, saying 'If you'd like, I'll remove a breast.'"[47]

Lowenstein stayed on the ballot, continued to bring in volunteers, and campaigned on Brooklyn's streets through the fall. It was his third campaign of 1972 against John Rooney. To a few Lowenstein disciples, his decision represented the ultimate act of heroism and commitment to principle at any price. "He's managed the triumphant feat of losing three times in a single summer," Jeff Robbins later commented. "He knew that. He knew all that. Yet knowing that, he chose to put himself through it . . . [and I] just . . . watched the beauty of [his] pressing on." To others, however, his decision simply reinforced a growing concern about where Al was going, and why. "It was the campaign that never ended," Jenny said.[48]

TRYING TO FIND A PLACE

Even for a congenital liberal optimist, the end of 1972 and beginning of 1973 offered little basis for hope. When Allard Lowenstein launched his "dump Nixon" youth crusade in the spring of 1971, he repeatedly declared that the nation was at the most important turning point in its history. It would either plummet further into cynicism, despair, and resignation or recapture the spirit of Robert Kennedy and leap forward to embrace a new coalition whose achievements would dwarf even those of the New Deal. "Which way we move from here, and likely for many years to come," he wrote, "devolves on the man who is elected [president] in 1972." That man was Richard Nixon; his opponent, George McGovern, won just a single state; and Lowenstein himself, in a campaign of "light against darkness," had gone down to defeat three times. What would he do now with his mission to reclaim America?[49]

During the next two years, Lowenstein pursued a series of sometimes frenetic efforts to find an answer to his own personal and political dilemma. He continued to jet across the country exhorting students to engage in political struggle and resist the evils of the Nixon administration, and he taught classes at Hunter, the New School, and Johnson State University in Vermont where his old friend Bill Craig was now chancellor. Between dividends from the family restaurant business, lecture fees, and teaching salaries, he managed—barely—to support his family. But beneath these concerns, a fire still burned propelling him to seek public office. He had become like an addict. Having staked his identity and career on a definition of himself as the embodiment of a new politics of righteousness, he could not retreat from the field of battle without vindication from the people in whose name he was fighting. Where and how he would find his salvation remained unclear. Frequently in 1973 and 1974 he seemed confused and bewildered by his options. But the quest would not end—could not end—until vindication was his.[50]

Lowenstein's most logical option was to stay where he was and run again from the fourteenth in 1974. By July, leaders of Brooklyn community groups were demanding that Rooney step down because he had answered only 3 of 319 roll calls; they talked in their press conference about Lowenstein as a logical replacement for Rooney. And by October, the Brooklyn Democratic machine had told Rooney it would not support another reelection bid. In addition, Rooney was aging and suffering from a series of health problems. Notwithstanding the debacle of the Liberal party race in November, Lowenstein was ideally situated to be the heir apparent. As Eileen Dugan remarked, "the district [would be] two years more liberal, [there'd be] new people coming in, [he'd have] roots, and [they] couldn't say he was a carpetbagger."

Repeatedly during the spring and summer of 1973, Steve Morgan reported, Lowenstein was told the seat was his if he wanted it. Perhaps sensing Lowenstein's troubled soul, Lawrence Spivak, the acerbic host of

NBC's "Meet the Press," urged his young friend to stop going off in so many different directions. "One of these days," he wrote, "you'll learn to limit your activities and target your goals, and if you do, I think you will be amazed at how much more you will accomplish." For the moment, it seemed that Lowenstein might take Spivak's advice. He opened an office in the fourteenth to provide assistance to constituents needing help (as if he were, in fact, their representative) and recruited a staff of volunteers to engage in community service.[51]

Yet already his gaze had shifted to the possibility of running for the Democratic nomination to oppose U.S. Senator Jacob Javits, who was up for reelection in 1974. Ever since 1968, Lowenstein had wanted that seat. Robert Kennedy and Steve Smith had urged him to run for it as "their" candidate, and he had almost done it; only the ultimately irreconcilable tensions between Kennedy and Eugene McCarthy prevented him. Again in 1970 Lowenstein toyed with the idea of a Senate candidacy, especially when his congressional district was gerrymandered. That year he probably could have won the primary and the general election in a three-way race with Republican Charles Goodell (whom Nixon refused to support) and Conservative James Buckley. But Goodell was Lowenstein's friend, and he had decided to run for reelection to the House. Now, by late spring 1973, Javits was up for reelection, the Watergate scandal had begun to explode, and Lowenstein started champing at the bit.[52]

Already, veteran Lowenstein staffers were wary. Harriet Eisman and Mimi Perr, two devoted and loyal aides, were apprehensive about another race beginning barely six months after the last Rooney election. Gary Hart and Jim Haas, two Stanford protégés, shared their concern. "Another defeat would be so hard to take," they wrote. Yet by the end of May, word was out that Lowenstein was interested. Using his credentials as a Democratic National Committee member, he embarked on a "fact-finding" mission upstate. The *Wall Street Journal, New York Times,* and other papers began to print reports that Lowenstein was considering a Senate campaign. Ironically, at just the moment Lowenstein was being reassured that the congressional nomination in Brooklyn was his for the asking, he started to walk away from it. "Take it, Al, take it," his friend Steve Morgan pleaded. But, "if Al didn't want to hear something, he didn't hear it." Thus, his Brooklyn allies were left holding their breaths in suspense—all the while risking the loss of the prize of the fourteenth congressional district nomination—as Al embarked on what amounted to a twelve-month flirtation with running for the U.S. Senate.[53]

What proved most maddening about Lowenstein's course of action was his total—and by now predictable—inability to make a decision. Unwilling to reject out of hand his dream of becoming a U.S. senator, he engaged in an almost endless "testing of the waters" for the Senate race. Yet he could not afford to renounce the Brooklyn possibility, lest he decide to end up there. The scenario was infuriating for supporters who were committed to one or the other alternative. "[I've] heard troubling things about the Senatorial bit," wrote Father Richard Neuhaus, one of his early 1972 backers in Brooklyn, "*and* about where things may be going with the Congressional race in the 14th." Some of Lowenstein's young devotees had even moved to Brooklyn, settling there almost solely because of their commitment to working for him in the fourteenth. The longer Lowenstein waited, the more likely it was that someone else would step into the vacuum. Already by the late fall of 1973, friends were alerting him to rumors of other possible candidates for Rooney's seat.[54]

Nor did the situation clarify with the passage of time. Indeed, if anything it became even murkier. Another round of redistricting was under way in Brooklyn and would inevitably affect the fourteenth. One criterion for redistricting was making it possible for a minority member to be elected. Running for the Senate, on the other hand, involved taking on a distinguished liberal Republican with a record on the war, social welfare, and even Richard Nixon that was more that of a progressive Democrat than of a conservative Republican. Javits boasted strong labor union support and, well in advance of other Republicans, had indicated he might support impeachment of Nixon over Watergate. A statewide senatorial campaign required huge sums of money and could not be run off peanut butter sandwiches and volunteers. Moreover, Lowenstein was no favorite of the state Democratic organization, which ever since 1968 had regarded him as a loose cannon. Most of Lowenstein's political allies still believed Brooklyn offered the best option, if only he would commit in time. Sensing Lowenstein's reservations, Andrew Tobias wrote: "It must be galling to have to run yet again for a seat that was rightfully yours before." Yet the odds of winning were overwhelming, especially compared with the Senate race.[55]

Then a new variable appeared. Lowenstein's old district on Long Island had also been reapportioned, and this time his home in Long Beach and the liberal Democractic Five Towns area were made part of the new district, now represented in Congress by the veteran Republican John Wydler. Although even more Republican demographically than the earlier

386

district had been, the new district had potentially more liberal Republicans, and Wydler seemed vulnerable on Nixon and Watergate. In one more manifestation of a classic Lowenstein draft, Democrats from Long Island pleaded with him to come back there and run. Or, as one Lowenstein staffer put it, "they were desperately eager to have him."[56]

If multiple options in the midst of chaos was his definition of happiness, Lowenstein was in his element. Three separate possibilities awaited him, he was the desired object of attention in all three, and infinite variations could be played with in the process of finally making a decision. For one who took perverse joy from the process of teasing out potential courses of action, it was a time of intrigue, concentration, and intellectual challenge. Never one to simplify, Lowenstein toyed with different ideas for preserving his freedom. Through an intermediary, for example, he suggested to Arnie Miller that *he* secure the Long Island designation for Congress with the understanding that if Al then decided not to run for the Senate or for Congress from Brooklyn, Arnie would step aside and let Al have the nomination. Similarly, Lowenstein broached to Brooklyn sources the idea of his taking the fourteenth congressional district seat for one or two terms, then resigning so that a black or Puerto Rican could take over. It was like the chess game that Lowenstein's aide used as a metaphor. Al took pure pleasure in plotting ahead eight or nine moves, calculating how everything might fall into place. The problem was that politics was not a chess game, there were other people involved, and they could not wait endlessly for all of Lowenstein's moves to work out.[57]

The New York State Democratic convention in June precipitated the crisis. Whatever his mixed signals to people on Long Island and in Brooklyn, the Senate was still Lowenstein's first choice. In his travels across the state over the preceding twelve months, he had met with an ambivalent response. Warmly received by former McCarthy backers and some Kennedy supporters, he nevertheless was perceived as marginal and something of an oddball by others. The field of candidates anxious to oppose Javits was not large. Lowenstein had won the endorsement of the peace-oriented New Democratic Coalition over the former attorney general Ramsey Clark, giving him a solid bloc of progressive delegates to the state convention. But the machine clearly wanted someone else, especially on a ticket that looked like it would be headed by gubernatorial candidate Howard Samuels and include Bronx politician Robert Abrams. "Look Al," the labor leader Victor Gottbaum allegedly told him, "can't you get it through your head? I need another Jew on this ticket like I need another asshole."

Faced with a possible slate of four Jewish males, party leaders pieced together a last-minute coalition backing the mayor of Syracuse, Lee Alexander, for the Senate nomination.

Fighting for his political life, Lowenstein pleaded with the delegates for their votes. His name had been placed before the convention well after midnight, and he did not take the podium until nearly 3:00 A.M. "Al was tired, and you could sense just how important this was to him," Harvey Lippman recalled, "and how desperate he was . . . to get the Democratic party designation and avoid having a costly, divisive primary," since with the legitimacy of party backing he could raise the money needed. "So he's screaming, he spoke faster than usual . . . [and] more loudly, and the line he kept repeating was, 'Let me at Javits, let me at Javits.'" Lowenstein's vote in fact was far higher than most people had expected. He won 39 percent of the delegates (Clark got 2 percent), but Alexander corralled the majority needed for the party designation. Lowenstein's percentage had qualified him for a place on the primary ballot should he choose to take his candidacy to the voters. But that would mean a long, expensive statewide campaign against Alexander and Clark (if Clark chose to run by petition) before he could even have the chance to "get at" Javits. Suddenly, things had gotten much more complicated, and Lowenstein had just two weeks to decide whether to have his name removed from the ballot.[58]

The pressure mounted. Lowenstein tried to strike a deal with Ramsey Clark and his manager Victor Navasky to drop out of the primary race, but Clark refused. (Al "absolutely despised" Clark, a Lowenstein confidant said.) That meant a three-way primary with two of the candidates going to the same financial well for resources. Lowenstein's friends from Congress weighed in. The overall situation, Don Riegle wrote, made it almost impossible to defeat Javits and go to the Senate. Moreover, Riegle pointed out, Lowenstein had to be aware of what such a race would mean "to your most dedicated workers and volunteers who would walk off cliffs on command. . . . I think one must protect others from harm. And I continue to worry greatly about the possibility of fruitless agony . . . that hits those less strong than ourselves." Others shared the same concern. "You had the courage and devotion to try to change things . . . at a fateful and critical time [in the 1960s] despite the conventional wisdom of cynical politicians," another associate wrote, "[but] one more loss and you are going to be called by many the Harold Stassen of liberal Democrats. That would be an especially cruel end to a political career which promised so much good." Why not stay in Brooklyn, the friend suggested, where there was abundant opportunity for success?[59]

There were few moves left on the chess board. Redistricting had been completed in Brooklyn. John Rooney had announced he would not seek reelection, and his campaign manager from two years earlier, a multimillionaire named Fred Richmond, had declared his intention to run. But Richmond was like Rooney; though younger and less identified with the machine, he could still be attacked effectively if Lowenstein based his campaign in the minority and white liberal communities. On Long Island, meanwhile, Wydler had placed some distance between himself and Nixon as Watergate hurtled toward a climax. And then there was the Senate. Lowenstein believed he could win the September primary, but would he have enough left to wage an effective race in only eight weeks against a liberal Jew?

Lowenstein's decision had to be conveyed to the state board of elections by a letter postmarked no later than midnight on June 30. He had convened a meeting of friends and campaign aides at his home to debate the choice. At 11:40, he dispatched Harvey Lippman to the Brooklyn post office with his official verdict: he would remove his name from the primary ballot in the U.S. Senate contest. Subsequently, he conveyed to others his decision about the other options. He would *not* seek the designation as the Democratic nominee to run for the seat vacated by John Rooney in the fourteenth. He *would* return to Long Island and accept the Democratic nomination to oppose John Wydler's reelection.

Most Lowenstein supporters were stunned. "I was livid," Jay Jacobson recalled. Jacobson met Lowenstein at the University of North Carolina in the 1960s, was a Vietnam combat casualty, and moved to Brooklyn to help Lowenstein in 1972. "Do you want to be in Congress or do you want to lose and be a martyr!" he exclaimed. "For crying out loud, get your shit together!" When Lowenstein responded that the redistricting was intended to choose a minority candidate, Jacobson said, "Bull shit. Fred Richmond is going to run and win unless you run and win. Do you want these people represented by Richmond or do you want them represented by you? That's the choice, that's the reality." To which Lowenstein responded: "No, that's not the reality unless I choose to make it the reality. . . . Case closed." Virtually all of Lowenstein's backers, past and present, shared Jacobson's assessment, including people from Long Island. "I cannot recall anybody of even mediocre intelligence," Jacobson concluded, "who didn't say, 'Run for Congress in Brooklyn' . . . [or] certainly run for the Senate before going to Long Island again." Yet the die was cast. The Lowensteins would change their residence once more. When the clock ran out and there was only one play left in the chess match, Lowenstein had made a move that, to most people, seemed inexplicable.[60]

He did, of course, have his reasons. Long Island offered the only contest in which Lowenstein could avoid a bruising primary battle. He would probably have defeated Richmond in the fourteenth district (although, had he opted for Brooklyn earlier that would not even have been necessary), and he might have prevailed as well against Lee Alexander and Ramsey Clark. (Clark won that race, suggesting that Lowenstein would have also.) On Long Island, by contrast, the party gratefully accepted his candidacy. Moreover, he was deeply loved by many people in the district. Name recognition was certainly no problem. Nor was money. And Wydler's mainstream Republican credentials—especially his association with Nixon—injected the moral element into the campaign that Lowenstein always needed. "If he didn't have an uphill battle," Steve Morgan noted, "he couldn't take it on. It had to be imbued with this sense of national significance or of great struggle." Or as Willie Vargas put it, "Maybe Al wanted to have a dragon to slay. . . . The dragon was [already] slain in Brooklyn."[61]

Yet even his most devoted followers felt little of the transcendent passion or exhilaration in the race against Wydler that they ordinarily associated with a Lowenstein campaign. The campaign workers might be the same as in the 1968 and 1970 races, but the atmosphere was not. The activist women in the community who literally had devoted their lives to the previous campaigns were now "wearing down," one campaign worker said. A large number of volunteers still appeared, but instead of excitement, Ellen Vollinger said, they displayed a sense of defeatism and asked, why was Al running here? "People got very petty, and [there] just wasn't [the same] sense of spirit." No one really thought the campaign could succeed, Vollinger observed, "and maybe that's because a lot of us had never given up the idea that we should have gone for some of the other [options]." The previous campaigns "were crusades," Greg Craig noted. "They were evangelical exercises." But now, as the *New York Times* declared, "Lowenstein has apparently outlived his radical reputation and emerged . . . as a low key candidate of 'middle-America.'"[62]

Worst of all, Lowenstein's decision to run on Long Island raised the carpetbagger issue to a new level, as though he intended to direct a spotlight on it. "I didn't like the move to Brooklyn and the move back again," one of his Long Island protégés said. "It's hard to accept someone's sincerity [about] trying to serve a constituency when the constituency is a moving target." Wydler played up his own association with Jewish causes and effectively defended his record in Congress. But his trump card was being able to say he was reliable and known, "[while] my opponent jumps around every two years." Disorganized, dispirited, and poorly run (there were three different campaign managers), the Lowenstein campaign could not escape its own credibility gap. "I don't care how you slice it," Art Kaminsky, one of the managers, said, "it's just a bad thing to have to say, 'I ran in district 1 in '66, district 2 in '68, district 2-A in '70, district 3 in '72, and now I'm back to district 4 in '74, plus I tried to run for the Senate a few times.' . . . It was a very difficult issue, particularly for a guy whose major appeal was his brilliance and his sincerity. He was really calling the sincerity into question."[63]

No matter how frenetically he raced across the district, prodded his volunteers, or tried to inspire his supporters, Lowenstein could not make this campaign work. His own energy level might have been the same; the ringing exhortations still conveyed a sense of moral urgency; but the campaign was like an empty shell, devoid of the substance and purpose that so often in the past had made a Lowenstein campaign special. On election day, John Wydler won 54 percent of the vote, Lowenstein 46 percent. There was no fraud—the voting machines had not broken down, nor had the board of elections conspired to deny the insurgent campaigner a fair chance. The voters had simply said no, leaving Allard Lowenstein to ponder what this meant for his vision of reclaiming America.

CONCLUSION

The early 1970s were not kind to Al Lowenstein or to American liberalism. Emerging from a devastating defeat at the hands of Norman Lent in 1970, Lowenstein had responded with a ringing reaffirmation of his faith in the American system and the power of rational debate and political principle to triumph over chicanery and manipulation. The journey that bullets had temporarily stopped in a Los Angeles kitchen in 1968 would be resumed, led by a generation of young Americans whose faith had been shattered by Robert Kennedy's death, but who now would lead the nation into an era of compassion, idealism, and political efficacy. If Lowenstein's defeat in 1970 symbolized victory for the forces of darkness, his role as champion of a youth crusade for political justice would symbolize resurgence and victory for the forces of light. It was a melodramatic script, almost destined to fail.

As events would have it, rather than win victory at the polls, Al suffered defeat four times in three years. Despite the rhetoric surrounding the voter registration drive, little had come of it. As had been the case with newly enfranchised women fifty years earlier, many of the prospective voters did not register, and those who did produced no political surprises. Lowenstein had prophesied that 1972 would be the most pivotal election in years. He was right, about both his own political history and that of the larger society. But it was a turning point not toward revitalization and victory but toward despair and defeat. The system had neither recovered nor been redeemed. Conservatism was in control.

Lowenstein responded to this series of developments in two ways. On the one hand, he began to entertain for the first time the possibility that the political process he had so fervently embraced might not be as pure and healthy as he had always assumed. On the other hand, he insisted—almost defiantly—that the more he and the country were victimized by manipulation and dishonesty, the greater was the need to commit even greater energy to the redemption of America and its electoral system. These apparently contradictory responses reflected the dynamics that would shape his political career for the rest of his life.

The first response grew from a personal sense of vulnerability, failure, and alienation. Going back to his feeling of physical inferiority as a child, Lowenstein had always been anxious about being accepted by other people. Now this string of defeats reactivated all his fears. "It was an embittering period for him," Steve Morgan recalled. On trips to explore the possibilities of a Senate race, "the Democratic leadership wasn't welcoming him the way he would have liked. . . . He was getting discouraged . . . about his own political opportunities." Harvey Lippman observed the same phenomenon traveling around New York City with Al. "He was beginning to be perceived as somewhat of a laughing stock in New York politics," Lippman said. "*Has-been* is too strong a word, but . . . he wasn't respected by people who clearly were not his equals. . . . I remember literally going with Al and watching him sneak into meetings where he wasn't invited—testimonial dinners and the like—where he wanted to be because he wanted to be seen. . . . It was sad, almost pathetic in a sense, to watch him have to go through that."[64]

In his own mind, Lowenstein made a connection between the way he was being regarded by the political establishment and the way he had been treated in the political process. He had been cheated out of victory in Nassau in 1970 by gerrymandering and smears; he had been cheated out of victory in Brooklyn in 1972 by voter fraud. In 1973, he learned that his name was number seven on Richard Nixon's "enemies list," a compilation by White House aides John Dean and Charles Colson—on Nixon's direct instructions—of those "who tried to do us in." "They are asking for it," Nixon told Dean in September 1972, "and they are going to get it." Lowenstein's name was on the list because of his leadership of the "dump Nixon" movement. Fascinated by the revelation, Lowenstein started to link his place on the enemies list with events of the preceding three years—the burglaries at the Pittsburgh and Austin voter registration offices, Murray Chotiner's role in the 1970 Lent campaign, rumors of J. Edgar Hoover's aid to John Rooney in the Brooklyn campaign, all the "screw-ups" that had occurred during the youth crusade.[65]

The linkage caused Lowenstein to speculate that he had been targeted by the "establishment," that his marginalization was no accident, and that a poison had been injected into the political system that threatened its basic integrity and health. "In the context of Watergate," one close aide recalled, "he began to develop . . . a set of concerns that led him to think he might have been naive in the past in dismissing possibilities about the misuse of power and the extent of sabotage of legitimate procedures . . . and that there might be a lot more wrong with how events transpired than he'd been prepared to accept." Jenny had the same sense, especially after Brooklyn. "What had begun to happen," she said, "was that with the revelations about the enemies list and stuff like that . . . there began to be [a feeling] that maybe we were—paranoia is too strong—but . . . fighting things you didn't know you were fighting." Lowenstein even told Steve Morgan that he had begun to question whether he was right to say that a person should work inside the political system. "It was the first cynicism about elective politics I ever heard from him," Morgan commented. In fact, Lowenstein was now entertaining the idea that the nation as a whole might be subject to powers totally beyond accountability. "This was a fundamental restructuring of his understanding of the political process," one personal aide concluded.[66]

On the other hand, there was a side to Lowenstein's personality that could view all these setbacks as perfectly logical. Far from challenging his worldview, they confirmed it, fitting right in with his perception that life was a constant struggle between good and evil, and that the more evil triumphed, the greater was the responsibility of good people to fight back. As far back as his election contests in college, Lowenstein had always seen defeat and victory as inextricably connected, defeat more often than not signifying moral victory, so that in a perverse way the prospect of winning actually signified moral defeat. Hence, his perpetual need to define issues in terms of light and darkness, and his utter inability to come to grips with short-term political realities—to do so would have been to call into question the very principles he stood for, to imply that winning was more important than standing fast for justice.

That offered at least a partial explanation for Lowenstein's political behavior in the early 1970s. "I think he lost elections because he probably chose areas that he couldn't have won in," Ann Feldman commented. "He always thought he could do the impossible and he came awfully close to it . . . but he just didn't choose easy things to do." Once a challenge was downgraded from the impossible to the doable, it became suspect. Hence, Lowenstein's otherwise inexplicable decision to say no to an almost certain win in the Brooklyn district where he had just spilled his blood and guts through three elections in four months. "Did the guy want to win?" his friend Jay Jacobson asked. "Maybe [not]. Maybe he always liked to tilt at a windmill. Maybe that was his motive for existence in life. Why go for something that is easy when you can have something harder, [even if you might] fail?"[67]

In that context, the key criteria for judging a political contest was how moral the issues were and how impossible the chances for winning. That was what made the "dump Johnson" movement Lowenstein's quintessential political act. As one of his protégés said, "He had to persist when everyone said, 'You're wrong.' . . . 'It can't be done.' . . . He ignored all of them and trusted himself and he persisted in spite of all the authorities." Ironically, once Lowenstein succeeded that one time, he was forever validated in *his* way of "doing" politics. He could ignore all the advice he received, no matter how high the authority. Who needed to plan as long as the cause was just? When Barney Frank or others pointed out that this time his choices really were impossible, Al would respond, "That's what they told me when I said we were going to dump Johnson." It was an airtight response, impenetrable by logic, sealed once and for all by Lyndon Johnson's abdication. Thus, while one side of Allard Lowenstein began to question for the first time the integrity of the political system, the other side simply took the experience of defeat as another sign that he was right and needed only to redouble his commitment to the struggle.[68]

More often than not, therefore, Lowenstein continued to preach the "impossible dream." "Now more than ever," he told an audience of Stanford students in 1973, "we must work to inform and arouse opinion." The odds against success had grown ever greater in light of the "desperate maneuverings of demagogues" in the White House and the power of assassins' bullets. "But the fact that these things are not easily done should propel us into working [even] harder to do them." Almost acknowledging the struggle in his own soul, Lowenstein admitted that some might call his reform goals unattainable. But with almost religious conviction, he affirmed that "we would have to work for them [anyway]." In a world where defeat meant victory, and victory defeat, part of him believed there was no other choice but to continue the struggle. "You are like Sisyphus pushing the rock eternally up the hill," a volunteer wrote him after the Brooklyn race, "and you will be out there by yourself doing it for the most part." Inspired by his example, Jeff Robbins declared that Lowenstein represented "the closest thing to good versus bad that I would ever see in my life. . . . In the course of knowing Lowenstein, I came to see what a special thing it is for people to give their all in an effort that, more likely than not, won't be successful. . . . Lowenstein was not afraid to lose."[69]

The early 1970s thus severely tested Allard Lowenstein's credo and identity. His vision of reclaiming America not only remained far in the distance; he had found his own association with that vision repeatedly challenged and rejected. To an ever increasing extent, he had become marginal in other people's eyes. It was almost as though his determination to shape his own destiny were under assault. "The more he got defeated," his friend Nancy Steffen said, "the more he got into a sort of . . . will struggle within himself." Was each defeat just one more trial to measure whether he, like Job, could retain his faith? Or was it a sign that who he was and what he believed were fundamentally open to question?[70]

In the midst of all this, Sandy Friedman wrote Lowenstein a letter. It was time, Freidman told his friend, for Al

> to renounce once and for all your father's old and altogether inappropriate image of you as an overly idealistic, somewhat dilettantish also-ran, and renounce as well the MacKinlay Kantor idyll [that you embody purity]. Neither notion was ever the least bit authentic—except as you yourself endowed them with authenticity. . . . You have made yourself into one of the most skillful and experienced politicians in the country. . . . For you to acknowledge that would in no way be arrogant, immodest, hubristic, or any of the other things you spoke of apprehensively last

night. On the contrary it is your absolute responsibility as a human being to recognize at last the "I" you have become, the "I" you are — to affirm unequivocally that "I" as yours. . . . To do otherwise would be to shirk your destiny. . . . And I hope it's clear that what I am talking about has nothing to do with winning or losing, but simply with being.

Friedman had zeroed in on the problem. It was all about who Allard Lowenstein was, not just politically but personally. The old answer that Lowenstein had given to that question of identity was now under severe scrutiny; it had been given "one last chance" and had not passed muster. As Jenny said, "There began to be a sense [in Al that] . . . you were fighting things you didn't know you were fighting. . . . That's a sense that grew . . . [and] I think it began to get to Al in ways that he didn't understand and couldn't face." Whether out of that confusion there could come a new answer was not clear.[71]

In 1963 and 1964, Lowenstein played a major role in recruiting hundreds of white students to go to Mississippi to help blacks fight racism. Bob Moses (pictured here) coordinated the Freedom Vote and Freedom Summer campaigns, but tensions over who should control the movement and who should participate eventually led to a split between Lowenstein and Moses. (Photograph copyright Danny Lyon/Magnum Photos)

By the second half of the 1960s, Lowenstein was devoting most of his time to protesting the war in Vietnam, seeking to persuade people like these to channel their energies into mainstream antiwar politics.

In 1966, Lowenstein met and married Jennifer Lyman, who became his political partner and confidante, as well as the mother of his children. A descendant of the New England aristocracy, Lyman fulfilled all of Lowenstein's dreams of a perfect mate.

In 1966 Lowenstein also began his close association with Robert Kennedy, who became his final political hero.

As leader of the Dump Johnson campaign in 1967–68, Lowenstein tried to persuade Robert Kennedy to run. Then when Kennedy did become a candidate, he sought—unsuccessfully—to win Lowenstein's endorsement. On a bus ride back from a New York state convention, Kennedy penned this note to Lowenstein in praise of his courage and character. Lowenstein treasured the note and showed it to all his friends as a testament to his closeness with Kennedy.

By the time Lowenstein served as congressman from Long Island's 5th district (1968–70), Jenny and Al had two children. Jenny campaigned for Al, and campaign literature featured pictures of the family, emphasizing their Long Beach roots.

After being gerrymandered on Long Island and losing his seat there in 1970, Lowenstein decided in 1972 to run against John Rooney in Brooklyn's 14th Congressional District—an area full of ethnic and racial tensions between Hasidic Jews, blacks, Poles, and Puerto Ricans.

In the Brooklyn race, as well as his 1970, 1974, and 1976 congressional runs on Long Island, Lowenstein attracted support from numerous celebrities. Pictured in the top photo are Warren Beatty, Andrew Young, and Coretta Scott King, and in the bottom photo, George Segal and Buck Henry.

Throughout the late 1960s and 1970s, Lowenstein appeared repeatedly on such shows as "Meet the Press," "Face the Nation," and as shown here, William F. Buckley's "Firing Line." Despite their philosophical and political differences, Buckley endorsed Lowenstein for Congress on multiple occasions, and had Lowenstein as a guest on his show more often than any other politician.

September 9, 1971

MEMORANDUM FOR: JOHN DEAN

FROM: CHARLES COLSON

I have checked in blue those to whom I would give top
priority. You might want to check someone else although I think you will find this is a pretty good list.
Right on!

6.   STEIN, HOWARD
     Dreyfus Corporation
     New York

     ✓

     Heaviest contributor to Mc Carthy in '68. If Mc Carthy
will receive the funds.

7.   LOWENSTEIN, ALLARD
     Long Island, New York

     ✓

     Guiding force behind the 18 year old "dump Nixon"
vote drive.

8.   _____

     Leading executive at Common Cause

     ✓

Suffering defeat after defeat, Lowenstein started to feel that he might be a victim of
international sabotage from the powers that be. His appearance as number 7 on
Richard Nixon's "enemies list" reinforced his suspicions.

15
Coming Apart

AFTER HIS DEFEAT IN THE 1974 CONGRESSIONAL RACE, ALLARD LOWEN-stein's world gradually disintegrated. Having already started to question whether the political system might be poisoned, he decided to focus his energies directly on the event that precipitated his own sense of despair—Robert Kennedy's assassination. With a logic that was both compelling and frightening, he reasoned that if evidence suggested a cover-up of the Kennedy assassination, then all that came after it might reflect the same unaccountable forces of evil that had derailed the "impossible dream" of 1968. In other words, Lowenstein decided to grapple with the demon of conspiracy. The Kennedy assassination became for him a test case of whether the system had fair and just answers or had been taken over by insidious agents. If the verdict were negative, he would have final confirmation that his own defeats were attributable to evil influences determined to crush anyone who stood up for the right. Hanging in the balance were his political identity and the worldview to which he had committed himself.

Even more at risk during these years was Lowenstein's personal identity. After almost three decades of incessant pursuit then avoidance of intimacy, Lowenstein had wooed and won the hand of a woman who matched perfectly his ideal—Jenny was witty, charming, attractive, and a Boston

Brahmin. But what did marriage and children mean? How did being a husband and father alter the personality of someone dedicated to a lifestyle of incessant motion? What about the young men in Lowenstein's life who for so long had provided a focus of attention even in the midst of his peripatetic wandering? Sometimes, Lowenstein dealt with these terrifying questions in a conscious manner, seeking answers to who he was and where he fit in. More often, he practiced denial and rationalization, finding ways of armoring himself that would ward off the necessity of making basic decisions. But ultimately, he could not escape the dilemma. The contradictions that drove him in different directions eventually ripped asunder his marriage as well.

All of this occurred in a context where the American liberal tradition, to which Lowenstein had so devoted himself, was also in the process of disintegrating. The personal and the political had always operated interdependently in Lowenstein, but rarely was their synergy so sharply focussed as at this time. The liberal creed of seeking racial and social justice along with an expanding economy seemed to lose its vitality and appeal in the 1970s—perhaps a function of its contradictory impulses to improve the lot of some without taking anything away from others. In the meantime, the personal lifestyle Lowenstein had clung to as a means of coping with his own contradictory impulses was slowly unraveling, precisely because those impulses had become so self-destructive. Instead of carrying him to safety, his drive to transcend the moment through constant motion turned upon itself. The result was a head-on collision that shattered the foundations on which he had built his life.

A POLITICAL QUEST FOR ANSWERS

Allard Lowenstein devoted more time and mental energy to ruminating about the death of Robert Kennedy than to almost any other political event of his lifetime. Kennedy's assassination both provoked in Lowenstein searching thoughts about the meaning of life and crystallized his deepest hopes and fears about "making a difference" through individual political activity. "One part of growing older is getting used to death," Lowenstein wrote. "We learn to live knowing our own lives may end at any moment . . . so we make peace with Death, accepting each loss as best we can . . . finding strength in hopes of a reunion beyond, or solace in memories of a shared past. . . . But these things have not helped in the death of Robert Kennedy. We are unprepared for a wound that does not ease, for a loss that grows more immediate and total as time passes, for a death more unacceptable now than when it occurred."

The meaning of Kennedy's death for American political life was enormous. "Not too long ago," Lowenstein said, "there was this man amongst us who thought it was never too late; who mocked odds and captured peaks, and took all of it and made it come out better for all whose lives he touched." This was the RFK who proclaimed after coming out of the iron mines of Chile that if he lived there, he would be a Communist, too, and who became speechless with rage after seeing one Mississippi child after another with a bloated belly from malnutrition. But there was a poignant personal identification as well. "He died . . . before he could help in my campaign or I in his. Like so many others . . . who were touched by his prophetic life, I find myself wondering what he would do if he were here, [and] wondering what he would think I should do. . . . What a wrong it would be if the ultimate monument to him, who more than anyone tried to show that an individual could make a difference, should be the end of individual effort to make a difference among those who shared his hopes and goals." Not only had Kennedy died before Lowenstein could join his crusade, but his death had also set in motion the decline of liberalism's appeal to the American people.[1]

How natural, then, that Lowenstein should seek the answer to what had transpired politically in America since 1968 by going back to that moment when the world turned upside-down, when Kennedy fell before an assassin's bullets in a Los Angeles hotel kitchen. The almost palpable victory for peace and insurgent reform had suddenly evaporated into thin air. Ever since, Lowenstein's efforts to carry the Kennedy torch and reclaim his vision had been frustrated, taken away by gerrymanders, political dirty tricks, and voter fraud. What if the lesson of the entire experience was that the political system itself had been taken away from the people by Kennedy's assassination? And if so, taken away by whom?

Lowenstein had been approached by people interested in the Kennedy assassination ever since his election to Congress. But for the most part, he dismissed them as crackpots. After all, Sirhan Sirhan had written explicitly of his hatred for Kennedy, and everybody had seen him fire the pistol. But then Lowenstein started to see a pattern of outside interference and malfeasance in his own political life, from the burglary of office files in the 1971 voter registration drive to alleged FBI intervention on behalf of John Rooney in 1972. "The enemies list was my personal trip wire," he later wrote. "I began wondering why I assumed that only obscure people could arouse illegal meddling. If the White House, the CIA, the FBI, the IRS, and other prime instruments of an impartial government could be used against civil rights groups, churches, members of Congress, and anyone else who incurred official displeasure, *clearly someone, somewhere, might have organized some of the events that had changed America.* The implications of that possibility were staggering, and drove me to take a belated look at the assassinations." Indeed, Lowenstein filed suit in federal court against the Nixon administration for depriving *him* of his constitutional rights.[2]

Lowenstein was aware of the behemoth he was taking on. "They are there," he wrote, "they are powerful . . . they have allies . . . in politics and the professions and the media and the banks." The very strength of this force was terrifying. "In the end, no one knows what is in the ultimate computer. . . . When it becomes unclear which are the forces of law enforcement and which of organized crime . . . then it is not difficult to understand why an atmosphere of fear develops. . . . It takes no imagination at all to understand that things can be planted in rooms that can be raided. . . . Who doesn't have something they don't want known? . . . Who doesn't have a relationship that can be made to look embarrassing?"

He also understood the potential price he might pay among friends and valued associates. The Kennedy family had always resisted inquiries into the assassinations because they reawakened painful memories. "I guess they felt that there's lots of ways you can turn your psychic energy," the Kennedy nephew Steven Smith, Jr., said, "and that turning it toward something that was obsessed with the past . . . was not the way to turn it." Smith recalled his father coming home after seeing Lowenstein and reporting, "[Al] was just . . . nutty about this." Running the risk of being shunned by the family whose favor he most prized was no small gamble. Nor was the danger that friends in high places might raise an eyebrow about this new "crusade." "He was involving himself with something that seemed like it was [lunatic fringe]," one of his young friends said. "Getting [identified with] this nonmainstream issue was hardly the kind of thing which was going to make him seem like a player among all the players."[3]

Yet in classic Lowenstein fashion, the very risks of the enterprise appeared to enhance its appeal as a morally compelling venture. "Those of us who preach the electoral process as the way to decide policies and leadership," he wrote, "have a special obligation to try to find out if somewhere there is a group (or groups) that has aborted the electoral process for its own purposes, and that could do so again." Shying away from asking the tough questions only made easier the triumph of those who might be wielding power in an unaccountable way. "In our agony we have instinctively recoiled from exploring the murky abyss in which may have been interred some of our most cherished assumptions . . . the fantasy that God somehow made all Americans immune to the evils of political murder, [or] that only loose nuts could possibly be involved in these crimes." Thus, to Lowenstein, it became the highest order of heroism to be willing to ask such unpopular questions. "To him," a close friend said, "this was . . . fundamentally [a question] about democracy. If you take any of the things he'd been involved in throughout his life—the 'dump Johnson' movement, the civil rights movement, Namibia [South-West Africa], Spain—it's all [about] people's right to determine their own fate. And in a free election, if your candidate is removed from that process [by violence], democracy is threatened." In Lowenstein's eyes, investigation of the Kennedy assassination was thus not an activity marginal to the mainstream, but a defense of the very heart of the political process.[4]

Lowenstein approached the inquiry from the framework of his training in the legal process, determined to give authorities in Los Angeles every opportunity to respond without facing sensational charges. "[Al] would have been an unbelievably good trial lawyer," his friend Gary Bellow, by then a Harvard Law School professor, noted. "What would happen to him is, he'd try on this new way of getting at [the case, finding] . . . the right combination of meaning and action." As he measured plausibility and evidentiary consistency, he used instincts and skills learned long before in law school. "He had a certain sense of pride of practice," Barney Frank recalled. Jenny agreed. "He could obsess for hours about the details of this," she said. "He would have made a brilliant detective. He loved evidence and mysteries."[5]

To demonstrate his bona fides as a responsible lawyer, throughout 1974 Lowenstein addressed questions about the assassination to the Los Angeles district attorney, Joseph Busch, and the Los Angeles Police Department (LAPD) without ever making a public statement. When it became clear that no adequate response would be forthcoming, however, Lowenstein moved his inquiries to the public arena. The day after his electoral defeat on Long Island in 1974, Lowenstein initiated contacts with the media that would soon make his questions a national news item. Paul Schrade, a close Kennedy associate who had almost been killed along with Kennedy, joined Lowenstein at press conferences in New York and

Los Angeles in December. Over the next few months, Lowenstein appeared on many televised talk and news programs, including interview shows with Tom Snyder, David Susskind, and Mort Sahl, and a CBS news special with Dan Rather. He also wrote articles for newspapers and magazines, initiated a lawsuit, and used every instrument at his command to compel a response from California officials. Investigating the RFK assassination was one of the longest sustained ventures of Lowenstein's life, a fact that reflected just how important it was in his eyes.[6]

The questions posed by Schrade and Lowenstein all revolved around a single issue: was Sirhan Sirhan the sole gunman in the kitchen of the Ambassador Hotel on June 5? A variety of evidence suggested that the question had never adequately been explored by the Los Angeles police. The autopsy report, for example, indicated that the fatal bullets had been fired at point-blank range into the back of Kennedy's neck, no more than two inches away. Yet not a single eyewitness placed Sirhan any closer to Kennedy than eighteen inches, and all said he was in *front* of Kennedy, facing him, not behind him. Sirhan's pistol could fire a maximum of eight bullets. Seven bullets were recovered, five from other wounded individuals, two from Kennedy. Yet police identified an additional three bullet holes in the ceiling tiles and another bullet in a door jamb. A bullet also exited Kennedy's chest, and another passed through the shoulder pad of his jacket. Police had removed the ceiling panels and the door jamb for evidence. If any bullets were embedded in these—as indicated in police photographs—it meant that anywhere between nine and thirteen bullets had been fired, prima facie evidence of a second gunman.

Reinforcing these questions were two other pieces of evidence. Contrary to every published report, eyewitnesses had identified a second pistol in the Ambassador kitchen, one that was drawn by a part-time security guard who was behind Kennedy. According to press reports, the guard had a right-wing past, and some witnesses claimed to have seen him fire his pistol. No tests were ever conducted on him or his gun to see whether the weapon had been fired. In addition, some ballistics experts testified that the bullet removed from Kennedy's neck could not have come from the same gun as the bullet removed from the bystander William Weisel. The Kennedy bullet featured only one cannelure—the concentric ring around the head of the bullet—and the Weisel bullet had two. The manufacturer of the bullets used by Sirhan indicated that it had never produced bullets with one cannelure, leading one forensic expert, the pathologist Professor Herbert MacDonnell, to conclude: "The bullet removed from Kennedy's neck could not have come from Sirhan Sirhan's revolver." Obviously, these questions were not frivolous.[7]

Some answers existed. Other eyewitnesses, for example, testified that just before Sirhan fired, Kennedy had turned to shake hands with someone, thereby putting his back to Sirhan rather than his front. If Sirhan had lunged forward, he might even have gotten very close to Kennedy. Police also explained that bullets that hit the ceiling might have ricocheted and wounded bystanders, reducing the total number of bullets in question. Finally, police declared that bullets fired from a gun identified as Sirhan's at the trial matched those recovered from Kennedy's body. Thus, the case for a cover-up, a second gunman, or a conspiracy was by no means as clear as the initial questions might suggest.

Yet the behavior of Los Angeles authorities simply spurred Lowenstein's suspicions. The gun test-fired by the police, allegedly to confirm that the fatal bullets came from Sirhan, had a serial number different from that listed in the court records as Sirhan's. When critics asked that the gun with the other serial number be retested, they were told it had been destroyed. For eighteen months, Lowenstein had pressed authorities to examine the ceiling panels and the door jamb, anticipating that doing so would at least clear up once and for all the issue of how many bullets had been fired. The LAPD made no response until August 21, 1975, when Police Commissioner Darryl Gates acknowledged that the panels and door jamb also had been destroyed—in June 1969, one month after Lillian Castellano stated in an article in the *Los Angeles Free Press* that two bullet holes were present in the door jamb. Lowenstein had requested nothing but routine criminal investigation procedures, all of them inexpensive and widely used. Yet he encountered only evasion and resistance.

Most infuriating and damning, from his perspective, was what appeared to be a common pattern of manipulation, distortion, and outright smear tactics, presumably designed to ridicule his inquiry and delegitimize the entire procedure. For example, the *Los Angeles Times* refused even to report the Schrade-Lowenstein press conference held in Los Angeles in December. But it then gave ample coverage to the district attorney's response, followed by an editorial condemning the Lowenstein operation as "wispy" and unwilling "to conclude that mundane facts can explain such fearful dramas." When the *Washington Post* published a story about Lowenstein's efforts, it misreported that one of the ballistics experts had changed his mind on the forensic evidence—thereby apparently discrediting Lowenstein—and then refused to correct the error. On a television panel, District Attorney Busch declared that "every eyewitness [agrees] . . . that Sirhan put that gun up to the Senator's ear and fired in there," then cited Karl Uecker as a primary case in point. Yet Uecker, the person standing closest to Kennedy, was Lowenstein's chief source for the assertion that Sirhan had never gotten within two feet of Kennedy. Finally, a CBS News report by Dan Rather on the assassination controversy was edited to cut Lowenstein off in midsentence, making him look like an irresponsible rabble-rouser. It was as if everyone was conspiring to sabotage Lowenstein's credibility and the seriousness of his mission. Whichever way he turned, Lowenstein found people apparently going out of their way to make him look like a fool.[8]

By the end of 1975, Lowenstein had become more convinced than ever that he was on to something, and that if nothing else, a conspiracy clearly existed to prevent him from pursuing his quest in a legal manner. Hilary Lieber, a former campaign aide, noted a "very dramatic change" in Lowenstein when he returned from working on the assassination; there were people out there, he told her, "trying to thwart social change." His writings reflected the shift. "No reasonable person who knows the facts can now profess to believe that the question of who murdered Robert Kennedy has been resolved," he commented in early 1976. "I do not know whether Sirhan acting alone murdered Robert Kennedy. I do know what happened when we tried to find out. Eventually, reluctantly, against all my instincts and wishes, I arrived at the melancholy thought that people who have nothing to hide do not lie, cheat and smear to hide it." As he deliberated on his experience, he drew his circle of logic ever tighter. "It's less and less a mystery whether there was a conspiracy," he wrote, "and more and more a mystery of why the truth must be distorted. There's no need for a conspiracy to conceal if there's no conspiracy to conceal." And then, as if to underline where he was heading in his thoughts, "There are people in this country who use murder to achieve political purposes."[9]

Beginning with a series of simple questions, Lowenstein had become enmeshed in a logic that brought him ever closer to the thinking of those he himself had once characterized as political crackpots. Now his inquiries had extended to the murders of John Kennedy and Martin Luther King, Jr., about which he found similar, equally compelling reasons to suspect cover-up and conspiracy. How could intelligent people not see the common patterns? he asked. "If there are forces that can wound democracy so cruelly, they are not likely to spring into existence simply on occasions of state murders." He then proceeded to link the assassinations of

Robert and John Kennedy to the mysterious disappearance of the Team-
ster boss Jimmy Hoffa and the murder of Sam Giancana—while "under
24 hour guard by the FBI"—because of his connection to John Kennedy
and the CIA. "The question," Lowenstein said, "is not really if there are
groups powerful enough to murder . . . famous people, but which of these
murders were committed by which groups, and which by none." Lowenstein was getting into "Mark Lane land," Jack Newfield said, as if he were
"paranoid after having an election stolen from him and being on Nixon's
enemies list." Other friends agreed. "The Sirhan thing became an idée
fixe," Nancy Steffen said, "[and] people who had known him for a long period of time sort of shook their heads."[10]

There were many, of course, who found Lowenstein's questions and lists
of connections completely coherent and persuasive. "Why is it," his aide
Greg Stone asked, "that all of the best leaders . . . all the most committed .
. . mobilizers of change . . . are no longer here?" Al had felt it "important
for someone in the political process . . . to address those kinds of issues."
Subsequently, others—including the Select House Committee on the Assassinations—would come to share the view that a conspiracy had probably existed, at least in the murder of John F. Kennedy, and another generation would appreciate even more Lowenstein's insight into the links between organized crime, the CIA, and political assassination. Lowenstein
had come a long way from the contention that the "system" was inherently
trustworthy, and that simply playing by the rules of the game would bring
justice and peace.

Perhaps most disturbing, he began to see himself as the victim of a
conspiracy as well. How else to explain what had happened in his political career over the past half decade? As Greg Stone commented, Al had
been "gerrymandered three times in a row because presumably he represented forces [that threatened] . . . the people in control"; he had been
dismissed by the media, which distorted his views and the evidence on
the assassinations; and in 1970 and 1972, his campaigns had been sabotaged by the Nixon administration's dirty tricks. *Everything* now became
explicable as part of a plot to get him. Lowenstein had begun his investigation of the Robert Kennedy assassination with the hope of ending, once
and for all, the notion that an all-powerful evil force existed and was committed to crushing the forces of good. By the end, he had concluded that
he was the latest victim of this conspiracy—the logical heir of his hero,
Robert Kennedy. Allard Lowenstein remained in his own mind a figure of
courage who had stood up—and would stand up again—to fight the good

battle. But no longer did he do so as a buoyant champion of the existing political process, celebrating its integrity and virtue.[11]

A PERSONAL QUEST FOR ANSWERS

One feature of Lowenstein's life that remained constant was his nearly insatiable appetite for intense relationships with the young people he met in the course of his travels. The number of lives he touched seemed almost infinite. Heartfelt, emotional attachments emerged wherever he went. Virtually without exception, they took the form of mentor relationships; as in the past, Lowenstein occupied the role of guru and inspirational leader. Ordinarily, the strongest bonds occurred with men. Sometimes, those relationships entered a physical phase; when that happened, it almost always involved someone who was not Jewish. Like a heartbeat, the drive for these ties accompanied Lowenstein wherever he went. Occasionally, he puzzled over the implications for other parts of his life. Usually, he just proceeded as if there were no conflict or problem. The only thing that was clear was that the drive would not go away.

In the late 1960s and 1970s, Lowenstein continued to play the confessor role he had developed to perfection during his own college years and his time at Stanford and Yale. Young people who were vulnerable, insecure, and in need of solace, support, and guidance would open their souls to him. "It filled a great need of mine just to have somebody that I could talk with [at that point in my life]," one former student noted. By offering a friendly ear, genuine interest, and the wisdom of experience, Lowenstein quickly drew such people to him. "Al could talk about personal things," Gary Bellow said, "[in a way] that would often just totally capture people." As a result of these conversations, young people continued to develop uniquely dependent and devoted relationships with him. "The only true good thing I have is our closeness," a student wrote him from Paris in 1967, "and it gives me some feeling of what might be. . . . Someday, some of us may give to you in return instead of always drawing on your strength." Another young friend expressed even more powerfully this sense of specialness. "I want to be back talking to you," he wrote.

> I am far away from the two days [we spent] and I suppose I really want to reaffirm the somewhat incredible fact of their reality. . . . I know when I read this over it will sound unusual to me and I will think perhaps I am overestimating our closeness, but I am going to say it anyway because

you told me I could. . . . I guess my fumbling around in the last few lines is my attempt to answer your question that day I left . . . as to how I felt. I feel so good and so bad, bad because I'm three thousand miles away [from you].[12]

The metaphor of "touch" ran throughout the discourse on these relationships. "Maybe what I will learn," one friend wrote, "is that all it takes to break down barriers is simply to reach out and touch—and maybe the things that reap the most rewards are the things that involve the most risk." Al was someone "hungry for touch and affection," his blind Stanford friend John Kavanaugh noted. "When you were with him, you were his and he was yours—[it was a] sense of almost merging that captivated so many people, that he thrived on."[13] It is not surprising that many of Lowenstein's relationships with male friends continued to end with hugging and sleeping in the same bed, a tangible expression of the closeness they had developed. As one of these men recalled, "It was something . . . that seemed very genuinely affectionate and close and mostly not sexual. . . . I felt that for me a certain amount of hugging and affection was consistent with the very intense experience I had of being a participant in his life, and of the interest that he seemed to take in mine."[14]

Yet the erotic overtones of these relationships posed a dilemma for at least some of Lowenstein's friends, especially those who knew Jenny or were themselves involved with wives and women friends. In the past, Lowenstein had told one friend "that physical relations of this very circumscribed type [were] just fine, but if ever they got [you] away from the primary relationship in your life, which was your wife or girlfriend, then you would have to choose." Another close friend described a similar scenario. The two had become close initially on a long drive during which they talked about the problem of sexuality. Lowenstein described a relationship he had with a man in Denmark in the 1950s, and his own feelings about being able to express physical affection with men. That night, they ended up in the same bed. "Al asked to embrace, and we did," the friend said. "I told him that I wasn't interested in anything sexual . . . and he said, fine, that's what he wanted, too. And that basically is what happened, that kind of embrace and staying in the same bed. It was never orgasmic . . . and I believed what he told me, that he wasn't interested in consummating sex, and that this was something that was wholly supportive and not undermining of his relationship with his wife."[15]

Through such justifications, Lowenstein deflected for the moment any conflict that he or his friends might experience over the fact that he had a wife and family. "I don't think getting married represented a break from who he was before," John Kavanaugh declared. At times during these years, Al told a friend with whom he shared a bed that he loved him; yet at the same time he affirmed his love for Jenny, as though there did not need to be any tension between the two loves, especially given the innocent nature of the physical contact.[16]

Yet there were layers of secrecy not revealed in the confidences Lowenstein had been willing to share. Sometimes his sleeping together with men did lead to sexual climax. Hugging was not always the limit. Moreover, at least a few of Lowenstein's friends did see a contradiction between marriage and their own close relationship with him. Announcing his engagement, one of these friends wrote Al, "From my point of view some changes in our relationship should [now] occur. . . . Would like to go into my feelings but for many reasons don't think this letter is an appropriate place."[17]

One problem that would not go away was the simple difficulty of sustaining the number of close friendships Lowenstein had initiated, whether or not they involved physical contact. Al was a whirling dervish, continually drawing people into his orbit, only to then move on to the next town or the next frenetic go-around. "What limits do you think there are to one person's capacity for deep love of those around him," one friend wrote, "in number and intensity?" Some were prepared to be satisfied with the time they had from him. "The nights spent with you do recharge some sagging batteries," another noted. "What has to be done has to be done and schedules are ridiculous. [For] those of us who love you, there is only sweetness left thinking of you." But for others, the rush of the intense encounter generated expectations that turned to frustration when there was no follow-through. "You wined and dined me, and then offered me a part of your personal life, laying bare your ego," one student intern commented, only to then leave the hopes for longer lasting ties unfulfilled. A person could achieve the height of gratification during a period of service to Lowenstein, only to be replaced the next instant by someone else. "He wasn't the greatest at letting you down," another protégé observed.[18]

The result was either pained bewilderment or angry recriminations. Those on the receiving end when Al became cold, distant, and unresponsive frequently expressed perplexity about what they had done wrong. "[You] express your disappointment in such an obtuse, indirect way," one wrote, trying to figure out why he was being singled out for the cold shoulder. Others, however, instinctively recognized what was happening and struck back. "I would be sarcastic with him in ways I observed other people being sarcastic with him," Jeff Robbins noted, "people who had been lieutenants at one point but who had since been supplanted by new lieutenants." In such circumstances, Lowenstein sometimes tried to win back the apostate by inviting him to dinner, just the two of them. "Yeah," Robbins once responded, alluding to Lowenstein's famous dinners at the family restaurant, "you, me, and the Washington Redskins."

At least one Lowenstein associate gave a name to the process. John Kavanaugh, a blind Stanford student whom Lowenstein befriended, subsequently became a psychotherapist. He called Lowenstein's serial relationships with special others a form of narcissism. "Al was capable of using people until they wore out," Kavanaugh said; he then moved on to others without even being aware of the impact of his actions. Narcissists are typically "good in engaging large groups and also good at maintaining very intense individual relationships, but not necessarily good at maintaining boundaries over a long period of time or over distance. . . . When he's there, he's very much there with you, and when he's not, you're left with whatever it is that you bring to the relationship. . . . He's just not going to be in it anymore."[19]

Friends at the time analyzed Lowenstein similarly, without the psychological terminology. "When you . . . cast people aside," one friend wrote,

they feel used. . . . Do you ever think about how many people there are all over this country who you were close to at one time and are no longer? I have heard it said that you run through people like water. My first reaction to your coldness [toward me] was coldness [toward you] . . . [but] really, I have trouble getting angry with you because I feel so sorry for you. You strike me as a very lonely man. If you keep running through people it has to be affecting more than the people you run through—it has to be affecting you too. I wonder if you are even willing to admit that to yourself.

This friend identified Lowenstein's Achilles' heel: by trying to multiply his options for close relationships, then moving on to the next possible object of attention, he was in fact precluding the chance for sustained intimacy with a chosen few and avoiding the truth telling and reckoning that alone could bring him peace.[20]

Lowenstein's painful awareness of his problem emerged in a series of conversations he had during the early 1970s. Prior to that time, he had shared his doubts about his sexual preferences with only a few individuals, preferring to tell most of the men he was attracted to that his impulses were not sexual in nature. But he had discussed his confusion with Bruce Payne, an old friend from Yale. "What do you call what I am?" Lowenstein asked. Now he went further, raising specifically with two individuals the issue of how someone who might be homosexual should handle that possibility in his own behavior and with those closest to him.[21]

In February 1974, Lowenstein attended a party in New York in honor of Dr. Howard Brown, a former New York City health commissioner who had recently announced he was homosexual at a New Jersey medical meeting. Another guest of honor was Bruce Voeller, who was prominently associated with the National Gay Rights Task Force. Lowenstein remained at the reception well after most of the guests had left and asked Voeller if he could seek his counsel. The two men subsequently met twice, then talked further by telephone. "The tenor [of the conversations]," Voeller reported, "was [that this] was more than just his fantasy life." Lowenstein was not interested in doing anything public, as Commissioner Brown had done, "but rather in dealing with his wife and his kids and others he was close to." Voeller had been married and had a family, so he was a particularly appropriate confidant. "He was very troubled about what the effect might be on his [wife] and kids," Voeller said, "and felt very much that he had . . . lived a lie, and that was rather foreign to his character. . . . His main concern . . . was, having dealt with it and reached a conclusion, did he stand to lose it all? What were the risks? What were the dangers? . . . How do you broach these matters?"[22]

Lowenstein also talked directly with his oldest friend, Sandy Friedman, who had been openly homosexual since adolescence. Despite that fact, they had never discussed Lowenstein's sexuality. Now, Friedman commented, "he is talking to me about how to . . . deal with his homosexual half. I think Allard, clearly, was bisexual," Friedman said, "and he just didn't know what to do about it." Lowenstein still carried around in his psyche "that MacKinlay Kantor thing," Friedman noted, "young, innocent, and dancing in the grass . . . and that is all churning in his brain, how to work this out and do it honorably and not be absolutely destructive."[23]

In his deepest self, therefore, Lowenstein not only was aware of the tensions and contradictions he had so persistently repressed, but was crying out for help. He was desperate to find a solution that would resolve his ambivalence about his sexual identity yet preserve and protect the woman and children he also loved deeply and would do anything to avoid hurting.

The deeper tragedy was that even as Lowenstein finally began to acknowledge the problem, his marriage and family were already in the process of coming apart.

THE MARITAL QUEST

When Al married Jenny, it seemed to everyone who knew him that doing so was the last piece necessary to complete a perfect life. Most if not all of his campaign workers were already in love with her. "Here's this wonderful person, with this wonderful sense of humor and a wonderful personality," Steve Cohen said, "and, of course, Al should have her for his wife. He's so brilliant, she's so perfect." Al himself was smitten. "I never thought I could be so lucky," he told Greg Craig, "I never thought . . . falling in love, getting married . . . could happen to me. . . . Surely, this is a dream, but for God's sake, don't please wake me up." When Jay Jacobson came to New York to help in Al's campaigns, Lowenstein exclaimed to him, "Isn't it extraordinary that [this] beautiful, smart woman could love me?" After they had gotten engaged, Douglass Hunt told Lowenstein, "the smartest thing that you can do is to let her know—by putting her and your marriage at the top of your priority list—that you . . . know how lucky you are." In his letters to Jenny, Al seemed intent on doing that. "One day I will do for you one millionth of what you do for me," he wrote in 1967, "not because one millionth is all I should or should like to [do], but because more than that no one ever could." A lilt of romance blossomed in his prose. "How much I wish I could hear [your voice]," he wrote from Berlin in 1969, "and see the beautiful things around where it comes out, like your face (and the rest of you)."[24]

Jenny reciprocated Al's love. In a "Dear Droopy" letter (their nickname for each other), she wrote:

> The whole house is like a movie with no soundtrack when you are not here. . . . Frankie and Tommy [who had been born in 1969] are both asleep with their bottoms in the air, and I am smiling at everyone as you would instruct me to do. . . . I just wish you could know what [these three] years have meant to me. I have had more happiness in this short time than anyone could possibly deserve. If only I could revise and extend myself to a point where you'd believe me. . . . But please know and remember that you are the dearest thing in the world to me and these few years of being with you have held all the love anyone could feel and receive in a lifetime.

(Her "revise and extend" comment refers to Lowenstein's by then famous penchant for "revising and extending" remarks he made on the House floor for reprint in the *Congressional Record.*)[25]

The first years of their marriage were full of excitement, fun, victory—almost a sense of magic. Despite the tragedy of Kennedy's assassination, it was generally an "up" time, from the success of "dump Johnson" and going to Washington to having children whose names read like a Lowenstein hall of fame—Frank Graham Lowenstein (1967), Thomas (after Norman) Kennedy Lowenstein (1969), Katharine (after Hepburn) Eleanor Lowenstein (1971). There were all the problems that might have been predicted—Al's lateness, his chaotic travel schedule, his tendency to invite ten people to dinner at the last minute. (At one point, Mimi Perr, his secretary, refused to call Jenny anymore at the last minute to announce there would be extras coming home for dinner. "I said, 'Al, I'm not doing it because it's cruel. You've got one meatball, and you're inviting twelve people.'") But enough joy dominated day-to-day life that the problems seemed like small blips on a radar screen, more like idiosyncracies to be commented on or joked about than signs of impending danger.[26]

The positive atmosphere largely reflected Jenny's own infectious spirit and the excitement of sharing in a community of friends devoted to common objectives. It was all kind of crazy and fun. Their next-door neighbor Susan Andrews recalled that when Al suddenly announced ten new guests for dinner, everyone chipped in. "Some of us would bring food, some of us would put something in a pot when we got there. Some of us just went there so we could greet people as they came in and . . . engage them while Jenny was doing whatever. . . . But there was always someone to do the serving and putting things together." A kind of playful hilarity filled the house. "Jenny and I were like school kids together," Andrews said. In the middle of a serious political discussion about tactics, something would strike them as funny and "we would laugh hysterically. . . . Sometimes when things became too bizarre . . . [we'd be laughing so hard] we'd have to go in the back room."

Jenny's sense of humor sparkled, making even tedious chores seem less burdensome. A testimonial dinner became a "$7.50 bowel movement"; writing hundreds of Christmas cards and thank-you notes after a campaign was "days and days of deeply grateful." Why, Susan Andrews asked, should Al stay on Long Island in 1970 and run again in the fifth congressional district? "Because you married Jenny—the *most* outrageous and beautiful girlchild in the country . . . because you are a Gilbert and

Sullivan fan . . . and because the brown envelope in the refrigerator does not contain bread and salt, but instead hundreds of FDR stamps." It was that kind of house, that kind of family.[27]

Ultimately, however, these were the "glory days," as Jenny called them, because she played the role of superwoman. No challenge was too great, no problem insuperable. When Al was two hours late for a political gathering at the house on Lindell Boulevard, she would charm the guests. When four times as many people arrived for dinner as she had expected, she would rush next door for a pound of ground chuck and trot out the Hamburger Helper. If she had to substitute for Al at a political meeting downtown and had no baby sitter, she would ask the plumber to stand by with a pacifier for an hour while she raced to the engagement. "It was incredible how you could tend to FGL [the baby Frankie] so well, campaign vigorously and effectively, and also put up with the chaos and incredible intrusions into your household," Emory Bundy wrote after the 1968 campaign, "plus the frustrations of living with a picky eater and . . . such an unorthodox campaigner. . . . I hope you will put your foot down now that the election is over." Obviously, it helped that these were days of victory, that neighbors and campaign workers chipped in, and that soulmates like Susan Andrews helped keep the merry-go-round moving with her companionship and humor. But what would happen when things turned bad?[28]

Arguably, the same behavior patterns that could be dismissed one moment as humorous foibles—"well, that's just Al"—might be transformed the next into infuriating and outrageous character flaws. Certainly to any objective observer, Lowenstein completely fit Emory Bundy's description as "one of the world's most difficult persons to be married to." Al apparently gave no thought to how difficult it might be for Jenny to accommodate his lifestyle, or the people he surrounded himself with. "You have no idea what their house was like," Art Kaminsky said. "There can't be anything like it in the history of mankind. The man was an adult—and it was like a clubhouse . . . 365 days a year, 52 weeks a year, kids and people, strangers and semistrangers and old friends constantly coming through the place, sleeping on the floor, sleeping in the basement. . . . It was just such a bizarre scene. We all wondered how anyone could live something resembling a normal life in that." Kaminsky exaggerated, but not much. Volunteers camped out in the house, staff members like Greg Stone lived there for years, and the front door was always left unlocked so that the next visitor would have easy access. "Here's a woman who had to put up with these hundreds of kids," Arnie Miller commented. "She never knew who the hell was going to be sleeping in her home, where her husband was, or what he was doing." Gina Galke, a virtual around-the-clock secretary at the Lowenstein house in the mid-1970s, echoed Miller. "Do you know what madness is?" she asked. "I tell you, wall-to-wall kids."[29]

At the heart of the problem was Al's presumption that he did not have to be accountable to Jenny or anyone else for his behavior, that he had a right to act as he pleased. The presumptuousness appeared in his attitude toward lateness, for example. Once during the South African venture, Sherman Bull and Emory Bundy kept Al waiting for them, and "he went bananas." When they responded, "Jeez, we wait for you a hundred times a day," he said, in essence, "Hey, your time is not important, and mine is." Thus, because Al's "mission" was so important, he claimed the right to do things that otherwise would have appeared utterly contemptuous of people—and was not even conscious of doing so. "A life lived as Al lived his," his old friend Judy Quine remarked, "was a driven life." Jenny just had to cope with it, however difficult that might be. "I don't think he was instructible when it came to personal matters," Sandy Friedman observed. "[Politics] was his life. . . . I don't think he ever thought, 'What could I contribute on the home front?' . . . [Rather], 'I will go there as I can . . . but it can't be very often, and they'll manage and I'll get there and we'll roll around the floor. . . . And someday we'll play softball on the beach like the Kennedys.' . . . And I don't think he had any guilt about it." Al might be cruel, Friedman said, "but I don't think [it] was a knowing cruelty. That was just the way things are."[30]

Therefore, Lowenstein could love his wife and children yet simultaneously be oblivious to the demands he was placing upon them. "I can't imagine what it would have been like for Jenny," Nancy Steffen said, "being with someone [like Al] who could never stop spinning like a dervish," yet always be expected to "be there" and respond, crisis to crisis. Longtime family friend Colleen Cuthbertson poignantly evoked how the scene could look when it featured fatigue and irritation rather than buoyancy and laughter. Al arrived home for dinner with his usual additional people, Cuthbertson said, and there was Jenny. "She took the cake out and tried to put another layer onto it. There wasn't enough meat, there wasn't enough anything. . . ."[31]

In the early 1970s, Jenny endured a series of her own crises that made "managing" this lifestyle far harder than it had ever been before. Jenny's family had always experienced more than its share of turmoil. There had been multiple divorces and some history of mental illness. In the mid-1960s, her stepfather had been murdered. Now in the winter of 1970, just weeks after Al's bitter defeat at the hands of Norman Lent, her younger brother committed suicide. "It was this whole awful ordeal," she said. "Al hung in there every second of the way" when they went to Maine to bury him, but she was crushed. Then, a year later, Jenny's mother died suddenly at the age of fifty-five. Two devastating personal losses, plus an agonizing political defeat—all experienced between the fall of 1970 and Christmas 1971. "I think I began to be somehow a more fragile person," Jenny said. More than anything else, she needed space, the opportunity to grieve, "to make a family," and to recover her sense of equanimity. "[We should have had a year off], and kind of lick our wounds, and do something to heal . . . and that just didn't happen." No matter how much help Al offered in the immediate crisis, as soon as it was over, "the politics were right there [again]. . . . I just think that for me, who wasn't necessarily the most strong, mature person . . . I just think that after a while, I didn't have it anymore."[32]

For Jenny as for Al, Brooklyn became pivotal. The campaign moved into full gear less than five months after her mother's death. They rented a three-room basement apartment in a marginal neighborhood; space was so cramped that she and Al had to sleep on a pullout sofa in the living room. The district was new, and there were so many complicated constituencies and ethnic tensions to be sensitive to, in addition to all the old problems of extra people showing up for dinner or to sleep on the floor. "I don't know how she stood it for so long," Steve Morgan said, "just being barraged with strange people . . . being in a dangerous neighborhood, and the unpredictability of Al and his feeling that it was a right for him to be gone as often as he was." Life was out of control. "I was always willing to do routine work," Jenny commented, "going and ringing doorbells in places that were war zones. I was just one of the troops that would have done anything for Al, until it got to be one campaign too many, and then I just sort of lost my heart for it."[33]

The "campaign that never ended" became a life force in itself as Al compulsively reentered the fray and refused to accept defeat by John Rooney. "I remember . . . running on the Liberal [party] line," Jenny said, "[thinking] . . . 'Oh God, do we have to go through this again? Do I have to canvass these precincts all over again?' . . . I mean, usually people get defeated once and then there's a two-year break before they can run again." But in Brooklyn, that did not happen. "Always get back up and fight," was Al's motto. "Go on, fight, fight, fight." The demands, the constant pressure to be "on," the lack of any open space or time—like dripping acid, eating away at a rock, it started to erode the foundation of their relationship. "This business of being defeated over and over again was devastating," Jenny said. "It made me feel sad and hurt . . . terribly hurt for Al. And angry that it kept happening, sort of irrationally. 'Why are we going through this again? Why do you want to hurt me again?'"[34]

In characteristic fashion, Al refused to acknowledge any problem in his political life. At the moment of defeat, he would say, "Let's get back to reality and go to the movies." After the Norman Lent victory in 1970, he gathered up the family, put on the Vietnamese cooley hat he had brought back from Saigon, and set off for the evening show, as if to say, "This is going to be fun, we're going to be okay, life is great." And when things got really bad, he would always say, "We have each other and our three lovely children." Al was an expert at denying pain. After a gall bladder operation in 1967, he insisted on getting out of bed and leaving the hospital early, refusing to admit he was in agony when he walked. "I never saw him collapse," Jenny said. "It just wasn't there. As a wife, maybe you want a tiny shred of that to be there . . . [to hear,] 'Oh God, I'm exhausted. I'm going to bed for two days.'"[35]

Worst of all, Al carried this refusal to admit vulnerability and pain into his home life, the personal and political once again becoming almost one. Although deeply frustrated at being victimized, Lowenstein could not be open even with Jenny. "It became hard to share that [anger and frustration]," she said, "and so we began to . . . get against each other, with me just saying, 'I can't do this anymore,' and he was saying, 'We have to do it again.' He could almost never let himself be sad when he lost. He'd go into some big new act—immediately, the next day. You sort of couldn't grieve."

Nor would Al provide the space or time for the two of them to heal their personal pain and conflict. "I can't imagine that, aside from their honeymoon, they ever had more than about five minutes of private time," Nancy Steffen said. "There would always be somebody in the house." Rick Saslaw, who, as a teenager took care of the children, later noted that in most families, tensions "were both discussed and resolved in the bedroom," but in the Lowenstein home, "I don't think . . . those opportunities were as frequent as Jenny would have liked . . . because he was off and running so much of the time and left her with the . . . children and a house and a horde of well-meaning friends. . . . I think Jenny craved a normal, stable, family environment. There was no way she was ever going to get it married to Allard Lowenstein."[36]

Indeed, Lowenstein's lifestyle seemed almost perniciously designed to preclude opportunities for Jenny and him to be alone. As early as college, he had established the pattern of bringing large numbers of people home so that he would not have to deal one on one with his father. "That was deliberate," his sister-in-law observed, "part of his defense mechanism." Similarly, Al appeared to go out of his way to bring people home with him to Jenny. He would be away for days, Ann Feldman commented, "and then it would be time to go home, [and] he'd say to me, 'Come with me. Jenny would love to [see you],' [and] I'd say, 'Jenny doesn't want to see me. She wants to see you,' [and he'd reply], 'No, no, no. She's so fond of you.' . . . It wasn't just me. He would have said it to anyone. It was like he was afraid to be alone with anybody for a long period of time . . . where there was going to be any intimacy."[37]

Presumably, a part of Lowenstein's fear of being alone with his wife involved his continuing ambivalence about his sexuality, an ambivalence he had just started to share with a few others in the early 1970s. In the eyes of many of Al's friends, it would have been impossible for Jenny not to have noticed the particular fascination preppy young men had for Al. "Every one of [those friendships]," Bruce Payne noted, "was a sort of crush and had [a kind] of erotic magic around it." On the other hand, Jenny may have been sufficiently unsure about the issue that it could remain the subject of speculation rather than confrontation, especially if she had few opportunities to deal with personal problems. Yet even if unacknowledged, Al's tension over sexual preference and identity seems to have been an important ingredient in his determination to surround himself with people in order to avoid the painful issues he sought to deny.[38]

As time went on, the accumulating burden of coping with Lowenstein's behavior patterns took its inevitable toll on their marriage. The seemingly nonstop Brooklyn campaigns had hardly come to their merciful end when Lowenstein embarked on his pursuit of the Senate seat. There was never any down time, never a chance to recover and heal. "[Al] never really understood this whole thing," Susan Erb, his personal assistant from the mid-1970s, said.

> Jenny had a lot of problems with the campaigns. . . . I spent a lot of time with Jenny, and there were people running in and out all the time. Every day she would wake up and there would be different people staying there for breakfast, and they weren't there to see her, they were there to see Al, but Al would run off and Jenny would be left with the people. It was just a constant influx, and they would be in her way, all the time. There was no place she could go, and she was upset about this whole thing. She would always say, "What am I going to do?"

As their friend, Franklin D. Roosevelt III observed, "Al [was] just not . . . there enough to meet her needs for some kind of a relationship."[39]

By the end of 1974, Jenny had begun to dig in her heels. Frustrated by her lack of an independent life, she began the long process of building a career of her own. "Maybe there was some sense," Jenny said, "that I . . . want[ed] to do all the things that the women's movement started to talk about." Encouraged by new friends, she began classes in psychology and social work, first at Brooklyn College, then at Adelphi. Because of her new interests, she was less available for campaign appearances, more distant from the political whirligig, readier to express resentment about the student volunteers and others who occupied her house. She had experienced defeat so often that the very thought of a new campaign became frightening. "I just didn't see how we could win," she said.[40]

Jenny also became more emotionally vulnerable from the repeated battering of her psyche. Colleen Cuthbertson noted that Jenny was likely to get upset "when Al wouldn't show up when he said he would." Friends referred to her "moodiness." In the eyes of some, including Al, Jenny began to exhibit symptoms of depression. "I was not the most emotionally self-controlled [person in the world]," she later said. "I was very moody, immature, not necessarily a day at the beach to be married to." Most people saw her emotional swings as a totally natural response to the pressures she had to live with day to day. Even those who believed they might be connected to a family history of depression saw the symptoms as reactive. As one friend said, "I think if she was depressive that could've reached a breaking point [by having to bear] all the responsibilities of that family." There had been too many losses, too many deaths, too many people, too little time to "just be a family." Without some dramatic change, total disintegration appeared imminent.[41]

For one brief moment in the late spring and summer of 1975, it seemed almost possible that such a change might occur. Jerry Brown, the newly elected governor of California, was visiting his next-door neighbors Paul and Monica Schrade one night when the conversation turned to their mutual friend, Al Lowenstein. Why not hire him? Schrade asked. "He could be my Kissinger," Brown responded, and at midnight California time, he called the Lowenstein house. Answering the phone at 3:00 A.M. on Long Island, Jenny turned to Al and said, "It's probably one of your kookie friends; he says he's Jerry Brown." Within days, Lowenstein had decided to take Brown up on his offer to become part of his "kitchen cabinet." For a number of years, he had speculated about moving to California and finding a congressional district there to run in. Now he could go there for the summer, coordinate a summer intern program for students, and at the same time explore, with Jenny and the children, the possibility of establishing a new home and a new base of operations. In contrast to New York's negative associations, California represented everything positive— a fresh start, bright sunshine, a different lifestyle.[42]

Jenny was enthusiastic. By going to work for Jerry Brown, she reasoned, "it seemed like we were doing something other than running, and maybe [Al] could get back into doing something that he enjoyed again, [and] that he'd be recognized for." She also clearly saw the move as a second chance for their relationship. By then, close friends were aware of problems in the marriage. "I hope," Steve Morgan wrote Al in May, "that the California trip turns out to be the godsend Jenny anticipates." Gary Hart expressed similar sentiments, saying that he hoped "you and Jenny are still pals." With typical Lowenstein overoptimism (or unreality), Al tried to rent a three-bedroom house in Marin County—with a pool—for $500, but when no such rental for that price materialized, Jerry Brown volunteered his residence in Los Angeles. They were on their way.[43]

Taking Harvey Lippman with him as his personal aide, Al flew to California in the late spring to set up the intern program. (It was a typical trip, Lippman said: Al barely made the plane in New York and almost missed it again during a stopover in Denver because he wanted to get a shave in the airport.) Jenny and the children, meanwhile, set out in their Toyota Corolla station wagon with another woman friend and her child—six people in a compact car. Each night, they were scheduled to stop and stay with a friend of Al's. Frank Lowenstein, eight years old at the time, recalled the trip as "just bedlam the entire way . . . one of the most bizarre journeys in history." The kids dubbed the car "the green dragon," its interior "packed to the hilt with our worldy belongings." "My image," Frankie said, "is arms and legs [and heads] hanging out the windows, screaming." Things were off to a flying—and hilarious—start.[44]

Politically, the California experience seemed to provide precisely the ego boost and revitalization Lowenstein needed. Brown was a new governor with grand ambitions, and Lowenstein was perfectly suited for the role of his éminence grise. David Bender, a close Lowenstein associate during these years, recalled that Al served as Brown's "chief adviser" and was definitely "the chief strategist for [what became] the [Brown] presidential campaign in 1976." Although in retrospect Brown described Lowenstein's role as somewhat less pivotal, he acknowledged Al's significant contribution. "To me, Al was like an energy source," he said. "Government . . . needs to be constantly agitated, pushed, confronted. . . . [He] was a source of inspiration . . . [and] had [a] quality of openness and playfulness and excitement. . . . [I thought] if we could just get these bright people in here . . . handling the levers of government, then good things would happen." In that framework, Al's task was to recruit forty student interns, set them to work in Sacramento and in the Los Angeles area on projects like a California conservation corps and gun control, and generate new ideas that would infuse government with both the creativity and energy of the young. A combination of teaching and role modeling, the job called forth Al's finest talents. He could dart in and out of various projects, challenge and excite the students with new ideas, create linkages that no one else had imagined possible, yet remain above the nitty-gritty of the day-to-day routine. He was in heaven.[45]

Lowenstein also had good reason to feel confident about his political future in California should he decide to relocate permanently. Ever since the early 1970s, he had discussed with local politicians the possibility of running for Congress there. His fingers were on the pulse of California politics. He knew which districts were most likely to become vacant (Tom Reese's in Los Angeles, Pete McCloskey's in the Bay Area); he had close friends who were well situated to help (Howie Berman in the state Assembly, Jerome Waldie and Pete McCloskey in Congress, Steven Reinhart and Mickey Kantor in the governor's office); and because of his preeminent role in the "dump Johnson" movement, he had a powerful popular base with members of the California Democratic Council, the leading progressive organization in the party. "It was such a refreshing change . . . when we arrived in California," Harvey Lippman said, "because Al was revered [there]. He was listened to, he was respected, people talked to him literally with awe in their eyes . . . [in contrast to] the way he was treated by political figures in New York." California politicians agreed. At a time when Lowenstein's political stock was falling in New York, Rick Tuttle said, "he was enormously strong in California. . . . He'd walk into . . . almost any room, even if he wasn't expected, and . . . you'd begin to hear . . . the applause." For the first time in years, the political future seemed bright.[46]

So, too, did relationships at home. Although not very much had changed in Al's peripatetic behavior—he commuted back and forth between Los Angeles and Sacramento and continued to surprise Jenny with unexpected dinner guests—being in a new place, especially California, created a fresh and optimistic atmosphere more like it had been in the first years on Long Island. There were new sights to see and trips to take with the kids. Instead of "all the oppression of East Coast politics," Jenny said, "[California] was a great place of freedom and joy. . . . It was so much fun." In a new milieu, Al seemed to become a different person. "It's like all the light side of him came out," Jenny observed. "Remember, there was a certain innocence about Al's sources of joy. . . . [I think] he had a real romance with California." The children also loved their time there. Known for his relatively ascetic lifestyle, Jerry Brown had few luxuries in his home and had forsworn the California landscaping fetish—prompting Frankie Lowenstein to ask, "How come the governor of California doesn't have a television set?" or, "Why does the governor of California live in a jungle?" Even the last-minute, hastily improvised dinners for twenty people were fun. Jenny would call the Schrades across the street, they would pool their food, and all of them together would settle in for a Sunday evening of intense discussion with the bright, young student interns about the unsolved problems of the universe.[47]

Yet in the end, California remained a sparkling hiatus rather than the new start both Al and Jenny had hoped for. The potential for something different was almost palpable. "He loved it here," David Bender said, "[and] it was sort of accepted that . . . as soon as Al said he was prepared to move back to Palo Alto . . . Pete McCloskey would stand down and support him. I mean, that was as close to a sure thing as one can have." Susan Andrews confirmed that Jenny very much wanted to stay in California and build from the start they had made in a fresh place. But staying would have required making a fundamental new commitment—settling in for two or three years until a congressional seat opened up, finding another job after the summer of advising interns, changing his life course in a definitive way. Al was not prepared to do that, however tantalizing the bright possibilities. Already he had begun conversations about running for Congress again on Long Island. His immersion in the Kennedy assassination controversy deepened, leading him to resign from his job working for Brown, who did not share his passion for investigating assassination conspiracies. But ultimately, Lowenstein refused to stay in California because he was unwilling—or maybe unable—to make the permanent life choices that could resolve his political and personal nightmares. Instead, he chose to plunge back into the morass that had created his political crises and exacerbated his personal ones. Perhaps he saw no other option. But even a brief look back would have told him that his decision spelled disaster.[48]

THE NADIR

Returning to Long Island was like a perpetual rerun of all the circumstances that had driven Jenny to personal despair and Al to political despair. The film never stopped, only a few of the characters changed, and the plot became so predictable that almost everyone knew the outcome well in advance of the conclusion. Lowenstein's obsession with the Kennedy murders drove him ever further into the marginalization he abhorred and feared. His compulsion to run for office persisted, even as those who had devoted their lives to his service began to shake their heads and withdraw from the fray. And the woman who had been the emotional anchor for Lowenstein's every public act finally had to leave lest she, too, be destroyed. The drama of the tragedy was in the pathos and poignancy of the players' inevitable pain, not in any suspense over how the story would end. It was all too familiar.

Despite the ample grounds Lowenstein had for being outraged by the response of the media and the Los Angeles police to his queries about the Robert Kennedy assassination, he never succeeded in winning significant support for his point of view. Some of his old friends—Bill Buckley, David Susskind, and James Wechsler—offered him forums, but even they felt he had gone overboard and was losing credibility. Lowenstein wrote powerful indictments of the official stance on the assassinations and described his own personal journey toward doubt and skepticism, but his articles were turned down by most established journals. Instead, they appeared in *Argosy* (February 1976), a men's magazine that specialized in hunting and wildlife stories, and *Oui* (March 1976), a monthly, devoted principally to sex, that featured *Playboy*-style photographs of men and women in erotic poses. (In 1977, Lowenstein did finally publish an article on the assassination in *Saturday Review*.) The questions Lowenstein asked remained pertinent and insightful, but clearly, he had lost much of the mainstream audience he so wanted to reach.[49]

At the same time, Lowenstein made the inexplicable decision to run again against John Wydler in the fifth congressional district. Nothing had changed significantly since Wydler had won by 14,000 votes two years earlier. Even Al's sister Dorothy, always a devoted supporter, urged him not to run. "I just really felt he was doing the wrong thing," she said. Although there were always fresh volunteers who could be recruited, many of Al's most loyal allies on Long Island expressed openly their dismay and disapproval at his decision. "We thought he was just nuts," Barbara Bernstein said. "I thought, he doesn't know when to quit." It all seemed so self-destructive. "It was like, 'Why are you doing this to yourself?'" Hilary Lieber commented. "'Why don't you write books and teach and do what you should be doing. Why do this?'"[50]

Especially why do this when Jenny had made it crystal clear she would not tolerate another campaign. "By '76," she said, "I . . . put my foot down." Instead of compromising or giving in, "I was just more willing to stomp out of the room and say, 'Sorry, tough! You're not going to have any kaffeeklatsches here." Once again, the house was full of people, many of them strangers to her. "Jenny would be there with the kids," Susan Erb said, "and a disaster would happen—things would be broken—and it was just a mess." And Al was not around. The tension between them grew greater; according to friends, Jenny told Al that she would leave if he ran but would stay if he promised not to run. But Al insisted on pursuing his quest, and as soon as the campaign began, Jenny went off to Maine for the summer with the children.[51]

Al's best friends had already warned him repeatedly that if he persisted in his course of action, he would destroy his marriage. Whether or not he listened, he had heard many times by 1976 how huge a gamble he was taking. "Al, you're going to lose your marriage if you don't get straightened out," one close friend told him over and over again in 1976. "He knew that I knew something [about their relationship] . . . but he didn't want to be told that . . . he just ran from it." Obviously, something was deeply wrong with their marriage. Not only was the magic gone, but she had even announced her intention not "to go through this again." Yet he persisted in his denial. "I don't know whether it was because he was inattentive to himself or to her to not have known [what was wrong]," Bruce Payne said.[52]

Instead, Lowenstein dealt with the problem by a combination of rationalization and repression. If people asked where Jenny was or what was going on, he would explain that she had a history of depression, and that "she was prone to this [kind of emotional disturbance]." Blaming "chemical imbalance" and the like became his way of avoiding the real issues. "He'd talk about how depressed she got at certain moments . . . how he'd have to cajole her out of it, and [how] it ran in the family," Jay Jacobson said, "[but] I didn't really want to listen to him when he talked about Jenny." Other friends had the same response. "I could just see him grasping at [straws]," Susan Erb said, "like it wasn't his fault. In point of fact, it was. Jenny put up a valiant effort to keep going. . . . It's just that he had a different set of priorities." Anyone who knew Al and Jenny, Nancy Steffen said, raised their eyebrows when Al started talking about genetic mental disorders. Such talk, she said, constituted "one of the most incredible conversations I had with him. . . . He was very vulnerable and he had to blame somebody."[53]

Reinforcing his rationalization was an ironclad armor of denial that prevented Lowenstein from probing his own accountability for what was transpiring. He refused to argue with Jenny or confront the problems. "He'd grown up with that [kind of anger in his parents' house]," she said. "He hated it. He would have gone through hellfire rather than to have an angry scene. . . . He'd say, 'It is so wrong to say things that can't be taken back, that people will remember.'. . . Sometimes by literally biting his lip, [he would say], 'I will not do this'. . . and that took a certain amount of self-control, because God knows, he was furious." Yet the apparent self-control deflected and denied the reality of what was happening, because the pain of exploring that reality was so potentially searing. "He just had to be in some ways profoundly self-protective," Jenny said, and denial offered the only way to stay armored against himself.[54]

In some ways, the campaign for the fifth congressional district seat—Lowenstein's fourth—also represented a form of denial. He sent out telegrams to students who had worked in previous campaigns, called in chits at campuses where he had a long track record, and sought to put back together the kind of coalition he had managed to mobilize in 1968, 1970, and 1972. Yet in doing so he was rejecting the advice of his best friends that he should stop running, as well as ignoring the fact that many of his old supporters had fallen away. "He just didn't hear negatives anymore," Hilary Lieber said, "he wanted so much to be back [in Washington]." Ann Feldman described her own decision to not participate anymore. Driving home after midnight with a student volunteer, "I suddenly remember sitting in the truck and thinking to myself, 'What am I doing here? I'm a [middle-aged] woman. . . . Why am I driving around in a truck with this crazy kid for no particular reason?' . . . I really had this . . . feeling like I was in something that was out of control." Other older people shared her feeling that their participation in Lowenstein's perennial campaigns had become "a little bit more than what was appropriate." As a result, Feldman said, his campaign attracted only "the losers of the world. That's who was helping him now, because the others had all dropped off. It was sort of sad to see."[55]

Lowenstein did his best to marshal the kind of diverse backing that would make him seem more mainstream. Bill Buckley endorsed him one more time, as did Leonard Garment, who had been White House counsel under Nixon, and Rita Hauser, the coordinator of Nixon's reelection committee in 1972. But Wydler then trotted out James Buckley. More to the point, he won the backing of rabbis in the liberal Five Towns area, which had always been a bastion of Lowenstein strength. As Susan Erb commented, "There were people deserting the camp." Wydler refused to debate, relying instead on ads that were by now tested, tried, and true. "Allard Lowenstein," they said, "has spent most of his adult life desperately and unsuccessfully trying to find a constituency that wants him as its Congressman." The ad then listed all Lowenstein's defeats, including his most recent loss as a delegate to the 1976 Democratic convention. "Like Harold Stassen," the ad concluded, "Lowenstein . . . just can't seem to get the message."[56]

The only bright political spot of the year was Lowenstein's involvement in Jerry Brown's brief but dazzling entry into the 1976 presidential sweepstakes. There was "an electricity" between the two men, one friend commented, and the two worked closely to build support around Brown's last-minute candidacy. Lowenstein's contacts throughout the country helped Brown piece together a campaign apparatus. Miraculously, they won a write-in vote in Maryland in April, momentarily rattling Jimmy Carter. Brown referred to Lowenstein as his "secret weapon," and one columnist, writing about Lowenstein's helter-skelter role, declared: "[He] holds no title in the campaign; he just runs it." But if the Brown run rekindled in Lowenstein some sense of being in the limelight of a crusade, it also reminded others of Lowenstein's political weaknesses. "It was a typical Lowenstein thing," California's Howie Berman said. "It started late without any serious vote counting [and] relied on the magic of the candidate."[57]

The election returns on Long Island proved that whatever magic Lowenstein might still have in Maryland or California, it no longer existed in the fifth congressional district of New York. Even as Lowenstein tried the old routine of bringing in celebrities to boost his chances, an air of resigned pessimism prevailed in the campaign. "I was just getting jaded," Ellen Vollinger recalled. Al blamed his campaign staff and would not acknowledge his part in the old problem of never being able to trust anyone to take charge and act as an equal. "For all his intellect," Harvey Lippman said, "I don't think he was the perfect judge of . . . people's abilities." The reality was that Lowenstein had only himself to blame. Running once more in a race he should not have entered, he added one additional defeat to his now lengthening record, cementing in many people's minds the impression that he was a political loser.[58]

Far worse from Lowenstein's point of view was the fact that he was about to lose his family as well. Harvey Lippman recalled the day Jenny returned from Maine. Jerry Brown was in the district campaigning for Al, who was jumpy all day and called repeatedly to see whether Jenny had arrived. "He knew things weren't right," Lippman said, "and I think he wasn't even sure if she was actually going to come back." For much of the next ten months, Al continued to entertain the hope that somehow things could be made right and Jenny would stay. To most of the world, he still pretended that everything was fine; at home, meanwhile, he persisted in his refusal to explore what was wrong, "to say things that can't be taken back." Not once, the Lowensteins' oldest son Frank recalled, did Al speak a cross word, either to the children or to Jenny. She would get mad and lose her temper; he would not.[59]

Yet nothing short of a dramatic transformation could stop Jenny from leaving. Al had made the decision for them when he came back from California determined once more to be a candidate, disregarding Jenny's ultimatum and the advice of friends. "I [just] couldn't stop him from running," she said. Jenny now was building her own life, finishing a degree in social work, ready to move to a new place, anxious to give her children a normal life. Frank recalled that, as a child, "I was . . . incredibly insecure. . . . I literally just wanted a house and a dog and a car, to be driven to my Little League games and taken to school and picked up." Jenny intended to make that happen by moving to a rural suburb of Boston and starting over. Al took the children to the beach to give them the news when it became clear that there was no other option. He had intended to tell Frankie about "the birds and the bees" as well, but Frankie indicated that was not necessary. "I love you," Al told them. "What happened between your mother and I is unfortunate but had nothing to do with you. You musn't blame yourself." Al also asked Susan Andrews to accompany him to a meeting, for once insisting that she be alone with him after it ended. Sitting in a diner for three hours, he told her the news and asked whether Jenny had already let her know. Jenny had not. "I've seen Al lonely in the past," she said, "but that was the loneliest I've ever seen him."[60]

Jenny and the children left the day Al was sworn in as one of five U.S. ambassadors to the United Nations. Despite his support for Jerry Brown in the presidential race, he had many friends in the Carter administration, including the White House aide Jack Watson and the U.N. ambassador,

Andrew Young. After serving as the U.S. delegate to the Human Rights Commission in Geneva, Al was offered an ambassadorship at the United Nations in New York. Finally, he had achieved recognition and legitimacy again. The children returned from camp and accompanied Jenny to the swearing-in ceremony. In his remarks, Al thanked his family for all they had done, singling out Jenny for her special contribution. Then, when the reception was over, Jenny and the children got into one car and headed for New England, while Al got in another and went back to the house on Lindell Boulevard. Except for intimate friends, no one was told of the separation. But the story had ended.[61]

CONCLUSION

Allard Lowenstein's life during these years of disintegration reflected two interrelated themes. The first had to do with his self-image as a hero, acting on behalf of moral principle, who became a victim of outside forces he could not control, but that he would never stop fighting. Central to that theme was Lowenstein's egomania. He alone knew the path of righteousness; hence, everyone must follow his lead, and anyone who did not was guilty of betrayal. The second theme represented the converse of the first—a summons to doubt, to self-examination and exploration, to reassessment. This theme suggested a growing awareness of the contradictions that warred for control of Lowenstein's life, a realization among friends and loved ones that his cherished persona was deeply flawed. This was the theme that asked for choices and commitments to be made, tensions to be explored, secrets to be confronted. Each theme embraced the personal and the political. For almost the entire period of the early 1970s, the first theme continued to prevail, virtually unchallenged. Yet by 1977, the second had begun to manifest itself, if for no other reason than that the first had imploded, bringing Allard Lowenstein's world to a crumbling heap at his feet.

Consistent with his egomania, Al's first response to Jenny's leaving was complete rage. According to virtually all his closest friends, he reacted with fury and righteous indignation. "He had this defensive attitude," Susan Erb said. "He would kind of put Jenny down to people . . . like she was the bad person and he was the innocent victim." He was helped in making that interpretation by the fact that Jenny developed a relationship with Nick Littlefield, one of Al's protégés, who had coordinated the voter registration campaign of 1971 and the first Brooklyn race against Rooney.

"He felt incredibly betrayed," Jay Jacobson said, as though Nick had made it happen. Indeed, focusing on Nick, Sherman Bull pointed out, "made it easier than trying to figure out if you were in any way responsible for the whole situation. . . . He didn't want to hear anything about [himself]." Furthermore, that way he could fantasize about Jenny coming back someday—as had happened with another friend whose wife had left him. And so, Jay Jacobson said, Al defined himself as the victim: someone else had stolen his wife, and he was not responsible. In addition to having been robbed of his congressional seat and the Brooklyn election, Ann Feldman said, he could now complain of being "robbed of his wife."[62]

Such an interpretation derived, in turn, from Lowenstein's prior sense that his political mission was so noble that it justified neglect of family responsibilities. Hence, he could not be held accountable because his primary obligation was to a higher cause—a cause that clearly compelled similar devotion from others, including the willingness of friends and family to accept without question his definition of the game and how he should play it. "We all live with some self-image and illusions," Sandy Friedman noted. "If you have that messianic impulse and you think you are really doing good . . . [and then] your wife doesn't see this [and] leaves you," rage is the only possible response. Anger was an attempt "to protect that image . . . so that you can go on being the person you yourself think you are."

On the other hand, the very dimensions of the devastation that befell him created the possibility that Lowenstein might pursue the second, albeit minor theme of these years—a willingness to explore the unknown, to entertain even the hardest questions of all. Until he married Jenny, Al had kept his life in constant motion—largely to escape such questions, but also to find temporary intimacy with the countless young protégés he recruited. With Jenny, he had found an anchor. Even though his frenetic motion continued, she had given him a home base, a foundation on which to build everything else—at least as long as she remained primary in his life, and he in hers. During the early years, Bruce Payne observed, that was the case. "Jenny was in every way more than anybody to him. . . . [He was] the one who could be with her, the one who could touch her, the one who could laugh with her . . . and share things with her. . . . It seemed to me a complete relationship." But then that completeness began to erode as Al's demands took precedence and he ignored her needs and her primacy. In the end, Lowenstein almost compulsively deflected or repressed the mounting evidence that things were falling apart, both politically and personally. He gave occasional indications of being confused and in pain, as when he talked to Bruce Voeller and Sandy Friedman about his sexual identity. But it was almost as though raising such questions was itself so frightening that, like Aladdin, he had to try desperately to put the genie back in the bottle. And so he just ran and ran, hoping to escape the need to face what was happening.[63]

Yet another instinct in him, crying to be recognized, kept pushing him toward that confrontation. It was fundamentally a self-destructive instinct: the very impulse to not stand still and make basic choices would eventually turn upon itself and force others to make the choices he insisted on avoiding. How else to explain his decision to move back to New York from California—to move away from putting down new roots, finding a different life, getting a second chance with Jenny? How else to explain his decision to run for election again on Long Island even though Jenny had announced she would not tolerate it? Lowenstein's continuing assumption that he could do it all without paying a price—hold on to Jenny and the family and still pursue his compulsive lifestyle—literally guaranteed that the price would have to be paid. And when Jenny left, the bill came due.

Allard Lowenstein had torn himself apart. Suddenly, the self that he had "willed" into existence at the age of sixteen in order to break away from his father and stepmother lay in tatters. Jenny's departure, Sandy Friedman said, "was an earthquake for him." For one of the only times in his life, "Allard was vulnerable, extremely vulnerable." No longer was he in control. No longer was he "calling the moves." Yet the destruction of one self created at least the possibility of discovering another one. The shattering of a way of life that had been built on illusions and denial could pave the way for a more honest, authentic, and fulfilling life. The closed book had been pried open—as much by Lowenstein's own drive to destroy the life he had created as by Jenny's insistence on saving herself. Whether Al could now gather the pieces together to take advantage of the opening and find a new self would occupy him for the remaining three years of his life.[64]

16

A Second Act?

WITH HIS HOME BASE NOW DESTROYED—LITERALLY AS WELL AS METAPHORI-cally—Allard Lowenstein was forced to confront a series of choices he had put aside when he married and started a family. Although he had never really altered his lifestyle of constant motion, marriage had created the illusion of stability and this illusion was sufficient to obscure or deflect fundamental questions about direction, meaning, and purpose. Now the illusion had been shattered. The divorce had been an "earthquake," Sandy Friedman said, and had thrown into disarray the psychic and intellectual arrangements that permitted Lowenstein to function. Each "aftershock," in turn, brought into ever clearer perspective the fissures that needed to be faced if he were to find a center for his existence.

In real life, of course, such defining moments are hidden in the flow of daily, routine activity. They may even exist more in the retrospective judgment of a biographer than in reality. Thus, for example, it can be argued that Lowenstein's public life at the United Nations, his endless quest for a congressional seat, and his immersion in Ted Kennedy's presidential candidacy in 1980 were simply extensions of his age-old patterns. Similarly, his ongoing exploration of the issue of his sexual identity (even as he considered remarriage to wealthy WASP women) could be construed as more of the same old behavior.

Yet such an assessment does not do justice to the pain, the searching, and the tentative new beginnings that marked the last years of Al Lowenstein's life. Even as he continued in his habitual behaviors, he began to re-examine the core questions of his life. Were some friendships more important than others? Did family responsibilities and some relationships require a different order of commitment than that entailed in hit-and-miss contact on the run? Was politics itself an activity that justified the sacrifice involved, and if so, were there new crusades that might make public service more redemptive and worthwhile? Above all, what mattered most when life was flying past and a sense of mortality could no longer be denied?

Allard Lowenstein may never have found answers to these questions. But he appears to have been asking them during the last three years of his life with unprecedented seriousness and directness. In some ways, the ordeal of divorce returned him psychically to the days during and just after college when Mimi Massey, Joan Long, and others challenged him to make some basic choices. It was now nearly thirty years later. He had turned fifty, a birthday that made him acutely aware of how much of his life had already passed by and highlighted the question of how long he could continue as the world's oldest student leader. Increasingly preoccupied with his own death, as well as intensely aware of what he had lost when his children moved to Boston, Allard Lowenstein was groping for new beginnings by asking old questions. That he was murdered by one of the most powerful figures from his past represented just part of the tragedy of his death. Even more poignant was how tantalizingly close he came on the eve of his assassination to finding a new life.

THE SAME OLD POLITICS?

Al Lowenstein quickly cultivated friends in the new Carter administration to secure a presidential appointment. Interestingly, he focused on foreign policy and the United Nations, perhaps because Andrew Young, his old friend and a close aide of Martin Luther King, Jr., had been selected as Carter's U.N. ambassador. Carter and Young promised to make concern for human rights the hallmark of their foreign policy, an ideal emphasis given Lowenstein's perspective. From his devotion to anti-Franco democratic insurgents in Spain to his struggle against apartheid in South Africa, Lowenstein had championed human rights throughout his life as the centerpiece of America's contribution to the world community. While he had no formal diplomatic training, his extensive travel abroad, as well as his leading role in creating an anti-Communist international student movement, made him a natural candidate for one of the U.N. positions. Almost immediately after the election, he began to lobby Carter aides Jack Watson and Hamilton Jordan for such a post. Once Andy Young was selected and became Lowenstein's advocate, the appointment became a foregone conclusion. Lowenstein friends were ecstatic. "We all liked the U.N. thing," Art Kaminsky said, "because it gave him a job."[1]

Asked initially to lead the U.S. delegation to the Human Rights Commission in Geneva, Lowenstein quickly made a mark with his aggressive and candid advocacy of human rights everywhere. Impressively, he succeeded in getting the question of Soviet mistreatment of dissidents on the U.N. agenda, largely through his directness and sincerity. Brady Tyson, one of his associates in the delegation, stunned diplomats by acknowledging publicly the U.S. role in overthrowing the Salvador Allende regime in Chile in 1973. Lowenstein's apparent willingness to support self-determination in Africa and Latin America as emphatically as in Eastern Europe signaled to many a "new departure" in U.S. foreign policy on human rights issues. The idealistic leader of the delegation was a perfect symbol for the new diplomacy.[2]

When Lowenstein was sworn in as ambassador in charge of special political affairs at the United Nations, he continued to focus primarily on human rights, although his responsibilities also included appropriations and assessments. Andy Young had five ambassadors under his control at the United Nations. All the others were Foreign Service officers accustomed to the detailed regulations and constraints of the State Department. Once a week, the entire team met to coordinate operations. The rest of the time, each ambassador pursued his or her area of specialization under the general supervision of Young's deputy, Ambassador James Leonard. Lowenstein got along well with Leonard and with Melissa Wells, the ambassador for social and economic affairs. With others, according to Young's aide Stoney Cooks, "[he] chose to look out the window."[3]

In fact, Lowenstein's career as a U.N. ambassador was a perpetual tug-of-war between his instinct to leap clear of all State Department constraints and his obligation to speak on behalf of the official policy of the country. Lowenstein chafed at the rules and regulations. Decision-making at the State Department, he observed, was like watching an elephant get pregnant. "Everything takes place at a very high level, there is a great commotion, and then nothing happens for twenty-two months." Accustomed to initiating contacts and developing arguments on his own, he detested having to report every conversation with a delegate from another country to a desk officer in Washington, and needing clearance and instructions before a follow-up contact could occur. Frequently, he tried to circumvent the process and went directly to the assistant secretary of state for international organizations, Bill Maynes, or even to the White House itself. Sometimes he would simply seize the initiative, hoping to get away with it before getting caught. "He was a free-wheeler," Stoney Cooks said, "and if he had a bee in his bonnet, he'd go whichever way he could." Lowenstein tried to have the CIA banned from the U.S. delegation (unthinkable even to Young, given the intelligence activities undertaken at the United Nations); sought to orchestrate a meeting between the head of the World Zionist League and the Palestinian leader Yassar Arafat on Belgian television; and hoped to intervene personally to bring peace to Northern Ireland. When ordered by an apprehensive State Department to cease and desist from such activities, Lowenstein fumed. "He wanted to be a Lone Ranger," Brady Tyson noted, "[and] he screwed up the whole bureaucracy . . . do[ing] his own thing." One associate estimated that, given his hatred for filling out forms and going through the proper channels, Lowenstein probably absorbed over $15,000 in travel expenses that he had never filed for before he left the United Nation.[4]

Nowhere was the tension more visible or important than in Lowenstein's efforts on behalf of independence for South-West Africa, the territory under South African control about which Lowenstein had written *Brutal Mandate*. Under U.N. auspices, five nations were in charge of the South-West Africa negotiations. So delicate were relations with South Africa that, by prior agreement, no official was to have any contact with authorities from that country unless representatives of the other countries were also present. Donald McHenry, a black, fairly conservative Foreign Service officer, was the U.S. ambassador in charge, and he insisted on going by the book. Lowenstein, on the other hand, believed that his intimate familiarity with South Africa gave him carte blanche to proceed as he wished. As one of his associates reported, "Al found a way to end up in South Africa and met the president and foreign minister [alone] and came back with different understandings [than everyone else had]." He was enormously successful in striking out over the heads of his superiors, but the result was endless frustration, for both him and others. After leaving the United Nations, Lowenstein undertook one more series of bold initiatives in Africa—seeking single-handedly to work out a solution for the independence of Zimbabwe (then Rhodesia). Here, as with the Biafran crisis ten years earlier, Lowenstein believed that he and he alone had the clout and the connections to tease a solution out of otherwise intransigent politicians. To some extent, he was correct. There were few people who could communicate just as credibly with white supremacists such as Ian Smith and Pik Botha as with black African leaders such as Kenneth Kaunda and Julius Nyerere. Yet the very maverick qualities that enabled Lowenstein to make such bold forays also sabotaged completely the bureaucratic processes of foreign policy management.[5]

Given his still unresolved obsession with elective office, Lowenstein took the first opportunity to reenter the political wars and leave his U.N. post. "I think that eight to ten months into it," Stoney Cooks said, "he [just] lost interest . . . because of the structures." Although he had been involved in some of the most productive and path-breaking foreign policy initiatives of the Carter administration, Lowenstein found it intolerable to function under someone else's control. "He was no team player," Cooks observed. Hence, when Congressman Ed Koch was elected mayor of New York in 1977, creating a vacancy in the eighteenth congressional district on the East Side of Manhattan, Lowenstein determined to throw his hat into the ring once more. It would be the fourth district in which he had been a candidate.[6]

Lowenstein actually ran twice in 1978 for Koch's former seat. In January, he sought the Democratic designation from county committee delegates for a special election to fill out Koch's uncompleted term. His Democratic opponent was the colorful, politically progressive former congresswoman Bella Abzug. Lowenstein entered the contest late after taking a leave of absence from his U.N. post. He had no campaign manager, no headquarters, no game plan. With his assistant Susan Erb, he worked the cocktail and kaffeeklatsch circuit in the days leading up to the county committee meeting. Pressed to comment on local conditions in the district, he responded: "I cannot win [by the criteria] . . . of who went to the most Christmas parties and what people think about block associations. One must discuss the direction of the planet. Not to do so is tawdry." Running on his past reputation, Lowenstein appeared to offer little new to the delegates. "Once again," *New York* magazine's Kenny Lerer wrote, "Lowenstein isn't taking care of business; he is his own worst enemy." When the county committee met, Lowenstein failed to win the party designation.[7]

Unwilling to give up, Lowenstein entered the race once more in June, this time competing in the Democratic primary race to determine who would oppose the Republican William Green (who eventually won Koch's seat at the beginning of the year). This time, Lowenstein's opponent was Carter Burden, an eight-year city council veteran with abundant financial resources and deep roots in the community. In what amounted to a revisit of his first race in 1966 against Ted Weiss, Lowenstein had to face the charge of not having down his homework in the district and of being far more concerned about the fate of the planet than about garbage collection or police protection on East Eighty-third Street. By now the carpetbagger charge had become a cliché, reinforced by Lowenstein's insistence on focusing on global questions, and shunning neighborhood concerns. "He never did polling or anything," Susan Erb said. "I think he may have been afraid to find out the truth." Lowenstein recruited celebrities like Dustin Hoffman and George Plimpton to appear on his behalf, but it was Burden who had the track record. Friends abandoned the cause, blaming Lowenstein for being so self-destructive. "I couldn't stand what he was doing," Ann Feldman said. "I thought it was just such a foolish thing." A volunteer accused Lowenstein of misusing the people who wanted to help him. "You should have won," she wrote, "and yet you arranged your own defeat." Some even attributed his eventual loss (45 percent to 40 percent) to his friends. "You would be surprised, and might even be shocked," Tom Mechling wrote, "at the size of the cadre of your erstwhile politically-sophisticated supporters who worked against you. You just used too many people along your political way, and they and the others caught up with you."[8]

Apparently intent on remaining mired in old patterns, Lowenstein blamed his defeat on external forces. The newspaper strike caused his defeat, he claimed, by preventing the voters of New York's affluent East Side from following their usual instinct to vote for the candidate endorsed by the *New York Times*. "Surely," Lowenstein's friend Hyman Bookbinder wrote reassuringly, "the endorsements would have made the difference." Howie Berman found such an explanation ludicrous. "The notion that he has to depend on how much he's mentioned in the *New York Times* . . . was absurd. Hey, control your own destiny, run your own campaign." One longtime Lowenstein watcher and well-wisher could not believe Al's capacity for denial. "[In] our phone conversation," he wrote, "you did not seem to admit an iota of culpability. . . . You refuse to forego running every two years in futile races. You move around from one district to the next . . . not doing your homework and not establishing credibility as a concerned resident. . . . Jimmy Wechsler's [columns] cannot elect you, try as he might. . . . You are 50 now; no more time for games."[9]

Lowenstein seemed condemned to repeat ad nauseam his patterns of self-deception and self-defeat. Ignoring political realities, eschewing local issues, and portraying himself as the innocent victim of cosmic forces beyond his control, he seemed trapped in a downward spiral and refused to be accountable for his own failures. Yet even as he went back to all the old excuses, he was examining these behavior patterns and reconsidering their appropriateness. Beginning with personal issues, he gave indications of thinking anew about his whole life, including politics.

REFLECTIONS ON THE PERSONAL

It is unlikely that Al Lowenstein ever got over his divorce. Even at the end of their marriage, he apparently could not conceive of the possibility that Jenny might leave, so fundamental was her presence as the anchor that made everything else possible. Like the money he had always received from his father, she and the children existed in his life as a given, as the foundation for everything else. Hence, her departure shattered more than just Lowenstein's ego. It reopened all the questions about who he was and what mattered that he had left in abeyance once he started his family. The fact that Jenny subsequently married Nick Littlefield, one of Al's protégés, simply dramatized the degree to which this event challenged him to look with new eyes at all parts of his life—his friendships, his children, his lifestyle, his career choices, and his sexual identity.[10]

Yet as the divorce destroyed, it also created—by instigating the process of renewal and reevaluation. Although Al did not talk to everybody about the breakup, he sought out those he trusted and reflected at length on what it meant and why it happened. Floss Frucher, a Stanford student he had maintained contact with, related that Al announced a ground rule when he came to dinner: no one was to say anything about the divorce—then he proceeded to talk about nothing else for forty-five minutes. He was hurt, bereft, confused, and distraught. But he shared that vulnerability and pain. Except when he had opened up about his sexual confusion a few years earlier, Sandy Friedman said, it was the first time Allard ever bared his soul. "In some perverse or ironic way, [it] brought him back to college or youth. . . . Certain new possibilities exist[ed] as a result of this." Bruce Payne had a similar experience. "Almost despairingly," Payne reported, "[Al would say] that he didn't know how to have a life." But these expressions of confusion and need were themselves a breakthrough, a new beginning. The person who had always played the role of confessor now had something that he needed to confess.[11]

With increasing frequency, Lowenstein sought solace—and a place to think—in his adopted second home, California. There existed in California another whole orbit of Lowenstein friends, politicos like Rick Tuttle and Howie Berman, celebrities like Robert Vaughn and Judy Quine, well-connected friends like Marcia Borie and Carol Moss, or new protégés such as David Bender and Alan Arkatov. Only now his visits, for at least a while, were less frenetic. After leaving the United Nations, Lowenstein had become associated with a New York law firm. Most of his earnings still came from lecturing, but occasionally a case would bring him to San Diego. Or he would parlay a lecture appearance into a longer stay. Frequently, he ended up in the Beverly Hills home of Carol Moss, a new friend he had met during his summer of work for Jerry Brown. Moss, too, was divorced; a mother of four children, she was trying to finish a law degree. She offered him her home as a place to escape to and make his home as well. Al would arrive, she said, and spend endless hours "lying out in the sun on the balcony." One hour a day he would lift weights and exercise, but the rest of the time he just absorbed the sunshine, sometimes singing, often just lying there, perhaps healing. "He loved it," she said. "Maybe part of it was we were very close. Our family had already become a family. . . . He liked to be warm in the sunshine. He got to hate New York."

California became for him a spiritual retreat as well. In an article, Lowenstein said, "I have marveled at a place so civilized and free-wheeling, a place at once healthy, stale and zany. . . . California, where splendor is natural, where pockets of misery interrupt the countryside rather than the other way around . . . [where there exists] diversity without trenches, ethnic heritages preserved but not often distorted [into bitter rivalries]." And above all, there was the sunshine. "He loved the sun more than anything," Al's son Frank recalled. "He was always saying, 'Like man, give me skin cancer. Give me blisters.' . . . He loved the sun." California, Sandy Friedman observed, "was a whole package."[12]

It was also one of the places Al took the children for vacation. They had enjoyed their time in California in 1975 and were the delight of Al's friends, who whisked them off on whale-watching trips or to Universal Studios. They also developed their own intimate friendships with people like David Bender, who became a surrogate older brother or uncle. Al brought them to Carol's house the winter after the separation to celebrate

Hanukkah and Christmas with her children and their California friends. In general, Al preferred to go places with the children; visiting them in Massachusetts, he said, was always "too orchestrated" and awkward. Hence, he would take the children to places like Sherman Bull's house in Connecticut, where there was a pool, or South Africa, where they stayed in first-class hotels (the trip was sponsored by a liberal antiapartheid businessman) and met such famous people as Winnie Mandela and Alan Paton.[13]

With the family now broken up, the children became Lowenstein's joy. In the past he had doted on them and bragged about them, but he had rarely been there with them. Now, Sandy Friedman said, "for the first time, he took real delight in his children. . . . He had time to play with them and be with them." Neither Friedman nor Frank Lowenstein thought that Al had "a clue" about how to be a father. In the past he had often been an absentee Dad. But with the divorce, time with the children became the most precious thing he had and the process of being a father a cherished opportunity. He planned trips, looked forward to their phone calls, and marveled at the children's response. "It was really touching," Susan Erb said. "[Al] used to come back and say, 'It's unbelievable, Tommy really loves me.'" Al found new ways to include them in his life, writing humorous postcards about his activities (on a visit to Colombia, he wrote the children that he had been rooting for Columbia University the previous week, and that both places were named for Columbus. "Who was Columbus and why didn't he ever make the majors?"); or referring to them in his speeches (at a Hyde Park ceremony honoring Eleanor Roosevelt, he quoted Kate's remark that God must have loved Mrs. Roosevelt to give the rain to make the flowers grow at her grave. Mrs. Roosevelt, he told Kate, was the U.S. representative to the Human Rights Commission. "Can you name another Representative of the U.S. on the Human Rights Commission?")[14]

As in any divorce, tension and strain frequently accompanied the efforts to get together. Although Al and Jenny had successfully kept the children out of their conflicts, the separation inevitably took a toll on them. One friend described Frankie as "very angry and very sullen" after the divorce. Kate was sometimes petulant, resisting Al's efforts to get her to travel to see him. Resettled in Massachusetts, the children were trying to build a new life with new friends; often they resented having to go visit their father in New York. "It was a big pain in the ass," Frank said. "We used to have to take a bus down to New York." Al would be late, and the kids would end up waiting in a bus station. In a campaign, Al might take the children leafleting on street corners. Tommy liked it, but Frank resisted. "I was too shy," he recalled. "I hated it. All I wanted to be was normal. . . . We sort of felt like freaks to begin with, because [we thought] we should have lived in suburbia with this father." One day, Al asked Harvey Lippman to drive with him to meet the children in New Haven to go to a Yale football game. But first, Al insisted on revisiting his old haunts in Long Beach to create the impression that he still lived there with his family and everything was fine. By the time they reached New Haven, the kids had been waiting for an hour and a half. Sometimes Al was so intent on the children having a good time that he tried to will them into happiness, just as he had willed himself into becoming physically fit. "I remember seeing Al . . . grab [the kids'] cheeks," Harvey Lippman said, "to force them to smile about something when they were obviously not in a smiling mood."[15]

Yet there were good times, too—times to talk and get to know each other. Frank remembers saying to his father, "'Dad, why don't you just go to work? Get yourself a goddamn job. Get up in the morning and go to work.' I always wanted to be normal, just have a normal family, and he would always say to me, 'Frank, that's the worst thing that could ever happen. Why would I ever want to get up at eight o'clock every morning and go to work from nine to five. . . . Everybody does that. That's the saddest and most pointless way to spend your life. You're not accomplishing anything.'" Tommy in particular appreciated his father's political activities, recalling with fondness a long drive in 1980 back to Massachusetts from the New Hampshire primary during which they had their first serious conversation about life and politics.

And all the children enjoyed the trips. After they visited South Africa, eleven-year-old Frank announced to his father that there should be a big war there and all the white people should die. He inquired whether Al would ever support violence, and Al replied that he would if all efforts at negotiation failed. Lowenstein boasted about that conversation for days. He was proud of his children and thought they were the smartest, funniest, most beautiful children in the world. He would write down their jokes, dwell on their idiosyncracies, and seek, during his time with them, to impart the lessons he cared about most. "Don't pout," he would say. "Wherever you go, whatever you do . . . be just 'Like wow, this is great.' . . . Try to have fun, try to be happy, try to be enthusiastic. . . . No foot dragging." Gabriel would have smiled.

But he was also sad, knowing how much he had lost. Al loved to laugh, to be funny himself, or have other people be funny. "He would embellish the hell out of a story," Frank said, and took special delight when his children did the same. "It was like, if he could videotape everything that we ever did, he would have. . . . He used to pay us for our quotes." One night, they were in New York having dinner at the Puffin Billy, the Lowenstein family restaurant on Madison Avenue where they always went to eat. "So somebody said something funny," Frank recalled. "He just looked at them for a second with a big smile, and then it slowly deteriorated and the sides of his mouth curled down and he started crying. And he got up and just walked away without saying anything. . . . It was just . . . heartbreaking. You could see that he just loved us kids, and it was just hard."[16]

Yet in acknowledging what he had lost, Lowenstein also was learning— through the pain—how much he had to gain by being with his children and loving them. Had the divorce and the geographical separation not happened, he might have gone on doing no more than dip into their lives. But now he appreciated how important they were to him and savored their time together, deriving from it a new sense of priorities, of what mattered and what did not. His new insight did not lessen Lowenstein's deprivation, but it did give him the ability to sort out and make choices that otherwise might never have emerged.

In similar fashion, he began to revise the way he carried on his friendships. For most of his life, he had moved from one intense relationship to another, seemingly afraid to linger for too long in one situation lest the demands and intimacy generated by sustained contact require a lasting commitment. Some of these relationships, of course, were renewed regularly over the years, offering some measure of continuity and depth. But more often than not, they were like incandescent lights that passed into the darkness when Al persisted in his endless wanderings and sought new contacts. Most characteristic of all had been the large number of friends brought together by Al. Instead of five, eight, or ten people as regular confidants and "best friends," Al had accumulated hundreds—even thousands—of friends who had received the "Lowenstein treatment" and thought of themselves as his intimates. But in fact they were almost indistinguishable from each other. Lowenstein's Long Island aide, Harriet Eisman, parodied this dimension of his personality when she said one evening, "Come on over here, Al, and give me two minutes of your innermost bullshit."

But now Al began to reach out to fewer friends, engaging them in more sustained contact, appearing to recognize that his pain required the healing nurture of in-depth relationships rather than transitory intensity. He regularly called Harvey Lippman late at night, arranging to meet him at an all-night Greek coffee shop equidistant from their apartments for Drake's cakes, Coke, and long conversations. He asked Floss Frucher to call Peter and Marian Wright Edelman so that these few old friends could meet for a quiet dinner and talk. More and more he relied on his oldest friend, Sandy Friedman, or one of his longest standing Stanford associates, John McPherson. "I think Al was . . . headed in that direction where he'd have a few close friends," Susan Erb commented, "which isn't really something he focused in on before that."[17]

Nowhere was this shift more noticeable than in Lowenstein's relationship with Sherman Bull, the protégé who had accompanied him to South Africa in 1959. The two had maintained contact over the years; indeed, Lowenstein had insisted that Bull, barely finished with his medical training, perform his gall bladder surgery in 1967. But their contact had not been frequent or deep. Bull had gone through a painful divorce at the same time Lowenstein did, and now they suddenly began to see more of each other. "Very often he would call up, and we would just meet," Bull said. "And it was very different. He wasn't into this frantic stuff anymore. He had really gotten over that. You would go for dinner, and there would be just Al." One night Al joined Bull and his new wife at an off-Broadway play that was about divorce. "And the three of us just came out of there crying, just weeping together. . . . He never had time for that sort of thing before. . . . I think he had changed in many ways . . . had gotten his priorities straightened out, and I think he realized that one of his problems was . . . [his] frantic lifestyle—a crazy, insane pace—[that] nobody could keep up with." Lowenstein would come to Bull's Connecticut house on weekends, sometimes with the kids, but sometimes alone, "just to get away and be quiet . . . and be out of this crazy maze." Clearly, something was changing in Lowenstein. "In the beginning [in 1959], I was kind of the student, and he was the teacher," Bull commented. "[Now] we were adults coping with personal crises and exchanging ideas and having fun together on a peer level."[18]

These shifts in Lowenstein reflected not only the devastation of his divorce but the new and excruciating awareness of his own mortality that accompanied turning fifty. Many birthdays carry substantial emotional freight, but perhaps none more than the half-century mark. At forty, one can still feel and look young and, if an optimist, continue to believe that life is only half over. But no matter what a person's appearance at fifty, the knowledge that life is now all downhill is unavoidable. It is a time for reflection about what has been, as well as for sober confrontation with what will come.

For someone who had devoted his entire career to leading and living among the young, that confrontation was likely to be especially poignant and difficult. "I think [Allard] was dumbstruck by middle age," Sandy Friedman said. "When he was fifty, [he saw himself] as failing in every department." His wife had left him, his kids were more than 200 miles away, he had suffered defeat after defeat in politics. For someone who thought "everything can be done by will . . . it was almost a sin to admit of depression"; yet no other word could describe the overwhelming sense of failure that gripped Lowenstein. "He had no platform, no showcase. . . . Fundamentally, a dream and an illusion had been shattered." Greg Craig recalled Lowenstein's plight as a classic midlife crisis, compounded by his unique circumstances. "He was not achieving the position in society and politics . . . that a man of his brilliance and past record [should have]." And the future did not look much better. "He would not have been a happy old person because he would have had to stop running at some point," Craig said. "It would have been embarrassing for a sixty-five-year-old man." Frank Lowenstein recalled his father addressing the problem directly. "He was about fifty . . . [and] sort of at a crossroads in his life," the younger Lowenstein said, and he told his son, "I don't want to just sit around and be fat, balding and fiftyish and not doing anything [important]."[19]

Less intimate friends shared the impression that Al was bewildered about how to proceed with the rest of his life. Floss Frucher noted that Al "seemed to be very isolated and alone again, a person without a place or a cause at the moment. . . . [There] was a sense of the most important things he had worked on having . . . passed; his family was gone . . . he was by himself again. There was almost a reversion back to the way I had known him in the beginning, which was being alone, having his family . . . be this huge network of people." A former Long Island protégé, Rick Saslaw, who spent Thanksgiving with Lowenstein and Carol Moss in Los Angeles, had the same sense. "Here was this brilliant man," he said, "who at fifty-one years of age . . . was experiencing a severe identity crisis. . . . He was a man who had moved mountains, but by the world's standards, he was a failure. He didn't have a [decent] place to host his kids during visitation rights. He didn't have a job to speak of. . . . He was lost." Ken Liberman, another activist from the 1960s, stayed at Lowenstein's apartment when he visited New York at the end of the 1970s. "He was busy like always," Lieberman said, "but he was like an automaton. . . . He would go to the law office, he would go to the Yale Club [to exercise], he would . . . make two or three talks every night." Yet when Lieberman asked him about politics, Lowenstein told him, "I'm just going through the motions. This is my life. I'm stuck, but it's too late to do anything."[20]

Lowenstein also exhibited during these years an increasing preoccupation with his own death. The subject was not entirely new. "He really had it on his mind all the time," Greg Craig observed; his father's death had created the fear that he would also die from a heart attack. The specific focus of Lowenstein's thoughts about dying, however, altered dramatically when Robert Kennedy was killed. When he drove around upstate New York with Steve Morgan in 1973 to explore the possibility of running for the Senate, Al talked at length about his funeral, giving Morgan a list of pallbearers and telling him that "Amazing Grace" should lead the list of songs to be sung. "Something's going to happen to me violently, I feel," he said. "It so stunned me that . . . I didn't want to hear it," Morgan recalled. "He was very serious . . . and maudlin about it, and I felt eerie. . . . It was one of several times that I started to think, 'This man doesn't think that he's going to live long.'"[21]

The morbid fears seemed to intensify during the late 1970s. On a trip to California, Lowenstein took Marcia Borie to dinner and started to write on a napkin a list of songs that included "The Battle Hymn of the Republic," "Amazing Grace," and a song by Peter, Paul, and Mary. "Here," he said, "if anything happens to me, these are the songs I want played at my funeral." On several occasions, Lowenstein took out a yellow pad while having dinner with Harvey Lippman at the Puffin Billy and wrote out a will, as well as detailed instructions for his funeral. He even worried whether the rabbi would allow "Amazing Grace" to be sung in a synagogue. While riding through the New Hampshire countryside in early 1980 with Steven Smith, Jr., Robert Kennedy's nephew, Lowenstein returned again to the topic of his death. Al thought, Smith remarked, "that something . . . had gone tragically wrong with the country, and . . . he felt he was going to be killed . . . violently. . . . He just said that . . . ever since Bobby died that . . . he had this feeling . . . that he was going to be killed also." Al told Carol Moss that he did not expect to live past fifty-five, and David Bender that he expected to be killed like Kennedy. During 1979, Susan Erb observed, Al "kept mentioning, 'This is the last year of my life.'" When she showed him pictures of himself at a kaffeeklatsch, he commented, "These look like Frank Porter Graham the last month of his life."[22]

One way to interpret such premonitions is to conclude that Lowenstein's sense of failure had led him into a profound depression, where the personal and the political were joined and the only exit he saw was that of the tragic hero, shot down like Robert Kennedy. Although it was natural for his friends to remember these remarks after Lowenstein died and raise them to a magnified level of prescient prophecy, the fact remains that Lowenstein talked much more about death than one might expect in a normal person, even one who had just turned fifty. Moreover, many friends commented specifically on Lowenstein's depression. "I thought he was a little bit lost," Nancy Steffen said. "He was having to go faster and faster with less and less effect." "It was a depressing period for him personally," Paul Schrade observed, "but also the politics of that period were so bad." Carol Moss noted that when they were alone together, Al seemed particularly downcast, and that he even stopped doing his daily hour of physical exercise. With everything important in his life falling apart, he found himself alone in the world, unappreciated and unrewarded for all his talents and achievements; it made sense in a melodramatic way for Lowenstein to conceive of his life as an existential drama now fated for a tragic end.[23]

Yet there is another possible interpretation, not necessarily incompatible with the first. Lowenstein seemed clearly to have come to a new appreciation of the importance of both his children and a few close friends. (Sherman Bull noted that at Al's fiftieth birthday party, there were only a few good friends rather than the usual hundreds of acquaintances.) More aware perhaps of how his constant motion undermined the possibility of finding a center for his life, he was groping for a new identity. Becoming fifty simply accentuated the symbolic nature of his own transition. The glory days of the 1960s might be over, but that did not necessarily mean there was nothing left to do. "I always thought," Nancy Steffen said, "[that Al] perceived of himself in very dramatic terms. . . . He saw his life as an ongoing [play]. . . . I don't think he was finished in terms of his own emotional growth. Even though he spent his whole life running away from himself . . . I always imagined he was someone who had the capacity to understand, to wise up about himself." The conversations with Sherman Bull and Harvey Lippman certainly suggested that potential, as did the intimate, smaller gatherings with friends. "He was turning fifty years old, which to him was cosmic," Nancy Steffen said. "For Allard not to be a kid was like Peter Pan not to be a kid. . . . He hadn't really figured out what to do when he ceased to be a student leader. . . . [But] my sense is that . . . he would have had a second act. . . . He would have figured out a second act." The question was what that act might consist of.[24]

SOME POSSIBILITIES

Inevitably, much of the answer would depend on how Lowenstein chose to deal with his ongoing dilemma over sexual identity. To some extent, he had become more open in his interest in men. During the 1978 race for Congress, for example, some staff members were concerned about Al becoming too visible when he frequented areas associated with gay activities. He continued to date a variety of women and ruminated out loud about the possibility of remarriage. Cheryl Tiegs, the model and entertainer, was one object of speculation; Shirley Oakes Butler, a multimillionairess who had been a law school classmate and bridesmaid for Jacqueline Kennedy, was another. Yet none of these relationships seemed that serious, and Al continued to be attracted to young men. One night, he asked out an old girlfriend, then left her with a male friend and went off on his own. After staying out all night, the two friends decided to stop off at Lowenstein's house the next morning. Al was coming out the door with a young man and seemed "dismayed" that they had seen him.[25]

Yet Lowenstein remained confused about his self-definition. Many of his homosexual friends, Al told Bruce Payne, thought he should identify himself as gay. "Maybe they're right," he said. "This is a weird way I have of living, and I don't know if there's anybody like me." In Payne's view, "Al didn't know what to make of himself." But he expressed interest in the possibility of living with a man. "We had a talk about coming out of the closet," Payne recalled, "[and] there was some kind of byplay about what closet could he come out of." Lowenstein read books like *The Dave Kopay Story*, an autobiography of a professional football player who declared he was gay. But he was not yet ready to do that himself. "All people aren't the same," Al said to Payne. Payne left the conversation with the sense that "there was more to find out, that life kind of opened up in front of him and that he didn't know where it was going to take him . . . [but] he was at least thinking about relationships down the road."[26]

Another associate saw the same perplexity in Al's approach to the issue. "He probably would have been very uncomfortable with the kind of gay sexuality that was prevalent at the time," the San Francisco gay activist and Democratic leader Jim Foster noted. "He may have had homosexual . . . tendencies that were expressed in . . . almost Victorian fashion, [but] . . . I'm sure that he did not identify with drag queens or people who . . . expressed their sexuality in rather extreme ways. . . . His homosexuality, I think, was a great deal more cerebral than it was physical and overt. Almost Grecian in a sense." In that situation, Foster remarked, "coming out" would have been very difficult, especially given Lowenstein's family concerns. "[The fact] that he came to where he [did] . . . was, I think, a great acknowledgment of his . . . ability to deal with his own reality."[27]

Whatever his eventual decision on declaring his sexual orientation, Lowenstein clearly was embarked on a quest for new alternatives. He continued to explore the possibility of moving to California. His friend Rick Tuttle, prominent in California education, hoped to find him a presidency of a community college. Carol Moss was involved in seeking faculty appointments for him at both UCLA and Berkeley. Lowenstein himself hoped that a month-long lectureship at the University of California at Santa Barbara might lead to a permanent position there, while Gary Hart speculated about a teaching position at Stanford. Harris Wofford, who was a college president himself at the time, was working for the same goal on the East Coast, recommending Lowenstein for a position at Haverford. Interestingly, Lowenstein seemed shy and insecure in interviews for academic positions, perhaps a legacy of his difficult departure from Stanford. Carol Moss, for example, reported that at a lunch with a UCLA faculty committee, Al was "like a meek, pathetic creature. . . . He just didn't know how to . . . sell himself. It was so poignant to see him sort of with his tail between his legs, because here was a man on a larger stage who was a powerhouse." Some of these academic possibilities came closer to fruition than others. In the end, none of them materialized. Yet the very number of such inquiries suggested a readiness on Lowenstein's part to think about new beginnings.[28]

In addition, he signaled at least some people that he was rethinking his position on political office. More and more of his friends took the risk of alienating Lowenstein by pleading with him not to run again. And while Lowenstein refused to bare his soul in response, the very number of moving pleas he received had to make an impact. To some people, Al confided a reluctance to keep running. He may have told Ken Liberman that "it's too late to do anything," but he also told his young aide Mark Childress "how nice it would be to really get out of the rat race and out of the New York-to-Washington shuttling and [instead] to go with the kids and spend a lot more time with them." Possibly with that in mind, Lowenstein changed law firms, moving to a smaller office headed by an old friend, and purchased a condominium in Florida. "We who love you are happy to see you moving into new places and spaces," Carol Moss wrote him.[29]

Even in that part of his life that remained explicitly committed to party politics, Lowenstein exhibited a range of concerns that reflected new departures. Lowenstein had always been supportive of human rights efforts to abolish discrimination based on sexual preference, but now he became specifically associated with gay rights political activity. When some California voters sponsored a referendum to pass the Briggs Amendment, a law requiring school officials to report on any gay activities among schoolteachers, Lowenstein volunteered to campaign actively against it. "I could tell when he visited me at headquarters that [it] was a very difficult decision for him," the gay rights leader David Mixner noted, but Lowenstein ended up committing himself fully to the effort. One of his former Stanford protégés who had recently "come out" recalled that in the mid to late 1970s, Lowenstein "had become somewhat of a caricature of himself . . . just sort of replicating the things that he had done before. . . . But then he began to get involved in the gay rights issue," and that was something new.

Lowenstein became enough a part of a gay rights political network that Rick Saslaw recruited him to come to the 1978 midterm Democratic convention at Memphis to lobby delegates for a gay rights platform provision. Not only did Lowenstein respond; he also effectively used his White House contacts to win a near victory. If being gay involved acknowledging "the politicization of one's sexuality," Democratic activist Jim Foster said, "I think Al had reached that point."[30]

Significantly, Lowenstein carried this new political emphasis into his last major campaign as a debater, strategist, and activist for Ted Kennedy's 1980 presidential candidacy. Lowenstein had become involved early in the Kennedy movement; he had made the difficult decision to turn down Jerry Brown's request for support of his presidential bid. Lowenstein performed many roles in the Kennedy campaign, but his activities focused on California and Florida. In the Miami–Ft. Lauderdale area, he concentrated much of his energy on mobilizing gay activists to Kennedy's banner. In California, he campaigned like he was on home ground. "At the state convention," his young aide Alan Arkatov said, "it was Al at his best . . . doing eight caucuses at once, each targeted. He'd be as brilliant in the black caucus as he was in the Hispanic caucus or in the women's caucus." But Lowenstein also worked effectively with the gay

Democratic clubs of Los Angeles and San Francisco. Kennedy's margin of victory in the straw vote was sufficiently narrow that it could be argued that gay delegates provided the decisive difference; in fact, when Lowenstein called Kennedy to tell him the results, he put Jim Foster, the gay Democratic leader on the phone, urging him to "tell Kennedy who did it." "It was sort of amusing," Foster said, "because here is Al, who everybody sort of knew was closeted, telling me, who can't be closeted, to haul out the flags and the band. . . . He was so tickled and proud." In Foster's view, Lowenstein had played a major part in shaping Kennedy's attitude toward homosexual rights. "[Al] was almost ready to take this [issue] on," he concluded, "having seen the difficulties of it."[31]

In many ways, Lowenstein's involvement in the Kennedy candidacy mirrored all the dilemmas he faced as he tried to chart the public course he might follow in his sixth decade. He had become so marginalized owing to his Stassen-esque runs for office that in many parts of the country—especially the New York–Washington corridor—he had lost credibility. Lowenstein's flirtation with assassination conspiracies had also distanced him to some extent from the Kennedy clan. (Lowenstein once told Carol Moss, for example, that even if Ted Kennedy won, he would not receive any important position because he had "transgressed" into forbidden territory with his investigation.) On the other hand, Lowenstein possessed a brilliant political mind, especially on the "big" issues, was a superb advocate, and in debate was perhaps the best spontaneous speaker in the Kennedy camp.[32]

Supersensitive to his standing in Kennedy's eyes, Lowenstein often felt resentful that he was being kept on the outside instead of being given a seat at the power tables in New York. He once called his old ally Joe Rauh from New Hampshire to ask whether he should stay stuck up there or come to Washington. "That was a very depressing conversation," Rauh said. "He sort of felt left out . . . and wasn't particularly happy with what he was doing up there." His friend Steve Morgan put it more directly. "He felt he was being shafted by the Kennedy people," Morgan said, yet he also desperately wanted to be included. Traveling with Lowenstein on many of his jaunts, Alan Arkatov observed the same pattern. Lowenstein would have Arkatov or Morgan call the Kennedy camp on his behalf to try to get funds for a plane ticket somewhere; he seemed afraid to put himself directly on the line in case his requests were rejected. He wanted the respect accorded a real "player" but could not count on that respect automatically. Almost like a Willy Loman, he craved the recognition that he believed his career warranted yet feared profoundly being discarded as "used goods."[33]

On the other hand, Lowenstein persisted in his struggle for acceptance until he won. With the tenacity of a tough wrestler, he kept coming back for more, making himself indispensable, proving by his good works that he merited the recognition and redemption he sought. Steven Smith, Jr., Ted Kennedy's nephew and the son of the campaign manager, served as one ally. Traveling together through New Hampshire and other states, they became fast friends. They also shared many ideas about what the campaign needed, and Smith became Lowenstein's advocate in family campaign counsels. "There was an element to Al that was perceived as a little bit ungovernable," Smith said, "and I think that was an error on their part." By taking Al's side, the younger Smith helped reinforce the bonds that already tied Lowenstein to the family. "He was sort of on the periphery of the campaign [in the beginning]," Smith acknowledged. "I was his way in, in a way." As the Kennedy candidacy met repeated adversity, from the candidate's disastrous interview with Roger Mudd on CBS News to the Iranian hostage crisis, which made it impossible to attack Carter, Lowenstein stood strong and tall, refusing to give up and exhorting others to keep fighting.[34]

That kind of loyalty transformed the perception of Lowenstein's persistence—his unwelcome pushiness became laudable courage. "[Al] maintained a sense of what his own personal convictions were," Smith commented, regardless of setbacks in Iowa and elsewhere. Kennedy and the senior Smith had known and appreciated Lowenstein from the "dump Johnson" days of 1968. He would walk in "with his briefcase falling apart" and try to convince Bobby to reconsider being a candidate. "He was irresistible in that sense." Now he did the same with Ted Kennedy, who recalled, "He just sort of squatted here. He just took over your house in a marvelous, wonderful way. . . . And you didn't have to know Al for a long time to be his friend. He was one of those rare people, when you sort of know him, you know right away he was a friend." Robert Shrum, a key Kennedy adviser, summarized what Lowenstein contributed besides his debating skills and brilliance. "He was most valuable," Shrum said, "because he combined two rare qualities: complete loyalty and complete honesty. And he had Kennedy's total trust."[35]

By the late winter of 1980, Lowenstein's determination had paid off. His contributions in California and Florida had boosted his currency in campaign circles. He had performed brilliantly as a Kennedy advocate on

William Buckley's "Firing Line" and on David Susskind's television show. The *Atlanta Journal* called him "the leading national campaigner for Ted Kennedy." And when he was in New York, Lowenstein became a nightly visitor to Steve Smith's home for dinner or late-evening conversation in which the top campaign aides discussed the day's events and laid out strategy for the next day.

Lowenstein was thus midstream in his exploration of new possibilities as the 1980s began. In many ways, he remained caught up in the vicious circle of constant motion, perpetual campaigning, and nearly reflexive repetition of old patterns. Yet there was also impressive evidence that he was changing. Not only was Lowenstein reevaluating the primacy he gave to time with his children and close friends, he also seemed intent on re-thinking how he would define himself sexually, both in his own life and as a political figure. Perhaps willing to give up his compulsion to run for Congress, he was even prepared—in the minds of some of his friends—to consider a new career as a crusading advocate for gay rights. In Nancy Steffen's words, Lowenstein may have been in the process of "organizing himself another act."

Such were the circumstances when Lowenstein flew in from the campaign trail the week of March 9 to help plan a new media blitz for the up-coming New York primary. He met with the Kennedy media people on Thursday, March 13, to sketch out new TV commercials; he was to join them again late Friday afternoon to put the finishing touches on the plans. He never made the meeting. Instead, he kept an appointment he had scheduled earlier with a former Stanford protégé, Dennis Sweeney.[36]

THE CIRCLE CLOSES

Born in Oregon to working-class parents, Dennis Sweeney survived a somewhat troubled childhood. His father was a pilot during World War II who subsequently separated from his wife. Dennis spent only one month with his father, when he was two; his father was later killed in Korea. Sweeney's mother remarried as he approached adolescence. Her new hus-band was a perfectionist who brooked no deviation from prescribed rou-tine. Serious and religious, Dennis performed well in high school, both in sports and in academics. Handsome, quiet, and reputed to be a natural leader, he won a scholarship to Stanford, where he quickly became a prominent figure on campus. Sweeney was attracted to the religion classes of Robert MacAfee Brown and became known for the intensity of his views. "I felt guilty in Dennis's presence," his classmate Patty Hagen said. "He had a way of making you feel that you weren't committed enough. He was a saint, sure of his beliefs." By 1963, Sweeney had been elected speaker of the Stanford Student Congress and was an honors student.[37]

Al Lowenstein immediately singled Sweeney out as a prime candidate for recruitment as a young activist. In Dwight Clark's typology, Sweeney was in the first circle of Lowenstein disciples—not a preordained and already acknowledged leader, but someone with enormous potential who could be cultivated, then groomed into greatness. Lowenstein poured enormous energy into these relationships, and Sweeney responded with alacrity. When Al went to Mississippi in the summer of 1963, one of the first people he called was Sweeney, urging him to come to Mississippi and get involved. It was exactly the kind of mission Sweeney saw as most consistent with his own sense of religious "calling." When he returned to Stanford for the fall semester, Sweeney became Lowenstein's chief lieutenant in mobilizing students to volunteer their money and bodies for the Mississippi Freedom Vote. Totally devoted to Lowenstein, Sweeney chastised those who did not react enthusiastically, acting almost as though Lowenstein were God. "Al's not going to be very happy," he said menacingly to one student who was resisting Lowenstein's appeals. As soon as the call came in October to go to Mississippi, Sweeney was in the first Stanford car, along with Fred Goff and John Bryson. "People respected the fact that [Dennis] was willing to toss things aside and simply jump into a crisis and not look back," former Stanford student Ken Stevens said.[38]

As taken as Sweeney was with Lowenstein, the older man's feelings for his new protégé were even more intense. "This is difficult to say, but it is in fact true," one close friend of Lowenstein's observed. "[Al] was in love with this man. . . . There was no one in his life at that time that had the same kind of hold on him as Dennis did. . . . He seemed so much more committed and clear in what he wanted to do with his life. He was an extraordinary personality sort of marching through your life. He stuck out instantly. . . . [Al] talked about Dennis all the time." Sweeney quickly became a hero to many civil rights workers, some of whom shared Lowenstein's fascination with him. "He was a wonder kid," Susan Goodwillie observed. Ed King saw Sweeney as the best that white youth had to contribute to the movement, "a very effective, quiet organizer who . . . accepted the Mississippi style of just quietly talking to the people." Marian Wright Edelman described him as the person who, in the purest way, lived out his commitment to the civil rights movement. When Greg Craig met Sweeney at the Atlantic City Democratic convention, he, too, was awed. "Out of his T-shirt and his blue workshirt," Craig said, "he had loafers on and slacks and a tweed jacket. . . . He looked smashing . . . a quiet, strong, and very charismatic sort of guy." Everyone who knew Sweeney, it seemed, felt drawn to him. But no one more than Lowenstein.[39]

It was all the more painful, then, when Sweeney turned against Lowenstein in the summer and fall of 1964. Sweeney had committed himself totally to the organizing style and political perspective of SNCC. Galvanized by the struggle of Mississippi blacks to overcome both rampant racism and white paternalism, Sweeney soon came to share SNCC's suspicions of northern white liberals—a suspicion he increasingly focused on Lowenstein. "Al's a very complicated guy," Sweeney told one mutual friend, "and I'm not sure I approve of the role he's played." Mendy Samstein, another white SNCC worker, saw Dennis's alienation as "the split that everybody was feeling with Al," a split based on Al being an outsider who was trying to tell people on the inside what to do. But there was another dimension as well. "Since Dennis and I had been quite close friends," Lowenstein told the civil rights historian Clayborne Carson, "it became a very, very personal thing. . . . During the period when I was becoming the villain in [SNCC's] eyes, [he] became the spearhead of their campaign against me."[40]

From the fall of 1964 through the spring of 1965, Sweeney suffered some of the traumas associated with combat experience. While working and living in a Freedom House in McComb—described by nearly everyone as the most brutal town in Mississippi—Sweeney was nearly killed when seventeen sticks of dynamite exploded six feet from his bed. Only a thick bed board saved him. He became more wary and suspicious, quieter, moodier. Instead of staying in one place and focusing on a single project, he moved from one location to another, avoiding long-term involvement. He retained contact with Lowenstein, asking for his help in securing a fellowship from the Eleanor Roosevelt Foundation to finance his work in Mississippi. But he also continued to express resentment toward Al. On a trip to Yale in the fall of 1964, he connected with Bruce Payne, who had also been part of the Freedom Vote venture. "There was something wrong there," Payne recalled. "I was troubled because at one level he was so open and so winning and so attractive, but his anger at Al was so irrational." John Steinbruner, a Stanford friend who had also been to Mississippi with Sweeney in 1963, recalled seeing him at a party and being disturbed by his appearance. "Uh-oh," he thought, "something [happened]."[41]

One possibility was that Sweeney had become a psychological victim of the stresses associated with the movement. In an article written at the time, Robert Coles—frequently called the movement's "staff psychiatrist"—described the fatigue that overcame activists who endured "almost impossible sacrifices of living conditions and freedom in towns whose existence and character in this nation are perhaps unbelievable if not seen." In the face of such conditions, Coles said, movement veterans often developed clinical signs of depression—"exhaustion, weariness, despair, frustration and rage. . . . The youth affected may take to heavy drinking, or become silent, sulky and uncooperative. Frequently, one sees real gloom, loss of appetite, withdrawal from social contacts as well as from useful daily work in the movement."[42]

Sweeney exhibited many of these symptoms. Rumor had it that, during 1964–65, he had started smoking marijuana heavily. In the course of the year, he fell in love with Mary King; the daughter of a Methodist minister, she worked on press relations for SNCC. The two got married in a home ceremony, with only Bob and Donna Moses present, and then returned to California, where they lived for six months with Bob Beyers, the director of the Stanford news bureau and also a veteran of Freedom Summer. "He wasn't the same person when he came back," Beyers said. "You could say, 'Well, none of us were,' but he was spent. . . . He would just sleep all day for days and days and days." Unfocused, he could not complete projects he started, became even moodier, and seemed without purpose. After less than a year of marriage, Mary King left him.[43]

The next year, an old Stanford ally, Armin Rosencranz, encountered Sweeney at an annual brunch that brought together activist friends in the Stanford community. "He looked different," Rosencranz observed. "His hair was short, his eyes were blazing." Rosencranz had heard the rumors about Sweeney's drug use and said to him, "There's something in your eyes that's different." Sweeney responded, "Well, I've had about 100 acid trips since we last saw each other, and that will do a lot to your head." Then Sweeney turned to Rosencranz and asked, "Do you know anything about Al Lowenstein being a homosexual?" Rosencranz remarked that he knew about the "single bed routine"—which he would not necessarily call homosexuality—and then asked Sweeney if he had experienced anything more than that. "No," Sweeney said, "but I know somebody who has." According to Sweeney, Al had once gotten a motel room with one bed and tried to hug Sweeney as he had many others, many of them Sweeney's classmates. In Rosencranz's view, that action was not unusual. Yet of all the people troubled by these episodes, he thought, "none [was] as troubled as Sweeney."[44]

By the end of 1966, Sweeney had become heavily involved in the antiwar movement, especially draft resistance. He moved into a commune of like-minded activists. David Harris, a former Stanford friend, was the most prominent member of the commune. Harris, too, had been a Lowenstein "groupie," experienced a brief infatuation with him, and been the object of a Lowenstein advance. Now he was most famous for his resistance activities and his relationship with the folk singer Joan Baez. Harris had broken with Lowenstein over the Vietnam War, accusing Lowenstein of "collaborating" with an evil system by asking people to stay within the electoral process and not break the law. Although Sweeney and Harris shared a common animus toward their former leader, they had their own disagreements. Sweeney thought Harris was hypocritical for living off Baez's money. Harris and others in the house got fed up with Sweeney's idiosyncracies. Sweeney took up acoustic guitar and for a few months played rhythm guitar in a resistance band. But he had little musical talent and was merely tolerated. He also attempted to make a film about Mississippi black life based on outtakes from a project he had worked on with Ed Pincus, a Boston filmmaker, in 1965. But it was criticized for being condescending. His old movement friend Mendy Samstein observed that "Dennis was struggling with some things he could not articulate." With no civil rights movement to provide an external focus for his drives, "there [remained] only the inner difficulty."[45]

To an increasing degree, that "inner difficulty" became visible to others. Sweeney participated in a 1967 antiwar trip to Bratislava, Yugoslavia, to meet with a North Vietnamese delegation. Stoney Cooks, a member of the U.S. team, thought that Dennis was "acting weird" and seemed particularly fearful on the way over. Richard Flacks, another member of the delegation, roomed with Sweeney in Paris. "What was very odd," he recalled, "was the almost complete silence he would lapse into of a kind I'd never experienced with any other person." When Flacks finally asked Sweeney about it, Sweeney replied, "Well, you know, I'm seeing movies in my head when that happens"; he attributed the condition to the aftereffects of having "dropped acid hundreds of times." By 1970, he confided in a friend that someone had implanted electrodes in his body to control him. Soon, these electrodes began to transmit messages as well. Eventually, Sweeney became convinced that the voices came from transmitters that had been placed in his bridgework by a "liberal do-good" dentist who worked on his teeth when he was on the SNCC staff. The dentist, Sweeney concluded, had been a CIA agent "and had doctored him up good." In a desperate effort to silence the voices, Sweeney filed down all his dental crowns, leaving only the tiny pointed posts that had anchored the crowns. Yet the voices would not stop.[46]

By the winter of 1973, Sweeney's symptoms had become so extreme that his parents and friends sought help. Moving back to Oregon in the summer of 1972, he lived with an old school friend, Charles Hinkle. At that point, he traced the voices back to 1967, when he had turned in his draft card. Frightened by his behavior, his parents sought to have him committed to a state mental institution for treatment, but in an era when institutionalization was believed to be ineffective and inappropriate, they dropped their effort to do so on the condition that Sweeney seek private psychiatric care. His mother asked Hinkle to write to Lowenstein and other friends for financial help to put Dennis in a private hospital, but to his regret, Hinkle could not bring himself to write the letters. After a few sessions with a psychiatrist, Sweeney left for Boston. "I feel powerless to do anything," Hinkle wrote Lowenstein in April. "Fifteen years ago, or even ten, [Dennis] was a man of such promise. A lot of people must have failed him—including me."[47]

Sweeney himself, meanwhile, desperately sought some answers and even expressed a willingness to do penance for his own role in creating his condition. Writing to SDS friends in 1973, he declared that the psychological warfare against him had started in 1971, and that he was carrying around "extra software" in his head. "I have done everything I can do to locate it and remove it," he said. "My efforts have all been failures and usually self-destructive. No doubt in the 60s, I was party to some behavior that was politically irresponsible. *If that incurred a social debt, then I am willing to pay it in reasonable terms* [rather than endure] the bureaucratic sadism and infinite guilt which is what I see confronting me" (italics added).[48]

Although Lowenstein was only one of a spectrum of "enemies" Sweeney suspected, he did not immediately single Lowenstein out as the source of his problems. Rather, it seemed at first that he wanted to reach out to Lowenstein for help. In his view, Lowenstein had played a major role in all the circumstances surrounding the onset of his difficulties. But Lowenstein's instrumentality might mean he had some clues about a solution. For his part, Lowenstein had continued to talk about Sweeney often, seeing him as a symbol of the sad fate of the civil rights movement. He had kept up with Sweeney's condition and knew from Hinkle's letter just how pathological it had become. Thus, when Sweeney called him in 1974 and asked to come see him at the house in Brooklyn, Al was eager to try to help. Al had told her repeatedly, Jenny said, "how wonderful Dennis had been, what a talented, bright, dedicated person, and how terribly sad it was." Jenny went to bed when Sweeney arrived, but after he left, Al woke her to share his concern about Sweeney's condition. "Dennis is just more wretched than ever," Al told her, "and he's hearing things transmitted through his teeth."[49]

By 1975, Sweeney had deteriorated further. He accused Ed Pincus, the civil rights filmmaker, and Pincus's wife and child, of "broadcasting" to him all day long. Confronting Pincus, Sweeney called him a member of the international Jewish conspiracy, seeking to destroy him via the transmitters in his head. Terrified by Sweeney's demeanor, Pincus sent his family out of state and purchased a pistol. The next time Sweeney faced Pincus, he assaulted him with his fists and screamed at him to stop the messages. Pincus had friends there to protect him, and Sweeney was pulled away. But Pincus remained fearful, convinced that Sweeney represented a profound personal threat.[50]

Sweeney also turned directly on Lowenstein. In 1975, he demanded that Lowenstein stop tormenting him and asked to see him. Lowenstein went to Philadelphia, where Sweeney was living temporarily, and met him on a dark platform of Pennsylvania Station. Stepping out of the shadows, Sweeney pleaded with Lowenstein to call off the voices. Lowenstein offered to get Sweeney psychiatric help and then left. He continued to talk about Dennis with everyone who knew him. Then two or three years later, Dennis called again to ask to meet him in Manhattan. Accompanied by his friend Judy Quine, Al walked with Dennis for twenty minutes on the Upper East Side, listening once again to Sweeney's pleas that he stop the voices. Afterwards Quine told Lowenstein, "Al, you can't do anything. There is nothing you will ever be able to do for him. With all the best intentions, you have to let go."[51]

By the end of the 1970s, Lowenstein seemed fully aware of both Dennis's desperate condition and his potential for violence. On a trip to Europe in 1978, Al met a former Stanford student whom both he and Dennis had known. "The subject that seemed to be most on Al's mind," Paul Strasberg recalled, "was Dennis, about whom he was very troubled."

Lowenstein described in detail his encounter with Sweeney in the Philadelphia train station, "how Dennis was fearful of him . . . [and] waiting sort of in the shadows . . . to talk to him and . . . ask him to stop." Al told Strasberg that Dennis had threatened to kill him. The last time Al saw Greg Craig, he returned once again to the subject of how crazy Dennis was, telling Craig that "people are worried about him being violent." But Lowenstein still took Sweeney's phone calls. "[He] was unfailingly sure that he could . . . fix it for Dennis," Judy Quine said. "You went out to fix whole parts of the society, [so] it's very hard to think that you can't fix it for one poor guy that was a devotee."[52]

Sweeney's descent into madness continued, with an ever sharper focus on Lowenstein as its source. His stepfather died in early February 1980, and he flew home to Oregon from New London, Connecticut, where he was working as a carpenter. Already persuaded that Lowenstein was responsible for the voices in his head that would not stop, he had also become convinced that Lowenstein had caused the killing of Mayor George Moscone in San Francisco and the American Airlines DC-10 crash in Chicago that had taken more than 250 lives. Now he fastened on the notion that Lowenstein was to blame for his stepfather's heart attack. Deciding to give Lowenstein one more chance, he called him for an appointment for Friday, March 14. He would ask Al for the last time to halt the voices. If Al agreed, he was ready to go back to Portland, live with his mother, and return to school. He had already packed his belongings and had transcripts sent to an Oregon community college. But he also had purchased a seven-shot semiautomatic .38 pistol and was determined to kill his tormentor if he refused to call off the voices.[53]

Lowenstein agreed to see Sweeney. "Everybody [else] had abandoned him, but Al wouldn't," Ann Feldman commented, "as though he had some responsibility to make the whole world happy." Sandy Friedman had a somewhat more complicated explanation. "It was very important for Allard to help people," he said, "and so apart from any love that he might have, [he had the] hubris to assume that he could somehow help this man. . . . If you are blinded by something like that [sense of power], then you don't see the danger because you are focused on what you are going to do to help this person." For years, Lowenstein had held the belief that there was nothing he could not shape and control. He had rescued the country from Lyndon Johnson; he had saved countless young people from despair and disillusionment; and he had lifted the civil rights movement in Mississippi out of failure to success. Surely he could also rescue his cherished friend Dennis Sweeney from the psychic trauma that had followed that movement.[54]

Sweeney came into the law office while Lowenstein was on the phone about Kennedy campaign business and trying to arrange a speech in Montana so he could take the children there for their spring vacation. Sweeney wore a green jacket and brown pants—"like Al would wear," Susan Erb said. After Lowenstein came out to greet him, he told Erb not to put through any calls and the two men went into his office. A few minutes later, Erb heard two pops. She thought they sounded like gunshots, then concluded it was the sound of the staple guns being used by workers putting in new phones. Then came five rapid-fire additional shots, and she knew what they were. Lowenstein was screaming. Sweeney walked out, put his gun in the receptionist's tray, and sat down. When Erb reached Lowenstein, he was still conscious, lying on his stomach. "Did they get the guy who did it?" he asked. Someone called 911, and the police arrived. Lowenstein had turned gray and gone into shock. "You know, he's really bad," the police said. Within five minutes, an ambulance had arrived with paramedics desperately trying to keep Lowenstein alive as they raced to St. Clare's Hospital in midtown Manhattan. The law office was in the same building as the Associated Press, and Erb knew that within minutes the story would be on the wires. Her first thought was to call Jenny so that she could be the one to break the news. Immediately, Jenny left Boston with the kids and Nick to come to New York. David Bender arrived from the Kennedy campaign, and shortly thereafter, Steve Smith called, wondering where Lowenstein was. They were waiting for him at the meeting to decide on new commercials.

The scene at the hospital was pure chaos. As doctors struggled to save Lowenstein's life in the operating room, family and friends gathered on a lower floor. Sherman Bull raced in from Connecticut. In an earlier conversation with Erb, he had been optimistic because she had told him Al was still conscious. Now he arrived at the operating room to discover that Lowenstein had been hit by five bullets. Two had struck his heart, and another fractured his left arm as he threw it up in self-defense. Lowenstein's left lung was shattered. "There was essentially zero potential to save the guy," he concluded. Still, the doctors frantically tried. Bull called the nation's leading trauma surgeon to get his advice. Doctors administered multiple transfusions while sewing up the holes in Lowenstein's heart and trying to stabilize his vital signs.

Downstairs, meanwhile, friends and family continued to gather. Steve

Smith came in with his son, Steve, Jr. "Having been through this," the younger Smith said, "my father . . . sort of [went] on automatic pilot. . . . I guess it [was] his way of dealing with it." The younger Smith went to Al's son Tommy, whom he had come to know. "I felt a lot of empathy for Tommy," he said, "just because my uncle had been killed, and I think, in a way, if you grew up with Al you grew up with Bobby, so it was like we were part of the same family." Peter Yarrow arrived and started to lead the group in songs. "To him," Yarrow said, "[music] was as real as touching somebody or hugging somebody. . . . [When we sing] we are all trans- formed . . . into a place where we can, for a moment, believe in ourselves in a different way." That night they needed to believe. "We had precedent in our lives," Yarrow later said, "[so] we sat there and we sang. And peo- ple wept and held each other."

Upstairs, the doctors were fighting a hopeless fight. Each time they stopped the bleeding one place, it started somewhere else. The doctors were massaging his heart by hand to keep it going. When their efforts be- came futile, they went to the family to convey the news and ask if anyone wanted to go in. "I'll go," Jenny said. Shortly thereafter, Sherman Bull went downstairs. "Jeez," he said, "I could see this was a horrible situa- tion. I just walked in the room and they all looked up at me and they knew right away what the story was." Peter Yarrow saw the doctors coming in. "When they entered," he recalled, "I was singing 'Blowing in the Wind,' and I knew the time had come." His voice wavering and crying, he went on, "[I] didn't want it, so I, I wouldn't let them stop the song. . . . And when we heard that he had died . . . we sang and we remembered our friend." There was nothing more they could do.[55]

THE END

There had always been drama to Allard Lowenstein's life, what his best friend Sandy Friedman referred to as his "theatricality." It was reflected in his efforts to cultivate an image the exact opposite of that projected by his bourgeois family: the shirttail hanging out, his shoes untied, his hair flop- ping all over, and his baseball hat on backwards. The same penchant for the dramatic informed his mad dashes for the airplane as the door closed; the bulging, unhitched briefcase, suggesting a mind overflowing with ideas; the crusading zeal of his rhetoric; and above all, his extraordinary talent for occupying center stage by intentionally arriving late, rushing in at the last minute. "That's called 'making an entrance,'" Friedman said.

Thus, there was something almost perversely ordained about Lowenstein's death. "I'm a great devotee of Greek tragedy," Friedman commented, "and I just can't think that was all so accidental." There were not only Lowenstein's own fantasies about suffering a violent death. There was also the reality of his life—a youthful hero reaches the crowning glory of deposing a sitting president, only to suffer the exasperation of struggling unsuccessfully each year thereafter to regain that power. What do you do when you've done it all? Alan Arkatov asked. And when the gleam of that achievement becomes tarnished by repeated defeats, and there is no longer a youth crusade to lead? Is there not a sense that the end to this drama was destined?[56]

Some would later argue that Lowenstein's death was indeed fated—but as the result of a genetic flaw in Sweeney rather than a tragic dynamic in Lowenstein's own life. According to psychiatrists, Sweeney was the victim of adult-onset schizophrenia, a disease that strikes an individual entering his twenties, when, because of the presence of an uncontrollable genetic time bomb, he loses his grasp of reality and begins to hallucinate, feel persecuted, hear voices, and turn violent. Lowenstein happened to be a pivotal figure in Sweeney's life when that time bomb started to explode, but it was the sickness, not Sweeney's relationship with Lowenstein or his feeling of alienation and betrayal, that caused events to follow the course that they did.[57]

Yet, even if such a diagnosis were completely accurate, there remains a deeper sense in which Friedman's description of Lowenstein's death as a Greek tragedy is profoundly true. Lowenstein's hubris made him believe, even with advance knowledge of Sweeney's capacity for violence, that he could save him. "The irony of Al's death," Peter Yarrow observed, "was that [he was] someone who let crazies into his life . . . [and] believed in his capacity to go into the den of wolves and emerge unscathed." As the ultimate rescuer, he was convinced he could handle any situation. "That grandiosity killed him," his friend John Kavanaugh said. Yarrow agreed. "In a sense," he said, "he was killed by his own hand."[58]

Even more important, that grandiosity played a pivotal role in Lowenstein's intimate relationships with his protégés—relationships so crammed with volatile emotion that each contained the potential to explode. The very nature of the interaction made it difficult to keep feelings within bounds. Young people, vulnerable and insecure, became devoted to someone who gave them the total attention and praise Lowenstein did. They then became obsessed with their new hero, venerating and following him with slavish devotion—until he moved on, leaving them with passions they no longer had a constructive outlet for. "People who are fairly well put together," John Kavanaugh observed, "take from the experience and integrate it into their lives, do something with the political commitment Al engendered . . . and appreciate who he was for them." But many had a difficult time with that transition. "I remember having absolutely murderous thoughts toward him," Nancy Steffen said, "as probably a last sort of breaking away." When Kris Kleinbauer heard the news of Al's death, she recalled thinking reflexively, "Oh God, they're going to think that I had something to do with it. . . . And I remember thinking that that was like a real possibility . . . and that bothered me for a long time, to be so alienated from somebody that really meant a lot to me." It was not an unusual response. "In retrospect," Kavanaugh said, speaking as a therapist, "[I found it] surprising that more people didn't have these kinds of psychic transferences to Al, because he developed such intense relationships with people." That it was Sweeney did not matter. "It was inevitable," one of Lowenstein's closest associates concluded, "that someone was going to get Al—because he really was a magnet, he was the sun . . . a bright sun."[59]

At the core of the Greek tragedy was the seed of self-destruction imbedded in the protégé relationship. As Bill Buckley observed, "He was killed by one of his children." But this was not an ordinary one of Al's children—the hundreds, perhaps thousands, whom he had inspired, galvanized, cultivated, and then perhaps left behind. Sweeney had been special, from beginning to end. "Al loved Dennis," commented someone who knew them both, "and pursued him [and] wanted to be his best friend. . . . And then he was killed by him." That was the essence of this Greek tragedy, the horror that prevented Al Lowenstein from ever discovering whether he would be able to organize the second act of his life.[60]

At his funeral, Allard Lowenstein received the recognition and appreciation that had eluded him the last few years of his life. With bravery and love, Jenny played the role of Al's widow and was acknowledged as such by friends and family alike. People poured in from all over the country—Jerry Brown's sister Kathleen on the red-eye flight from California, with Robert Vaughn, Marcia Borie, and Judy Quine; a planeload of officials from the Carter administration, including Jack Watson, Secretary of Transportation Neil Goldschmidt, and Anne Wexler; old and dear friends from Congress who had continued to revere Lowenstein for what he had done for congressional self-esteem during his one term there; the godparents of his children; and all the hundreds of friends whose lives he had changed—Clint Deveaux from Atlanta, Greg Craig from Washington, Rich Hammond from Marin County, Franklin Roosevelt III from New York. Harvey Lippman presided over the arrangements, taking from his files all the versions of the holographic wills Lowenstein had scribbled out over those dinners at the Puffin Billy, and all the instructions for what should be done at his funeral, who should serve as pallbearers, who as ushers. Al had been right: the rabbi did not like the idea of singing "Amazing Grace" at the synagogue.

More than 2,000 people crowded into the Central Synagogue on Manhattan's East Side, with another 500 massed on the street outside to hear the ceremony on loudspeakers. It was a funeral graced by the royalty of Lowenstein's lifelong associations, as well as by the average people he had touched. Coretta Scott King and Jacqueline Kennedy were there. Ted Kennedy, who had flown back from Chicago to go to the hospital the night of the shooting, sat next to Bill Buckley, who had jetted in from a vacation in Switzerland. There in the synagogue also was Jo Ann Molnar, a cerebral palsy victim who idolized Al and for whom he always kept a special place—calling her on the phone, encouraging her in her academic ventures, jotting her notes on current political gossip. And also in attendance were the staff people who had served him with such devotion, working more hours than there were in the day—Gina Galke, Harriet Eisman, Susan Erb, Greg Stone.

As Lowenstein had hoped, singing provided the transformative spirit that made acknowledgment of his death a time to celebrate struggle rather than descend into despair. Peter Yarrow joined Mary Travers, his partner in Peter, Paul, and Mary, and Harry Chapin, the brilliant singer and composer, to carry out Al's wishes. They sang "Amazing Grace," the soaring hymn that had brought comfort and strength to black Americans during their decades-long quest for freedom, and "Stewball Was a Race Horse," one of Al's favorite Peter, Paul, and Mary songs; he had always asked that it to be sung when an election was lost, spirits were at their lowest, and the banner of hope and struggle needed to be raised once more. Pete McCloskey and Andy Jacobs spoke from Congress, Andy Young on behalf of all Al had meant to the battle for human rights, and Al's nephew, Douglas Lowenstein, for the family.

It was Ted Kennedy and William Buckley, however, who articulated most powerfully the meaning of Al Lowenstein's life and the significance of the occasion. Reciting a litany of Lowenstein's achievements, Kennedy declared:

> There are black people in Mississippi who can vote because he was there in the civil rights movement. . . . There are American sons living out normal lives who did not die in Vietnam because he was there in New Hampshire in 1968. . . . There are political prisoners in the Soviet Union whose cause was heard . . . because he was there in the United Nations. . . . For me he was more than a friend, though his friendship was rare. He was more than a counselor, though his counsel was wise. For me and for so many others, he was our brother. . . . It is the last and the least we can give to Al . . . [to] pledge that we shall . . . strive as he so tirelessly did to do better. Our brother left us his love. He goes with ours.

"How did he live such a life," William Buckley asked,

> so hectic with public concern, while preoccupying himself so fully with the individual human being. . . . His rhythms were not of this world. His days, foreshortened, lived out the secular dissonances. "Behold, Thou hast made my days as it were a span long: and mine age is even as nothing in respect of Thee; and verily, every man living is altogether vanity." The psalmist spoke to Al on Friday last—"I became dumb, and opened not my mouth, for it was Thy doing." To those of us not yet dumb, the psalmist also spoke, saying, "The Lord is close to the brokenhearted; and those who are crushed in spirit, He saves." Who was the wit who said that Nature abhors a vacuum? Let Nature then fill this vacuum. That is the challenge which, bereft, the friends of Allard Lowenstein hurl up to Nature and to Nature's God, prayerfully, demandingly, because today, Lord, our loneliness is great.

Lowenstein's ashes were taken to Arlington National Cemetery, where they were interred at a gravesite equidistant between the tombs of Robert F. Kennedy and John F. Kennedy. Peter Yarrow sang "The Marvelous Toy," for himself and Al's children and everyone else: "We look for love and we look for light, even in the darkest of moments." The tragedy had ended.[61]

Epilogue

WHAT IS ONE TO MAKE OF SUCH A LIFE? HOW IS IT POSSIBLE TO FIND A label for Allard Lowenstein within the conventional vocabulary of American politics? Did his liberalism speak to the larger themes of the American political tradition? Or was it so much a product of the peculiarities of his personality that it deserves to be called sui generis—unrelated to the larger political culture of which he was a part?

First, it seems clear that, however much Allard Lowenstein differed from a typical liberal like Hubert Humphrey, his actions and values illuminate both the weaknesses and strengths of liberal activism in postwar America. Like other liberals, he preached and personified a commitment to saving democracy by devoting himself to the electoral processes of mainstream politics. Nevertheless, Lowenstein lived on the margins of traditional liberalism, and more than most, he identified personally with victims of oppression—whether Spanish Republicans, African nationalists, or Mississippi blacks. But his political stance ultimately was not that of the outsider sympathizing with revolution, but that of the insider, speaking on behalf of the best of the liberal tradition. Calling Lowenstein a prophet, William Sloane Coffin noted that, "if he opposed American behavior, it was in the name of American ideals." Lowenstein was "the last and best liberal," Jack Newfield said, "one who always goes into revolutionary situations, yet always stays a liberal." If he could be a prophetic voice against

465

evil and simultaneously preserve and defend the democratic system, Lowenstein would earn both the mantle of the Just Man and the plaudits and legitimacy conferred by established authority.[1]

In this role, Lowenstein—like most liberals—found it more plausible to act on behalf of the highest ideals of the prevailing system than to align himself with those who sought to alter that system fundamentally. Thus, in South Africa, he saw his primary mission as making an appeal to the better side of whites—even though he espoused the cause of black Africans. Elite white students were his primary audience there, and his goal was to inspire them to save the land they were in danger of losing. So, too, in Spain, where his constituency consisted, in his words, of the sons of "aristocrats and grandees, with lives of almost guaranteed success ahead of them," whom he tried to persuade to act on "their conscience . . . [and] throw away" privilege on behalf of restoring democracy to their homeland. And in America, Lowenstein appealed to "the best and the brightest," the Ivy League children of the "establishment," to rise above their comfortable status to serve a higher cause—reclaiming America. However he differed from other liberals, Lowenstein shared with them a vision of the task of reform as something the best people in society do *for* those unable to fend for themselves.[2]

If preserving America from within by galvanizing its "best" side was one part of Lowenstein's role, identifying the outside enemy that embodied evil was a second part. All his life, Lowenstein knew that enemy to be communism and those he considered its dupes, the radical left. Here, too, Lowenstein exemplified the values of the "liberal consensus" he shared with so many. "If substantial . . . change could always be brought about by democratic means, without bloodshed—as Lowenstein's generation of liberals insisted," Paul Cowan wrote, "it followed that revolutionaries presented as deep a threat to progress as did reactionaries." In the Spanish civil war, the formative moment of Lowenstein's political history, he was convinced that the Stalinists had betrayed the loyalists and were as much if not more the villain than the Fascists, especially since they were *supposed* to have been on freedom's side. Ever since, he had believed—with most liberals—that Communists were more of a threat to justice than were rightists.

In both the civil rights and antiwar movements, that obsession with communism divided Lowenstein from those he had initially recruited to those struggles. So concerned was he with the involvement of the National Lawyers' Guild in Freedom Summer, and of New Left organizations in the

Moratorium and Mobilization rallies, that an outright break with these movements seemed to him preferable to conciliation. Lowenstein and most liberals wanted to reform America. SNCC wanted to radicalize it. In Lowenstein's view, allowing a role to organizations like the Lawyers' Guild guaranteed that reform would be destroyed. "So far as he was concerned," a disenchanted, though once admiring Paul Cowan wrote, "persons who talked publicly about their disgust with the American government . . . were dangerously disloyal. . . . [He believed in the existence of] a well-planned conspiracy, [which] he fought . . . in a way that made him resemble the McCarthyites he despised."[3]

In critical ways, then, Allard Lowenstein shared the values and assumptions of mainstream American liberalism. Given his role in initiating the NSA's cold war crusade and in leading the fight within the civil rights movement against the National Lawyers' Guild, it could be said that he set an important part of liberalism's anti-Communist agenda, even as he also led the way in liberalism's fight for civil rights and peace. But perhaps the most important characteristic he shared with other liberals was a desire to channel insurgent protests into existing political processes, and to deny them the resources and support to attack policies from below or from outside. Lowenstein—and most liberals—believed that they should define the left. Hence, anyone who espoused a program beyond that which they embraced was potentially subversive.

On the other hand, Allard Lowenstein defied typical liberal behavior in his eagerness to incite rebellion against authority and challenge conventional norms of behavior. There was no role he prized more than that of enfant terrible, particularly if he could occupy the position of leader of the insurgents. Lowenstein reveled in making college presidents uncomfortable, in identifying with student groups that wanted to break out of old routines, and in marching at the head of youthful battalions of protesters who idealistically sought to change policies through teach-ins, voter registration projects, or nonviolent sit-ins. Lowenstein thought and wrote more cogently about the problems of sustaining liberal democracy than did most of his peers. And as long as he was not threatened by competition from the left, he sustained a skepticism toward those in power that considerably exceeded that of most liberal activists.

In his suspicion of conventional wisdom and authority, Lowenstein exhibited the qualities that allowed him to try to link two generations of activists by reaching out to the young. He shared with the new generation of the 1960s and 1970s a desire for something more than politics as usual.

Indeed, he had helped to stimulate that desire in them. If only they would accept his definition of the "new politics," then perhaps liberalism could survive, infused with a new energy and the freshness of youthful idealism yoked to experienced leadership.

But the tensions were too great, the agendas and perspectives of the different generations too different. By the 1970s, the liberal banner that had once united labor leaders, civil rights activists, and youthful dissenters had become frayed and tattered by radical-liberal splits. As the larger liberal community lost its coherence and vitality, its declining fortunes mirrored Al Lowenstein's inability to bridge the gap between competing generations of activism, even through his own inimitable methods of outreach.

Could Al Lowenstein have done anything different? Was there a way in which he could have shaped his liberal activism to make less likely the divisions that eventually destroyed his dream? Perhaps. At a pivotal moment in the civil rights struggle of 1964, he might have set aside his suspicions of SNCC and committed his resources instead to working together with Bob Moses on Freedom Summer. Lowenstein's split from the movement at that point both signified and hastened the growth of black/white antagonism and of liberal/radical polarization. If ever there was a time in the 1960s when a different direction might have been possible, that was it. Certainly, other white activists of similar persuasion—such as Michael Harrington—later regretted the degree to which their concern with fighting putative remnants of the communist left had kept them from joining broader coalitions for social change.

Lowenstein could also have pursued a different course in his political career. From college all the way through the late 1970s, he eschewed acting intelligently in his own interest. He was unwilling to do the preplanning, the dogged leg work, the pragmatic laying of foundations that would have made possible political success. At almost every turn, he made the wrong decision. He entered the 1966 reform fight too late; then, instead of building a base in Manhattan for a 1968 run, he moved to Long Island. Rather than campaign for the Senate in 1970, he took on the nearly impossible task of overcoming the gerrymander of his congressional district. Then in 1974, instead of opting for surefire election for Rooney's old seat in Brooklyn, he went back once more to Long Beach. It was almost as though his success in the "dump Johnson" fight caused him to believe that from that moment forward, the more impossible the battle, the greater the need to take it on. Clearly, Lowenstein had enormous talents as a behind-the-scenes tactician and strategist. But it was a side of himself that he refused to assert or acknowledge in any public manner. Had he been willing even once to pursue his logical self-interest, he would easily have found the secure seat in Congress he so desperately seemed to crave.

Yet in the end, Lowenstein could not choose these alternative courses because of the personality he was. He could not keep running if he were to settle down in one place; nor could he scale the next mountain if he gave priority to values of security and pragmatism.

It was in his style, his attitudes, and his mode of operation that Lowenstein's politics most directly reflected his distinctive personality. Lowenstein saw himself playing the role of a hero. In a world starkly split between the forces of good and evil, he would identify the good and then, with the authority of one "called" to intervene, provide the individual leadership that would make the difference in the triumph of good over evil. In that scenario, it was no accident that the hero was an "ugly duckling" who might even find an answer to his quest for love and fulfillment in the struggle to overcome evil. And if victory in the struggle sometimes required defeat, that necessity simply made the role of hero all the more tragic and dramatic.

The hero role was tied directly to Lowenstein's private insecurities and needs. He identified so readily with pure and righteous causes because they enhanced his self-worth and provided him with an authority he felt would otherwise have been in doubt. He needed such help because he thought of himself as unattractive. But "ugly" was not just physical. It was also ethnic—being the child of immigrants and, even worse, being Jewish, with a last name and a nose with a certain shape that signified being outside the circle.

Yet his feeling of strangeness involved even more than ethnicity and physical appearance. It was also attributable to the secrets Allard had that could never be shared because they were taboo. First there was the secret of Augusta—discovering on the cusp of adolescence that his mother was not his mother, and that a conspiracy of silence, authored by his father Gabriel was to prevent him forever from talking about his mother with his father. Augusta's absence from their conversations—the fact that she could not even be named in Gabriel's presence—meant that all other important issues between them had to be avoided also. In a profound way, Gabriel's refusal to address Augusta's death represented a violation of trust that then made impossible communication about other hopes, fears, and differences of opinion. No wonder that Allard learned to "scoot around" his father, or that he absorbed early the lesson of how to avoid conflict—with Douglass Hunt, Mimi Massey, and countless others, not the least of whom was Jenny.

The second great secret that made Allard feel so unacceptable was his torment over how to deal with his sexual interest in men. He decided to cope with his "uncontrollable urges" by seeking "very good friendships." In the best platonic tradition, these friendships would be intimate relationships with the erotic component sublimated to the larger connections between two people. "He would try to establish a very close involvement," John Steinbruner said, "in terms of political purpose . . . emotional identification, political philosophy, and some sign of quasi-sexual identification. . . . [But] it's easy to overvalue . . . the sexual dimension. . . . It was really an element in a much larger bonding, and the bonding was important."[4]

There would be no single "best friend." Rather, his quest became peripatetic—the key to Lowenstein's method of political recruitment—and thousands of young people became enmeshed in his political and personal mission. With twenty or thirty or forty of them, the linkage was longer lasting and they became part of the network of complicated, intense, and conflict-ridden relationships that ran, like an emotional cardiogram, through Lowenstein's life. Almost always Al gave the "other" the message that he was a special person—the "best" student government leader, the funniest storyteller. Then came his invitation to share confidences; a meditation on how rare and important "best friends" were; the conclusion that a deep and lasting bond had been established; and then, perhaps, a physical expression of that intimacy.

The romance and intensity of Lowenstein's peripatetic lifestyle was a magnet that drew countless people. Local New York politicians might enjoin him to stay put and "flush his toilet" on the West Side of Manhattan. But such a course could not hold a candle to the adrenalin rush he got from inspiring 500 students with a spellbinding speech, then spending five hours after midnight in an intense bull session before rushing to the airport for the next stop in a car driven by the latest and newest convert to the Lowenstein mystique. Although many friends suggested, in the words of one of them, *"Why don't you just stop* . . . and reflect on your life?" Al neither wanted nor could afford to stop, especially to reflect. That would have diluted his appeal and confounded his purpose. As Kris Kleinbauer observed, "Al was . . . always in the wind. . . . He was hard to catch."[5]

In the end, Lowenstein seemed to feel he had no other option. If he stayed in one place, he would have had to deal with all the issues—including the secrets—from which he was running. Homosexuality was still a taboo issue in America. If you stayed in one place, enough people might start to talk that your life and career would be destroyed. "One was always afraid of being exposed or being discovered," David Mixner had said. "They couldn't catch you if you moved fast enough." That was Al. As Kris Kleinbauer said, he was "hard to catch." To never stop running seemed the only option as long as confrontation and truth telling were too dangerous and frightening. The tragedy of Lowenstein's last years was that he may have been almost ready to stop running. He had begun to sort out his priorities and to make commitments to valued individual friends; he had even started down the painful path process of dealing with his deepest secret. American culture and society had not offered him that opportunity before. Now, through the actions of countless others, it had become a possibility. Then the play ended. F. Scott Fitzgerald once wrote that Americans are too immature to have a second act, that we have too far to go in acquiring wisdom and insight. Allard Lowenstein may have been ready to confound that assertion.[6]

The key remaining question is whether Lowenstein could have made so extraordinary an impact on the history of his time without the personal dilemmas that made escape and constant motion the metaphors of his life. Was his capacity to inspire by embracing the noble and the ideal dependent on his need to avoid the darker, less attractive side of himself? Could he have mobilized so many to join the crusades to achieve racial justice and end the Vietnam War were he not impelled to seek out the young as a means of satisfying his desire for a "best friend?" And could he have mobilized the young in other ways that might have minimized the hurt of disillusionment? Would it have been possible for him to be part of a movement that was bigger than a single individual, instead of having to define the movement by making it an extension of himself? Above all, could he have helped shape the critical battles of his era had he stopped running, as his friends asked him to?

In all likelihood, the answer to these questions is no. On one occasion, as a way of asking Al to reflect on himself, David Bender inquired whether Eleanor Roosevelt had ever found a way to be content with her family and personal life as well as her public life. No, Lowenstein responded, he did not think Mrs. Roosevelt had ever achieved happiness.

Perhaps Al Lowenstein saw himself destined to a similar fate. Had he grown up in a different time, one that was more open to people confused over their sexual identity, his life might have been different. But Lowenstein himself would probably have said that he chose his lot, was prepared to live with the consequences, and could not have achieved what he did achieve without the demons that drove him.[7]

What he did contribute to his world was a remarkable ability to reach high and to inspire others to do the same. "He had the ability to bring out the best of our angels," his NSA friend Bill Dentzer said. And if sometimes those angels became his demons—because Al placed such demands on people and insisted they act *his* way—they had still had the experience of being the best, for at least a while. Reflecting on his own experience with Lowenstein, Paul Strasberg—who had resisted the call to become a Lowenstein disciple—observed that he had not been "sucked in, hook, line, and sinker . . . because I was not strong enough to have withstood that." But he also said that the 1960s were "the most important period of our lives [and] I have always regretted that I [didn't] go into it more deeply than I did." Most of those Lowenstein touched did not resist. They enlisted voluntarily in his crusades. And if eventually they withdrew, as perhaps the only way they could save themselves from being destroyed, almost all look back now on the experience as among the most challenging, exciting, and rewarding of their lives. As Greg Craig observed, "Anyone who is interested in life and cares about other people . . . [is] going to be grateful for their relationship [with Al], and choose it, choose it, choose it."[8]

In all of this, Lowenstein did what he felt he had to do. Like Dr. Rieux in Albert Camus's *The Plague* (1947), he determined to take his stand, "to do what is necessary," in order to forestall pestilence and defeat oppression. "I never saw him spend one hour in . . . regret or self-doubt," Pete McCloskey said. "He just looked for the next fight and went forward. He never looked back." Although he could never stop trying to taste again the fruits of victory he had tasted in 1968, Lowenstein also knew—with Camus in *The Myth of Sisyphus* (1942)—that victory is never won. The rock will always tumble down the hill again. What makes human beings different from other species is the knowledge that pushing it back up the hill represents the meaning of existence—to do what has to be done. What Al Lowenstein taught, Steve Smith, Jr., said, was that "humanity is won by struggling in the face of certain defeat."[9]

"As you go along," Lowenstein said,

you build a life . . . in which you do many different kinds of things. But it all has a common denominator that gives it some sense, some direction— the sense that your total activity is going to make a better situation for people to live in. . . . A lot of times people think things are impossible because they don't try them. It becomes a case of self-fulfilling impossibles. If you seek to achieve only things which you think are supposed to be possible, you may end up achieving things that aren't even very useful. The question should be, is it worth trying to do, not can it be done? . . . You don't just set goals and when you reach them, find that they equal happiness. . . . Within the quest itself, much of the fullness of life exists.[10]

Because of that philosophy, Allard Lowenstein helped to shape a generation. Failure more often accompanied his efforts than did success. The determination to never stop running brought personal devastation and tragedy. But by his own measure of "standing up for something and being effective for it," Lowenstein had made contributions that were inestimable. John Kenneth Galbraith wrote Robert Kennedy after John Kennedy's death that there had been two major issues during the Kennedy presidency, nuclear war and civil rights, and Jack Kennedy had made a difference on both. There were at least three major issues during Allard Lowenstein's lifetime that he affected—South African apartheid, racial injustice in America, and the war in Vietnam. On these issues, Allard Lowenstein also made a critical difference. "[Everyplace he went] he left his mark," Alan Arkatov remarked. "Some of [those he touched] are in business, some are in the arts, some are still doing politics . . . but they all keep that little spark in them, and if you know that they knew Al, and you touch them with that, they open up . . . they get a glimmer in their eye." For more people than could possibly be counted, Al Lowenstein had made it possible to be—and to want to be—an engaged citizen.[11]

In effect, Lowenstein wrote his own legacy in "Angus," his 1965 novella and screenplay about the civil rights movement. With extraordinary insight, he described the dilemma of a white liberal, clearly modeled after himself. No matter how well intentioned he was, no matter how hard he worked, Angus knew that he could not control the black revolution. Nor could he control his own fate, including the vicious effort by white racist authorities to destroy his reputation by suggesting he was a homosexual. What he could do was to keep on waging the struggle, doing whatever he had to do to "stand against the wind" and work for justice.

Just prior to descending to the streets, where he would be slain in a race riot, Angus had dictated a memo to his secretary announcing his candidacy for the governorship of Mississippi. "I am through with silence," he said. "I will talk about what happens to people who live on the backs of another race, who are fed hate disguised as virtue until they do not know the difference. . . . I do not suppose that saying these things is likely to get me elected . . . but it may be that one man speaking up can help change the atmosphere. In any event, I intend to try."

Then—in the conclusion to his statement—Angus went on to a final issue. In the novella's final scene, Al did not speak of sexuality (though he might have). But he did address the question of family. "I must . . . refer to one other matter," Angus said. "[It] should not have to be discussed in public. . . . [I am not] sure that my wife, whose love has been my life for so long, will understand. I hope she will forgive the ugliness and distress that I may be causing her. I am sure my children one day will understand, because nothing is more certain than that, as there is a God, this cause will prevail. I hope they will be proud that their father, late—but not, I hope, too late—joined with those who have been working for a better world."[12]

They were words that Allard Lowenstein might as easily have penned on March 14, 1980, as he prepared to raise the curtain on his second act.

Notes

INTRODUCTION

1. Godfrey Hodgson, *America In Our Time* (New York: Doubleday, 1976). Hodgson's book explores the ramifications of this "liberal consensus" for the 1950s, 1960s, and 1970s.

CHAPTER 1

1. Interview with Jennifer Littlefield, Wayland, Mass., October 8, 1987, and Washington, D.C., January 28, 1991; AKL, autobiographical statement for Yale Law School application 1949, Augusta Lowenstein diary [n.d.], and Florence Lowenstein diary, all in the Allard K. Lowenstein Papers (hereafter referred to as AKL Papers), Southern Historical Collection, Wilson Library, University of North Carolina at Chapel Hill. Unless otherwise stated, all interviews have been conducted by the author. The original tapes and transcripts are on file at the Allard K. Lowenstein Collection, Columbia University Oral History Collection, Butler Library, Columbia University. Copies of the transcripts are also included in the AKL Papers.
2. The biographical data on Gabriel Lowenstein has been gathered from the following sources: interviews with Lawrence Lowenstein, Chapel Hill, June 20, 1986, and New York, September 25, 1987, and Dorothy (Lowenstein) DiCintio, New York, September, 1986; interview with Jennifer Littlefield;

Men of Science in America (New York: Simon & Schuster, 1944); and scattered obituary clippings, AKL Papers.

3. *Men of Science;* interviews with Marie Lowenstein, Chapel Hill, June 20, 1986, and New York, September 25, 1987, and Sanford Friedman. The Friedman interview is in the author's possession and has not been deposited, at the request of the interviewee.

4. Gabriel Lowenstein to AKL, August 7, 1944, AKL Papers; interviews with Sanford Friedman and Dorothy DiCintio.

5. Interview with Ruth Goldberg, New York, April 6, 1990; Augusta Lowenstein diary, entries for March 15, June 20, October 28, and December 2, 1929; Augusta Lowenstein to Grace [surname unknown], July 7, 1929, all in AKL Papers.

6. Interviews with Ruth Goldberg; Lawrence and Marie Lowenstein, and Jennifer Littlefield; Florence Lowenstein to AKL, January 7, 1948, AKL Papers. Florence would later comment to Allard that "Dad was lamenting the fact that he gave up teaching at Columbia. Now that he has tasted of all the temporary pleasures of material wealth he realizes that some things have much more permanency and one of those is teaching." In spite of the family legend that Doc had sacrificed the certainty of a distinguished academic career, that was not necessarily the case. Most of his teaching was done as a graduate assistant; he held only a brief appointment as an assistant professor. His major interest—nutritional science—was not a prestige research concern in biochemistry at Columbia. Furthermore, Columbia at that time was not known as a place where Jewish professors found a ready home. Hence, notwithstanding his affection for scholarship, Doc Lowenstein may also have opted for the restaurant business because it represented a more viable career path.

7. Florence Lowenstein autobiography, "Now It's Funny," typescript, [n.d.] AKL Papers; interview with Jennifer Littlefield.

8. Interviews with Lawrence and Marie Lowenstein, Dorothy DiCintio, and Ruth Goldberg; Florence Lowenstein to AKL, March 20, 1945, AKL Papers. Bert Lowenstein practiced medicine in a variety of locales during his life. As discussed later, he experienced a series of mental breakdowns. He suffered a stroke in the 1980s and was largely disabled until his death in 1992.

9. Florence Lowenstein to AKL, October 23, 1946, and May 16, 1947, AKL Papers; interview with Lawrence Lowenstein. When Larry gave his stepmother a box of candy, she was astonished. "There were no ifs or ands," she wrote to Allard. "This is the very *first time* he has done this in all his life" (AKL Papers).

10. Interview with Dorothy DiCintio; Florence Lowenstein diary, August and September 1930 entries, AKL Papers; interviews with Jennifer Littlefield and Marie Lowenstein.

11. Interviews with Marie Lowenstein, Lawrence Lowenstein, Dorothy DiCintio, and Ruth Goldberg.

12. Interviews with Dorothy DiCintio, Jennifer Littlefield, Regina Galke, New York, May 11, 1992, Lawrence and Marie Lowenstein, Ruth Goldberg, and Sanford Friedman; AKL to Ruth Goldberg, July 23, 1944, and Ruth Goldberg to AKL, [n.d., 1944], both in AKL Papers.

13. Sanford Friedman has characterized Gabriel Lowenstein as distant and unaffectionate, especially in physical terms, with almost every expression of approval conditioned on performance and achievement by his children.

14. Interviews with Dorothy DiCintio and Marie Lowenstein. One teacher in Dorothy's school, for example, asked her whether Bert was the only son Gabriel had in his first marriage. Al wrote to a college friend in the late 1940s about having finally told Dorothy about the "two marriages" (AKL to Mimi Massey, [n.d.], AKL papers).

15. Florence Lowenstein to AKL, August 18, 1948, August 17, 1944, and January 26, 1949, AKL Papers.

16. Interview with Dorothy DiCintio.

17. Interviews with Dorothy DiCintio, Marie and Lawrence Lowenstein, and Jennifer Littlefield. Both Al and Dorothy commented about the conflicts between their parents in letters. In a letter to his mother and father from camp, Al expressed the hope that they could all "try to understand each other better," then added: "And while I'm delivering a sermon, no more fights." Offering a dollop of humor (and advice), the 14-year-old proceeded to tell about a 105-year-old man who attributed his long life to his vow not to fight with his wife. When she got mad at him, he left the house. He lived so long, he said, because of all the fresh air he got by standing outside. Dorothy would write Al in 1945, "Mom and Dad haven't argued since yesterday, ain't it wonderful," then in a subsequent letter said that when she did not play golf with her parents, "Dad was furious (per usual)." Later, Dorothy wrote Al at college, "I didn't hear what the argument was about [tonight], since I wasn't particularly interested, though it was probably money. . . . When the hell are you coming home? It's boring to have me home all alone. Mom and Pop have no one else to yell at, so I get it all." AKL to Gabriel and Florence Lowenstein, July 27, 1943, and miscellaneous letters from Dorothy Lowenstein to AKL, [n.d., 1945], all in AKL Papers.

18. Miscellaneous letters between AKL and his Goldberg grandparents, [n.d., 1943], and Ruth Goldberg to AKL, [n.d., 1944], all in AKL Papers; interviews with Ruth Goldberg and Jennifer Littlefield.

19. Florence Lowenstein to AKL, July 19, 1943, November 27, 1945, October 30, 1945, and [n.d., 1945], AKL Papers.

20. Interviews with Marie and Lawrence Lowenstein, and Dorothy DiCintio; Gabriel Lowenstein to AKL, July 10, 1945, AKL Papers.

21. Interviews with Dorothy DiCintio, and Lawrence and Marie Lowenstein. Larry Lowenstein to AKL, November 10, 1942. (AKL Papers).

22. Interviews with Jennifer Littlefield and Dorothy DiCintio.

23. Interview with Dorothy DiCintio.

24. Interviews with Dorothy DiCintio and Lawrence Lowenstein; annual evaluations of AKL from Ethical Culture School, 1936–38, Ethel Bratton to Mr. and Mrs. Lowenstein, February 14, 1936, both in AKL Papers.

25. "A Day with Bodo," typescript, 1937, AKL Papers.

26. Ethical Culture School newspaper, miscellaneous letters between Chet McCall and AKL, [n.d. 1941], Caroline Whiting to AKL (about his critique of *The Nation*), and AKL, letters to the editors of the *New York Times* and *PM*, all in AKL Papers.

27. Gabriel Lowenstein to AKL, August 4, 1943, and Larry Lowenstein to AKL, August 10, 1942, both in AKL Papers.

28. Interview with Sanford Friedman.

29. Florence Lowenstein diary, March 25, 1935, entry, AKL Papers; interviews with Jennifer Littlefield and Sanford Friedman.

30. Rex Freeman to AKL, March 1, 1942, [n.d., 1943], and August 11, 1944, AKL Papers. Freeman said that a "blank wall" always seemed to keep whites from trying to understand blacks, but that with Al, this wall did not exist. W. E. B. DuBois had written about a "veil" descending between whites and blacks once early childhood was over (*The Souls of Black Folk: Essays and Sketches* [Chicago: A. C. McClurg, 1903], p. 23).

31. Interview with Sanford Friedman; see also a short story written by Lowenstein (February 28, 1943, AKL Papers) in which he tries to imagine how a black man on a New York subway comprehends the hostile glances he is getting from white passengers.

32. *Horace Mann Record*, miscellaneous issues (esp. October 11 and 18, 1943, and November 24, 1943), Anthony Lewis to AKL, January 13, 1949, Bunny Davidson to AKL, [n.d.], all in AKL Papers.

33. AKL, "Pericles: Dictator or Democrat," high school term paper, AKL Papers; see also AKL, "Paul Revere III," high school term paper, May 12, 1940, and "Victory Done," high school term paper, [n.d. 1943], AKL Papers.

34. Florence Lowenstein to AKL, August 13 and July 19, 1943, July 24, 1944, and November 20, 1945, AKL Papers.

35. Gabriel Lowenstein to AKL, July 7, 1943, and July 5, 1945, AKL Papers.

36. Gabriel Lowenstein to AKL, July 5, 1945, AKL Papers.

37. Gabriel Lowenstein to AKL, July 24, 1943, AKL Papers.

38. Interview with Marie Lowenstein; Florence Lowenstein to AKL, [n.d., 1949], AKL Papers.

39. Gabriel Lowenstein to AKL, July 7 and 13, 1944, and AKL to Gabriel Lowenstein, July 27, 1943, all in AKL Papers.

40. Gabriel Lowenstein to AKL, August 22, 1945, AKL Papers.

41. Gabriel Lowenstein to AKL, October 12, 1948, and [n.d., 1946], AKL Papers.

42. Interviews with Lawrence and Marie Lowenstein, and Dorothy DiCintio.

43. Interviews with Jennifer Littlefield and Sanford Friedman.

44. AKL diary [n.d., 1943], AKL Papers; interview with Sanford Friedman. For an excellent historical discussion of how homosexuality was viewed in America during these years, see John D'Emilio, *Sexual Politics, Sexual Communities: The Making of a Homosexual Minority in the United States, 1940–1970* (Chicago: University of Chicago Press, 1983). Martin Duberman has written vividly of what it was like growing up with homosexual urges in a New York Jewish home in the 1930s; see *Cures: A Gay Man's Odyssey* (New York: Dutton, 1991). His story is very similar to Lowenstein's. See also Paul Monette, *Becoming a Man* (New York: Harcourt, Brace, Jovanovich, 1992). Alfred Charles Kinsey's research showed that despite the social pressures to view homosexual activity as abhorrent, 37 percent of American men had experienced at least one orgasm with another man, and approximately 10 percent were practicing homosexuals; see *Sexual Behavior in the Human Male* (Philadelphia: Saunders, 1948).

45. Interview with Alice Popkin for the documentary film *Citizen*, transcript in author's possession (hereafter referred to as *"Citizen* interview with . . . "); miscellaneous AKL correspondence with high school classmates, 1941–45, AKL Papers; interviews with Sanford Friedman. Popkin described the social life of the time as, in retrospect, quite "backward." Once she was supposed to go to the junior prom with Al and he told her he had to go with another date, not because the other girl was more beautiful or because he preferred her, but because "he thought he meant more to [the other girl]. She was not invited out very much and therefore he would take her to the dance. . . . [That] was the start of my profound understanding of Al's desire to include people." Judy Quine, another high school acquaintance, also described Lowenstein as an "extraordinarily kind boy . . . [who] never failed to say hello to me." Interview with Judy Quine, Los Angeles, December 19, 1988. I am indebted to Lawrence Lowenstein for providing me with all the *Citizen* interview transcripts, which are now deposited with the AKL Papers.

46. Interviews with Sanford Friedman and Jennifer Littlefield.

47. See a series of letters from Robin Fau to AKL, esp. November 12, 1944, and February 16, 1945, AKL Papers. Fau talked about "what we had together that night [at camp in Vermont]," and about their special song. But she acknowledged that she had changed a great deal since the summer of 1944. "I don't think we could ever pick up where things ended," she said, expressing the hope that they could be "friends" instead.

48. Gabriel Lowenstein, miscellaneous letters to AKL, 1943–49, Douglass Hunt to AKL, September 1946, Jean Teller to AKL, [n.d., 1945], Sanford Friedman to AKL, July 2, 1945, all in AKL Papers. See also interviews

with Douglass Hunt, Chapel Hill, January 24, 1990, Sanford Friedman, and Miriam (Massey) Johnson, Eugene, Oregon, March 5, 1988. On a visit to Lowenstein's Westchester home, Douglass Hunt, a college friend, shrewdly observed the family dynamics between the Goldbergs and the Lowensteins. In a letter to his friend, Hunt noted how amazed he was that "you could take so many pains to be diplomatic with Ruth (who is not the closest person to you in the world by a long shot) and be at almost equal pains to be tactless with your parents."

49. Interview with Sanford Friedman.

50. Interview with Lawrence Lowenstein.

51. Gabriel Lowenstein to AKL, July 20 and October 30, 1945, AKL Papers.

52. Bert Lowenstein to AKL, November 1, 1944, and Lawrence Lowenstein to AKL, December 3, 1944, both in AKL Papers; interview with Lawrence Lowenstein. Allard would later tell friends that he thought Harvard had ruined his brother Bert, and that it was a terrible place to go to school.

53. Bert Lowenstein to AKL, January 16, 1945, AKL Papers.

54. Interviews with Jennifer Littlefield and Sanford Friedman; AKL to Sanford Friedman, June 23, 1945, AKL Papers.

55. Interview with Marie Lowenstein. On Lowenstein's machinations over college applications, see Edna Livingston to AKL, March 3, 1945, Loretta Jacobs to AKL, April 17, 1945, Samuel Heyman to AKL, May 10, 1945, and a series of letters from AKL to Sanford Friedman, June 14, 16, 19, 23, and 25, 1945, all in AKL Papers. Lowenstein told Friedman in June he had not yet heard from Yale and was preparing—with great anxiety—to set off for Chapel Hill. In talking about Yale, Lowenstein said "prospects of the bargain"—presumably with his father—now seemed nil because "suddenly the new cry seems to be, 'the individual, not the college, is what counts,'" suggesting that Gabriel had given up on Yale as a possible alternative to Chapel Hill.

56. Interviews with Sanford Friedman, Jennifer Littlefield, Dorothy DiCintio, and Themistocles Michos, Palo Alto, November 23, 1991. Michos was Al's closest friend in the army during the 1950s, and reported later on how much Al wanted to neutralize his Jewishness at college.

57. Dorothy Lowenstein to AKL, [n.d.], AKL Papers.

58. Interviews with Jennifer Littlefield, Sanford Friedman, and Marie Lowenstein.

59. Interview with Sanford Friedman.

60. Interview with Sanford Friedman; Gabriel Lowenstein to AKL, August 22, 1945, AKL Papers.

61. Florence Lowenstein to AKL, [n.d., 1942], Sanford Friedman to AKL, July 2, 1945, and Ruth Silver to AKL, [n.d., 1945], all in AKL Papers.

CHAPTER 2

1. Interview with Dorothy DiCintio.
2. Interview by Eugene Pfaff with Douglass Hunt and James Wallace, transcript in author's possession; interview with Douglass Hunt, Chapel Hill, January 24, 1990. I am grateful to Eugene Pfaff for sending me transcripts of the interviews he conducted with UNC people about Lowenstein.
3. James Wallace to AKL, July 12, 1949, AKL Papers.
4. Pfaff interview with Hunt and Wallace; interviews with Dorothy DiCintio, Jennifer Littlefield, and G. Benton Johnson, Eugene, Oregon, March 6, 1988.
5. Pfaff interview with Hunt and Wallace; Douglass Hunt to Frank Porter Graham, [n.d., fall 1945], AKL Papers.
6. Pfaff interview with Hunt and Wallace; interview with William Mackie, Chapel Hill, [n.d.]; AKL, draft statement on fraternities, [n.d.], AKL Papers.
7. V. O. Key, *Southern Politics in State and Nation* (New York: Knopf, 1949), p. 209; Warren Ashby, *Frank Porter Graham, a Southern Liberal* (Winston-Salem, N.C.: J. F. Blair, 1980), pp. 232–36; John Ehle, *The Free Men* (New York: Harper & Row, 1965); Pauli Murray, *Song in a Weary Throat: An American Pilgrimage* (New York: Harper & Row, 1987); Chapel Hill Civil Rights Collection, Duke Oral History Archives, Perkins Library, Duke University.
8. Pfaff interview with Wallace and Hunt; interview with Douglass Hunt.
9. Ashby, *Graham*, pp. 231–32; Pfaff interview with Wallace and Hunt; *New York Post*, December 12, 1945; see *Raleigh News and Observer* coverage, December 10–11, 1945.
10. Alice Gilbert to AKL, December 11, 1945, Ruth Silver to AKL, December 11, 1945, and Gabriel Lowenstein to AKL, December 18, 1945, all in AKL Papers; Pfaff interview with Wallace and Hunt. Lowenstein's father suggested he write up the episode for *The Nation*.
11. Ashby, *Graham*, pp. 99–232; Pfaff interview with Wallace and Hunt. See also *Raleigh News and Observer* coverage, December 10–11, 1945, and *Daily Tar Heel* coverage, December 10–15, 1945.
12. Gabriel Lowenstein to AKL, December 4, 1945, and James Wallace to AKL, December 4, 1948, both in AKL Papers; interviews with Douglass Hunt, G. Benton Johnson, Miriam Johnson, Dorothy DiCintio, and Jennifer Littlefield.
13. Pfaff interview with Wallace and Hunt; Douglass Hunt to AKL, September 30 and November 11, 1945, Gabriel Lowenstein to AKL, December 12, 1945, and Thelma Cohen to AKL, April 3, 1946, all in AKL Papers.
14. Pfaff interview with Wallace and Hunt; interviews with Miriam Johnson, G. Benton Johnson, and Dorothy DiCintio.

15. AKL to Sanford Friedman, June 29, 1945, and Bunny Peek to AKL, August 29, 1945, both in AKL Papers; Pfaff interview with Wallace and Hunt.

16. Pfaff interview with Wallace and Hunt; interview with Douglass Hunt; AKL to Sanford Friedman, July 2, 1945; AKL Papers.

17. Interviews with Douglass Hunt, Junius Scales, Durham, November 1, 1988; miscellaneous letters between Douglass Hunt and AKL, fall 1945, AKL Papers.

18. AKL stationery, AKL Papers.

19. Charles Sellers to AKL, February 26, 1946, and Rabbi Elmer Berger to AKL, February 25 and March 6, 1946, all in AKL Papers.

20. Mindy Berlowe to AKL, February 25, 1946, Thelma Cohen to AKL, April 3, 1946, Charles Sellers to AKL, February 26 and March 30, 1946, and Douglass Hunt to AKL, October 27, 1945, all in AKL Papers.

21. Douglass Hunt to AKL, October 27, 1945, AKL Papers; interviews with G. Benton Johnson and Themistocles Michos.

22. Allan Milledge to AKL, January 8, 1950, and Florence Lowenstein to AKL, [n.d.], both in AKL Papers; interview with G. Benton Johnson.

23. Fred Prince to AKL, March 4, 1947, and Betty Ragland to AKL, [n.d., 1946], both in AKL Papers. Conference delegate Leon Thompson wrote repeatedly (see, for example, July 9, 1946) asking for follow-up on the conference.

24. Ruth Silver to AKL, February 15 and 23, 1946, Douglass Hunt to AKL, November 6, 1946, Louis Wheaton to AKL, June 10, 1947, Pat Knight to AKL, January 11, 1948, G. Benton Johnson to AKL, January 18, 1948, Miriam Massey to AKL, January 28, 1948, and Beth Safir to AKL, January 29, 1948, all in AKL Papers.

25. Pfaff interview with Wallace and Hunt; interviews with Douglass Hunt and Junius Scales.

26. Interview with Junius Scales.

27. Miriam Massey to AKL, [n.d., 1948], James Wallace to AKL, January 3, 1948, Lowell Beveridge to AKL, April 28, 1948, Betty Ragland to AKL, [n.d., 1948], G. Benton Johnson to AKL, October 19, 1948, AKL to *New York Star*, October 25, 1948, Howard Beale to AKL, December 9, 1948, all in AKL Papers; *Daily Tar Heel*, March 31, 1948.

28. Interview with Miriam Johnson; Bob Sicular to AKL, November 6, 1947, and Lois Turner to AKL, August 14, 1947, both in AKL Papers.

29. Liz Taylor to AKL, [n.d.], Lois Hunt to AKL, September 9, 1947, Bob Sicular to AKL, November 6, 1947, all in AKL Papers; interview with Miriam Johnson.

30. Interviews with Miriam Johnson, Lawrence Lowenstein, and Dorothy DiCintio.

31. Interviews with Miriam Johnson and Dorothy DiCintio.

32. Lois Turner to AKL, August 14, 1947, and January 11, 1948, Lois Hunt to

AKL, September 9, 1947, [unidentified correspondent], September 4, 1947, all in AKL Papers.

33. Interview with Sanford Friedman; James Wallace to AKL, December 4, 1948, and Ruth Silver to AKL, August 21, 1946, both in AKL Papers.

34. James Wallace to AKL, February 11, 1948, AKL Papers.

35. G. Benton Johnson to AKL, February 24, 1949, Douglass Hunt to AKL, May 12, 1947, James Wallace to AKL, January 30, 1948, and Charles Sellers to AKL, April 14, 1947, all in the AKL Papers.

36. James Wallace to AKL, May 11, 1948, AKL "Ruminations," handwritten notes, [n.d., 1947], AKL to Miriam Massey, January 14, 1949, and Douglass Hunt to AKL, September 26, 1946, all in AKL Papers; interview with Miriam Johnson. During one critical episode at UNC involving the chancellor and President Graham, Lowenstein displayed the following circular—and paralyzing—sequence of thoughts. If he were to reveal that the chancellor "is a bastard and has been caught with his pants down . . . it may expose Frankie . . . since Frankie is too honest to stand up with the [chancellor] if we should tell him the true course of affairs; and for Frankie to turn now on the [chancellor] might prove fatal." The result? Nothing was done.

37. Douglass Hunt to AKL, September 26, 1946, and Gabriel Lowenstein to AKL, December 6, 1945, both in AKL Papers; interview with Dorothy DiCintio.

38. Helen Jean Rogers to AKL, April 8, 1949, Richard Murphy to AKL, January 17, 1950, John Sanders to AKL, January 21, 1950, all in AKL Papers; interviews with Miriam Johnson, G. Benton Johnson, and Sanford Friedman. Sanders wrote Lowenstein: "You see . . . [your opponent] thought that you took advantage of him under the guise of friendship, and that when expedient, you turned on him."

39. Interview by Eugene Pfaff with John Sanders.

40. Robert Lindsay to AKL, May 1949, AKL Papers.

41. Pfaff interview with Wallace and Hunt; interview with Douglass Hunt.

42. Pfaff interview with Sanders; interviews with Miriam Johnson and William Mackie.

43. Mickey McNutt to AKL, May 24, 1949, Gabriel Lowenstein to AKL, April 5, 1949, James Wallace to AKL, February 11, 1948 (citing AKL's comment to him), all in AKL Papers; interviews with Miriam Johnson and G. Benton Johnson, and Alice Popkin.

44. Pfaff interview with Sanders.

CHAPTER 3

1. AKL to Sanford Friedman, July 31, 1945, and Sanford Friedman to AKL, [n.d., probably 1946], both in AKL Papers.

2. Gabriel Lowenstein to AKL, July 5, 10, 13, and 30, and October 30, 1945, January 11, 14, and 31, and June 21, 1946, and January 8, 1948, AKL Papers.

3. Florence Lowenstein to AKL, April 28, 1946, and October 23 and November 5, 1945, AKL Papers.

4. Florence Lowenstein to AKL, October 5, 1946, and Lawrence Lowenstein to AKL, January 6, 1947, both in AKL Papers; interview with Lawrence and Marie Lowenstein.

5. Florence Lowenstein to AKL, October 9 and 18, 1945, AKL Papers; interview with Lawrence and Marie Lowenstein.

6. Florence Lowenstein to AKL, January 14, 1947, and March 1947, Dorothy Lowenstein, miscellaneous letters to AKL, 1947, and AKL diary entry, January 13, 1948, all in AKL Papers; interview with Lawrence and Marie Lowenstein.

7. Florence Lowenstein to AKL, January 14, 1947, AKL Papers; interview with Lawrence and Marie Lowenstein. This is the period when "Doc" wrote his poignant letter to Al, reaching out to him for help (see ch. 1, n. 40). Dorothy's letters to Al during this period comment on how much her father doted on Bert. Dorothy Lowenstein to AKL, [n.d.], AKL Papers.

8. Florence Lowenstein to AKL, November 12, 1945, and Dorothy Lowenstein, miscellaneous letters to AKL, 1946–47, all in AKL Papers.

9. Florence Lowenstein to AKL, March 2, May 25, and October 28, 1947, August 24, 1949, and January 8, 1950, AKL Papers. Suggesting her own sample of potential brides (one, she said, "would do you honor, be a helpmate and a beautiful hostess"), Florence wanted to make sure her son understood a "little philosophy." "The spokes of a wheel make a complete article only when they fit perfectly (thus, Marie into our family)," she said. "There is complete understanding, feeling, pleasure, because there is the same background."

10. Florence Lowenstein to AKL, [n.d., 1947], AKL Papers. It should be noted that an anchor is also something that weighs a person down.

11. Florence Lowenstein to AKL, April 29, 1947, AKL Papers.

12. AKL, school papers, [n.d.], AKL Papers. Lowenstein was also prepared to engage in the tactic historians have dubbed "plantation sabotage." Since direct resistance and escape were not options for slaves, they frequently adopted ploys designed to so frustrate and impede their masters that protest, in the guise of accommodation, dominated the plantation. Breaking tools, participating in slow-downs, acting dumb—all worked brilliantly to undermine the system. Lowenstein did not go to these lengths, but he had his own arsenal of responses—staying in bed all morning, coming home in the wee hours, leaving his room a total mess, repeatedly appearing late for engagements with his parents, and, above all, dressing in his own bizarre fashion. Visiting in the Lowenstein home and observing these tactics, Douglass Hunt concluded: "One of two things must be true: 1) you're trying to

make a point; or 2) you're being exceedingly foolish." Trying to prove that he was "a more than mildly obstreperous mental case" seemed stupid, since it could only convince his parents that if they could not watch over him, they needed to hire someone who could. "I must conclude, therefore," he wrote, "that unwittingly, or perhaps a little peevishly, you allow yourself to create family crises over such small things as a worthless hat . . . [or] a new tie ruined." Douglass Hunt to AKL, September 12, 1946, AKL Papers.

13. Interviews with Lawrence and Marie Lowenstein, and Miriam Johnson; Frances Gidens to AKL, March 8, 1948, and Helen Lowenstein to AKL, October 20, 1947, both in AKL Papers.

14. Interviews with Sanford Friedman, Miriam Johnson, and G. Benton Johnson.

15. AKL diary entry, early 1950, AKL Papers.

16. Grey Sanders to AKL, February 2, 1950, and Alice Gilbert to AKL, August 13, 1948, both in AKL Papers; interviews with Sanford Friedman and Dorothy DiCintio.

17. James Wallace to AKL, July 12, 1949, AKL Papers.

18. Jerry Davidoff to AKL, March 13, 1950, and James Wallace to AKL, September 18, 1945, both in AKL Papers; interview with G. Benton Johnson. In a letter to Lowenstein, Si Newhouse, a Horace Mann classmate, said that a friend of his had met Hunt and described him as "a very brilliant, and very handsome and startling young fellow."

19. Pfaff interview with Wallace and Hunt.

20. Douglass Hunt to AKL, August 30, 1945, AKL Papers.

21. Douglass Hunt to AKL, September 30, 1945, AKL Papers.

22. Douglass Hunt to AKL, October 20, 1945, AKL Papers.

23. Douglass Hunt to AKL, October 27, 1945, AKL Papers.

24. Douglass Hunt to AKL, December 22 and 25, 1945, and March 21, 1946, AKL Papers. In response to Lowenstein's protestations that Hunt was doing too much for him while Lowenstein was ill, Hunt said, "I wanted to do it; I enjoyed it; and I don't feel like a 'martyr' for having done it."

25. Douglass Hunt to AKL, March 21, 1946, AKL Papers. Hunt's reference is to Emerson's meeting with Carlyle when he visited the United Kingdom. Although Carlyle did not know Emerson, he had heard of him, and when Emerson came to call after a long journey by coach, the two found an immediate rapport and sharing of spirits that seemed almost magical to both.

26. Douglass Hunt to AKL, September 17 and 25, and October 2, 1946, AKL Papers. At one time, Hunt complained that he had fourteen people to write to, including family, and declared that their letters had become "like a two-sided monologue, rather than a conversation, or like shadow-boxing." Al's letters, Hunt said later, were "the most obtuse, oblique, and obscure letters I think I ever tried to decipher."

27. Interview with Lawrence and Marie Lowenstein. See also the Robin Fau correspondence, 1944–45, AKL Papers (see ch. 1, n. 47).

28. Loretta Jacobs to AKL, [n.d. 1944–45], AKL Papers. Indeed, Al was receiving a flurry of different messages from home. His stepmother wanted him to marry a nice Jewish girl. His brother, probably acting on instructions from Doc, urged him to stay away from sex and liquor altogether. "Be careful of who you play around with," Larry wrote. "VD is no joke. . . . Remember, if women play with you they play with anybody else that comes along. . . . [So] stay away from women and keep the pants on at all times—that's the only certain preventative. . . . This is all from me." (Presumably, Al understood exactly where such advice had come from.)

29. Iris Bost to AKL, July 27, 1949, Betty Ragland to AKL, [n.d.], and Ruth Silver to AKL, August 21, 1946, all in AKL Papers; interview with G. Benton Johnson. Al's own confusion about the "dating game" was reflected in a note he wrote to himself reconstructing a "typical" conversation with a coed. "If I invited you to supper would you maybe accept sometime," he asks. "I'm sorry," she responds, "but I go steady." "With whom," he persists. "Even at meals? I know what—we'll talk politics." All Cashion [a dormitory] girls, he concludes, "go steady from the day before I meet them." See dialogue in AKL's handwriting on the back of a mimeographed assignment sheet, AKL Papers.

30. Interview with Miriam Johnson; Bob Sicular to AKL, November 6, 1947, AKL Papers. See also the correspondence on the Encampment cited in chapter 2, notes 29 through 32.

31. Connie Dyregov to AKL, October 2, 1947, Jim Kruskopf to AKL, November 7, 1947, Miriam Massey to AKL, [n.d., summer 1947], Douglass Hunt to AKL, November 26, 1947, Florence Lowenstein to AKL, May 2, 1948, and Dan McFarland to AKL, May 16, 1948, all in AKL papers.

32. Interview with Miriam Johnson.

33. Interviews with Miriam Johnson and G. Benton Johnson; Miriam Massey to AKL, December 1947, and [n.d., summer 1948], AKL Papers.

34. Miriam Massey to AKL, June 11, 1948, AKL Papers.

35. Miriam Massey to AKL, [n.d., autumn 1948], and December 25, 1948, AKL Papers.

36. G. Benton Johnson and Miriam Massey to AKL, January 3, 1949, AKL Papers. The Massey-Johnson letter took the opportunity both to kid Lowenstein about his own political machinations and to alert him to what was going on between them. "He won't have to try too hard to cement relations on this end," they wrote, Mimi adding, "that'll scare him." When Benny then asked, "Does he or does he not want us to be solidary?" Mimi replied: "The old concept of ambivalence arises. He doesn't want me, but he wants me to [not be tied to someone else]." But Al had plenty of chances "to get attached and stay attached," Benny responded, "to people like you, Mimi." Yes, she agreed, but she no longer cared about Al, "at least in an erotic sense."

37. AKL to Miriam Massey, May 16 and 24, 1949, AKL Papers.

38. AKL to Miriam Massey, July 3 and 30, 1949, AKL Papers.

39. AKL to Miriam Massey, July 3 and 30, 1949, and Miriam Massey to AKL, [n.d., summer 1949], AKL Papers.

40. AKL to Miriam Massey, October 13, 1949, AKL Papers.

41. Pfaff interview with Sanders.

42. Harding Menzies to Joan Hammond, January 11, 1953, AKL Papers.

43. Mary Ellen Knight to AKL, February 10, 1951, AKL Papers.

44. Interviews with Marcia Borie, March 14–15, 1989, Los Angeles, Dorothy DiCintio, Themistocles Michos, Palo Alto, November 23, 1991, and Sanford Friedman; AKL, handwritten notes on Florence Lowenstein's letter to him of July 9, 1949, and AKL diary entry, [n.d. 1950], both in AKL Papers.

45. James Wallace to AKL, September 18, 1945, and February 11, 1948, AKL to Miriam Massey, January 2, 1949, AKL Papers; interviews with Miriam Johnson, G. Benton Johnson, and Douglass Hunt.

46. Miriam Massey to AKL, four letters, [n.d., summer 1947, and summer 1948], AKL Papers.

47. Interviews with Miriam Johnson and G. Benton Johnson.

48. Carroll Smith-Rosenberg, "The Female World of Love and Ritual: The Relations between Women in Nineteenth-Century America," *Signs: Journal of Women in Culture and Society* 1 (1975): 1–30.

49. Anthony Rotundo, "Romantic Friendship: Male Intimacy and Middle-Class Youth in the Northern United States, 1800–1900," *Journal of Social History* 23, no. 1 (Fall 1989): 1–25.

50. Interview with Sanford Friedman.

51. Grey Sanders to AKL, July 18, 1949, Eugene Schwartz to AKL, February 19, 1950, Betty Ragland to AKL, [n.d.], and Miriam Massey and G. Benton Johnson to AKL, January 31, 1949, all in AKL Papers.

52. AKL to Miriam Massey, May 16, 1949, and Miriam Massey to AKL, [n.d., summer 1949], both in AKL Papers; interview with Miriam Johnson.

CHAPTER 4

1. Ashby, *Graham*, pp. 3–98.

2. Some of the correspondence discussing Lowenstein's move to Washington as Graham's aide includes Sara Tillett to AKL, February 10, 1950, and Florence Lowenstein to AKL, May 10, 1949, both in AKL Papers; see also Pfaff interview with Wallace and Hunt. Senator Wayne Morse characterized Graham in 1949 as "one of the most Christ-like men I have ever met." Ashby, *Graham*, p. 245.

3. Ibid., pp. 171–256.

4. Ibid., p. 261. On the campaign, see also Samuel Lubell, *The Future of American Politics* (New York: Harper, 1952).

5. Ashby, *Graham*, pp. 257–271.

6. Ibid., pp. 161–163, 235–239; Robert Kelley to AKL, May 7, 1949, and AKL to Robert Kelley, May 7, 1949, both in AKL Papers.

7. Ashby, *Graham*, pp. 252–263.

8. Ibid., pp. 263–271. The Graham campaign is generally viewed as the most pivotal in modern southern history since it set the precedent for the race-baiting and red-baiting tactics that were later employed so widely by politicians like Orval Faubus, George Wallace, and Jesse Helms. Helms, of course, helped invent these tactics through his role in the Willis Smith campaign.

9. Pfaff interview with Wallace and Hunt; Peter Jones, "History of NSA/IUS Relations," AKL Papers.

10. Jones, "History."

11. Ibid., NSA congress report, First National Student Congress, Chicago, in AKL Papers.

12. Helen Jean Rogers to AKL, July 1, 1949; preface to NSA congress report, First National Student Congress; NSA congress reports, Second (1948, Madison, Wisc.) and Third (National 1949, Student Congresses); NSA resolution, September 3, 1947; Jones, "History," all in AKL Papers. See also *New York Times*, August 23, 1949; and Pfaff interview with Wallace and Hunt.

13. Miriam Massey to AKL, September 9, 1949, Alice Gilbert to AKL, May 31, 1949, Elmer Brock to AKL, April 4, 1952, Lucille Kohn to AKL, August 22, 1949, and Helen Jean Rogers to AKL, [n.d., 1949], all in AKL Papers. See also interview with Alice Popkin, New Haven, Connecticut, April 7, 1990.

14. NSA congress report, Third National Student Congress; Elmer Brock to AKL, April 4, 1952, and AKL, typescript on NSA presidency, [n.d.], both in AKL Papers.

15. AKL, mimeographed statement on the *Maroon* affair, [n.d.], AKL Papers.

16. AKL, press release on behalf of NSA, May 15, 1951, AKL Papers.

17. AKL to NEC, December 4, 1950, and foreword to 1950 report on international activities by NSA, both in AKL Papers. It should be noted that Herbert Eisenberg, the NSA's international vice-president, opposed dividing the student world into two camps.

18. AKL diary, [n.d., fall 1950], and AKL to Dean Acheson, September 17, 1950, both in AKL Papers; *Raleigh News and Observer*, October 16, 1950.

19. "A New Role for the American Student: Reports from Stockholm, S.E. Asia, the U.S., USNSA," AKL Papers. Among those present at the Stockholm meeting was the president of the Swedish student association, Olaf Palme, who would subsequently become prime minister of Sweden. The head of the opposition IUS was Enrico Belinguer, subsequently the head of Italy's Communist party, and the person identified with the liberal approach dubbed "Eurocommunism."

20. Jones, "History," Peter Eckstein to AKL, May 7, 1963, and press release

and minutes, ISC Conference, all in AKL Papers. Eckstein was apparently responding to Lowenstein's anger at Peter Jones's description of the response of other delegates to his speech at the ICS meeting. Jones suggested in his "History" that the delegates had censured Lowenstein.

21. Ade Thomas to *World Student News,* March 1951, "open letter to AKL" from his opponents, [n.d., letter to the editor] reports on NEC and NSA congresses, February and August 1951, Elmer Brock to AKL, October 23, 1951, and Joan Long to AKL, [n.d., 1951], all in AKL Papers. Long noted that at least Lowenstein had not been called a Fascist, in her view the customary epithet applied to opponents of the IUS.

22. "New Role for American Student. . . "

23. AKL to Gertrude Anderson, February 21, 1951, AKL speech draft, 1951, and AKL to James Conant, July 5, 1951, all in AKL Papers.

24. NSA, "International Affairs Reports," 1950–51, and Paul Pitner to AKL, July 26, 1951, both in AKL Papers.

25. Marcia Borie to AKL, December 22, 1951, and William Dentzer to AKL, November 17, 1951, both in AKL Papers.

26. William Holmes to AKL, March 18, 1951, NSA congress report, Fourth National Student Congress, 1950, Ann Arbor, Mich., and William Birenbaum speech, June 10, 1951, all in AKL Papers.

27. *New York Times,* February 16, 1967; *Washington Post,* February 16, 1967; NSA press release, February 15, 1967, AKL Papers; Sol Stern, "A Short Account of International Student Politics and the Cold War," *Ramparts* (March 1967); *Village Voice,* July 6, 1967.

28. Interviews with William Dentzer, New York, December 9, 1989; Rick Stearn, Boston, November 21, 1989; Karen Paget, Stanford, Spring 1990; and Curtis Gans, [n.d.]. See also the *Ramparts* and *Village Voice* citations. Dentzer, Stearn, and Gans were NSA officers in these years, and Paget was closely involved with the NSA. The CIA connection began during Dentzer's term of office; subsequently, he supervised the CIA's relationship with the NSA for a number of years. As international vice-president in the 1960s, Stearn was involved in terminating the relationship. Overseeing that process was Phil Sherburne, NSA president in 1966–67. See Ken Metzler, "Covert Action Division No. 5," *Old Oregon* (May–June 1967).

29. Interviews with William Dentzer and Curtis Gans. Robert Kiley, another NSA president who subsequently took over Dentzer's role as CIA overseer of the relationship with the NSA, also denies that Lowenstein was in the loop, citing the same reasons. Interview with Robert Kiley, New York City, September 11, 1990.

30. Penciled notes on two mimeographed sheets discussing the CIA revelations, and AKL to James Conant, July 5, 1951, both in AKL Papers; interviews with Philip Sherburne, Rick Stearn, and Karen Paget. Sherburne said that he was called to a breakfast meeting in a Washington hotel where Lowenstein and a CIA officer were present. Lowenstein attempted to per-

suade Sherburne not to corroborate the forthcoming news stories about the CIA connection, arguing that to do so would place in physical danger hundreds of innocent foreign students who might have been recipients of CIA money without knowing it. Stearn said that, in conversations about it, Lowenstein displayed a degree of factual familiarity with the CIA-NSA connection that was inconsistent with having no prior awareness of it. Lowenstein, in turn, acknowledged to a *Village Voice* reporter in 1967 that he had been asked by the parties involved to "facilitate" the dissolution of ties between NSA and the CIA. That in his role as facilitator he would have had access to the kind of information Stearns alludes to is dubious. See *Village Voice*, February 23, 1967.

31. Interviews with Michael Horowitz, Washington, D.C., April 25, 1989; and Gary Bellow, Boston, December 11, 1990; Jeanette Sacks to AKL, November 24, 1952, Marianna Milray to AKL, September 1, 1951, Bob Kelley to AKL, September 16, 1952, and Jan [surname unknown] to AKL, September 11, 1956, all in AKL Papers.

32. Interviews with Gary Bellow and Michael Horowitz.

33. David Broder, *Washington Post*, March 19, 1980.

CHAPTER 5

1. For discussion of Lowenstein's uneasy contemplation of the law school dilemma, see Benny Johnson to AKL, August 31, 1951, Douglass Hunt to AKL, April 25, 1949, Howard Beale to AKL, November 11, 1951, and Jerry Davidoff to AKL, January 21, 1949, all in AKL Papers.

2. Harding Menzies to Joan Hammond, January 11, 1953, Douglass Hunt to AKL, January 23, 1949, Benny Johnson to AKL, August 31, 1951, and Iris Bost to AKL, October 8, 1951, all in AKL Papers. Lowenstein's stepmother summarized the family position. "You will *never* be satisfied," Florence wrote, "if you do not study law. Somewhere in your makeup is a feeling that you should do this. And from my point of view you should. This does not mean that you will practice law, but . . . it must be there for you to use when needed. You are a little afraid of the confinement of law school. You must accustom yourself to think of the study as a responsibility of yours and in your usual way, make yourself content until it is over." The family message was clear: repress your instincts once more and do the right thing. But so was the political message: "Get law behind you and then push it into the background to bring forth only to serve you." Florence Lowenstein to AKL, February 2, 1950, and November 10, 1952, AKL Papers.

3. AKL to Gabriel and Florence Lowenstein, July 16, 1950, AKL Papers.

4. AKL diary entry, October 18, 1951, miscellaneous AKL letters to friends, October 1951 through January 1952, Mary Ellen Knight to AKL, December 2, 1951, and January 16, 1952, William Friday to AKL, [n.d., 1952], Helen Jean Rogers to AKL, November 16, 1951, and Howard Beale to

AKL, November 9, 1951, all in AKL Papers. See also subsequent Lowenstein diary headlines: "Asks Self if Three Years Might Not Be Better Spent Elsewhere" (October 25, 1951), and "A. L. Tells Dad of Doubts About Law as a Career" (December 9, 1951).

5. Interviews with Alice Popkin, New Haven, April 7, 1990; Ann Feldman, Brooklyn, October 7, 1991; and William Taylor, Washington, D. C., June 2, 1989; Florence Lowenstein to AKL, September 3, 1952, AKL Papers.

6. Eleanor Roosevelt to AKL, October 1, 1951, AKL Papers; interviews with Ann Feldman, Alice Popkin, William Taylor, and Gary Bellow.

7. Howard Beale to AKL, November 11, 1951, and Florence Lowenstein to AKL, [n.d., 1953], both in AKL Papers; interviews with Alice Popkin, William Taylor, and Ann Feldman.

8. Note from speed-reading instructor, [n.d.], AKL Papers.

9. AKL to Benny and Miriam Johnson, February 14, May 23, and June 16, 1955, AKL, miscellaneous notes on army training, Sanford Friedman to AKL, [n.d.], all in AKL Papers; interview with Themistocles Michos. Michos noted that Lowenstein "was absolutely useless for virtually any conceivable task that the Army could perform." Lowenstein spent most of his time, according to Michos, providing help to a black officer, Captain Ellison Wynn, and striving to promote better race relations at the army post. Michos said that Al had also helped persuade another army sergeant to marry a German woman whose child the sergeant had fathered.

10. Interviews with Themistocles Michos, Carol Hardin, New Haven, November 28, 1989; Mary Lynch (Muffie Grant), Greenwich, Connecticut, February 14, 1989; and Judy Quine; AKL to Norma and Ken Johnson, September 1, 1954, Muffie Grant to AKL, [n.d., 1955–56], Carol Hardin to AKL, [n.d., 1955–56], and Jim Rial to AKL, January 23, 1958, AKL to Florence Lowenstein, May 17, 1956. For an example of Lowenstein's endless machinations to get an early release from the army, see his May 17, 1956 letter to Florence Lowenstein giving her detailed instructions on how to write various people so that the army would get the impression that he was desperately needed back in the States for important work. Lowenstein also tried to get Governor Stevenson and various officials at UNC and Yale to intervene, as well as friends in the media, who might say he was needed for a radio or television show. Although minor, the episode reveals how devious Lowenstein could be in his behind-the-scenes politicking—a trait that in other situations raised serious questions about his character and motivation. AKL to Douglass Hunt, October 24, 1955, AKL to Lucille Kohn, [n.d., 1956], and AKL to Marietta Tree (Gov. Stevenson's assistant), January 18, 1956, all in AKL Papers; *Seattle Post-Intelligence*, April 20, 1956.

11. Dorothy Lowenstein to AKL, assorted letters, [n.d., 1951–52], and AKL, notes on his grandfather's interment, both in AKL Papers. Dorothy at one point bemoaned the fact that she and Al had ceased "communicating" as they used to. She also observed in a 1950 letter regarding her father and

Bert: "I never know what to believe when Daddy says something. It's always based on the truth, but the truth is so far buried under the layers Dad puts on that it is very hard to uncover it. It's down there somewhere sort of like the foundation of a house."

12. Gabriel Lowenstein to AKL, October 30, 1955, and miscellaneous letters from Gabriel Lowenstein and Florence Lowenstein to AKL, 1953–55, all in AKL Papers.

13. See miscellaneous letters to AKL from army buddies, 1956–57, Peter Goldschmidt to AKL, September 28, 1958, Gary Bellow to AKL, October 1, 1958, and miscellaneous letters to AKL from college classmates, 1950–55, all in AKL Papers.

14. Marty Bennet to AKL, February 9, 1950, Mary Kay Perkins to AKL, August 18, 1952, Benny and Miriam Johnson to AKL, August 25, 1952, and Grey Sanders to AKL, [n.d., 1954], all in AKL Papers; interview with Themistocles Michos.

15. Helen Jean Rogers to AKL, November 16, 1951, and [n.d., 1951], AKL Papers.

16. Helen Jean Rogers to AKL, December 23, 1951, and May 17, 1952, and Lucille Kohn to AKL, March 20, 1955, all in AKL Papers.

17. Katherine White to AKL, miscellaneous letters, [n.d., 1958], Judy McMichael to AKL, miscellaneous letters [n.d., 1957], all in AKL papers; interview with Frances (Suzman) Jowell, London, June 18, 1987; Katherine White signed her letters, "love, Snuggles."

18. AKL to Sanford Friedman, November 7, 1955, AKL Papers.

19. Interviews with Mary ("Muffie" Grant) Lynch, Carol Hardin, and Rob Redpath, London, January 10, 1990.

20. Interview with Mary Lynch; Muffie Grant to AKL, [n.d., 1956], AKL Papers.

21. Muffie Grant to AKL, [n.d., 1956], AKL Papers; interview with Mary Lynch.

22. Norman Buck to AKL, May 12, 1953, and counselor reports, 1953–54, all in AKL Papers. Buck was in the dean's office. One of Lowenstein's UNC classmates with whom he was close sometimes wondered about their relationship. "So many times I have seen you do things for others simply out of consideration for their feelings," he wrote Al, "that I can never be sure whether your kindnesses to me can be thusly categorized, or whether they have deeper meanings." (John Sanders to AKL, January 18, 1951, AKL Papers).

23. Interview with Bruce Payne, Durham, June 9, 1989; Archie Richards to AKL, December 1954, David Lapham to AKL, November 1954, and Jonathan [surname unknown] to AKL, April 26, 1954, all in AKL Papers.

24. Interview with Gary Bellow.

25. Letters to AKL, [n.d.], AKL Papers.

26. The questionnaire is in the AKL Papers. A significant number of respondents indicated they had experienced heterosexual contact with prosti-

tutes, and some had had homosexual relationships. See also interview with William Taylor.

27. See previously cited correspondence, footnote 25. This pattern of talking with some intimacy about sexual issues—which would recur throughout Lowenstein's life—often focused on "girlfriend" problems. One person, for example, wrote Lowenstein from the army that he was not having as much success as Lowenstein in relating to enlisted men and having them come sit on his bed to confide their successes and failures with women.

28. David Lapham to AKL, November 1954, and March 22, 1955, AKL Papers.

29. David Lapham to AKL, [n.d., summer 1955], AKL Papers.

30. Mr. Lapham to AKL, September 9, 1955, Eleanor Roosevelt to AKL, November 25, 1955, Mrs. Lapham to AKL, January 9, 1956, "Phil" [full name unknown] to AKL, January 1956, all in AKL Papers. Phil wrote: "Your letter only made me realize the more how close you were to Dave—it brought back different things—the way you and he gabbed about each other and all." See also interviews with Mary Lynch and Carol Hardin.

31. Interviews with Mary Lynch and Marcia Borie; John Sanders to AKL, October 2, 1951, AKL Papers.

32. AKL to Ken Johnson, May 1, 1956, AKL Papers.

33. Interviews with Bruce Payne and Curtis Gans; Dennis Hill to AKL, [n.d.], AKL Papers. This theme will be dealt with in greater length in chapter 9.

34. Douglass Hunt to AKL, October 2, 1946, Miriam Massey to AKL, [n.d., 1949], Muffie Grant to AKL, November 28, 1956, and Joan Long to AKL, [n.d., 1951], all in AKL Papers.

35. Muffie Grant to AKL, [n.d., 1956], and Kenny Nelson to AKL, May 11, 1956, both in AKL papers; interview with Marcia Borie.

36. AKL to Muffie Grant, [n.d.], AKL Papers; Norma (Nelson) Johnson to AKL, [n.d.], AKL Papers.

CHAPTER 6

1. As one of Al's friends put it, "There were too many problems in the world for him to show up on a regular basis." Eugene Pfaff interview with Anne Queen.

2. For a discussion of his first trip to South Africa, see Allard K. Lowenstein, *Brutal Mandate: A Journey to South-West Africa* (New York: Macmillan, 1962), pp. 29–33.

3. Hubert Humphrey to AKL, February 11, 1959; AKL to Hubert Humphrey, [n.d.]; AKL, draft for Humphrey's speech of April 15, 1959; all in AKL Papers.

4. AKL's notations on a memo pad, [n.d., spring 1959], AKL Papers.

5. Interview with Emory Bundy, Seattle, May 21, 1988; Lowenstein, *Brutal Mandate*, pp. 3–4.

6. Interviews with Emory Bundy and Mary Benson, London, June 19, 1987;

Lowenstein, *Brutal Mandate,* pp. 4–7. Benson was a longtime South African white insurgent, eventually forced into exile by the regime there.

7. Lowenstein, *Brutal Mandate,* pp. 32–33; interview with Frances (Suzman) Jowell.

8. Dan Verwoerd to AKL, October 27, 1958, AKL Papers; Lowenstein, *Brutal Mandate,* pp. 8–9.

9. Interviews with Sherman Bull, New Canaan, Connecticut, February 24, 1991; and Emory Bundy.

10. Interview with Emory Bundy.

11. Emory Bundy to AKL, April 26, 1957, AKL papers; interview with Emory Bundy.

12. Interviews with Emory Bundy and Sherman Bull.

13. Frank Porter Graham to Dorothy Schiff, May 13, 1959, Hubert Humphrey to Dorothy Schiff, May 13, 1959, Eleanor Roosevelt to Dorothy Schiff, May 18, 1959, Dorothy Martin (Schiff's secretary) to AKL, May 15, 1959, Willard Johnson to AKL, May 1, 1959, Tom Kendrick to AKL, December 24, 1958, and Nina Wallace to AKL, May 18, 1958, all in AKL Papers. It is noteworthy that the NSA's international vice-president, who was working for the CIA, once again asked Lowenstein to do some student government chores while in South Africa.

14. Perrin Henderson to AKL, June 23, 1959, AKL Papers; interviews with Frances Jowell and Emory Bundy.

15. Interview with Emory Bundy; Lowenstein, *Brutal Mandate,* pp. 42–63.

16. Interview with Emory Bundy; Lowenstein, *Brutal Mandate,* pp. 32–57.

17. Interview with Emory Bundy; Lowenstein, *Brutal Mandate,* pp. 75–79.

18. Emory Bundy testimony before the United Nations, October 13, 1959, AKL Papers; interview with Emory Bundy; Lowenstein, *Brutal Mandate,* pp. 81–85, 93–102.

19. Interview with Emory Bundy; Bundy U.N. testimony, Lowenstein, *Brutal Mandate,* pp. 129–146.

20. Sherman Bull, who was also under surveillance, had an equally close call. Frances Suzman was to bring his ticket to the airport; racing there, she barely arrived before Bull's plane was to leave. From Johannesburg, Bundy and Lowenstein eventually went on to the Vienna youth festival.

21. Emory and Mary Bundy to AKL, November 24, 1959, Sherman Bull testimony before the United Nations, October 13, 1959, Bundy U.N. testimony, AKL testimony before the United Nations, October 16, 1959, Phyllis Green to AKL, October 27, 1959, and Ethel Grossman to AKL, November 26, 1959, all in AKL Papers; interviews with Emory Bundy and Sherman Bull.

22. Interview with Emory Bundy.

23. Emory Bundy to AKL, November 19, 1959, Evelyn [surname unknown] to AKL, September 16, 1959, and Donald Rumsfeld to AKL, October 18, 1959, all in AKL Papers.

24. Nathan Straus to AKL, December 2, 1959, Lucille Kohn to AKL, November 16, 1959, Ronnie Dugger to AKL, [n.d. 1960], and Ethel Grossman to AKL, November 27 and December 12, 1959, all in AKL Papers.

25. Frank Porter Graham to AKL, October 8, 1959, AKL Papers; interviews with Emory Bundy, James Nash, Seattle, May 21, 1988; and John Wilson, Seattle, May 21, 1988.

26. Ronnie Dugger to AKL, September 24, 1960, Douglass Hunt to AKL, October 17, 1960, Douglas Sante to AKL, November 1, 1960, Fred Weaver to AKL, August 2, 1960, Frank Porter Graham to AKL, August 2, 1960, Marge MacNamara to AKL, August 4, 1960, Lucille Kohn to AKL, August 12, 1960, Roland Giduz to AKL, September 19, 1960, and Lucille Kohn to AKL, November 16, 1960, all in AKL Papers.

27. Everet Chapman (USIA) to AKL, May 18, 1961, Lucille Kohn to AKL, February 2, 1961, Chester Bowles to AKL, February 7, 1961, Peter Lapham to AKL, January 22, 1961, Douglass Hunt to AKL, February 16, 1961, Gladys Tillett to AKL, February 16, 1961, Douglass Hunt to AKL, March 17, 1961, and Ethel Grossman to AKL, March 14, 1961, all in AKL Papers; see also interview with Barbara Boggs Sigmund, Princeton, New Jersey, June 23, 1989.

28. Interview with Emory Bundy.

29. Douglass Hunt to AKL, February 15, 1961, and Gary Bellow to AKL, [n.d., 1961], both in AKL Papers.

30. Emory Bundy to AKL, March 2, 1961, and Ethel Grossman to AKL, January 24, February 27, March 19, and April 8, 1961, all in AKL Papers.

31. Ethel Grossman to AKL, January 29 and 24, February 24, and May 11, 1961, AKL Papers.

32. Orville Prescott, reviewing the book in the daily *New York Times* on July 16, 1962, called Lowenstein "a capable writer [and] a fiery idealist, a zealous crusader for social and political righteousness. . . . As an account of the plight of natives in Southwest Africa, it is horrifying, and as a prolonged editorial, sermon, and denunciation, it is eloquent." Gwendolyn Brooks's review in the *New York Times Book Review* of November 7, 1962, was more mixed: she praised Lowenstein for helping to prompt the UN hearings but said that "the pages of commentary on the South African situation . . . need more sophisticated analysis."

33. Jim Reese to AKL, [n.d., 1961], AKL Papers; Christopher Lasch, *Haven in a Heartless World: The Family Besieged* (New York: Basic Books, 1977).

34. Perrin Henderson to AKL, November 13, 1959, and Sarah [surname unknown] to AKL, [n.d., 1960], both in AKL Papers.

35. Sarah [surname unknown] to AKL, [n.d.], and Ethel Grossman to AKL, [n.d.], both in AKL Papers.

36. Beth Brod to AKL, February 24, 1960, AKL Papers.

37. Interview with Barbara Boggs Sigmund; Ethel Grossman to AKL, January 27 and 29, 1961, Gabriel Lowenstein to AKL, March 8, 1961 (on how "Mr. Boggs is engineering a very clever delaying action with the hope that

things will work out differently"), John Boettiger to AKL, May 17, 1961, and Barbara Boggs to AKL, May 23, 1961 (about lengthy conversations with her father), all in AKL Papers.

38. Barbara Boggs to AKL, June 12, 1961, AKL Papers.
39. Barbara Boggs to AKL, July 27 and August 1, 1961, AKL Papers.
40. Barbara Boggs to AKL, August 1 and 8, 1961, Florence Lowenstein to AKL, August 7, 1961, and Ethel Grossman to AKL, August 9, 1961, all in AKL Papers. For letters on the delay in announcing the engagement and more on his visits to her parents, see Barbara Boggs to AKL, September 29 and November 1 and 12, 1961, Ethel Grossman to AKL, October 8, 1961, and Cokie Boggs to AKL, November 24, 1961, all in AKL Papers. In her November 12 letter, Boggs wrote:

> I have never known such joy and humility as I did when you explained to [my parents] your feeling for me. I remember that the first time you ever told me you loved me, I said thank you and you laughed, but I still can't think of anything more appropriate to tell you—if I ever prove worthy of your love, I'll be a very blessed woman. As for my love for you, per usual, my words are inadequate. You said something to M & D during the course of your talk about your feelings when we're separated, prefacing it with, "I don't know how she feels when we're apart, but." Well, this sounds silly, but I always feel as if I have an arm missing. It sounds ridiculous, but the feeling of incompleteness is that acute. I know it's not poetic or beautiful, but it's *exactly* the way I feel.

In reality, of course, Barbara wrote as beautifully and poetically as anyone.

41. Interview with Barbara Boggs Sigmund; Barbara Boggs to AKL, June 12, 1961, and February 18, 1962, AKL Papers.
42. George Hazelrig to AKL, February 9, 1962 (about the church questionnaire), Barbara Boggs to AKL, February 18, 1962, Ethel Grossman to AKL, March 1962, Helen Stancill to AKL, May 5, 1962 (about postponing the wedding from June until September), and Barbara Boggs to AKL, August 2 and September 9, 1962, all in AKL Papers. Lowenstein sent Boggs a telegram on the day they were to have been married. Boggs, in turn, wrote Lowenstein:

> fundamental differences between us are so great, that no matter what tit for tat arrangement we made before we got married, we would never believe that we were raising our children in the way we thought best for them, and . . . we both care about children too much ever to put ourselves in this position. But besides this . . . I have come to realize over the past year how great a gulf religion creates between us. Much of this is hidden to you, because I have not told you the hurt I feel when you make little barbed remarks about the church, both publicly and privately, nor have I told you how uneasy or unnatural I feel about saying the simplest religious

or "Catholic" things to you. . . . But I could not stand this uneasiness for long in my home. . . . I want religion to be positive and all-pervading, not negative and niggardly and a cause for tension and unhappiness. . . . I was not up against some external structure, but against myself.

AKL to Barbara Boggs, September 9, 1962; Barbara Boggs to AKL, September 9, 1962, both in AKL Papers.

43. Interview with Barbara Boggs Sigmund; Barbara Boggs to AKL, September 9, 1962, AKL Papers. Boggs subsequently married Paul Sigmund, a Princeton professor; she remained very friendly with Lowenstein. She was elected mayor of Princeton and ran unsuccessfully in the Democratic primary for governor of New Jersey in 1988. She died of cancer two years later. Deeply devoted to her family and religious faith, she wrote a volume of poetry—published after her death—that included a beautiful, warm, and humorous salute to "Christopher Sullivan Lowenstein," the child she never had with Al.

44. Interviews with Barbara Boggs Sigmund and Curtis Gans.

45. Interviews with Curtis Gans, Barbara Boggs Sigmund, and Greg Craig, Washington, D.C., October 14, 1988, and February 16, 1989.

46. Ethel Grossman to AKL, January 13 and 24, 1961, July 2 and December 28, 1962, Lucille Kohn to AKL, January 13, 1961, and Ethel Grossman to AKL, December 31, 1960, all in AKL Papers. Grossman did write one of the most eloquent passages of *Brutal Mandate*, the description of Michael Scott.

47. Ethel Grossman to AKL, January 13 and 15, 1962, July 2, 1962, January 13, 1961, [n.d., 1961], February 27, 1961, and March 23, 1962, AKL Papers. Lowenstein suggested to many people that he would dedicate the book to them; in the end, he dedicated it to no one, instead mentioning scores of people in his acknowledgments.

48. Ethel Grossman to AKL, January 29, August 9, and May 11, 1961, AKL Papers.

49. Ethel Grossman to AKL, January 22, 1960, May 31 and September 20, 1961, and July 2, 1962, AKL Papers.

50. Ethel Grossman to AKL, September 11, 1962, AKL Papers.

51. Ethel Grossman to AKL, September 27 and 30, 1962, AKL Papers.

52. Brookes Aronson to AKL, March 2, 1962, AKL Papers.

53. Ethel Grossman to AKL, [n.d., 1962], AKL Papers; interview with Curtis Gans.

54. Interview with Frances Jowell.

CHAPTER 7

1. Interviews with William Craig, San Diego, December 11, 1988; Armin Rosencranz (a Stanford student at the time), Inverness, California, August 20, 1988; Robert Beyers (director of Stanford's press service), Palo Alto,

February 21, 1990; Colleen and Kenneth Cuthbertson (a senior administrator and his wife), Saratoga, California, August 20, 1988; and Patti
Hagen (a Stanford student at the time) New York, October 4, 1988; Stanford University orientation materials, 1961, and statement on residential
policy to the Stanford Board of Trustees, February 21, 1957, both in AKL
Papers.

2. Interviews with Robert Beyers, Stanford, Feb. 21, 1990, Colleen and Kenneth Cuthbertson, and Floss Frucher (Stanford student at the time), New
York, Oct. 4, 1988; B. (William) Craig to R. (Robert) Wuert, January 9,
1962. Criticizing the house system, the faculty member Wilfred Stone told
the trustees in 1958 that Stern and Wilbur halls gave the students the message that "you are here to be processed, your individual freedom is on pro-
bation, and therefore you are afforded the comforts . . . of a well-appointed
prison." Wilfred Stone, "Stanford's House System: Spaces for Freedom,"
1958, both in AKL Papers.

3. Interviews with William Craig, and Colleen and Kenneth Cuthbertson; B.
Craig to AKL, March 20 and May 31, 1961, AKL Papers.

4. Interview with Fred Goff (a Stanford student at the time); Stern Hall freshman questionnaire, AKL Papers.

5. Interviews with Colleen and Kenneth Cuthbertson, and William Craig;
Stern Hall newsletter, February 16, 1962, AKL Papers.

6. Interviews with William Craig and Dwight Clark (a Stanford assistant dean
at the time), Stanford, December 14, 1988.

7. Interviews with Patti Hagen, Floss Frucher, New York, October 3, 1988;
and Kris Kleinbauer, Los Angeles, June 1, 1988 (all Stanford students at
the time).

8. Interviews with Colleen and Kenneth Cuthbertson, Patti Hagan, and Kris
Kleinbauer.

9. Interview with John Steinbruner (a Stanford student leader at the time),
Washington, D.C., October 16, 1988.

10. Interviews with Dwight Clark, John Steinbruner, and Skip Martin, Washington, D.C., October 15, 1988.

11. Interviews with Nancy Steffen (a Stanford student at the time), Brooklyn,
November 14, 1988, Patti Hagen, Armin Rosencranz, and Dwight Clark;
Stanford Daily, [n.d.], AKL Papers. Frequently, Lowenstein used compar-
isons with Yale, especially regarding literary magazines and political ac-
tivism, to spur Stanford students on (AKL typed statement, January 1962,
AKL Papers).

12. John Foresberg to AKL, March 8 and May 31, 1962, John Balch (Lowenstein's assistant), two letters to AKL, [n.d., 1962], Bill Craig to Robert
Wuert, February 9, 1962 (re: "petty rules"), Bill Craig to AKL, [n.d.,
1962], and minutes of March 1, 1962, meeting regarding jukebox funds, all
in AKL Papers.

13. Interviews with Kris Kleinbauer, Fred Goff, Armin Rosencranz, and

Colleen and Kenneth Cuthbertson.

14. Interviews with Colleen and Kenneth Cuthbertson, Bill Craig, Dwight Clark, and Armin Rosencranz; John Cahill to AKL, September 16, 1965, AKL Papers.

15. Interviews with Armin Rosencranz, and Colleen and Kenneth Cuthbertson.

16. Interviews with Armin Rosencranz, John Steinbruner, and Susan Goodwillie (a Stanford student at the time), Washington, D.C., January 22, 1989. An ally of GRIP was GLOP—the Group with Loose Outside Power.

17. Copy of Rosencranz address, AKL Papers.

18. Armin Rosencranz to AKL, November 26, 1962, Dwight Clark to AKL, October 7, 1962, and Tom Boysen to AKL, October 12 and 3, and December 19, 1962, all in AKL Papers.

19. See, for example, the rash of correspondence surrounding one of these visits: John Steinbruner to AKL, January 17, 1963, Tom Boysen to AKL, January 12 and 25, and February 13, 1963, Colleen Cuthbertson to AKL, [n.d., 1963], and Armin Rosencranz to AKL, February 6, 1963, all in AKL Papers. See also the *Stanford Daily*, January 28–31, 1963. Rosencranz remarked on how much the "first string" enjoyed having him there.

20. Interviews with Patti Hagen, Nancy Steffen, Floss Frucher, Skip Martin, and John Steinbruner. Lowenstein's impact on Stanford was sufficiently great—and stressful—that the president and his top aides later sought to blackball Lowenstein when he was about to be hired as a consultant on student concerns at the Ford Foundation (see chapter 9).

21. *New York Times*, March 20, 1960; Casey Hayden to AKL, [n.d., 1960], AKL Papers.

22. On Lowenstein's employment at NC State, see George Gullette to AKL, April 2 and 18, 1962, AKL course outlines and syllabi, James Stewart to AKL, May 4, 1964, all in AKL Papers. Lowenstein was hired at $7,000 a year.

23. For discussions of the Raleigh demonstrations, see transcripts of Jesse Helms's WRAL-TV editorials, May 3 and June 14, 1963, *The Technician*, May 1–3, 1963, and *Raleigh News and Observer*, April 30–May 20, 1963, all in AKL Papers. State Senator Clarence Stone, a conservative defender of segregation, launched a campaign to have Lowenstein fired because of his civil rights activities. He was supported in that venture by Jesse Helms.

24. For Lowenstein's recollections of this first visit, see his comments in the *Stanford Daily*, May 28, 1965. For other recollections of the visit, see interview with Ed King, Chapel Hill and Washington, March 10 and May 26, 1988; *Citizen* interview with Aaron Henry; and Ed King's transcript of a Lowenstein speech at Millsaps College in 1979 commemorating the Mississippi struggle, in the author's possession (hereafter referred to as Millsaps speech). See also AKL to Franklin Delano Roosevelt III, July 27,

1963, and Aaron Henry to AKL, July 13, 1963 (thanking Lowenstein for coming), both in AKL Papers. Henry wrote, "You were one of many persons in my lifetime that comes to mind with no effort as I sometimes think of the good old days of yesterday." For general background on these years, see Doug McAdam, *Freedom Summer* (New York: Oxford University Press, 1988); Clayborne Carson, *In Struggle: SNCC and the Black Awakening of the 1960s* (Cambridge: Harvard University Press, 1981); James Forman, *The Making of Black Revolutionaries: A Personal Account* (New York: Macmillan, 1972); Mary Aickin Rothschild, *A Case of Black and White: Northern Volunteers and the Southern Freedom Summers, 1964–1965* (Westport, Conn.: Greenwood Press, 1982); Joseph Sinsheimer, "The Freedom Vote of 1963," *Journal of Southern History* 55, no. 2 (May 1989): 217–44; John Dittmer, "The Politics of the Mississippi Movement, 1954–1967," in Charles Eagles, ed., *The Civil Rights Movement in America: Essays* (Jackson: University Press of Mississippi, 1986).

25. Interviews with Ed King and Robert Moses, Stanford, October 7, 1989; *Stanford Daily,* May 28, 1965; *Citizen* interview with Aaron Henry. See also interview with Lawrence Guyot, Washington, D.C., March 20, 1989, one of those who saw the repression as just another part of the process of building a movement.

26. *Stanford Daily,* May 28, 1965; Millsaps speech; interview with Ed King.

27. Millsaps speech; Robert Moses to AKL, October 18, 1963, Ed King to AKL, October 2, 1963, "Statement from Allard K. Lowenstein" (as chairman of the Aaron Henry for Governor Advisory Committee), all in AKL Papers; interviews with Ed King and Robert Moses.

28. Interviews with Floss Frucher, Patti Hagen, Nancy Steffen, and Colleen and Kenneth Cuthbertson.

29. Interview with William Sloane Coffin, Washington, D.C., May 11, 1989; the Moses and Wright speeches received extensive coverage in the *Yale Daily News,* October 16–17, 1963.

30. Dennis Sweeney to AKL, October 8, 1963, AKL Papers; *Stanford Daily,* October 2, 1963; *Yale Daily News* coverage, October 14–30, 1963. Bingham later became famous because of his alleged involvement in the Angela Davis–George Jackson Soledad prison killing; he was forced to go underground for a number of years. (The charges subsequently were dropped.) Lieberman became a U.S. senator, Payne a lecturer on ethics at Duke University, and Else a widely known documentary filmmaker.

31. Millsaps speech; AKL to Franklin D. Roosevelt III, October 27, 1963 (apologizing for the phone call), transcript of AKL speech in August 1963 to the National Council of Churches conference on civil rights, all in AKL Papers; see also interviews with Ed King and Franklin D. Roosevelt III, New York City, November 18, 1988.

32. Freedom Vote news releases, October 23–November 2, 1963, Kenneth

Klotz to Sen. Birch Bayh, October 28, 1963, *Yale Daily News* coverage and *Stanford Daily* coverage, October 20–November 4, 1963, all in AKL Papers; interviews with Bruce Payne and Nicholas Bosanquet.

33. Frank Porter Graham to AKL, October 23, 1963, and Sheryl Arnold to Jack Sundine of the *Moline Daily Dispatch*, [n.d.], both in AKL Papers; *New York Times* coverage, October 20–November 4, 1963.

34. *Stanford Daily*, May 28, 1965; Stanford University press release after Lowenstein's death, March 17, 1980.

35. Interviews with Ed King and Robert Moses; McAdams, *Freedom Summer*; Carson, *In Struggle*.

CHAPTER 8

1. The staff member's quote is cited by John Dittmer in a personal communication with the author, April 5, 1992. See also Nicholas Bosanquet to AKL, December 11, 1963, AKL Papers; and interviews with Ed King and Robert Moses.

2. Millsaps speech; interviews with Ed King and Lawrence Guyot. James Forman talks about the Yazoo incident and other sources of anger at Lowenstein in his book, *The Making of Black Revolutionaries*, pp. 356–358. Lowenstein discussed seeking refuge in the hamburger joint, and Moses's defense of him, in his Millsaps speech. John Dittmer recalls a meeting after the Freedom Vote campaign when Dona Richards reminded Bob Moses of "a situation where a kid . . . wouldn't take orders from you. He said his orders came from Al Lowenstein." On the volunteers, see Rothschild, *A Case of Black and White*.

3. Interviews with Ed King, Lawrence Guyot, and Robert Moses; Forman, *The Making of Black Revolutionaries*, pp. 89, 356; Robert Moses to AKL, [n.d., late 1963 or early 1964], AKL Papers.

4. Interviews with Barney Frank, Washington, D.C., April 25 and May 1, 1989, Nancy Steffen, and Bruce Payne; David Curtin to AKL, March 17, 1964, Ilene Strelitz to AKL, March 17, 1964, Jim Scott to AKL, January 23, 1964, John Bundy to AKL, January 17, 1964, and Bob White to AKL, [n.d.], all in AKL Papers.

5. Susan Goodwillie to AKL, January 7, 1964, and Robert Moses to AKL, [n.d., early 1964], both in AKL Papers. In a more personal postscript, Moses asked whether Lowenstein would be willing to come to Mississippi to "handle the program to unseat the Mississippi Democratic Party" in the event he lost his teaching position in North Carolina—a strong possibility given the controversy there over Lowenstein's activities. In this letter, Moses appears to place a higher estimate on Lowenstein's role and value than he did in his subsequent recollections.

6. Interviews with Lawrence Guyot, Washington, D.C., March 20, 1989, Ed

King, and Courtland Cox (a SNCC staff member), Washington, D.C., April 26, 1989.

7. Interviews with Joseph Rauh, Washington, D.C., June 9, 1988, Ed King, John Lewis, Washington, D.C., April 25, 1989, and Michael Harrington, by telephone, November 26, 1988; Carson, *In Struggle*, pp. 67, 105–107, 137, 182.

8. Interviews with Ed King, Joseph Rauh, Michael Harrington, and Nancy Steffen.

9. Interviews with Ed King, Lawrence Guyot, Joseph Rauh, Michael Harrington, and Kris Kleinbauer; AKL diary, [n.d., spring 1964], AKL Papers.

10. Interviews with Lawrence Guyot, Robert Moses, and Ed King. The reference to a "casual invasion" appears in a letter from Ilene Strelitz to Robert Moses, May 2, 1964, AKL Papers. Strelitz was attempting to mediate between Lowenstein and Moses and appears, in this instance, to have been paraphrasing Moses's impression of Lowenstein's recruiting practices. SNCC staff member Dorothy Zellner certainly had the same impression. See Dorothy Zellner to Mendy Samstein, February 27, 1964, and Zellner to Lois Chafee and Mendy Samstein, March 1, 1964, both in the Jan Hildegas Collection, State Historical Society, Jackson, Miss. I am deeply indebted to John Dittmer of DePauw University for bringing these letters to my attention.

11. Emory Bundy and AKL to John Bundy, April 30, 1964, AKL Papers.

12. Ilene Strelitz to Robert Moses, May 2, 1964, AKL Papers; interview with Robert Moses.

13. *Stanford Daily*, May 3, 1964; Bruce Campbell (*Daily* reporter) to AKL, May 4, 1964, AKL Papers; interview with John Rosenberg, Washington, D.C., October 16, 1988. The remark about Moses being "run by Peking" was reported to me by John Dittmer.

14. Marian Wright to AKL, May 9, 1964, AKL Papers; interview with Ed King.

15. Bob Malone to AKL, June 4, 1964, AKL Papers.

16. Interview with Nancy Steffen; Irene Strelitz to AKL, [n.d., late April] and July 14, 1964, AKL Papers.

17. Norman Thomas cablegram to AKL, and Nicholas Bosanquet to AKL, June 1 and July 20, 1964, both in AKL Papers; interviews with Nancy Steffen and Skip Martin.

18. Jim Haas to AKL, July 27, 1964, AKL Papers.

19. AKL speech to August civil rights conference, typescript in AKL Papers.

20. Interviews with Joseph Rauh, Robert Moses, and Ed King; for more on Atlantic City, see Carson, *In Struggle*, pp. 123–139; Forman, *The Making of Black Revolutionaries*, pp. 386–396; and William H. Chafe, *The Unfinished Journey: America since World War II* (New York: Oxford University Press, 1986), pp. 311–313.

21. Interviews with Ed King, Joseph Rauh, Robert Moses, John Lewis, and Michael Harrington; Nancy Adams to AKL, September 9, 1964, AKL Pa-

pers. Jack Newfield writes about the meeting cited by Harrington. According to Newfield, it took place on February 1, 1965 and was convened by
Bayard Rustin. Newfield's report focuses on the persistent split between
white liberals and SNCC. Liberals, he said, charged that in Freedom Summer, "SNCC made all the decisions, got all the glory, and indoctrinated
800 of the best college students in the country with their line." Although
he does not attribute that sentiment to Lowenstein, it reflects almost word
for word what Lowenstein was saying at the time. Jack Newfield, *Cavalier*
(June 1965). Rustin was in communication with Lowenstein about this
meeting and their common concerns about SNCC. The FBI evidently had a
tap on Rustin's phone, and a December 1964 conversation is cited in
Lowenstein's Freedom of Information Act (FOIA) file.

22. Interviews with Ed King, Robert Moses, and Barney Frank. Frank empha-
sizes how upset Lowenstein was that the MFDP was not allowed to select
its own delegates as part of the compromise. "That always bothered him,
that people didn't keep in mind that distinction."

23. Interviews with John Lewis, Floss Frucher, and Fred Goff, Oakland, December 14, 1988.

24. Interview with Robert Moses.

25. Interviews with Ed King, Robert Moses, Lawrence Guyot, and Courtland
Cox, Washington, D.C., April 26, 1989. A partial transcript of the New
York meeting appears in Forman, *The Making of Black Revolutionaries*, pp.
399–405.

26. Interview with Ed King; Aaron Henry to AKL, October 4, 1964, Connie
Curry to AKL, October 4, 1964 (regarding his critique of SNCC and
COFO), internal memorandum from Arthur Schiff and AKL (on William
Miller), October 8, 1964, Kim Ingram to AKL, October 24, 1964, and
Clarence Greenburg to AKL, November 3, 1964, all in AKL papers.

27. Kris Kleinbauer to AKL, December 13 and 19, 1964, AKL Papers.

28. *Stanford Daily,* May 28, 1965; interviews with Nancy Steffens, Fred Goff,
and Armin Rosencranz.

29. *Stanford Daily,* May 28, 1965; mimeographed press release with AKL's
penciled notations, AKL Papers; interviews with Ed King and Michael
Horowitz. Horowitz recalls that Lowenstein "invented" the concept for
Freedom Summer during a car ride from New Orleans to Mississippi.

30. Carson, *In Struggle,* pp. 97–99; interview with Robert Moses.

31. Interviews with Ed King, Robert Moses, Lawrence Guyot, Joseph Rauh,
Michael Harrington, Geoff Cowan, Los Angeles, March 15, 1989, and
Michael Horowitz. Moses did state in 1965 that, "while [Lowenstein]
wasn't sufficient to [the Freedom Vote campaign], he was certainly neces-
sary to bring it off, and without him it would never have come off as it did."
Stanford Daily, May 28, 1965.

32. *Citizen* interview with Ivanhoe Donaldson; interview with Casey Hayden,
Atlanta, October 28, 1988.

33. Interviews with Lawrence Guyot and Ed King.
34. AKL notes on a Freedom Summer brochure, [n.d., 1964], AKL Papers; interview with Robert Moses.
35. Interviews with Joseph Rauh, Michael Harrington, and John Rosenberg.
36. Interviews with Robert Moses, Lawrence Guyot, and Skip Martin.
37. Interviews with Ed King, Robert Moses, and Lawrence Guyot.
38. Interview with Robert Moses.
39. Interview with Ed King.
40. Interview with Casey Hayden; Dick Van Wagener to AKL, [n.d.] (regarding a *Yale Daily News* article on SNCC and Lowenstein), AKL Papers.
41. Interviews with Ed King, Robert Moses, and Geoff Cowan. Cowan, who was associated with the newspaper project, has said that Lowenstein blocked a Field Foundation grant to the project and later apologized to him for having done so.
42. Interviews with Armin Rosencranz and Skip Martin.
43. Interviews with Geoff Cowan, Armin Rosencranz, and John Rosenberg.
44. Interviews with Nancy Steffen, Skip Martin, Fred Milhiser, and Patti Hagen; Clayborne Carson, interview with AKL, transcript in author's possession. I am grateful to Clayborne Carson for sharing this interview with me.
45. Sam Beard to AKL, [n.d.], AKL Papers.

CHAPTER 9

1. Interviews with William Dentzer and Greg Gallo, Palo Alto, June 5, 1990; Sara Evans, *Personal Politics: The Roots of Women's Liberation in the Civil Rights Movement and the New Left* (New York: Knopf, 1979; Vintage Books, 1980).
2. Interviews with Jennifer Littlefield and Rich Hammond, San Francisco, August 19 and December 15, 1988. See also Paul Cowan, "What Makes Al Lowenstein Run?" *Ramparts* (September 7, 1968). The cultural linguist Robin Lakoff, whose work has focused on women's speech patterns, has observed that those who end their sentences with a question mark frequently are manifesting low self-esteem and lack of confidence. See Robin Lakoff, *Language and Woman's Place* (New York: St. Martin's, 1975).
3. Interviews with Nancy Steffen and with a confidential source. In this and subsequent chapters, where some of the material is of a sensitive nature, the citation will be to confidential sources and, occasionally, to letters. Ordinarily, such information was obtained in interviews. There are thirteen such confidential sources.
4. Interviews with Kris Kleinbauer, Nancy Steffen, Ronnie Eldridge, New York, April 7, 1988; Greg Craig, Armin Rosencranz, Barbara Boggs, and Steve Roberts, Washington, D.C., December 19, 1990.
5. Interviews with Patti Hagen, Fred Goff, Jeff Robbins, Boston, October 3, 1988, Jim Haas, San Francisco, August 21, 1988, Nancy Steffen, and Gary

Hart, Los Angeles, December 11, 1988. Hart was a Stanford student who played a major role in Lowenstein's political campaigns during the late 1960s. He is now active in California politics. He is *not* the Gary Hart who managed George McGovern's 1972 presidential race, served as Democratic senator from Colorado, and ran for president in 1984 and 1988.

6. Interviews with Greg Craig and Jeff Robbins; Kris Kleinbauer to AKL, [n.d., late 1964], AKL Papers.

7. Interview with Rich Hammond; Rich Hammond to AKL, September 15, 1966, AKL Papers.

8. Interviews with Bruce Payne, Harold Ickes, New York, December 10, 1990, and Jim Haas. Ickes came to know Lowenstein during his 1966 race for Congress and in the antiwar movement.

9. Interview with Greg Craig; see also interview with Jeff Robbins.

10. Four confidential letters to AKL, all in AKL Papers; interview with Bruce Payne. For discussion of the Yale experiences, see chapter 5.

11. Interviews with Armin Rosencranz, Patti Hagen, Nancy Steffen, and assorted confidential sources.

12. Interview with confidential source.

13. Interviews with confidential sources.

14. Interview with Armin Rosencranz.

15. Interviews with confidential sources.

16. Interviews with Nancy Steffen, Steve Roberts, and Dwight Clark.

17. Interview with Armin Rosencranz; Rotundo, "Romantic Friendship." In his article on male bonding in the nineteenth century, Anthony Rotundo makes the point that intimacy between men was acceptable as long as it was perceived as a stage—a step on the way to "mature heterosexual relations." Likewise, it is possible to imagine Lowenstein telling himself that his desire to remain in a college setting to initiate relations with young men was a "phase" rather than a life choice.

18. Miscellaneous EFC papers, including roster of participants, schedule of lectures, evaluation forms, and outside activities, in AKL Papers; interviews with Nancy Steffen, Greg Craig, John Steinbruner, Bruce Payne, and Barney Frank. Twenty years later, Barney Frank acknowledged that he was gay, but in the mid-1960s, according to statements he subsequently made, he was still denying his sexual preference by making himself so busy he had no time to deal with the issue.

19. Interviews with Greg Craig, Bruce Payne, and Nancy Steffen; Karen [surname unknown] to AKL, October 18, 1965, and John Ewell to AKL, [n.d.], AKL Papers.

20. Interview with confidential source; Pugh [surname unknown] to AKL, October 1965, John Cahill to AKL, September 16, 1965, and Karen [surname unknown] to AKL, October 18, 1965, all in AKL Papers.

21. Interview with Bruce Payne; two letters from "Harry" to AKL, [n.d.], AKL Papers.

22. Interview with Bruce Payne.

23. Interview with confidential source.

24. Interviews with confidential source and with Armin Rosencranz. Rosencranz, though he was close to Lowenstein, was not someone to whom Lowenstein made sexual advances.

25. Interviews with confidential source, Bruce Payne, and Armin Rosencranz.

26. Kinsey, *Sexual Behavior in the Human Male*, see also D'Emilio, *Sexual Politics*, and Duberman, *Cures*.

27. Interview with David Mixner.

28. Interview with David Mixner. For further discussion of some of these pressures, see Duberman, *Cures;* Monette, *Becoming a Man*; and John D'Emilio, *Making Trouble: Essays on Gay History, Politics, and the University* (New York: Routledge, 1992).

29. Interviews with confidential sources.

30. Confidential to AKL, [n.d.], AKL Papers.

31. Interviews with Armin Rosencranz and confidential sources.

32. Interview with Colleen and Kenneth Cuthbertson.

33. Gabriel Lowenstein to AKL, [n.d., 1963], and June 1, 1961, AKL Papers.

34. Florence Lowenstein to AKL, July and August 1964, AKL Papers.

35. Elise Lapham to AKL, April 17, 1965, and Ilene Strelitz to AKL, April 17, 1965, both in AKL Papers.

36. Interviews with Nancy Steffen and Gary Bellow.

37. Marcia Borie to AKL, March 9, 1965, AKL Papers.

38. The best summary of this episode is contained in an April 27, 1965, letter to Paul Ylvisaker of the Ford Foundation from John Ehle, a program officer with the Foundation. Deeply distressed at what he saw as the shabby and unethical treatment of Lowenstein, Ehle defended him, buttressing his case with multiple testimonials on Lowenstein's behalf. Although he refused to be interviewed by this author, Fred Glover—Sterling's assistant at Stanford—confirmed in a telephone conversation that Sterling had called Lowenstein a liar and a fraud. Some have speculated that Sterling's animus toward Lowenstein went back to his feeling that he had been humiliated by Lowenstein during the latter's time at Stanford. The question of whether Lowenstein did in fact serve as a writer-in-residence at Stiles College is one of the more fascinating subplots of this episode. Lowenstein's FOIA file reveals that in January 1965 the FBI checked to see whether Lowenstein had ever received mail at Ezra Stiles College. Interestingly enough, there is *no* material on Lowenstein in the Sterling papers at Stanford except for routine mention of his appointment in 1961. For further documentation, see Fred Glover to J. Wallace Sterling (regarding Lowenstein's consultancy with Ford), Paul Ylvisaker to AKL, April 1, 1965 (confirming his appointment as a consultant), Paul Ylvisaker to AKL, May 3, 1965 (terminating the consultancy), John Ehle to Nancy Steffen, May 7, 1965 (explaining AKL's termination), Richard Sewall to AKL, December 4, 1964 (regarding a dinner at Yale

where Al talked about his writing experience there), and Barney Frank to AKL, December 2, 1964 (on the same subject), all in AKL Papers; see also interviews with Colleen and Kenneth Cuthbertson, and Bruce Payne.

39. Interviews with John Rosenberg and Nancy Steffen; Ilene Strelitz to AKL, July 14, 1964, and AKL to Ilene Strelitz, November 4, 1965, both in AKL Papers.

40. Interview with Kris Kleinbauer; Kris Kleinbauer to AKL, December 27, 1964, [n.d., 1965], AKL Papers. Mary Benson wrote AKL (December 31, 1964) to say that Ethel Grossman had told her that Al and Kris were engaged.

41. Nancy Adams to AKL, September 8, 1964, and AKL to John McPherson, April 9, 1964, both in AKL Papers; interview with confidential source.

42. Marcia Borie to AKL, April 15, 1964, Lucille Kohn to AKL, April 15, 1964, and Tom Boysen to AKL, April 22, 1964, all in AKL Papers.

43. Interview with Nancy Steffen. Curtis Gans, who was close to Lowenstein at the time, agrees that Gabriel's death was a watershed event for him and dramatically affected his political activities thereafter, especially the extent to which he put himself forward as a political celebrity instead of operating behind the scenes.

44. Interview with Jennifer Littlefield; *Long Island Press*, November 13, 1968.

45. Interviews with Nancy Steffen, Bruce Payne, and Harold Ickes.

46. Interviews with Rich Hammond and Nancy Steffen.

47. Interviews with Jennifer Littlefield and Bruce Payne.

48. Interviews with Jennifer Littlefield, Bruce Payne, and Ronnie Eldridge.

49. Interviews with Harold Ickes, Jennifer Littlefield, and William Sloane Coffin.

50. Interview with Rich Hammond.

51. Interviews with Greg Craig, Susan Goodwillie, Harold Ickes, Bruce Payne, and William Sloane Coffin. Susan Andrews, a Long Island friend of the Lowensteins, recalls going to see Woody Allen's movie *Annie Hall* with Al and Jenny. Afterwards, she said, Al commented on the scene in the movie where the Woody Allen character goes to Annie Hall's midwestern Protestant home to meet her parents. Allen imagines that Annie's parents are seeing him as an orthodox Jew, dressed in a black coat with a black hat and *payess* hanging down over his cheeks. "That's how it was when I met Jenny's family," he said.

52. Interviews with Jennifer Littlefield and Sanford Friedman. Sandy Friedman noted how astonished he was when he discovered Jenny was pregnant. "I simply did not know," Friedman said humourously, "[that] Allard knew how to [do that]."

53. AKL to Jennifer Lowenstein, July 27, 1968, AKL Papers.

54. Interview with Clinton Deveaux, Atlanta, October 31 and November 1, 1990.

55. AKL, "Angus," typescript in AKL Papers.

56. Interview with Gary Bellow.

CHAPTER 10

1. *West Side News*, December 30, 1965; *New York Times*, December 19, 1965; interviews with Ronnie Eldridge, New York, April 7, 1988, Dora Friedman New York, January 30, 1988, Tedda Fenichel, New York, January 30, 1988, and Martin and Kathleen Berger, New York, January 30, 1988. All of these individuals were active in West Side politics in the 1960s. I was also a participant-observer as an antiwar activist in West Side politics at this time.

2. Interviews with Gary Bellow, Martin and Kathleen Berger, and Dora Friedman.

3. Interviews with Barney Frank, Ronnie Eldridge, Harold Ickes, Jack Newfield, New York, December 9, 1989, Dora Friedman, and Sara Kovner, New York, November 15, 1988. Barney Frank telegraphed Lowenstein on December 8, 1965, saying he would convene a meeting of campaign workers; Steve Roberts did a memo for the *Times* that was the basis for the paper's December 19 story (Steve Roberts to AKL, December 22, 1965); and Frank Porter Graham met with local district leaders (see Marian Graham to AKL, December 8, 1965); all in AKL Papers. See also *Village Voice*, March 3, 1966.

4. Interview with Harold Ickes.

5. Michael Harrington, *New York Herald-Tribune*, March 6, 1966; James Wechsler, *New York Post*, February 2, 1966; *New Yorker*, March 12, 1966; various campaign brochures, and Aaron Henry to AKL, December 18, 1965, both in AKL Papers.

6. Interviews with Barney Frank and Jack Newfield; *West Side News*, December 30, 1965.

7. Interviews with Ronnie Eldridge, Jack Newfield, and Dora Friedman.

8. Interview with Dora Friedman.

9. *West Side News*, March 10 and 17, 1966; *New York Times* coverage, March 11–12, 1966; *New Yorker*, March 12, 1966. One of the more divisive issues was who would win the endorsement of the reform congressman William Fitts Ryan. Weiss and Lowenstein connived to leave the impression that Ryan favored them, although in fact he was neutral; it was only members of his staff who endorsed one or the other. See Geoff Cowan interview.

10. Larry Lowenstein to AKL, April 14, 1966, AKL Papers.

11. Interviews with William Sloane Coffin and Greg Craig.

12. *Washington Post*, October 26, 1965; *New York Times*, October 26, 1965; Norman Thomas to AKL, October 5 and 28, 1965, AKL Papers; interviews with William Sloane Coffin and Greg Craig.

13. For David Harris's account of this encounter, see his book *Dreams Die Hard* (New York: St. Martin's Press, 1982), pp. 150–155. See also interviews with Greg Craig and Rick Weidman, New Haven, April 7, 1989.

14. Interviews with Greg Craig and Rick Weidman; *Daily Tar Heel*, January 5, 1967.

15. Interviews with Greg Craig, Clinton Deveaux, and Steven Cohen, Washington, D.C., January 8, 1991.

16. *New York Times*, December 30, 1966; *Washington Post*, December 30, 1966.

17. Interviews with Steven Cohen, Greg Craig, and Rick Weidman.

18. Interviews with Greg Craig and William Sloane Coffin.

19. Interviews with Robert Kiley and William Dentzer; *Village Voice*, February 23, 1967; *New America*, March 22, 1967.

20. Interviews with Rick Stearn, Phillip Sherburne, Robert Kiley, William Dentzer, and Greg Gallo. Lowenstein's FOIA file does not clarify the issue. According to an FBI investigation, a source at Stanford reported to the Justice Department on February 5, 1962, that Lowenstein had boasted on two occasions of a CIA affiliation. But a March 29, 1962, FBI report concluded that Lowenstein was never connected to the CIA, noting that as early as January 9, 1961, the CIA had advised the FBI that Lowenstein never had a relationship with the intelligence agency. A series of memos indicates that Lowenstein was under FBI surveillance during these years, but with no results. In March 1985, Lee Hamilton, chairman of the House Intelligence Committee, said: "Based on representations made to me, I can say that Mr. Lowenstein was never an agent of the CIA." None of this evidence is definitive, nor does it alter the overall interpretation offered here: that Lowenstein was in all likelihood not witting in the 1950s but became so in the 1960s, and that he would have had to be obtuse or blind not to have suspected some connections between the NSA and the government. See FBI memos, December 13, 1961–February 18, 1965, AKL Papers.

21. Interviews with Greg Gallo, Steve Robbins, telephone interview, June 4, 1990, and Fred Goff; Sol Stern, "A Short Account of International Student Politics and the Cold War," *Ramparts* (March 1967); Todd Gitlin and Bob Ross, "The CIA at College: Into Twilight and Back," *Village Voice*, July 6, 1967.

22. Theodore Draper, "The New Dominican Crisis," *New Leader*, January 31, 1966; *Stanford Daily News*, May 23 and 26, 1966; Norman Thomas, memorandum to members of the Committee on Free Elections in the Dominican Republic, June 20, 1966, AKL Papers; James Wechsler, *New York Post*, June 6, 1966; Ruth Sherif, "The Committee for Free Elections in the Dominican Republic," *Liberation* (November 1966); Ruth Shereff, "Liberals in Wonderland," *Commonwealth*, May 5, 1967; interview with Fred Goff. Shereff's name is spelled differently in the two journals cited here.

23. Transcripts of AKL sessions with Juan Bosch, AKL Papers; *Stanford Daily*, May 24, 1966.

24. Shereff, "Liberals in Wonderland."

25. Interview with Fred Goff; James Wechsler, *New York Post,* June 6, 1966; Sherif, "Committee for Free Elections."

26. Interviews with Fred Goff and Bruce Payne; Wechsler, Shereff, "Liberals in Wonderland." Bruce Payne, who was working for Lowenstein and Thomas at the time, reported that Bosch's wife was angry and wanted to denounce the election results, but that Lowenstein and Thomas persuaded her to go along with their assessment. According to Payne, Lowenstein agreed that it was unfair that Balaguer had won but thought Bosch had been a weak candidate. After Goff and others on the committee had protested Lowenstein's actions, Goff was let go from his staff position. Subsequently, at a large social gathering at Lowenstein's home, Goff was introduced to someone who agreed with Lowenstein's stance on the Dominican situation. When that person started to engage Goff in conversation, assuming Goff was an ally on the issue, Lowenstein interrupted and said, "He's on the other side." Goff has devoted his life to analysis of Latin American politics and economics as head of a nonpartisan, nonprofit research center. His testimony on this episode appears, to this observer at least, highly credible.

27. Sherif, "Committee For Free Elections,"; and Shereff, "Liberals in Wonderland."

28. Interview with Jennifer Littlefield.

CHAPTER 11

1. Interviews with David Hawk, New York, September 10, 1990, Clinton Deveaux, and Sam Brown, San Mateo, California, May 29, 1990. David Hawk has remained a peace activist for more than two decades, working for resolution of fratricidal wars in Cambodia and elsewhere. Clinton Deveaux is a judge in Atlanta. After holding political office in Colorado, Sam Brown now lives in California, where he remains involved with such issues as developing affordable housing.

2. Interview with Allard K. Lowenstein, Eugene McCarthy Oral History Collection, Princeton University (hereafter referred to as AKL interview), also in AKL Papers; interviews with Curtis Gans, Washington, D.C., March 30, 1989, David Hawk, and Clinton Deveaux. The Curtis Gans interview was not taped, at his request, and therefore no transcript exists. My handwritten notes of the interview will be deposited with the AKL Papers.

3. Andy Young to mobilization organizers, with copy to AKL, [n.d., early 1967], AKL Papers; AKL interview; interview with Curtis Gans. Lowenstein had been appointed to the SCLC board the previous year. There is no evidence that his selection had anything to do with his ongoing differences with SNCC.

4. AKL interview; interview with Curtis Gans.

5. Interviews with Greg Craig, Barney Frank, David Hawk, Clinton Deveaux, and Steven Cohen.

6. Interviews with Joseph Rauh and Leon Shull (longtime executive director of ADA), Washington, D.C., February 11, 1992; ADA minutes of board meetings, May 1966 and April 1967, Gus Tyler to John Kenneth Galbraith, May 25, 1967, Richard Miller to John Kenneth Galbraith, May 31, 1967, Joseph Rauh memorandum to ADA board, July 28, 1967, ADA statement, October 6, 1967, SANE (San Francisco chapter) memorandum [n.d., spring 1967], and Douglas Dowd to Donald Keyes, June 18, 1966, all in AKL Papers.

7. *New York Times,* August 15, 1967; *Washington Post,* August 15, 1967; interviews with Clinton Deveaux, David Hawk, Greg Craig, Sam Brown, and Steve Roberts.

8. Sanford Gottlieb, "Report on National Conference for New Politics Convention," AKL Papers; see also the *New York Times* and *Washington Post* coverage, August 29–September 5, 1967.

9. Interviews with David Hawk and Sam Brown; AKL interview. Despite Lowenstein's strong advice to stay away from Chicago, Brown went to the NCNP gathering. Hawk did not. Brown later concluded that Lowenstein had been right.

10. "Bailey Laird" [Richard Goodwin], *New Yorker,* September 16, 1967.

11. Interviews with Clinton Deveaux, Sam Brown, David Hawk, Harold Ickes, and Curtis Gans; AKL interview. Jim Farley managed FDR's campaigns and was legendary for his political legerdemain. Larry O'Brien was JFK's chief organizer; his card files on potential supporters made him the envy of other politicians.

12. Interviews with Harold Ickes, Curtis Gans, David Hawk, and Clinton Deveaux; AKL interview.

13. AKL interview; interviews with Harold Ickes and Curtis Gans.

14. Theodore H. White, *The Making of the President, 1968* (New York: Atheneum, 1969), pp. 71–80; Lewis Chester, Godfrey Hodgson, and Bruce Page, *American Melodrama: The Presidential Campaign of 1968* (New York: Viking, 1969), pp. 58–67, 76–77, 87–89; *New Republic,* September 30, 1967; David Halberstam, "The Man Who Ran against Lyndon Johnson," *Harper's* (December 1968); interviews with Clinton Deveaux, Curtis Gans, Sam Brown, and Greg Craig.

15. Arnold Kaufman and Allard K. Lowenstein, "The Time Is Ripe to Dump Johnson," *War-Peace Report* (November 1967).

16. Interview with Jack Newfield; AKL interview; *Citizen* interview with David Halberstam; Arthur M. Schlesinger, Jr., *Robert Kennedy and His Times* (Boston: Houghton Mifflin, 1978), pp. 824–825, 841; Halberstam, "The Man Who Ran against Lyndon Johnson."

17. AKL interview.

18. Jack Newfield, "The First Hurrah for a Quiet Senator," *Village Voice,* November 16, 1967; Hodgson, *American Melodrama,* pp. 63–67; White, *Making of the President,* pp. 75–76, 80.

19. Interviews with Greg Craig and Cynthia Samuels, New York, September 10, 1990.
20. *Citizen* interview with David Halberstam.
21. Interviews with Curtis Gans, Harold Ickes, and Greg Craig.
22. *Citizen* interview with David Halberstam.
23. *Newsweek*, November 27, 1967; interview with Steven Cohen.

CHAPTER 12

1. Interviews with Sara Kovner, Sam Brown, Rick Tuttle, Los Angeles, December 19, 1988, Rick Saslaw, Los Angeles, November 16, 1990, and William Sloane Coffin. Tuttle was a teacher and politician from California. Saslaw was a Long Island teenager who worked in Lowenstein's campaign and also drove Eugene McCarthy on occasion. He subsequently moved to California, where he was active in Democratic politics.
2. AKL interview; *Newsweek*, November 27 and December 4, 1967. For a survey of the entire McCarthy campaign operation, see Jerry Tallmer, "Gene's Team: How It Grew," *New York Post*, March 18, 1968; and Jeremy Larner, *Nobody Knows: Reflections on the McCarthy Campaign of 1968* (New York: Macmillan, 1969).
3. Interviews with Clinton Deveaux, Jennifer Littlefield, and Harold Ickes. Lowenstein's speech was improvised and spontaneous, and no text of it exists.
4. Interviews with Gary Hart, Harold Ickes, Curtis Gans, Jack Newfield, and Howard Berman, Los Angeles, November 15, 1990. See also Steve [surname unknown] to AKL, December 24, 1967, Jake [surname unknown] to AKL, December 10, 1967, both in AKL Papers; and the *New York Times* and *Washington Post* coverage, December 3–4, 1967. Berman subsequently went to Congress.
5. Interviews with Harold Ickes, Clinton Deveaux, and Curtis Gans.
6. AKL interview.
7. Interview with Rich Hammond.
8. Interview with Curtis Gans; Jack Newfield, "A Time of Plague, A Season for Courage," *Village Voice*, December 28, 1967. McCarthy might well have also resented Lowenstein's continued notoriety as creator of the "dump Johnson" movement; Lowenstein appeared on NBC's "Meet the Press" the day after the Chicago speech, and on the "Today" show shortly thereafter.
9. Interviews with Curtis Gans and Sam Brown.
10. Interviews with Jennifer Littlefield, Nancy Steffen, Curtis Gans, Harold Ickes, and Sam Brown.
11. The history of Lowenstein's relationship with Kennedy is recounted by Lowenstein in an oral history he provided for the Robert F. Kennedy Pa-

pers at the John F. Kennedy Presidential Library, Boston. See also Schlesinger, *Robert Kennedy*, p. 745; David Halberstam, *The Unfinished Odyssey of Robert Kennedy* (New York: Random House, 1969), pp. 3–9; and Jack Newfield, *Robert Kennedy: A Memoir* (New York: Dutton, 1969), pp. 134, 177–188. These words from Robert Kennedy's South Africa speech are inscribed on his tomb. On the manuscript of the speech, many of the interlinear additions appear to be in Lowenstein's handwriting.

12. Interviews with Harold Ickes, Jennifer Littlefield, and Jack Newfield. Edward Kennedy, in an oral history interview for the film *Citizen*, recalled how Lowenstein would come to Robert Kennedy's home, squat on the floor, and try to persuade him one more time to run.

13. Newfield, "A Time of Plague."

14. AKL interview.

15. AKL interview; Schlesinger, *Robert F. Kennedy*, p. 841. Lowenstein had many allies on Kennedy's staff who also believed the senator should run. Adam Walinsky gave Kennedy his notice after the "unforeseeable circumstances" comment, and Peter Edelman also announced his plans to leave; neither actually left. Rick Tuttle, a Kennedy supporter in California, recalls Lowenstein appearing at Los Angeles Airport where Tuttle, Paul Schrade, and Jess Unruh just happened to be having a meeting to put together a Kennedy slate. Schrade was a Kennedy friend and union official (later shot when Kennedy was assassinated), and Unruh was the most powerful politician in the California legislature.

16. AKL interview; Schlesinger, *Robert Kennedy*, pp. 854–855.

17. AKL interview.

18. AKL interview; interviews with Curtis Gans, Harold Ickes, and Ronnie Eldridge; *Los Angeles Times*, March 17–18, 1968.

19. *Los Angeles Times*, March 18, 1968; AKL interview; interviews with Ronnie Eldridge, Sara Kovner, and Harold Ickes. On the possibilities of a Lowenstein Senate race, see Eleanor Clark French (of CDA) to AKL, February 10, 23, and 27, 1968, and Donald Shaeffer to AKL, March 13, 1968, both in AKL Papers. See also *New York Times*, March 14, 1968, and *Washington Post*, May 19, 1968.

20. AKL interview; interview with Sara Kovner.

21. *Washington Post*, March 17, 1968; interviews with Skip Martin and Harold Ickes. It was no secret that Lowenstein had been at Hickory Hill the night Kennedy made his decision, and that he had helped draft Kennedy's announcement. The *Washington Post* reported Lowenstein's presence there, and Lowenstein himself seemed to relish the role he had played, both then and later.

22. Interviews with Sam Brown and Curtis Gans; Terry Smith to AKL, [n.d., spring 1968], AKL Papers. Curtis Gans described Lowenstein's conduct as follows: "[After Wisconsin] he adopted the position of public endorsement

of McCarthy, not getting involved in any campaign between the two, and privately doing everything he could to condemn McCarthy and all he could do to advance Kennedy."

23. AKL interview. Lowenstein held onto Kennedy's quote and showed it to everyone, until finally one of his aides became concerned that it would tear into shreds and had it framed.

24. Carol Kimball to AKL, July 1966, Ed Gold to AKL, March 24, 1966, and Jackie McDuff to AKL, March 18, 1967, all in AKL Papers.

25. Larry Maxwell to AKL, February 7, 1968, Willis Steinitz to AKL (inviting him to Oceanside Concerned Democrats), November 1, 1967, and Donald Shaeffer to AKL, March 13, 1968, all in AKL Papers; interview with Kathleen and Martin Berger (who heard Lowenstein tell Jenny how much he loved her); *New York Times*, April 11 and June 17, 1968; *New York Post*, April 12, 1968.

26. Interview with Harold Ickes. Lowenstein's "drafts" would become legendary; each race he ever ran in allegedly involved one, but all were Lowenstein-generated.

27. Interview with Gary Hart.

28. There are two typescripts on the campaign in the AKL Papers. One is by a student, the other by Herbert Kramer (hereafter referred to as Kramer typescript).

29. Kramer typescript; *Newsday* coverage, March 31–April 10, and June 1, 1968; *South Shore Record*, May 16, 1968; Vorspan campaign literature, AKL Papers; interview with Steve Roberts.

30. Interviews with Clinton Deveaux, Greg Craig, Nancy Steffen, Jim Haas, Gary Hart, Rick Weidman, and Fred Milhiser, Washington, D.C., January 22, 1989.

31. Interviews with Mimi Perr, Long Island, December 9, 1990, Rick Weidman, Jim Haas, Rich Hammond, Gary Hart, Arnold Miller, Cambridge, Massachusetts, November 8, 1990 and Fred Milhiser. The staff regularly put events on the schedule half an hour before they were actually to start, hoping that they could thereby get Lowenstein to the designated site, but Lowenstein invariably confounded them. He would tinker with his schedule, trying to squeeze other things in. At different times, Gary Hart, Paul Offner, and Kirby Jones held the title of campaign coordinator, but Lowenstein never ceded authority to anybody. There was also tension between the storefronts and the central office; some local women refused to let the central office interfere with their operations.

32. Kramer typescript; *South Shore Record*, May 16, 1968; Vorspan literature, AKL Papers.

33. Interviews with Mimi Perr, Gary Hart, and Rick Weidman.

34. *Citizen* interview with David Halberstam; *Newsweek*, June 10, 1968; interview with Gary Hart.

35. AKL interview.

36. Interview with Ronnie Eldridge; Schlesinger, *Robert Kennedy*, p. 913. Kennedy had already reached John Kenneth Galbraith, enlisting his help, and Lowenstein was reported to have said that if Galbraith was ready to switch to Kennedy, he was also.

37. Interviews with Ronnie Eldridge, Gary Hart, Jennifer Littlefield, and Skip Martin; Schlesinger, *Robert Kennedy*, p. 913.

38. Interviews with Marcia Borie, Ronnie Eldridge, Aino Juppala, Helsinki, April 21, 1990. According to Marcia Borie, he had taken a Kennedy luggage tag as a way of holding on to some tangible remnant of his ties to his friend. (Similarly, Lowenstein's Finnish au pair reported that he had a pair of Kennedy's sunglasses.)

39. Albert Vorspan interview, typescript, AKL Papers (hereafter referred to as Vorspan interview); *Oceanside Beacon*, June 13, 1968.

40. Kramer typescript; Vorspan interview; *New York Times*, June 16, 17, 19, and 20, 1968.

41. Interviews with Ronnie Eldridge and Jack Newfield. There seems to be a solid basis for thinking that Lowenstein redefined the purpose of Kennedy's phone call. Virtually every source in close proximity to the principal figures agrees that Kennedy was indeed calling to discuss reconciling the Kennedy and McCarthy camps, *not* with the message "now it's time to help Al."

42. AKL interview; interview with Clinton Deveaux; *New York Times*, June 30, 1968.

43. *Washington Star*, June 29, 1968; Mary McGrory, *Washington Post*, July 1, 1968; Flora Lewis, *New York Post*, June 25, 1968; *Time*, July 12, 1968; interviews with Gary Hart and Clinton Deveaux.

44. *Time*, July 12, 1968; *London Times*, *Washington Star*, July 1, 1968; Richard Celeste to AKL, July 1, 1968, AKL Papers.

45. Interviews with Clinton Deveaux and Kenneth Liberman, Eugene, Oregon, March 6, 1988; White, *Making of the President*, pp. 280–285; AKL interview; *New York Times*, August 10 and 18, 1968.

46. Flora Lewis, AKL interview.

47. AKL interview; *New York Times*, July 4 and August 15, 1968.

48. Interview with Harold Ickes; AKL interview.

49. AKL interview; interview with Rick Tuttle. Lowenstein said in his interview for the Eugene McCarthy Oral History Collection that he had explored the Kennedy option "to the point that I was satisfied that, given certain conditions, the Kennedy thing could occur."

50. AKL interview.

51. AKL interview.

52. Paul Cowan, *Village Voice*, September 10, 1968.

53. AKL interview.

54. Kramer typescript.

55. Interviews with Rod Boggs and Greg Craig; Kramer typescript.

56. Interviews with Rick Weidman, Jeff Robbins, and Greg Craig.
57. Kramer typescript; interviews with Rod Boggs, Greg Craig, and Rick Weidman.
58. Kramer typescript; interviews with Gary Hart, Fred Millhiser, Rich Hammond, and Mary Louise Oates, Washington, January 9, 1991.
59. Interviews with Rick Saslaw and Jeff Robbins; Leonard Schecter, "Teenie Power," *New York* (December 1968).
60. Interviews with Steve Morgan, Boston, February 19, 1991, and Jennifer Littlefield.
61. Interviews with Jennifer Littlefield, Sue Andrews, Mimi Perr, and Barbara Bernstein.
62. Interviews with Gary Bellow and Jennifer Littlefield; *Village Voice*, September 26, 1968.
63. Interviews with Rick Weidman, Steven Cohen, Rich Hammond, Fred Millhiser, and Gary Hart.
64. Interviews with Arnold Miller and Rick Weidman; Rowland Evans and Robert Novak, *New York Post*, September 26, 1968.
65. *New York Times*, September 2, October 30, and November 3, 1968; Kramer typescript; interviews with Lanny Davis, Washington, D.C., February 25, 1992, Rick Weidman, Rod Boggs, Jennifer Littlefield, and Gary Hart.
66. Kramer typescript; *New York Times*, November 7, 1968; *Newsday* and *Long Island Press* coverage, November 5–9, 1968; Marcia Borie to AKL, [n.d., November 1968], AKL Papers.
67. *Citizen* interview with David Halberstam.
68. Interview with Gary Bellow.
69. Ronnie Dugger to AKL, April 3, 1968, Frank White to AKL, April 9, 1968, and Nancy Braumel to AKL, June 18, 1968, all in AKL Papers.
70. *Washington Post*, May 19, 1968; interview with Rick Tuttle.
71. Interview with Jack Newfield.

CHAPTER 13

1. *New Yorker*, January 10, 1970; James Wechsler, *New York Post*, January 9, 1970. See also Mary McGrory, *New York Post*, (January 3, 1969) on Lowenstein's role as a representative of the new politics, and Herbert Mitgang, *New York Times*, (January 6, 1969) on the same theme. In Mitgang's view, if Lowenstein and others could succeed in reforming the administration's policies on the draft and the war, "the political equation would be radically changed. That could blunt the radical direction of the new politics and turn it back to old-style liberalism." That certainly was Lowenstein's hope.
2. Interview with Jennifer Littlefield; Daniel Mandel to AKL, November 14, 1968 (urging him to respond to every constituent request and use local staff), and Gary Bellow to AKL, December 3, 1968, both in AKL Papers.
3. *New York Times*, January 18 and 22, 1969; *Newsday*, January 18 and 22,

1969; *Washington Post,* January 18 and 22, 1969. Lowenstein made the Calcutta analogy repeatedly. See *Progressive* (August 1969); and *Look* (August 25, 1970).

4. *New Yorker,* January 10, 1970; *Citizen* interview with Doug Walgren; *Long Island Press,* February 1, 1969. Lowenstein also made the geriatric charge a constant theme.

5. Mary McGrory, *New York Post,* January 3, 1969; Lewis, *New Yorker,* January 10, 1970.

6. Interview with Rod Boggs; Larry Cheek, *Greensboro* (North Carolina) *Record,* April 13, 1969. Because of his identification with North Carolina, the press there devoted much more attention to Lowenstein than to other out-of-state congressmen.

7. *Citizen* interview with Andy Jacobs; interviews with Rod Boggs and Susan Tannenbaum (another member of Lowenstein's staff), Washington, D.C. April 26, 1989.

8. *Citizen* interview with Pete McCloskey.

9. *Long Island Press,* December 4, 1968, and February 3, 1969; *Merrick Life,* May 1, 1969; *Newsday,* March 3, 1969; Lewis, *New Yorker,* January 10, 1970; interviews with Rod Boggs and Arnold Miller; *Citizen* interview with Greg Stone.

10. Interviews with Rod Boggs, Jennifer Littlefield, and Eugene Goldman, Washington, D.C., April 26, 1989.

11. Interview with Fred Millhiser, a former NC State student of Lowenstein's and subsequent staff member; *Look,* August 25, 1970.

12. Interviews with Marcia Borie, Mimi Perr, Barbara Bernstein, and Susan Tannenbaum; *Look,* August 25, 1970.

13. Interviews with Rod Boggs, Susan Tannenbaum, Emory Bundy and Roger Poole, San Francisco, December 16, 1988. Bundy was Lowenstein's first administrative assistant, Poole was his legislative assistant, Tannenbaum handled his schedule.

14. Interviews with Emory Bundy, Roger Poole, Susan Tannenbaum, and Arnold Miller. Miller was in charge of Lowenstein's district office.

15. Interviews with Jack Watson, Emory Bundy, Roger Poole, Susan Tannenbaum, and Fred Millhiser; Bundy, Lowenstein's old friend from NSA days and the trip to South-West Africa, was teaching political science at Oberlin. He gave up his academic career for a salary of $10,000 (only $750 more than he had been making at Oberlin), with the expectation that he would play a major role in policymaking and staffing the office. In particular, he wanted to be in charge of African issues. But before Bundy could even consult with Lowenstein on these issues, Lowenstein was off to Biafra and took charge of his own appointments. In typical fashion, he wanted to secure good assistants, but never to cede authority. See Emory Bundy to AKL, December 7, 1968, AKL Papers.

16. John Curtis, "The Ballad of AKL," "The Dump Al Movement," and staff

birthday greetings, January 1970, all in AKL Papers; interviews with Roger Poole and Susan Tannenbaum.

17. Interviews with Roger Poole and Susan Tannenbaum; Barry Farber, [interview with Allard Lowenstein], *Penthouse* (August 1970). Farber's interview and another article Lowenstein did for *Glamour* (June 1970) are extensive explorations of Lowenstein's political philosophy.

18. For Lowenstein's involvement on the Biafran situation, see Natalie Zinboboy's telegram to AKL, July 25, 1968, and copies of telegrams to Secretary of State Dean Rusk, AKL Papers; *New York Times*, August 14, 1968; *Newsday*, February 6, 1969; *Long Island Press*, February 19, 1969; and *Newsweek*, March 24, 1969. See also interview with Greg Craig. On Vietnam, see *Merrick Beacon*, February 13, 1969; AKL, speech before the House of Representative, [n.d.], AKL Papers.

19. *Long Island Press*, March 27, 1969; *Washington Post*, April 23, 1969.

20. *New York Times*, September 24, 1969; *Washington Post*, September 24, 1969.

21. *South Shore Record*, October 1, 1968; *Citizen* interview with Bobby Mueller.

22. Jay Jacobson to AKL, April 23, 1968, AKL Papers.

23. Interviews with Rich Hammond and Rick Weidman; Rick Weidman to AKL, October 26, 1969, AKL Papers. The letters in the AKL Papers from soldiers in Vietnam as well as from antiwar protestors are a powerful documentary record of what the Vietnam War did to the American psyche.

24. Interviews with Sam Brown, David Hawk, David Mixner, Los Angeles, March 15, 1989, and Arnold Miller.

25. Interviews with David Mixner, David Hawk, and Sam Brown. Greg Craig and Clint Deveaux, who were on the other side of this issue from Mixner, Hawk, and Brown, basically confirm this account of what happened.

26. Interviews with Greg Craig, Clinton Deveaux, David Mixner, David Hawk, Sam Brown, and Rick Saslaw. Clint Deveaux to Eli Evans (a Revson Foundation official and old friend of Lowenstein's), May 26, 1969, AKL Papers.

27. Interviews with David Mixner, Sam Brown, David Hawk, and Jack Newfield. Newfield's book *A Prophetic Minority* (New York: New American Library, 1966) addresses the issues associated with the youth movement.

28. Interviews with David Mixner, David Hawk, Sam Brown, Greg Craig, Clinton Deveaux, and Jack Newfield; *Citizen* interview with Andy Jacobs; *Newsday*, October 7 and 10, 1969; *Newark Evening News*, October 7, 1969; *Newsweek*, October 6 and 20, 1969; *Los Angeles Times*, October 16, 1969; *New York Times*, October 16, 1969.

29. Interviews with David Hawk and David Mixner; Mary McGrory, *New York Post*, November 7, 1969. For discussions of what was going on in the New Left during these years, see Todd Gitlin, *The Sixties: Years of Hope, Days of Rage* (New York: Bantam Books, 1987); and James Miller, *Democracy Is in the Streets: From Port Huron to the Siege of Chicago* (New York: Simon and

Schuster, 1987). Both written by former SDS leaders, these books chroni-
cle—as memoirs and analysis—the turbulent history of the late 1960s.

30. *Nassau Herald,* December 25, 1969; AKL, "Polarize or Persuade," draft of
Glamour article, in AKL Papers, hereafter referred to as AKL, "Polarize."

31. *Newsday,* November 7 and 10, 1969; *Washington Post,* November 11,
1969.

32. *Newsday,* October 28 and November 5, 7, 8, and 10, 1969; *Long Island
Press,* October 28, 1969; *Nassau Herald,* December 25, 1969; *Washington
Post,* November 11, 1969; AKL, "Polarize"; interviews with David Hawk
and Sam Brown.

33. AKL, "Polarize."

34. *Long Island Press,* February 14, 1969; *Newsday,* April 24, 1969; Harvard
Class Day speech, manuscript, in AKL Papers; *Boston Globe,* September
27, 1969.

35. *Minneapolis Star,* March 31, 1969; *Progressive* (August 1969); *Penthouse*
(August 1970); *Newsday,* May 2, 1969; *Stanford Daily,* April 17, 1969; interview with Sam Brown.

36. *Penthouse* (August 1970); *Glamour* (June 1970); *Newsday,* October 24,
1970.

37. *Glamour* (June 1970); *Penthouse* (August 1970); *Newsday,* May 7, 1970;
interview with Greg Craig.

38. *Newsday,* May 7, 1970; *Long Island Press,* 1970.

39. *Penthouse* (August 1970); *Glamour* (June 1970).

40. AKL speech to Congress, June 1970, AKL Papers.

41. Interview with Jeff Robbins; *Penthouse* (August 1970).

42. *Richmond Times-Dispatch,* February 17, 1970.

43. *Newsday,* October 1 and December 9, 1969; *New York Times,* December
30, 1969, and January 20, 1970.

44. *Newsday,* December 9, 1969, and December 26, 1969; *Merrick Life,* February 5, 1970; Fred Shapiro, term paper, in AKL Papers (hereafter referred to
as Shapiro paper).

45. *Newsday,* February 17, 1970; *New York Times,* February 16, 1970; *New
York Daily News,* February 2, 1970; *Washington Post,* March 4, 1970.

46. *Long Island Press,* March 2, 1970; *Washington Post,* March 4, 1970. Not
everyone on Lowenstein's staff agreed that the resignation and special election was a good idea. "This was another example," Arnie Miller later said,
"of the annoyance I think a lot of people must have felt with this guy constantly bothering them with stuff."

47. *Newsday,* April 6, 1970; Mary McGrory, *New York Post,* December 15,
1969; *Long Island Press,* December 17, 1969; *Citizen* interview with Greg
Stone.

48. Susan Andrews to AKL, [n.d., 1970], AKL Papers; *Newsday,* April 14,
1970; *New York Times,* April 14, 1970; *Long Island Independent,* April 16,
1970; *Long Island Graphic,* April 16, 1970.

49. *Long Island Press,* March 5, 1970; Shapiro paper.

50. Frank Mankiewicz and Tom Braden, *Washington Post,* October 13, 1970; Judith Coburn, "Dump Lowenstein," draft article in AKL Papers; *Newsday,* September 11 and October 6, 1970; Republican ad, "Responsible Americans Can No Longer Be Silent," *Washington Evening Star,* September 22, 1970. Richard Dean McCarthy in *Elections for Sale* (Boston: Houghton Mifflin, 1972) alleges that Nixon singled out Lowenstein for attack.

51. Interviews with Jennifer Littlefield and Jeff Robbins; Shapiro paper.

52. *Long Island Graphic,* October 8, 1970; *Long Island Press,* October 11–12, 1970; *Penthouse* (August 1970).

53. *Long Island Press,* October 11–12, 1970; *Newsday,* September 11 and 1970; October 14, 1970.

54. Interviews with Jennifer Littlefield and Jeff Robbins; *Merrick Life,* February 5, 1970.

55. *TV Guide,* January 24, 1970; interview with William Buckley, New York, September 16, 1991.

56. *Long Island Press,* August 27 and October 14, 1970.

57. Bill Wilka, "How I Helped Lose an Election," in AKL Papers; *Newsday,* September 2, 14, and October 12, 1970; interviews with Steve Morgan, Marcia Borie, and Susan Andrews.

58. Charles [surname unknown] to AKL, AKL Papers; interviews with Rich Hammond, Arnold Miller, and Jeff Robbins; *Citizen* interview with Hamilton Richardson. Jeff Robbins recounts how Al would handle bad news. "He'd look at you and his glasses would slide down the nose. He would burp. He would think about it for a moment . . . and [then] would say, 'Well, that's a blow.' . . . and with a flicker of a smile say, 'But we're going to have to press on.'"

59. Interviews with Arnold Miller and Jeff Robbins; *Newsday,* May 1, 1970.

60. Interviews with Rich Hammond and Arnold Miller; *Long Island Press,* October 16, 1970; *Newsday,* October 24, 1970.

61. Interviews with Arnold Miller and Emory Bundy; *Citizen* interview with Hamilton Richardson.

62. *Look,* August 25, 1970; *Newsday,* October 31, 1970; Evans and Novak, *New York Post,* October 20, 1970. *Newsday* pointed out that even if Lowenstein was hated by SDS activists, he was still identified with the student movement; that identification, plus his own voluminous comments on every conceivable subject, made him vulnerable to attack.

63. Interviews with Jennifer Littlefield and Lanny Davis; *Long Island Express,* October 14, 1970; Robert Sherrill, "De-escalator of the War on Poverty," *New York Times Magazine,* December 13, 1970.

64. Interviews with Arnold Miller and Gary Bellow; *Washington Post,* October 19, 1970; *Massapequa Post,* October 22, 1970; *Long Island Press,* October 28, 1970.

65. *New York Times,* October 23, 1970; *Newsday,* September 23, 1970; *Penthouse* (August 1970); interview with Eugene Goldman.
66. *Newsday,* October 14, 1970; *Long Island Press,* October 15, 1970.
67. *Long Island Press,* November 4, 1970; *Newsday,* November 4, 1970; *New York Times,* November 4, 1970; Shapiro paper.
68. *Newsday,* November 4, 1970; interviews with Jennifer Littlefield and Jeff Robbins.
69. Interview with Jennifer Littlefield; Jerome Waldie to AKL, December 1970, AKL Papers.
70. John Gilligan to AKL, [n.d.], AKL Papers; interview with Eugene Goldman; *Citizen* interview with Pete McCloskey; *Citizen* interview with Thomas Downey.
71. Interview with Arnold Miller.
72. Wilka, "How I Helped"; "The Diary of a Loser," *Notre Dame Observer,* November 19, 1970, AKL Papers.
73. *Newsday,* January 19, 1971.
74. Interview with Marcia Borie.

CHAPTER 14

1. *Newsday,* November 4, 1970; Patrick Owens, *Newsday,* December 7, 1970.
2. *Newsweek,* October 25, 1971. On women's voting experience, see Nancy Cott, *The Grounding of Modern Feminism* (New Haven: Yale University Press, 1987); J. Stanley Lemons, *The Woman Citizen: Social Feminism in the 1920s* (Urbana: University of Illinois Press, 1973); and William H. Chafe, *The Paradox of Change: American Women in the Twentieth Century* (New York: Oxford University Press, 1991).
3. *Harvard Independent,* October 9, 1969.
4. *Harvard Independent,* October 9, 1969; Jules Witcover, *Long Island Press,* April 3, 1971; *Citizen* interview with Greg Stone; interview with Nick Littlefield.
5. Jennifer recalls that Al was not that happy with the ADA post, but "it gave him the chance to talk about issues." His correspondence with Adlai Stevenson III and Leon Shull, ADA's executive director, also suggests that he was reluctant to be chair of the ADA again, and that during his two-year stint there were difficult moments. Interview with Jennifer Littlefield, Adlai Stevenson III to AKL, April 26, 1972, and Leon Shull to AKL, May 23, 1973, both in AKL Papers. On Lowenstein's election as chair of the ADA in 1971, see James Wechsler to Joe Duffy, March 31, 1971, AKL Papers. For an overall assessment, see interviews with Joseph Rauh, Leon Shull, Washington, D.C., February 11, 1992, and Art Kaminsky, New York, September 17, 1991. Shull noted that Lowenstein seemed initially to suspect him, and that there was tension because Lowenstein was trying to

have young people take over. "There were all kinds of machinations going on around me," he said, but after Shull insisted that they air their differences, a closer relationship developed.

6. Interviews with Nick Littlefield, Art Kaminsky, Clinton Deveaux, and Lanny Davis; *Newsweek,* August 23 and October 25, 1971; David Broder, *Washington Post,* March 28, 1971; *Los Angeles Times,* April 4, 1971; *Indianapolis Star,* May 23, 1971; *New York Times,* May 23, 1971. Much of the voter registration campaign was bankrolled by two liberal Democrats, Abraham Feinberg and Marvin Rosenberg.

7. *Look,* June 1, 1971; *Newsweek,* October 25, 1971; *Time,* July 19, 1971; *New York Times,* September 26, 1971. See also Lanny Davis, *The Emerging Democratic Majority: Lessons and Legacies from the New Politics* (New York: Stein and Day 1974), pp. 113–122. Davis notes that, as a personal favor to Lowenstein, he had persuaded Muskie to speak.

8. Bella Abzug, clipping, AKL Papers; *Newsweek,* August 23, 1971.

9. *Newsweek,* May 24, 1971; *Newsday,* June 14, 1971.

10. The plan was for Lowenstein to dictate sections, then Anson would edit and polish them. The problem, Art Kaminsky, one of Lowenstein's young aides, noted, was that Anson could never catch up with Lowenstein so that they could work on the book. The two received an advance of $12,000. *McCall's* planned to print an excerpt in its December 1971 issue, and the entire book was to be delivered in January for spring 1972 publication. John Gallagher to AKL, October 27, 1971, Kenneth Gross to AKL, September 7, 1971, Susan Stanward to AKL, November 17, 1971, and Hy Cohen to AKL, April 9, 1974 trying to get Saturday Review Press's advance back, all in AKL Papers; see also interviews with Art Kaminsky and Jennifer Littlefield.

11. Quotations in this section are from Allard Lowenstein, "Reclaiming America," unpublished book manuscript, in AKL Papers.

12. The two best books for understanding the inside history of the New Left are Gitlin's *The Sixties* and Miller, *Democracy Is in the Streets.*

13. Interviews with Steve Morgan, Greg Craig, Nick Littlefield, and Art Kaminsky; *Texas Observer,* August 27, 1971; Don Siegelman to AKL, September 13, 1971 (regarding disagreements over the campaign), AKL Papers.

14. Interviews with Arnold Miller and Art Kaminsky; Robert Frisbee to AKL, September 20, 1971 (regarding a failure to get speakers and entertainers committed), AKL Papers; *Indianapolis Star,* May 23, 1971. The confusion also extended to staffing. A Brown student, for example, accused Lowenstein of letting him down twice regarding a promised job in the campaign. "In this light, it is easy to see how most of your local and national efforts have been failures, and why so many of your own staff people distrust or dislike you." Student to AKL, May 27, 1971, AKL Papers.

15. *New York Post,* April 19, 1971; *Newsweek,* August 23, 1971; *Look,* June 1,

1971; *Time,* July 19, 1971; Lanny Davis, *The Emerging Democratic Majority,* pp. 113–122; interview with Lanny Davis.

16. Interviews with Steve Morgan, Greg Craig, and Barney Frank; *Newsweek,* October 25, 1971.

17. Interview with Jennifer Littlefield.

18. Interviews with Arnold Miller, Art Kaminsky, Nick Littlefield, Ann Feldman, Brooklyn, October 7, 1991, John Mulvern, New York, February 18, 1991, Father Richard Neuhaus, New York, September 17, 1991, and Willie Vargas, New York, October 7, 1991. John Mulvern was a priest at the time and heavily involved in community affairs. Father Richard Neuhaus was a Lutheran minister who at that time was strongly identified with liberal reform causes; he is now more closely associated with neoconservative positions. Commenting on Lowenstein's penchant for creating drafts, Art Kaminsky observed: "There were all sorts of sham events that he stimulated, that would invite him to come. . . . He couldn't just stand up and say, 'I want to do this.' That would be too self-promoting, too risky . . . too clear, too honest."

19. *Congressional Quarterly,* May 13, 1972; interviews with Father Richard Neuhaus, John Mulvern, Willie Vargas, and Ann Feldman. See also Ron Tabak, unpublished manuscript, in AKL Papers, hereafter referred to as Tabak manuscript.

20. Interview with Ann Feldman; *Congressional Quarterly,* May 13, 1972.

21. Interviews with Ann Feldman, Lanny Davis, Jennifer Littlefield, and Carol Bellamy, New York, October 8, 1991; *Citizen* interview with Greg Stone; Tabak manuscript.

22. Interviews with Nick Littlefield, Arnold Miller, Art Kaminsky, and Steve Morgan.

23. Lanny Davis, "Why Lowenstein Lost: Ethnics, Crooks and Carpetbaggers," *Washington Monthly* (September 1972); advertisement for John Rooney, *Brooklyn Heights Press,* June 8, 1972; *Indianapolis Star,* April 13, 1972.

24. Tabak manuscript; Lowenstein campaign literature, in AKL Papers; interviews with Ann Feldman, Steve Morgan, Art Kaminsky, Eileen Dugan, Brooklyn, October 8, 1991, Father Richard Neuhaus, John Mulvern, and Jennifer Littlefield.

25. Interviews with Arnie Miller, Steve Morgan, Nick Littlefield, Eileen Dugan, John Mulvern; Tabak manuscript.

26. Interviews with Willie Vargas, Eileen Dugan, and John Mulvern.

27. *Village Voice,* June 29, 1972; Tabak manuscript; interviews with John Mulvern, Ellen Vollinger, Washington, D.C., September 6, 1991, Willie Vargas, and Eileen Dugan.

28. Davis, "Why Lowenstein Lost"; Tabak manuscript; interview with Ann Feldman.

29. Russ Levitt to AKL, [n.d., 1972], and Debbie Wise to AKL, November 8, 1972, both in AKL Papers; interview with Ann Feldman.

30. Eleanor Curtin to AKL, September 23, 1972, AKL Papers; Tabak manuscript; Ken Sobol, *Village Voice*, September 30, 1972.

31. *Village Voice*, June 29, 1972; September 30, 1972.

32. Davis, "Why Lowenstein Lost"; *New York Times*, June 21, 1972; interviews with Gary Bellow, Harvey Lippman, New York, February 23, 1991, and Jennifer Littlefield; Tabak manuscript.

33. Interviews with Eileen Dugan, Steve Morgan, and Art Kaminsky.

34. Tabak manuscript; interviews with Eileen Dugan, Carol Bellamy, Ann Feldman, and Art Kaminsky; *Village Voice*, September 30, 1972.

35. Interviews with Art Kaminsky, Ann Feldman, and Jennifer Littlefield.

36. Interview with Harvey Lippman; *Nation*, September 25, 1972; *New York Times*, July 25 and September 6 and 13, 1972.

37. *New Yorker*, September 30, 1972; *New York Times*, September 18, 1972; *Village Voice*, September 30, 1972.

38. *New Yorker*, September 30, 1972; *New York Times*, September 20, 1972; interviews with Steve Morgan, Art Kaminsky, and Ann Feldman; Tabak manuscript. Kaminsky said that Lowenstein knew about the fried chicken. Ann Feldman agreed. When someone told her Lowenstein's people were trying to buy votes with chicken, she went to Lowenstein and told him. "He said, 'I know nothing about it,' and as soon as he said it, I knew . . . the way he said it . . . that it was his idea. . . . [That] was a turning point for me, because I couldn't believe he would do something so tacky and so basically racist."

39. Interview with Ann Feldman; Tabak manuscript. Lanny Davis came back for the second election, having experienced a typical cycle of emotions with Lowenstein. After initially being asked to serve as Lowenstein's campaign coordinator, he suddenly found himself "cut off at the knees wherever I went" and was eventually replaced by a series of new coordinators, none of whom was given any real authority. Eventually, Davis became a precinct captain and, after the first primary, wrote a cogent analysis of the results for *Washington Monthly*. He then discovered that Lowenstein was furious at him for writing the piece. "I had 'betrayed' him was the word [Ann Feldman] used." Still, Davis went back to work in the rerun. "I was trying to prove to him that he was wrong in the way he had treated me." Davis went up to Al and said, "Al, I'm here, I'm sorry. I just wanted you to know I worked real hard and I wanted to try to talk to you." Lowenstein stared at him, turned, and walked away. The message, in Davis's view, was that anything less than total devotion was unacceptable.

40. Pete Hamill, "The Last Hurrah," *New York Post*, September 20, 1972.

41. *Village Voice*, September 30, 1972.

42. Interviews with Ann Feldman and Steve Morgan; Tabak manuscript.

43. Interviews with Ann Feldman, Steve Morgan, Lanny Davis, and Gary Bellow; Tabak manuscript.

44. Interviews with Barney Frank and confidential source.

45. Interviews with Rick Saslaw and Howard Berman.

46. Interview with Eileen Dugan.

47. Andrew Roffe to AKL and Jenny, [n.d., 1972], AKL Papers; interview with Steve Morgan.

48. Interviews with Jeff Robbins and Jennifer Littlefield.

49. AKL, "Reclaiming America."

50. Interview with Regina Galke and Susan Erb, Long Island, February 24, 1991; AKL tax returns, in AKL Papers. Lowenstein ordinarily received $500–1,000 for lecturing and usually about $30–40 per hour for teaching. His net taxable income in these years ranged from $18,000 to $35,000. Jennifer also received some income from a trust. Lowenstein's tax returns suggest that he was never affluent. Indeed, one of the primary tasks of his aides was to keep American Express from canceling his card since usually his account was overdue.

51. Interviews with Eileen Dugan, Steve Morgan, Jay Jacobson, Little Rock, Arkansas, November 21, 1991, Willie Vargas, and John Mulvern; Lawrence Spivak to AKL, January 16, 1973, and Greg Stone and James Brogan to Andrew Tobias, September 24, 1973, both in AKL Papers; July 4, 1973; *New York Times*, October 3, 1973.

52. AKL interview; interviews with Steve Morgan and Ronnie Eldridge. As early as April 26, 1973, *Newsday* had indicated Lowenstein was actively considering a Senate candidacy.

53. Gary Hart to Harriet Eisman and Mimi Perr, May 13, 1973, Gary Hart and Jim Haas to AKL, [n.d.], Peter Deurio to AKL, October 2, 1973 (about announcing for the Senate), Jo Ann Molnar to AKL, [fall 1973], and Jerome Wilson to AKL, November 8, 1973, all in AKL Papers; interview with Steve Morgan; *Citizen* interview with Greg Stone; *Wall Street Journal, New York Times*.

54. Richard Neuhaus to AKL, September 17, 1973, and Susan Cohen to AKL, November 8, 1973, both in AKL Papers; interviews with Jay Jacobson, Arnold Miller, and confidential source; *New York Times*, January 7, 1974; *Newsday*, January 18, 1974.

55. Robert Boehm to AKL, February 2, 1974, Tom O'Brien to AKL, March 27, 1974, Jim Haas to AKL, April 8, 1974, and Andrew Tobias to AKL, January 1, 1974, all in AKL papers; interview with Steve Morgan.

56. Robert Boehm to AKL, February 2, 1974, AKL Papers; *New York Times*, March 3, 1974; interviews with Mimi Perr, Ellen Vollinger, and confidential source.

57. Interviews with Arnold Miller and Ann Feldman.

58. Selma Galton to AKL, May 12, 1974, Ron Tabak to AKL, May 28, 1974, France Hubbard to John Hatt, June 17, 1974, all in AKL Papers; *New York Times*, March 6, May 12, and June 7 and 16–20, 1974; interview with Harvey Lippman.

59. Interviews with Harvey Lippman and Greg Craig; Don Riegle to AKL, June

17, 1974, and William Hoffman to AKL, May 12, 1974, both in AKL Papers.

60. Interviews with Harvey Lippman, Jay Jacobson, Ann Feldman, Steve Morgan, Arnold Miller, Art Kaminsky, Ellen Vollinger, and Rick Saslaw; *New York Times*, July 1, 1974; *Village Voice*, July 4, 1974; *Long Island Press*, July 15, 1974. Harvey Lippman returned from the post office and, as a practical joke, told Lowenstein he had missed the midnight deadline.

61. Interviews with Steve Morgan and Willie Vargas.

62. Interviews with Ellen Vollinger, Mimi Perr, Barbara Bernstein, Sue Andrews, Art Kaminsky, and Greg Craig; *New York Times*, October 15, 1974.

63. Interviews with Rick Saslaw and Art Kaminsky; New York *Times*, October 15, 1974.

64. Interviews with Steve Morgan and Harvey Lippman.

65. Richard Nixon to John Dean, September 15, 1972, quoted in Daniel Schorr, *Clearing the Air* (Boston: Houghton Mifflin, 1977); p. 89; Judith Coburn, press release, "Dump Lowenstein"; Steve Roberts, *New York Times*, July 16, 1973 (reporting that Lowenstein had asked for an inquiry as to whether there was a conspiracy to destroy him politically).

66. Interviews with Steven Morgan, Jennifer Littlefield, and confidential source.

67. Interview with Jay Jacobson.

68. Interviews with Steven Cohen, Arnold Miller, Barney Frank, and Lawrence Lowenstein. Lowenstein's brother Larry commented, "He never took time during a campaign . . . to sit down and actually plan what [he was] going to do." Barney Frank noted that when Lowenstein trotted out the Dump Johnson argument, Frank would respond, "Yes, once you were right, and most of the time, it is impossible."

69. AKL, Stanford speech, May 15, 1973, Mary [surname unknown] to AKL, [n.d., 1972], both in AKL Papers; interview with Jeff Robbins.

70. Interviews with Ann Feldman and Nancy Steffen.

71. Sanford Friedman to AKL, March 19, 1974, AKL Papers; interview with Jennifer Littlefield.

CHAPTER 15

1. AKL, "Reclaiming America" (introduction).

2. AKL, "Personal Odyssey" draft, AKL Papers; AKL, "Personal Odyssey," *Argosy* (February 1976); *New York Post*, April 18, 1974; *Newsday*, April 19, 1974; interview with Jeff Robbins.

3. AKL, "Personal Odyssey" draft, (introduction), AKL Papers; interviews with Steven Smith, Jr., Cambridge, January 28, 1990, Jeff Robbins, David Bender, Los Angeles, March 15, 1988, and Jennifer Littlefield.

4. AKL, "Personal Odyssey" draft; interviews with David Bender and Jeff Robbins.

5. Interviews with Gary Bellow, Barney Frank, Jennifer Littlefield, David Bender, and Greg Stone.

6. Interviews with Paul Schrade, Jeff Robbins, David Bender, and Regina Galke; *New York Times*, December 17, 1974; *Washington Star*, May 4, 1975; *New York Post*, May 13–19, 1975; *Washington Post*, July 13, 1975. Lowenstein signed a book contract with Putnam's to coauthor a book on the assassinations and received a $12,000 advance. See Ned Chase to AKL, October 15 and 27, and November 24, 1975. Lowenstein also had a contract with a lecture bureau. See also letters from William La Forge, December 18, 1974, Ed Koch, December 26, 1974, Frank Boch, December 28, 1974, John Christian, January 17, 1975, and Sylvia Meagher, November 13, 1974, all in AKL Papers.

7. *Washington Star*, May 5, 1975; *Boston Globe*, July 13, 1975; *Los Angeles Times*, August 15, 1975; *New York Post*, May 19–23, 1975. Professor MacDonnell was part of a panel at the American Forensics Association examining ballistics evidence from the Kennedy case. In *Computers and Automation*, (September 1972), Richard Sprague asserted that two eyewitnesses saw the hotel guard shoot Kennedy. Another piece of evidence cited by assassination aficionados was that auditory tests showed that microphones could not pick up the sounds of gunshots fired from Sirhan's position but did pick up the sound of three other shots, presumably nearer the tape recorders held by radio and television reporters. The hotel guard was nearer these tape recorders. William Harper, a forensic expert, stated that the autopsy established two firing positions, one from Sirhan in front, the other in close proximity to Kennedy but behind him and to his right. Of the four shots allegedly fired from behind, all produced powder residues; there was no powder residue from the bullets fired from Sirhan's position.

8. See newspaper articles cited in notes 6 and 7. See also Lillian Castellano, *Los Angeles Free Press*, May 23, 1969; Steve Morgan to AKL, January 10, 1976 (about Lowenstein interview with Dan Rather), AKL Papers.

9. AKL, assorted unpublished articles on the Kennedy assassination, in AKL Papers, hereafter referred to as AKL assassination articles; interview with Hilary Lieber, Washington, D.C., September 6, 1991.

10. AKL assassination articles; interviews with Jack Newfield and Nancy Steffen. Robert Anson writes about the Giancana episode in *New Times*, January 23, 1976.

11. *Citizen* interview with Greg Stone; interview with confidential source.

12. Interviews with confidential source, Gary Bellow, and John Kavanaugh, New York, September 16, 1991; letters to AKL, July 18, 1967, [n.d., 1968], October 13, 1968, and October 28, 1975, in AKL Papers.

13. Letter to AKL, November 8, 1973, AKL Papers; interview with John Kavanaugh.

14. Interviews with confidential sources.

15. Interviews with confidential sources.

16. Interviews with John Kavanaugh and confidential sources.

17. Interviews with Bruce Payne, and confidential sources; [confidential], letter to AKL, [n.d.], AKL Papers.

18. Confidential letters to AKL, 1969–75, AKL Papers; interview with confidential source.

19. [Confidential], letters to AKL, 1972, AKL Papers; interviews with Jeff Robbins and John Kavanaugh.

20. Larry [surname unknown] to AKL, January 2, 1973, AKL Papers.

21. Interview with Bruce Payne.

22. Interview with Bruce Voeller, Los Angeles, December 12, 1988; *Village Voice*, March 23, 1974, on the party; *New York Times*, October 3, 1973, (on Howard Brown disclosing he was gay); Robert Livingston to AKL, February 28, 1974, AKL Papers.

23. Interview with Sanford Friedman.

24. Greg Craig to AKL, July 20, 1974 (on the occasion of his own marriage and recalling Lowenstein's comments to him), Douglass Hunt to AKL, July 8, 1966, and AKL to Jennifer Lowenstein, September 2, 1967, and September 2, 1969, all in AKL Papers; interviews with Jay Jacobson and Steven Cohen.

25. Jennifer Lowenstein to AKL, August 15, 1969, AKL Papers.

26. Interviews with Jennifer Littlefield and Mimi Perr.

27. Interviews with Mimi Perr, Barbara Bernstein, Susan Andrews, and Jennifer Littlefield; AKL to Sanford Friedman, November 10, 1972, and Susan Andrews to AKL, January 26, 1970, both in AKL Papers.

28. Emory Bundy to AKL and Jennifer Lowenstein, November 7 and to AKL, December 7, 1968, AKL Papers; interviews with Susan Andrews and Jennifer Littlefield. In a letter to her husband, Bundy expressed amazement at Jenny's "serenity in the midst of prolonged crisis and chaos and her devotion to you."

29. Emory Bundy to AKL, December 7, 1968, AKL Papers; interviews with Art Kaminsky, Arnold Miller, Regina Galke, and Floss Frucher. Jenny told Floss Frucher that at the Democratic convention in Chicago in 1968, there were never fewer than twenty people in their room.

30. Interviews with Sherman Bull, Judy Quine, and Sanford Friedman.

31. Interviews with Nancy Steffen, and Colleen and Kenneth Cuthbertson.

32. Interview with Jennifer Littlefield.

33. Interviews with Steve Morgan and Jennifer Littlefield.

34. Interview with Jennifer Littlefield.

35. Interviews with Sherman Bull and Jennifer Littlefield.

36. Interviews with Jennifer Littlefield, Nancy Steffen, and Rick Saslaw.

37. Interviews with Marie Lowenstein and Ann Feldman.

38. Interviews with Bruce Payne and two confidential sources.

39. Interviews with Susan Erb and Franklin D. Roosevelt III. Susan Erb de-

scribed further the scene at the house: "People were supposed to work down in the basement, but they never did. They all used to hover around the first floor, so they were always underfoot, in the kitchen, and Jenny would come down and they would always be there. Al would be off someplace else." When Erb pointed out the problem to Al, he would respond, "Oh, I thought everyone liked her," to which Erb would reply: "It wasn't a question of whether everyone liked her or not, but they were there to see you, not her."

40. Interview with Jennifer Littlefield; Mrs. Ronald Lyman to AKL, April 7, 1974, AKL Papers.

41. Interviews with Colleen and Kenneth Cuthbertson, Jennifer Littlefield, Sanford Friedman, Jay Jacobson, and Steve Morgan; Steve Morgan to AKL, [n.d., late 1973], and Jennifer Lowenstein to AKL, [n.d., 1967], both in AKL Papers. Colleen Cuthbertson noted that Jenny was likely to get upset "when Al wouldn't show up when he said he would."

42. Interviews with Paul and Monica Schrade, Los Angeles, March 16, 1989, Jennifer Littlefield, Jack Newfield, and Harvey Lippman; see also Michael Berman to AKL, January 24, 1972, AKL Papers. Berman was on the California assembly's committee on elections and reapportionment, and he was writing Lowenstein about possible districts to run in.

43. Interviews with Jennifer Littlefield, and Paul and Monica Schrade; Steve Morgan to AKL, May 9, 1975, Gary Hart to AKL, June 30, 1975, and June Degnan to AKL, May 15, 1975, all in AKL Papers.

44. Interviews with Harvey Lippman, Frank Lowenstein, Washington D.C., December 18, 1990, and Jennifer Littlefield.

45. Interviews with David Bender, Jerry Brown, San Francisco, November 23, 1990, Harvey Lippman, Rick Tuttle, and Steven Reinhart. Jerry Brown initially described Lowenstein as just one among a large number of "idea" people he recruited. "He would just come around," Brown remarked, saying there were "relatively few conversations over a period of a couple of years." When reminded that Lowenstein had lived in his house and been intimately involved in his decision to run for the presidency, Brown's recollection of Lowenstein's role improved significantly. Perhaps the most accurate description of Lowenstein's role is to call him a "minister without portfolio." Steven Reinhart, a Lowenstein classmate at Yale Law School and now a federal judge, described the relationship between Brown and Lowenstein as somewhat strained, because they were close yet had different ideas. Reinhart served as an intermediary between this "odd couple," as he described them. Judy Quine recalls how Lowenstein and Brown drove around one day after deciding Brown would run for the presidency to announce the decision to their friends.

46. Michael Berman to AKL, January 24, 1972, AKL Papers; interviews with Rick Tuttle, David Bender, Harvey Lippman, and Steven Reinhart; see

also *Citizen* interviews with Jerome Waldie and Pete McCloskey. Howard Berman noted that some politicians in California saw Lowenstein as a threat because of his popularity.

47. Interviews with Jennifer Littlefield, Frank Lowenstein, Paul and Monica Schrade, David Bender, and Harvey Lippman.

48. Interviews with David Bender, Susan Andrews, Harvey Lippman, and Rick Tuttle. Virtually everyone agreed that Lowenstein could have had a future in California, and that his decision to leave was hard to understand.

49. AKL, "The Murder of Robert F. Kennedy: Suppressed Evidence of More Than One Assassin," *Saturday Review*, February 19, 1977.

50. Interviews with Dorothy DiCintio, Barbara Bernstein, and Hilary Lieber.

51. Interviews with Jennifer Littlefield, Susan Erb, Ann Feldman, and Susan Andrews.

52. Interviews with confidential source, Bruce Payne, and Susan Erb; Steve Morgan to AKL, [n.d., 1976], AKL Papers. Steve Morgan wrote to Lowenstein about the tension between public and private priorities, suggesting that "you, Jenny and the kids ought to have the opportunity to get to know each other a bit more."

53. Interviews with Steve Morgan, Jay Jacobson, Susan Erb, and Nancy Steffen.

54. Interview with Jennifer Littlefield.

55. Interviews with Hilary Lieber, Ellen Vollinger, Barbara Bernstein, Susan Andrews, Mimi Perr, and Ann Feldman.

56. *Newsday*, September 17, 1976; *Pennysavers*, October 4, 1976; *Congressional Quarterly*, October 9, 1976; interview with Susan Erb.

57. Interviews with Judy Quine, Robert Kiley, New York, September 11, 1990, and Howard Berman; *New York Post*, May 24, 1976; Don Siegelman to AKL, April 12, 1976, Bill [surname unknown] to AKL, April 18, 1976, and David [surname unknown] to AKL, April 15, 1976, all in AKL Papers.

58. Interviews with Ellen Vollinger, Hilary Lieber, and Harvey Lippman.

59. Interviews with Harvey Lippman, Jennifer Littlefield, and Frank Lowenstein.

60. Interviews with Jennifer Littlefield, Frank Lowenstein, and Susan Andrews.

61. Interviews with Stoney Cooks and Susan Erb; Bert Lowenstein to AKL, November 21, 1976, AKL Papers.

62. Interviews with Greg Craig and Bruce Payne.

63. Interviews with Sanford Friedman, Susan Erb, Jay Jacobson, Sherman Bull, and Ann Feldman.

64. Interviews with Sanford Friedman and Sherman Bull.

CHAPTER 16

1. Interviews with Stoney Cooks, Brady Tyson, Washington, D.C., February 11, 1992, James Leonard, Washington, D.C., February 25, 1992, David Bender, and Art Kaminsky. Although it was clear early in the Carter administration that Lowenstein would have a position, bureaucratic infighting blocked the actual appointment until the summer. See the *New York Times,* April 20, 1977 (Young introduces Lowenstein as part of his staff), then the *New York Post,* September 17, 1977 (Midge Costanza of the White House staff pushes through Lowenstein's appointment when it is stalled).

2. Interviews with David Bender, Brady Tyson, Stoney Cooks, and James Leonard; *New York Times,* March 9 and February 9, 1977; *New York Post,* March 29, 1977.

3. Interviews with Stoney Cooks, James Leonard, and Brady Tyson.

4. *New York Post,* July 14, 1978; interviews with Stoney Cooks, James Leonard, and Brady Tyson.

5. Interviews with Stoney Cooks, James Leonard, and Brady Tyson; Consulate General of the U.S. Embassy in Johannesburg to AKL, May 1, 1978, U.S. Embassy in Lusaka to U.S. State Department (marked secret), February 20, 1979 (cable regarding Lowenstein's conversations with Muzorewa, Botha, Smith, and Kaunda on possible terms of a settlement in Zimbabwe), Mary Benson to AKL, April 24, 1979 (on the same matter, and opposing his support for Muzorewa), Homer Jack to AKL, May 1, 1979 (also opposed), George Houser to AKL, May 3, 1979 (also opposed), and Congressman Howard Pollock to AKL, May 10, 1979 (urging Lowenstein's support for lifting economic sanctions against Rhodesia), all in AKL Papers. Lowenstein was part of a Freedom House delegation to observe elections in Rhodesia. The panel found the elections to be relatively free of fraud. The only problem was that they took place under a constitution that had been passed and ratified by whites only; hence, the structure under which the elections occurred was fundamentally flawed and reflected racist assumptions. In what seemed at times like a replay of his involvement in the Dominican Republic elections of 1966, Lowenstein ended up supporting the idea of a process—free elections—even when the structure surrounding that process was skewed so that truly free and autonomous elections were not possible. In Rhodesia, Lowenstein eventually played a constructive role. He did not ultimately support a lifting of sanctions (although that was the point he started from) but rather endorsed retaining them until further progress was made on the fundamental questions of representation and autonomy. On the other hand, through some of this haggling, he occasionally found himself in the anomalous position of being on the same side as Jesse Helms. Both were deeply suspicious of Robert Mugabe, the Zimbabwe leader Lowenstein opposed for being, he thought, a Marxist and too close to the Communists. Andrew Young, on the other hand, consistently felt that

Mugabe was a more representative figure and that he would eventually end up on top. Young was right, and Young prevailed within the Carter administration. The episode exemplified what Brady Tyson called Lowenstein's "Lone Ranger" approach to policy: although he played his role with consummate skill, Lowenstein's behavior demonstrated once more his belief that he alone could pull all the chestnuts from the fire and find a miracle answer.

6. Interviews with Stoney Cooks and James Leonard; Martha Darling to AKL, May 11, 1978, and Pearl Bitker to AKL, May 25, 1978, both in AKL Papers; *New York Times*, December 19, 1977, and January 5 and May 11, 1978; *New York Post*, January 5, 1978.

7. New York *Times*, December 19, 1977; January 5, 1978; May 11, Kenny Lerer, *New York*, January 16, 1978; interview with Susan Erb.

8. *Village Voice*, September 11, 1978; *New York*, September 11, 1978; *New York Post*, August 15, 1978; *Soho Weekly*, August 31, 1978; *Herald*, September 1, 1978; interviews with Susan Erb and Ann Feldman; AKL to Dustin Hoffman, August 22 1978, Judy Greenfield to AKL, June 21 and October 4, 1978, and Tom Mechling to AKL, September 13, 1978, all in AKL Papers.

9. Hyman Bookbinder to AKL, October 20, 1978, and Halton Adler Mann to AKL, December 3, 1978, both in AKL Papers; interview with Howard Berman.

10. Jenny married Nick Littlefield in the fall of 1979. Al wrote the children asking them to convey his good wishes "to Mom as she goes down the aisle." He would not speak with Nick; Steve Morgan wrote Al that he hoped they could "break the silence [and] communicate with one another. Too many lives are involved for the two of you not to speak with one another." Al and Nick eventually did resume communication. AKL to the Lowenstein children [n.d., fall 1979], and Steve Morgan to AKL, April 12, 1978, both in AKL Papers.

11. Interviews with Floss Frucher, Sanford Friedman, Bruce Payne, and Rick Tuttle. Lowenstein also talked at length about the divorce with Harvey Lippman, Sherman Bull, and the Cuthbertsons.

12. Interviews with Carol Moss, Susan Erb, Frank Lowenstein, and Sanford Friedman. Lowenstein's expenses had declined. He paid $425 a month for an apartment; his utility bill was practically nonexistent since he was almost never home; and he ate most of his evening meals at the family restaurant.

13. Interviews with Carol Moss, Los Angeles, June 1, 1988, Paul and Monica Schrade, David Bender, Alan Arkatov, Los Angeles, December 18, 1988, Sherman Bull, and Frank Lowenstein; *Citizen* interview with Mark Childress.

14. Interviews with Sanford Friedman, Susan Erb, and Frank Lowenstein; AKL

to the Lowenstein children, fall 1977, and AKL to Kate Lowenstein, December 2, 1978, both in AKL Papers.

15. Interviews with Clinton Deveaux, Harvey Lippman, Jennifer Littlefield, and Frank Lowenstein.

16. Interviews with Frank Lowenstein and Thomas Lowenstein.

17. Interviews with Floss Frucher, Sanford Friedman, Susan Erb, and Harvey Lippman.

18. Interview with Sherman Bull.

19. Interviews with Sanford Friedman, Greg Craig, and Frank Lowenstein.

20. Interviews with Floss Frucher, Rick Saslaw, and Ken Liberman.

21. Interviews with Greg Craig and Steve Morgan.

22. Interviews with Marcia Borie, Harvey Lippman, Steve Smith, Jr., Carol Moss, and Susan Erb.

23. Interviews with Nancy Steffen, Paul and Monica Schrade, and Carol Moss. Similar comments were made by Ken Liberman, Floss Frucher, and Rick Saslaw.

24. Interviews with Nancy Steffen, Sherman Bull, and Harvey Lippman.

25. Interviews with confidential source, Steven Reinhart, and Nancy Steffen.

26. Interview with Bruce Payne.

27. Interview with James Foster, San Francisco, December 14, 1988.

28. Interviews with Rick Tuttle and Carol Moss; Harris Wofford to AKL, March 8, 1978, Gary Hart to AKL, July 7, 1979, and Bill Edwards to AKL, August 21, 1979, all in AKL Papers.

29. David Bender talked movingly about his request to Al to cease running; see also interview with Nancy Steffen; Bill [surname unknown] to AKL, October 16, 1976, and Carol Moss to AKL, October 16, 1979, both in AKL Papers; interview with Ken Liberman; *Citizen* interview with Mark Childress.

30. On the Briggs Amendment, see interviews with David Mixner, Rick Tuttle, and Jim Haas; on the Memphis convention, see interview with Rick Saslaw; interview with Jim Foster; John Vecsey (director of a foundation committed to fighting antigay discrimination) to AKL, October 17, 1977, and Margie Bernard to AKL, December 11, 1978, AKL Papers.

31. *New York Times*, November 7, 1979; *Atlanta Journal*, January 14, 1980; Barney Frank to AKL, February 1980, and Harold Kwalwasser to AKL, January 21, 1980 (on Al's critical role in the straw ballot), both in AKL Papers; interviews with Harvey Lippman, Alan Arkatov, Steve Morgan, and Jim Foster.

32. Interview with Carol Moss.

33. Interviews with Joseph Rauh, Steve Morgan, Susan Erb, and Alan Arkatov.

34. Interview with Steven Smith, Jr.

35. Interview with Steven Smith, Jr.; *Citizen* interviews with Edward Kennedy and Robert Shrum.

36. Interview with Steven Smith, Jr.; *Citizen* interview with Robert Shrum.

37. On Sweeney's early life, see Harris, *Dreams Die Hard*, pp. 8–9, 14–15; and Teresa Carpenter, "From Heroism to Madness," *Village Voice*, May 12, 1980; interview with Patti Hagen.

38. Interviews with Dwight Clark, Fred Goff, Ed King, and Ken Stevens, Brooklyn, November 14, 1988.

39. Interviews with confidential source, Susan Goodwillie, Ed King, Floss Frucher, and Greg Craig. Edelman's comment was reported by Floss Frucher.

40. Interviews with confidential source, Mendy Samstein, Brooklyn, September 9, 1990, Ed King, Lawrence Guyot, and Bob Moses. Clayborne Carson, interview with AKL. I am indebted to Clayborne Carson for sharing this interview with me.

41. Harris, *Dreams Die Hard*, pp. 92–96, 102–4, 106–8; and Carpenter, "From Heroism to Madness"; Dennis Sweeney to AKL, [n.d., fall 1964], AKL Papers; interviews with Bruce Payne and John Steinbruner.

42. Robert Coles, "Social Struggle and Weariness," *Journal for the Study of Interpersonal Processes* 27, no. 4 (November 1964):305–15.

43. Carpenter, "From Heroism to Madness"; interview with Robert Beyers, Stanford, February 21, 1990; Mary King, *Freedom Song: A Personal Story of the 1950s Civil Rights Movement* (New York: Morrow, 1987).

44. Interview with Armin Rosencranz. In Rosencranz's view, the "somebody" Sweeney referred to as having had sex with Lowenstein had probably just described a classic Lowenstein advance in more vivid detail.

45. Harris, *Dreams Die Hard*, pp. 124–25, 130–31; Carpenter, "From Heroism to Madness"; interview with Mendy Samstein.

46. Interviews with Stoney Cooks and Richard Flacks, Santa Barbara, December 13, 1988; Charles Hinkle to AKL, April 1, 1973 (asking for help), AKL Papers; Harris, *Dreams Die Hard*, pp. 295–97; Carpenter, "From Heroism to Madness."

47. Charles Hinkle to AKL, April 1, 1973, AKL Papers.

48. Dennis Sweeney to Leni Wildflower and Paul Potter, quoted in Carpenter, "From Heroism to Madness"; and Harris, *Dreams Die Hard*, p. 298.

49. Interviews with Jennifer Littlefield, Greg Craig, and Paul Strasberg, Stanford, November 22, 1991; Harris, *Dreams Die Hard*, pp. 300–305; Carpenter, "From Heroism to Madness."

50. Harris, *Dreams Die Hard*, pp. 300–305.

51. Interviews with Bruce Payne and Judy Quine.

52. Interviews with Paul Strasberg, Armin Rosencranz, Greg Craig, and Judy Quine.

53. Harris, *Dreams Die Hard*, pp. 315–23; Carpenter, "From Heroism to Madness."

54. Interviews with Ann Feldman and Sanford Friedman.

55. Interviews with Susan Erb, Sherman Bull, and Steve Smith, Jr.; *Citizen* in-

terview with Peter Yarrow; *New York Times* coverage, March 15–19, 1980; *New York Daily News* coverage, March 15–19, 1980; *Washington Post* coverage, March 15–19, 1980.

56. Interviews with Sanford Friedman and Alan Arkatov.
57. E. Fuller Torrey, *Psychology Today* (October 1980.)
58. Interview with John Kavanaugh; *Citizen* interview with Peter Yarrow.
59. Interviews with John Kavanaugh, Nancy Steffen, Kris Kleinbauer, and confidential source.
60. *Citizen* interview with William Buckley; interview with confidential source.
61. AKL funeral service, tape recording, AKL Papers; *New York Times*, March 18, 1992.

EPILOGUE

1. Interviews with William Sloane Coffin and Jack Newfield.
2. Allard Lowenstein, "Spain Without Franco," *Saturday Review*, February 7, 1976.
3. Paul Cowan, "What Makes Al Lowenstein Run?" *Ramparts*, September 7, 1968.
4. Interview with John Steinbruner.
5. Interview with Kris Kleinbauer.
6. Interview with David Mixner.
7. Interview with David Bender.
8. Interviews with William Dentzer, Paul Strausberg, and Greg Craig.
9. "Citizen" interview with Pete McCloskey; interview with Steven Smith, Jr.
10. *The New Yorker*, March 12, 1966.
11. John Kenneth Galbraith to Robert Kennedy, January 21, 1964, John F. Kennedy Library, Boston, Massachusetts; interview with Alan Arkatov.
12. Allard Lowenstein, "Angus," a screenplay, AKL Papers.

Index